THE LAND OF THE BIBLE

The Land of the Bible

A Historical Geography

Revised and Enlarged Edition

YOHANAN AHARONI

Translated from the Hebrew and
Edited by
A. F. Rainey

The Westminster Press
Philadelphia

First edition published in Great Britain 1967
Revised and Enlarged edition 1979

Second edition

Published by The Westminster Press®
Philadelphia, Pennsylvania

PRINTED IN THE UNITED STATES OF AMERICA
9 8 7 6 5 4 3 2 1

To
Professor Benjamin Mazar
who enlightened my path into
the Land of the Bible

Library of Congress Cataloging in Publication Data

Aharoni, Yohanan, 1919-1976.
The land of the Bible.

Translation of Erets-Yiśrael bi-teḳufat ha-Miḳra.
Includes bibliographical references and indexes.
1. Bible. O.T.—Geography. 2. Jews—History—To 70 A.D. I. Title.
BS630.A4213 1979 221.9′1 80-14168
ISBN 0-664-24266-9

Contents

CONTENTS

CONTENTS

List of Maps

Preface to the first edition

The historical geography of the Holy Land is as old as the Bible itself, since it was to an already ancient and venerated land that the Israelites came. The ancient mounds—the *tells*—which dot the land of Palestine today, commanding attention and giving the landscape an enduring dignity and to the traveller a continuing sense of history, were there when the Israelites arrived. Some were never resettled, and on others the last centuries of Israelite occupation have added only a few feet to the masses of earlier debris.

The great antiquity of the land, and the continuing awareness that here was the locale of so many vital crises in human history unquestionably influenced the Hebrews in their developing consciousness of the meaning of history. Out of this emerged, humanly speaking, their unique conviction that the God of Israel acts through history. His deeds are manifest in all human events, but particularly and significantly through His mighty acts in His dealing with the Children of Israel. Canaan was the land of His choice for His people. This was the stage for His dramatic and redemptive acts. Without an awareness of the stage, the action of the drama cannot be fully understood. Thus, the historical geography of the Holy Land is a reflection of the mutual relation between God and Israel as understood and interpreted by Israel's national faith. It is no accident that the history of cities and regions and their people is a subject common to many a biblical story. And examining them in their broader connections inevitably deepens our understanding of the ancients and of the Scriptures.

Geography has a way of lending to history some of her more enduring motifs. Certain geographic considerations combined to place the history of the little land of Palestine in the very heart of the ancient Near East. Located on the bridge between three continents, it became involved in almost every event of importance in the history of the ancient Fertile Crescent. It is not too much to say that the geographical position of this little land has always dominated its history.

Thus, in the land of the Bible, geography and history are so deeply interwoven that neither can be really understood without the help of the other. To portray this mosaic of history and geography, with the aid of all available sources, is the aim of this book.

We walk in the footsteps of innumerable savants and scholars, of whom only those of recent generations could usually be mentioned in the bibliographical footnotes accompanying the text. The Church father Jerome, who at the beginning of the fifth century translated into Latin the Greek *Onomasticon* of Eusebius, wrote in the introduction to his commentary on Chronicles:

> Just as those who have seen Athens understand Greek history better, and just as those who have seen Troy understand the words of the poet Virgil, thus one will comprehend the Holy Scriptures with a clearer understanding who has seen the land of Judah with his own eyes and has come to know the references to the ancient towns and places and their names, both the principal names and those which have changed. For this reason we have also been concerned to take this work upon ourselves, together with Hebrew savants, and to describe the country.

Eusebius, Jerome and the Jewish savants mentioned above, as well as many others, did mainly literary work. The Jewish scholar Eshthori ha-Parḥi, who lived in Beth-shean during the first half of the fourteenth century, carried his investigations further, and combined a mastery of biblical and talmudic sources with his knowledge of Hebrew and Arabic as he engaged in topographical research. In his *Kaphtor Wapherah*, he explains his method for the identification and description of ancient places:

> . . . I will make known what has disappeared in this generation since it does not know about the land of Israel, the boundaries of the tribes or their towns, as the good hand of God is upon me . . . to the advantage that we shall know whenever we pass over them: here we shall work a wonder and a marvel and we will thank God for them. I will mention the name in the sacred tongue and in Arabic, admitting it when it is impossible, due to a slight change in a few of them. And this is the inquiry I like better than searching for the places of the stars in the sky, although the subject resembles that today, and everyone knows that there are in the sky twelve constellations and twenty-eight stations of the moon, and eight forms . . . and there are also seven planets . . . and the wheel turns and turns and the same stars pass over us continually and few are they that recognize them. Just so the towns are known in the land of Israel and the sons of men pass by and return, ascend and descend, without knowing a thing about this. Therefore, I come, poor and humble, to tell my brothers and my people what I have found of that which has been sought. And the advantage of my achievement is not over the achievement of one who does not speak about this but rather the advantage of my investigation over his investigation and my movement over his movement. Thus I was about two years in Galilee inquiring and

investigating, and another five years in the rest of the land of the tribes; I did not restrain myself one hour spying out the land, blessed be the One who helps.

Many of Eshthori ha-Parḥi's identifications have been confirmed by subsequent investigation, even though some of them were "discovered" anew by modern scholars unfamiliar with his work.

Scholarly investigation flourished during the nineteenth century. With Edward Robinson, who carried out researches in Palestine during the years 1838 and 1852, historical geography became a sound science based on a critical analysis of the ancient sources in the light of modern philology and topographical surveys. Starting with Sir Flinders Petrie's epoch-making excavation of Tell el-Ḥesi in 1890, pottery chronology developed into a sensitive medium by means of which the periods of settlement of an ancient site can be determined with remarkable accuracy. The history and character of various important biblical cities are today well known to us, and modern archaeological survey enables us to study the process of settlement over whole regions. However, what is unquestionably the greatest contribution towards the understanding of the history of Palestine and its general setting is due to the rediscovery of Ancient Near Eastern civilizations. Once meaningless and dubious biblical terms have become names of well-known countries, peoples and rulers. How could we suppose, e.g. from the biblical stories alone, that the Land of Canaan at the period of the Conquest was nothing more than an Egyptian province?

It is now possible to evaluate most of the biblical traditions in the light of their authentic, historical and geographical setting. Whole chapters of the country's history have been illuminated; and indeed in some instances we now possess even foreign counterparts to various biblical accounts. However, the very abundance of available material inevitably makes its review increasingly difficult, with the result that it becomes more and more the possession of various specialists.

Our aim has been to assemble all this material, and to unite it into one flowing account of the history of the country and its people, with a dual purpose: to make it easily available to the more general reader, and to draw it to the attention of scholars of various related subjects.

This volume is not intended as a contemporary repetition of George Adam Smith's *Historical Geography of the Holy Land*. As a general introduction to the subject, and as a beautifully and vividly coloured description of the Land and its environs, his book remains unrivalled. With the vast minutiae of material now available to us, it is difficult indeed in our age to match the classical outlook and the broad mind of the previous century. This volume is intended to be rather a text-book. It gleans from source to source on a long, long road. Sometimes one is almost overwhelmed by the wealth of the material. If it has some poetry, it is the song of perception. It is the struggle with the material in its minute details which brings a person suddenly to summits of broad insight and enlightenment.

As Eshthori ha-Parḥi phrased it, I have perhaps one advantage over many scholars: my profound aquaintance with the country itself. I feel that in a very real way this book began during my many excursions as a schoolboy, rambling into the most remote corners of the country, and then suddenly standing breathless and fascinated before the huge stone walls of a long-deserted city. In those days I was fortunately able to visit many of the areas which were closed later to the Jewish visitor. I am keenly aware of the limitation forced upon me in recent years in not being able to visit the other side of the Jordan, and it is my hope that the time may soon come when peaceful conditions will return to the country.

But aside from this unfortunate restriction, it has always been my privilege to combine theoretical research with field work and surveys, which opened my eyes to many hidden problems and question marks.

It is my pleasant duty to mention the eminent scholars of our generation from whom I learned most: W.F.Albright and B.Mazar, who made level the path to the understanding of the history of Palestine in the light of the Ancient Near East; A. Alt and M. Noth, who laid the foundations of *Territorial-geschichte* with the help of the rigid analysis and examination of original source *materia*; S. Klein, who drew to our attention the talmudic and midraschic literature; F. M. Abel and M. Avi-Yonah, who greatly enriched the earlier periods by the study of classical and early Christian sources.

The dedication of this book to my teacher, Professor Benjamin Mazar, is only a small expression of my obligation and the depth of my gratitude. He opened for me the gates of research, influenced fundamentally my working methods and devoted to me numerous hours of his time discussing most of the problems dealt with in this book. Many of his opinions and ideas are imbedded in these pages—consciously or unconsciously—though of course not in every matter do we agree. But in my attitude to the historical sources, and the utilization of archaeological research in the understanding of historical-geographical processes, I adhere throughout to the principles developed by him.

The original Hebrew version of this book was published in the fall of 1962 by the Bialik Institute in Jerusalem. The English version, which I am glad to offer now to a wider circle of readers and scholars, is more than a mere translation. The material has not only been brought up to date and fully revised, but various chapters have been rewritten and enlarged, and in some the material has been regrouped in a more appropriate way. The book has been considerably improved by the work of Dr A.F.Rainey, who made the English translation. He advanced many significant remarks and checked carefully the foreign names and the various problems connected with philology and linguistics. My wife shouldered, as usual, the bulk of the work, assisting me in preparing the manuscript and maps. Finally, my thanks and appreciation are due to the University of North Carolina, where I am spending part of my Sabbatical leave from the Hebrew University. In the environment of its hospitality I am adding the final touches to the book; and its Professor of Biblical Literature, Prof. Bernard Boyd, has been most helpful in the realization of this English version.

Y.A.

Chapel Hill, North Carolina, February 24, 1966

Preface to the Second Edition

Just three years ago Yohanan Aharoni departed this life. His career was tragically cut short, leaving a vacuum in the hearts of his friends and colleagues and also in historical geography as a discipline. During the final weeks of his life Aharoni worked incessantly on the present revision. He managed to complete his insertions for the main text of both the Hebrew and the English editions. It remained for the present editor to put those passages into proper English and to devise the documentary apparatus for the footnotes. Here and there some additional annotations and insertions have been added to bring the work up to date. Thus some references and observations deal with publications that appeared during the 1976 academic year. In most cases, the information in these new publications was known to Aharoni beforehand; they are frequently the work of his own disciples and colleagues who had discussed their work with him before submitting it to the press.

The difficulties encountered in working with this material without being able to counsel with Aharoni have been eased to some extent by the use of his personal files. These were placed at the editor's disposal by Mrs Miriam Aharoni whose co-operation in the preparation of the revised edition has been considerable. For that and many other kindnesses, not to mention permission to edit the book, I am deeply grateful.

Many teachers of Old Testament and Israelite history have told me how useful they have found the first edition. It undoubtedly provided the geographic-political-social dimension so lacking in the standard histories. The historical geography of *The Land of the Bible* is a necessary correlate to the ideological and theological emphases which generally dominate this field.

Yohanan Aharoni was a very down-to-earth person. Few scholars have enjoyed such a common-sense grasp of the various lines of evidence that must be co-ordinated in historical geography. He was an archaeologist who knew how to digest an historical source; he was an historian who saw his people as human beings who had lived in a real physical environment. His work was a happy marriage of the field and the library.

Although the first edition was well received and widely used, I have become painfully aware that historical geography has yet to come into its own as a core subject in biblical studies outside Israel. More than ever before we are in a position to push forward the frontiers of knowledge in this sphere. Archaeological, ecological, linguistic and philological studies are in full swing and have at their disposal new techniques and source materials. The present work not only represents Aharoni's final thoughts on the subject; it is in a sense a status report on the discipline. The reader will find numerous changes; Aharoni was not afraid to relinquish a pet theory when new evidence required it. He was well aware that the future would also bring many alterations in our understanding. There is no doubt that many changes will take place in our knowledge during the ensuing years; sometimes they seem to flow daily from the oral reports of colleagues active in the field. Nevertheless, we are confident that *The Land of the Bible* will continue to serve as a springboard for current research and, hopefully, for classroom instruction.

The dimension of historical geography is essential for a well-rounded grasp of life in ancient Israel. Even the prophets dealt with geographic and geo-political entities. If the present edition can make a contribution to bringing biblical studies down to earth, then Aharoni's efforts will not have been in vain.

A.F.R.

10 February, 1979

PART ONE

Introductory Survey

CHAPTER I

The General Setting

The history of any land and people is influenced to a considerable degree by their geographical environment. This includes not only the natural features such as climate, soil, topography, etc., but also the geopolitical relationships with neighbouring areas. This is especially true for Palestine, a small and relatively poor country, which derives its main importance from its unique centralized location at a juncture of continents and a crossroads for the nations.

1. The Bridge between Continents and Civilizations

The trend of Palestinian history has been determined in large measure by that country's place in the geopolitical and political framework of the ancient Near East.[1] As a geographical unit, about 350 miles in length, it extends from Sinai in the south to the Amanus and Taurus mountains in the north, while its width from the Mediterranean shore to the fringes of the inland desert averages only about 60 miles. This long, narrow strip beside the Mediterranean has the most exceptional climate and topographical structure in all the region. Only here does one find an appreciable rainfall during the winter months, which is increased by the high altitude of the mountain ranges that bisect the area longitudinally. In contrast to the barren desert which borders it on the east, the Levant comprises an important segment of that inhabitable region happily defined by Breasted as the "Fertile Crescent" (cf. map 1).

This crescent is hedged in on all sides by natural barriers: the sea on the west, arid wastelands in the centre and on the south, high mountains to the north and east. Its eastern and northern arm is known as Mesopotamia, the land of two rivers of which the northern segment was called Aram-naharaim after the settlement there of the Aramean tribes; the character of this region is determined largely by its two great rivers, the Tigris and the Euphrates. These two rivers originate in the highlands of Armenia and descend to the Persian Gulf. At the beginning of their courses they diverge widely from one another, the Tigris turning south-east and the Euphrates south-west; at their most widely separated points, when they are about 450 miles apart, the upper Euphrates is at the apex of the Fertile Crescent while the Tigris is on its eastern edge. However, near Aleppo in North Syria the Euphrates swerves sharply

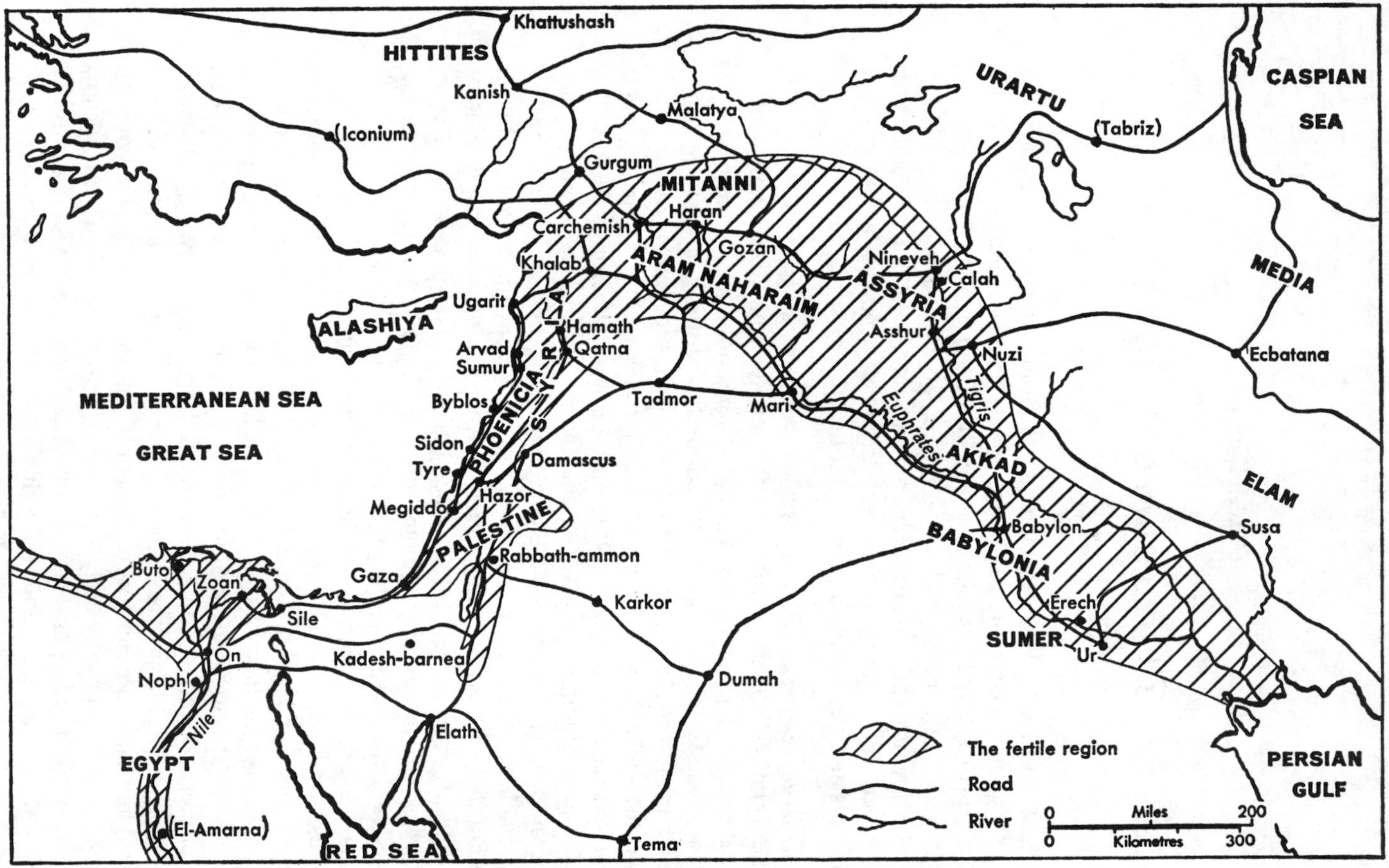

Map 1. The Fertile Crescent.

around to the south-east and continues to approach the Tigris until the two rivers are only about 20 miles apart at Baghdad, just slightly north of the site of ancient Babylon. Today the two rivers unite at a point 180 miles north of the Persian Gulf, which marks the south-eastern limit of the Fertile Crescent. In antiquity the Gulf extended somewhat farther north, and the two rivers poured into it at separate points. Ur of the Chaldees in that region and Niṣṣana (el- 'Auja) in the south of Palestine are located at the same latitude (30° 50″).

Palestine comprises the south-western arm of the Fertile Crescent and is the poorest and smallest of all of its countries. Its main geopolitical importance lies in its role as a passageway to the second great centre of ancient civilization, Egypt, the land of the Nile. The strip of desert separating Palestine from Egypt is about 120 miles in length, but it served not only as a partition but also as a corridor between Egypt and the lands of the Fertile Crescent. It constitutes the only land bridge between the two continents of Asia and Africa.

Towards the end of the fourth and the beginning of the third millennia B.C. the foundations of human civilization were laid in the two lands of the great rivers, Mesopotamia and Egypt. These two regions saw the rise of the first mighty kingdoms which succeeded in imposing an organized and unified government over their respective populations, and in various periods even spread their authority to areas beyond their natural borders. The birth of these two civilizations was aided by similar economic and geographical factors in their respective regions. Each contained broad expanses, the fruitfulness of which depended upon the great rivers passing through them. The river is the main force for integration and unification in these lands; it is a convenient and inexpensive artery for transportation and irrigation, which stimulated the local populations to take advantage of its blessings. However, this required well-organized manpower to carry out extensive building projects such as canals and dams.

Factors such as these do not exist in Palestine and Syria where the geographical features tend to separate the land into smaller districts and serve as serious stumbling blocks to unification. Not one but three rivers flow across it lengthwise: the Orontes going north, the Litani and the Jordan whose streams run southward. Of course these river valleys are conducive to the development of urban settlements. Such was the case in the 'Amuq Plain (Antiochia) in northern Syria, the Lebabese Beqa' between the Lebanon and Anti-Lebanon ranges, as well as certain areas in the Jordan rift, such as the valleys of the Yarmuk and Beth-shean and the plains of Succoth and Jericho. The excavations at Jericho have, in fact, demonstrated that one of the most ancient urban settlements in the Middle East was founded there, dating back to the Neolithic period, apparently in the eighth millennium B.C., at the dawn of human civilization in this part of the world.

These characteristics are brought to mind when one reads the description of the Jordan Valley in the patriarchal narratives: "And Lot lifted up his eyes, and saw that the Jordan Valley was well watered everywhere like the garden of the Lord, like the land of Egypt" (Gen. 13. 10). Evidently the circumstances here were quite favourable to human occupation and the establishment of a permanent agricultural settlement. But the possibilities for irrigation and the areas available for settlement were limited, and external factors to encourage extensive political unification were absent.

Thus Palestine and Syria became a middle ground between Mesopotamia and Egypt from both the economic and the political point of view. The mighty kingdoms on both sides of the Fertile Crescent considered this strip of land a thoroughfare; and both of them laboured to impose their authority over it, mainly so as to control the trade routes passing through it and to use it as a bridgehead for defence or offence. The position of Palestine as a land bridge between the great world powers surrounding it has made an indelible impression upon its history. For long periods it was subjugated to foreign rulers. Cultural influences from both the north and the south met here, being carried by the many peoples who traversed its length. This made it very difficult for any kind of independent economic and political development, but it also gave access to all the accomplishments of ancient civilization. In this melting pot of cultural contact some of the greatest human cultural achievements came into being, e.g. alphabetic writing and monotheistic faith.

2. *The Table of Nations*

The geopolitical situation of Palestine as a meeting place between continents and civilizations was indelibly impressed on the minds of the ancients and received its clearest expression in the biblical "Table of Nations" (Gen. 10; 1 Chron. 1. 1–23).[2] This roster is a brief survey of the lands and peoples within the horizon of Israelite knowledge during the biblical period. It takes the form of a genealogical tree in which all the peoples of the world are related to one ancestor, Noah. The order generally followed is political and territorial; besides tongue and race the homeland of each people is defined in terms of its geographical position and political dependence (cf. map. 1).

All of the human family is divided into three main groups, which surrounded Palestine: the sons of *Shem* to the east, the sons of *Ham* to the south and the sons of *Japheth* to the north and west. Shem included the Semitic-speaking peoples to whom the Israelites felt themselves most intimately affiliated; the ancient traditions emphasize the association between ethnic and linguistic relationships. However, Canaan was related to Ham, despite its Semitic and Hebrew-like language, obviously because of its long political association with Egypt. Japheth was the least affiliated with Palestine; to him belong the northern, mainly Indo-European-speaking peoples, including the Greek and Pre-Greek inhabitants of the Mediterranean.

The survey begins with the most distant and concludes with the nearest. First comes the genealogy of the sons of *Japheth*: Madai on the east, Ashkenaz and Gomer in the north and Tiras (the Etruscans?) and Tarshish in the west. The sons of Japheth include Anatolia (Togarmah, Tubal, Meshech), Javan (Greece) from Asia Minor to the land of Greece itself, and the islands of the sea from Elishah (Cyprus; Alashia in cuneiform sources). Rodanim (according to 1 Chron. 1. 7 instead of Dodanim; Rhodes), Kittim (Caphtor and the other islands), including Tarshish (Sardinia ?), which are subsumed under the expression "islands of the peoples" (MT as against RSV; Gen. 10. 5).

The second group contains the sons of *Ham* who come from the Egyptian political sphere, viz. Cush in the south (Nubia), Egypt itself, Put on the west (Lybia) and Canaan in the north. The sons of Cush include some of the lands in South Arabia which have affinities with Africa, viz. Seba, Havilah, Sabtah, Raamah, Sheba and Dedan. Some of these peoples also appear in the list as sons of Shem.

It is extremely difficult to identify the various peoples associated with Egypt, but the last of these can be easily understood if one accepts the following emendation: "and the Caphtorim from whence came the Philistines". Even the Philistines who dwelt in the southern coastal region of Palestine were reckoned as the sons of Egypt, in spite of the fact that they came from Caphtor (Crete), one of the "islands of the peoples" belonging to Japheth. To Canaan are related, besides the well-known peoples of Canaan (Heth, the Jebusites, the Amorites, the Girgashites and the Hivites [Horites?], the main cities of Phoenicia: Sidon, which also served as a general term for Phoenicia, including Tyre and Byblos, 'Arqat (the Arkites), Sin (the Sinites), Arvad and Ṣumur (the Zemarites). And finally Hamath on the Orontes is also reckoned with the sons of Canaan, although its occupants were Hittites.[3]

To the Hamites was also reckoned a group of major Mesopotamian cities, even though Asshur is also assigned to the sons of Shem. These cities appear here because of their connection with Nimrod, who is associated with Cush. The group includes Babel, Erech, Akkad and Calneh (as against RSV) in the land of Shinar (southern Mesopotamia), and Nineveh, Rehoboth-Ir, Calah and Resen in the land of Assyria (northern Mesopotamia).

The third section of the Table of Nations concerns the sons of *Shem*, "the father of all the children of Eber" (the Hebrews!) to which the Israelites are also related. As mentioned above, this group contains Semitic-speaking peoples whose languages are related to Hebrew, except for Elam in the east and Lud in Asia Minor (Lydia ?). The Semites are divided into three groups: Asshur in Mesopotamia (here belong the Mesopotamian towns listed with the Hamites); Aram which extended from northern Mesopotamia to middle Syria and northern Transjordan; and finally the various tribes of South Arabia who are connected with Joktan the son of Eber and who are therefore, from this point of view, the closest relations to the Israelites. The best known of these tribes are Hazarmaveth, Sheba and Havilah, who have already been mentioned among the sons of Cush.

The composition of the list fits best the early phase of the Monarchy, especially the enumeration of the South Arabian countries.[4] This date is indicated not only by its contents but also by its general outlook. On the one hand, we can hardly imagine that all these peoples could come within the purview of the tribes before their unification and active participation in the commerce and politics of the Middle East. On the other hand, the political affiliations of the nations which influenced their arrangement in the list still belong to the period of the conquest and settlement. The association of Canaan with Egypt preserves the memory of its status as an Egyptian province. The same is true with the Philistines, who are reckoned as sons of Egypt since they were allowed to settle in the southern coastal area which was a centre of Egyptian influence. The Hittites, however, are no longer reckoned as residents of Anatolia; the reference here is to the Neo-Hittite elements within the Canaanite sphere.

The Table of Nations reflects the ethnic and geographic world known to Israel during her apogee, and it gives a faithful sketch of Palestine's position among the peoples and kingdoms of the ancient Near East where the three spheres of Shem, Ham and Japheth intersected.

3. Between Sea and Desert

A factor no less important in the history of Palestine is its geographical position between the sea and the desert. The climate of Palestine is best defined as the outcome of the struggle between these two divergent powers.[5] Palestine is located in a sub-tropical zone, having a rainy season in the winter and a dry season in the summer. The westerly winds bring the wet storms of winter and the refreshing summer breezes from the sea, while the easterly winds bring with them the dust and dryness of the desert, hot and burning in summer and cool but dry during the winter. The spring is early and short. The rainy season begins during October or November (sometimes as late as December), and a few weeks after its beginning a green carpet covers the hills and valleys, providing plentiful pasture for the flocks. During February and March everything blossoms, and thistles spring up taller than a man. Near the end of March the hot desert winds, called "sirocco" or "khamsin" usually begin. These generally last from a few days to a week or more and are most common during April–May and September–October. With their beginning everything dries up rapidly and the blossoming landscape turns yellow and desolate almost overnight.

Not only the seasonal pattern but also the differing climate of the respective regions is an outcome of the contest between desert and sea. The amount of precipitation varies greatly in different parts of the country due to their geographical location and is intensified by the great differences in altitude.

Only a narrow strip along the Mediterranean coast enjoys any appreciable degree of rainfall, and the transition to arid desert country is quite sharp in the east and on the south. Therefore, the places receiving the largest amount of rainfall are the coastal strip and the northern highlands. To the degree that a particular region is lower, southerly, or removed from the sea its rainfall diminishes accordingly.

Since the precipitation is associated with climatic instability and barometric depressions which come and go during the winter, a great percentage of the rain falls during a limited number of days; likewise the difference may be very great from one year to another, and drought years are frequent. Deluge and drought do not balance out against one another, because on a rainy day the streams rise up and great currents of water overflowing from the hills suddenly flood into the plains; this may be followed by a series of warm days when the ground dries up rapidly under the hot rays of the sun, pouring down from a cloudless sky. Most of the streams are intermittent and contain water only on rainy days.

Perennial streams which flow toward the Jordan Valley are the Yarmuk, the Jabbok and some smaller tributaries on the east, and the Wadi Jalud on the west; the Arnon and the Zered empty into the Dead Sea. The Yarkon is the only river flowing to the Mediterranean; it runs its brief course from a rich and constant source at the foot of the ancient Aphek-Antipatris. The remaining streams, including the Kishon, carry water over short distances only and usually in small amounts.

The influence of the Mediterranean (the "Great Sea" in biblical terminology) on population and economy is not so pronounced in the history of Palestine as one might deduce from its long coastline. The main reason for this is the lack of convenient harbours and natural anchorages. The shoreline is almost straight, and in many places a high ridge rises up sharply from behind a narrow strip of beach which makes approach to the shore most difficult. Furthermore, a large percentage of the shoreline, especially in the south, is backed by a strip of shifting sands, often several miles in width, which also blocks the approach to the shore and deflects the highway from the coast inland so as to by-pass the sands. Therefore, most of the small anchorages were located in antiquity at the mouths of streams, which gave some measure of protection to small boats and from which one could advance eastwards for some distance towards the mainland. In spite of the fact that there have always been harbours along the Palestinian coast, some of which enjoyed a certain measure of importance, e.g. Ashkelon, Joppa, Dor and Acco, maritime commerce remained limited during most periods. Thus the harbour towns did not serve to introduce much cultural influence from over the sea.

On the other hand, the coastline enjoyed special importance in the development of Syria. Along the Syro-Phoenician coast there are many excellent natural harbours, several on off-shore islands, e.g. Tyre and Arvad which were important bases for maritime activity. Therefore, sea trade was highly developed on the Canaanite-Phoenician coast from even the most ancient periods. Ships of Byblos were famous during the third and second millennia, and Canaanite Tyre and Sidon became the most important sea powers in the Mediterranean during the early centuries of the first millennium B.C.

The *desert*, on the other hand, which surrounds Palestine on the east and the south, exercised a much stronger influence on the country and its population. There are no natural barriers to protect the settled areas from nomadic tribes except for the desert expanses themselves. Of course, the desert population was quite sparse, so that there was plenty of room for the Bedouin to occupy extensive areas and to utilize them as pasturage, albeit poor, for their flocks and cattle. However, the mighty wastelands are a never-ending source for tribal migrations that exert constant pressure on the populated areas.

The conflict between the desert and the sown land is unceasing.[6] The desert dwellers are always half starved, and thus they gaze longingly at the delights of the settled country. They take advantage of every opportunity to invade the sown lands, requiring the frontier dwellers to be constantly on their guard. In their respective periods the desert raiders—Amalekites, Midianites, Ishmaelites, *et al.*—were the Israelite farmers' most dangerous enemies in biblical times; one of the major accomplishments of Saul, the first King of Israel, was to relieve his people from the danger of these marauders (1 Sam. 14. 48). The line of Egyptian border forts in the eastern delta, the biblical Shur, was intended first and foremost to keep close watch over the movements of such Bedouin tribes.

Palestine possesses a long mutual boundary with the desert which provides plenty of opportunity for invasion and infiltration. Obviously this was more strongly felt in those districts adjacent to the desert, viz. the Negeb and central and southern Transjordan.[7] These areas, which are wide open to incursions from the desert, suffered long periods of domination by the nomads with their flocks, which prevented any form of permanent settlement.

But enmity and strife were not the only relations that could prevail between the nomads and the sedentary population. Transactions were sometimes carried out concerning trade and the use of seasonal pasturage during the summer months when the desert oases do not suffice. Penetration by Bedouin with their flocks, especially in the regions of Gilead, the highlands of western Palestine, the Negeb and the delta region of Egypt, was a frequent phenomenon in all periods, often permitted by the masters of the land who allowed the nomads to pasture their flocks in forested or swampy regions and even in their own stubble fields after the harvest.

The continual pressure by Semitic nomads from the desert so influenced the composition of the populace in Palestine that it remained predominantly Semitic, in spite of several invasions by other peoples from the north. The large majority of geographical names in Palestine is Semitic. This is clear evidence concerning the early residents who founded these settlements during the fourth and third millennia B.C., since the place names usually withstand even the passage of time and the recplacement of whole populations by invasion and migration. The historical sources record at least two tremendous Semitic waves that inundated Palestine and the other lands of the Fertile Crescent in the biblical period: the Amorite wave at the end of the third and the beginning of the second millennia B.C. and the Hebrew-Aramean wave in the last centuries of the second millennium. The Arab-Islamic invasions must be viewed as the latest wave of this ethnic migration from the desert into the sown land of the Fertile Crescent.

4. *The Geological Foundations*

The sea and the desert are also the basic forces which created the rock of Palestine and its soil.[8] Most of its rock consists of various limestones, formed as sedimentary deposits of the sea during relatively late geological periods: the Cenomanian, Turonian and Senonian, which are the last phases of the Secondary era, and the Eocene, which starts the Tertiary era.

The composition of the karstic limestone permits a rapid seepage of water which is absorbed to great depths until it reaches a solid, non-porous stratum of rock where it is then forced to flow horizontally. Only a part of this water breaks through to the surface in springs, which are especially prevalent in the geological rifts forming the valleys. This phenomenon increased the dryness in antiquity, because only during modern times have the really deep waters been exploited by pumping.

The Cenomanian, Turonian and the younger Eocene form hard rocks, capable of withstanding erosion. They are quarried into excellent building stones, one of the natural resources of Palestine; and they weather into a fertile red-brown soil, the famous *terra rossa* of the Mediterranean sphere. Fortunately, they comprise the main part of the west-Palestinian hill country and of central Transjordan, which owe to them their richness and fertility. The intermediate Senonian rock, on the other hand, has completely different qualities. It forms a soft chalk which is easily eroded into a light grey, infertile soil. It is very porous, dries quickly, and is poor for agriculture. The Judean Desert above the western shore of the Dead Sea consists mainly of this Senonian chalk, and its qualities combined with the influence of the steep eastern descent transformed this area into a complete desert. However, Senonian valleys are the most suitable for traffic, as the soft rock quickly develops a smooth surface, undisturbed by boulders, usually dry even during the winter. The Senonian strips exposed at the base of the hills became therefore the most important thoroughfares through the hill regions, cf. especially the roads from the Sharon to the Jezreel Valley like the famous Megiddo pass or the Darb el-Ḥawarnah which crosses Lower Galilee (*infra*, pp. 50 f., 60).

The valleys of western Palestine are covered with a deep alluvial soil, washed down from the hilly regions. The largest and most important are the coastal plain and the Jezreel Valley (usually referred to as "The Valley"), which are the richest agricultural areas of the country. The western part of the coastal region is mostly covered with sand brought in by the sea, which extends inland over a strip of three to four miles or more. These are comprised partly of hard sandstone layers (called *kurkar*) and partly of shifting sand dunes, which threaten to cover more and more of the cultivated area. In the western Negeb, where they encountered no resistance, they penetrated inland up to a distance of 30 miles and more. The central part of the Sharon is covered by a special red sand as a result of weathering by later geological deposits in the area. Though it has now become the soil *par excellence* for citrus cultivation through irrigation and fertilization, it was virtually useless for agriculture in antiquity and for the most part remained forested until recent times. The major part of the northern Negeb is covered by layers of *loess*, a very fine yellow-brown dust carried by the desert winds. If adequately cultivated and watered it is a rich and fertile soil (cf. e.g. Gen. 26. 12). However, with the first rain it develops a hard crust, rather impermeable to water, across which the rains glide as if on oil. This factor increases considerably the danger of flash floods during the winter downpours to further aggravate the dryness of this semi-arid area. On the other hand, it facilitates the direction and collection of run-off water.

Large parts of southern Transjordan and the environs of the River Jabbok in central Transjordan are covered by a thick layer of red sandstone, desposited during long periods of early desert conditions. Its orange to dark red colour gave the name to the huge, steep mountains of Edom (which means *red* in Hebrew). It is a hard sandstone, resistant to erosion and to the penetration of water, which has brought about the formation of the beautiful cliffs of Edom and Moab and the abundance of vegetation and water in areas of sufficient rainfall. This so-called Nubian sandstone contains the copper deposits of the Arabah. Only in the southern portions of the Arabah does one find protrusions of more ancient granites, not covered by later strata, whose wild spikes remind one of the huge granite mountains in the southern Sinai Desert.

The later phases of the Tertiary, the Miocene, the Pliocene and especially the Pleistocene eras left considerable traces of volcanic eruptions, mainly in northern Palestine. Particularly in northern Transjordan (Bashan) and in the eastern portions of Lower Galilee does one find areas of volcanic rock created by the action of extinct volcanoes. These cone-shaped hills still dominate the landscape of Bashan, and famous representatives of their kind in Lower Galilee are the Hill of Moreh and the Horns of Ḥaṭṭin (Qarn Ḥaṭṭin). The basalt rock weathers into a rich grey-black soil, to which Bashan owes its proverbial fertility (Amos 4. 1; Psalms 22. 12, etc.). In various areas, however, unweathered basalt boulders remain which are a serious obstacle to traffic and agriculture. This is true for the steep eastern slopes of Lower Galilee and for the mountainous eastern reaches of Bashan, Hauran or Jebel Druze. Its north-western, lower portion, el-Leja, is a desertlike area of basalt boulders.

These periods of volcanic eruptions also saw the main tectonic activity which shaped the topography of Palestine. Mountains were pushed up, and deep crevices sank between them. The largest and deepest of these rifts is the Jordan Valley, which is only one segment of a great rift running from the Lebanese Beqa' to the Red Sea and on into Africa. Its sinking continued during the Pleistocene period when the most ancient race of man, the "Pebble Culture", was already inhabiting part of it.[9] The area of the deep rift is sensitive to tectonic activity to this very day, as evidenced by the numerous hot springs and by frequent earthquakes.

5. *The Pastoral-Agrarian Economy*

The economy of Palestine is largely determined by natural geographic features: (1) its narrow dimensions; (2) its varied topography; and (3) its position as a land bridge between the great cultural centres.

Agriculture was the basis for the economy of most countries in antiquity including Palestine. Not only villagers but many "city dwellers" made their livelihood from agriculture, and farmers were the majority and the backbone of the population.

Palestinian agriculture was mainly natural farming without irrigation.

In this there are both advantages and disadvantages. Egypt and appreciable portions of Mesopotamia are actually deserts whose fertility depends upon the exploitation of water from their respective rivers through human effort. By contrast, it is possible in Palestine to sow and to reap a good harvest like a gift from heaven coming down in the form of rain and dew. However, the rains are limited mostly to the winter season and are not always sufficient in all parts of the country. Furthermore, drought years are not infrequent when the rain is insufficient everywhere. Years of drought and famine run like a scarlet thread through the ancient history of Palestine. In such times it often happened that part of the population was compelled to seek refuge in Egypt which is supported by a permanent water supply from the Nile. Only in parts of the Jordan Valley, especially the eastern sectors, rich in wells and tributary streams, was there irrigation in ancient times. The fertile land and the warm climate permitted lucrative irrigational farming (Gen. 13. 10). Nevertheless, this called for organization and diligence; since the Jordan Valley was close to the frontier, it was open to frequent depredations by desert marauders, making it a desolate waste for many centuries.

The contrast between the natural farming conditions in Palestine and Egyptian irrigation is expressed quite clearly in the Bible:

> For the land which you are entering to take possession of it is not like the land of Egypt, from which you have come, where you sowed your seed and watered it with your feet, like a garden of vegetables; but the land which you are going over to possess is a land of hills and valleys, which drinks water by the rain from heaven, a land which the Lord your God cares for; the eyes of the Lord your God are always upon it, from the beginning of the year to the end of the year (Deut. 11. 10–12).

Here the feeling finds expression that the land is dependent upon God throughout the whole year, as portrayed in the festivals which are related to the agricultural seasons. Its limited area and varied topography are also described ("a land of hills and valleys"), in contrast to the broad plains of Egypt and Mesopotamia.

The main agricultural products are included in the description of the seven species for which the country was renowned:

> For the Lord your God is bringing you into a good land, a land of brooks of water, of fountains and springs, flowing forth in valleys and hills, a land of wheat and barley, of vines and fig trees and pomegranates, a land of olive trees and honey . . . (Deut. 8. 7–8).

The most important products of horticulture and aboriculture are singled out, the former mainly in the valleys and the latter in the hills. The honey is probably not from bees but from dates, a typical product of the

Jordan Valley and the Dead Sea area during antiquity, though not mentioned here specifically by name. A more concise expression of praise used frequently in the Bible is "a land flowing with milk and honey", referring to the produce of the two most important agricultural activities: milk—dairy farming, flocks and herbs; honey—the cultivation of trees. Cattle-raising was continued even after the Israelite tribes had settled down. It occupied an important place in the economy of various regions, especially Transjordan (Num. 32. 1 ; 1 Chron. 5. 9, *et al.*), the fringe of the desert, and the Negeb (1 Sam. 25. 2 ff ; 1 Chron. 4. 38–41; 2 Chron. 26. 10).

A description similar to this appears in one of the more ancient Egyptian documents, viz. the story of Sinuhe from the mid-twentieth century B.C. Sinuhe flees from Egypt and finds refuge in a land of Upper Retenu, a region on the border between the settled and the nomadic populations, perhaps in the Yarmuk Valley and on the slopes of Golan.[10]

> It was a good land, named i-3-3 [Araru ?]. Figs were in it, and grapes. It had more wine than water. Plentiful was its honey, abundant its olives. Every (kind of) fruit was on its trees. Barley was there, and emmer. There was no limit to any (kind of) cattle.

Sinuhe recounted the wealth which he left behind on his return to Egypt: "My serfs, all my cattle, my fruit, and every pleasant tree of mine."[11] The picture as seen through this Egyptian's eyes does not differ from that of the Bible, both of them stress the agricultural wealth of the land, cattle and fruit trees, i.e. "a land flowing with milk and honey".

The same situation is reflected by the list of David's officers in charge of the royal estates. They included supervisors

> . . . over those who did the work of the field for tilling the soil . . . over the vineyards . . . over the produce of the vineyards for the wine cellars. . . . Over the olive and sycamore trees in the Shephelah . . . over the stores of oil. . . . Over the herds that pastured in Sharon . . . over the herds in the valleys,

and finally

> . . . over the camels . . . over the she-asses . . ., [and] . . . over the flocks . . . (1 Chron. 27. 25–31).

Camels and she-asses are not directly related to agriculture but rather to the trade routes. Control over the main arteries of commerce in the Middle East, which passed through Palestine, assured that trade would be an important branch of the economy, especially in those sectors transversed by the roads. This commerce was partly in the hands of nomads and semi-nomads and partly a monopoly of the kings and rulers. Up until the end of the Bronze Age transport was mostly by asses. It would seem that only towards the end of the second millennium B.C. was the camel domesticated in sufficient numbers so as to become the typical "ship of the desert".[12] Commercial caravans of nomads are even mentioned in the Patriarchal narratives ("a caravan of Ishmaelites coming from Gilead, with their camels bearing gum, balm and myrrh, on their way to carry it down to Egypt" [Gen. 37. 25]). This, like most other local data in the patriarchal narratives, cannot antedate the period of the Israelite conquest. We are also informed from the El Amarna letters about merchant caravans passing through Canaan (*EA*, 7.73; 8. 13; 52.37; 226. 15; 225.8). At the beginning of their period of settlement the Israelite tribes were cut off from most of the important commercial routes dominated by Canaanites and Philistines, but this situation changed with the conquest of the plains by David. Solomon's great wealth was based on his control of these important trade arteries (1 Kings 4. 21–34; 9. 15–18) including the Via Maris and the King's Highway, clear out to such distant centres as Tadmor and Tiphsah (1 Kings 4. 24; 9. 18; 2 Chron. 8. 4). The traffic in precious goods was a royal monopoly and the Bible stresses the great international trade connections of King Solomon's merchants as suppliers of war chariots from Egypt and horses from Kue in Cilicia (1 Kings 10. 28–9).[13] Control over Elath was also quite important since it opened the trade routes to southern Arabia, Africa and even the Indian Ocean. The Queen of Sheba's visit to Solomon (1 Kings 10. 1–13) and the dispatch of "ships of Tarshish" from Ezion-geber (1 Kings 10. 22, etc.) are connected with the development of this traffic which brought into the royal treasury gold, silver, precious stones, perfumes and other expensive luxury items.

After the division of the kingdom, Israel continued to control a certain section of the *Via Maris* and in some periods even parts of the King's Highway in Transjordan. Judah sought to maintain control over the Arabah, Edom and Elath, in particular during the reigns of Jehoshaphat and Uzziah (1 Kings 22. 29; 2 Kings 14. 22, etc.). It is no accident that meagre biblical citations from the chronicles of the kings of Judah and Israel include a disproportionately large amount of information about the fate of Elath, a place so important for the economy of Judah. Evidence for trade with South Arabia was found in the excavations at Ezion-geber (Tell el-Kheleifeh)[14] and perhaps in a South Arabian seal that has turned up at Bethel.[15]

Besides transport commerce, in which Palestine enjoyed the role of intermediary between the adjacent lands, especially with regard to valuable luxury items, we also have information about imports and exports. In antiquity the country exported mainly its agricultural surpluses, e.g. grain, oil, wine and honey (1 Kings 5. 11; Ezek. 27. 17), and also perfume and medicinal balm (Gen. 37. 25; 43. 11; Ezek. 27. 17). The balm was extracted from certain trees in the forests of Gilead (Jer.

8. 22). Imports included luxury wares and garments from Egypt (Ezek. 27. 7), lumber and fish from Phoenicia (Neh. 13. 16), as well as the above-mentioned luxuries and perfumes from South Arabia. Evidence for imports of this type from Egypt appears as early as the El Amarna letters. In a message from Pharaoh to the King of Gezer he affirms the dispatch of silver, gold, garments, precious stones and ivory-inlaid chairs in exchange for a shipment of beautiful handmaidens from Gezer.[16]

Navigation never held a very important place in Palestine's economy, in spite of its long coast. The main reason for this was a lack of harbours suitable for anchorage, in addition to the strip of shifting sand dunes that prevented the main highways from approaching too near the shore. Quite the opposite is true on the Phoenician coast where harbour cities flourished such as Tyre, Sidon, Byblos, Arvad, *et al.* Fishing in the Mediterranean and in the Sea of Galilee was doubtless practised in most periods, especially as the smaller fishing boats do not need a deep anchorage.[17] However, the sources are extremely meagre and its extent and importance was probably limited.

Of course, there were some harbour towns established in Palestine taking advantage of small harbours or rocky coves. The most important of these were Acco, Dor, Joppa and Ashkelon. Between them, there were some additional anchorages, especially at the river mouths, providing a certain amount of protection to the small coastal boats used in antiquity. Among these minor seaports three are known from excavation: Tell Abu Huwam near the mouth of the Kishon,[18] Tell Qasileh at the Yarkon estuary[19] and Tel Mor (Tell Kheiḍar) at the mouth of Wadi Sukreir.[20]

Not a great deal is known about sea trade in Palestinian ports during the Bronze Age. Tables recently found at Ugarit do bear witness to commercial relations with various towns on the Levantine coast, e.g. Arvad, Byblos, Tyre, Acco, Ashdod and Ashkelon. Some of the commodities imported to Ugarit include fish, milk, wool, fabrics and clothing.[21] A more explicit testimony comes from the story of Wenamon dated to the beginning of the eleventh century B.C. It mentions that a fleet was stationed at Dor belonging to the Tjeker (Sekel), one of the Sea Peoples.[22] It may be assumed that similar fleets of ships were also at the disposal of the other Philistine cities along the coast. However, Dor is the only one of the four main seaports mentioned above that passed into Israelite hands and must have served as a port for the kingdom of Israel. We do not have any detailed evidence on this point, but the prominence of Dor stands out in the list of Solomon's district commissioners where it appears as a special district and its commissioner is the king's son-in-law (1 Kings 4. 11). Acco was under Israelite control in David's reign (Josh. 19. 29; 2 Sam. 24. 7), but in

Solomon's day it was returned to Tyrian jurisdiction (1 Kings 9. 11). The hint about maritime activity on the part of Zebulun and Asher (Gen. 49. 13; Judg. 5. 17) apparently testifies to their penetration into the Plain of Acco, doubtless under the patronage of the Canaanite cities at first (cf. Judg. 1. 31–2). Ashkelon became one of the five Philistine capitals, and Joppa was also included in their territory, although we have no definite information about its lot. It is clear that Joppa itself remained outside the Israelite boundary (Josh. 19. 46), and it is interesting to note that in Sennacherib's time it was under the jurisdiction of Ashkelon rather than nearby Ashdod.[23] Perhaps it was because Ashkelon was the major Philistine sea power that it ruled over Joppa and its vicinity. It is also possible that we generally do not hear about conflicts between Ashkelon and Israel because the latter did not entertain maritime aspirations.[24] A list of annual tribute paid by Ashkelon to Assyria was found at Nimrud containing among other things an appreciable quantity of woven fabrics, coloured cloth and fish.[25] From this we deduce that, in addition to the fishing industry, the manufacture of woven goods and their dyes were important branches of Ashkelon's economy. The lumber for building the temple was transported by sea from Tyre to Joppa both in the days of Solomon and of Zerubbabel (1 Kings 5. 9; Ezra 3. 7). This may be a reference to the Yarkon estuary. Perhaps Israel required the services of Philistine sailors. Jonah the prophet set sail from Joppa in a ship of Tarshish (Jonah 1. 3). During the Persian period the various harbours of Palestine were handed over to Tyre and Sidon as bases for coastal shipping. From the inscription of Eshmunezer, King of Sidon, we learn that he received Dor and Joppa as grants from the Persian King.[26]

King Solomon inaugurated shipping on the Gulf of Aqabah with the help of Phoenician sailors, and for this purpose he built Ezion-geber close to the Elath (1 Kings 9. 26; 2 Chron. 8. 17).[27] Jehoshaphat (and apparently Uzziah as well) followed his example (1 Kings 22. 49; 2 Kings 14. 22; 2 Chron. 20. 36; 26. 2). The only competitors to Israelite shipping on the Red Sea were the Egyptians, and it is possible that one of Shishak's objectives in his campaign after Solomon's death was to put an end to Israelite maritime activities on the Gulf of Aqabah.[28]

Palestine is not rich in raw materials. Nevertheless, Scripture does connect a wealth of iron and copper with the country ("a land whose stones are iron, and out of whose hills you can dig copper" (Deut. 8. 9). A few iron mines have been discovered in Transjordan,[29] and the text may have meant to include the iron mines in the Lebanon region. Copper mines have been discovered in the Arabah between the Dead Sea and the Gulf of Aqabah. We have no positive evidence for the utilization of salt from the Dead Sea. But perhaps we are entitled to see hints to this effect in the stories about pillars of salt in its vicinity as well as the settlement named "the City of Salt" located in that region (Josh. 16. 61), apparently Khirbet Qumran.[30] From the el-Amarna tablets we hear about shipments of raw material for the manufacture of glass being sent to Egypt from Tyre (EA, 148), Lachish (EA, 331), Ashkelon (EA, 323) and elsewhere (EA, 327) in southern Canaan. The techniques of the glass industry seem to have developed in the Levant during the 15th century B.C.[31]

Some of the urban settlers must certainly have engaged in various crafts, but information on this subject is quite scanty. It would appear that most of the crafts were passed by inheritance from father to son, the professions remaining within the clan or guild. In the Bible we find occasional references to families of artisans, e.g. potters (1 Chron. 4. 23; cf. Jer. 18. 2), builders (1 Chron. 4. 14); weavers (*ibid.*, 4. 21) and scribes (*ibid.*, 2. 55). Several dyeing plants were discovered in the excavations at Tell Beit Mirsim. This seems to have been the main occupation of the local inhabitants there.[32] Along the coast people were engaged in extracting valuable purple and violet dyes from various kinds of shellfish (*Murex*). That industry was a major source for the wealth of the Canaanites,[33] and for a time the tribe of Zebulun seems to have engaged in it (Deut. 33. 19).

With all this the economy of the country remained principally pastoral-agrarian during the biblical period: "He who tills his land will have plenty of bread . . ." (Prov. 12. 11).

[1] Cf. especially G. A. Smith, *The Historical Geography of the Holy Land* (London, 1894); F. M. Abel, *Géographie de la Palestine,* I (Paris, 1933); W. B. Fisher, *The Middle East* (London, 1950).

[2] Maisler (Mazar), *Untersuchungen,* pp. 74–76; A. Hermann, *Die Erdkarte der Bibel* (Braunschweig, 1931); G. Hölscher, *Drei Erdkarten* (Heidelberg, 1949); J. Simons, "The Table of Nations", *Oudtestamentische Studiën,* 10 (1954), pp. 155–84.

[3] The absence of Byblos is most surprising, because it is difficult to assume for the roster a period of major decline of this important Phoenician city, which was most intimately connected with Egypt. May we perhaps see in the following word "border" (Hebrew *Gebul* which has the same consonantal spelling as *Gebal*) a corruption of its name, and amend the text in the following way: "And the Arvadite, and the Zemarite, and the Hamathite, and the Gebalite; and afterwards were the families of the Canaanites spread abroad from Sidon, and thou comest to Gerar, etc." I owe this suggestion to Prof. Mazar.

[4] K. Elliger, *PJb,* 32 (1936), pp. 63 ff.; Albright, *SAC,* p. 191.

[5] H. Klein, *ZDPV,* 27 (1914), pp. 217–49; 297–327; D. Aschbel, *Das Klima Palästinas* (Berlin, 1930); *idem, Ha-aqlim be-erets Yisrael u-shekhenoteha* (Tel Aviv, 1948) (Hebrew); D. Baly, *The Geography of the Bible* (London, 1957), pp. 41–82.

[6] A. Reifenberg, *The Struggle between the Desert and the Sown* (Jerusalem, 1954).

[7] Cf. N. Glueck, *The Other Side of the Jordan* (New Haven, 1945).

[8] G. S. Blake, *The Stratigraphy of Palestine and its Building Stones* (Jerusalem, 1935); L. Picard, *Structure and Evolution of Palestine* (Jerusalem, 1943); Baly, *op. cit.* (note 5) pp. 14-40.

[9] M. Stekelis, *IEJ,* 10 (1960), p. 118.

[10] *ANET*, p. 19; B. Mazar, *EI*, 3 (1954), p. 21 (Hebrew).

[11] *ANET*, p. 21.

[12] W. F. Albright, *SAC,* pp. 120 ff.; *idem, Archaeology and the Religion of Israel* (Baltimore, 1942), pp. 132 f.; *BASOR,* 163 (1961), p. 38; R. Walz, *ZDMG,* 104 (1954), pp.

45–87; W. G. Lambert, *BASOR,* 160 (1960), pp. 42 f.

[13] W. F. Albright, *BASOR,* 120 (1950), pp. 22–25; H. Tadmor, *IEJ,* 11 (1961), pp. 143–50.

[14] N. Glueck, *BASOR,* 71 (1938), pp. 15–17.

[15] G. W. van Beek and A. Jamme, *BASOR,* 151 (1958), pp. 9–16; 163 (1961), pp. 15–18; but cf. also Y. Yadin, *BASOR,* 196 (1969), pp. 37–45; G. W. van Beek and A. Jamme, *BASOR,* 199 (1970), pp. 59–65; J. L. Kelso, *ibid.,* p. 65; R. L. Cleveland, *BASOR,* 209 (1973), pp. 33–36.

[16] *ANET,* p. 487 (*RA*, 31, pp. 125-36).

[17] M. Nun, *Fishing and Fishes in the Bible and the Talmud* (Tel Aviv, 1964) (Hebrew).

[18] R. W. Hamilton, *QDAP,* 4 (1934), pp. 1–69.

[19] B. Maisler (Mazar), *IEJ,* 1 (1950–51), pp. 61–76, 125–40, 194–218.

[20] M. Dothan, *IEJ,* 9 (1959), pp. 271–72; 10 (1960), pp. 123–25.

[21] C. F. A. Schaeffer, *Ugaritica,* IV (Paris, 1962, p. 142; J. Nougayrol, *Le Palais Royal d'Ugarit,* VI (Paris, 1970), Nos. 79, 9, 16 and 156; A. F. Rainey, *Israel Oriental Studies,* 3 (1973), pp. 60-61.

[22] *ANET,* p. 26.

[23] *ANET,* p. 287.

[24] H. Tadmor, *BIES,* 24 (1960), pp. 173–74 (Hebrew).

[25] B. Parker, *Iraq,* 23 (1961), p. 42.

[26] *ANET*[2], p. 505.

[27] N. Glueck, *BASOR,* 72 (1938), pp. 2–13.

[28] S. Yeivin, *JEA*, 48 (1962), pp. 75-80.

[29] K. Galling, *Biblisches Reallexikon* (Tübingen, 1937), Sp. 95–8.

[30] Noth, *Josua,* p. 72; F. M. Cross and J. T. Milik, *BASOR,* 142 (1956), p. 16.

[31] A. L. Oppenheim, *JAOS*, 93 (1973), pp. 259–66.

[32] W. F. Albright, "Tell Beit Mirsim III", *AASOR,* 21–2 (1943), §§36–40.

[33] Galling, *op. cit.* (note 29), Sp. 153; B. Maisler (Mazar), *BASOR*, 102 (1964), pp. 7 ff.

CHAPTER II

The Land of Many Contrasts

Palestine, in spite of its limited area, is divided into many smaller districts which differ radically from one another. Most of the Jordan Valley, including the Sea of Galilee, down to about 40 miles south of the Dead Sea is below sea level. Its depression culminates at the Dead Sea, the surface of which is 1,275 feet below sea level, the lowest point on earth. Due to this deep cleavage the country is divided longitudinally into four distinct geographical strips: the coastal plain, the central mountain range, the Jordan rift and the Transjordanian highlands.

The differences of altitude between these neighbouring regions is enormous. The mountains of western Palestine rise in several points to a height of more than 3,000 feet, i.e. in Upper Galilee, in the Hebron area and Mount Ramon in the Negeb. In most areas their height is not less than 1,500-2,000 feet. The mountain plateau of Transjordan is even higher than this. Its average level is 2,000–2,500 feet, and its peaks reach more than 3,000 feet at many points, exceeding 5,000 feet in Edom. The snow-capped heights of Lebanon and Anti-Lebanon, which achieve altitudes of 8,000–9,000 feet, are the towering summits of the whole Levant but are separated from one another by the steep descents of the deep cleft between them. Due to these extreme variations of altitude over small distances, combined with the fluctuations of climate between desert and sea, the main characteristic of Palestine is its mountainous and chopped up appearance. Though in itself quite small, it is divided into many tiny regions, each possessing its own peculiar geographical features.[1]

Smaller fissures cut latitudinally across the country, especially in the north, and divide the principal longitudinal sections into their main subdivisions. The most prominent of these is the Jezreel Valley, separating Galilee from Mount Ephraim, which bisects the longitudinal barriers and thus comprises the most direct west–east passage through Palestine.

The four longitudinal zones of Palestine are subdivided, therefore, into the following subdivisions (cf. map 2):

I. THE COASTAL ZONE

This strip is narrow at the north but broadens considerably towards the south as the coastline swings westward. The shore line is generally characterized by a strip of shifting sand dunes which has forced the *Via Maris* to move farther inland. Consequently, the major towns in the coastal region were not generally situated directly on the shore but grew up along the highway farther east. This international trade route (cf. *infra,* pp. 45 ff.), combined with the rich alluvial soil, the abundance of springs and the high ground-water level, have made of the coastal plain the richest region of Palestine as well as the most densely populated in most periods. This is also true for the Jezreel Valley, which may best be reckoned as an eastern continuation of the coastal zone.

1. The Plain of Acco

This northernmost coastal plain is delimited by two steep mountain ridges which rise abruptly from the Mediterranean: the white, wave-beaten cliff of Rosh HaNiqra (Ras en-Naqurah) "the Ladder of Tyre", to the north; and the venerated and forested Carmel to the south. In the south-east it is connected with the Jezreel Valley by a narrow strip between the Carmel and the hills of Lower Galilee, through which the Kishon River winds its way.

Acco, one of the most important harbour cities of Palestine, lies on the northern end of the broad Acco-Haifa bay, protected somewhat from the north-west winds. The city divides the plain into two approximately equal parts, both of which were densely populated in antiquity. In the northern part the shore is rocky and without sand dunes; thus both the arable lands and the road approach the coast. Second in importance to Acco was Achzib, the northern harbour town which is situated on the mouth of the dry Nahal Keziv (Wadi Qarn) and protected from the sea by rocks and small islands.

The Haifa bay is made shallow by heavy deposits of sand which also cover the southern part of the Acco Plain to an extent of several miles. These sand dunes block the outflow of the rivers and thus tend to create marshes, thereby pushing the roads and limits of cultivable soil farther to the east. The only additional harbour was therefore at the southern end of the bay, i.e. Tell Abu Huwam on the mouth of the Kishon River. It flourished during the end of the Canaanite period and the early days of the Monarchy. The other perennial river of the south plain is the Na' aman, which rises in the centre of the plain and flows northward until it breaks through to the sea near Acco. Its main spring is dominated by Tell el-Kurdaneh, probably ancient Aphek (Josh. 19. 30; Judg. 1. 31). The most important city of the southern Acco Plain in the biblical period was Achshaph, which has been identified only tentatively with Khirbet Harbaj seven miles south-east of Haifa.

2. The Jezreel Valley

This is the largest valley bisecting the central mountain range and the

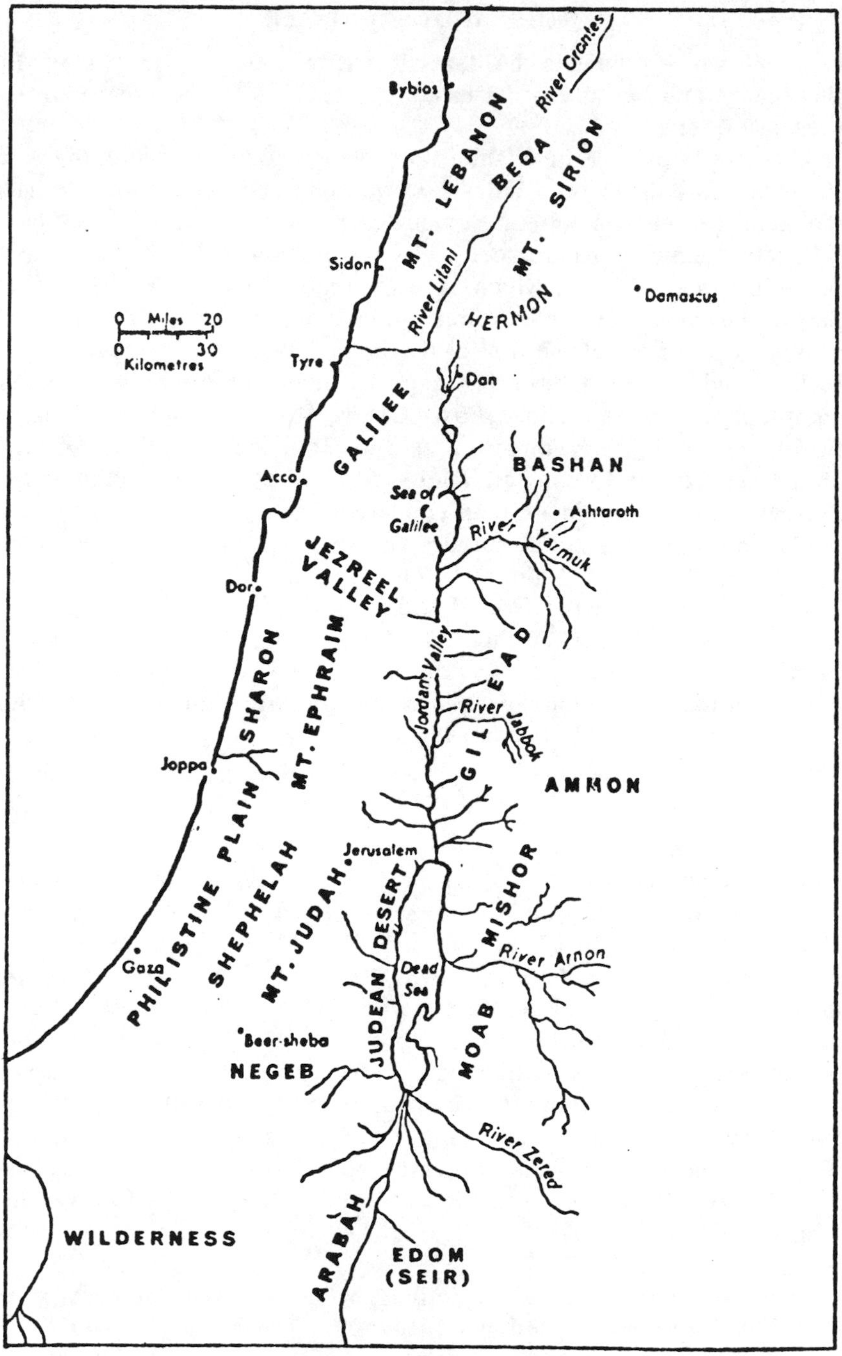

Map 2. The Geographical Regions of Palestine.

only one which connects the coastal area with the Jordan Valley. For this reason and because of its basic features it is best enumerated with the coastal zone.

The narrow pass of the Kishon River which connects it with the Acco Plain is guarded on both sides by two relatively small but obtrusive mounds, Tell el-'Amr (Geba-Somen ?) on the west and Tell el-Qassis (Helkath ?) on the east. Jezreel, a city of Issachar and the winter capital of the Omride Dynasty, which gave the valley its name in the Israelite period, lies at its eastern extremity, rather high up on a spur of Mount Gilboa. Opposite it at the foot of the Hill of Moreh is Shunem, and the high ground between them was the most convenient link between Mount Ephraim and Lower Galilee. East of Jezreel rises the spring of Harod, flowing in an easterly direction to the Beth-shean Valley, which is already part of the Jordan rift. The Jezreel Valley proper, to the west of Jezreel, forms approximately an equilateral triangle, each side about 20 miles long. Ibleam is at its southern vortex, and its two upper points are Jokneam to the west and Mount Tabor to the east.

The importance of the Jezreel Valley lies in its rich alluvial soil and the principal branches of the *Via Maris* which crossed it in several directions (cf. *infra*, pp. 52 f.). Its main cities were along the western side, guarding the various passes from the Sharon: Jokneam, Megiddo, Taanach and Ibleam. Between Megiddo and Mount Tabor many crucial battles were fought during the long history of Palestine, and the control of *The Valley* was always a major objective of the rival powers.

3. *The Sharon*

The coastal plain from the Carmel range to the vicinity of Joppa is called the Sharon. This name, which also applied to other regions in Palestine (e.g. 1 Chron. 5. 16), is taken by some to mean "level country", but more likely means "forested region", which aptly describes its nature in antiquity and fits well the various biblical allusions (Isa. 33. 9; 35. 2, etc.).[2]

The Sharon Plain is dominated by the strip of Mousterian red sand which covers its central part to a distance of seven-eight miles from the shore. In this area grew the famous oak trees (the Sharon withstood deforestation because of the uselessness of the red sand for agriculture in antiquity). Between it and the coast there is a range of *kurkar* hills which are an obstacle to the drainage of the river valleys, thus promoting swamps.

These conditions restricted settlement in the western part of the Sharon, which concentrated mainly along the few stream beds that wind their way to the coast. Most of the area remained free for "the herds that pastured in Sharon" (1 Chron. 27. 29). The principal segment of the *Via Maris* was forced to swing to the east, and here, between the red sand and the hilly region, there also lay the chain of important cities from Aphek (Antipatris) on the sources of the Yarkon in the south to Socoh (1 Kings 4. 10), Yaḥam, and Gath(-padalla) farther north.

The two main harbours of the Sharon were at its northern and southern extremities, viz. Dor and Joppa. Dor commanded two small bays enclosed by rocks. It was probably founded as a naval base during the New Egyptian Empire, enjoyed prosperity as a centre of navigation under one of the Sea Peoples (the Tjeker/Tjekel [Sicel ?]) and became the main harbour city of northern Israel. The sea at Joppa (2 Chron. 2. 16; Ezra 3. 7) was poorly protected by a chain of rocks, but this important city served as the main harbour for Jerusalem and Judea in most periods.

4. The Philistine Coast

The southernmost coastal area is named after the Philistines. They settled there during the twelfth century B.C. and became henceforth the dominating population of the southern coast. Eventually their name came to be applied to the whole country (Palestine) through the mediation of the classical world.

The coastal plain broadens in the south, the red sand disappears gradually, and the heavy alluvial soil is more and more mixed with wind-borne loess. This made traffic much easier, and the roads moved unhindered in all directions, separated from the shore only by the strip of sand dunes. Rainfall decreases in the south; however, as far down as the Gaza region it still suffices for growing good crops of grain on the plains. These virtues combined with the important trade routes made the Philistine coast one of the richest and most desirable regions of the country.

Gaza, the southernmost coastal city, was the metropolis of the area for long periods and served as a regional capital of Canaan during its domination by Egypt. It was rivalled by Ashkelon and Ashdod. Only Ashkelon lay on the coast proper, because of a gap in the dunes. It became, therefore, the main Philistine harbour, though the other cities also had anchorages on the shore. Farther inland lay Gath (Tell eṣ-Ṣafi ?) and Ekron (Khirbet el-Muqanna‘), which were the main rivals in the Judean Shephelah.

5. The Shephelah

Between the southern coastal plain and the Judean mountains there is a hilly region built of Eocene limestone called the Shephelah, i.e. "Lowland" from the standpoint of the Israelite mountain population. It was famous for its olives and especially sycamore trees (1 Chron. 27. 28; 1 Kings 10. 27, etc.) and was densely settled in antiquity.

The Shephelah was a most valued part of the Judean kingdom, fortified by a chain of fortresses against the Philistines and more distant enemies. Its most important fortified cities stood on the various valleys through which the roads led to the mountains of Judah: Gezer, Aijalon and Beth-horon on the Valley of Aijalon; Beth-shemesh, Timnah and Zorah on the Valley of Sorek (Wadi Ṣarar); Socoh and Azekah on the Valley of Elah; Lachish and Mareshah on the road to Hebron. The frequent references to these cities in the Bible are due to the many battles fought in their vicinity.

6. The Western Negeb

The 300-mm. annual rainfall line which passes 10–15 miles north of Beersheba marks the border of the Negeb, the "Dryland" in the south. Beer-sheba and Raphia on the coast have an average annual rainfall of 200 mm., and south of them humidity declines rapidly into arid desert conditions. The Negeb proper is the strip of about 30 miles between the 300- and 100-mm. lines, with Beer-sheba in the centre.

In this territory settlement and agriculture are still possible, but only under special conditions. It is a level area, rising slowly up to 800–900 feet near Beer-sheba, covered mostly by the fine and fertile loess. The problems of settlement are water and the nomads of the adjacent deserts. Rainfall varies greatly from year to year and therefore droughts are frequent. Even in different areas of the Negeb itself variations may be drastic, and so we find the patriarchs at Gerar in the western Negeb during years of drought. In addition to this climatic difficulty there is constant danger from the marauding Bedouin; the looting of various Negeb settlements by the Amalekites during David's absence from Ziklag (1 Sam. 30) is a typical example. Settlement in the Negeb was possible therefore only under a strong and interested government which was able to resist the Bedouin and assist the settlers in times of drought, and this occurred only during restricted periods. Even in modern times the Negeb lacked any permanent settlement until the foundation of Beer-sheba by the Turks with German help at the beginning of this century and the resettlement of the area by the State of Israel.

More continuous settlements existed only along the great river beds of the northern Negeb. These usually dry wadies collect water on rainy days from vast areas. The situation is also aggravated by floods from the desert mountains and southern Judah. For a day or two or, more frequently, for only a few hours they turn into dangerous torrents, and "the water-courses in the Negeb" (Psalm 126. 4) became proverbial for their sudden coming and disappearance. Most of these floods swept into the Mediterranean and were useless in antiquity; however, along these river beds are located most of the springs and wells of the Negeb which were essential for permanent habitation, especially in early periods.

The two major wadies of the western Negeb are Wadi esh-Shari' ah (the biblical Valley of Gerar) and Wadi Shallaleh (the biblical Besor ?), which join in their last segment. Along them lay the important centres of the area: Tell esh-Shari' ah (Ziklag ?) and Tell Abu Hureireh (Gerar) on Wadi esh-Shari' ah; Tell el-Far' ah (Sharuhen) and Tell Jemmeh (Yurza ?) on Wadi Shallaleh.

II. THE CENTRAL MOUNTAIN RANGE

This ridge of hills rises sharply from the coastal plain and the Shephelah, and its highlands are generally more spacious and convenient in the north but relatively narrower in the south. Appreciable portions of this region were forested in antiquity, but most of the forests were cut down when settlement took place, being replaced by fruit trees planted on terraces buttressed by stones to prevent erosion. With the devastation of the country and the decline of its population, many of the cultivated slopes fell into neglect, the terrraces collapsed, and much of the fruitful soil was swept down the now-barren hillsides. Many of these slopes are presently only fit for reforestation where the process of creating new top soil has begun anew.

The mountain range is divided from north to south into four main regions: Galilee, Mount Ephraim, the mountains of Judah and the mountains of the Negeb.

1. Galilee

As the highest and northernmost of the mountain regions, Galilee is the coolest and most lush of them all, reminding one of the densely vegetated Lebanon. Spotted with small villages, blanketed by olives and various fruit trees, it was relatively isolated from the main arteries of commerce and centres of government. Its role as a kind of *hinterland* was much more important than would appear from the historical sources.

Galilee is divided into northern Upper Galilee which reaches elevations of more than 3,000 feet and southern Lower Galilee, the highest peaks of which remain below 2,000 feet. The border between both is most strikingly marked by a steep slope which rises almost vertically 1,500–2,000 feet, making communications between them most difficult.

Upper Galilee is a mountain plateau, having its highest portions in the south and sloping gradually to a level of 1,500–1,800 feet in the north. It extends as far as the deep gorge of the River Liṭani-Qasimiyah which separates it from the mountains of Lebanon. The highest southern parts are difficult mountainous terrain which raised many obstacles to habitation and were thickly forested in antiquity. The northern areas consisted of spacious tablelands with a multitude of springs offering ample opportunities for settlements, which were much more numerous here in most periods; however, little is known about them from our sources. Perhaps the largest and most important of them was "Kedesh in Galilee in the hill country of Naphtali" (Josh. 20. 7, *et al.*), which lay in its eastern zone, overlooking the northern Jordan Valley. It is now just inside Israel territory on the Lebanese border, which leaves most of the Upper Galilean tableland in the modern State of Lebanon.

Lower Galilee is the most level of all the hill regions and it is actually an intermediate zone made up of low mountain ranges with shallow, broad expanses between them. Four major valleys bisect it latitudinally from east to west; however, none of their names is known from the Bible. They are from north to south: the Valley of Beth-Kerem (esh-Shaghur) in which is located biblical Ramah (Josh. 19. 36); the Valley of Sakhnin; the valley of Beth-netopha (Sahl el-Baṭṭof) with Hannathon (Josh. 19. 14) guarding its western outlet; the Valley of Tur‘ an with the extinct volcano, the "Horns of Ḥaṭṭin", at its eastern end. Except for the isolated Mount Tabor this latter is the most distinct landmark of Lower Galilee. On top of it stood the largest and strongest city of the area, possibly Shemesh-adam of the Egyptian sources, Adamah of Naphtali (Josh. 19. 36). Southeast of it stretches Arḍ el-Ḥima, the biblical valley of Jabneel (Josh. 19. 33), through which ran the most important thoroughfare of Lower Galilee, the Darb el-Ḥawarnah, connecting the Jordan Valley with Acco (cf. *infra,* p. 60). The most important early cities lay along this road, while other parts were mostly forested up to the Israelite period. Between the Jabneel and the Beth-shean valleys lies the rather low basaltic plateau of Issachar, drained in its centre by the Nahal Tavor (Wadi Bireh). Its settlement was rather sparse, due to the decreasing amount of rain. Its most imposing site is Kokab el-Hawa, the Belvoir of the Crusaders. Though less than 1,000 feet high, it is about 1,500 feet above the Jordan Valley and offers a magnificent view of Northern Gilead. It was possibly Jarmuth of Issachar (Josh. 21. 29), and the whole region is called Mount Jarmuth in an Egyptian stele from Beth-shean (cf. *infra*, p. 179).

Due to the many mountain ranges and faults which cross Galilee, traffic in a north–south course is most difficult. Roads of more than local significance only traversed Galilee in an east-west direction.

2. Mount Ephraim

This is the central part of the hill region and the most important from the standpoint of settlement.

The tribe of Ephraim, who gave it his name,[3] actually occupied only its southern part. The northern portion was inhabited by Manasseh, both tribes being sons of Joseph. To the south of Ephraim settled Benjamin, whose name in Hebrew means "the son of the south". Its eponymous ancestor was reckoned as the younger brother of Joseph. Though Manasseh was the first-born, Ephraim became stronger according to the blessing of Jacob (Gen. 48. 14 ff.). These genealogical relations obviously reflect the actual situation of the tribes in the central hill country. Later in the period of the Monarchy, with the founding of

Samaria, the name of this new capital gradually replaced the name of Ephraim as the general designation for the whole area.

Quite distinct geographical differences exist between the tribal areas of Ephraim and Manasseh, i.e. the southern and northern sections of Mount Ephraim. The southern part is the higher one, comprising a mountain plateau rising to more than 3,000 feet at its highest point, viz. Baal Hazor (Tell'Aṣur) north of Bethel. Like central Judea it is built of Cenomanian limestone, resistant to erosion and weathering into the fertile *terra rossa*; hence its extensive vegetation and the dense habitation which followed its deforestation. The main north–south road follows the watershed, which is near the eastern side of the plateau. The western and still more the eastern slopes are cut by many deep stream beds, which comprise a serious obstacle to passage. It is therefore a most fertile area, traversed by a good longitudinal road and guarded on both sides by difficult approaches. Its main cities, like Mizpah, Bethel and Shiloh, stood along or near the principal mountain road (cf. Judge. 21. 19, etc.).

The northern part of Mount Ephraim is lower, built mainly of less fertile Eocene limestone and broken by quite extensive Senonian valleys. Though less fruitful, it was traversed by convenient roads in all directions, enjoying the benefits and disadvantages of easy communications. Its urbanization was therefore earlier and more extensive, and its main cities developed at the principal road junctions: Shechem, between Mount Ebal and Mount Gerizim, Tappuah at the border of Ephraim (Josh. 17. 8), Tirzah at the head of the eastern descent of Wadi Far' ah, Dothan in the north and later Samaria in the west. Shechem, the ancient capital of Mount Ephraim, is actually the first city of Palestine mentioned in the description of an Egyptian military campaign (cf. *infra*, p. 147), a fact which fits well its situation and importance.

3. *The Judean Hill Country*

In its main features the mountainous area of Judah is similar to southern Mount Ephraim: it is a Cenomanian limestone plateau, guarded by steep slopes and traversed by a good north–south road near its eastern edge, along which lay its main cities, like Jerusalem, Bethlehem, Beth-zur and Hebron. It, too, has fertile soil, excellent for fruit trees, vines and other plants, if it is retained by terraces built on the slopes. Towards the south rain diminishes, and the land gradually becomes suitable mainly for pastorage.

Almost immediately east of the watershed begins the Judean Desert. Jerusalem and the other principal cities actually lie on the edge of the desert, and from high points one enjoys a magnificent view across the yellowish wilderness to the blue of the Dead Sea with the reddish-violet mountains of Moab beyond.

The eastern slopes of the Judean mountains are an almost complete desert because of the steep descent of more than 3,000 feet over a distance of only 10–15 miles. Most of this is an outcrop of soft and porous Senonian limestone, which intensifies the consequences of the minimal rainfall. Due to the steep slope most of the wadies do not join, but have cut for themselves deep stream beds, forming vast canyons and cliffs in areas of harder Cenomanian rock. The last "stage" above the Dead Sea consists of almost vertical cliffs, rising to a height of 1,500 feet and more, broken every few miles by grandiose canyons. This shelf is a most serious obstacle to roads, which can climb it only via difficult and treacherous passes. Besides the oasis of En-gedi and some smaller, less-permanent forts and settlements, the wilderness of Judah never possessed any permanent habitation. Its western zone was used mainly as pasture for small cattle during the spring, and its various sections were called after the neighbouring villages, like the wilderness of Tekoa, of Ziph, of Maon, etc. However, this nearby desert with its chasms and hidden caverns played an important role during many periods as a place of refuge for rebels, fugitives and hermits. Its dry caves have become, during recent years, one of the principal treasuries for ancient scrolls and manuscripts. Thanks to this frightful wilderness the mountains of Judah are a rather isolated and closed country: the desert not only serves as an impassable guardian from the east, it also prevents a west–east passage through Judah. The Dead Sea by itself was indeed not a total obstacle to traffic, as there was a shallow ford opposite the Lisan and navigation may also have existed. However, combined with the difficulty of the Judean Desert, the various tracks leading eastwards had no more than local importance.

This makes the significance of Jerusalem more intelligible. Hebron lies in the centre of the Judean hills at its highest point (almost 3,000 feet) and was its ancient capital. Jersualem is situated near the northern border of Judah, actually on the same latitude as the northern end of the Dead Sea, and therefore its territory served as the southernmost thoroughfare to Transjordan. This line of communication, ascending to Jerusalem from Gezer, Aijalon and Beth-horon and descending to Jericho, was dotted with important cities from early times. Among these we should mentioned the cities of the Gibeonites northwest of Jerusalem, which were the prime factor in one of the major early clashes between the Israelites and the Canaanite city-states of Judah (Josh. 10). Jerusalem itself preserved its independence as a Jebusite town up to the days of David. This foreign stronghold constituted a border between Judah and Mount Ephraim, from which developed the antagonism between Judah and Israel, and Jerusalem always remained near the northern border of Judah. The boundary between Judah and Mount Ephraim was therefore created mainly by history, and no natural dividing line is visible in the mountainous terrain.

4. The Eastern Negeb

The eastern part of the Negeb is a continuation of the central mountain range. As in the west, its border is clearly defined by climatic conditions. About 15 miles south of Hebron the level of the terrain declines quite abruptly to only *c.* 1,500–1,800 feet. From this line begins the typical semi-arid climate of the Negeb, the rainfall diminishing quickly as one goes south. In spite of the relative height the loess-covered area is generally level, similar to the extensive plains of the western Negeb. However, even small differences in temperature and moisture increase the possibilities of agriculture and pasturage. This is proabably the reason that the eastern Negeb enjoyed somewhat more continuity of settlement than the lower Beer-sheba region. Its main cities were Arad and Hormah, situated on the eastern section of the large Nahal Be' er Sheva (Wadi Meshash). However, this part of the Negeb also saw long intervals without settlement when the only population was nomadic. Even today it lacks any permanent settlement, except for the construction of modern cities.

Ancient Aroer, *c.* 15 miles south-east of Beer-sheba, is near the border of permanent settlement even in the heyday of this area. Farther south the large desert wastes begin; these were not reckoned as part of the Negeb but are called in the Bible the wilderness of Zin, of Paran, of Sinai, etc. The mountains rise gradually until they reach a level of more than 3,000 feet at Răs Raman, 55 miles south of Beer-sheba. The higher tablelands of this region enjoys a relatively larger amount of rainfall, which allows some farming. However, in the biblical period it was mainly the roads leading to Egypt, Sinai and Edom that were of importance. They were guarded by a chain of fortresses, and under their protection there developed here and there some temporary settlements, widely dispersed over vast areas.

The eastern part of the southern mountains is broken by three magnificent depressions: Wadi Ḥaḍireh (the Little Makhtesh, "mortar"), Wadi Ḥathireh (the Great Makhtesh) and the still larger Wadi Raman (Makhtesh Ramon). They mark the end of any settlement or agriculture. East of them is the completely barren and wild desert, cut by large stream beds and gorges created in the Pluvial period. This is the wilderness of Zin on the southern border of the land of Canaan.

III. THE JORDAN RIFT

This great fissure is the main factor that has shaped the Palestinian landscape. It is a long and deep depression with an average width of 10 miles, in the centre of which the Jordan flows down from the base of Hermon to the Dead Sea. From an altitude of about 300 feet in the north it descends to 1,200 feet below the Mediterranean at the shore of the Dead Sea, the lowest point on earth. From here the valley floor rises again gradually to about 750 feet above the sea, the highest point of the Arabah, and then slopes down again to the shore of the Red Sea. Still more important than this absolute level is its relative depth *vis-à-vis* the mountains on both its sides. The slopes are generally steep and sudden, sometimes forming huge precipices. To the west the mountain range rises in many places 3,000 feet and more above the rift, and the eastern mountains are still higher. This has made the Jordan rift a sharp dividing line between the two mountainous areas and is the reason for its completely different climate. Even in the north it is relatively warm and dry and in the south there are desert conditions, and the temperatures are the highest in the country. Wherever there exist springs or rivers a tropical vegetation develops. The Jordan rift may be conveniently divided into the following five areas:

1. The Huleh Valley

Its northern portion begins with biblical Ijon and consists of a valley (albeit at *c.* 1,800 feet elevation) bounded on the west by the Liṭani River and on the east by snow-covered Mount Hermon. This fertile and well-watered district with its cool and refreshing climate lies mostly in the modern State of Lebanon. It is probably the biblical land or valley of Mizpeh (Josh. 11. 3, 8), the border between Israel, Phoenicia and Aram in biblical times.

Nine miles south of Ijon was Abel-beth-maacah, situated just south of Metulla, the modern frontier village of Israel. To the east of it lay Dan with its royal sanctuary, which symbolized the ancient Israelite boundary. These are the Israelite-Aramean frontier posts mentioned on several occasions (1 Kings 15. 20; 2 Kings 15. 29, etc.).

In the vicinity of Abel the valley descends quite suddenly to a level of about 300 feet. One of the smaller sources of the Jordan which passes near Abel leaps over this step in a gushing waterfall. The main sources of the Jordan originate in the north-eastern part of the valley, fed by the melting snows of Hermon. One major spring starts below the ground at Dan and the other three miles east of it below Caesarea Philippi (Baniyas), today in Syrian territory.

The various sources of the Jordan flow through the central part of the Huleh Valley, joining and then parting once again farther down where marshes abound. Near its southern end was the small Lake Huleh, blocked in the south by masses of basalt, now mainly dried up by an artificial deepening of the Jordan outlet.

South-west of the lake lay Hazor, dominating the southern edge of the Huleh Valley. It drew its main importance from the junction between the north-south road and the route to Damascus which crossed the Jordan at the only possible fording place just below the lake, today marked by the Bridge of Jacob's Daughters.

2. Chinnereth

Below Lake Huleh the valley makes another sudden descent through a rocky basaltic area in which the Jordan has cut a deep channel bed. The shore of Lake Huleh is 210 feet above sea level, that of the Sea of Galilee, the biblical Chinnereth, is 630 feet below sea level, and the distance between them is only 10 miles. After the draining of the small Lake Huleh, the Sea of Galilee is today the only natural sweet-water lake of Palestine. Its length is 13 miles, and its maximum width reaches seven miles. Its waters are usually smooth and dark blue, and its abundance of fish was probably exploited from most ancient times. However, it is also famous for its sudden storms which blow down from the surrounding mountains and transform it into a boiling cauldron.

The Sea of Galilee is surrounded by narrow valleys, broadening only a little in the north and the south. Though small, their fertile alluvial soil, the abundance of water and the hot climate make these valleys some of the most densely and continuously populated areas of the country. The city of Chinnereth, situated on the north-western shore above the "seven springs" of Heptapegon (Ṭabghah) on the main road to Hazor, gave the lake its name in the biblical period. Later it was called Lake Tiberias after the main city which was founded farther to the south between ancient Hammath and Rakkath. At the south-western edge of the lake there once flourished the tremendous site of Beth-yeraḥ, guarding the outflow of the Jordan. This was one of the country's major cities in the third millennium B.C. During the second millennium the smaller mound of el-ʻAbeidiyeh, situated on the Jordan two miles south of the lake, took its place. This latter was probably ancient Yenoʻ am, which dominated the roads bisecting the area. A few miles farther south the Jordan is joined by the Yarmuk, which carries about the same amount of water. The triangle between the two rivers and the lake is a most fertile and populated area; near Yenoʻ am prehistoric remains have been discovered which rank among the most ancient in the world.

The beautiful scenery of the lake and its surroundings, the warm climate, rich vegetation and several hot mineral springs make the vicinity of Chinnereth a veritable healing resort for both body and soul.

3. The Jordan Valley

The Jordan Valley proper is the strip approximately 70 miles long between the Sea of Galilee and the Dead Sea. The river has carved a deep and winding course for itself through the centre of the valley; it is not navigable and flows too deeply for its waters to have been exploited by primitive methods. Only a narrow strip close to the river's course, sometimes up to one mile broad, is occasionally flooded. There one finds a dense and entangled vegetation. This is the *Zor* in Arabic, *ge' on hayyarden* in biblical Hebrew, i.e. "the pride" or the lush region of the Jordan, also rich in fauna, where lions were still to be seen in biblical times (Jer. 49. 19, etc.). Above it lies the main part of the Jordan Valley, the *Ghor,* divided from the *Zor* by a broken and desolate slope. This area is quite desertlike due to its scanty rainfall, with the exception of sections watered by springs or tributaries of the Jordan. Of course, the water has to be caught on higher ground and brought to the fields by canals or aqueducts. This is the reason for the different appearance of the Jordan Valley in various periods, sometimes dismal and yellow, like a desert, and at other times green and lush with rich, tropical foliage (cf. Gen. 13. 10).

Only a very few perennial rivers come down from the west. The most important is the Jalud River in the Beth-shean Valley, the eastern continuation of the Jezreel Plain. This valley was most densely settled in the Canaanite and Israelite periods, and its principal city was Rehob, situated five miles south of Beth-shean. This city is not mentioned in the Bible; however, it appears frequently in Egyptian sources. Farther south and of some importance was Wadi Far‘ ah, which leads down from Tirzah to the ford at Adam. This was the best road connecting Mount Ephraim with Transjordan, and the vicinity of Adam was famous for the occasional landslides which dammed the floods of the Jordan (Josh. 3. 16). From here down to the Jericho oasis near the Dead Sea the western Jordan Valley is a virtual desert.

The eastern side of the Jordan Valley is watered by many more rivers and therefore we find here a chain of important cities from the Sea of Galilee in the north to the Dead Sea in the south. The largest river, besides the Yarmuk, is the Jabbok, which reaches the Jordan at Adam. Along its course were Succoth and Zarethan (probably Tell Umm Hamad) and farther to the east Penuel and Mahanaim (eastern and western Tulul edh-Dhahab).

North of Succoth was Zaphon, probably Tell es-Sa‘ idiyeh on the Wadi Kufrinjeh. Still farther north, on Wadi Malawi opposite Rehob, was ancient Peḥel, the Pella of the Decapolis, which also remained unmentioned in the Bible in spite of its importance. This is also the case with other mounds situated on the various smaller rivers, like the river of Jabesh (Wadi Yabis), named after ancient Jabesh-gilead which was situated higher up in the mountains.

South of the Jabbok were Beth-nimrah on the waters of Nimrin (Wadi Nimrin), Abel-shittim on Wadi Kafrein, Beth-haram on Wadi Rameh and near the Dead Sea Beth-jeshimoth on Wadi ‘Aẓeimeh. The region around these latter is called the "plains of Moab", where the Israelites encamped before crossing the Jordan (Num. 33. 49, etc.).

4. The Dead Sea

The Jordan empties into the biblical Salt Sea, better known as the Dead Sea because its high salt content resulting from the lack of a natural outlet except for evaporation prevents any sort of marine life. The hot, stifling climate at this inland sea makes most normal vegetation impossible along its shores. Its minerals, particularly the potash, extracted in large artificial pools through evaporation, is today one of the most valued raw materials of the country. In antiquity only salt and the precious bitumen, which appears occasionally on its surface, were exploited. The sea is divided into two parts by the *Lisan,* a boot-shaped peninsular extending out from the eastern shore. The larger northern part, approximately 30 miles long, reaches a depth of 1,200 feet. On the other hand, the southern part, about 15 miles long, is only 30–35 feet deep. Geologists believe that this part was still shallower and only sank in relatively recent times. At the south-western point of the *Lisan* the sea is only 2.5 miles broad, and here was a passable ford which is attested in written sources as late as 1846.[4]

High cliffs rise on both sides of the Dead Sea, broken frequently by tremendous canyons. The shore is mostly narrow, especially on the eastern side where the Nubian sandstone rises immediately from the sea at many points, preventing any passage. Most of the soil is salty marl, and at the south-western corner of the sea stands Jebel Usdum (Mount Sedom), a salt mountain with strange shapes and projections, apparently reflected in the story of Lot's wife (Gen. 19. 26).

The general picture of the area is therefore a heavy, dead sea, surrounded by a salty desert and gigantic heights, covered by a dusty haze and an almost unbearable heat during most of the year (cf. Gen. 19. 28). Nevertheless, wherever rivers or springs of fresh water combine with arable land, oases of inexpressible beauty are found. On the western shore En-gedi is the only great oasis; its beauty and fertility is celebrated in the Song of Songs (1. 14). On the south-eastern corner was Zoar (eṣ-Ṣafi), situated on the delta of the River Zered (Wadi Ḥesa), and farther north-east of the *Lisan* is Mazra', possibly ancient Eglaim. To these oases of the Dead Sea we may also add Jericho, seven miles north-west of the sea, apparently the most ancient city of Palestine. The peculiar importance of these places lies in their tropical vegetation and especially the priceless spices grown there such as the henna blossoms and the famous *opobalsamon.*

5. *The Arabah*

The Arabah is the continuation of the Jordan rift between the Dead Sea and the Gulf of Elath (Aqabah). It is about the same length as the distance between Dan and the Dead Sea, i.e. about 110 miles. Today the name is restricted to this region, while in the Bible parts of the Jordan Valley were also called Arabah, and even the Dead Sea appears as "the sea of the Arabah" (Deut. 3. 17, etc.). The term Arabah is used as a virtual synonym for desert, and such it is. Enclosed between the mountains of the Negeb and the lofty slopes of Edom, it has a hot climate with only sporadic and fitful rainfalls. Just a few scanty springs which can support small oases occur here and there, mostly on the eastern side, and no perennial river exists in this area.

The main economic importance of the Arabah stems from the copper mines and the road which passed through it to Elath. Copper ore appears in the Nubian sandstone, and its main centres were in the north-eastern part of the Arabah at Punon (Feinan) and Ir-nahash (Khirbet Naḥas) and in its south-western corner in Wadi Mene' iyeh (Nahal Timna'). In the Iron Age and later in the Nabatean and Roman periods there was a chain of fortresses along the Arabah, guarding the strategic points and the water supply along the main highway. Its destination was Elath (Aqabah), the Red Sea port and transit station for the profitable trade with South Arabia and the East African coast. Control over Elath was therefore a prized objective of Israel, Edom and other rival powers. It was secured during the days of Solomon and later Judean kings by a strong fortress built at the centre of the Gulf of Elath that has been identified with "Ezion-geber, which is near Eloth on the shore of the Red Sea, in the land of Edom" (1 Kings 9. 26).

IV. THE TRANSJORDANIAN HIGHLANDS

In Transjordan the shape of a genuine mountain tableland, built up mainly from strata of Cenomanian and Senonian limestone, is preserved better than elsewhere. Below them are deep layers of hard Nubian sandstone laid bare mainly in the south and occasionally at the western edge of the plateau. The latter are barely porous to water; thus the presence of many perennial rivers in Transjordan is mainly attributable to the existence of the lower rock formations.

On the west the country is bordered by steep slopes descending to the Jordan rift. These high ridges arrest and cool the atmosphere, causing the large amount of rainfall which most parts of Transjordan enjoy. On the east the highlands gradually blend into the Syrian-Arabian Desert, and there exists no natural border but the wilderness itself. This is the reason why the fate of Transjordan is so closely intertwined with the desert. Burning siroccos in the spring and fall, and icy desert winds in winter sweep undisturbed over the tableland, rendering most difficult the cultivation of olive groves and vineyards, which are so common in western Palestine. The character of the country is therefore mainly pastoral, and wherever rain is sufficient wheat is the primary crop. Not only the winds but also the desert nomads sweep over Transjordan whenever central authority is weak, which explains the long intervals between periods of permanent occupation in its history, most strongly observable in the southern sections.

Most of the rainfall in Transjordan flows to the Jordan rift, due to its double watershed. One is near the western edge of the plateau, from whence the many short but deep rivers flow to the west. Most of the shallower easterly-directed rivers do not reach the desert but are caught on their way by one of the four great rivers: the Yarmuk, Jabbok, Arnon and Zered. These rivers and their main tributaries flow at their upper courses near the border of the desert in a south-north direction, breaking suddenly to the west, and finally reaching the Jordan or Dead Sea through deep gorges. They are the main obstacles to the roads in this area (cf. *infra,* pp. 54–56) and form the natural divisions of the country. It is no wonder, therefore, that they serve occasionally as political, ethnic or administrative boundaries. Thus the Zered is the border between Edom and Moab (Deut. 2. 13 f.), the Arnon between Moab and Israel (Deut. 3. 8, 16 etc.) and the Jabbok between Ammon and Israel (Num. 21. 24, Deut. 2. 37, etc.) as well as between Gad and the half-tribe of Manasseh (Deut. 3. 16, etc.). However, the two latter valleys actually cross and bisect geographical units which show no real topographical differences on both sides of the respective valleys. Therefore, most of the above-stated borders were only temporary, and the Bible emphasizes the geographical unity of these topographical zones. The area north of the Arnon is an integral part of Moab in various periods; Gilead stretches north and south of the Jabbok, and they are called the two halves of Gilead (Josh. 12. 2, etc.).

1. Bashan

Bashan is the northern district of Transjordan, situated mainly north of the Yarmuk. However, it is not clear if the Yarmuk was its actual border, and Edrei, one of its early capitals (Num. 21. 33; Deut. 3. 10, etc.), was situated on one of the eastern tributaries of the Yarmuk. Its southern border was apparently not far from the modern border between Syria and Jordan, which coincides with the Yarmuk in its lower course and follows its southern tributaries farther east.

Bashan is a most fertile basaltic tableland and the "cows of Bashan" were proverbial for carefree prosperity (Amos 4. 1, etc.). One of its areas, probably in the centre, was Argob, famous for its many great cities "with walls and bronze bars" (1 Kings 4. 13; Deut. 3. 4 f., etc.). Unfortunately, no major archaeological excavation has so far been carried out in the region; however, ancient sources and sporadic archaeological surveys indicate that settlement was early and continuous in contrast with the more southerly parts of Transjordan. The reason for this was probably not only the fertility of the soil but also Mount Hauran (Jebel Druze) which rises east of Bashan and guards it from the desert. This mountain range, whose snow-capped points reach heights of more than 5,000 feet, enjoys a large rainfall in spite of its eastern location. Because of its masses of basaltic rocks from geologically recent volcanoes, it is an isolated area, difficult to penetrate, famous for its independence in various periods. North-west of Mount Hauran lies the Leja, the Hellenistic Trachonitis. This area is a virtual basaltic desert, lacking almost any soil, which remained unsettled and untouched by roads. It was in all periods an ideal asylum for rebels and bandits, and hence its modern name of el-Leja, "The Refuge". Mount Hauran is probably the biblical Mount Bashan (Psalm 68. 15), ranking with Lebanon and Carmel (Isa. 33. 9; Jer. 22. 20, etc.) and famous for its oaks (Isa. 2. 13; Ezek. 27. 6, etc.).

The ancient capital of Bashan was Ashtaroth, which was later rivalled by neighbouring Karnaim. Its western part, the later Gaulonitis, was the country of Geshur, which kept its independence even during the reign of David (2 Sam. 13. 37 f.) and later became tributary to Aram. Bashan itself was a prized plum between Aram–Damascus and Israel, which was able to hold it only in major periods of strength.

2. *Gilead*

Gilead is a higher and more rugged mountain region which reaches altitudes of over 3,000 feet north and south of the Jabbok. It is made up mainly of hard Cenomanian limestone, and the red Nubian sandstone is exposed only in the Jabbok ravine. The mountainous area and the western slopes comprise therefore the larger, dominating part of the country, while the actual tableland is relatively narrow. The absence of any mountains to the east comparable to Mount Hauran brings the desert much nearer, about 25–30 miles from the Jordan rift, and the same situation prevails farther south.

The western slopes of Gilead and its mountainous regions were largely forested in antiquity, especially north of the Jabbok. Therefore, only a few early cities developed, mainly on the eastern plateau. The foremost among them was Rabbath-ammon ('Amman), situated near the desert fringe, which occupied an isolated and naturally well-fortified hill on one of the most south-easterly sources of the Jabbok. To the west of it lay Jaazer (Khirbet eṣ-Ṣar ?), and at the southern end of Gilead was Heshbon. The last two were conquered by the Israelite tribes of Reuben and Gad, which occupied mainly the southern half of Gilead. Due to the difficult terrain their economy remained principally pastoral. Reuben in particular preserved his semi-nomadic life on the edge of the desert (1 Chron. 5. 9). Rabbath-ammon, on the other hand, continued to serve as the capital of the small Ammonite kingdom. In spite of its limited territory between the desert and the mountainous area of southern Gilead, its importance and wealth was significant for its unrivalled domination of the King's Highway (cf. *infra,* p. 55). In certain periods it was well organized and fortified (cf. Num. 21. 24) and tried to enlarge its domain by annexing various parts of Gilead.

Northern Gilead, and especially the region near the Jabbok, remained largely forested even after the Israelite occupation (compare "the forest of Ephraim" near Mahanaim, 2 Sam. 18. 6) and formed, therefore, a limit for the Gadite settlement. Only farther north do we find settlements such as Jabesh-gilead in the mountainous area and Ramoth-gilead on the eastern plateau. The latter became one of the main Israelite border strongholds in the struggle against Damascus. Northern Gilead was settled, therefore, by various tribes, like Jair, which evidently occupied its north-western portions. During the period of the Judges it became a main colonization ground for the surplus population of the West-Palestinian tribes. The foremost among them was Manasseh (Machir), who became the dominant power of northern Gilead.

Gilead was the centre of the Israelite population in Transjordan and its name is sometimes extended to include virtually the whole Israelite zone of Transjordan. Its isolation from the western tribes is often felt in the biblical stories; however, the constant danger from the desert and the various rival kingdoms stimulated their interest in a united and strong monarchy. For this reason it became a land of refuge for various Israelite kings in times of political crisis.

3. Moab

Like the two halves of Gilead divided by the Jabbok, there are also two parts of Moab, divided by the deep river bed of the Arnon, which becomes near the Dead Sea one of the largest and most impressive ravines of Palestine. Both are basically similar: they consist of high tablelands, formed of Cenomanian limestone resting on Nubian sandstone, which is broadly exposed at its western side. They lie high above the Dead Sea, whose whole eastern shoreline forms the western border of Moab, separated from it by steep and frightening ascents. At the south the Wadi Ḥesa, probably the River Zered, divides it from Edom. Only in the north is there no natural border between Gilead and Moab, which are blended into one another along an approximate line ascending from the northern end of the Dead Sea, between Heshbon and Medeba.

For this reason the northern zone was always under dispute between Israel and Moab. This is a level tableland, 2,000–2,400 feet high, called in the Old Testament *the Mishor,* i.e. "the Plain" (Deut. 3. 10; 4. 43, etc.). Its main cities were Medeba in the north and Dibon in the south, both stations on the King's Highway. South-east of Dibon lay Aroer, the traditional border city of Israelite Transjordan, overlooking the passage of the highway through the Arnon (Josh. 12. 2; Jer. 48. 19, etc.). In spite of this Dibon was the native city and one of the capitals of Mesha, King of Moab, who took all the Mishor up to the vicinity of Medeba, as did previous and later rulers of Moab.

The nucleus of Moab to the south of the Arnon is higher, rising in the south to more than 4,000 feet. Little is known about its cities and villages from history, except for its capital Kir-hareseth or Kir of Moab, situated high up in an excellent strategic location overlooking the southern part of the Dead sea.

The economy of Moab remained virtually pastoral, as stated categorically by the narrator: "Now Mesha King of Moab was a sheep breeder . . ." (2 Kings 3. 4).

4. Edom

The last region of Palestine to be enumerated is Edom or Mount Seir, pointing like an outstretched finger into the desert. It consists of the high mountains to the east of the Arabah, built mainly of the red Nubian sandstone on a foundation of granite. Their altitude exceeds 5,000 feet in many instances and occasionally reaches heights of 5,600 feet and more. For this reason they enjoy an adequate rainfall in winter, but only on the western ascents and the western edge of the plateau. This long and narrow area which is fit for cultivation was largely covered by thick shrub-forests, which have been partly preserved even up to recent times. Due to them the region was called Mount Seir, "the hairy mountain".

Edom played a significant role in the earliest history of Israel, because its affiliations with the southern deserts were close. It is a difficult area, not easily accessible, and its many crevices and natural strongholds provide excellent places of refuge for the population in time of emergency. A chain of fortresses on the fringe of the desert gave added protection. Thus in both early and later periods it enjoyed considerable strength and independence.

However, these defences did not save the country from subjugation by a united Israel or by Judah in periods of strength. Their main purpose in the occupation of Edom was domination of the southern end of the King's Highway and the Arabah road, including control over the Red Sea port of Elath. These most important trade routes with South Arabia and the East African coast were the main source of wealth for Edom. The copper mines on both sides of the Arabah were probably of only secondary importance.

Foreign conquest was apparently facilitated by the broken and longitudinally extended nature of the country. Indeed we are not sure which was the capital of Edom, and at least in the early stages it probably moved from one city to another (Gen. 36. 31–9). Even in later periods there apparently existed two centres: Teman, near Rekem (Petra), in the south and Bozrah, between Sela (es-Sela') and Punon, in the north. The northern part was the first to be annexed in the days of Amaziah, who "took Sela by storm, and called it Joktheel . . ." (2 Kings 14. 7). Only his son Uzziah (Azariah) completed the conquest of

Edom, and "He built Elath and restored it to Judah, after the king slept with his fathers" (vs. 22).

Many passages in the Bible prove that the country's sharp division into these natural topographical units was quite clear to the early generations of settlers; each region had its own geographical designation. This is especially clear in western Palestine where the different areas are described in various summary passages (Deut. 1. 7; Josh. 10. 40; 11. 16; 12. 8; Judg. 1. 9). In these descriptions seven geographical units are mentioned: the hill country, the Shephelah, the sea coast, the slopes, the Arabah, the desert and the Negeb.

The Hill Country—the central mountain range, including mainly the hill country of Judah and Mount Ephraim.

The Shephelah—the range of low-lying hills running north and south between the Judean hill country and the coastal plain.

The Sea Coast—the coastal strip west of the Shephelah.

The Slopes—the steep descent from the hill country of the Jordan rift.

The Arabah—the Jordan rift, including its southern continuation to the Gulf of Aqabah, which is still referred to by that name today.

The Desert—in these biblical passages this refers to the wilderness of Judah which lies between the Judean hill country and the Dead Sea; as a wild, desolate and extremely broken region in close proximity to the settled areas, it played an important role in the history of the country.

The Negeb—the dry country; this refers to the southern regions south of the Judean hill country and the Shephelah beginning slightly to the north of Beer-sheba in the region where the annual rainfall decreases rapidly the farther south one goes (cf. map 2).

Between the hill region and the Negeb one finds the land of Goshen (Josh. 11. 16), which seems to be an exception to the general geographical designations in this description. Here we evidently have a reference to the broad intermediate zone designated as a border region between the hill country and the Negeb, because of the way that the Judean hills slope off in that direction.

Parallel descriptions of Transjordan are missing; the two inclusive geographical terms, Bashan and Gilead, referred to both the slopes and the tableland. Only in the south does the Bible recognize a geographical distinction of this nature between the plateau and the slopes descending towards the Dead Sea, as we learn from the expression "the slopes of Pisgah" at the north-eastern end of the Dead Sea (Deut. 3. 17; 4. 49; Josh. 12. 3; 13. 20).

To sum up, in spite of its limited size, Palestine is characterized by great variations in topography. Only short distances apart we find areas that differ from one another in nearly every respect, e.g. the mountainous, rain-swept Galilee and the tropical Jordan Valley, the fertile Transjordanian highland over against the barren Negeb and the wild Judean desert. The mountain slopes are steep, comprising natural divisions between the different regions. Therefore, it is no surprise that in the various periods of its history the population of each region was often quite different from that of the next, both in density as well as in social and ethnic composition. This situation was never conducive to national or political unity.

[1] For a description of the various regions cf. particularly G. A. Smith, *The Historical Geography of the Holy Land*[25] (London, 1931); F. M. Abel, *Géographie de la Palestine, I* (Paris, 1933); A. J. Braver, *Eretz Yisrael* (Tel Aviv, 1949) (Hebrew); D. Baly, *The Geography of the Bible*[2] (London, 1973).

[2] B. Maisler (Mazar), *Jerushalayim*, 4 (1952), pp. 16 f. (Hebrew).

[3] It is not impossible that this was the original name of the mountain, cf. *infra*, p. 210.

[4] T. J. Salmon and G. T. McCaw, *PEQ*, 1936, pp. 103–11.

CHAPTER III

Roads and Highways

In the history of Palestine and its various regions the network of roads was of prime importance because of their value as arteries for international commerce in the ancient Near East. Unlike the country's geographical structure which tended to induce fragmentation, the network of important roads crossing it encouraged political and economic unification, often under the authority of a foreign power.

The broken landscape of Palestine makes it so difficult to develop new routes or to modify the old ones that the pattern remained more or less fixed at all times. At key points dominating the major road junctions important cities were founded whose fate became inexorably linked with the economic and military development of their respective routes. Inasmuch as these roads passed through particular sectors and ignored others, they must be reckoned as one of the decisive factors in the development and concentration of the population into certain regions.

In a "land bridge" such as Palestine three types of route may be distinguished according to function and measure of importance: (1) international highways; (2) intra-regional roads; (3) local trails. Obviously this classification is quite schematic because the international routes changed according to historical circumstances, and even the "intra-regional roads" might be used by foreign caravans under certain conditions.

The routes may be recognized mainly by the stations that grew up along them. In the biblical period preparation of road beds was limited to removing rocks and levelling the surface where necessary with grading only at very difficult spots.[1] Road-making in this sense is mentioned in the Bible, e.g. "build up, build up the highway, clear it of stones" (Isa. 62. 10; cf. also 40. 3; 57. 14; 49. 11; Jer. 18. 15). Testimony similar to this apparently exists in the Amarna tablets, e.g. in the letter of a ruler from Bashan who declares that he has prepared the king's roads as far as Busruna (EA 199). The Egyptian Pharaoh probably required the Canaanite rulers to look after the repair and strengthening of roads in their respective regions. The fords of Nahr el-Kalb near Beirut were graded by pharaohs of the New Kingdom and renewed by conquerors who followed them. Likewise, Mesha, King of Moab, boasts

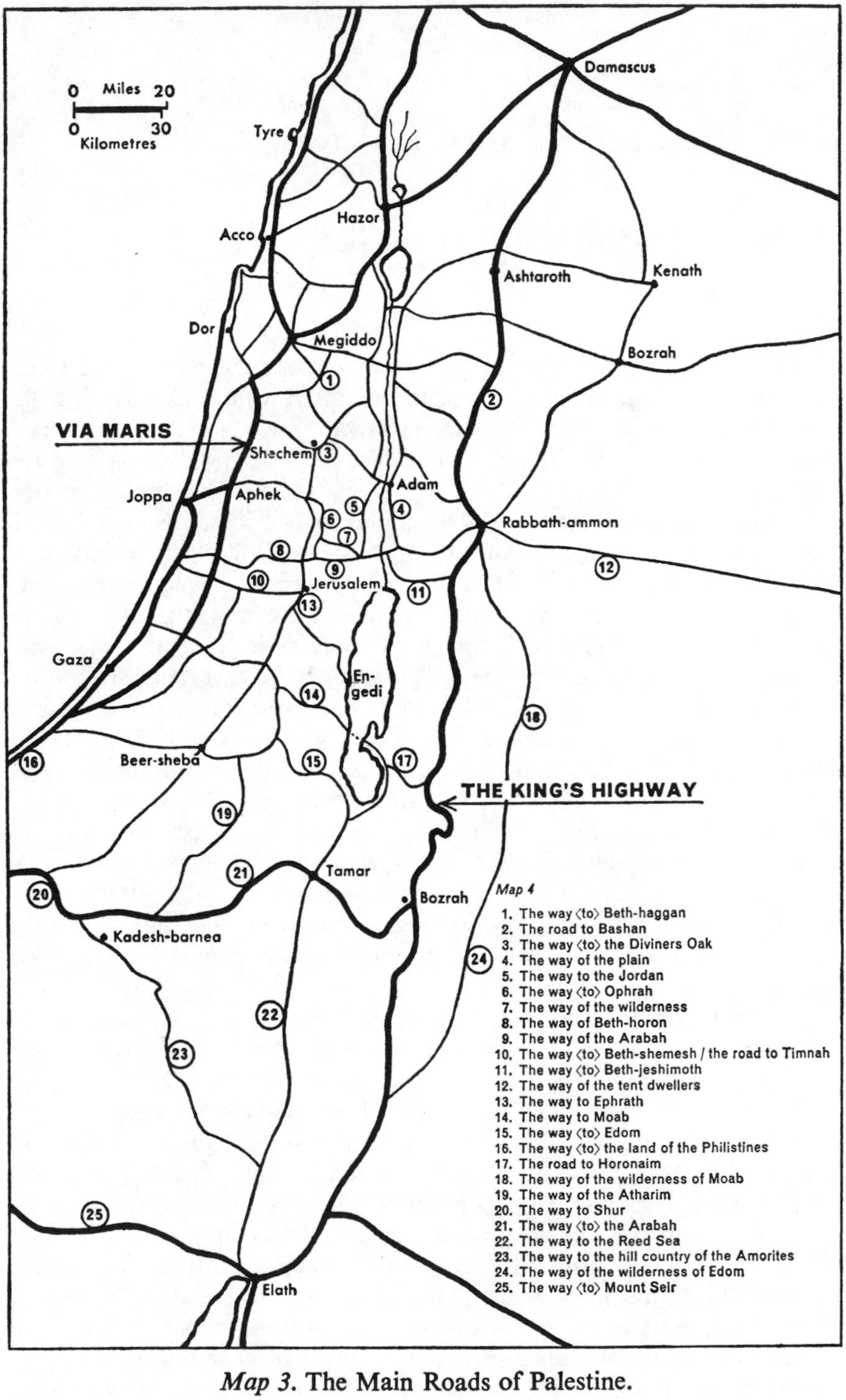

Map 3. The Main Roads of Palestine.

in the inscription on his stele that he built Aroer and prepared a highway at the Arnon (line 26), i.e. he constructed the Arnon crossing beside Aroer.

For reconstructing the road network three types of sources are at our disposal: (1) The names of the roads and their descriptions in the Bible and other ancient inscriptions, especially Egyptian and Assyrian. Here the information pertaining to this subject usually appears incidentally in connection with the description of journeys by people, caravans and armies. It must be stressed that routes which are given names in the Bible are usually designated by their terminal point, e.g. "the way to Shur" (Gen. 16. 7), viz. the road leading to Shur; "the way to Edom", the road going up to Edom (2 Kings 3. 20; RSV "the direction of Edom"), etc. It should be observed that most English translations take the Hebrew word road (דרך) only as a preposition, like towards or the direction of, etc. Although it is not always a proper name, it is at least a designation of a road leading to a certain locale. Examples are very rare of roads being named after some special feature or according to the vicinity through which they passed, e.g. the King's Highway. (2) Archaeological investigation which has revealed chains of settlements along the various routes. (3) The courses followed by later routes, e.g. Roman and even modern, on the assumption that in many sectors the road network remains fixed due to topographical conditions.

I. INTERNATIONAL HIGHWAYS

The important international highways are "The way of the sea", and "The King's Highway" (cf. map 3). The former, which runs the length of the country's coastline, is the most important of these; this is the *Via Maris* of later periods. It was in use during all historical periods, and along it there arose the most important and most ancient cities of the country. Over it passed messengers, caravans and countless military expeditions in every age. This route and its branches were always the great powers' prime objective in their conquests of Palestine-Syria. On the other hand, the King's Highway, as it is called in the Bible (Num. 20. 17; 21. 22), ran along the length of the Transjordanian range, close to the desert fringe. For long periods this route was the exclusive possession of nomads, who kept it free of any settlement or fortification. But at other times a chain of important settlements also developed along its length which were able to compete with those on the *Via Maris*.

1. The Way of the Sea

It is only natural that many testimonies concerning this route should have come down to us, especially in Egyptian and Assyrian records. The term "way of the sea" appears in the Bible only in the book of Isaiah (9. 1), which lists in succession: "the way of the sea, the land beyond the Jordan, Galilee of the nations". This passage concerns the conquest by Tiglath-pileser III and refers to the coastal region, Gilead and Galilee in which were founded the Assyrian districts of Dor, Gilead and Megiddo respectively. Isaiah calls the Israelite coastal region by the name of the important route which passed through it—"the way of the sea". North of the Plain of Sharon it splits off into several branches, and only the westernmost of these continues northward for the whole length of the Phoenician coast. The eastern branches pass through the Plain of Jezreel and go up from there to the Lebanese Beqaʿ, to Damascus and thence to Mesopotamia. This so-called "way of the sea" is called "the way to the land of the Philistines" in the Exodus story (Exod. 13. 17), i.e. the way to the Philistine coast. We shall deal with the route and its branches together, though it is doubtful that the term "way of the sea" applied to all of them as an entity. Latin versions of the Bible render Isaiah's "way of the sea" by the term *Via Maris.* During the Middle Ages the route from Damascus to the sea was known by this Latin name though no ancient Roman source ever used it as such. Perhaps in the medieval tradition, modern scholars have sometimes used *Via Maris* to denote the great trunk route coming from Egypt and crossing the land of Canaan towards Mesopotamia via Damascus. It is in this latter sense that we will use it in our ensuing discussion.[2]

The most inclusive document, which actually describes all the main branches of the *Via Maris,* is the geographical section in the letter by the Egyptian scribe Hori during the reign of Ramses II (Papyrus Anastasi I)[3]. In this epistle the Phoenician cities from Ṣumur in the north to the Plain of Acco in the south are listed first. From here the description turns inland to Hazor and Yenoʿ am which dominate the main fords in the Jordan Valley. It continues northwards to the Lebanese Beqaʿ as far as Kadesh, reaches the Damascus region, returns via the Golan to the Beth-shean area. From here the scribe turns his attention to Megiddo, describes the Wadi ʿAra, and continues to Joppa. In the last part of the letter, the desert section of the road from the Egyptian border to Raphia is described. These were the most important routes passing through Canaan during the New Kingdom period, the *Via Maris* and its various branches, and the Egyptian scribe was quite well acquainted with them.

The starting-point of this route from the Egyptian border is Sile (Egyptian: *ṯ-r*), perhaps *Silu* in the Amarna letters (EA 288), and *Sele* or *Selle* in Byzantine sources, today Tell Abu Ṣeifeh nearly two miles east of Qanṭarah.[4] This place is mentioned as the jumping-off point for many Egyptian campaigns, and one of the eastern Nile canals ran out to it.[5]

In Papyrus Anastasi I the place is called "the fortress of the ways of Horus", i.e. the ways of Pharaoh, the living embodiment of the god Horus on earth. The name "the ways of Horus" is applied to it in the Sinuhe story from the Middle Kingdom (twentieth century B.C.), and from here Sinuhe returns to the capital of Egypt by boat. Thus it would seem that the southern section of the *Via Maris* connecting Egypt with Palestine was called "the ways of Horus" by the Egyptians, i.e. Pharaoh's route, like the "King's Highway", because it was the established line of march for Egyptian troops heading northward.

This section was most essential to Egypt; and therefore a chain of forts was established on it, way stations and wells at fixed distances, to facilitate the passage of caravans and the army and to protect the route. Thus it is not fortuitous that from this segment of road the earliest itenary is preserved in Papyrus Anastasi I as well as a series of reliefs from the reign of Seti I describing the various stations. These latter may be considered a preliminary attempt at map making.

Both documents have been studied by Gardiner who arranged the stations in the two descriptions side by side[6]:

LIST OF STATIONS BETWEEN SILE AND GAZA

Bas Reliefs of Seti I	*Papyrus Anastasi I*
1. "The dividing waters"	
2. "The fortress of Sile"	"The Ways of Horus"
3. "The dwelling of the Lion"	"The dwelling of Ram Ses"
4. "The Migdol of Menma' rē' (Seti I)"	
5. "The well of *Ḥ-p-n*"	*Ḥ-ṯ-y-n**
6. "Buto of Sety-merenptaḥ"	"Tract of Buto of Ram Ses"
7. "The well tract of . . ."	
8. "The castle of Menma' rē' (Seti I)"	
9. "The stronghold of Sety-merenptaḥ"	"In his stronghold is Usima' rē' (Ramses II)"
10. "Town which his majesty [built] newly"	*s-b-ỉr**
11. "The well *'Ib-s-q-b*"	*'Ib-s-qb*
12. "The well of Sety-merenptaḥ"	*'-y-n-n**
13. "The well Menma' rē'-(is)-Great in Victories" (Seti I)	
14. "The well (called) sweet"	*Ḥ-b-r-t*
15. "The town which his majesty built newly at the well *Ḥ-b(?)-?-t*	
16. "The stronghold of Menma' rē', heir of R'" (Seti I)	
17. *?-b(?)-r-b-t*	
18. "The well of Menma rē " (Seti I)	
19. "*N-ḫ-s* of the prince"	*N-ḫ-s*
20. "The town of [Raphia]"	Raphia (*r-pḥ*)
	Gaza (*q-ḏ-t*)

* Matching this station with one in Seti's reliefs is most problematic.

The "map" of Seti is more detailed than the "itinerary" of Papyrus Anastasi I, but most of the names are parallel. The probable reason is that Seti designates the forts and their adjacent water sources by separate names while Papyrus Anastasi I only gives one name at each station. Among the places listed by Seti which are not mentioned in Papyrus Anastasi there is a fort called *m-k-t-r*, the second station after Sile, which is also mentioned in other Egyptian documents and later sources as well.[7] It is very probable that this is the Migdol of the Exodus narratives (Exod. 14. 2; Num. 33. 7; cf. also Jer. 44. 1; Ezek. 29. 10). The rest of these names are not mentioned in the Bible because the Israelites did not continue along the "way to the land of the Philistines" which was well guarded and fortified. From the description of Thut-mose III's campaign we know that he went from Sile to Gaza (*c.* 150 miles) in ten days.[8] This is an appreciable speed which was achieved only by virtue of the route's perfect organization. The many difficulties encountered by an enemy coming to attack Egypt are vividly described in the annals of Essarhadon, King of Assyria, concerning his Egyptian campaign in 671 B.C.[9] He recounts that, in spite of the name "the Brook of Egypt", there is no river on the whole route so that he was compelled to obtain water for his troops by drawing it from wells, using ropes, chains and buckets. The kings of Arabia also furnished them with water-bearing camels. Farther on he describes the horrors of the desert, a land covered with desolate rocks, full of strange and awesome creatures.

Great importance was attached to the cities along the southern border of Canaan which become the strongholds of Egyptian authority, viz. Raphia (Tell Rafaḥ), Laban (Sheikh ez-Zuweid ?), Sharuhen (Tell el-Far'ah), Yurza (Tell Jemmeh ?), Beth-'eglaim (Tell el-'Ajjul) and especially Gaza, the Egyptian capital in Canaan. The *Via Maris* did not pass right along the shore line because of the strip of creeping sand dunes near the beach. For this reason most of the major towns were founded at a distance of three to four miles from the coast, along the line of the highway. The most important of these cities had a small harbour town on the shore opposite, e.g. the harbour of Ashdod, which is called "Ashdod of the Sea" (*Asdudimmu*) in Assyrian sources.[10] The only southern cities situated right on the shore were Ashkelon and Joppa where the line of coastal sand dunes was interrupted. This has given them special importance as the main harbour cities in southern Palestine.

The most complete description of the towns along the *Via Maris* in the northern Shephelah and the Sharon is preserved in Thut-mose III's list. From his "annals" we only learn that he covered the distance of about 75 miles between Gaza and Yaḥam (Khirbet Yemma in the Sharon) in eleven or twelve days. The decrease in his rate of progress to an average of seven miles per day must have been due to some resistance encountered along the way.

Most of the cities which he passed in this region, and which he subdued, appear in Thut-mose's list of Canaanite towns. This is the only segment of the list in which places are arranged in strict geographical sequence, perhaps because these cities were well known to the Egyptians in this order. The segment under discussion includes the following names[11]: (61) Mahoz (*m-ḫ-ś*), apparently Tell Abu Sulṭan near Jabneh; (62) Joppa; (63) Gath, perhaps the biblical Gath-rimmon (Tell el-Jerisheh on the Yarkon ?) or the later Philistine town (Tell eṣ-Ṣafi ?); (64) Lod; (65) Ono (Kafr 'Ana); (66) Aphek (Tell Ras el-'Ain at the sources of the Yarkon); (67) Socoh (Khirbet Shuweiket er-Ras); (68) Yaḥam; (69) *ḫ-b-ḏ-n* (unidentified); (70) Gath (the Gath-padalla of EA 250; modern Jatt in the Sharon); (71) Migdal (perhaps Tell edh-Dhurur near Khirbet Mejdel which preserves the ancient name; cf. map 9, p. 155).

This section emphasizes the special importance of Aphek as a key point on the *Via Maris*. In the Shephelah there are several branches of this route, one near the coast, and others farther east. On one hand, Thut-mose's list follows the line Mahoz-Joppa-Gath(-rimmon) which is close to the coast, and on the other, it gives the road Gath-Lod-Ono-Aphek to the east of it. The Yarkon constitutes a serious obstacle to traffic, compelling the western branch to turn eastward so that the two run together again. For that reason Aphek is mentioned in many military campaigns; in the Bible it is the starting-point for Philistine expeditions (1 Sam. 4. 1; 29. 1).

Additional information concerning the two branches of the *Via Maris* between Ashdod and the Yarkon comes from Assyrian sources and the Bible. On the eastern branch, south of Lod, was located Gath-Gittaim (Ras Abu Ḥumeid beside Ramleh), Gibbethon (Tel Melat), Ekron (Khirbet el-Muqanna') and Gath (Tell eṣ-Ṣafi). Sargon followed this route to Ashdod and declares that he conquered Ashdod, Gath and Ashdod-yam[12] Uzziah had followed a similar line, "and broke down the wall of Gath and the wall of Jabneh, and the wall of Ashdod" (2 Chron. 26. 6). The great importance of Gibbethon lies in its being a key point on this eastern branch of the *Via Maris* at the northern extremity of the Philistine kingdom of Ekron so that its possession became a matter of controversy between Israel and the Philistines (1 Kings 15. 27; 16. 15).

By contrast, Sennacherib took the western approach.[13] After he had taken Joppa and its "hinterland" (Beth-dagon, Bene-barak and Azor—mostly towns of the "Danite inheritance", Josh. 19. 45), he advanced southward and smote Eltekeh (Tell esh-Shallaf, north of Jabneh).[14] From here he turned eastward following the Valley of Sorek (Wadi eṣ-Ṣarar) and conquered Timnah (Tell el-Baṭashi) and Ekron.

From Aphek northward along the Sharon Plain there was actually only one route. It ran along the eastern side skirting the hill country at an average distance of about eight miles from the coast. The western part of the Sharon was full of forests, swamps and sand dunes, a formidable obstacle to any traffic[15] An enlightening description of this section comes from Amen-hotep II, son of Thut-mose III, in the record of his second campaign to Canaan (*c.* 1428).[16] The first city conquered on this campaign was Aphek. From here he continued north past Yaḥam, but then he turned and conquered two settlements west of Socoh, from which he took considerable booty, especially cattle and flocks. From Yaḥam he went a bit farther north and once again swung westward to engage two more towns, Migdal and Adorain. In this description the main line of the route is prominent as it passes from Aphek, through Socoh and Yaḥam, to Gath whence Amen-hotep carried out raids against the western settlements in the forested and swampy region. Along this same line Pharaoh Shishak returned southward from the Plain of Jezreel during his Palestinian campaign (*c.* 924 B.C.). In his list he mentions ʻAruna (Kh. ʻAra, 32), Borim (Khirbet Burin, 33) and Gath-padalla (34), Yaḥam (35) and Socoh (38).[17]

From the Sharon the *Via Maris* turns north-eastward across the Plain of Jezreel. At times there certainly must have been a second branch continuing directly to the Plain of Acco around the Carmel range. Its trail passed Dor (Khirbet el-Burj beside Ṭanṭurah) which became the main Israelite port on the Sharon from the beginning of the Israelite period. However, the passage here was very difficult because of the forests and swamps and the sands in the western part of the Acco Plain; therefore, references to the use of this route are quite rare. This branch came into use only at the end of the Bronze Age with the rise of Dor and other harbour towns, e.g. Tell Abu Huwam at the mouth of the Kishon, as stations for the developing sea travel and with the decline of security on the inland routes. The first and only document describing a campaign following this branch is the list of Ramses II from Amara in which the following cities are mentioned along the coast[18]: (66) Raphia; (67) Sharu[hen]; (69) Mahoz; (70) Socoh; (71) A[dora]in; (77) Dor; (78) Rehob. Ramses passed, therefore, through the Sharon, reaching Dor, and from there continued directly to Rehob which is known from the Bible as one of the Canaanite towns on the Plain of Acco (Josh. 19. 30; Judg. 1. 31).

The passes of the *Via Maris* from the Sharon to the Plain of Jezreel through the ravines of the northern Ephraimite hill country were the most sensitive points on this route because they were easily blocked. The main pass followed Wadi ʻAra (N. ʻIron, pronounced *ee-rón*) between ʻAruna (Khirbet ʻAra) and Megiddo. It had the advantage of being the shortest, along with the disadvantage that in places it passed through very narrow defiles between ranges of hills covered with thick forests in antiquity. Herein lies the special importance of Megiddo at the entrance of the *Via Maris* into the Jezreel Plain from whence its various branches separate from one another and continue northward.

We have two Egyptian descriptions of this pass which emphasize its character. The first appears in the chronicles of Thut-mose III (1468 B.C.) in the words of Pharaoh's commanders[19]:

> What is it like to go [on] this [road] which becomes (so) narrow ? It is [reported] that the foe is there, waiting on [the outside, while they are] becoming (more) numerous. Will not horse (have to) go after [horse, and the army] and the people similarly? Will the vanguard of us be fighting while the [rear guard] is waiting here in ʿAruna, unable to fight?

The second passage is from the letter of the Egyptian Scribe Hori during the reign of Ramses II (Papyrus Anastasi I) who describes a lonely charioteer's passage through the Wadi ʿAra on his way from Megiddo to the Sharon[20]:

> Behold the ambuscade is in a ravine 2,000 cubits deep, filled with boulders and pebbles. . . . The narrow valley is dangerous with Bedouin, hidden under the bushes. Some of them are four or five cubits from their noses to the heel, and fierce of face. Their hearts are not mild, and they do not listen to wheedling. Thou art alone; there is no *messenger* with thee, no army behind thee. Thou findest no scout, that he might make thee a way crossing. . . . Thy path is filled with boulders and with reeds, thorns and brambles, and "wolf paw". The ravine is on one side of thee and the mountain rises on the other. Thou goest on jolting, with thy chariot on its side, afraid to press thy horse hard. If it should be thrown towards the abyss. . . . Thou startest to trot. The sky is opened [i.e. he has reached the end of the forest]. Then thou thinkest that the foe is behind thee. Trembling seizes thee. If only thou hadst a hedge of *shrubs* that thou mightest put it on the other side! The horse is *played out* by the time thou findest a night-quarters. . . .

This latter passage portrays the state of affairs that prevailed at the beginning of the thirteenth century with the entrance of the Hebrew tribes into the hill country threatening the thoroughfares wherever they passed through the hills.

Besides the Wadi ʿAra there were a number of alternative passes somewhat easier but longer. These routes are mentioned by Thut-mose's chronicle in the passage about the conference that took place at Yaḥam when his commanders recommended choosing one of them:

> . . . two (others) roads are here. One of the roads—behold it is [*to the east of*] us, so that *it* comes out at Taanach. The other—behold it is

to the north side of Zephath, and we will come out to the north of Megiddo. Let our victorious lord proceed on the one of [them] which is [satisfactory to] his heart, (but) do not make us go on that difficult road![21]

The southern branch turns eastward from Yaḥam to the Valley of Dothan and reaches the Plain of Jezreel south of Taanach. It would appear that the caravan of Ishmaelites took this road on its way from Gilead to Egypt (Gen. 37. 25). The northern branch goes up along Wadi Timsaḥi north of Zephath (Khirbet Sitt Leila),[22] which guarded the entrance to the pass on the Sharon side, reaching the Plain of Jezreel via Wadi el-Milḥ beside Jokneam. The three major tells on the south-western edge of the Jezreel Plain—Taanach, Megiddo and Jokneam—guarded these three important passes of the *Via Maris*.

Going north from here, the *Via Maris* divides into several branches. One route turns north-westward to the Plain of Acco and goes up from thence along the Phoenician coast to Ugarit in the north, and on to Anatolia. The most instructive list about this road is again in Papyrus Anastasi I,[23] which begins its description at Ṣumur, a Phoenician coastal city near the River Eleutheros north of Byblos, which was a border fortress for the Egyptian province of Canaan at the beginning of Ramses II's reign. After it the scribe lists in north–south order: Byblos, Beirut, Sidon, Zarephath, the River Liṭani (*n-ṯ-n*), Usu on the shore opposite Tyre, then Tyre itself on an off-shore island, the pass of the "cliffs" (*d-r-ʿ-m*=צלעם; Ras en-Naqurah), Acco and Achshaph (spelled with *ayin* by mistake). Concerning the latter city, he asks: "Where does the Achshaph road come? *At* what town?" Apparently he is referring here to a branch of the *Via Maris* coming from Megiddo past Jokneam and reaching the Plain of Acco near Achshaph (probably Khirbet Harbaj), and he is asking about one of these towns which controlled the road.

The cities of the Phoenician coast and the Plain of Acco are mentioned in connection with many military expeditions, both from the north and from the south. The father of Ramses II, Seti I, mentions Acco, Usu, Tyre and also Ullasa in the neighbourhood of Ṣumur in the campaign of his first year (*c.* 1300 B.C.).[24] It is most instructive to compare the expedition of Sennacherib, King of Assyria, in 701 B.C. when he captured such places on the Phoenician coast as Great Sidon, Little Sidon, Beth-zaith, Zarephath, Mahalab, Usu, Achzib and Acco.[25]

Across the Plain of Jezreel runs the most convenient thoroughfare to the east via Transjordan, Damascus, the Lebanese Beqaʿ and thence north-eastward to Mesopotamia. North of this plain rise the high mountains of Galilee and Lebanon, and only north of them does one find easy passage again, through the valley of the Eleutheros leading north from the Lebanese Beqaʿ to Kadesh. As a matter of fact, the roads which turned east and north-east from Megiddo were of no less importance than the coastal road. These were actually the most direct routes connecting the two great centres of the ancient East, Egypt and Mesopotamia.

Two main branches may be noted, with secondary branches belonging to each. One route crossed the plain opposite Megiddo, passed through the Chesulloth Valley between the Hill of Moreh and Tabor, finally descending to ancient Chinnereth (Khirbet el-'Oreimeh near the north-western shore of the Sea of Galilee). This segment of the road was dominated by the tell at Qarn Ḥaṭṭin, which was apparently Adamah or Shemesh-adam,[26] known not only from the Bible but also from the list of Thut-mose III, and especially from the first royal campaign of Amen-hotep II, *c*. 1430.[27] A fragment of an Egyptian stele from one of these two pharaohs was found at Chinnereth,[28] which dominated the ascent of this route northward into the Jordan Valley to Hazor. Hazor is a key-point on this route, being near the Jordan ford on the direct road to Damascus. Another road went northward from Hazor to Abel-beth-maacah, Ijon and the Lebanese Beqa'. Amen-hotep II followed this line up to the Orontes River, and Ramses II took the same route on his famous campaign against Kadesh. This place was also a convenient entry for invading Palestine from the north. Ben-hadad, King of Aram of Damascus, used it when he conquered "Ijon, Dan, Abel-beth-maacah, and all Chinneroth . . . (1 Kings 15. 20), and so did Tiglath-pileser III, King of Assyria, when he took Ijon, Abel-beth-maacah and Hazor (2 Kings 15. 29).

The second branch turns eastward from Megiddo and descends through the Jezreel Valley to Beth-shean. From here it goes up past Ashtaroth, capital of Bashan, where it joins the King's Highway coming northward to meet it across Transjordan. A secondary branch running the length of the Jordan Valley and leading from Beth-shean past Chinnereth to Hazor passes by Yeno' am (el-'Abeidiyeh)[29] which was located at a key position dominating the roads in the northern Jordan Valley to the south of the Sea of Galilee. This route, known from the expedition of Seti I, who set up two victory stelae at Beth-shean, went from this latter place past Yeno'am to Hazor. It is described in Papyrus Anastasi I in which are mentioned the Jordan fords opposite Rehob and Beth-shean, and the ascent to Megiddo. The section from Rehob and Beth-shean is also mentioned in the list of Shishak which makes reference to "The Valley" (i.e. the Valley of Beth-shean), Rehob, Beth-shean, Shunem, Taanach and Megiddo. Another route went up from Yeno'am to Bashan passing by Aphek. It is also mentioned in connection with the wars between Israel and Aram-Damascus (1 Kings 20. 26 ff.; 2 Kings 13. 17).

From Damascus the route goes out to the important desert oasis of

Tadmor and thence to the Euphrates region. Another important route extended northward through the Lebanese Beqa' to Hamath and Aleppo reaching the northern Euphrates district in the vicinity of Carchemish.

The various branches of the *Via Maris* converge, therefore, like the spines of a fan at Megiddo and unite to form one chief route. Thus we can understand the great value of the Palestinian coast for controlling this important international route, as well as the decisive position of Megiddo at the main junction.

2. The King's Highway

Next in importance to the *Via Maris* is the King's Highway, which runs the length of Transjordan. This name is taken from the biblical story (Num. 20. 17; 21. 22) and may not be a special name for that route but only a reference to an official main road otherwise known simply as "the highway" (Num. 20. 19). In the Bible its northern section is also called "the way of Bashan" (Num. 21. 33; Deut. 3. 1), because it went from Heshbon to Ashtaroth, capital of Bashan.

The King's Highway runs the length of the Transjordanian highlands and extends to Damascus. Therefore, this trail was a competitor to the *Via Maris* because it, too, was capable of serving international commerce. It was of special importance because it facilitated the export of precious perfumes from the countries of South Arabia.[30] The topography of Transjordan limits the possibilities for north-south movement to two parallel lines. A double watershed exists along the whole length of Transjordan: most of the wadies descending westward from the highlands are short, and the watershed between them and those running eastward is only 13 to 16 miles from the Arabah and the Jordan Valley. Along with these Transjordan also has four large wadies with much longer stream beds which have carved deep canyons for themselves 25 to 30 miles in length. These wadies, which divide Transjordan into its principal geographical sectors, are: the Yarmuk (its name is first mentioned in the Mishnah), the Jabbok, the Arnon and the Zered. The route which circumnavigates these deep canyons follows a line some 25 to 30 miles from the Arabah along the most convenient topographical course. The railroad still follows this track today. The disadvantage of this route is that it is so far out as to be already in the desert. On the other hand, there is another line running along the secondary watershed farther west. This one has the advantage of passing through a region replete with settlements and water sources, but it suffers the disadvantage of the difficult fords across the large wadies. The various historical records and especially the remains of settlements prove that the western course was the main one during most periods and that the ford crossings, such as the Arnon trail, received special attention. At Rabbath-ammon the two lines meet, hence the decisive position of that city for ruling the King's Highway.

Since the King's Highway runs near the desert and passes through the regions in which the population and government were not always fixed, it served first and foremost as a trail for nomadic caravans. The ancient non-biblical sources say very little about expeditions carried out along its length. Therefore, we do not really have much on this subject except what we learn from the Bible. The most ancient campaign along the King's Highway is described in Genesis 14 and associated with Abraham, but the chronology of this campaign is still shrouded in mist. The four kings of the north under the leadership of Chedorlaomer, King of Elam, on their expedition against the cities of the valley traversed eastern Transjordan from north to south. From Ashtaroth, capital of Bashan, and Karnaim, its neighbour (which eclipsed the former in importance during a later period), they came to the city Ham in northern Gilead (four miles south-west of Beth-arbel—Irbid), then on to Shaveh-kiriathaim on the Moabite plateau (Kiriathaim in the list of Reubenite cities, Josh. 13. 19), and to "Mount Seir as far as El-paran on the border of the wilderness", apparently Elath at the edge of the great Paran Desert. That is the extreme southernmost point of the expedition. From here they turn back to En-mishpat (viz. Kadesh[-barnea]). Therefore, the description of this campaign only mentions the capitals or the key points of the main sectors along the length of Transjordan: Bashan, Gilead, the Moabite plateau and Seir-Edom, as far as the key point in the south, Elath on the Gulf of Aqabah. Karnaim and Ashtaroth are located on the King's Highway; Ham is close to it. Kiriathaim is apparently more to the west (Qaryat el-Mekhaiyet); however, the identification of ancient Shaveh is unknown.

Various stations along the southern section of the King's Highway are mentioned in connection with the Israelites' march from Kadesh-barnea to the plains of Moab opposite Jericho. They asked permission to pass by the King's Highway (Num. 20. 19; 21. 22), and when it was refused they went "by the way of the Reed Sea, to go around the land of Edom" (Num. 21. 4), i.e. they went up from Elath to the southern end of Edom and from there continued along the border of the desert on the line of the eastern route which is called "the way of the wilderness of Moab" (Deut. 2. 8; not according to RSV). The Bible also preserves a list of stations along the length of the King's Highway in Edom and in Moab: Zalmonah, Punon, Oboth, Ije-abarim on the Brook Zered, Dibon-gad, Almon-diblathaim, the mountains of Abarim before Nebo and the plains of Moab by Jericho (Num. 33. 41–9; cf. *infra.*, pp. 201–2). This list follows the line of the main route from Kadesh-barnea to northern Moab. From Kadesh-barnea the Israelites descended to the Arabah, doubtless via the Wadi Zin (Wadi Fuqrah), crossed the Arabah in the vicinity of 'Ain Ḥusḅ (Tamar?) and ascended from here by way of

Punon in the vicinity of Khirbet en-Naḥas (which may have some relation to the story of the brazen serpent [Heb. *naḥaš*], Num. 21. 4–9), reaching the King's Highway in central Edom, south of Bozrah and Sela. From here they turned northward with the King's Highway and crossed the Brook Zered, the border between Edom and Moab, at Ije-abarim. There is no station in this list from central Moab between the Zered and the Arnon, e.g. Kir-hareseth (el-Kerak) the capital of Moab which was situated on the King's Highway. Nevertheless, it is clear that this road is meant since the station mentioned after the Brook Zered is Dibon, which was on this same road north of the Arnon. This latter town appears here with an added designation, Dibon-gad, an anachronism related to the Israelite tribe that settled in this region. From here they continued northward along this route and near Medeba they turned westward to the plains of Moab in the southern part of the Jordan Valley.

The important settlements of Transjordan were always located along the King's Highway: Naveh, Karnaim and Ashtaroth in Bashan; Ramoth-gilead, Gerasa and Jogbehah in Gilead; Rabbath-ammon, the Ammonite capital and Heshbon, the ancient capital of Sihon, King of the Amorites; Medeba and Dibon on the Moabite plateau north of the Arnon; Madmen and Kirhareseth in central Moab; Sela and Bozrah in northern Edom. From here two branches go out across the desert to Egypt: (1) the northern route passes through the wilderness of Zin to Kadesh-barnea and reaches Egypt via "the way of the wilderness of Shur"; (2) the southern route continues southward through the Edomite hill country in close proximity to Teman and Rekem and descends to the southern end of the Arabah at Elath. From here it crosses the wilderness of Paran via eth-Themed[31] and Qal' at en-Nahl, arriving at Egypt near the present-day Suez.

The King's Highway therefore went a much greater distance into the desert than the "way of the sea". Archaeological research in Transjordan has proven that settlements did not flourish along this route during every period, in contrast to the general picture with regard to the "way of the sea". In biblical times a thriving population is indicated along the length of the King's Highway in two periods: first, at the end of the third millennium B.C.., and second, with the occupation of the Hebrew tribes from the thirteenth century to the end of the Iron Age. During the long period of occupation decline there were mainly nomadic tribes here.[32] On the other hand, in northern Gilead near the junction of the "way of the sea" and the King's Highway, no such habitational gap exists. From the vicinity of Ramoth-gilead northward one again finds the continuous settlement as in the other regions of the "way of the sea". Here the influence of this important route on the founding, growth and historical continuance of settlement is clearly seen. The periods of settlement in the central Negeb highlands (south of the biblical Negeb) are even shorter, being limited to a brief space of time at the end of the third millennium, and to a later period from the eleventh or tenth to the seventh centuries.

The King's Highway was of special importance, therefore, mainly in the particular historical periods when those sectors were settled. However, even in the absence of a permanent settlement it was a competitor to the *Via Maris*, since the desert nomads used it not only in their wanderings but also for the transport of their own commercial caravans and the exchange of agricultural and manufactured products between the settled areas. During the Israelite Monarchy a special importance was attached to the King's Highway by virtue of the commerce with South Arabia that passed over it. There was stiff competition between Israel and Aram-Damascus over control of the King's Highway, and at every opportunity the Arameans tried to gain control of this region (2 Kings 10. 33; 16. 6).[33] So with the Assyrian conquest of Damascus we usually hear about invasions of Transjordan and Arabia as well.

II. INTERNAL ROADS

The internal network of roads which served to connect the various regions of the country is also fixed mainly in accordance with the two main routes on the west and east which served both for international and internal needs (cf. map 3). Most of the internal roads are latitudinal, connecting the main routes to one another. Because of the topographical difficulties, longitudinal roads crossing the country from north to south parallel to the main roads are few.

One longitudinal road of some importance is that through the hill country (cf. Judg. 21. 19) which runs along the length of the north–south mountain ridge. In the section between Hebron and Shechem it follows a single track corresponding approximately to the watershed, and the deep wadies on both sides prevent any deviation to the right or left. The main cities in the hill country are situated either near or on this route, e.g. Debir, Hebron, Bethlehem, Jerusalem, Mizpah and Bethel. The section near Bethlehem is called "the way to Ephrath" (Gen. 35. 19; 48. 7). The highway from Bethel to Shechem is mentioned in the description of Shiloh (Judge. 21. 19). From Shechem the road forks out into two branches: the western one passes through Samaria, Dothan, Ibleam and Beth-haggan to the Plain of Jezreel; and the eastern reaches the Valley of Beth-shean via Tirzah and Bezek. The segment of the western branch between Jezreel and Beth-haggan is called "the way of Beth-haggan" [not RSV] and passes through the "ascent of Gur" (2 Kings 9. 27). South of Hebron the road also forks to form additional branches: the westernmost descends via Debir and Madmannah to Beer-sheba, whence it continues southward past Niṣṣana towards the "way to Shur" which leads to Egypt. The eastern branch turns from Hebron towards Juttah and Eshtemoa and descends towards Arad and Hormah. From here it extends southward through the heart of the Negeb past Aroer, Oboda and Bir-Ḥafir to Kadesh-barnea. A chain of forts dating to the Israelite Monarchy was discovered along this line. Therefore, one may assume that this is the biblical "way of the Atharim" leading from Kadesh-barnea to Arad (Num. 21. 1).[34]

A second longitudinal trail runs along the deep Jordan rift from Jericho to the Valley of Beth-shean. In fact, there are two parallel roads here on opposite sides of the Jordan. However, the eastern one was more important because of the many settlements situated on it, e.g. Adam, Zarethan, Succoth, Zaphon and Pella. This is the biblical "way of the plain" (2 Sam. 18. 23). A similar route also ran down the Arabah south of the Dead Sea connecting Zoar and Tamar with Elath on the Gulf of Aqabah. Therefore, it is called in the Bible "the way of the Reed Sea" (Exod. 13. 18; Num. 14. 25; 21. 4; Deut. 1. 40; 2. 1; Heb.). The Dead Sea forms a partition between these two routes because the steep vertical cliffs prevent passage along its shore. We have no information as to whether there was sea traffic in the biblical period such as existed later.

One may assume that, like "the way of the wilderness of Moab" (Deut. 2. 8; Heb.), the section east of Edom was called "the way of the wilderness of Edom", which appears in the Bible (apparently by mistake) instead of "the way of Edom" (2 Kings 3. 8, 20). One must assume that the routes leading from Judah to Edom and Moab were called "the way to Edom" and "the way to Moab" respectively and that the roads on the east running through the desert were called "the way of the wilderness of Moab" or "the way of the wilderness of Edom".

Additional longitudinal routes of some importance also existed in the Shephelah of Judah where the topographical difficulties are few. Of special importance was the road running from Lachish to the Valley of Aijalon eastward of the mountainous ridge, on which were situated Tell el-Judeideh (Moresheth-gath?) and Azekah. A strong fort was built on this route in the days of the Judean kings (the southern Khirbet Rasm eḍ-Ḍab ʿ),[35] serving as a lookout post to maintain contact between three important Judean tells in this region: Azekah, Tell el-Judeidah and Khirbet Tell el-Beiḍa (Achzib?). It was along this route that Joshua pursued the five Amorite kings after his victory at Gibeon (Josh. 10. 10), and by it Nebuchadnezzar ascended to Jerusalem after destroying Lachish and Azekah (Jer. 34. 7 and the Lachish letters).

Latitudinal roads crossing the country from east to west and connecting the *Via Maris* with the King's Highway are much more numerous. We will indicate the most important ones in their respective regions:

1. In the Negeb

(1) The road connecting Kadesh-barnea with the southern Arabah evidently "the way to the hill country of the Amorites" (Deut. 1. 19)[36];

(2) The road descending from the vicinity of Arad to the northern end of Jebel Usdum and thence to the Arabah. Israelite forts were discovered at both ends, and one of them, the large Khirbet Ghazzeh, probably Ramoth-negeb, which resembles in plan the fort at Kadesh-barnea, is a testimony to the great importance of this route. This is doubtless the "way to Edom" (2 Kings 3. 20), because this is the main route leading to Edom[37];

(3) A latitudinal route certainly must have connected Gaza, Gerar, Beer-sheba, Hormah and Arad, although there is no evidence for it in the written sources.

2. In Judah

Concerning the various routes going up to the Judean hill country, we learn mainly from the settlements built along these trails and by comparison with later roads. The most important of them are:

(1) The road from Lachish to Hebron;

(2) Via the "Valley of Elah" to Bethlehem;

(3) Via the "Valley of Sorek" to the "Valley of Rephaim" and to Jerusalem; its western segments are called "the way to Beth-shemesh" (1 Sam. 6. 9, 12; Heb.) and probably "the road to Timnah" (Gen. 38. 14);

(4) Via Rabbah and Kiriath-jearim (Baalah) to Jerusalem;

(5) The "way of Beth-horon" is not only the northernmost but also the most important strategic road and is the only one mentioned by name in the Bible (1 Sam. 13. 18; Heb.).[38] Unlike the more southerly routes which generally ascend via stream beds, this road climbs up the steep "ascent of Beth-horon" and thence to Gibeon and Jerusalem on the central ridge. This was its advantage from the standpoint of security and usefulness for commerce; its most obvious weak point was the "ascent of Beth-horon" (Josh. 10. 10), also called "the descent of Beth-horon", depending upon one's direction (Josh. 10. 11; Heb.). Beth-horon was therefore a key point in the ascent to the hill country of Judah and Ephraim and was fortified at least by Solomon's time (1 Kings 9. 17; 2 Chron. 8. 5). This fort did not prevent Pharaoh Shishak from going up to the hill country via this route on his way from Gezer and Aijalon towards Gibeon.

A few roads descend from the hill country of Judah to the southern Jordan Valley and the Dead Sea:

(6) The most important of these is the road from Jerusalem to Jericho and eastward to Transjordan. It ran through the "ascent of Adummim" (Josh. 15. 7; 18. 17) and is also called "the way to the Arabah" (2 Sam.

4. 7; 2 Kings 25. 4; Jer. 39. 4; 52. 7), although this is not a special name for that road but only a designation for the various routes leading down to the Arabah, even that one which descended from the Negeb to the area south of the Dead Sea (Deut. 2. 8). The section from Jericho eastward is called "the way to the Jordan" (Josh. 2. 7).

(7) From the vicinity of Hebron a road descends to En-gedi. The story of the expedition during the reign of Jehoshaphat shows that this route continued on to Moab, probably via the shallow ford opposite the Lisan (2 Chron. 20).[39] This road's steep ascent in the vicinity of En-gedi is "the ascent of Ziz" (2 Chron. 20. 16). The Israelite fort above En-gedi[40] was built on this route, perhaps because of the attempted Moabite invasion. The two Judean forts discovered in the vicinity of Wadi Saiyal[41] indicate that a road also descended here to the shore of the Dead Sea. This was the shortest and most convenient route to Moab.

3. In the Hill Country of Ephraim

(1) The most important latitudinal road ascends from the vicinity of Socoh in the Sharon to Samaria and Shechem. From here it joins the longitudinal road and goes north-east as far as Tirzah, whence it descends via the Wadi Far'ah to the important fords of the Jordan near the city of Adam. This is the most convenient line by which one may cross the central hill country and helps to explain the rise of important cities on the sites of Shechem and Tirzah, and later also Samaria, at major highway junctures.

(2) A route farther south ascended to Bethel from the vicinity of Aphek. The Antipatris(Aphek)–Gophnah line was of prime importance during the Roman period, but we do not know whether the road followed this same track in biblical times. From the vicinity of Bethel the route continued eastward to the Jordan Valley near Naarath and Jericho. This is the biblical "way of the wilderness" (Josh. 8. 15; Judg. 20. 42; Heb.). Apparently this road is also described as "the way of the border" (1 Sam. 13. 18). If this is not a textural error, it would seem that the road ran more or less along the traditional boundary between Benjamin and the House of Joseph (Josh. 16. 1–2; 18. 12–13), which later became the boundary line between the kingdoms of Judah and Israel. A branch of this road is apparently mentioned in 2 Samuel 2. 24 also. The "way of Ophrah", running east of the main highway from the vicinity of Michmash to Ophrah and Baal-hazor is also mentioned in the Bible (1 Sam. 13. 17), but this road had only local significance.

4. In Galilee

A road of great importance crossed Lower Galilee from the Jordan Valley south of the lake to the Plain of Acco. Until very recent times it was known by the name Darb el-Ḥawarnah, because this was the main route connecting Hauran and the northern sectors of Transjordan with the coastal region. The road runs through the Valley of Jabneel and the western portion of the Sahl el-Baṭṭof. Along its length was discovered a chain of Israelite and Canaanite settlements from el-'Abeidiyeh (Yeno' am?) on the fords of the Jordan near the mouth of Wadi Fajjas to Jabneel and Adami-nekeb in the Jabneel Valley and as far as Hannathon in the Sahl el-Baṭṭof.[42] In the biblical period this route sometimes served as an alternative to the branches of the *Via Maris* passing through the Plain of Jezreel, perhaps mainly during the rainy season when the plain was difficult to cross. Therefore, we have witnesses to the use of this road even in Egyptian sources from the New Kingdom. Note that it is mentioned in Papyrus Anastasi I, which normally lists only the most important roads. After the scribe reaches Yeno'am from Hazor via the Jordan Valley he asks: "If one is travelling to Adamim (*ỉ-d-m-m*), which way is the face?"[43] The experienced Egyptian scribe needed to know that Yeno' am was at the junction of two roads from whence the "Darb el-Ḥawarnah" turned westward towards Jabneel and Adami-nekeb. In one of the Amarna tablets (EA 8) the King of Babylon writes that his caravan travelling through Canaan was attacked and plundered by the Kings of Acco and Shim' on near the city of Hannathon. Hence it is clear that this road also served as an international caravan route. In one of his letters the King of Megiddo writes (EA 245) that the king of Acco had taken Lab'ayu, King of Shechem, from Megiddo in order to send him by ship to Egypt according to pharaoh's command, but while on the way he had accepted a bribe and permitted Lab'ayu to escape from Hannathon. Thus we learn that sometimes they also used the Megiddo-Shim' on-Hannathon-Acco road to go from the Plain of Jezreel to the Plain of Acco.

The roads in Upper Galilee may be reconstructed mainly by following the chains of sites discovered in archaeological surveys.[44] The most convenient ascent from the east passed by Kedesh, which explains the special importance of this city during the Canaanite and Israelite periods. From here a chain of tells leads westward via Yiron, Iqrit and Abdon to Achzib in the northern Plain of Acco. Evidently, a more important route turned north-westward leading to Tyre via Tibnin (the talmudic Taphnit) and Kanah. This route was the principal line of communication from the northern Jordan Valley to the Phoenician coast, between Hazor and Tyre. It is especially from the campaign of Tiglath-pileser III in which Kedesh, Merom (Marum), Yiron and Janoah are mentioned that we discern the existence of a route leading from Kedesh to the Plain of Acco.[45]

5. *In Transjordan*

Besides the branches of the "way of the sea" and the King's Highway mentioned above, a few other roads ascended to the Transjordanian highlands; and three of them, evidently the most important, are mentioned in the Bible:

(1) From the Plain of Succoth a road followed the valley of the Jabbok to Penuel and nearby Mahanaim, from whence it ascended in a southerly direction towards Jogbehah and Rabbath-ammon. Along this route Gideon pursued the Midianites (Judg. 8. 5 ff.) and reached the "way of the tent dwellers" (Judg. 8. 11; Heb.), evidently the main route used by nomads, viz. Wadi Sirḥan;

(2) The eastern continuation of the road from Jericho, which ascended from Beth-jeshimoth to Heshbon, is mentioned in the Bible as the "way of Beth-jeshimoth" (Josh. 12. 3; Heb.);

(3) The road ascending from Zoar to Horonaim and Kir-hareseth is the "road to Horonaim" (Isa. 15. 5) or "the descent of Horonaim" (Jer. 48. 5). By this route the Kings of Israel and Judah went up on their campaign against Mesha, King of Moab (2 Kings 3), when they chose "the way to Edom" that goes around the Dead Sea on the south.

The remaining roads mentioned in the Bible had only local significance, e.g. the "way of the Diviners' Oak" beside Shechem (Judg. 9. 37; Heb.) and the "ascent of the Mount of Olives" beside Jerusalem (2 Sam. 15. 30).

[1] The statement by Josephus that King Solomon paved all of the roads leading to Jerusalem with black stones (*Antiq.*, VIII, vii, 4) is an anachronism.

[2] R. Hartmann, *ZDMG*, 64 (1910), pp. 694 ff., *idem*, *ZDPV*, 41 (1918), p. 53; G. A. Smith, *op. cit.*, p. 279; F. M. Abel, *Géographie de la Palestine*, II (Paris, 1938), p. 219; Z. Meshel, *IEJ*, 23 (1973), pp. 162–66.

[3] *ANET*, pp 476–78; Aharoni, *Settlement*, pp. 120–25 (Hebrew); cf. *infra*, pp. 182.

[4] Gardiner, *Anc. Eg. On.*, II, pp. 202* ff.

[5] Cf. the drawing of the canal in the reliefs of Seti I, *ANEP*, No. 323.

[6] A. H. Gardiner, *JEA*, 6 (1920), pp. 99–116.

[7] *ANET*, pp. 259, 292; Abel, *Géogr.*, II, p. 387; now Tell el-Ḥeir.

[8] *ANET*, p. 235.

[9] *ANET*, p. 292.

[10] *ANET*, p. 286.

[11] Simons, *Handbook*, p. 117.

[12] *ANET*, p. 286.

[13] *ANET*, p. 287 f.

[14] B. Mazar, *IEJ*, 10 (1960), pp. 72 ff.

[15] Y. Karmon, *PEQ*, 1961, pp. 43–60.

[16] *ANET*, pp. 246 f.

[17] Simons, *Handbook*, p. 181.

[18] B. Mazar, *BIES*, 27 (1963), pp. 1939–44 (Hebrew) = *idem*, *Cities and Districts in Eretz-Israel* (Jerusalem, 1975), pp. 154–59 (Hebrew).

[19] *ANET*, p. 235.

[20] *ANET*, pp. 477 f.

[21] *ANET*, p. 235.

[22] Y. Aharoni, *IEJ*, 9 (1959), pp. 110–22.

[23] *ANET*, p. 477; Aharoni, *Settlement*, pp. 120 f. (Hebrew).

[24] Simons, *Handbook*, pp. 139 f., 143, 145; M. Noth, *ZDPV*, 60 (1937), p. 213; Aharoni,

Settlement, pp. 57 ff. (Hebrew).

[25] *ANET*, p. 287

[26] Y. Aharoni, *JNES*, 19 (1960), pp. 177-83.

[27] This branch also enjoyed great importance in later periods, cf. R. Hartmann, *ZDPV* 41 (1918), pp. 53–56.

[28] W. F. Albright and A. Rowe, *JEA*, 14 (1928), pp. 281-87.

[29] Cf. Aharoni, *Settlement*, pp. 125–29 (Hebrew).

[30] Cf. G. W. Van Beek, *JAOS*, 78 (1958), pp. 141–52; *BA*, 23 (1960), pp. 70 ff.

[31] On the Roman *Tabula Peutingeriana* eth-Themed is called Phara (i.e. Paran). It is probable that this name is given here with the addition of the name of the desert in which it was located, like El(ath)-Paran, and that on the Roman map only the second part of the name is preserved. A similar development may have occurred with relation to Feiran in the southern part of the Sinai peninsular (cf. *infra*, p. 199).

[32] N. Glueck, *The Other Side of the Jordan* (New Haven, 1940), pp. 114 ff.

[33] B. Mazar, *BA*, 25 (1962), pp. 102 ff.

[34] Y. Aharoni, *IEJ*, 10 (1960), p. 109.

[35] This fortress, which is similar in plan to the fortresses of Kadesh-barnea and Khirbet Ghazzeh, was discovered by L. Y. Rahmani, cf. *Yediot*, 28 (1964), pp. 209–14 (Hebrew).

[36] Y. Aharoni, *Tur-Sinai Vol.* (Jerusalem, 1960), pp. 43–46 (Hebrew).

[37] Y. Aharoni, *IEJ*, 8 (1958), p. 35.

[38] Th. Oelgarte, *PJb*, 14 (1918), pp. 73–89.

[39] T. J. Salmon and G. T. McCaw, *PEQ*, 1936, pp. 103–11.

[40] Y. Aharoni, *BIES*, 22 (1958), pp. 30–32 (Hebrew).

[41] *Id.*, *IEJ*, 11 (1961), pp. 15 f.

[42] A Saarisalo, *The Boundary between Issachar and Naphtali* (Helsinki, 1927).

[43] *ANET*, p. 477.

[44] Aharoni, *Settlement*, pp. 6 ff. (Hebrew).

[45] *Ibid., pp. 129 ff.*

CHAPTER IV

Boundaries and Names

On three sides Palestine is surrounded by natural borders: to the west the Mediterranean, "the Great Sea" of the Bible; on the east and south the desert. It is obvious that the most permanent boundary is the sea on the west. The desert served as an eastern boundary in times when Transjordan was occupied. But when Transjordan became an unsettled region, a pasturage for desert nomads, then the Jordan Valley and the Dead Sea formed the natural eastern boundary of western Palestine.

The desert is not a boundary whose line is clear and permanent like the sea. Not only is it varied by nature but it also moved back and forth from generation to generation according to the population's ability to expand. The need was never felt for fixing a precise border on the east because the vast expanses of the desert were beyond any governmental control. Not so in the south; Egypt was not far away, and the important international "way of the sea" passed through here. Therefore, it was always necessary to determine a clear boundary between Palestine and Egypt, especially near the coast. The southern limits of population were not reckoned as a borderline in this area because the frontier cities dominated great expanses in the Negeb, and even the boundaries of the populated areas themselves were not fixed but were moved according to prevailing circumstances a few miles south or north. The most prominent natural geographic feature south of the populated areas of Palestine is the great Wadi el-ʿArish that empties into the sea about 30 miles south of Raphia. This stream drains the northern part of the Sinai Desert (about 10,000 square miles), and during the rare rainy days its bed fills up with a mighty stream of water. It is the only geographicl obstacle in this area besides the desert itself, and for this reason the Wadi was considered the natural border between Palestine and Egypt. Thus it was called "The Brook of Egypt". This name is known not only in the Bible but also in Assyrian records (*Naḫal Muṣur*), and there it serves also as a designation of the border region in which several cities were located, including Raphia.[1]

A more distant boundary demarcation is beside Sile (*ṯr* in Egyptian sources), on the eastern edge of the delta where Egypt borders on the Sinai desert. In antiquity the easternmost branch of the Nile passed this point; and reliefs from the reign of Seti I picture Sile as a fortress built on two branches of a canal which is called "the dividing water".[2] This locale also appears in biblical boundary descriptions as "the river of Egypt" (Gen. 15. 18) or "Shihor of Egypt" (1 Chron. 13. 5), since it is part of the Nile.

On the other hand, it is difficult to point out a natural boundary in the north between Palestine and Syria. The high Lebanon mountains on the west and Mount Hermon and Mount Sirion (Anti-lebanon) on the east served as a boundary in some sense, but the Phoenician coast and the Beqa‘ (Valley of Lebanon) extend on northward without real obstacles, and only the Taurus and Amanus mountains on the north and the wide Euphrates on the northeast form a natural boundary to the north of Syria.

In fact, it is especially the northern boundary of Palestine that changed from time to time according to the ethnic and political circumstances. In reality the border itself was a result of these circumstances, and in some periods no definite border existed between Palestine and Syria. Its final establishment was due mainly to the rise of Israel on the Palestinian stage, because never before in the history of the country had there been a united internal force, successful in the integration of the various sectors into one political or national unit. However, in the eyes of the great powers to the north and south Palestine and Syria were one unit over which they sought to impose their authority.

The question of the country's name at different stages of its history is intimately related to the question of its boundaries in the various periods. At certain times the name differed according to the viewpoint of the observer, whether from within or without. These ancient names are known to us from either Egyptian or Mesopotamian records. Most of these sources subsume Palestine and Syria under one geographical designation.

In Egyptian sources from the Old Kingdom there appears the name Ḥariu-sha‘ (*ḥryw-š‘*), i.e. "(the land of) the Sand Dwellers". This refers to the desert and perhaps also to the sandy coast of Palestine which was seen for the first time by the Egyptians coming up the coast to Palestine, whether by sea or land.[3] But we do not know the real extent of this name. The inhabitants of Asia are called in the earliest Egyptian sources by the name ‘Aamu (*‘ȝmw*), and Phoenicia was known by the name Fenḫu (*fnḫw*). However, the meanings of these names are still obscure.[4]

In Mesopotamian inscriptions from the third and second millennia B.C. we find "the land of Amurru" (*māt Amurri, Amurru;* written ideographically: *kur* MAR.TU), meaning "the West", "the West-land", and designating all of the country west of the Euphrates as far as "the Sea of

Amurru", viz. the Mediterranean.[5] Although this name was primarily intended for northern Syria, it includes all of Syria and Palestine, and its people are "men of Amurru", Amorites. The geographical names and the regions of Palestine mentioned in Sumerian and Akkadian sources, and also early Babylonian and Assyrian records, are almost negligible because the extent of their rule had not yet reached to such distances. Gudea, the King of Sumerian Lagash of the twenty-first century B.C., tells how he brought cedars from the mountains of Amana (Amanus) and building stones from two mountains, one of which was "Basalla in the Amorite mountain".[6] According to the Mari letters (from the end of the eighteenth century B.C.) Amurru was a definable political unit south of Qaṭna, and in matters concerning it Hazor holds a prominent place.[7] During the New Kingdom period in Egypt a principality by the name of Amurru was known which had its centre in the Lebanon region and whose boundaries were from Ṣumur on the Phoenician coast to the Beqa'.[8] Evidently, this is none other than the last remnant of the more extensive Amurru from an earlier period.[9] One of the biblical names of Palestine was also "the land of the Amorite", derived from the ancient name which in its day had included Palestine and at least a part of Syria.

During Egypt's Middle Kingdom the name Retenu (*rṯnw*) appears in Egyptian sources. It continued in use through the New Kingdom period, and it also included Palestine and Syria, which were at that time within the Egyptian sphere of influence and bordered on the land of Mitanni (Naharina) in the northern Euphrates region. Some records divide the land of Retenu into two parts: Upper Retenu and Lower Retenu, like Upper and Lower Egypt. It is difficult to say just where the boundary was between these two areas of Retenu, or if this was a geographically definable division. Possibly the border region was in the vicinity of the Plain of Jezreel.[10] Likewise, different conjectures have been made concerning the derivation and interpretation of this name; because the three Egyptian consonants *r-ṯ-n* could be transcriptions of the Semitic consonants *r/l-t/d/z-n,* and therefore its correct reading is uncertain. In Alt's opinion,[11] the name is related to the city Lod (*ldn*) on the Palestinian *Via Maris*, and according to Albright,[12] with the city Luz (*lzn*), viz. Bethel (or its ancient neighbour Ai?). However, it is difficult to understand how the name of one of these cities could have served as an all-inclusive title for Palestine and Syria since, as far as we know, they never enjoyed more than a local importance. More attractive is the older suggestion discussed by Gardiner[13] to equate Retenu with biblical Lotan (Gen. 36. 20, 22, 29; 1 Chron. 1. 38 f.), the eponym of Southern Transjordan, though semantic and phonetic problems exist. Most unlikely is the proposal of Mazar, viz. that the name should be read Razanu (*rznw*), meaning "the land of the rulers" (Heb. רוזנים).[14] The Egyptian title *ḥqꜣ-ḫꜣśwt* would then be a semantic parallel, i.e. "the ruler of a foreign land". One of the rulers of Retenu bears this title in the Sinuhe story (twentieth century B.C.), and the term Hyksos (the Hellenistic form of *ḥqꜣ-ḫꜣśwt*) remained in Egyptian tradition as the name of the foreigners who had once overrun Egypt.

In the New Kingdom period two new terms appear: Djahi (*ḏ-h*) and "the land of Hurru" (*ḫ-r*). The origin of Djahi has not been clarified: it evidently served as a general name for Palestine and Syria.[15] "The land of Hurru", i.e. the land of the Horites, is a result of ethnic changes that took place in Palestine under the Hyksos rule. This receives confirmation from the various documents of the fifteenth and fourteenth centuries B.C. in which many rulers of the Canaanite city-states have Hurrian names. It is clear, therefore, that various districts and cities of Palestine fell into the hands of Hurrian rulers who probably came from the north.

The common denominator in all these terms is the manner in which they are used: in spite of the fact that they do not have the same linguistic derivation or the same meaning, they include Palestine *and* Syria as one political and geographical unit under the influence and domination of Egypt on one hand and the Mesopotamian kingdoms on the other. This concept is reflected in the Bible by the boundary descriptions in the Patriarchal narratives. They include Palestine and Syria in one unit from the River of Egypt or the Brook of Egypt to the Great River, the Euphrates and from the desert and the Sea of Reeds to the Great Sea or the Sea of the Philistines, the Mediterranean (Gen. 15. 18; Exod. 23. 31; Deut. 1. 7; 11. 24; Josh. 1. 4).

I. THE LAND OF CANAAN

An additional name that is found in full use during the New Kingdom period is the "land of Canaan." The ethnicon, "Canaanites," first appears, according to the present state of our knowledge, in a text from Mari (18th cent. B.C.). There a military commander reports to the king of Mari that the "marauder" (*ḫabbātum*) and the "men of Canaan" are in the town of Rāḫiṣum while he and the troops of Mari are posted nearby, confronting them.[16] At least one can now say that Canaan as a geopolitical entity did exist in the Middle Bronze Age even though our documentation is still restricted to this one reference. The next allusion to Canaan is in the inscription on the stele of Idrimi, the king of Alalakh (mid-fifteenth century B.C.), who had found refuge during his exile at Ammiya in the "land of Kin' ani(m)", a city on the Phoenician coast known from the Amarna tables.[17] Canaanites also appear as foreigners on rosters from the kingdom of Alalakh in North Syria.[18] They are first mentioned in Egyptian documents on a list of booty taken by Amen-hotep II (*c.* 1430 B.C.) where they appear among the various nobles of Retenu.[19] In the Bible also there remain a few verses where the term Canaanite has the meaning "nobles and merchants" (Isa. 23. 8; Hos. 12. 7; Zeph. 1. 11; Zech. 11. 7, 11; Job. 41. 6), and now it is evident that the ancient meaning of the term is preserved here. From the Hurrianized Nuzi inscriptions (fifteenth century B.C.) it has been shown that a word *kinaḫḫu* had the meaning, "purple".[20] Between the spelling of this word and the Akkadian spelling of Canaan in the Amarna letters (*Kinaḫna, Kinaḫḫi*) there is no significant difference. The consonant *ḫ* in those documents serves as the reflex for *ayin* which does not exist in Akkadian script. Since the extraction of purple from sea shells (*Murex*) was one of the established vocations on the Phoenician coast and fine garments coloured with this valuable dye were in great demand throughout the ancient east, there must be some connection between the name Canaan and this special term. Therefore, it was suggested that the Phoenician coast was called "the land of the purple" by the Hurrians and that this name became accepted along with the term Hurru, at first only a name for the Phoenician coast, though in time its significance was broadened. We see a similar development in the name Phoenicia, which is derived from the Greek word Φοῖνιξ "purple". Even in the Bible there are still some traces of this usage of the term Canaan with that limited geographical sense. Joshue 5. 1 distinguishes between "the kings of the Amorites that were beyond the Jordan to the west" and "the kings of the Canaanites that were by the sea" (cf. also Isa. 23. 11). However, B. Landesberger has now shown that *kinaḫḫu* should probably be read *qinaḫḫu* and that it derives from Sumerian *gìn* = Akkadian *uqnû*, Ugaritic *iqnu,* Syrian *q'nâ '(a)/qun'(a)* and Greek κύανος [21] The connection between *kinaḫḫu* and Canaan must therefore be abandoned. Several passages in the Bible attach the northern Jordan Valley to the coastal region and unite these two districts under the name Canaan: "the Canaanites dwell by the sea, and along the Jordan" (Num. 13. 29; cf. Josh. 11. 3). The connection between the Jordan Valley and the Phoenician sea coast is alluded to in the story about the conquest of Laish by the Danites (Judg. 18. 7, 28).

The term Canaan (*Kinaḫḫi, Kanaḫna, Kinaḫni*) appears quite frequently in the El Amarna letters from the first half of the fourteenth century. Here, too, the reference is primarily to the Phoenician coastal area, but the name also occurs with a wider significance as a general term for the whole region of Egyptian rule in Palestine and part of Syria, which is designated in one text (*EA,* 36. 15) as "the province of Canaan" ([*p*]*iḫati ša Kinaḫi*). This is even more prominent in a letter of the King of Babylon to Aḫ-en-aton, in which he complains that a Babylonian caravan was plundered and its people murdered near Hannathon (*Ḫinnatuni*) in Lower Galilee; he demands reparations and the punishment of the criminals and argues: "[Ca]naan is your land and [its kin]gs are [your servants]!" (*EA*, 8. 25). In fact, Canaan has been transformed into a political concept and has become the official name of the Egyptian province which included Palestine and southern Syria. In the north it extended up to the boundary of the Mitanni, later Hittite, sphere of influence, those two kingdoms being successively Egypt's strongest opponents in this period. Some have assumed that even Ugarit was reckoned with Canaan, depending on a letter of the King of Tyre in which he reports concerning what has been heard in Canaan and tells, among other things, about a conflagration that has ravaged Ugarit (*EA*, 151. 49–58). However, it is now clear from the Ugarit texts themselves that Canaanites were considered to be foreigners there.[22] In the inscriptions of Seti I from *c.* 1300 B.C. there appears the form *p-kn 'n,* i.e. "*the* Canaan",[23] referring to Gaza, which was the capital of the Egyptian province of Canaan. In Merneptah's poem from *c.* 1225 B.C. the form *p-kn 'n* appears as a general term for the entire district under Egyptian rule.[24]

The biblical description of the borders of "the land of Canaan" at the time of the conquest defines the exact same area (Num. 34. 1–12; cf. map. 4). This is one of the most interesting geographical documents in the Bible, which bears witness to the most ancient and reliable traditions incorporated in the various sources and stories.

In the Bible there are two passages which parallel the list under discussion: (1) the southern border appears again in the description of the southern boundary of Judah's inheritance (Josh. 15. 1–4); (2) Ezekiel uses the same list to describe the borders of the land of Israel as revised in terms of geographical concepts from his own day (Ezek. 47. 15–20; 48. 1, 28).

The boundary description begins at the south-eastern extremity of the Dead Sea. Beginning here the four directions of the border are described in a strict geographical order. Thus it makes a full circle and comes back to its point of departure.

The Southern Boundary

For purposes of comparison the three relevant passages are listed below:

Numbers 34, 3–6 (RSV)	*Joshua 15, 1–4 (RSV)*	*Ezekiel 47. 19; 48. 28*
Your south side shall be from the wilderness of Zin	Southward to the boundary of Edom, to the wilderness of Zin	On the south side, it shall run
along the side of Edom,	at the farthest south.	from Tamar
and your southern boundary shall be from the end of the Salt Sea on the east;	And their south boundary ran from the end of the Salt Sea, from the bay that faces southward;	
and your boundary shall turn south	it goes out southward	

of the ascent of Akrabbim,	of the ascent of Akrabbim,	
and cross to Zin, and its end shall be south of	passes along to Zin, and goes up south of	
Kadesh-barnea; then it shall go on to Hazar-addar, and pass along to Azmon;	Kadesh-barnea, along by Hezron, up to Addar, turns about to Karka, passes along to Azmon,	as far as the waters of Meribath-kadesh,
and the boundary shall turn from Azmon		
to the Brook of Egypt, and its termination shall be at the Sea.	goes out by the brook of Egypt, and comes to its end at the sea.	thence along the Brook of Egypt to the Great Sea.

Noth's opinion seems to be correct, viz. that only the geographical names along the border have been taken from the original list[25] and that the verbs used in the description were a later addition, because those in the two parallel passages are different. The delineation of the boundary begins, as we said, along the south-eastern edge of the Dead Sea. The location of "the ascent of Akrabbim (scorpions)", is unknown; and there is no evidence for identifying it with Naqb eṣ-Ṣafa. Zin is also unknown, unless we assume that it is a general name for the wilderness of Zin which extended as far as Kadesh-barnea and was already mentioned at the beginning of the description. At this point, the book of Ezekiel mentions Tamar which was the most important station in the northern Arabah, evidently the modern 'Ain Ḥusḅ, 20 miles south-west of the Dead Sea.[26] From all this it is clear that the starting-point of the boundary from the south-eastern edge of the Dead Sea includes the north-eastern portion of the Arabah with Zoar and perhaps other settlements as well (cf. Gen. 10. 19; Judg. 1. 36). The general importance of this area was very great due to the copper mines in its vicinity and because of the routes connecting it with the king's Highway and with Elath. It is possible that the Canaanite Zoar is mentioned in the El Amarna texts (*Ṣuḫru; EA*, 334; 335).

The next point on the border is "south of Kadesh-barnea". In all probability Kadesh-barnea is 'Ain el-Qudeirat, the richest and most centrally located of a group of springs on the southern edge of the Negeb, in spite of the fact that the ancient name was preserved at 'Ain Qedeis, a small well five miles farther south.[27] One may surmise that the whole region was called Kadesh-barnea, with the name being preserved only at the southernmost well. The book of Numbers, chapter 34, lists only two points here (Hazar-addar and Azmon) as against four places in Joshua 15 (Hezron, Addar, Karka, Azmon). In the vicinity of 'Ain el-Qudeirat there are three additional wells Taking the order of these

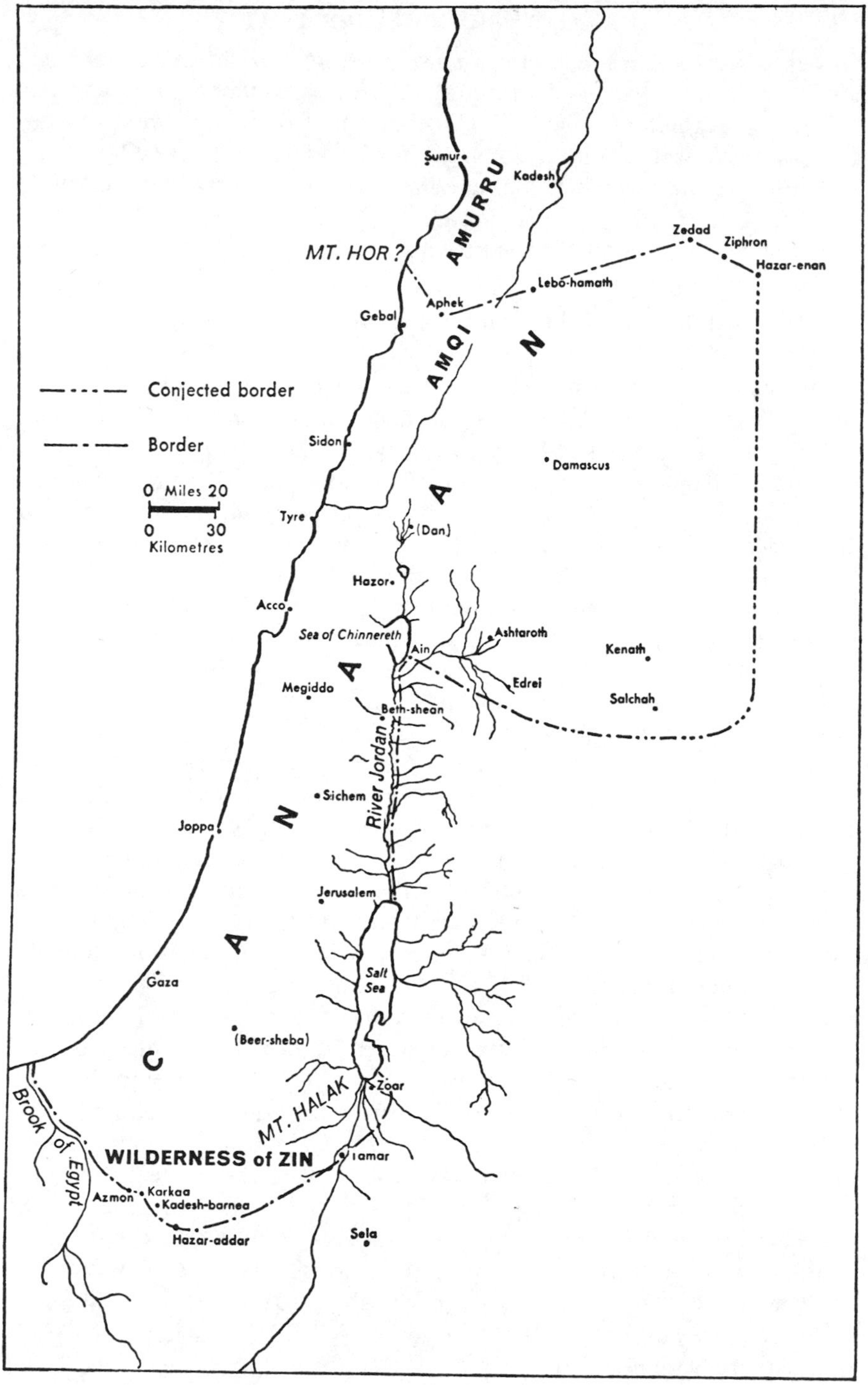

Map 4. The Borders of the Land of Canaan.

border stations from east to west, the following identifications are probable: ‘Ain Qedeis—Hazar-addar; ‘Ain Qeṣeimeh—Karka; ‘Ain Muweiliḥ—Azmon. Above ‘Ain Qedeis a fort from *c.* the tenth century B.C. was discovered; possibly it can be identified with Hazar-addar.[28]

From here the boundary continued on to the Mediterranean, following the “Brook of Egypt”, the great Wadi el-‘Arish, i.e. the natural geographical boundary between Palestine and Egypt.

The Western Border

“The Great Sea”, i.e. the Mediterranean.

The Northern Border

The keys to establishing the northern border are Lebo-hamath and Zedad. Many scholars have assumed that Lebo-hamath is not the name of a city but only a general expression which should be translated “the entrance of Hamath” (e.g. RSV), referring to Hamath on the Orontes.[29] However, there is really no doubt that Lebo was an important city on the border of the kingdom of Hâmath and is to be identified with Lebweh situated on one of the sources of the Orontes north of Ba‘albek.[30] The Hebrew phrase לבוא חמת might be interpreted linguistically as “the entrance to Hamath”, but the expression מלבוא חמת, “*from* Lebo-hamath” (Amos 6. 14), cannot be so construed. Neither does it seem proper to use an inclusive term in a list of border stations. But most important of all is the information about a city by this name in the region south of Kadesh on the Orontes which is preserved in both earlier and later sources. The city is probably mentioned in the Egyptian execration texts from the end of the nineteenth century B.C. (No. 31. *r-b-ỉ*) close to Sirion (*Ś-ꜣ-y-n*).[31] In Thut-mose III’s list it apparently occurs in the form *l-b-n* (*r-b-n,* No. 10) beside other towns in the Lebanese Beqa‘ (or perhaps *r-b-ꜣ*, No. 82). This spelling corresponds to *Labana* of the El Amarna tablets, which is mentioned with Kadesh, Damascus, and the land of ‘Amqi in the Beqa‘ (*EA*, 53). The clearest geographical testimony is from the annals of Amen-hotep II which speaks about a hunting expedition carried out in the forest of *r-b-ỉ*. Before this, Kadesh on the Orontes is mentioned and afterwards we find *ḫ-š-b* which is in the land of ‘Amqi, south of Ba‘albek (Ḫašabu of the El Amarna tablets).[32] The forest of Lebo also occurs in Ramses II’s memorial inscription about the battle of Kadesh. It occurs in the story before the battle.[33] In a city list of Tiglath-pileser III *Lab’u* in the land of Hamath is mentioned.[34] Furthermore, in the itinerary of Antonius *(Antonini Placentini,* sixth century A.D.), a place by the name of Libo occurs on the main route through the Beqa‘ between Laudicia (Kadesh) and Heliopolis (Ba‘albek).[35]

All of these sources suit Lebweh quite well, and a large tell has been found there containing remains from the Bronze Age up to the Arab period.[36] It is situated north of the watershed between the Orontes and the Liṭani. This region was forested and only sparsely settled in antiquity; it served in all periods as a natural boundary in the middle of the Beqa'. South of it was the land of 'Amqi, and a Hittite invasion of this sector in the Amarna Age was regarded as the violation of a recognized boundary.[37] When the Assyrians organized this area into provinces the southern boundary of the Hamath province passed by here; and Riblah, on the Orontes between Lebo and Kadesh, was in the land of Hamath during the reign of Nebuchadnezzer (2 Kings 23. 33; 25. 21). "The border of Hamath", which coincides with the northern border of Canaan according to Ezekiel, is none other than the boundary of the Hamath province in his own day (Ezek. 47. 16; 48. 1). Beside Lebo-hamath he mentions Berothah, a city of Hadadezer, King of Aram-zobah, in the Beqa' (2 Sam. 8. 8). It is usually identified with Bereitan south of Ba'albek.

These identifications are also confirmed by the next point, Zedad, whose name is preserved to this day in the village Ṣadad east of Sirion (Anti-lebanon), near the Damascus–Homs highway, 35 miles north-east of Lebweh. Zedad is situated on the edge of the desert and it is therefore likely that the next two places after it are the two desert oases found east of Zedad,[38] Ḥawwarin (Ziphron)[39] and Qaryatein (Hazar-enan).

To the west of Lebo-hamath only one point is mentioned on the northern border, viz. Mount Hor, indicating a sacred peak like the Mount Hor in the Negeb. This is doubtless a reference to one of the northern summits of the Lebanese range in the vicinity of the coast, approximately on a geographical line from Zedad to Lebo-hamath. The various conjectures for identifying it with one of the Lebanese mountains such as Jebel 'Akkar (7,016 feet) east of Tripolis or Jebel Makmel (10,046 feet) a bit farther south are without foundation, especially since these ridges are far from the sea coast. Here we get some assistance from the description of the northern border of "the land that remains" (Josh. 13. 4), which included the region of Byblos and extended to Aphek on the Amorite border, i.e. the kingdom of Amurru in the northern Lebanon (cf. *infra,* pp. 171). Therefore, it seems that Mount Hor is one of the north-western summits of the Lebanese range, north of Byblos, such as Ras Shaqqah, the hallowed Theouprosopon between Byblos and Tripolis.[40]

The Eastern Boundary

The first two points, Shepham and Riblah, are completely unknown. The second of these should not be confused with the Riblah mentioned earlier, which is in the Lebanese Beqa' north of Lebo. It is possible that Ain is the Ḫayanu in the land of Gari (Geshur?) of the Amarna letters (*EA*, 256), today Khirbet 'Ayyun, *c.* three miles east of the Sea of Galilee, north of the River Yarmuk. In any case, it is clear that the boundary came down to the south-eastern edge of the lake. "The shoulder of the sea of Chinnereth on the east" is the steep eastern slope.

From here the boundary follows the Jordan River to the Dead Sea and thus returns to its original starting-point. Along this portion the book of Ezekiel indicates the Assyrian-Babylonian districts of its day, describing it in two segments: between Hauran and Damascus on one hand and between Gilead and Israel (i.e. Samaria) on the other. By "the eastern sea" Ezekiel means the Dead Sea.

Although some doubts remain about particular details, the general location of the Canaanite borders is clear to us from the biblical description (cf. map 4). In the north are included the mountains of Lebanon and Sirion, with the boundary passing through the Lebanese Beqaʻ at Lebo-hammath south of Kadesh. In the north-east the border reached the edge of the desert and included the environs of Damascus. Likewise, it is clear that Bashan was also included, but we do not know if the oldest description included Mount Hauran (Jebel ed-Druze) as well, since it was excluded by Ezekiel. From here the boundary descends south-westward to the shore of the Sea of Galilee approximately along the Yarmuk Valley so that Gilead and all of the southern sectors of Transjordan are excluded from the limits of Canaan. On the south the boundary is the Brook of Egypt and Kadesh-barnea, the most important oasis in the northern wilderness of Paran.

All of the attempts to interpret these boundaries in the light of political or ethnic conditions in the Israelite period have failed.[41] The Israelite occupation never extended that far; and although one may point to periods in which the hand of Israelite authority reached the Lebanese Beqaʻ and Damascus, e.g. in the reign of David, the boundary never passed north of Sidon on the Phoenician coast. And on the contrary, Gilead was always an integral part of the Israelite population and remained within the boundaries of the kingdom of Israel during most periods. However, why should we struggle to explain the boundaries of Canaan in terms of later Israelite occupation, seeing that they conform in every respect to "the land of Canaan" seized by the Israelite tribes during the thirteenth century B.C.?[42]

During the fourteenth and thirteenth centuries B.C. the name Canaan became the official and accepted title of the region under Egyptian authority in Palestine and Syria which bordered on the Hittite kingdom in the north. The title appears with this significance, not only in the passage under discussion but in other ancient biblical sources as well. All of our information about the Egyptians' Canaan matches the biblical description and can be used to complete the boundary lines at certain points which remain unclear.

In the twenty-first year of Ramses II (*c.* 1270 B.C.) a peace pact was signed between Egypt and Hatti according to which the sphere of authority in Asia was divided between these two kingdoms.[43] We know that Kadesh on the Orontes was not conquered by Ramses and remained in Hittite hands.[44] We also know that, farther east, Damascus and evidently the area of Bashan stayed under Egyptian authority.[45] But this was not the case with Gilead and the southern sectors of Transjordan, which are never mentioned before the thirteenth century in Egyptian sources, and the archaeological survey showed that these regions were practically unoccupied in this period.[46]

In Papyrus Anastasi I from the beginning of Ramses II's reign Ṣumur is mentioned as the northernmost city on the Phoenician coast in which an Egyptian garrison was stationed.[47] Ṣumur was a well-known town on the coast of Phoenicia, situated north of Byblos near the mouth of the Eleutheros River (Nahr el-Kebir);[48] its inhabitants are mentioned in the Bible: the Zemarites in the Table of Nations, one of the sons of Canaan alongside the Arvadites (Gen. 10. 18; cf. also 1 Chron. 1. 16). We also know from the Amarna letters that in Ṣumur there were Egyptian government buildings and that the city was controlled by the Kings of Amurru. The kingdom of Amurru was theoretically an Egyptian province until the battle of Kadesh, but after that it became a Hittite dependency (cf. *infra,* pp. 171., 190). Therefore, the boundary was fixed between Ṣumur and Byblos at this time. We have seen that precisely in this region we must look for the Mount Hor on the northern border of Canaan.

It is also clear that this border was not an innovation in the days of Ramses II. During the reign of Thutmose IV the treaty made with Mitanni recognized that Kadesh was the southernmost domain of the northern power.[49] Though no copy of that treaty exists, the status of Kadesh is demonstrated later by the Hittite sources which state that Suppiluliuma took Kadesh from Mitanni (!).[50] Furthermore, a treaty was then made between the Hittites and Egypt, the agreement concerning the people of Kurustama, and the border between the Hittite and Egyptian spheres of influence was south of Kadesh. Again, the text of the treaty is missing, but Mursili, the son of Suppiluliuma, blamed his father for breaking the treaty with Egypt by invading the land of Amqi, i.e. the Liṭani Valley south of Lebo-hamath.[51]

In fact, the biblical description matches perfectly the boundaries of the Egyptian district of Canaan during the second half of the thirteenth century. This is one of those most instructive examples of ancient sources being preserved among the geographical texts of the Bible, because we have here a document that makes no sense whatever in later periods. By virtue of its resemblance to the description of the tribal boundaries one may conjecture that this document was preserved at the covenant centre of the Israelite tribes at Shiloh (cf. *infra,* p.254), where it served as a sort of deed and testimony for the tribes, who considered themselves the rightful heirs of Canaan.

Canaan appears with the same significance in various stories from the period of the settlement. Therefore, it does not include the sectors of Israelite population in Transjordan (e.g. Gen. 13. 12; 33. 18; Num. 32. 32; 35. 14). This is most prominent in the ancient story about an altar constructed by the Transjordanian tribes "at the frontiers of the land of Canaan, in the region about the Jordan, on the side that belongs to the people of Israel" (Josh. 22. 9 ff). They return and depart from "Shiloh, which is in the land of Canaan, to go to the land of Gilead" (vs. 9). The emissaries return "from the Reubenites and the Gadites [only these two tribes were included in the original story] in the land of Gilead to the land of Canaan, to the people of Israel" (vs. 32). The argument put forth for building this altar is most revealing: ". . . but we did it from fear that in time to come your children might say to our children, 'What have you to do with the Lord, the God of Israel? For the Lord has made the Jordan a boundary between us and you, you Reubenites and Gadites; you have no portion in the Lord . . .' " (vss. 24–5). Here the ancient viewpoint is quite clear, viz. that Gilead is outside the borders of Canaan. Therefore, the fear existed that it would also remain outside the boundaries of the Israelite inheritance with all the secular and sacred significance which that entailed.

The description of Canaan in the Table of Nations (Gen. 10. 15 ff.) also conforms to this idea. The first-born of Canaan is Sidon which had come to exercise such power over the other more southerly Phoenician cities by the period of the Conquest that the term Sidonians was now synonymous with Phoenicians-Canaanites. "And the territory of the Canaanites extended from Sidon, in the direction of Gerar, as far as Gaza, and in the direction of Sodom, Gomorrah, Admah and Zeboiim, as far as Lasha" (vs. 19); i.e. all of the coastal sector from Phoenicia to Gaza, the most important southern city near the Egyptian border, and eastward to just beyond the ancient cities located according to tradition at the southern end of the Dead Sea.

The tradition of the Canaanite boundaries from the Negeb to Lebo-hamath shows up in other biblical boundary descriptions, e.g. "from the wilderness of Zin to Rehob, near Lebo-hamath" (Num. 13. 21). The Israelite conquests are also described within this framework. On the one hand, the southern conquests were "from Kadesh-barnea to Gaza, and all the country of Goshen, as far as Gibeon" (Josh. 10. 41). On the other hand, the general conquest was "from Mount Halak, that rises toward Seir, as far as Baal-gad in the valley of Lebanon below Mount Hermon" (Josh. 11. 17; cf. 12. 7). Since the Israelite occupation did not reach the northern limits of Canaan, there arose the concept of "the land that remains" which was not conquered and whose borders extended "from Baal-gad, below Mount Hermon to Lebo-hamath" (Josh. 13. 5; cf. Judg. 3. 3; cf. *infra*, pp. 236f.).

The political and ethnographic situation in "the land of Canaan and its borders" changed with the occupation by the Israelite tribes and other related peples and with the cessation of Egyptian authority in Canaan. However, the ancient boundary delineation which existed in the country when the tribes came was not forgotten in the biblical tradition, and its echoes continue to the end of the Kingdom period. Lebo-hamath remains the desired boundary mark in the north as mentioned in the story of the spies (Num. 13. 21). During the reigns of David and Solomon (1 Chron. 13. 5; 1 Kings 8. 65; 2 Chron. 7. 8) and of Jeroboam II (2 Kings 14. 25; Amos 6. 14), Lebo again became the dividing point between the kingdom of Israel and Hamath, the Neo-Hittite kingdom in northern Syria. It was in this period that Lebo received the additional designation -hamath, which brought about the erroneous interpretation "the *entrance* of Hamath" for the city Lebo-hamath. Besides the actual extent of the Israelite occupation as expressed in the idiom "from Dan to Beer-sheba", there existed a wider concept founded upon the traditional boundaries of Canaan: from Lebo-hamath to the Brook of Egypt (Solomon); from Shihor in Egypt to Lebo-hamath (David); from Lebo-hamath to the sea of the Arabah (viz. the Dead Sea) or the Wadi Arabah (the border of Israel during the reign of Jeroboam II). As previously mentioned, Ezekiel also uses the traditional terminology of the Canaanite boundaries for his messianic vision of the return, infusing them with contemporary concepts, and thereby arranging a schematic model for the tribes of Israel (Ezek. 47–8).

II. THE LAND OF ISRAEL

The term "the land of Israel" came into use with the Israelite occupation, but its significance changes according to the historical situation. At first the term designated only the sectors populated by the Israelite tribes in contrast to the Philistine and Canaanite sectors (1 Sam. 13. 19). In the days of the kingdom the term broadened its frame of reference (cf. 1 Chron. 22. 2; 2 Chron. 2. 17; and also "the land of the sons of Israel", Josh. 11. 22). However, Judah and Israel are generally mentioned side by side (e.g. 1 Kings 4. 20) and the division of the land into districts which Solomon imposed "upon all Israel" (1 Kings 4. 7) took in only the northern tribes. The northern tribal alliance was designated by the term Israel, and afterwards this region became the kingdom of Israel as against the kingdom of Judah. Thus was created a certain dualism in the use of the term Israel, which could have either a limited or a wider significance. The borders of the land of Israel and its main sectors are described in the vision revealed to Moses: "and the Lord showed him all the land, Gilead as far as Dan, all Naphtali, the land of Ephraim and Manasseh, all the land of Judah as far as the Western Sea, the Negeb, and the Plain, that is, the valley of Jericho, the city of palm trees, as far as Zoar" (Deut. 34. 1–3). As a boundary designation for the land of Israel the phrase was eventually coined "from Dan to Beer-sheba" (2 Sam. 24. 2; 1 Kings 4. 25), indicating the main centres in the north and in the south. In Transjordan the borders are "from the valley of the Arnon to Mount Hermon" (Josh. 12. 1). The most detailed description of the boundaries of the "land of Israel" in this sense is given in the census taken of the Israelite tribes "from Dan to Beer-sheba", which was carried out by Joab during David's reign (2 Sam. 24. 5–7; cf. *infra*, pp. 297 f.).

In the days of the divided kingdom the term Israel served only in the limited sense (e.g. 2 Kings 5. 2; 6. 23; 2 Chron. 30. 25) as against Judah which was the geographical name of the southern kingdom under the Davidic Dynasty (e.g. 2 Kings 23. 24; Isa. 26. 1, *et al.*). The boundaries of these two kingdoms changed in accordance with historical circumstances. Only after the fall of Samaria, and during the last days of the kingdom of Judah particularly, with the great expansion under Josiah did the term Israel return to its wider and more ancient usage. Even so, Ezekiel still uses it in juxtaposition to Judah (Ezek. 27. 17).

With the triumph of Assyrian influence in the ninth and eighth centures B.C. a new term arises which once again includes Syria and Palestine as a single unit, viz. "beyond the river" (Assyrian: *eber nāri*), i.e. the region beyond the Euphrates. Naturally, from the Palestinian point of view, Mesopotamia is beyond the Euphrates; therefore, one finds verses in the Bible where the term "beyond the River" expresses this meaning (Josh. 24. 2–3, 14–15; 2 Sam. 10. 16). But in the course of time "beyond the river" became the standard designation for Syria-Palestine, and with this meaning it even occurs in the Bible (1 Kings 4. 24). During the Persian period the Aramaic form of this term (עבר נהרה/א) became the official title of the Fifth Satrapy (Ezra 4. 10; 5. 3, *et al.*), which included all the provinces in Syria, Phoenicia and Palestine, Judah being one of them (in Aramaic: *Yehud*).

"The land of Judah" was at first limited to the region of Judah's inheritance, the centre of which was between Jerusalem and Hebron.[52] Eventually it came to include all of the southern tribes; and with the division of the kingdom, it became the official designation of the southern kingdom. During the post-exilic period Judah became the official name of the Persian province, and with the expansion of the Hasmonean kingdom it was enlarged to include all of Palestine; in fact it assumed the meaning formerly attached to Israel. This name was even accepted by the Roman conquerors who transformed the country into the *Provincia Judaea*.

After the Bar-Kokhba revolt was quelled Hadrian changed the name to *Provincia Syria Palaestina*, and this term was shortened with the passage of time to simply *Palaestina*. Syria is a new term appearing in Hellenistic sources in place of "beyond the River". It apparently originated from (As)syria, signifying at first the Arameans who comprised the bulk of the Syrian population.[53] On the other hand, *Palaestina* is nothing but the Hellenistic form of Philistia, "the land of the Philistines" (Gen. 21. 32, 34; Exod. 13. 17; 1 Kings 4. 21, *et al.*), i.e. the area of Philistine population in the southern coastal sector of the land of Israel, and the term *Palashtu* occurs in Assyrian records with this meaning. The Greek historian Herodotos was the first to use this name Παλαιστινή in a wider sense, because at first the western world was mainly familiar with the Levantine coast. Philo of Alexandria and Josephus took this term from him. Hadrian adopted it in order to expunge the name Judah, and his effort was successful. Nevertheless, Jerome (fifth century A.D.) was still well acquainted with the broader political usage of the term Judah, and in his commentary on Ezekiel 27. 17 he says: *Judaea quae nunc appellatur Palaestina,* "Judah which is now called Palestine".

[1] E.g. *ANET*, pp. 286, 290, 292.

[2] *ANEP*, No. 323.

[3] B. Couroyer, *RB*, 78 (1971), pp. 558–75, takes this view and shows that the Sand Dwellers are the sedentary population of the southern Levant and not nomads, *contra* S. Yeivin, *JEA*, 51 (1965), p. 205.

[4] These terms, as well as the appellation, "God's Land," have been restudied in detail by B. Couroyer, *RB*, 78 (1971), pp. 59-70, 558-75; 80 (1973), pp. 53-75, 264-76; 81 (1974), pp. 481–523.

[5] *RLA*, I, pp. 99 f.; II, pp. 362–67.

[6] *ANET*, p. 269; this is evidently a reference to the Jebel Bishri, cf. D. O. Edzard, *Die "Zweite Zwischenzeit" Babyloniens* (Wiesbaden, 1957), p. 35.

[7] J. R. Kupper, *Les Nomades en Mesopotamia au temps des rois de Mari* (Paris, 1957), pp. 49, 179; A. Malamat, *JBL*, 79 (1960), pp. 12–19; *idem*, apud J. A. Sanders, ed., *Near Eastern Archaeology in the Twentieth Century* (New York, 1970), pp. 164–72; *idem*, *IEJ*, 21 (1971), pp. 31–38.

[8] Gardiner, *Anc. Eg. On.*, I, pp. 187* ff.

[9] Concerning the conjectures about the main centre and the extent of the ancient kingdom of Amurru, cf. *infra*, p. 149.

[10] For discussion of the various sources, cf. Gardiner, *Anc. Eg. On.*, I, pp. 142*–49*. According to the "annals" of Thutmose III, Yeno'am (apparently el-'Abeidiyeh just south of the Sea of Galilee) was in Upper Retenu; cf. *ANET*, p. 237.

[11] A. Alt, *ZDPV*, 47 (1924), pp. 169 ff.

[12] W. F. Albright, *The Vocalization of the Egyptian Syllabic Orthography* (New Haven, 1934), p. 9, note 23.

[13] Gardiner, *op. cit.*, I, pp. 148* f.

[14] B. Maisler (Mazar), *EI*, 3 (1954), p. 21 (Hebrew) = *Canaan and Israel* (Jerusalem, 1974), pp. 18–19; cf. A. F. Rainey, *IOS*, 2 (1972), p. 373 n. 22 and the remarks by Gardiner, *loc. cit.*

[15] Gardiner, *op. cit.*, I, pp. 145 ff.; Rainey, *UF*, 5 (1973), p. 281.

[16] G. Dossin, *Syria*, 50 (1973), pp. 277 ff. [This Rāḫiṣu might possibly be the later Ruḥiṣṣi (*r-g-ḏ*; for Rōǵiṣi), No. 79 of Thutmose III's list. A.F.R.]

[17] S. Smith, *The Statue of Idrimi* (London, 1949), pp. 72 f.; W. F. Albright, *BASOR*, 118 (1950), p. 16; *ANETS*, p. 557 [121]. For the most recent summaries of the evidence concerning the Canaanites, cf. R. de Vaux, *JAOS*, 88 (1968), pp. 23–29; *idem*, *Histoire ancienne d'Israël* (Paris, 1971), pp. 123–48; A. R. Millard apud D. J. Wiseman, *Peoples of the Old Testament* (Oxford, 1973), pp. 29–52.

[18] D. J. Wiseman, *The Alalakh Tablets* (London, 1953), Nos. 48, 5; 154, 24; 181, 9; *idem*, *JCS*, 8 (1954), p. 11.

[19] *ANET*, p. 246; B. Maisler (Mazar), *BASOR*, 102 (1946), pp. 7–12.

[20] E. A. Speiser, *Language,* 12 (1936), pp. 124 f. = *Oriental and Biblical Studies* (Philadelphia, 1967), pp. 327–29.

[21] *JCS,* 21 (1967), pp. 166 f.

[22] Rainey, *IEJ,* 13 (1963), pp. 43–45; 14 (1964), p. 101; *idem, BA,* 28 (1965), pp. 105–6; *idem, IOS,* 5 (1975), p. 26.

[23] *ANET,* p. 254.

[24] *ANET,* p. 378.

[25] M. Noth, *ZDPV,* 58 (1935), pp. 185 ff. (= *Aufsätze,* pp. 229 ff.); perhaps the original source was in Egyptian or Akkadian and was translated into Hebrew in different ways.

[26] Y. Aharoni, *IEJ,* 13 (1963), pp. 30 ff.

[27] Cf. recently B. Rothenberg and Y. Aharoni, *God's Wilderness* (London, 1961), pp. 33 ff., 121 ff.

[28] Y. Aharoni, *ibid.,* p. 138.

[29] Abel, *Géogr.,* I. pp. 300 ff.

[30] K. Elliger, *PJb,* 32 (1936), pp. 34 ff.; B. Maisler (Mazar), *BJPES,* 12 (1946), pp. 91 ff. (= *BIES Reader* B, pp. 60–71; Hebrew).

[31] B. Maisler (Mazar), *Revue d'histoire juive en Egypte,* 1 (1947), pp. 33 f.; *idem, EI,* 3 (1954), p. 26 (= *Canaan and Israel,* p. 31, Hebrew).

[32] *ANET,* p. 246.

[33] E. Edel, *ZDPV,* 70 (1954), pp. 153 f.

[34] Luckenbill, *AR,* II, § 821.

[35] K. Elliger, *PJb,* 32 (1936), pp. 34 ff.

[36] A Jirku, *ZDPV,* 53 (1930), p. 159; A. Kuschke, *ZDPV,* 70 (1954), p. 128; 74 (1958) p. 96.

[37] Y. Aharoni, *IEJ,* 3 (1953), pp. 153-61.

[38] Elliger, *loc. cit.* (note 35).

[39] In place of Ziphron, Ezekiel reads Sibraim which some have taken to mean Sepharvaim in Syria (2 Kings 17. 24, 31; 18. 34; 19. 13).

[40] In place of Mount Hor, Ezekiel reads "(the) way of Hethlon" (47, 15; 48. 1). It has been suggested by some that Hethlon be identified with Ḥeitela, north-east of Tripolis, two and a half miles south of Nahr el-Kebir; on this basis one might conjecture that Ezekiel meant the important Eleutheros road, but the matter is far from clear.

[41] According to K. Elliger, *PJb,* 32 (1936), pp. 34–73, these are the boundaries of the kingdom of David; according to M. Noth, *PJb,* 33 (1937), pp. 36–51, they are the boundaries of the Israelite settlement.

[42] B. Maisler, *loc. cit.* (note 30).

[43] *ANET,* pp. 199–203.

[44] Breasted, *AR,* III, §§ 298–351.

[45] According to Papyrus Anastasi III from the reign of Ramses II (1, 9–10; Gardiner, *LEM,* p. 21) and a letter of Ramses II to Hattusili III which mentions the Egyptian commissioner of the land of Upe-Damascus (E. F. Weidner, *KUB,* III, 57. 2, 8; E. Edel, apud *Geschichte und Altes Testament,* Tübingen, 1953, pp. 55 ff.; cf. A. Alt, *Kl. Schr.,* 1, p. 226 n. 3; III, pp. 107 n. 1, 189).

[46] N. Glueck, *The Other Side of the Jordan* (New Haven, 1940), pp. 114 ff.

[47] *ANET,* p. 477; Aharoni, *Settlement,* p. 120 (Hebrew).

[48] Cf. A. Alt, *ZDPV,* 68 (1951), pp. 117 ff. (= *Kl. Schr.,* III, pp. 125 ff.).

[49] M. S. Drower, *CAH,* II², Pt. I, pp. 463, 467; Helck, *Beziehungen*², p. 164.

[50] E. F. Weiden, *PD,* pp. 14–15; H. G. Güterbock, *JCS,* 10 (1956), p. 93; A. Goetze, *CAH,* II², Pt. II, p. 15. Helck, *Beziehungen*², pp. 176–77.

[51] *ANET,* p. 395; Güterbock, *op. cit.,* p. 94.

[52] Some are of the opinion that at the beginning the "hill country of Judah" was a geographical term for the southern sector of the mountainous area like the "hill country of Ephraim"; cf. Noth, *Geschte,*³ pp. 56. f.; L. Waterman, *AJSL,* 55 (1938), pp. 29 ff.

[53] B. Mazar, *BA,* 25 (1962), pp. 119 f. The Persians had already adopted the term Athura (Assyria) as a synonym for "beyond the River", thus providing the precedent for the Greek writers, cf. *infra,* p. 422, n. 95.

CHAPTER V

The Historical Sources

The sources from which we derive our information for the study of historical geography are of three main types: the Bible, epigraphic texts and archaeological research.

I. THE BIBLE

After all the many epigraphic discoveries of recent times the Bible still remains the main source for historical geography of Palestine during the Israelite period. Its narratives and descriptions reflect their geographical environment as well as the historical events that took place. It contains references to some 475 local geographical names, many of them in contexts which supply pertinent details about the nature, location and history of the place. Of course, not every part of the country is described with equal clarity; the Bible is neither a textbook on geography nor an encyclopedia. Instead it is concerned with the spiritual and the everyday life of the Israelite people in its homeland. Therefore, we find much more information about the central regions of the country and considerably less about frontier areas. Districts populated by non-Israelites, e.g. Philistia, receive relatively little attention, even though they, too, were reckoned as part of the "land of Israel". Greater than all the rest is the amount of detail preserved concerning Judah and Benjamin; there is not as much known about Mount Ephraim and even less concerning Galilee and Transjordan; about the Negeb and the coastal regions we know very little. Except for the five Philistine capitals there is practically no information about other population centres in Philistia; important towns in that region such as Beth-'eglaim (Tell el-'Ajjul) and Yurza (Tell Jemmeh?) are not mentioned at all. Even in the Israelite Sharon we know of important towns from other sources which continued to exist during the Iron Age, e.g. Yaḥam (*y-ḥ-m*), Gath(-padalla), Migdal and Zephath (*ḏ-f-t*), to which no allusion is made in the Bible. An inscription from Shishak, Pharaoh of Egypt, lists many settlements in the Negeb whose names do not appear in the biblical text. Therefore, when discussing a particular place or region in the light of it biblical references, we must always keep in mind the extent of its representation in the biblical narrative—it may be purely accidental.

Besides incidental references of a general nature the Bible also contains some specifically geographical texts, the majority of which have been taken from everyday administrative and governmental records and woven into the historical narrative. There are also a few documents which were evidently composed for the purpose of geographical-historical description, e.g. the Table of Nations (Gen. 10). However, we can seldom be certain on this point; various passages are considered by different scholars to be purely utopian or literary creations having no political, geographical or practical basis whatsoever. We seriously question the validity of this opinion; it appears that most of the geographical texts are taken from life situations, while only our faulty understanding and insufficient information prevent us from establishing their historical context.

From this it is clear that with regard to the understanding of the geographical texts in the Bible their utilization as historical-geographical sources depends upon two decisive questions: (1) The list's primary function and (2) the date of its composition. From whence was the document taken and was it originally used for the same purpose for which it has been inserted in the historical narrative? Does it really belong in the period to which it has been assigned by the biblical wrtier? Inasmuch as these are not epigraphic texts whose date can be established by paleographic considerations but are, rather, literary-historical compositions which have passed through the hands of many editors and copyists, we have no other way but to evaluate the various documents according to their structure and contents, disregarding the framework in which they are presently found.

Neither is the higher critical division of biblical sources in vogue among scholars today of any help to us. These geographical texts do not originate in the various "documents" which critical scholars distinguish; instead they have been taken from more ancient sources and inserted into these historical collections. If we establish, for example, that the descriptions of the tribal inheritances were collected by the Deuteronomist, we have proved nothing regarding the original nature of the lists—from whence were they taken and why were they composed? In this instance two documents from different times were brought into the framework of the book of Joshua in order to serve the same purpose, and from their position in this book we can learn nothing about their original dates and functions. Today there is no doubt that even the historical-geographical texts which appear in the late book of Chronicles were taken from ancient sources. Their inclusion in a relatively later book establishes nothing as far as their original importance is concerned. With regard to their evaluation as historical and geographical witnesses, their association with the various biblical sources neither enhances nor detracts. Therefore, we will not discuss this problem, which is itself the subject of so much disagreement.

Of course, the question arises as to whether the various documents may have undergone a certain amount of editing which would have resulted in omissions and additions. It must be stressed that, as far as this problem can be investigated critically by comparison of non-biblical sources or parallel lists in the Bible, it is obvious that the biblical editors treated their ancient source(s) with great caution and respect. They doubtless considered their text as being in some sense canonical, being accepted as such by their contemporaries; therefore, any radical changes in the document would weaken its authenticity and authority. Naturally one finds explanatory annotations here and there, e.g. the identification of an ancient place by the addition of a later name (cf. Gen. 14. 2–8; Josh. 15. 8, *et al.*), or an associational explanation regarding a place or a region (cf. 1 Kings 4. 13, 19). Likewise there are certain ellipses (*anacolutha*) of which the different style and content show that they have been inserted from some other source (e.g. Josh. 15. 45–7; 1 Kings 9. 16). However, it should not be assumed that alterations of a substantial nature have been made in geographical lists in accordance with later viewpoints or circumstances; the idea must be rejected that there was a scribal school that busied itself with the invention of geographical documents solely on the basis of their own imagination and comprehension.

On the other hand, it must be assumed that in most of the biblical documents some recognizable omissions and conflations have occurred. This is why one finds both detailed and laconic passages in the same source. The former should not be considered as later expansions; quite the contrary, the latter are intentional condensations. This is especially notable in the tribal boundary descriptions which are quite brief for some of the tribes and extensive for others. The same boundary may even be described in slightly different terms; for example, that between Benjamin and Judah is noticeably detailed in the vicinity of Jerusalem (Josh. 15. 8; 18. 16), but not because this section is a later addition; the rest of the border description has simply been abbreviated. Therefore, no chronological assumptions can be derived from the verse except as concerns the time and special intersts of the editor. This conclusion is made probable by the basic nature of administrative geographical lists which had to be both detailed and precise in their original form. By contrast, it was sufficient to present them in a partial and condensed form within the framework of a historical narrative.

The geographical documents in the Bible may be divided into three main types according to their source and function: (1) historical-geographical descriptions; (2) territorial administrative lists; (3) itineraries of expeditions and conquests.

1. Historical-geographical Descriptions

There are a few documents preserved in the Bible which, by their very essence, could never have been used for practical administrative purposes; they were composed purely as historical-geographical descriptions. To this class one may assign at least two documents with certainty:

(*a*) The Table of Nations (Gen. 10). This passage gives an ethnogeographic description of the lands and peoples with which Israel had come into contact. It apparently dates to the United Kingdom (cf. *supra,* p.8). Obviously such an all-encompassing list as this could not have served any practical administrative function. It is simply a literary and historical creation based on the principle that all of the peoples known to Israel had descended from one ancestor. Therefore, this list takes the form of a genealogy patterned after the traditional patriarchal viewpoint. The text belongs, then, to the body of Israelite historiography.

(*b*) The roster of conquered Canaanite kings (Josh. 12). This chapter is a summary of the royal Canaanite towns mentioned in the narratives of conquest and settlement (cf. *infra,* p. 230). Here, too, we have an obvious geographical composition dependent upon the historical narrative.

(*c*) The "Land which Remains," namely the area of the Land of Canaan which remained outside territory actually settled by the Israelites. This is an illuminating example of one ancient source that is utilized twice, each time in a different context and with a different rationale. In Josh. 13. 1-6, it is presented as the land that remains to be divided among the tribes, evidently a fiction. In Judg. 3. 1–4, the same territory is given in terms of its ethnic populations which are said to have been unconquered by Israel. This latter explanation is basically correct. Neither passage gives the complete source; each abbreviates it in a different manner. The heading in Josh. 13, "the Land that Remains," must have belonged to the original source, but the editor of Joshua misunderstood it. However, he used his ancient source without altering its form except to abbreviate it somewhat. Thus, we have here a classic example of how the later biblical editors utilized authentic historical-geographical sources for their own purposes.

(*d*) Itinerary of the wandering Israelites (Num. 33). This geographical list seems to belong to the same type, although opinions differ widely as to its proper interpretation (cf. *infra,* p. 201). It is evidently a summary of the various stopping-places referred to in the exodus and wilderness wanderings. Some places not mentioned in the earlier accounts which were nevertheless known to be in that region may possibly have been added; however, there is no basis for the assumption that this list served any functional purpose.[1]

The definition of these documents determines their interpretation and function. We cannot consider them as authentic records of the period which they describe but rather as historical-geographical compositions of a later age founded on earlier sources and traditions. For example, in the list of Canaanite kings we can deduce something about the conquest narratives which the author had at his disposal. Likewise we cannot simply reconstruct the Israelites' line of march through the wilderness according to Numbers 33; but that list doubtless represents a logical route based on way-stations known to exist in the areas relevant to the narrative, though the itinerary thus defined must be dated somewhat later.

2. *Administrative Territorial Lists*

The only administrative document pertaining to the official organization of the kingdom is the list of Solomon's district commissioners (1 Kings 4. 7–19). However, there do exist certain other lists, both boundary descriptions and rosters of towns, which have been inserted into the biblical narrative in various ways. Only an analysis of the passages themselves can determine whether or not they originally played some practical role in Israelite administration. Of course, there is a great deal of disagreement about the degree of authenticity to be found in such documents, and some scholars hold the view that even these texts are nothing but literary creations. But inasmuch as the real purpose of several lists in this group is now proved beyond all doubt, one has the right to assume that all of the boundary delineations and town lists in the Bible originated in the country's administration. In fact, all of them can be associated with reasonable certainty to the historical reality of some particular period.

These administrative-territorial lists fall into two main categories: boundary delineations and rosters of towns. The difference between them is made clear by their respective functions. The boundary descriptions are based upon agreements between states or tribes, while the town lists were part of the administrative division of the country. From the standpoint of topographical analysis there is also a practical difference between these two types. Only in border delineations, especially those pertaining to a continuous line, do we find a consecutive geographical order. Reference to a place on a boundary line is therefore extremely important for determining its exact location, and sometimes it is decisive for identifying a particular site. But this is not always true for lists of towns; even though they usually consist of places located near to one another, they do not necessarily follow a simple geographical sequence. The mention of several towns, one after another, serves to indicate that they are all in the same area but the order need not be geographical. However, a list of towns usually does assure that these places should be sought in a certain region, and this is a factor of primary importance that cannot be ignored. For example, the accepted identification of Libnah with Tell eṣ-Ṣafi is rendered impossible by the list of Judean towns, because that city is mentioned alongside Mareshah, Keilah and Nezib in the south-eastern Shephelah (Josh. 15. 42) and not in association with towns adjacent to Tell eṣ-Ṣafi.

(*a*) Boundary descriptions. The delineations of boundaries are included in the narrative for the purpose of defining the areas occupied by states or tribes; therefore, the emphasis is on territorial borders. They doubtless have their origin in agreements between kingdoms or tribes intended to establish good relations, and sometimes mutual obligations, between the neighbouring groups.[2] The main paragraph in a covenant of this nature dealt with respect for all borders of the parties concerned. Therefore, it was of primary importance to define these boundaries exactly. Borders were fixed according to the four points of the compass in one of the following ways: the fixing of terminal points or the recording in sequence of points along the border.

The first method, which adopts the formula, "from . . . to . . .", is known outside of the Bible from treaties between ancient kingdoms of the Middle East. The clearest example is the Aramaic inscription on a stele from Sfiré in North Syria. The text is a treaty between Matti' el, King of Arpad and Barga' yah, King of Katka, in the mid-eighth century B.C. Here we find a description of "the whole of Aram"(ארם כלה)which defines the territory included in the alliance:

> [From ʿA]rqu to Yaʿd[i], and. . .
> from Lebanon to Yab[rud and Damas]cus and ʿArʿaru and Ma[n-ṣ]uate, [fr]om the Vale (of Lebanon) to Katka.[3]

This formula defines the political and geographical centres on the borders of the kingdoms from ʿArqu (Arkath), on the Mediterranean shore at the Phoenician border, in the south-west to Ya"di (Sam' al) and another place whose name is not preserved, at the border of Anatolia in the north; from Mount Lebanon at the Phoenician border in the west to Yabrud on the fringe of the desert in the east and Damascus and the adjacent ʿArʿaru (Aroer; cf. Isa. 17. 1–2, Heb.) on the Israelite border in the south-east; from the Lebanese Beqaʿ at the Israelite border in the south (cf. the boundary at Lebo-hamath in the reign of Jeroboam II; 2 Kings 14. 25) as far as Katka, which is evidently at the northern extremity of Syria.

Formulae of this type are plentiful in the Bible. Sometimes they contain only the two extreme reference points, e.g. the territory of Israel "from Dan to Beer-sheba" (2 Sam. 24. 2, *et al.*); others furnish reference points in all four directions of the compass, e.g. the ancient concept of the promised land whose bounds extended "from the Red Sea to the Sea of the Philistines, and from the wilderness to the Euphrates" (Exod. 23. 31); and occasionally several points are designated in different directions, e.g. on the tribal boundary of Gad "from Heshbon to Ramath-mizpeh and Betonim, and from Mahanaim to the border of Lidebir" (Josh. 13. 26).

In the Bible these descriptions are based upon the following territorial concepts: "the land of the Amorites" in the patriarchal period (Gen. 15. 18; Exod. 23. 31; Deut. 1. 7; 11. 24; Josh. 1. 4); the land of Canaan (Num. 13. 21); the extent of the Israelite conquest (Josh. 10. 41; 11. 17; 12. 7) as opposed to "the land that remains" (Josh. 13. 5; Judg. 3. 3); the areas of Israelite settlement (Deut. 34. 1; Josh. 12. 1; 2 Sam. 24. 2, *et al.*); the kingdom of David and Solomon (1 Kings 4. 24; 8. 65; 1 Chron. 13. 5; 2 Chron. 7. 8); the northern kingdom under Jeroboam II (2 Kings 14. 25; Amos 6. 14) and the kingdom of Judah under Josiah (2 Kings 23. 8). Also included in this class are the boundary descriptions pertaining to the Transjordanian tribes, Reuben (Josh. 13. 16) and Gad (Josh. 13. 26).

The second method, listing a series of border points in sequence, is used in only two documents: the boundaries of the land of Canaan (Num. 34. 1–12) and the tribal inheritances (Josh. 15. 1–12; 16. 1–8; 17. 7–9; 18. 12–20; 19. 10–14, 26–7, 29, 33–4).[4] These two boundary descriptions are related not only as regards to their method but also their structure and composition, since the tribal inheritances are defined within the framework of the land of Canaan so that some of the borders described in the two documents correspond exactly to one another.

The great attention to detail in both cases proves that they are founded on a historical reality. The boundaries for the land of Canaan are those of the Egyptian province in Palestine (called Canaan) which were encountered by the Israelite tribes during the conquest period (cf. *supra,* pp. 74 f.). The tribal boundaries sprang from an alliance between the tribes in Mount Ephraim and Galilee, i.e. Israel in the limited sense of the term, which regarded itself heir to the land of Canaan (cf. *infra,* pp. 248–260).

(*b*) Town lists. Lists of various towns which appear in the descriptions of regions or tribal inheritances are derived from the administrative organization of the kingdom. This is explicitly stated only with regard to the list of Solomon's district commissioners (1 Kings 4. 7), but the same is unquestionably true for the roster of towns in Judah and at least part of those in Benjamin (Josh. 15. 21–62; 18. 25–8); analysis of all the remaining lists strengthens the probability that they have similar derivation. An administrative division of the kingdom was obviously intended to facilitate conscription and tax collection; it was doubtless based upon a cadastral and population census. Unlike an alliance between kingdoms or tribes, an administrative act of this sort was less concerned with the boundaries than with the settlements and the population included within each district. Even if the new administrative division followed the traditional boundaries to some extent, it gave them a new territorial significance. The following town lists are preserved in the Bible:

(1) The Solomonic districts (1 Kings 4. 7–19; cf. *infra,* p. 309ff.–half of which are named after tribes while the rest are defined by groups of cities. Comparison with the roster of towns in Judah makes it probable that both parts of Solomon's list are only excerpts defining the respective districts by name or by their principal towns. There doubtless existed a detailed list of settlements in each district. But in our text it is the names of the commissioners that receive special emphasis (1 Kings 4. 7–8), while the regions are defined with the utmost brevity. Some parts of the more complete city rosters may have been preserved for us in the description of the northern tribal inheritances. As we have previously noted, the administrative function of this list is most probable, and its contents fit best with the Solomonic period, to the second half of his reign to be more exact, after the construction of Hazor.

(2) The districts of Judah (Josh. 15; 18; cf. *infra,* p. 347ff.)–this is the most detailed roster of towns in the Bible. It no doubt reflects the administrative division of the Judean kingdom into twelve districts. Thus it obviously cannot be earlier than the division of the kingdom.

(3) The towns of Simeon and Dan (Josh. 19; 1 Chron. 4; cf. *infra,* p. 298 ff.)—these town lists become comprehensible only against the background of the period of Judges 14 as suggested by the allusion in 1 Chronicles 4. 31. These appear to have been town lists within the framework of the old tribal league and they were inserted bodily into the description of the tribal inheritances in the book of Joshua, since these tribes were missing from the boundary delineations. No other information concerning these ancient tribes was available to the editor.

(4) The town lists of the Galilean and the Transjordanian tribes and the northern city-group of Benjamin (Josh. 13; 18; 19; cf. *infra,* p. 349 ff.)—these rosters seem to belong to the administrative division of the Israelite kingdom, the foundations of which were laid by Solomon. The inclusion of Hazor among the towns of Naphtali (Josh. 19. 36) proves that this list cannot be older than the Solomonic period, inasmuch as Hazor was rebuilt only in the middle of Solomon's reign (1 Kings 9. 15), a fact also demonstrated by the excavations there.[5] The city lists for Naphtali, Issachar and Asher correspond to the Solomonic districts, and the abbreviated list pertaining to Zebulun (Josh. 19. 15) was evidently

part of the Asher district (1 Kings 4. 16; perhaps Bealoṯh should be corrected to Zebulun?). The northern (Israelite) list of Benjaminite towns (Josh. 18. 21–4) apparently defines the Benjamin district in that kingdom after the division of the monarchy, while the main part of Benjamin was annexed to the kingdom of Judah. The cities of Reuben and Gad (Josh. 13) probably correspond to the districts of Mahanaim and Gad (following LXX instead of MT which reads Gilead). From the stele of Mesha, King of Moab, we know that part of these towns had already been annexed to Moab by the beginning of the ninth century B.C.; thus it would seem that these rosters cannot be later than the United Monarchy. The list of Transjordanian towns in Joshua 13 portrays a well-ordered geographical division, Reuben in the south and Gad in the north, which does not represent the actual settlement pattern of these two tribes. A different scheme is described in the list of towns belonging to Gad and Reuben in Numbers 32. 34–8, where the Reubenite towns are grouped around Heshbon while the Gadite settlements are spread over the whole of southern Transjordan from Aroer and Dibon in the south to Jaazer, Jogbehah and Beth-nimrah which are north of Heshbon. This list appears to represent the actual settlement pattern of the two tribes at about the time of David, who relied upon the existing tribal divisions. Gad was also located in the southern part of Israelite Transjordan according to the census carried out by Joab at David's behest (2 Sam. 24. 5). On the other hand, Solomon preferred to adopt a territorial principle since Reuben had been reduced to a small pocket of settlement within Gad, and the description is abbreviated as usual. The editors of the book of Joshua did not take these terms into account; instead they used the list of the southern towns to describe the inheritance of Reuben and the list of the northern towns to describe that of Gad.

The absence of town lists in the inheritances of Ephraim and Manasseh for which we only have boundary descriptions is a serious problem. Certain scholars have sought to derive far-reaching conclusions from this situation. Alt assumes that there are two documents here, the first represented by the town lists of Judah, including those of Dan and all of Benjamin,[6] the second being an integrated roster of Galilee which he associates with the Assyrian province of Megiddo[7]; but he has no explanation for the origin of the Transjordanian lists. Noth practically denies the existence of town lists in the northern tribes and sees all of the rosters as border descriptions to which connecting verbs have not been added.[8] Except for the cities in the Judean kingdom there remain, according to his viewpoint, only the towns of Transjordan; this area he conjectures to be a thirteenth district of the Judean kingdom which was established after its annexation in the reign of Josiah.[9]

All of these explanations are forced and fraught with many difficulties.

As a matter of fact, town lists are preserved from all of the tribes except Ephraim and Manasseh. The texts pertaining to the various tribes cannot be combined to form a realistic and integrated administrative list when the central district of Mount Ephraim is lacking. One should also observe that the border descriptions of Ephraim and Manasseh are preserved in a very abbreviated form. For this reason it is more probable that the absence of town lists from these two tribal areas is an intentional omission, because the kingdom of Judah was always more interested in Galilee and Transjordan where an Israelite-Jewish population maintained its continuity rather than in Mount Ephraim, its competitor and adversary, where a mixed populace prevailed after the destruction of Samaria.

(5) The Levitical cities (Josh. 21; 1 Chron. 6; cf. *infra,* p.301 ff.)—here we seem to have two exemplars of the same list, the original of which contained forty-eight towns, four for each of the twelve Israelite tribes. The roster apparently dates to the reign of David, and those towns in which Levitical clans from Judah were settled were frontier colonies and other key centres. They were located mainly in newly annexed territory for the purpose of strengthening the monarchy and the loyal Israelite elements in these areas.

(6) The unconquered Canaanite cities (Judg. 1. 21, 27–35)—this roster, which also appears in part among the descriptions of tribal territories in the book of Joshua, lists the various Canaanite cities that had succeeded in maintaining their independence against the tribes in their respective areas. The list is not hypothetical in essence, as Alt assumes,[10] because it describes reciprocal relationships and situations of partial enslavement which differ with each group of towns. On the other hand, Alt is correct in pointing out the close connection between it and the tribal boundary descriptions. This is true not only from the standpoint of a similarity in outlook but also from the fact that the same tribes are described in both documents: Benjamin, Manasseh, Ephraim, Zebulun, Asher and Naphtali. At the end reference is made to the cities which had "pressed the Danites back into the hill country", though the tribe of Dan does not appear in the boundary lists. Nevertheless, according to Judges 1. 35 these towns were finally subjugated to the House of Joseph and no longer associated with Dan.

Like the boundary lists, this roster is also connected with the alliance of the tribes in Mount Ephraim and Galilee. In the region of the unconquered Canaanite towns it was not possible to establish precise inter-tribal boundaries. Therefore, the various Canaanite territories were indicated with respect to the tribe under whose influence they eventually fell (cf. *infra,* pp. 233 ff.).

(7) The list of Judean towns in the genealogical tables (1 Chron. 2–4; cf, *infra,* pp. 246 ff.)—the genealogical table of Judah contains a special

roster listing the dwelling places of the various clans according to a formula in which the clan becomes the "father" of the place. In this manner a special town list is obtained, being organized according to the chief clans of Judah: Shelah, Hur (the first-born of Hezron and Ephrathah), Caleb and Ephrathah, and the other sons of Caleb. It is probable that this situation originated from an alliance of the southern tribes in which Judah and Caleb were prominent.

(8) Towns of the Babylonian exiles (Ezra 2; Neh. 7; cf. *infra,* p. 416)—this list, preserved in two exemplars, is doubtless an official document dating to the return from exile and pertaining to the various clans returning to their proper homes.

(9) Builders of the wall of Jerusalem under Nehemiah (Neh. 3; cf. *infra,* p. 418)—this roster should also be accepted as it is, but the towns mentioned in it seem to represent the administrative centres of the Judean province at that time.

(10) "The rest of Israel" in the post-exilic period (Neh. 11; cf. *infra,* pp. 410 f.)—this list includes towns in Benjamin, the Negeb and the Shephelah, of which the majority were outside the bounds of the Judean province during the Persian period. Evidently these are the principal towns where a Judean population had been able to remain throughout the Babylonian exile.

(11) Lists of fortified towns—a special type of geographical roster is represented by the records of fortified towns, viz. fortresses and store cities built by the various Kings of Judah and Israel.

Only two lists of this nature have been preserved in the Bible: the fortresses of Solomon (1 Kings 9. 15–19; 2 Chron. 8. 1–6) and those of Rehoboam (2 Chron. 11. 5–12). These passages are doubtless extracts from the royal chronicles. Certain allusions give indication that the ancient editors had other lists before them of this type, viz. the cities built by Asa (2 Chron. 14. 6), Uzziah (2 Chron. 26. 6–10) and Hezekiah (2 Chron. 32. 29). What a pity that the editors did not attach sufficient importance to these "dry" lists to cite them fully!

There is no reason to doubt the date and function of these rosters as assigned to them in the Bible. Proof of this was recently furnished with regard to the first three of Solomon's fortified cities—Hazor, Megiddo and Gezer (1 Kings 9. 15). At all three of them gates identical in form and dating to the Solomonic period have been discovered.[11] There are some, of course, who object to assigning our second list to Rehoboam.[12] However, there is no reasonable answer to why the editor of the book of Chronicles should assign to Rehoboam a list from the reign of Josiah or some other king, and the text itself contains nothing incompatible with a date in Rehoboam's reign.

3. Expeditions and Conquests

Various texts pertaining to expeditions, especially during war but not infrequently in peacetime, are important geographical documents, having many parallels in external sources from the Egyptians, the Assyrians, the Babylonians, the Hittites, *et al.*[13] Descriptions of military campaigns and conquests doubtless originate from royal chronicles; therefore, there is no reason to doubt the authenticity of such passages in the Bible. Unfortunately, only a few brief exerpts from documents of this nature have been preserved in the biblical record; generally we only have a factual, unembellished statement that the campaign took place. Campaign descriptions containing specific geographic data are: the conquest of Abijah (2 Chron. 13. 19); the campaign of Ben-hadad, King of Aram-Damascus (1 Kings 15. 20); Uzziah's victories in Philistia (2 Chron. 26. 6); the campaign of Tiglath-pileser III (2 Kings 15. 29); the Philistine conquests during the reign of Ahaz (2 Chron. 28. 18). All of the other passages in this category mention only one or two places at the most and cannot be considered as geographical lists.

The Bible also preserves descriptions of two very ancient military campaigns: the expedition of the four kings from the north against the erstwhile cities in the Valley of Siddim (Gen. 14; cf. *infra,* p. 140), a passage containing important topographical information which is connected in the biblical story with the days of Abraham, although its date and historical circumstances are difficult to ascertain; the victory song of Sihon, the Amorite King of Heshbon (or the lament over defeated Moab), which refers to several places in Moab that had been conquered by Sihon (Num. 21. 27–30), purporting to be a composition from the period of the Israelite conquest in the thirteenth century B.C.

To this category also belong the oracles of doom against various regions and countries that we find in the prophetic books. Some of them concern Judah, while others have to do with neighbouring kingdoms. Most of them were evidently written after their respective districts had been devastated by an expedition, and they contain extremely valuable geographic material pertaining to their respective regions during the later phases of the Judean kingdom. The following passages are of this type: Isaiah's description of the land of Benjamin (Isa. 10. 28-32) and Micah's lament over the towns of the Shephelah (Micah. 1. 10–15), which evidently belong to the campaign of Sennacherib (cf. *infra,* p. 392); the denunciation of the Philstine capitals by Amos (Amos 1. 6–8) and by Jeremiah (Jer. 47. 1–7); the towns of Moab (Isa. 15–16; Jer. 48) and Edom (Jer. 49. 7–22); and finally Ezekiel's description of Tyre and the cities of Phoenicia which was evidently derived from an earlier source (Ezek. 26–8).

II. EPIGRAPHICAL DOCUMENTS

A double importance is attached to epigraphical documents: they provide the general Near Eastern background which greatly enhances our understanding of Palestinian history, and they furnish us with many direct parallels to the biblical sources, especially in regard to literary types, which is helpful even when the text in question does not pertain directly to Palestine; they contain a considerable amount of supplementary information concerning the history and topography of Palestine during various periods. Here in this brief review we will concern ourselves only with the main types of sources, those which have direct bearing on Palestine. As to the many texts which shed light upon the historical and cultural background of the Bible, we will deal with them when discussing their respective historical periods and only when they have direct relevance to our subject.

The epigraphical documents may be classed in three groups according to their country of origin: Egyptian, Mesopotamian and Palestinian.

1. Egyptian Sources

Most of the Egyptian sources date to the second millennium B.C. and provide the foundation for our understanding of the "land of Canaan" before its occupation by the Israelites. Though we have a few Middle Kingdom inscriptions from the Twelfth Dynasty (twentieth–nineteenth centuries B.C.), most of the Egyptian material belongs to the New Kingdom, especially the eighteenth (fifteenth–fourteenth centuries B.C.) and the nineteenth (thirteenth century) Dynasties. The Egyptian texts can be classified according to literary genre into seven categories: expedition journals ("annals"), bas reliefs, topographical lists, literary papyri, administrative papyri, execration texts and correspondence archives.

Expedition Journals ("Annals"). The Egyptians carried out frequent military campaigns to Palestine and Syria. Descriptions of many of these expeditions have been preserved in official inscriptions carved on temple walls; a few records of this type have also been discovered in the tomb inscriptions of officers who took part in the campaigns.[14]

Contributions of great significance to Palestinian geography are found in the following texts: the tomb inscription of Weni from the reign of the Old Kingdom Pharaoh Pepi I (twenty-fourth century B.C.; *infra,* p. 135); the stele of Khu-Sebek from the reign of Sen-Usert III (nineteenth century B.C.; *infra,* p. 147); the tomb inscription of Aḫ-mose concerning the expulsion of the Hyksos (*c.* 1550 B.C.; *infra,* p. 152); Thut-mose III's conquest of Megiddo (*c.* 1468; *infra,* p. 153); the campaigns of Amen-hotep II (*c.* 1445–1430; *infra,* p. 166); Ramses II's expedition to attack Kadesh (*c.* 1285; *infra,* p. 181); the victory hymn of Merneptah (*c.* 1220; *infra,* p. 184); Ramses III's battles against the Sea Peoples (*c.* 1170; *infra,* p. 267).

The two Egyptian stelae from the reign of Seti I discovered at Beth-shean (*c.* 1300 B.C.; *infra,* pp. 177, 179) also belong to this class.

They contain brief references to battles carried out in the country around Beth-shean.

Bas Reliefs. Besides inscribing them with annals the Egyptians ornamented their temple walls with bas reliefs depicting their campaigns and especially the conquests of important towns.[15] Most of these reliefs are rich in details concerning warfare but very poor in topographical information. However, those of Seti I (*c.* 1300 B.C.) are especially valuable for topography, since they also describe the many fortresses and wells along the route from Egypt to Palestine (cf. *supra,* p. 47). The reliefs of Ramses II (thirteenth century; *infra.* p. 181) also show us certain conquered towns in the land of Canaan, but the pictures conform to stylized patterns and thus do not furnish any unique details about a particular place. Ramses III's war with the Sea Peoples is also extensively portrayed in reliefs (*c.* 1170; *infra,* p. 267).

Topographical Lists. To this class belong the reliefs containing a series of geographical names.[16] In these reliefs a great deal of space is devoted to rows upon rows of oval rings symbolizing the fortification walls of the conquered towns, the names of which they contain. Above the oval name-ring is a partial figure of the local chieftain, the head and shoulders with the arms tied behind. The necks of these rulers are all bound by a long rope, one end of which is grasped by the deity who is presenting the prisoners to Pharaoh.

The earliest topographical list, which served as a prototype for all those that followed, is that of Thut-mose III. It contains 119 names of the places conquered by him in Palestine after his victory at Megiddo (*c.* 1468; *infra,* p. 154 ff.). This text is also the most complete and most important of all from a topographical standpoint. Following his example, most of the pharaohs of the Eighteenth to Twentieth Dynasties immortalized their deeds of valour in the form of topographical lists. However, of Thut-mose's successors Seti I (*infra,* p. 178) and Ramses II (*infra,* p.182) have made the most important contributions to our topographical information. The long lists of Ramses III have little independent value, since it is clear from their composition that many of the names were simply copied from his predecessors. Only the inscription of Pharaoh Shishak (*c.* 924 B.C.; *infra,* p. 323) provides details concerning Palestine in the Israelite period.

Undoubtedly there is a direct connection between the expedition journals and the topographical lists. This has been demonstrated most clearly by the rosters of Seti I, which contain the same series of geographical names as those mentioned in his stele from Beth-shean (cf. *infra,* p. 178). This relationship can also be demonstrated by comparing the introduction to the "annals" of Thut-mose III with his topographical lists. He states that the whole land had rebelled from Yurza to "the end of the earth", though an Egyptian garrison was still holding out at

Sharuhen. Thus Yurza appears in the topographical list (No. 60), while Sharuhen is not mentioned. One may also compare Shishak's list with the biblical description of his campaign (cf. *infra,* p.323) since we do not have Shishak's own journal of the expedition. The biblical narrative stresses that Jerusalem was not conquered (in return for a heavy ransom); and Shishak does not include Jerusalem in his roster, though he does mention several places near by.

At the same time, one should not always expect to find a logical and continuous line of march in the order of names so inscribed. The places are not generally listed in consecutive geographical order. Noth's attempts to reconstruct the courses followed by Thut-mose III and Seti I according to the sequence of names on their respective inscriptions cannot be maintained under critical examination (cf. *infra,* p.157). The only section in Thut-mose III's lists where the names appear in proper geographical order is that group of towns located in the northern Shephelah and the Sharon (Nos. 61–71). It may be that the actual line of march taken on this military expedition is preserved in this passage, while the fall of the other towns may have come as a result of Thut-mose's over-all victory at Megiddo or from separate operations carried out afterwards at the various places. Certain geographical districts of the country are noted, and here and there one finds neighbouring towns grouped together in a manner similar to the biblical lists; in such cases the scribe is evidently following previously established patterns with which he was familiar. Even the references to various towns in the "annals" does not always follow the order in which they were conquered; an illuminating example of this is Seti I's stele and his topographical list (cf. *infra,* p. 177 f.). The main parts of Shishak's list are evidently arranged in the geographical order of the expedition, but in the fifth line certain names have been added without regard to their proper place in the sequence.

Literary Papyri. Some literary passages containing descriptions of Palestine have been preserved,[17] but these are characterized by all the advantages and disadvantages of a literary creation. They are later in date than the subjects discussed in them and lack the historical authenticity of documents contemporary with the events. On the other hand, they are not so dry and matter-of-fact as most epigraphical texts; and some passages provide illuminating descriptions of districts, places and peoples in various periods. Furthermore, they are not too far removed from the periods in which they purport to deal, since some of their contents are attested in papyri as old as the Middle and Late Kingdoms.

The most important documents in this class are: The Tale of Sinuhe, twentieth century B.C. (cf. *infra,* p. 142 ff.); The Taking of Joppa in the reign of Thut-mose III; The Epistle of the scribe Hori, Papyrus

Anastasi I, thirteenth century B.C. (cf. *infra,* p.182 f.);The Onomasticon of Amenope, eleventh century B.C. (cf. *infra,* p. 270); The Story of Wen-Amon, early eleventh century B.C. (cf. *infra,* p. 269).

Administrative Papyri. Only a few papyri are known which have bearing on the Egyptian administration of the land of Canaan during the Late Kingdom.[18] The main texts in this group are: a list of emissaries from various Canaanite towns dating to the fifteenth century B.C. (cf. *infra,* p. 165); administrative papyri from the border fortresses of Egypt which served as practice texts for budding Egyptian scribes (cf. *infra,* p. 184).

Execration Texts. A unique class of documents is the collection of texts inscribed with the names of rulers over various towns and ethnic groups of Palestine during the Middle Kingdom. The names are accompanied by curses and execrations directed against these rulers.[19] From these documents which date partly to the twentieth and partly to the end of the nineteenth century B.C. we receive the earliest information of any importance concerning the make-up of the population in the land of Canaan.

Correspondence Archives. The royal archive discovered at El Amarna is the only collection of Egyptian documents containing extensive correspondence with the Kings of Canaan. It dates to the first half of the fourteenth century B.C.[20] The letters are written on clay tablets in the Akkadian language, which was the *lingua franca* of that time (cf. *infra,* p. 169 ff.).

2. *Mesopotamian Sources*

Palestine is both geographically and politically closer to Egypt than to Mesopotamia. Therefore, the number of Mesopotamian documents pertaining to Palestine is proportionately less. Except for general references to Palestine and Syria (Amurru), the Mediterranean (the Sea of Amurru) and several mountains in Syria (Lebanon, Amanus and perhaps Bashan), the only Akkadian documents earlier than the first millennium to mention a town in Palestine are the tablets from Mari on the Euphrates dating to the eighteenth century B.C.[21] These are letters and administrative records from the royal archive. Though they contain a few meagre allusions to Hazor and Laish, it is not possible to derive much information from them about those cities (cf. *infra,* p. 149).

More detailed Akkadian documents are available only from the period of expansion by the new Assyrian kingdom in the ninth to seventh centuries B.C.[22] These sources are limited primarily to stelae, reliefs and passages from military annals dating to the reigns of Shalmaneser III, Adad-nirari III, Tiglath-pileser III, Sargon II, Sennacherib, Esarhaddon and Ashurbanipal. Really detailed topographical information is found only in the inscriptions of Tiglath-pileser III, Sennacherib and Esarhaddon (cf. *supra,* p. 48, *infra,* pp. 372, 388 ff.). Concerning the provincial centres in the Assyrian period, we are aided by the Assyrian eponym lists and a few other rosters of important towns (cf. *infra,* pp. 374 ff.).

3. Palestinian Sources

The epigraphical texts discovered in Palestine itself are limited in number and only a few of them contain topographical information. Isolated Akkadian tablets similar to those in the El Amarna archives furnish a certain amount of geographical detail; such letters have been discovered at: Taanach (*infra,* p. 169), Gezer (*infra,* p. 174) and Tell el-Ḥesi (Eglon?, *infra,* p. 174). Besides the Egyptian stele from Beth-shean mentioned above in relation to similar Egyptian sources, the only stele bearing an important historical inscription discovered in Palestine is that of Mesha, King of Moab, from the mid-ninth century B.C. (*infra,* p. 336 ff.). The only administrative documents of substantial geographic significance found in this country are the Samaria ostraca from the early eighth century B.C.; they provide very important details about the Samaria region (*infra,* p. 356 ff.). The royal seal impressions stamped on the handles of storage jars from Judah dating to the end of the eighth and the beginning of the seventh centuries B.C. fall into a special class. Though each impression bears only one of four place names, this collection of inscribed jar handles is very useful for geographical purposes (*infra,* p. 394 ff.). Finally, the Lachish letters also contain occasional geographic allusions (*infra,* p. 407).

III. THE CONTRIBUTION OF ARCHAEOLOGY

Today archaeology is one of the foundation stones in our historical and geographical research. It is precisely because Palestine is poor in contemporary epigraphical material that the archaeologists have learned to prize every small remnant from the ancient material culture. By combining all these scraps of information they strive to fill in the gaps in our historical knowledge about settlements and regions. These data put our knowledge on a realistic footing, and sometimes they are the main source at our disposal. Archaeological research consists of two specialized activities which complement one another, viz. excavation and survey.

1. Excavation

Thanks to scientific archaeological excavations we know a great deal today about the nature and history of ancient settlements. We are acquainted with the structures typical of an ancient town: its general layout and fortifications, public and private buildings, systems for water supply and drainage, as well as the material culture and commercial relationships with other lands. Archaeology draws heavily upon the exact sciences and strives constantly to approach their standards of accuracy. To this end it seeks above all else to establish accurately the material facts. However, when it comes to historical or historio-geographical interpretation, the archaeologist steps out of the realm of the exact sciences, and he must rely upon value judgements and hypotheses to arrive at a comprehensive historical picture.

The basis of scientific archaeological work is stratigraphic investigation, the discernment of the different occupation levels within a particular mound. The excavator must distinguish carefully between the various strata of his tell and, as much as is practicable, he must analyse each one separately in terms of its respective "finds". This is usually not an easy task, because the actual levels in a particular tell are not uniformly laid one above the other. However, since the pioneering stratigraphic work of Petrie at Tell el-Ḥesi in 1890, methods of excavation have been considerably refined to permit the achievement of quite satisfactory results.

A stratigraphic excavation furnishes us a chronological frame of reference for the interpretation and understanding of the finds. The dates established are only relative at first; certain objects can be shown to be older or younger than others from the same site. These provisional conclusions become increasingly more refined with every new excavation which confirms or corrects the earlier results and increases the degree of accuracy. The relative dates gradually become more and more absolute as the relationship between the particular discoveries and finds from other excavations become better established, especially when Egyptian inscriptions or comparisons of the material culture in Palestine with vessels of known date from other countries can be utilized. Historical considerations also play a role in this process. Unlike the relative chronology, which is more or less certain for an orderly stratigraphic excavation, one must exercise extreme caution in seeking to establish an absolute chronology. Usually inscriptions only furnish a *terminus a quo* for their own stratum because the possibility always exists that the inscribed objects saw a long period of use, or even re-use, after being discarded by the original owners. This is particularly true of scarabs bearing the names of pharaohs which were kept, perhaps as amulets, for remarkable periods of time. Comparison with other countries is also sometimes dangerous, for one may fall into a vicious circle where the objects in the other culture may have been dated by their relationship to the Palestinian, without sufficient regard for the circumstances of discovery and the relative chronologies involved. It goes without saying that historical considerations are especially risky, since they always involve certain presuppositions and subjective attitudes.

We must always remember, therefore, that not all dates are absolute and are in varying degrees suspect. However, by cautious utilization of all the most recent data obtained from every new excavation one may achieve considerable precision today. A good example of how a precise date can be established by utilizing all available archaeological data in combination with historical information may be drawn from the excavations at Hazor. There it was possible to distinguish eight Iron Age strata, which were designated as levels X–V (including XA–XB and IXA–IXB). Comparison with other excavations indicated that the pottery in these levels belonged to approximately the tenth to eighth centuries B.C. Then in the earliest stratum (XB) the great gate was discovered, bearing an amazing similarity to the gates at Megiddo and Gezer. Thus the historical conclusion was reached, with almost complete certainty, that this level was Solomonic in date, its structure having been built in *c.* 950 B.C. (cf. 1 Kings 9. 15). The latest Iron Age level (V) showed signs of massive destruction and burning, which brought an end to the great fortified city. Again it seemed quite certain that this conflagration must be assigned to the campaign of Tiglath-pileser III in 733–732 B.C. (cf. 2 Kings 15. 29).

To these decisive arguments certain secondary and derived considerations may be added. In level VIII large public buildings were built and the city's fortifications were strengthened and expanded; these are probably the works of Ahab in *c.* 870 B.C. Level IXB was destroyed by fire and part of the Solomonic wall was dismantled, never to be re-used; these are more than likely traces of the campaign by Ben-hadad, King of Aram-Damascus, in *c.* 885 B.C. (cf. 1 Kings 15. 20). Level VII had also suffered destruction, so much so that many of the great public buildings went out of use. There is good reason to assign this calamity to the campaigns by Hazael, King of Damascus, towards the end of Jehu's reign in *c.* 815 B.C. From all indications level VI was demolished by an earthquake, probably the one mentioned as having taken place during the reign of Uzziah, King of Judah, in *c.* 760 (cf. Amos 1. 1; Zech. 14. 5). Though not all of these assumptions are of equal certainty, it would appear that the dates of these levels are accurate within a range of 30 to 40 years.[23]

Most of the major excavations have been carried out at the larger and more centrally located sites in the country and give us a representative picture of the ancient settlements in various regions (cf. map 5). Most of them have been made in the valleys: the Valley of Jezreel—Megiddo, Taanach, 'Afula and Beth-shean; the Jordan Valley—En-gedi, Jericho, Teleilat el-Ghassul, Tell Deir 'Allah, Tell es-Sa' idiyeh, Peḥel, Khirbet Kerak, Hazor; the coastal plain—Achzib, Acco, Tell Kisan, Tell Abu Huwam, Shikmonah, Tell edh-Dhurur, Aphek, Tell Qasileh, Joppa and Ashdod; the Judean Shephelah—Gezer, Beth-shemesh, Lachish, Tell Beit Mirsim, Tell el-Ḥesi and Tell en-Nejileh; the Negeb—Tell el- 'Ajjul, Tell Jemmeh, Tell el-Far 'ah, Tell esh-Shari 'ah, Beer-sheba,

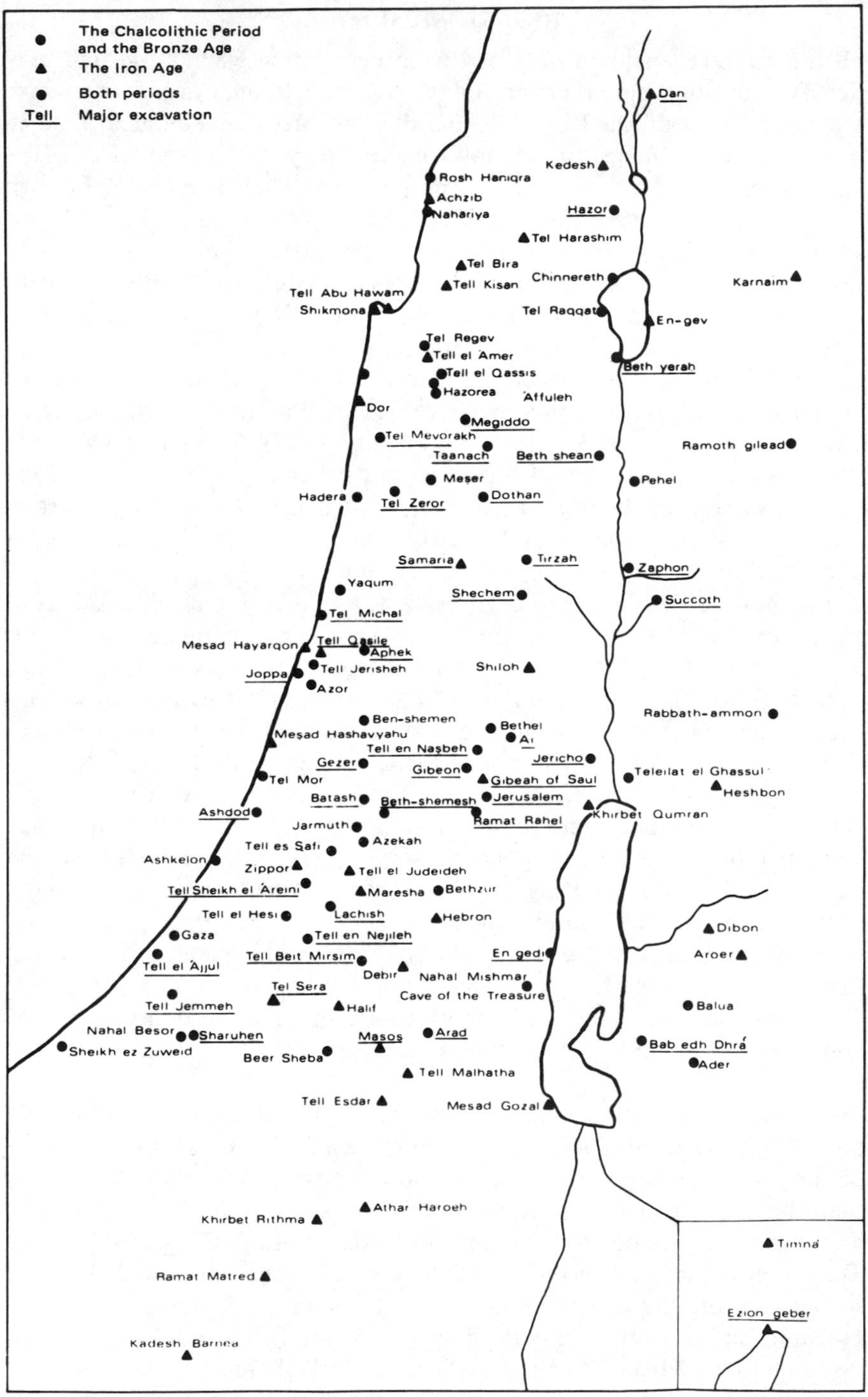

Map 5. The Archaeological Excavations

Tell Meshash, Tell el-Milh (Malhata) and Arad; in the Judean hill country—Beth-zur, Ramat Raḥel, Jerusalem, Tell el-Ful and Gibeon; Mount Ephraim—Tell en-Naṣbeh, Bethel, Shechem, Tell el-Far'ah, Samaria and Dothan; in Transjordan—Heshbon, Aroer, Buşeirah, Tawilan, Ezion-geber (Tell el-Kheleifeh). In certain areas the excavations have been few and on a very small scale, e.g. Transjordan and Galilee.

2. Surveys

For the historical geography of Palestine the archeological survey is no less important than the excavation. Excavation is limited, of necessity, to one main site, because it involves great expense and time. As a result, one obtains a picture of the one settlement located at that site, which is usually the chief city of the entire area.

On the other hand, an archaeological survey can provide a picture of the whole area and the occupational changes that have taken place in it. The one main settlement may not necessarily reflect all of these processes; since it was a main centre it was proabably occupied during most historical periods, even when other changes were taking place in the vicinity. The city itself does not always reflect these changes, because new settlers are most likely to appear at first in small villages or encampments. Before they gained occupancy in the city many modifications may have already come about in their utensils and manner of life as they adapted themselves to their new environment. Furthermore, the principal town may have seen periods of expansion or decline which were due to special causes and not typical of the adjacent region.

Therefore, the value of an archaeological survey is much greater when it takes in most or all of the antiquity sites in the area being examined, albeit of narrow compass. Obviously, the larger the area surveyed the greater the importance attached to the results. In an exacting survey one may not only establish the general features of a site, e.g. its size and the nature of its fortifications, one may also record the main periods of its occupation by means of the potsherds scattered on the top and slopes of the tell. The forces of nature, e.g. wind, rain, cold and heat, and the activities of man, e.g. ploughing, digging, building etc., have accomplished for us the task of uncovering sherds from the various periods. We need only to search patiently and scupulously on the top and slopes (which are especially convenient for sherding). Sometimes one must repeat the survey during different seasons of the year. In this manner we can usually assemble a sufficient quantity of sherds from each phase of the site's occupation to establish the periods in which settlement existed there and also when it was more extensive. The progress in stratigraphic excavation and typological classification of pottery provide the means for defining our assembled sherds with remarkable precision. Thus a systematic archaeological survey can produce an occupational map for the different periods in a certain area and shed much light on the processes of decline and increase in settlement which can never be achieved by excavation.

Modern archaeological surveys of this type have been carried out thus far only in a few areas of Palestine. The surveys of Conder and Kitchener[24] and of Schumacher in Transjordan[25] were made before the development of stratigraphic excavation when pottery as a means of dating was still unknown. Therefore, they were only able to fix precise dates for the later sites where they found buildings or inscriptions. The more ancient sites received only a brief and stereotyped description, covering building remains, stones and sometimes cisterns or graves. Thus these reports are lacking in chronological discernment and the ability to distinguish clearly between the ruin of a fortified town and that of a small unwalled settlement.

Extensive modern surveying has been done by Glueck in the central and southern regions of Transjordan.[26] He demonstrated the many latent possibilities for research in such a survey by examining hundreds of ancient sites in the southern sectors of Transjordan. It was proved that there were certain periods of occupation separated by noticeable gaps during which there was no permanent settlement in those regions. This is because Transjordan is open towards the desert on the east and the south; thus it was always the first area falling prey to tribes invading from the desert, who often left it in ruins for long periods of time. Of course, since Glueck published a report of his survey, remains have been discovered here and there from the Late Bronze Age, but this requires only slight modification of his results. The existence of isolated settlements does not alter the general historical outline of the occupational picture. From this standpoint the outline of an extensive survey is much more faithful than that of an isolated settlement or accidental discovery.

Except for the work in Transjordan only partial surveys in limited areas have been carried out thus far. However, every survey that has covered a complete district has proven immediately its great importance for understanding the process of settlement in the region. In later years Glueck continued his work by making extensive explorations in the Negeb,[27] which have subsequently been supplemented by other scholars. Saarilaso, in his survey of Lower Galilee, discovered the courses followed by the ancient trade routes in that area.[28] He also did some surveying in western Galilee[29] and the Shephelah.[30] The author has made a survey in Upper Galilee which brought to light traces of the Canaanite and Israelite occupation there and made possible the typological classification of the pottery shapes that developed in the young Israelite settlements.[31] One should also mention the surveys by

Zori in the Valley of Beth-shean and its vicinity[32] and Kaplan in the Tel Aviv area and the Shephelah[33] as well as many smaller surveys of more limited scope. In recent years a systematic survey of Israel has been launched; thus far several maps have been completed in the areas around Haifa, the southern coast and the Negeb. A further survey, not as minute but concentrating on endangered sites, has been conducted in Judah, Samaria and the Golan with many important results.[34]

All of this material helps us to understand the processes of settlement and occupation in the various parts of Palestine. One must hope that the near future will see excavations in those areas which have not been concretely investigated as well as an up-to-date systematic survey of the whole country. By this means our knowledge will be greatly deepened and enriched.

[1] Contrary to the opinion of M. Noth, *PJB*, 36 (1940), pp. 5-28.

[2] Compare S. Langdon and A. H. Gardiner, *JEA*, 6 (1920), pp. 179–205; V. Korosec, *Hethitische Staatsverträge* (Leipzig, 1931); M. Noth, *ZDPV*, 77 (1961), pp. 138 ff.

[3] Inscription published by A. Dupont-Sommer, *Les inscriptions Araméennes de Sfiré* (Paris, 1958); the translation and restoration adopted here are those of B. Mazar, *BA*, 25 (1962), p. 118; cf. most recently the remarks by J. A. Fitzmyer, *The Aramaic Inscriptions of Sefire* (Rome, 1967), pp. 62–64.

[4] For the second document cf. A. Alt, "Das System der Stammesgrenzen im Buche Josua", *Sellin Festschrift* (Leipzig, 1927), pp. 13–24 (= *Kl, Schr.*, I, pp. 193–202).

[5] Y. Yadin *et al.*, *Hazor*, II (Jerusalem, 1959), p. 3.

[6] A. Alt, *PJb*, 21 (1925), pp. 100–16 (= *Kl. Schr.*, II, pp. 276–88).

[7] A. Alt, *ZAW N.F.*, 4 (1927), pp. 59–81.

[8] M. Noth, *ZDPV*, 58 (1935), pp. 215–30.

[9] *Ibid.*, pp. 230–55.

[10] Alt, *op. cit.* (*note 4*),, *p. 17 f.* (=*Kl. Schr.*, I, p. 197).

[11] Y. Yadin, *IEJ*, 8 (1958), pp. 80-86.

[12] E. Junge, *Der Wiederaufbau des Heerwesens des Reiches Juda unter Josia* (Stuttgart, 1937), pp. 37 ff.; A. Alt, *Kl. Schr.*, II, pp. 306–15.

[13] *ANET*, pp. 227 ff.

[14] *ANET*, pp. 227 ff.

[15] W. Wreszinski, *Atlas zur altägyptischen Kulturgeschichte*, I–II (Leipzig, 1923–35); *ANEP*, pp. 90 ff.

[16] J. Simons, *Handbook for the Study of Egyptian Topographical Lists Relating to Western Asia* (Leiden, 1937); *ANET*, pp. 242 f.

[17] *ANET*, pp. 18 ff.

[18] *ANET*, pp. 258 f.

[19] *ANET*, pp. 328 f.; cf. *infra*, pp. 144–147.

[20] J. A. Knudtzon, *Die El-Amarna Tafeln* (Leipzig, 1915); S. A. B. Mercer, *The Tell El-Amarna Tablets* (Toronto, 1939); *ANET*, pp. 483 ff.

[21] *ANET*, pp. 482 f.

[22] *ANET*, pp. 265 ff.

[23] Hazor, II, p. 3.

[24] C. R. Conder and H. H. Kitchener, *The Survey of Western Palestine. Memoirs of the Topography, Orography, Hydrography and Archaeology*, I-III (London, 1881-83).

[25] G. Schumacher, *Unsere Arbeiten im Ostjordanland*, I-X (Leipzig, [*ZDPV*] 1913-17); *idem*, *Across the Jordan* (London, 1886).

[26] N. Glueck, *Explorations in Eastern Palestine* I-IV, *AASOR*, 14 (1934); 15 (1935); 18-19 (1939); 25-28 (1951).

[27] N. Glueck, *Rivers in the Desert* (New York, 1959).

[28] A. Saarisalo, *The Boundary between Issachar and Naphtali* (Helsinki, 1927).

[29] A. Saarisalo, *JPOS*, 9 (1929), pp. 27–40; 10 (1930), pp. 5–10.

[30] A. Saarisalo, *JPOS*, 11 (1931), pp. 98–104.

[31] Aharoni, *Settlement*, pp. 8–34 (Hebrew); *idem, Antiquity and Survival*, 2 (1957), pp. 146 ff.

[32] N. Zori in *Remnants of the Past* (Tel Aviv, 1951), pp. 82–92 (Hebrew); *idem, BIES*, 18 (1954), pp. 78–90; 19 (1955), pp. 89–98 (Hebrew); *idem*, in *The Beth Shean Valley*, Jerusalem, 1962, pp. 135–98 (Hebrew).

[33] J. Kaplan, *BIES*, 17 (1953), pp. 138–43; 21 (1957), pp. 199–207 (Hebrew).

[34] M. Kochavi, ed., *Judaea, Samaria and the Golan, Archaeological Survey 1967–1968* (Jerusalem, 1972); G. Barkay, Z. Ilan, A. Kloner, A. Mazar, D. Urman, *IEJ*, 24 (1974), pp. 173-84. [Future research should follow the example of the Aphek and Tel Mikhal expeditions where excavation is accompanied by a regional archaeological and ecological survey. A.F.R.]

CHAPTER VI

The Study of Toponymy

Every independent settlement in the Bible is called a town, without distinction as to its nature and size. The characteristic feature of most real towns was their fortifications, and the "daughters" of a particular town were doubless dependent upon it in this respect. However, not all towns were fortified, and the lists of places assigned to the various tribes include many unwalled settlements, some of which were certainly quite small.

In antiquity there was no clear-cut distinction between a town and a village. Agriculture was always one of the important branches of the economy even in urban settlements. Thus we often read about the town and its fields. Part of the urban residents even spent a certain season of the year living in the daughter settlements scattered about the city's territory. Every town which dominated a particular region must have possessed such "daughters", even though they are not always mentioned.[1] Unfortunately we do not know even one name of such a subsidiary settlement. We are not even informed as to whether there were separate names for each one or whether they were simply suburbs or individual dwellings subsumed under the name of the mother city (cf. 2 Sam. 20. 19).

I. THE CONTINUITY OF ANCIENT SITES

Towns were usually built on fixed locations throughout the course of long periods, and their names have been preserved with amazing consistency. The many tells in Palestine and the neighbouring countries represent the remains of settlements that stood "on their mounds" for an extended period, and their distinguishing shape was created by the mighty fortifications surrounding them, especially during the Bronze Age.

This continuity of the settlement was in force throughout the Bronze and Iron Ages, in spite of long intermissions in the respective histories of various settlements. The ancient towns were destroyed frequently as a result of the country's shifting fortunes. The new city was not always built immediately after the destruction of its predecessor. Most of the towns that have been excavated saw periods of abandonment lasting hundreds of years during the second half of the third millennium B.C., between the Early and Middle Bronze cultures. Even in the Late Bronze Age, particularly between the Canaanite and Israelite occupations, settlement was suspended on many tells. Nevertheless, the new settlement was nearly always founded on the same ancient hill, the old name being preserved in spite of all the changes in the population's composition.

The main causes determining the original choice of the site and its subsequent community may be classed under four headings:

(1) Strategic. The ancient settlement was primarily dependent upon its own arrangements for defence. During the Bronze Age there were no major kingdoms in Palestine. Instead, the political units were small city-states. Even during those periods when the Egyptians dominated the country the value of the security factor was not diminished, because every town had to defend itself without depending upon the Egyptian authorities. Therefore, the ancient settlers frequently chose the same hill since it lent itself more readily to fortification.

(2) Water supply. Especially during the Bronze Age the urban populations were made dependent upon a spring or well of fresh water because of the difficulty in storing up a quantity sufficient for the whole year. The need for a natural water supply manifestly conflicts with the security factors, because springs never break forth from the top of a hill but at the foot. Therefore, the settlers endeavoured to choose a place as near as possible to the water source, and on various tells impressive tunnelling operations have been discovered, shafts which brought the water from the spring into the town, e.g. in Jerusalem, Megiddo, Gezer, *et al.*

Of course there are Bronze Age tells which today do not have springs at their feet, but it is possible that in antiquity there were water sources in the vicinity of some of them. In Palestine the outlets of a spring (especially of the smaller ones) sometimes change due to alterations in the sub-surface limestone formations, doubtless because of earth tremors in many cases. At the foot of Megiddo's tell there are two springs today, but there is none at all near the mouth of the water tunnel that leads into the city. There are a few exceptions to this rule, for a small number of tells have never had springs or wells near by, e.g. Tell ʿArad in the Negeb or Gath (Jatt) in western Galilee. These settlements were located on hills consisting of rock that is resistant to water seepage, so it was possible to carve out cisterns and pools for the collection of rain water.

(3) Thoroughfares. Highways always played an important role in the history and economy of the country, especially the international thoroughfares. Thus the most important towns were established and flourished along the main lines of travel and their principal junctures. We find a continuous chain of settlements marking the *Via Maris* in

particular; at the entrance to every pass leading from the Jezreel Plain to the Sharon there was an ancient settlement; e.g. Jokneam, Tell Abu Zureiq, Tell Abu Shusheh, Megiddo and Taanach.

(4) Agricultural land. Since a major portion of the town's economy was based upon agriculture, the nearness of fertile lands was an important factor in choosing an urban site. Access to the fields had to be as convenient as possible.

It is the combination of these elements that explains why the same hill was repeatedly chosen for settlement in period after period. They were the most convenient and most desirable places to realize these objectives.

Certain fundamental changes are noted in the Israelite period. The means for preserving security were different among the incoming tribesmen. In the earlier stages the existence of tribal leagues guaranteed security. No longer did a town stand alone, and we almost never hear about settlements being besieged. Instead the tribal forces were called together in times of danger. Similarly, during the Monarchy a standing army was maintained to protect the kingdom's borders and all of its settlements. Nevertheless, the fortified towns still had an important role to play, so most of the Canaanite tells were occupied again and refortified after a certain lapse of time. Early in the Israelite period the plastered and whitewashed cistern came into wider use, thus making it possible to store an entire year's water supply.[2] This innovation permitted the establishment of settlements independent of the springs. Thus we find many small villages springing up in regions hitherto unoccupied. But this decreased measure of dependence notwithstanding, springs of fresh water were still a great benefit to urban residents in subsequent ages.

Circumstances changed completely during the Hellenistic and Roman periods. The small tell no longer sufficed for meeting the needs of the greatly expanded town that was laid out according to plan. Therefore, most of the tells were abandoned and the population usually transferred to a more spacious area round about. In many cases the ancient name was carried over to the new settlement.

II. THE ORIGIN OF PLACE NAMES AND THEIR MEANINGS

The names of places and regions were preserved in Palestine throughout thousands of years with surprisingly few changes. This is apparently due to two main causes: (1) During the various periods of its history the country's residents spoke Semitic languages more or less closely related to one another. (2) In spite of the changes that took place in the population's composition, there was usually a continuity of settlement so that each new wave of residents inherited the older names from their predecessors.

With the aid of Egyptian sources we may trace the history of various place names from the beginning of the second millennium B.C. The great majority of these names are Semitic. As to the remainder, it is not always possible to establish with absolute certainty the meaning or the root of a name. Therefore, one finds it most difficult to determine its linguistic affinity.

On the basis of this decisive percentage of Semitic names dating back to the earliest sources, it is usually assumed that from the very beginning of historical times, i.e. starting with the Early Bronze Age when a considerable number of settlements were founded, a Semitic tongue was spoken in Palestine. Of course one must not forget that there is a certain occupational gap between the end of the Early and the beginning of the Middle Bronze Ages. In all the towns that have been excavated signs of destruction are noted for this period. They were left in ruins for some time until a new settlement arose in the twentieth century B.C. Although we really do not have definite information about place names in the third millennium, it is probable that most of them did not differ appreciably from those we find in the second. There are at least two ancient names that bear witness to a continuity: Byblos appears in Egyptian inscriptions as early as the middle of the third millennium; Beth-yeraḥ flourished in the third millennium, but only after a tremendous lapse was occupation renewed in the Hellenistic period. This latter name is known to us only from later sources, but there is little doubt that it is much more ancient. Therefore, it seems likely that the name came into being during the Early Bronze Age.

It is not always possible to arrive at a conclusive interpretation of geographical names. One can, however, explain many of them with reasonable certainty. These latter fall into the following categories according to their meaning and origin[3]:

(1) Divine names. Most of the ancient names containing the word *beth* ("house") are related to the temple of some god which gave its name to the locale, e.g. Bethel, Beth-dagon, Beth-haram (Variant: haran), Beth-horon, Beth-anoth, Beth-anath, Beth-shean, Beth-shemesh, Beth-rapha, *et al.* Beth-baal-meon also appears in the form Baal-meon, and thus it is possible that some or all of the other theophoric place names originally stood in combination with the word *beth*, e.g. Jericho, Anathoth, Ashtaroth. Likewise, many names consist of various descriptive combinations concerning Baal, e.g. Baal-gad, Baal-hazor, Baal-peor, Baal-perazim, Baal-zephon (cf. also Zaphon), Baal-shalishah, Baal-tamar, Baalath-beer and also Baalath or Bealoth.

(2) Names of men or clans. Only a few place names are clearly related to men or to clans, e.g. (Elon-)beth-hanan, (Beth-)ʿazmaveth, Ananiah, Beth-pelet, Bene-barak, the Valley of (the son[s] of) Hinnom (Gehenna via Greek transcription). It would appear that all of these

names came into being during the Israelite period. Some which resemble personal names are derived from the combination of a verb and a theophoric element. At least a portion of these names were already in existence during the Bronze Age, and it is difficult to say whether they derive from a patronymic or are simply theophoric. To this class belong Jabneel, Jezreel, Iphtahel, (Je)kabzeel, Joktheel, Irpeel, Ibleam, Jokmeam, Jokneam, (Beth-)arbel and Penuel.

(3) The definition of a region or an area. Names which define the nature of a site and its surroundings are quite widespread, e.g. Geba, Gibeah, Gibeon, Gibbethon, Ramah, Merom, Mizpah (also Mizpeh), Zephath, Tyre, Beth-zur, Sela, Sansannah, Beth-emek, Rehoboth. Some describe the geographical location, e.g. Kedemoth, Zedad. Others indicate the existence of ancient ruins upon which the settlement has been built, e.g. Hattel, Ai, Aiath and Ije-abarim.

(4) Agricultural features. Many names indicate the nature of the soil, e.g. Tob, Naaman, Shaphir, Tirzah, Ahlab, Daberath, Madmen, Madmannah, Hepher, Ophrah, Jabesh, Beth-jeshimoth, the City of Salt. Others denote local produce, e.g. Abel-keramim, Beth-haccerem, Beth-gannim, En-gannim, Netaim. A number of place names denote central agricultural installations, e.g. Goren, Addar, Gath, Gittaim. Names related to water sources are also widespread, e.g. Abel, Aphek, En, Beer, Beeroth, Gebim, Giah, Hammath, Nahalal, Achzib.

(5) Special buildings. Many places are named after particular buildings characterizing the settlement in its earlier stages or after the general form of its dwellings, e.g. Dor, Mahanaim, Maon, Succoth, Kir, Kerioth, Ataroth, Hazeroth, Hazor and names derived from the word *ḥāṣēr,* "court", which are especially typical of the Negeb. Other names are connected with the city's fortifications, Migdal, Bezer, Geder, Beth-gader, Gederah, Gedor, Gederothaim, Shomron (Samaria), Shimron. A few of these concern special parts of the fortifications' structure, e.g. Shaaraim, Rehob. Likewise, some names indicate special cultic installations, e.g. Bamoth, Gilgal, Beth-gilgal.

(6) General characteristics. Some names are associated with general features of the site such as its circumference, e.g. Rabbah, Rabbath, Rabbith, Zair, Zoar. Others serve to define possession, e.g. Helkath, Manahath, Moresheth-gath, Gezer or sanctity, e.g. Kadesh, Adam, Adamah, Achshaph, Eshtaol and Eshtemoa.

(7) Names of animals. The names of many settlements are connected with animals, e.g. the Stone of Zoheleth, Aijalon, Beth-hoglah, Beth-lebaoth, Beth-nimrah, Gob, Hazar-susim, Hazar-shual, Chephirah, Laish, the Tower of Eder, Nimrim, Eglon, Beth-eglaim, En-eglaim, En-hakkore, the Jackal's Well, Etam, Zeboim, Zeboiim.

(8) Names of plants. Also quite widespread are the names of plants, e.g. (Abel-)shittim, Beth-shittah, Beten, Betonim, Beth-arabah, Beth-

tappuah, Rimmon, Rimmono, Gath-rimmon, the rock of Rimmon, En-rimmon, Senaah, the City of Palms, Tamar, Anab, Kanah, Kiriath-jearim, Sorek, Socoh, Shamir, Taanath-shiloh.

As mentioned above, we are far from certain about the original meaning of numerous place names; therefore, we have excluded many from this list, and even those which we have included are often somewhat uncertain. However, doubts about individual cases do not change the general picture of their common Semitic origin. Although many settlements were only founded upon the arrival of the Israelites, we are unable to detect any special flavour to the new place names they established. The new sites were given names similar to those of the Canaanites, and the Israelites usually accepted the old names inherited from their predecessors. These latter terms influenced the type of names given to the new settlements.[4]

Instances of changing the former name by the Israelites are quite rare. The only certain example is Canaanite Laish (Leshem) which was called Dan after the tribe which conquered and occupied it (Judg. 18. 29); the name Laish is actually mentioned in second millennium sources.[5] Even in cases of intentional change, such as that of Kenath in Bashan, which was captured by Nobah and named after him (Num. 32. 42), or of the Edomite Sela, which was called Joktheel after its submission to Amaziah (2 Kings 14. 7), the new names were unsuccessful in supplanting the old.[6]

The same is true concerning the names of various regions. Most of them are related to their natural features and several already appear in pre-Israelite sources. The name of the Lebanese Beqaʻ is written *b-q-ʻ-t-m* in the Egyptian execration texts from the nineteenth century B.C. (E-20).[7] Thut-mose III's list includes Negeb (No. 57), Emek (no. 107), Har ("mountain", No. 77), perhaps Galilee (*k-r-r,* No. 80) and also Sharon (*s-r-n,* No. 21) although, according to the context, this is not a reference to the coastal plain but rather to a place in the Bashan region (apparently the "pasture lands of Sharon", in 1 Chron. 5. 16).[8] On the other hand, the coastal Sharon does appear in the Annals of Amen-ḫotep II.[9] Only with regard to the Shephelah is it possible to conjecture that the geographic term was coined by the Israelites, because it corresponds to the viewpoint of hill dwellers looking down at the lower hilly region.

Ancient names of mountains and streams in Palestine that are known to us from non-biblical sources are very few. The mountains of Lebanon, Sirion (Shenir) and the Amanus appear already in Hittite sources, in texts from Ugarit, and in early Assyrian inscriptions. By contrast, not one of the more southerly mountains is known. Perhaps this is because these latter are relatively much smaller. In Papyrus Anastasi I from the reign of Ramses II (thirteenth century B.C.) a few hills and rivers are mentioned, e.g. Mount User (*wśr*, an Egyptian term meaning "strong, mighty") which may refer to Mount Carmel. It would seem that the prominent Carmel range was known to Egyptian sailors from remotest times, which would account for its having an Egyptian name.[10] Mount Shechem apparently included the entire range of the Ephraimite hill country, which was dominated by Shechem at that time. Similarly, Mount Beth-anath also appears in the inscriptions of Ramses II, evidently with reference to the Galilee region.[11] The River Liṭani is called *n-ṯ-n* in Papyrus Anastasi I, but the name of this river is not preserved in the Bible or in other sources. The River Jordan is also mentioned here. Concerning the derivation of this latter name opinions are divided. Some hold that it comes from the Semitic root *yrd* and means "the descending (river)". Others point an Indo-European derivation because there exist several rivers by the name Ἰάρδανος in Greece and elsewhere.[12] The names of other streams in the Bible are mainly associated with plant life, e.g. the Yarkon ("green" or "yellow"), and brooks such as the Kanah, the Sorek, the Elah and the Eshcol. The Brook of Egypt denotes the boundary between Egypt and Palestine. It is also mentioned in Assyrian texts (*naḫal Muṣur*).[13] The names of some other streams appear to be Semitic, but it is difficult to define their meaning, e.g. the Arnon, the Zered, the Jabbok and the Kishon.

III. THE ORIGINAL FORM OF THE NAME

We cannot always be certain about the original form of the ancient name because of two limitations in our sources: questions of transcription and of text.

Problems in transcription exist mainly in the non-biblical sources, especially the Egyptian and the Akkadian. These languages and their respective systems of writing did not possess all of the same consonants (or consonantal symbols) that correspond to the Canaanite-Hebrew sounds. Therefore, the scribes had no choice but to use symbols that were as close as possible. For this reason we cannot always be sure which original phonemes they intended to transcribe; some signs served to represent several Canaanite-Hebrew letters.

This problem is especially acute with regard to Egyptian, which cannot be classed as a Semitic language. Though it contains some Semitic elements, it differs considerably from Canaanite-Hebrew. Many names appearing in Egyptian inscriptions can be transcribed in each of several ways. The dental consonants, for example, often seem to interchange with one another in transcription. Furthermore, the Egyptians did not distinguish between *r* and *l* in their script; to represent the Semitic *l* they usually used the signs which Egyptologists traditionally transcribe with *r*. But sometimes they transcribed Semitic *l* by *n*. It must be stressed, on the other hand, that these documents usually display a concern for precision, and observable spelling mistakes are very few. Most of the inscriptions are concerned with expeditions, either military or political and commercial; these were usually accompanied by an expert scribe who recorded the geographical names with considerable exactness. The broad education and great skill of the qualified scribe are portrayed in a very instructive and entertaining manner by Papyrus Anastasi I, a literary treatise in the form of a satirical letter from one scribe to a colleague whose knowledge he is trying to belittle.[14] Among all the geographical names mentioned in this papyrus, it is possible to ascertain only one spelling mistake, viz. Achshaph, spelled with *ayin* instead of *aleph* (cf. *infra,* p. 182).

Like the Phoenician writing system adopted later by the Hebrews, the Egyptian system contained a series of symbols to represent individual consonants (from which the Phoenician signs were most probably derived), and it did not express vowels. But unlike the Phoenician script it had many signs expressing more than one consonant, not to mention word signs and determinatives. For the transcription of foreign words or etymologically obscure names a special system known as "group-writing" was devised and was in use at least as early as the Middle Kingdom (with some traces already in the Pyramid Texts). This involved the use of certain bi-lateral signs, viz. those containing a consonant plus a weak consonant or semi-vowel (ꜣ, ỉ ,*w, y*). The use of these "syllabic" signs is thought by some to be a representation of vowels,[15] but they often are combined with purely consonantal ones. We have chosen to use dashes in transcribing words written by this method.

When dealing with Egyptian transcriptions one must also take into account the date of the inscription; some of the consonantal equivalents used during the New Kingdom differ from those of preceding periods. We have summarized the various possibilities for transcribing the consonants of Egyptian script in the table on pp. 114 f. This graphic representation is based upon those place names which have been identified with a considerable degree of certainty.[16]

In many instances it is impossible to establish the identification of a name appearing in the Egyptian lists unless its association with a form found transcribed into some other script can be proved, either in the Bible or Akkadian texts. The spelling *m-k-t*, for example, might represent one of several Semitic combinations, e.g. *m-k-t, m-k-d,* or *m-g-t*, and only its equation with Megiddo on the basis of various contextual indications fixes its correct reading. On the other hand, it could not have been taken to represent *m-q-d* (Makkedah) because *q* is never represented by *k*. Some names can readily be explained by comparison with other Semitic nouns, even when they do not appear in other sources as place names, e.g. *m-k-t-r*, Migdal, or *k-n-t*, Ginti (Gath). In spite of all such possibilities, one must exercise great caution with regard to any suggested identification that goes against the general pattern of well established phonetic correspondences.

The problems of Akkadian transcription are simpler since it is a Semitic language (although its script was first designed for writing the non-Semitic Sumerian). There is also the great advantage that vowels are written.[17] One major difficulty arises with regard to the transcription of certain guttural consonants (', *h*, *ḥ*, ', *ǵ*), because they did not exist in Sumerian and therefore are not represented in the script. In Assyrian inscriptions these consonants are most generally transcribed by signs with ' ; in the El Amarna tablets the *h*, *ḥ*, *ǵ* and sometimes even ' and ' are represented by signs with *ḫ*, e.g. Ḫaṣura (Ḫazor), Ḫazati and also Azzati (Gaza), Akka (Acco), Akšapa (Achshaph), Naḫrima (Naharaim), Taḫ[nuk]a (Taanach), etc. The polyphony so characteristic of Akkadian script (and even more pronounced in Middle Babylonian texts such as those from Nuzi and El Amarna) admits of numerous possibilities for transcription. For instance, a particular syllabic sign containing *b* may also represent a syllable containing *p* (*ba* can be read *pá*, *ab* is also *ap*, etc.); by the same token other phonetically related consonants are represented by the same signs, e.g. the sibilants *s*, *ṣ*, *z*, the dentals *d*, *t*, *ṭ* and the velars *g*, *k*, *q*. The writing of doubled consonants and long vowels was optional (in our examples above one should read Ḫaṣūra and Ḫazzati on the basis of the Hebrew form). Since there were no special signs for "*o*" vowels (either long or short), they were represented by "*u*"-class signs; most signs containing *i* could also be read with *e*. The El Amarna letters from Canaan usually follow a spelling tradition closer to classic Babylonian. On the other hand, those from N. Syria and Boghazkoi contain Assyrian and Hurrian influences so that the consonant groups are even less precisely distinguished. It should also be noted that Assyrian texts usually represent *š* by *s* and *s* by *š*. Thus Sennacherib's annals have *Ushu* for *Usu* and *Lakisi* for *Lakiši*. Furthermore, the novice should be warned not to depend on older editions of cuneiform texts for the correct phonetic transcription. Today the Assyriologist has at his disposal a standard syllabary by which to distinguish the various phonemes, something which J. A. Knudtzon regretted not having.[18] Only a new transcription direct from cuneiform is valid for scholarly discussion.[19]

Transcriptions of the same name in another script may be used as controls for determining the correct reading in an Akkadian text. For instance, both Egyptian and Ugaritic transcriptions demonstrate that the correct consonants of the famous term usually written *ḫa-bi-ru* in Akkadian texts are ' *-p-r*. By supplying the vowels from the Akkadian form we can reconstruct the original form * '*apiru* (though the vowel lengths are still in dispute). When the same name is found in both Egyptian and Akkadian texts, it is possible to determine the original

Egyptologists' Transcription	*Semitic values Hebrew*	*Proto-Sem.*	*Egyptian*	*Examples Hebrew*	*English*
ꜣ Middle Kingdom	ל	l	i-ś-q-ꜣ-n	אשקלון	Ashkelon
	ר	r	ỉ-ꜣ-ḥ-b-w-m	(א)רחב(ם)	Rehob
Late Kingdom	(vowel sign)		ʿ-k-ꜣ	עכו	Acco
ỉ	א		ỉ-t-r-ʿ	אדרעי	Edrei
y	י	y	ỉ-y-r-n	אילון	Aijalon
ʿ	ע	ʿ	ʿ-y-n	עיון	Ijon
w (vowel or semi-vowel)	ו	w	y-p-w	יפו	Joppa
	י	y	r-w-ś	ליש	Laish
b	ב	b	b-t-ʿ-n-t	בית ענת	Beth-anath
	ב	b	ỉ-b-r	אבל	Abel
p	פ	p	p-ḥ-r	פחל	Peḥel (Pella)
	פ	p	ỉ-p-q-n	אפק(ן)	Aphek
note also	ב	b	k-p-n	גבל	Gebal (Byblos)
f	פ	p	ḏ-f-t	צפת	Zephath
m	מ	m	y-b-r-ʿ-m	יבלעם	Ibleam
n	נ	n	k-n-n-r-t	כנרת	Chinnereth
note also	ל	l	k-p-n	גבל	Gebal (Byblos)
n͡w	נו	no, nu	ỉ-n͡w	אנו	Ono
n͡r	ל	l	ỉ-s-q-n͡r-n	אשקלון	Ashkelon
r	ר	r	r-ḥ-b	רחוב	Rehob
	ל	l	r-t-n	לד(ן)	Lod
note also	נ	n	b-t-s-ỉ-r	בית שאן	Beth-shean
h	ה	h	n-h-r-y-n	נהרין(ם)	Naharain(m)
ḥ	ח	ḥ	b-t-ḥ-w-r-n	בית חרון	Beth-horon
ḫ	ח	ḫ	ỉ-n-ḫ-r-t	אנחרת	Anaharath
ś	שׂ	ṯ	ʿ-ś-t-r-t	עשתרת	Ashtaroth
	שׂ	ś	ś-w-k	שכה	Socoh
s (= ś)	שׂ	ṯ	ʿ-s-t-r-t	עשתרת	Ashtaroth
š	שׁ	š	m-š-i-r	משאל	Mishal
late (Shishak)	שׂ	ś	š-ỉ-k	שכה	Socoh
q (ḳ)	ק	q	t-m-ś-q	דמשק	Damascus
	ג	g	q-b-ʿ	גבע	Geba
	ע	ǵ(gh)	q-ḏ-t	עזה	Gaza (Ghazzeh)

Egyptologists' Transcription	*Semitic values* *Hebrew*	*Proto-Sem.*	*Examples* *Egyptian*	*Hebrew*	*English*
k	כּ	k	ᶜ-k-ꜣ	עכו	Acco
	כ	k	t-ᶜ-n-k	תענך	Taanach
	גּ	g	k-b-ᶜ	גבע	Geba
	ג	g'	m-k-t	מגדו	Megiddo
g	ג	g	n-g-b	נגב	Negeb
	ע	ġ(gh)	g-ḏ-t	עזה	Gaza (Ghazzeh)
t	ת	t	ḥ-m-t	חמת	Hammath
	ד	d	m-k-t-r	מגדל	Migdal
	ט	ṭ	t-b-y	טוב	Tob (Ṭūbu, *EA*)
ṯ (tj)	ת	t	k-n-ṯ	גת	Gath
	ס	s	ỉ-nr-ṯ	—	Ullasa ?*
d	ד	d	q-d-š	קדש	Kadesh
	ט	ṭ	d-b-ḫ	טבח(ת)	Tibhath (Ṭubiḫi, *EA*)
ḏ	צ	ḍ or ẓ	ḫ-ḏ-r	חצור	Hazor
	צ	ṣ	ḏ-f-t	צפת	Zephath
	ז	z	q-ḏ-r	גזר	Gezer
late (Shishak)	גּ	g	ḏ-d-p-t-r	גת (פדל)	Gath-padalla (*EA*)

*In Semitic loan words and in place names where the original conconant can be checked, this sign (*ṯ*) represents Semitic *s* and not *z*. Unlike our practice in the first edition, we have given up the conventional spellings of some place names, e.g. Hasi for Hazi, Usu for Uzu, Ullasa for Ullaza.

form with reasonable accuracy even without examples from Canaanite-Hebrew script, e.g. *ḫ-ṯ-y*—Ḫasi, *ḫ-š-b*—Ḫašabu, and note especially forms like ʿ *r -n* and Ḫalunni which complement one another in confirming *ʿ*alunni*. However, this method is insufficient for analysing some forms, e.g. *y-r-ḏ*, written syllabically *yu-ur-za* may represent either *Yurza* or *Yurṣa*. The historical development of Hebrew phonology must also be taken into account when comparing a Massoretic Hebrew form with an ancient transcription in some other language.

The main textual problems confronting us have to do with the Bible. The Egyptian and Assyrian documents were contemporary with the settlements and events described in them and, since the work of composition was usually scrupulous about details, mistakes are very few. On the other hand, the biblical sources have undergone a long process of oral and written transmission. Therefore, it is clear that, in spite of the great care taken in transmitting the biblical text, some errors with regard to place names have crept in. This is especially true of places mentioned only once or twice in the Bible whose occupation had already ceased in the preceding period. Sometimes it is possible to trace the errors in biblical place names, particularly in those instances where several copies of the same list are preserved. As an example, the towns of Simeon are listed in Joshua 19. 2-8; 1 Chronicles 4. 28-33; and Joshua 15. 26–32; while a few of them also appear in Nehemiah 11. 25–9 and 1 Samuel 30. 27–30. Comparison of these lists reveals that errors and changes have taken place in some of the names, especially those known only from these same texts.[20] Towns like Beer-sheba, Hormah and Ziklag appear in all the lists without change. A few names can be explained as variants of one another, e.g. Hazar-susah (Josh. 19. 5) and Hazar-susim (1 Chron. 4. 31), Beth-lebaoth (Josh. 19. 6) and Lebaoth (Josh. 15. 32), and also Eltolad (Josh. 15. 30; 19. 4) and Tolad (1 Chron. 4. 29). However, other names are errors for one original form, e.g. Baalah (Josh. 15. 29)—Balah (Josh. 19. 3)—Bilhah (1 Chron. 4. 29) in which instance we are unable to determine the original form with any certainty. Baalah is a common name, but precisely for this reason Albright was inclined to accept Bilhah as the original.[21] Another name which has been corrupted in various forms is Bethul (Josh. 19. 4)—Bethuel (1 Chron. 4. 30)—Bethel (1 Sam. 30. 27)—Chesil (Josh. 15. 30). After comparison of the various forms Albright prefers Bethuel.[22] In any case, Chesil is completely out of harmony with the other forms. One may also note the corruption of (Beth-)lebaoth to Beth-biri in one instance (1 Chron. 4. 31).

There is another double list for the Levitical cities in Joshua 21 and 1 Chronicles 6. Between the two rosters the following discrepancies may be noted: Ain—Ashan, Gibeon—Geba, Taanach—Aner, En-gannim—Anem, Helkath—Hukok, Dimonah—Rimmono; and other differences that may be interpreted as variations on the same name, e.g. Almon—Alemeth, Be-eshterah —Ashtaroth, Jarmuth—Ramoth, Mishal—Mashal, Hammoth(-dor)—Hammon and Kartan—Kiriathaim. These examples serve to demonstrate the great need for caution and careful scrutiny in studying biblical place names, in particular those that are rare.

Therefore, when we have textual problems concerning geographical names, we must endeavour to establish the original form using all available parallels and being guided by the following toponymic considerations:

(1) One must examine the text presented in the LXX, which is often based on parallel Hebrew traditions as demonstrated by certain fragments among the Dead Sea Scrolls. In order to do this one must compare all of the most important MSS of LXX to determine the most likely readings of this version.[23] Even if we succeed in doing so it is not certain that the form we finally deduce is the closest to the Hebrew original; but it might be and therefore must be taken into consideration.

(2) Comparison of the biblical form with that appearing in other sources, if there is any topographical or historical evidence pertaining to this identification.

(3) Comparison of the name with the Arabic form attached to the present-day tell or ruin (providing that there is sufficient reason for accepting the geographical equation).

(4) Historical and topographical considerations with reference to the mention of a specific place in a particular text and the spelling errors that are possible paleographically. The following examples are illustrative of the problem:

Eder—In the Negeb district of Judah the town Eder appears second on the list (Josh. 15. 21). A place by this name is otherwise unknown to us; on the other hand, Arad (same Hebrew consonants only with two of them reversed), which is known in this region from the Canaanite period, is missing from the list. The archaeological finds at Tell ʿArad prove that the settlement there flourished especially during the Israelite Monarchy and that even afterwards it was one of the most important towns in the region. Likewise, the interchange of the Hebrew letters *daleth* and *resh* (which have quite similar forms in the older Phoenician script and still more so in the later Aramaic script) was a common error in the transmission of the biblical text as illustrated by many examples. In this particular passage the LXX Codex Vaticanus has the reading ʿΑρα. All of these factors together make it probable that Eder is simply a mistake for Arad.

Ebron—this is a town from the tribal inheritance of Asher (Josh. 19. 28) which appears as Abdon in the list of Levitical cities (Josh. 21. 30; 1 Chron. 6. 74). Topographical considerations strongly suggest an identification with Khirbet ʿAbdeh, 10 miles north-north-east of Acco, thus favouring the originality of the form Abdon.

Adadah—There is supposed to be a town by this name in the Negeb of Judah (Josh. 15. 22), but it appears in the form Aroer in 1 Samuel 30. 28, and LXX (Vaticanus) reads ʾΑρουηλ. The name is preserved up to the present day in Khirbet ʿAr ʿarah, thus showing that the original form was Aroer—Ararah.

Sarid—It is a town on the border of Zebulun (Josh. 19. 10, 12). In some MSS of the LXX the form Σεδουδ appears.[24] Five miles south-east of Nazareth there is a Tell Shadud. It seems likely then that the original form of this name was Sadud.

Madon—a Galilean Canaanite city by this name participated in the battle of Merom (Josh. 11. 1; 12. 19). Scholars usually identify it with Khirbet Madin about one-third of a mile south of Qarn Ḥaṭṭin, an equation dependent entirely upon the similarity of names. However, we never hear about a Canaanite town so named in any other context and the LXX reads Μαρρων, i.e. Maron, thus identifying the town with a place in the vicinity of "the waters of Merom" (ὕδωρ Μαρρων). The town Merom is known from various sources, both Egyptian and Assyrian. In the absence of other data a final solution cannot be reached; but it is obvious that the accepted identification of Madon, based only on the resemblance between the Hebrew and Arabic names, must be considered as suspect.

Shimron—again we have to do with a town in Zebulun's tribal inheritance (Josh. 19. 15) which also is mentioned among the Canaanite cities taking part in the battle of Merom (Josh. 11. 1; 12. 20). The LXX reads Συμοων. The city is known from the execration texts and the list of Thut-mose III in the form *š-m-ʿ-n*. In the El Amarna letters it is written *Šamḫuna*. Josephus gives the form Σιμονιας and the Hebrew Tosephta has סימוניא There is a tell five miles west of Nazareth called Khirbet Sammuniyeh, and as early as the Jerusalem Talmud (*Megilla* 70a) we find the equation: "Shimron—Simonia", based on a simple deduction from the context by Rabbi Yosi bar Haninah. Thus, all of the witnesses testify to *Shimʿon as the original form.[25]

IV. PRESERVATION OF THE NAME

Many of the ancient place names have been preserved among the local residents up to the present time, in spite of all the historical convulsions and population changes that have taken place.[26] The great majority of sure identifications were made possible by the presence of the ancient name, either at the site itself, on a nearby ruin or tomb, or attached to a village in the immediate vicinity. The following table presents the transcriptions from Arabic generally accepted by linguists today. However, it must be pointed out that allowances have to be made for occasional deviations from this pattern:

ḍ	ض	ʾ	ا
ṭ	ط	b	ب
ẓ	ظ	t	ت
ʿ	ع	th	ث
ǵ (gh)	غ	j	ج
f	ف	ḥ	ح
q	ق	ḫ (kh)	خ
k	ك	d	د
l	ل	dh	ذ
m	م	r	ر
n	ن	z	ز
h	ه	s	س
w	و	š (sh)	ش
y	ي	ṣ	ص

Of course most place names have been subjected to certain phonetic and linguistic processes during the course of their transmission. Biblical Hebrew was very close to the Canaanite language that had prevailed in

Palestine before it; therefore, one does not find appreciable differences of form for geographical terms between the Bronze and Iron Ages. But from the Persian through the Roman periods Aramaic was used extensively here, and after the Islamic conquest even this latter tongue was displaced by Arabic. Many names underwent modifications as a result of these changes in the spoken language. Some of these alterations have to do with differences in the pronunciation of certain consonants while others are the result of different methods of word formation in Aramaic and Arabic.

The principal rules governing these changes were established by Kampffmeyer.[27] He based them upon a scrupulous comparison of the ancient and modern geographical names in cases where the identification is certain. The various mutations are explained by him in terms of linguistic and phonetic law. For establishing the exact spelling and pronunciation of Arabic names Kampffmeyer was especially dependent upon the work of Eli Smith, who travelled through the country with Robinson. He likewise made use of the Palestine Exploration Fund Map and Palmer's *Name List* which is based on it. Today additional material may be added, particularly that assembled by the Survey Department under the British Mandate[28] and the list of antiquity sites published by the Mandatory Department of Antiquities which was based upon the investigations of its own regional supervisors.[29]

The following are the main principles governing the mutations that have taken place in geographical names:

(1) Channels of transmission. Kampffmeyer tried to establish a rule for the transmission to Arabic with the Islamic conquest in the seventh century A.D. According to him the name passed through one of these channels: (*a*) Rapid bodily adoption of the name by the Arab conquerors in the main population centres where they had settled—Kampffmeyer called this transmission "by Arabic mouth". (*b*) Gradual mutation by "the Syrian mouth". That is, the local "Syrian" population had to learn Arabic and thus its native tongue, usually Aramaic, passed through a gradual process of transformation into Arabic.

The former channel of transmission is mainly phonetic. The Arabic speaker pronounced the name as he heard it and made use of the closest sounds possible in his own language. On the other hand, the gradual process is influenced by historical phonology. The Aramaic letters and words were replaced by their Arabic cognates. These differences find expression with regard to three consonants in particular: *shin* (*sh,* written *š*) becomes an *s* sound in the gradual transmission, usually *sin* in Aramaic (though once in a while examples of *samekh* show up; a phenomenon already known from a few Hebrew examples, cf. Michmash—Michmas) and always in Arabic (which has the value of *samekh*), e.g. Ashdod—Esdud, Heshbon—Ḥesban. However, in rapid transmission, by "the Arabic mouth", the *shin* is preserved, e.g. Ashtaroth (*Ashtarah)—Tell ʿAshtarah; Beer-sheba—Kh. Abu esh-Sheba.

Khaph (*kh*, aspirated *k*) is retained in the gradual transmission, albeit in its unaspirated form, e.g. Taanach—Tell Tiʿinnik. In the immediate transmission it was replaced by Arabic *kha* (ḫ) whose pronunciation approximates to that of the aspirated Hebrew *k* (i.e. *kh*), e.g. Michmas—Muḫmas (not from Michmash, which would have been Muḫmash by direct borrowing).

Pe (unaspirated *p*), when coming by the gradual process, appears in Arabic as *fa* (*ph*), e.g. (Beth-)tappuah—Taffuḥ, Ṣippori (Sepphoris)—Ṣaffuriyeh. In the immediate borrowing *pe* becomes *beit* (*b*) in Arabic, e.g. Mizphah—Tell en-Naṣbeh, Pharpar—Barbar. By the same token Greek *pi* (π) in Hellenistic names always becomes Arabic *beit*. This is not a matter of rapid or gradual transmission but rather a straight phonetic shift in the transcription of non-Semitic words, e.g. Tripolis (Τρίπολις)—Ṭarabulus, Neapolis (Νεάπολις)—Nablus, Paneas (Πανιάς)—Baniyas.[30]

The great majority of Arabic place names show evidence of a gradual linguistic transmission; there are only a few examples of immediate phonetic borrowing.

(2) Sufformatives were not permanent elements of the name, that is to say, many names were formed by the addition of sufformatives which can be changed without altering the geographic meaning of the term, e.g. Geba, Gibeah, Gibeon; Gader, Gaderah, Gederoth, Gederothaim; Ramah, Ramoth, Ramathaim, *et al.* Therefore, these sufformatives should not be considered as grammatical elements expressing feminine gender, plural or dual number, etc. It is more likely that they possessed locative force and could be altered or dropped without affecting the basic significance of the name.

Thus the sufformatives are usually changed in the Arabic form. In many instances this would seem to be due to an ancient secondary form of the name that is seldom preserved in the sources. We will content ourselves with only a few examples: Almon, Alemeth—Khirbet ʿAlmit; Shaalbon, Shaalabbin, Shaalbim—Selbiṭ; Dothan, Dothain—Tell Dothan; Shiloh (*Shilon)—Seilun; Adoraim (*Adora)—Dura; Betonim—Khirbet Baṭneh; Chesalon—Kesla; (Beth-)nimrah—Nimrin; (the waters of) Nimrim—Wadi eṇ-Numeirah. Sometimes the sufformative disappears entirely, e.g. Chesulloth—Iksal; Beth-horon—Beit ʿUr.

(3) Additional elements. Sometimes the name appears in Hebrew with the definite article, e.g. הרמה "the Height" (Ramah), etc. This usage stems from the name's original significance as an appellative; therefore, the article is not an integral part of the proper name. Even in the Bible one can discern a tendency for the article to disappear, e.g. it is used

with Chephirah in Joshua 9. 17 and 18. 26 but is dropped in Ezra 2. 25 and Nehemiah 7. 29. On the other hand, the definite article is sometimes added to the Arabic form of the name even though it was not a part of the original, e.g. Bir es-Seba' (Beer-sheba), el-Kirmil (the Judean Carmel), etc.

Various names appear in combination with the dependent element Beth- ("the house of"), e.g. Beth-shemesh, Beth-shean, Bethlehem, Beth-horon, *et al.* This element, which sometimes is dropped even in the Bible, may appear in Arabic as Beit (also "the house of"), but usually it is dropped; cf. Beth-horon—Beit 'Ur, Bethlehem—Beit Laḥm with Beth-tappuah—Taffuḥ, Beth-baal-meon—Ma'in, Beth-nimrah (Nimrah)—Nimrin.

(4) The change to an Arabic form. Frequently a Hebrew element is replaced by a similar Arabic word which may have the same meaning, e.g. Beth-shemesh— 'Ain Shems, Jabesh(-gilead)—Wadi Yabis; or the result of folk etymology, e.g. Beth-horon—Beit 'Ur ("House of the Blind"), Dibon—Dhiban ("Wolf"), etc. The original form may even be broken down into several words, e.g. Adullam—Khirbet 'Id el-Ma ("The Feast of the Waters") or 'Id el-Mi'ah ("The Feast of the Hundred"). In this latter process a consonant may even be transposed, e.g. Shephar'am (known from later Jewish sources)— Shefa 'Amr.

The regular Arabic diminutive form is widely used, e.g. Socoh—Shuweikeh, Jogbehah—Jubeihat. Likewise, the Arabic suffix *-iyeh* is frequently appended to the original, sometimes replacing a Hebrew sufformative, e.g. Adam, Adamah, Adamim—Damiyeh; Daberath—Daburiyeh; Ṣippori (Sepphoris)—Ṣaffuriyeh.

(5) Alteration to a more familiar name. As a clear example of this process, one may cite the Judean Jarmuth which appears as Khirbet Yarmuk, a change probably influenced by familiarity with the well-known River Yarmuk.

(6) Translation. Direct translations into Arabic words that are not cognate to the original Hebrew term are most rare. It is possible to cite only one apparent example: Dan ("He judges, judged")—Tell el-Qaḍi ("Mound of the Judge"), and perhaps Moladah—Khereibet el-Waṭen.

(7) Euphemism. A rule concerning euphemism (changing a bad element to something good) was established by Hartmann[31] with reference to the name Ophrah. Names from the roots *'pr* or *ḥpr* resemble the Arabic word *'ifrit,* "demon". Therefore, they are frequently changed to Ṭaiyibet el-Ism, "The Favour of the Name", or eṭ-Ṭaiyibeh, "the Favour". For example, the site of Ophrah, Ephraim north of Bethel is today called eṭ-Ṭaiyibeh.

The following is a summary of the general rules pertaining to various consonants:

Aleph—often dropped from the beginning of a word (Adoraim—Dura,

Adami—Damiyeh, Edrei—Der ʿa) or added in other cases (Chesulloth—Iksal, Bezek—Khirbet Ibziq, Bene-barak—Ibn Ibraq). It tends to drop out of the middle of a word, especially after the Hebrew semi-vowel, *shewah* (Beth-shean, Beth-shan, Beishan—Beisan; Beth-arbel—Irbid; Jezreel—Zer ʿin; Bethel—Beitin; Yiron—Yarun). At the beginning of a word it may shift to the stronger guttural *ayin* (Ashkelon— ʿAsqalan; Ono—Kafr ʿAna; Jattir [*Attir]— ʿAttir).

Beth—generally unchanged (but note that Arabic *b* can stand for original *p*). In a few cases *b* has become *m*, e.g. Jabneel (*Yabneh) in Galilee which appears in the Talmud as Yammah—Khirbet Yemma; Jebneel, Jabneh in Judah whose Hellenistic form was Ιαμνια, although the modern Arabic name is Yibna. The opposite shift from *m* to *b* is represented by Timnah—Khirbet Tibneh

Gimel—no change.

Daleth—usually unchanged, but one may note an occasional shift to Arabic *dhal* (Dibon—Dhiban) or *tha* (Hadid—Ḥaditheh) under the influence of similar-sounding Arabic words.

He, waw, zayin—no change.

Heth—it is possible that in biblical times a distinction was still made between ḥ and ḫ (which has since shifted to ḥ in MT). This might be thought to explain why ḥ is sometimes transcribed by LXX as χ while in other cases it is dropped entirely. However, such a correlation is not really in evidence. By a later period the ḫ has certainly shifted to ḥ; therefore, Massoretic ḥ (<ḫ) is often represented in modern place names by Arabic ḥ (Manahath-Malḥah, Janoah [in Galilee]—Yanuḥ). However, there are some exceptions (Ḥaluṣah—el-Ḫalaṣah). Occasionally ḫ appears as *ayin* (Beth-horon—Beit ʿUr; Zanoah—Zanu ʿ; Hali—Ras ʿAli; Baal-hazor—Tell ʿAṣur). Like all the guttural consonants it has a tendency to disappear at the end of a word (Janoah—Yanun, [the waters of] Nephtoah—Lifta), and sometimes even from the middle (Yaḥam [*y-ḥ-m*]—Yemma).

Teth—no change.

Yodh—preserved at the beginning of a word before a long vowel (Joppa—Yafa; Janoah—Yanun). Before a short vowel at the beginning of the word it often shifts to a vowel (supported by prothetic *aleph*; Jordan—Urdunn, Jericho—er-Riḥa; note Jezreel [*Izreel]—Zer ʿin where even the vowel is subsequently dropped) though sometimes it is preserved (Jabneh—Yebna; Jarmuth—Yarmuk; Juttah—Yaṭṭa).

Kaph—usually preserved as *k* whether originally aspirated or not (Kabul—Kabul, Acco— ʿAkka, Taanach—Ti ʿinnik). In rare cases it is supplanted by Arabic ḫ (Michmas—Muḫmas [note that the Arabic form was not derived from Michmash], Sakhnin–Saḫnin).

Lamedh—sometimes prone to appear as *n* or *d*, especially at the end of a word (Jezreel—Zer ʿin, Bethel——Beitin, Arbel—Irbid).

Mem—may shift to *n* (Mizpah—Tell en-Naṣbeh, Merom—Meirun or Marun), or *b* (Timnah—Tibneh), though such cases are rare.

Nun—occasionally shifts to *l* (Shunem—Solem, Manahath—Malḥah, [the waters of] Nephtoah—Lifta), or *m* (Jabneel [*Yabneh]—Yemma, Jokneam—Qeimun, Sansannah—Shamsaniyat). It is liable to drop from the beginning of a word (Capernaum [Kfar Naḥum]—Tell Ḥum, Neiel—Ya ʿnin).

Samekh—usually remains unchanged, but note one instance of its shifting to *š* (sh) (Sansannah—Shamsaniyat).

ʿAyin—in ancient Hebrew there must have been a distinction between ʿ and *ǵ* (*ghayin*). Therefore LXX sometimes transcribes Hebrew ʿ by γ, though in other cases they drop it altogether. In line with this the *ǵ* sometimes appears in the Arabic name (Gaza [Heb. ʿAzzah]—Ghazzeh, Zoar—Ṣughr). Occasionally it has shifted to ḥ (Azmaveth—Ḥizmeh, Aiath—Khirbet Ḥaiyan). Sometimes it disappears altogether (Jokneam—Qeimun, En-dor—Indur, Shaalbim—Selbiṭ, Keilah—Khirbet Qila).

Pe—rarely *p* shifts to *b* (Mizpah—Tell en-Naṣbeh, Pharpar—Barbar).[31a]

V. TRANSFERENCE OF NAMES

Not every name that has been preserved on the map of Palestine has remained fastened to the site of the original settlement, i.e. the tell or the ruin whose archaeological remains suit the period of the historical town. There are cases where the name has been transferred to a nearby location.[32] It is therefore possible to establish two rules:

(1) Preservation of the name on a nearby geographical feature, i.e. although the original site may have undergone a change of name the ancient name may still be found in the vicinity. It may show up as the title of a venerated sheikh's tomb which is on the tell or close by, e.g. Sheikh Jezari on Tell Abu Shusheh (identified with biblical Gezer) or Sheikh Riḥab beside Tell eṣ-Ṣarem (Rehob in the Beth-shean Valley). The name may be preserved in an adjacent spring, e.g. ʿAin Shems at the foot of Tell Rumeileh (Beth-shemesh) or ʿAin Ṣeridah at Deir Ghassaneh (Zeredah). On occasion it may only be found ascribed to a stream bed passing close to the tell, e.g. Wadi Yabis which bears the name of Jabesh(-gilead) or Wadi el-Qeini which points to the nearby location of biblical Kinah. Once in a while the name may have become attached to a mountain or hill in the immediate vicinity, e.g. the name of Merom in Jebel Marun; or as one element in it, e.g. Ẓahrat eṣ-Ṣafi beside Khirbet Sitt Leila which contains the name of Zephath.

(2) Transference of the name to a younger site. This phenomenon is easily understood where the settlement itself has moved over to a new location for various reasons. Such occurrences were widespread in Palestine from the Hellenistic period onwards. Many examples may be

given: ancient Jericho was situated on Tell es-Sulṭan and the name is preserved in the village of er-Riḥa close by; at modern 'Akka settlement has existed since the Hellenistic period, but the biblical Acco was on Tell-el-Fukhkhar east of the town; the tell of Beth-shean is called Tell el-Ḥuṣn and the adjacent village bears the name Beisan; the talmudic Jabneel is identified with Khirbet Yemma and its biblical predecessor with Tell en-Na 'am; Timnah is apparently to be found at Tell Baṭashi, though the name is preserved in Khirbet Tibneh some three miles to the south; Eglon is identified with Tell el-Ḥesi which is close to Khirbet 'Ajlan.

Shifting of the settlement and with it the place name are, of course, related to the special historical and geographical circumstances attending each individual case; fixed rules governing these movements cannot be established. It is clear that such shifts seldom took place over a distance of more than a few miles and that the new settlement usually remained on land that had belonged to its predecessor. However, in some special cases longer jumps were taken, particularly when a shift from the plain to an adjacent hill or vice versa was involved. Late examples of this phenomenon are plentiful. But when the distance concerned is great, it is not easy to determine for certain whether we have a simple case of name similarity or a bonafide transference. For example, the ancient name Ekron bears a great resemblance to that of the village 'Aqir, but the biblical site has been identified with considerable certainty at Khirbet Muqanna' , about six miles south-south-east of it. It is not unthinkable that the name has jumped such a distance via some intermediate station in the Hellenistic-Roman period, but evidence supporting such a move is lacking at present.

It is possible to state one general rule, viz. that the high tell was usually abandoned in the Persian or Hellenistic periods when the settlement moved to a site in the surrounding fields that was wider and more convenient. This phenomenon is especially prominent along the wadies of the southern Jordan Valley.[33] Tells containing remains from the Iron Age are found at the foot of the mountain slopes close to the springs so prevalent there, while the settlements that preserve the ancient name are further to the west amid the cultivated fields: Beth-jeshimoth—Tell el- 'Aẓeimeh and to the west Khirbet es-Seweimeh; Beth-haram (or -haran)—Tell Iktanu and to the west Tell er-Rameh; Beth Nimrah—Tell el-Bleibil and west of it Tell Nimrin.

VI. PRINCIPLES OF IDENTIFICATION

In order to identify an ancient settlement we must give scrupulous attention to three factors: (1) location of the proper general vicinity in accordance with the ancient sources; (2) analysis of the name, its development and its preservation in the area; (3) the archaeological evidence.

Most sources permit the localization of a settlement in a general vicinity only and seldom provide us with more exact geographical details. Of course there are instances when certain details about the town which aid in its identification are mentioned, but usually we are faced with lists of geographical names or incidental references to the place in relation to some other matter without its location being accurately fixed. Therefore, one must examine the source itself very carefully in order to extract what is possible, but no more than that. If this is a description of boundaries or of some particular road that requires a continuous geographical order or a list of towns that may be localized to some definite region, one still should not expect a geographical arrangement that is perfectly clear and orderly.

However, one may not only learn something about the location of a settlement from the historical records. Sometimes it is also possible to obtain details about its nature which have bearing upon the identification: for which periods is its existence attested and for which is it unattested; when did it reach its greatest expansion and importance so as to occupy a prominent place in the sources; and when is it mentioned only incidentally; is it a large, main settlement or a small, subsidiary one; is it a fortress or a sanctuary, etc.? On occasion one may learn something from the place name itself about certain topographical factors, especially when they are associated with water sources. An outstanding example of this is the name Aphek, which appears frequently in widely scattered areas of Palestine. Aphek, in the Sharon is identified with reasonable certainty as the tell of Ras el-ʿAin beside the sources of the Yarkon, Aphekah (Josh. 13. 4) is apparently Afqa on the sources of the River Ibrahim east of Byblos. On the basis of such considerations it has been suggested to identify the Aphek-Aphik from the tribal inheritance of Asher with Tell Kurdaneh near the sources of the River Naʿaman on the Plain of Acco.[34]

It is important to check all of the texts, both earlier and later, in which the name is mentioned, naturally keeping in mind the possibility that the settlement may have moved some distance away from its original site during the course of time. A continuous attestation of the name from the biblical period through the Roman, the Byzantine and even the Arab and Crusader periods up to the present greatly strengthens any conjectured identification.

Nevertheless, one must exercise extreme caution in handling later sources whose avowed aim is the identification of historical sites, viz. talmudic passages, Eusebius, Jerome and especially the medieval *itineraria*. Generally one cannot trust the traditions about places already ancient that were available to them; the main value of these texts lies in the contemporary place names which they mention and describe. Here are a few examples:

Jerusalem Talmud, *Shibiith* IX, 7—"And in the valley Beth-haran and Beth-nimrah and Succoth and Zaphon [Josh. 13. 27], Beth-haran—Beit Ramta, Beth-nimrah—Nimrin, Succoth—Dar'allah [Tar''alah], Zaphon— 'Ammethan ['Ammathu]". Beit Ramta and Nimrin serve as connecting links between the ancient names and the modern, viz. Tell er-Rameh and Tell Nimrin. On the other hand, two names are preserved in this text for which the talmudic sages suggested identifications requiring further examination. The equation of Succoth with Dar'allah, today Tell Deir 'Alla, is generally accepted since that is the most important site in this immediate vicinity and the sages themselves may have taken that into account.[35] Their conclusions about Zaphon were similarly based; 'Ammethan—Ḥammath, today Tell 'Ammata, was the main city in that region during the Roman-Byzantine period. Therefore, Glueck identified Zaphon with the nearby Tell el-Qos. However, it seems more likely that this is actually the ancient Ḥammath which took over Zaphon's prominent role in that neighbourhood. Zaphon itself was more probably located at Tell es-Sa'idiyeh slightly to the north-west. We must distinguish clearly between the essential facts presented to us by the sages, e.g. concerning the existence of 'Ammethan (Ḥammath) in that region, and their own opinions, e.g. the equation of Zaphon with the town known to them. These latter are always subject to separate critical examination.

A tradition about this same region appears in the Jerusalem Talmud, *Sotah* VII, 4—"Rabbi Yohanan said, 'Adam is a town and Zarethan is a town; they are 12 miles from one another'." In the light of the ancient sources which describe these two cities as close neighbours it is difficult to accept the tradition of Rabbi Yohanan. Although there are some scholars who rely upon it for making an identification, we must remember that this is not a testimony about the locale itself but only an attempt to interpret the ancient sources, perhaps supported by certain traditions.

The passage about the towns in Naphtali and Zebulun is most instructive (Jerusalem Talmud, *Megillah*, I, 77a): "Rabbi Yosi, son of Haninah, said, '. . . and their border is from Heleph and so forth (Josh. 19. 33), from Heleph—Ḥelef, from Allon—Ayalon, in Zaanannim—Agnaya belonging to Kedesh, and Adami—Damin, the Nekeb—Saydatha, and Jabneel—Kfar Yamma, as far as Lakkum—Luqim, and Kattath—Qeṭonith, and Nahalal—Mahalul, and Shimron—Simonia, and Iralah—Ḥeireiah (Ḥaureiah), Bethlehem—Beit Leḥem Ṣorayah (the Tyrian)'." Here we are provided with a collection of place names that still existed in that region during the talmudic period but have since disappeared: Ḥelef, Ayalon, Luqim and Qeṭonith are gone without a trace. Damin is an intermediate form (Aramaic) between the biblical Adami(m) and the Arabic Damiyeh. Kfar Yamma still exists in Khirbet

Yemma. Of the others, Mahalul is Maʿlul, Simonia is Tell Sammuniyeh, and the Tyrian Beit Leḥem is Beit Laḥm. These forms seem to have preserved the ancient names and the Talmud has provided us with evidence for intermediate forms that lay behind them. As concerns the rest, one must exercise a great deal of caution. Agnaya ("the valley"?) of Kedesh is equated here with Ṣaydatha—today Khirbet Ṣayadeh, Ḥeireiyah—Khirbet Ḥuwwareh. Khirbet Ṣayadeh, for example, is a late ruin which has no ancient tell near by; it is probable that "the Nekeb" is not an ancient name but rather an appellative to Adami—Adamim. Here Rabbi Yosi indicates a location close to Damin, but nothing can be learned from this concerning the ancient name.

The following are examples from the *Onomasticon* of Eusebius:

"Dan [Gen. 14. 14]: A village four miles distant from Paneas on the road to Tyre is called thus. It is also the northern boundary of the land of Judah and from thence the Jordan has its beginning" (Klostermann, p. 76 lines 6 ff.). Apparently at that time there was still preserved in the vicinity of Tell el-Qaḍi the ancient name of Dan, of which nothing remains today except a faint memory in the name of the River Liddan, a tributary of the Jordan that has its source near the tell. The village that was actually called Dan in Eusebius' day seems to have been located slightly west of the tell whose distance from Baniyas is only about two and a half miles, i.e. less than four Roman miles. However, Eusebius is to be trusted when he is reporting a distance along a main Roman road on which the milestones were accurately placed and registered on a chart.[36]

"Harosheth [Judge. 4. 2]: Town of Sisera, commander of the army of Jabesh ('Ιαβις instead of 'Ιαβιν). Today Jabesh is a very large city in Transjordan six miles distant from Pella [Peḥel] as you go up to Gerasa" (Klostermann, p. 32 lines 5 ff.).

"Jabesh-Gilead [Judg. 21. 8]: There the children of Israel fought. And today it is a village in Transjordan situated in the hills six miles from the city of Pella as you go (towards Gerasa)" (Klostermann, p. 110 lines 11 ff.).

Obviously Eusebius erred by substituting Jabesh for the name of Jabin, King of Hazor. Nevertheless, in both paragraphs he gives us information of the utmost importance for identifying Jabesh. Today the ancient name is preserved only in that of the Wadi Yabis along which several tells are located. But in Eusebius' own day there was still a village by that name, and his description leads us to the vicinity of Tell el-Maqlub which is situated on the heights of Mount Gilead at the proper distance along the road from Pella to Gerasa. The testimony of Eusebius is decisive in this instance, not because of his opinion about Sisera's relation to Jabesh but on account of the notice that a village by that name still existed in his day precisely in the region corresponding to the other sources and beside the wadi that bears the name in question.

Any site proposed for a historical identification must also be suitable archaeologically. Two main requirements must be satisfied:

(1) Its periods of occupation as determined by survey or excavation must conform to the settlement's appearance in the written sources. For example, a place mentioned in the list of Thut-mose III and also in the Bible must contain remains from the Late Bronze and Iron Ages. Furthermore, since it is unlikely that a town was only founded on the eve of Thut-mose's expedition, one should also expect to find Middle Bronze evidence as well.

(2) The site must meet the expected requirements from the standpoint of the size and nature of its settlement. For instance, a royal Canaanite city should be sought on one of the tells typical of that period. i.e. one whose prominent artificial slopes comprise the city's fortification. By way of illustration, one may point to Hazor and Ekron which were identified each with the largest tell in its respective area. In both cases there was no other site of such magnitude in the vicinity, and it is clear from the written sources that each was the largest and most influential city in its own region.

Sometimes one may point to more exact data for making an identification, especially in places where excavations have been carried out. The identical Solomonic gates at Hazor, Megiddo and Gezer, three towns mentioned together as fortifications of that kind (1 Kings 9. 15), are a case in point. Another good illustration is the identification of Sharuhen with Tell el-Far ʿah in the light of Flinders Petrie's excavations. Hyksos fortifications and an Egyptian stronghold from the New Kingdom period were discovered, features which corresponded so well with the information about Sharuhen that Albright was led to make the identification.[37]

At the same time, one must evaluate critically the periods in which, according to the ancient texts, a particular settlement was in existence. This is especially true with regard to the Bible. One cannot always unreservedly accept information from the Patriarchal or Conquest narratives as conclusive evidence for the existence of a settlement. An outstanding example is Ai. From the story of its conquest we can assume with certainty only that the place existed as a ruin during the Israelite period, "a heap of ruins as it is to this day" (Josh. 8. 28). But one may not accept the account iself without critical analysis; thus the fact that at et-Tell no traces were found of a Canaanite city from the Conquest period is no conclusive proof against the identification of that site with Ai.

However, in the final analysis the most certain identifications are still those dependent upon preservation of the ancient name, albeit with careful examination of written sources and archaeological data. Out of approximately 475 place names mentioned in the Bible[38] only about 262 have been identified with any degree of certainty, i.e. 55 per cent. Of these 190 are based upon preservation of the name, viz. 40 per cent of the over-all total, of which 158 (33.3 per cent) are places still bearing the name, and 32 (6.7 per cent) where the name was found somewhere in the vicinity of the ancient site. Only 72 places (15 per cent of the over-all total) have been identified in situations where the ancient name is not to be found somewhere in the vicinity, of which only about half carry a degree of certainty, the remainder being more or less conjectural.

[1] For the problem of the city and its dependents cf. M. Weber, *Ancient Judaism*, translated and edited by H. H. Gerth and D. Martindale (New York), pp. 13–27, condensed from *idem, Gesammelte Aufsätze zur Religions-Soziology,* III (Tübingen, 1921), pp. 16–45; also W. Caspari, *ZAW*, 39 (1921), pp. 174–80.

[2] W. F. Albright, *APB*, p. 132.

[3] The fundamental material has been collected by W. Borée, *Die alten Ortsnamen Palästinas* (Leipzig, 1930).

[4] B.S.J. Isserlin, *PEQ*, 89 (1956), pp. 133-44.

[5] G. Dossin, *RA*, 64 (1970), p. 98, line 21; for the correct reading of this name in the Execration Texts cf. A. F. Rainey, *IOS*, 2 (1972), p. 395; *contra* A. Malamat, *IEJ*, 21 (1971), p. 35.

[6] The passage in Num. 32. 38, translated by RSV, "their names be changed", has yet to be properly explained, cf. R. de Vaux, *Vivre et penser,* I (Paris, 1941), pp. 16 ff.

[7] B. Mazar, *EI*, 3 (1954), p. 25 (Hebrew); Helck, *Beziehungen*, p. 56.

[8] Simons, *Handbook*, pp. 117 f; Aharoni, *Settlement*, pp. 36-39 (Hebrew).

[9] *ANET*, p. 246.

[10] Aharoni, *Settlement*, p. 122 (Hebrew).

[11] Simons, *Handbook*, p. 149.

[12] *Enc. Bib.* (Hebrew), III, col. 787; L. Koehler conjectures that the word is derived from an old Persian combination of *yar,* "year", and *dan,* "river", meaning a perennial river (*ZDPV*, 62 [1936], pp. 115–70).

[13] *ANET*, pp. 286, 290.

[14] *ANET*, pp. 475–79.

[15] W. F. Albright, *The Vocalisation of the Egyptian Syllabic Orthography* (New Haven, 1934); Borée, *op. cit.* (note 3,), pp. 17 f.; cf., however, W. F. Edgerton, *JAOS*, 60 (1940), p. 473.

[16] My thanks are due to R. Grafman for checking the table of the Hebrew edition. The present table was checked by Prof. Rainey, who made many valuable suggestions; cf. also Helck, *Beziehungen*, pp. 589 ff.

[17] The Akkadian vowels were of the standard Semitic classes: *a, i, u,* with a secondary *e*. Dipthongs had all been reduced to long vowels. Two vowels falling together were usually contracted. However, as discussed below, vowel length is not always discernible from the script.

[18] J. A. Knudtzon, *Die El-Amarna Tafeln* (Leipzig, 1915), I, pp. 979 ff.

[19] Cf. A. F. Rainey, *AOAT*, 8 (Neukirchen-Vluyn, 1970, 2nd revised edition, 1977), pp. 1–2; *idem, UF*, 6 (1974), pp. 295–96.

[20] W. F. Albright, *JPOS*, 4 (1924), pp. 149–61.

[21] *Ibid.*, p. 150.

[22] *Ibid.*

[23] Basic textual research of this nature for part of the book of Joshua was done by M.L. Margolis, *The Book of Joshua in Greek,* Paris, 1931.

[24] *Ibid.*, pp. 364 f.

[25] A. F. Rainey, *Tel Aviv*, 3 (1976), pp. 57-69.

[26] It must be emphasized that research in Palestinian toponymy can only be done by recourse to the original languages involved. The biblical names in this chapter are

presented in their accepted English form. Therefore, the reader may find some puzzling differences between them and the Arabic names with which they are being compared. The non-specialists must realize that the English spellings have undergone such a process of transmission that they are almost unrecognizable in many cases. To aid the English reader we have assembled here a few of the most important corruptions that have taken place: Hebrew *yodh* at the beginning of a word usually appears as *j*—Yerushalaim becomes Jerusalem; initial *aleph* is not expressed in English, therefore, its vowel becomes the first English letter and names are alphabetized accordingly—Adam and Edom have the same Hebrew consonants; this also holds true for *ayin*—Aphrah and Ophrah both begin with Hebrew ʿ ; two Hebrew letters, *he* and *heth* usually appear as English *h*—Haran, the brother of Abraham and Haran the place in northern Mesopotamia are spelled with different consonants and are linguistically unrelated; Hebrew *kaph* may appear as English *ch* or *k*—Chephirah and Kephirim; Hebrew *qoph* shows up as *c* or *k*—Carnaim and Kedesh; English *s* (not *sh*) can represent both Hebrew *samech* as in (Timnath-)serah and *sin* as in Serah the daughter of Asher; Hebrew *tsade* can appear in English as *s* (Sidon), *z* (Ziklag), or in an exceptional case as *t* (Tyre); English *z* can also stand for Hebrew *zayin* (Ziph). In this edition biblical names are spelled in accordance with common usage; others are in a "biblicized" form whenever possible, otherwise they are "Anglicized" from the original.

[27] G. Kampffmeyer, *ZDPV*, 15 (1892), pp. 1-33, 65-116; 16 (1893), pp. 1-71.

[28] Survey of Palestine 1: 100,000.

[29] "Schedule of Historical Monuments and Sites", Suppl. No. 2, *Pal. Gaz. Extraord.*, No. 1375 (1944); *Yalqut Hapirsumim*, 1091 (1964), 1164 (1965), 1327 (1967), 1583 (1969), 1925 (1973).

[30] Kampffmeyer conjectured that in the rapid process aspirated *b* would become Arabic *f* and unaspirated *g* would become *k* but there is no evidence for this. Apparently these letters were always pronounced more like Arabic *b* and *g* respectively.

[31] R. Hartmann, *ZDMG*, 65 (1911), pp. 536-38.

31a Note also:

Ṣade—normally unchanged but in rare instances shifts to *s* (Zalmon—Khirbet Sallameh).

Qoph, resh—no changes.

Taw—the aspirated *t* (*th*) is occasionally represented by Arabic *tha* (Dothan—Dotha, Dothan). There are a few examples of final *t* shifting to *d* (Zephath—Ṣafed, Zarephath [*Ṣarefant]—Ṣarafand, and perhaps Salchah [*Salkhat]—Salkhad).

Vowels—Sometimes the vowel length has been preserved correctly: *Ḥalḥûl–Ḥalḥûl* (Halhul); *Ašdôd–Esdûd* (Ashdod); *Yâfō–Yâfā* (Joppa); *ʿAkkō–Akkā* (Acco). However, as Eli Smith pointed out, the quality of the vowels in Arabic, especially the colloquial, varies considerably in accordance with position, stress, etc. An originally long vowel which is not accented is usually shortened in the vernacular. Diacritical signs on Arabic names have been added in Appendix 2.

[32] Cf. M. Kochavi, *Tel Aviv*, 1 (1974), p. 3.

[33] N. Glueck, *BASOR*, 91 (1943), pp. 7-26.

[34] A. Alt, *PJb*, 24 (1928), pp. 58 ff.; B. Maisler (Mazar), *BIES*, 6 (1939), pp. 151 ff.=*BIES Reader B* (Jerusalem, 1965), pp. 36 ff. (Hebrew).

[35] It has been suggested to identify this biblical town with Tell Ekhṣaṣ, the name of which is an exact translation of Succoth ("booths"), but instances of exact translation are very rare and Tell Deir ʿAllah remains the dominant site in the region (cf. *infra*, p. 284 n.224).

[36] P. Thomsen, *ZDPV*, 40 (1917), pp. 1-103; M. Avi-Yonah, *Historical Geography of Palestine* (Jerusalem, 1949), pp. 73 ff. (Hebrew).

[37] W. F. Albright, *BASOR*, 33 (1929), p. 7.

[38] It is difficult to establish the exact number, because we are not always sure if a place name is meant, and there may be variations of the same name.

PART TWO

Palestine during the Ages

CHAPTER I

The Canaanite Period

In order to properly understand the biblical periods we must first examine briefly the beginnings of culture in Palestine. Then we will trace the growth of source material from a small trickle in the third millenium B.C. to the abundance of texts which shed a flood of light on the country at the eve of the Israelite invasion.

I. THE PROTO-HISTORIC PERIOD

The earliest written documents pertaining to Palestine that are available today come from the beginning of the second millennium B.C. (Middle Bronze Age). All information concerning earlier periods of the country's history must be derived from archaeological research.[1] Such is not the case for Egypt and Mesopotamia where a great deal is known from inscriptions about events of the third millennium B.C. Historical texts may one day be discovered in Palestine or its neighbouring lands to transform the Early Bronze Age of these countries into a historical period. Meanwhile, the centuries preceding the second millennium B.C. must, as far as Palestine is concerned, remain in the realm of pre-history. Inasmuch as this was not a prehistoric age in the usual sense of that term, we have chosen to call it proto-historic, since it stands at the dawn of Palestine's long history.

The earliest Palestinian town to be discovered thus far is Jericho.[2] The most ancient fortifications there date to the Natufian period. Carbon-14 tests point to a time in the eighth millennium B.C. From then and throughout the Neolithic period, i.e. until the end of the fifth millennium B.C., a large and well-developed town existed there with impressive fortifications, public buildings and a relatively high standard of material culture. In other parts of the country the contemporary settlements discovered thus far have usually been in caves or in a few simple huts built on small terraces. We still do not know what caused this surprising cultural advance at Jericho, which anticipated most other towns in the country by 3,000 years or more, nor do we know whether it was a unique phenomenon or, what is more reasonable to assume, simply one of the largest and most elaborate of the early settlements in Palestine. The warm climate and perennial springs throughout the

Jordan Valley provided the conditions conducive to settlement by ancient man, including an agriculture based on irrigation and an organized society to enjoy its fruits. Perhaps the Jordan may be reckoned among those river valleys that gave birth to civilization in its early stages. But if so, the small towns founded there could never have attained the heights of certain other Near Eastern cultures because of the Jordan Valley's limited area and isolated geographical position. Though its description in the Bible doubtless reflects a later period, it was probably appropriate for an earlier age as well: "And Lot lifted up his eyes, and saw that the Jordan Valley was well watered everywhere like the garden of the Lord, like the land of Egypt . . ." (Gen. 13. 10). However, as long as Jericho is our only example, one should not draw general conclusions from it concerning the occupation of the country in earliest times.

The first period to enjoy an extensive occupation throughout Palestine is the Chalcolithic, i.e. the fourth millennium B.C. Many Chalcolithic settlements have been discovered, not only along the Jordan but also in the Jezreel Valley, beside the stream beds in the northern Negeb, and even in the hill regions of Galilee and Mount Ephraim. The colonies were usually widely dispersed and unfortified. And, of course, several stages of developments are observable in the Chalcolithic culture as well as differences between various sections of the country. Nevertheless, there is a certain continuity throughout the entire period which finds expression in a relatively peaceful expansion and some amazing material accomplishments.

Traces of Chalcolithic settlement have been noted at a considerable number of Palestinian tells, e.g. Megiddo, Beth-shean, Gezer and Lachish. However, there was no historical continuity between these colonies and the towns of the Early Bronze Age.

The third millennium B.C., the Early Bronze Age, is the first great period of expansion and development in the history of the country. Most of the large Canaanite towns were founded at this time. Of course it cannot be proved, but it seems likely that they bore the same names which we find at a later period, the majority of which remained unchanged so long as the town was in existence (cf. *supra,* pp. 107 f.). Since most of these names are of Semitic origin, it would appear that the residents of Palestine were already speaking a Semitic language.

Apparently the population was mainly concentrated in large towns at this time instead of small, unwalled settlements. In the tells that have been excavated, e.g. Megiddo, Khirbet Kerak and Ai (et-Tell), large public buildings have been discovered from various phases of the Early Bronze age; and the towns were encompassed by strong fortifications, even in the earliest stages. Especially in E.B. II do we find the construction of huge walls made of brick on a stone foundation; at Megiddo and Khirbet Kerak they reached the thickness of some 30 feet. Great building operations such as these testify to the existence of city-states in the fullest sense of the term. However, since we have no written documents, we can tell nothing of their history; neither do we know what necessitated such huge fortifications, whether an external enemy threatening the country or internal rivalries between the various states.

In E.B. III a new culture appears which was first discovered at Khirbet Kerak, hence the term Khirbet Kerak Ware for its characteristic pottery. This particular pottery originated in northern Anatolia and the Caucasus region; and since these vessels make their appearance all at once and in great quantity, it would appear that their import is related to a wave of new conquerors from the north. The ware is widely diffused in the northern part of the country but quite scarce in the south, so the invaders may have reached only a limited area. Its manufacture ceased abruptly at the end of E.B. III, and this type of material culture vanished without leavng a trace. Again the absence of sufficient material prevents us from deciding whether the new settlers had become assimilated into the local culture or had abandoned the country at this time.

The only Egyptian document from the Early Bronze Age discovered thus far which seems to have bearing on Palestine is a tomb inscription from the Sixth Dynasty.[3] It is the biography of an Egyptian officer named Weni who describes a military campaign in the reign of Pepi I (*c.* 2325–2275 B.C.):

This army returned in safety,
  After it had hacked up the land of the [Sand]-Dwellers.
This army returned in safety,
  After it had crushed the land of the Sand-Dwellers.
This army returned in safety,
  After it had thrown down its enclosures.
This army returned in safety,
  After it had cut down its fig trees and its vines.
This army returned in safety,
  After it had cast fire into all its *dwellings*.
This army returned in safety,
  After it had killed troops in it by many 10-thousands.
This army returned in safety,
  [After it had taken troops] in it, a great multitude as living captives . . .

When it was said that *rebels* because of *some affair* were among these foreigners *at the Nose of the Gazelle's Head,*[4] I crossed over in transports with these troops. I made a landing at the rear of the heights of the mountain range on the north of the land of the

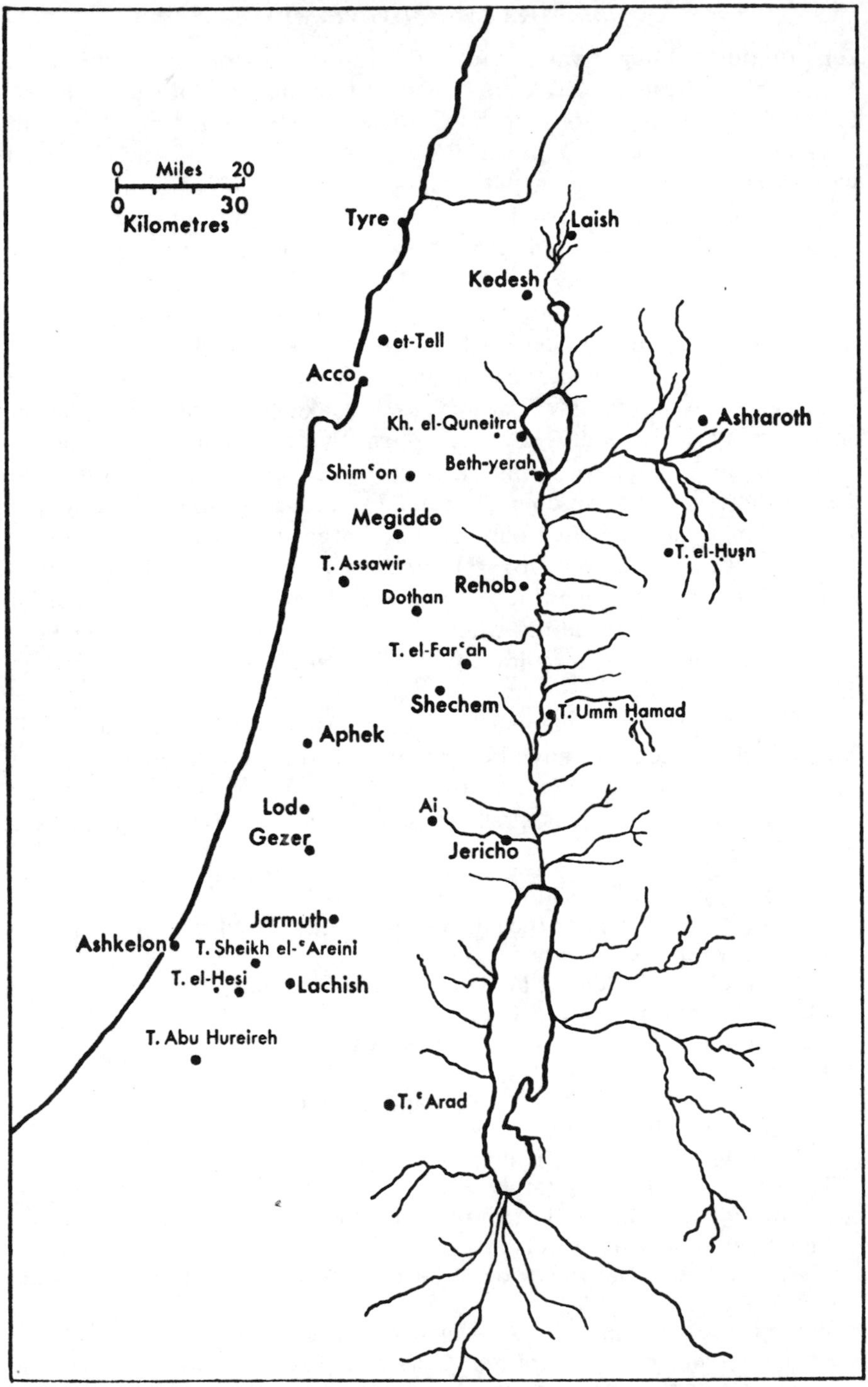

Map 6. Major Sites of the Early Bronze Age.

> Sand-Dwellers. While a full half of this army was (still) on the road, I arrived, I caught them all, and every *rebel* among them was slain.

"The Land of the Sand-Dwellers" (*tꜣ ḥryw-š* ʿ) is the ancient Egyptian expression for the region to the east of Egypt.[5] In describing the campaign Weni does not furnish any place names, but he does mention a prominent mountain ridge called "The Nose of the Gazelle's Head". The part of the Egyptian forces coming by sea evidently went around or beyond this ridge to make their landing. Although we cannot be absolutely certain, it would seem that Weni is referring here to the Carmel range, the "Nose" of which juts out into the sea. It is possible, therefore, that the Egyptians landed on the Plain of Acco from whence they attacked the Valley of Jezreel. Here they found villages and fortified towns with vineyards and orchards, especially figs, in the vicinity. From his description we learn something about the general nature of the country's settled regions, in particular about the valleys. It is also an indication that the Egyptians were seeking to exercise control over certain regions to which end they dispatched successive military expeditions into the country. Weni himself was sent to the "the land of the Sand-Dwellers" five times in order to put down what the Egyptians termed "insurrection." Even under the last pharaoh of the Sixth Dynasty, an officer named Khnum-hotep reported that he had made eleven trips to Byblos (*Kbn*) and Punt.[6]

The great population centres during the Early Bronze Age were in the valleys, especially along the important *Via Maris* (cf. map 6). One of the largest towns in that age was at Khirbet Kerak beside the Sea of Galilee which covered an area of some 50 acres. It was located in the fruitful Jordan Valley area near the most important branches of the *Via Maris*. However, major settlements are also found in various parts of the hill country, e.g. Upper Galilee, Mount Ephraim and Bashan. But in these latter regions the population was somewhat sparse, particularly among the forested district, e.g. parts of Upper and Lower Galilee and the Judean and Ephraimite hill country. Virtually unpopulated were the southern regions of Transjordan, the southern Shephelah, the Negeb and the forested hill regions.

The publication of the vast archive from Ebla (Tell Mardikh) in northern Syria will undoubtedly add a whole new chapter to the historical geography of the Levant.[7] Unofficial reports suggest that many cities in Canaan are mentioned in the Ebla archives (Jerusalem, Ashkelon, Acco and Hazor among them) and that Ebla ruled over the entire Levant and had contacts with Egypt and the kingdom of Akkad.

II. THE AMORITE WAVE

The excavations in all of the major tells pertaining to these ancient periods have revealed a destruction layer at the end of the Early

Bronze Age, followed by a certain occupational gap. At the end of E.B. or the beginning of M.B. settlement was renewed on different sites. The material culture changes completely, with only a few isolated elements being carried over from the older to the newer culture.

It is clear, therefore, that a new occupational wave had swept over the country at this time, putting an end to the E.B. population and laying the foundations for the eventual rise of new settlements in M.B. and L.B. This was one of the greatest and most decisive migratory movements in the history of Palestine. After it one finds occupational continuity in most parts of the country down to the end of the Bronze Age.

A nomadic wave of this kind, coming at the end of the third and the beginning of the second millennia B.C. is not a phenomenon unique to Palestine but is observable in all lands of the Fertile Crescent. Similar pressures were exerted from the West upon Mesopotamia which put an end to the kingdom of Akkad and the final remnants of the Sumerian kingdoms. Akkadian texts refer to these new Semitic-speaking invaders as the men of Amurru, i.e. westerners, who were known in the Bible as Amorites. Palestine and Syria were called the land of Amurru, the West Land, and the Mediterranean was known as the Sea of Amurru, the Western Sea. There is, therefore, no doubt that the invading wave at the beginning of M.B. was part of the Amorite migration. In other words, they represent a population speaking a West Semitic language who came in as nomads and gradually settled down to a sedentary life. Archaeological research has shown that the occupants of the country in that period belonged to several groups which took over, one after another, the various regions of the land.[8] For a while they evidently preserved their semi-nomadic way of life, and settlement after settlement fell before them. It is interesting that remains from this period are found not only on the previously occupied sites but also in the areas that had hitherto remained unsettled. The first great wave of settlers in southern Transjordan is dated to the end of E.B. and the first stage of M.B. (*c.* 23rd–20th centuries B.C.). On hundreds of tells surveyed in southern Gilead and the regions of Ammon, Moab and Edom one finds pottery from this period, after which there follows an occupational gap of nearly 600 years.[9]

A similar situation prevailed in the Negeb.[10] In all of its southern desert expanses one finds many sites from the M.B. I period, some of which may have come into being at the end of E.B. This wave of occupation was much shorter here than in Transjordan, and it was followed by a longer gap of nearly 1,000 years until *c.* the twelfth-eleventh centuries B.C. The intensive concentration of this culture in the Negeb is therefore even more startling. Here it is possible to gain some measure of information about its nature even without excavation. In the parched and barren Negeb, which never enjoyed a thickly settled occupation that could damage older remains, it is possible, in most cases, to distinguish the main lines of construction on an ancient site without having to dig. The great majority of M.B.I sites in the Negeb were seasonal settlements of semi-nomads, consisting mainly of large circles, apparently corrals for flocks, and smaller circles which were evidently protective walls for tents and huts. Most of these little colonies are made up of no more than ten to twenty circles, and a few are even smaller. However, some of the sites are larger, containing dozens of these circles. Here and there one sees rectangular, more substantial buildings, and a few of the colonies containing rectangular dwellings give the impression of being permanent settlements. The largest occupation site of this type to be discovered so far is near Bir Rekhmeh (today Beer Yeroḥam).[11] It contains dozens of closely crowded rectangular houses, surrounded by a sort of outer wall or fence against which the rooms are built.

In spite of the temporary nature of most of these sites, their material culture is not primitive. On the contrary, it is clear that they brought with them a great deal of technical know-how in the fields of ceramics, building construction and the manufacture of copper utensils. The pottery is uniform at all the sites, consisting of finely made, well-fired vessels. Near the settlements we find contemporary megaliths, usually in the form of circular tumuli, evidently funerary stelae for honoured members of the community. In conjunction with these tumuli there are long lines built of stone, fences or walls 4 to 5 feet thick and built in sections. These "walls" continue for hundreds of yards in a line straight as a ruler without regard for topographical obstacles.[12] The function of these "walls", which may have something to do with the funerary monuments, is as yet unexplained. Nevertheless, they are a testimony to the great technical ability of their builders.

A similar phenomenon is observable in the hill country. In the very regions of Upper Galilee that were unoccupied during the Bronze Age remains are found from M.B.I.[13] On one site where an excavation was carried out it was demonstrated that the settlers in this period actually lived in a cave.[14]

In all areas this was only a short lived wave of settlement which disappeared at the end of M.B. I. (*c.* 2000 B.C.). It was distinctly an intermediate wave having almost nothing in common with the preceding and succeeding cultures. Its evidently northern origins are still shrouded in mystery and it remained a transitory episode of semi-nomadic occupation which cannot be associated with historical data.[15] The usual view that it is the beginning of the Amorite wave is lacking in foundation.

The real Amorite wave evidently comes at the beginning of the second millennium B.C., i.e. the M.B. II in archaeological parlance.

This new nomadic wave is not a phenomenon unique to Palestine but is observable in all lands of the Fertile Crescent. Similar pressures were exerted from the West upon Mesopotamia which put an end to the kingdom of Akkad and the final remnants of the Sumerian kingdoms. Akkadian texts refer to these new Semitic speaking invaders as the men of Amurru, i.e. westerners, who were known in the Bible as Amorites. Palestine and Syria were called the land of Amurru.[16] There is, therefore, no doubt that the invading wave at the beginning of M.B. was part of the Amorite migration. In other words, they represent a population speaking a West Semitic language who came as nomads and gradually settled down to a sedentary life. They had shaft graves cut in the rock generally with single burials, in contrast to the family graves used in earlier and later periods.[17] This situation is similar to that of the Israelites and the peoples related to them who entered the country 1,000 years later.

Genesis 14 contains the ancient tradition about a military expedition to Transjordan and the Negeb. The historical background of the campaign has yet to be sufficiently clarified; the participating kings have not been successfully identified, and no external sources are available for fixing the date of this event.[18] Nevertheless, this is obviously an ancient tradition, the antiquity of which is evidenced by the many supplementary names which have been added to define the locale and to indicate the new centres that had inherited the roles of the older sites which were already archaic and not well known. Therefore, contemporary names were appended to them to facilitiate identification of the place or its region, frequently introduced by the phrase "that is", or else by use of a double name. The Valley of Siddim where the engagement took place is equated with the Dead Sea area; Ashtaroth, capital of ancient Bashan, is near Karnaim which inherited its place as the regional capital under Aramean and Assyrian rule. Shaveh, mentioned only here, is identified with the Kiriathaim of Reuben (Num. 32. 37; Josh. 13. 19), which later became Moabite (Jer. 48. 1; Ezek. 25. 9). "El-paran on the border of the wilderness" is apparently Elath on the fringe of the Paran Desert; En-mishpat is associated with Kadesh(-barnea). Hazazon is located at Tamar on the southern border of Canaan (Ezek. 47. 19; 48. 28; cf. also 1 Kings 9. 18), though at a later period it was identified with En-gedi (2 Chron. 20. 2) which is inconsistent with the campaign as described in Genesis 14.

The expedition's objective was the five cities of the plain, the last of which was Bela, identified by the text with Zoar on the south-eastern shore of the Dead Sea. In line with this the field of battle, the Valley of Siddim, is identified with the Salt Sea, which, according to the biblical tradition, covered the cities of the plain that met a violent overthrow. The expedition of the four kings followed the King's Highway along the

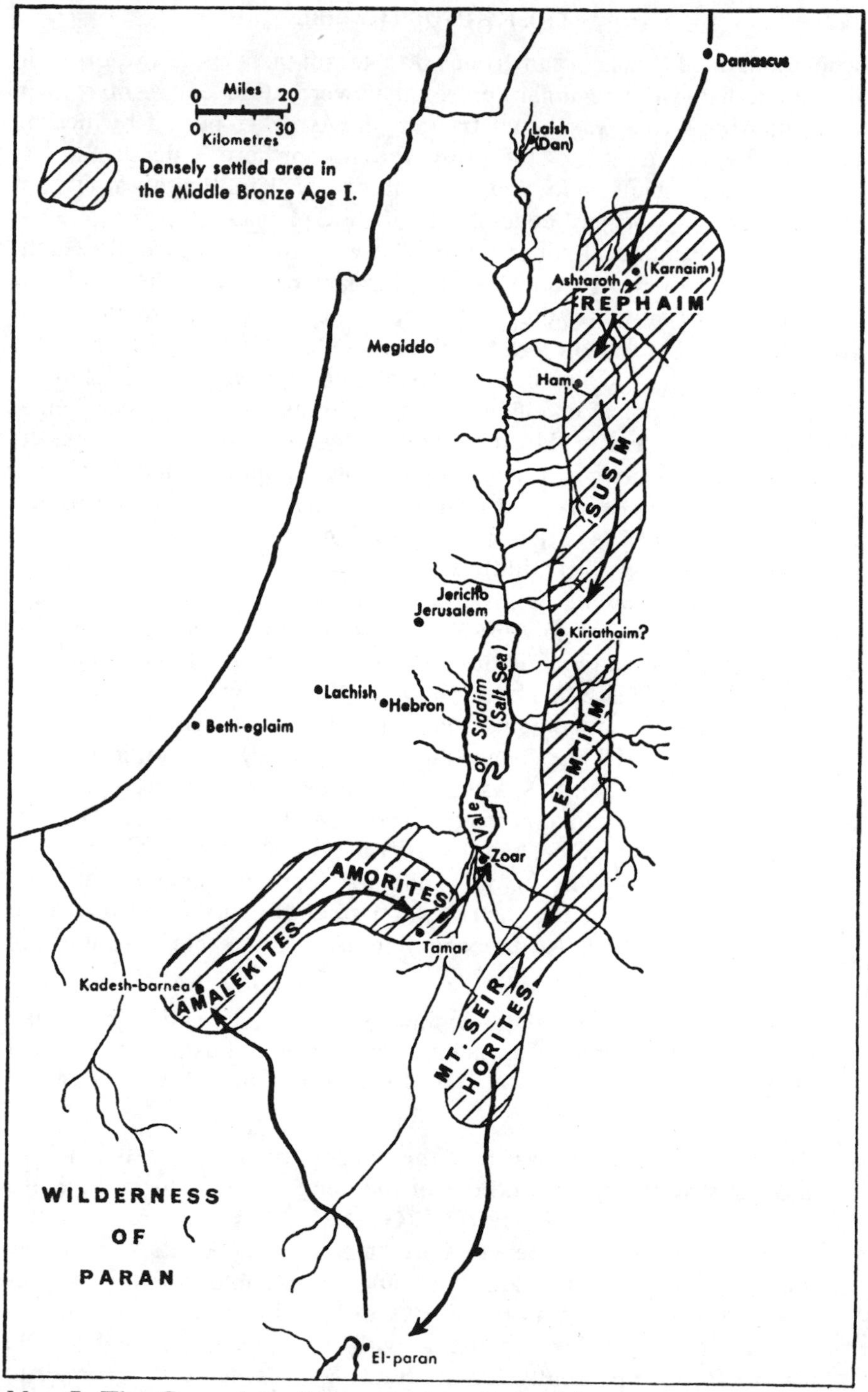

Map 7. The Campaign of Genesis 14 and the Spread of Middle Bronze Age I Settlements.

whole length of Transjordan from north to south. This is the order in which are listed the regional centres that were attacked: Ashtaroth in Bashan, whose role was taken over in the Israelite period by nearby Karnaim; Ham, a name still preserved in northern Gilead; Shaveh which, though itself unknown, is defined by Kiriathaim, a city of Reuben near the northern edge of the Moabite plateau (cf. *infra,* p. 337); Mount Seir (Edom); El-paran beside the wilderness, apparently Elath, on the border of the Paran Desert. This last place was the southernmost point; from there they returned to En-misphat, equated with Kadesh-barnea, and thence to Hazazon, identified with Tamar south of the Dead Sea in the northern Arabah, and finally to the Valley of Siddim. The peoples dwelling in these areas are also mentioned: Rephaim, Zuzim, Emim, Horites, Amalekites and Amorites. However, these appellatives belong, at least in part, to the populace that was living in these regions on the eve of the Israelite conquest; so it is doubtful that they were integral parts of the ancient tradition.

This itinerary describes faithfully the main centres of occupation along the King's Highway in Transjordan and also those in the Negeb. Therefore, the text probably has preserved a memory of the event that put an end to the settlement there during the twentieth century B.C., although the broad historical background is still unknown.

The first Egyptian documents concerning Palestine also date from the twentieth century. Of these the oldest is the story of Sinuhe from *c.* 1950.[19] The narrative begins with the death of Amen-em-het I (*c.* 1971 B.C.) and continues into the reign of Sen-Usert I (*c.* 1971–1929 B.C.). This is an autobiographical tale by an Egyptian officer named Sinuhe. He fled from Egypt when a new pharaoh was assuming the throne, found refuge in one of the districts of Upper Retenu and returned to Egypt at a ripe old age. At the beginning of his flight reference is made to:

> the Wall-of-the-Ruler, made to oppose the Asiatics and to crush the Sand-Crossers. I took a crouching position in a bush, for fear lest the watchman upon the wall where their day's (duty) was might see me.

Thus in this document we find the earliest reference to the line of fortifications on the eastern border of the delta, referred to in the Bible as "Shur, which is opposite Egypt" (Gen. 25. 18; 1 Sam. 15. 7). After crossing this barrier Sinuhe encountered a caravan of Asiatics, evidently on their way from Egypt to Palestine, and he was able to join it. On his course northward he got as far as Byblos, the Phoenician coastal city which had enjoyed close relations with Egypt ever since the Old Kingdom. It was apparently for this reason that Sinuhe was forced to wander on. For a year and a half he remained in the land of Qedem, the wilderness region to the east of Palestine and Syria. He finally found refuge with ʿAmmi-enshi, a ruler of Upper Retenu, who placed him in charge of one of his districts. The name of this region was evidently Araru[20] and may be a reference to the Yarmuk Valley to which Sinuhe's description is well suited. In the Amarna archives there is a reference to a town by that name in the land of Gari (Ga<shu>ri—the biblical Geshur? *EA,* 256. 25).[21] The text contains a most illuminating description of the region:

> He let me choose for myself of his country, of the choicest of that which was with him on his frontier with another country. It was a good land, named Araru. Figs were in it, and grapes. It had more wine than water. Plentiful was its honey, abundant its olives. Every (kind of) fruit was on its trees. Barley was there and emmer. There was no limit to any (kind of) cattle.

From the list of the "seven kinds" for which the land of Israel was renowned only the pomegranate is missing. Therefore, it is clear that the biblical passage is founded upon an ancient tradition defining the outstanding products of the land: fruit trees, field crops and cattle.

The residents of Palestine were still organized into tribes whose livelihood was still essentially pastoral:

> I spent many years, and my children grew up to be strong men, each man as the restrainer of his (own) tribe. The messenger who went north or who went south to the Residence City stopped over with me, . . . when the Asiatics became so bold as to oppose the rulers of foreign countries,[22] I counselled their movements. This ruler of (Re)tenu had me spend many years as commander of his army. Every foreign country against which I went forth, when I had made my attack upon it, was driven away from its pasturage and its wells. I plundered its cattle . . .

Thus it would seem that Egyptian influence was strongly felt in the country, since its emissaries were travelling along the main highways. But this was still not an absolute domination, because an honoured refugee from Egypt was still able to find political asylum. Apparently in most parts of the country the occupants were herdsmen who dwelt in close proximity to the wells, but this passage may refer mainly to Transjordan. Even in the duel which Sinuhe fought against one of his enemies (a story similar to that concerning the fight between David and Goliath) the booty which he took was of this type: "Then I carried off his goods and plundered his cattle. What he had planned to do to me I did to him. I took what was in his tent and stripped his encampment."

Further on in the story he mentions three rulers and their respective lands whom he suggests as references concerning his conduct: Maki from Qedem, Khenti-iaush from southern Cush and Menus from the lands of the Fenkhu. Fenkhu was probably Phoenicia or one of its regions. The tribes of Cush apparently had populated southern Transjordan and the Negeb (cf. *infra*, p. 146).

III. THE EXECRATION TEXTS

The most important information concerning Palestine in the twentieth to nineteenth centuries B.C. is derived from the Egyptian execration texts[23] (cf. map 8). These execrations, or curses, were composed in order to bring disaster on the heads of pharaoh's enemies, and in this manner a whole list of towns and tribes with which Egypt was concerned are preserved for us. Two collections of execration texts are known from different dates in the Twelfth Dynasty. The first is from the late twentieth and the second from the end of the nineteenth or the early eighteenth century B.C.

The first group of names[24] is inscribed upon sherds along with the appropriate curses. The inscribed sherds were smashed and buried in a holy place. The collection includes about twenty names of towns or regions in Palestine and Syria plus the personal names of more than thirty rulers. Most of these names are not known from other sources; we must assume that they represent tribes which had settled in particular areas. Among the towns known to us there are references to Jerusalem, Ashkelon, and Rehob in Palestine; Byblos, ʿArqat and Ullasa on the Phoenician coast. For each place we usually find the names of three rulers, though sometimes there are only two, and in one instance there are four. This picture is typical of a nomadic society caught up in the process of settlement wherein the tribe is still the basic form of social organization. This is doubtless the reason for the very small number of recognizable towns in proportion to the many unfamiliar tribal names. With regard to the latter there is at least one tribe known from other sources, viz. the Shutu (cf. Num. 24. 17 ?), for whom the names of three rulers are preserved.

The second group[25] consists of inscriptions on small figurines in the form of prisoners. There is a total of sixty-four place-names, mostly of well-known towns; generally only one ruler, or sometimes two, is listed for each place. In addition there are seven names of countries in Asia. All the identifiable place-names of the earlier group appear in these texts also, but most of the tribal names have disappeared, while many more towns have been added. The following is a list of the identifiable names arranged according to region:

Phoenician coast: Byblos, Ullasa, ʿArqat, Tyre.
Lebanese Beqaʿ and Damascus region: the Beqaʿ (*b-q-ʿ-t-m*), Lebo, Sirion,
Apum (Damascus).
The Plain of Acco: Acco, Mishal, Achshaph and perhaps Rehob.

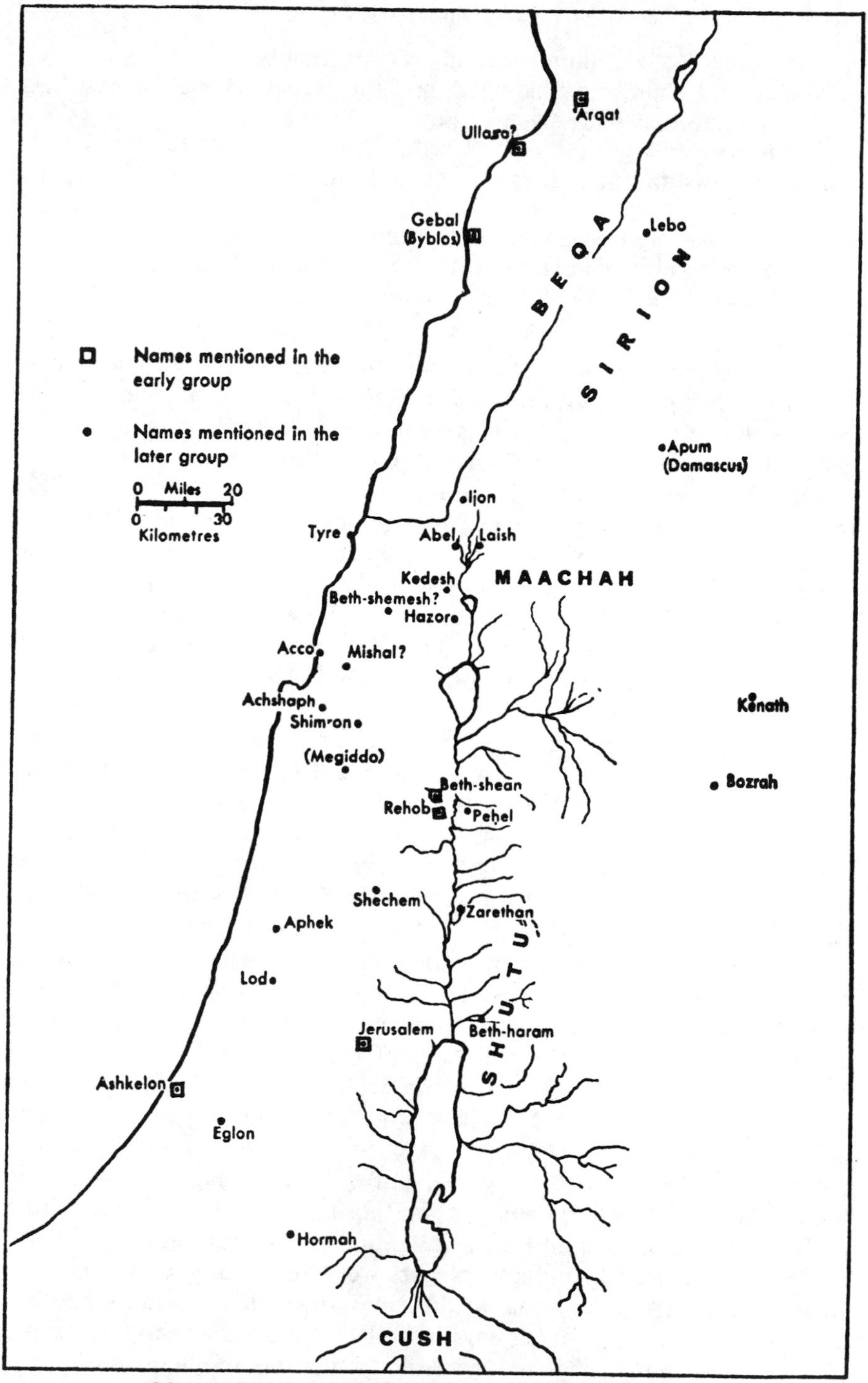

Map 8. Palestinian Cities in the Execration Texts.

The Jezreel Valley: Shim ʿon, and perhaps Rehob.
The coastal plain, the Shephelah and the Negeb: Aphek, Ashkelon, Eglon, Hormah and perhaps Lod.
The Jordan Valley: Ijon, Abel, Laish, Hazor, Peḥel and (Beth)-haram.
Bashan: Ashtaroth, Bozrah, Zer, Kenath (*q-n-ʾ*) and perhaps Maachah.
Galilee: Possibly Kedesh and Beth-shemesh.
Ephraimite and Judean Hill Country: Shechem and Jerusalem.
The tribes of Cush and Shutu also appear.

The differences between these two collections of execration texts reflect the changes that took place in Palestine during the twentieth to nineteenth centuries B.C., viz. transition from a nomadic to a sedentary way of life and a shift from patriarchal rule by three or four tribal leaders to an urban autocracy, usually under only one ruler. Archaeological research has shown that the new population flourished mainly in the same regions of concentration as during the Early Bronze Age, i.e. in the principal valleys and in Bashan with very little in the hill countries. Nevertheless, Shechem and Jerusalem have now become major centres. These two towns may have enjoyed special importance as key points on the connecting routes leading to the King's Highway, which seems to have had unusual prominence at that time.[26]

The picture of a caravan arriving in Egypt, perhaps via the King's Highway, is preserved in a wall painting from a Twelfth Dynasty Egyptian tomb at Beni Ḥasan (early nineteenth century B.C.).[27] The group is comprised of thirty-seven Asiatics (*ʿAamu, ʿȝmw*) from the land of Shutu who are delivering black eye-paint to Egypt. Their leader has an apparently Semitic name, Ibsha (*ʾi-b-šȝ*), and bears the standard Egyptian title "ruler of a foreign country" (*ḥqȝ ḫȝst*).

It is probable that the land of Shutu is the ancient term for Gilead and that the Cushites were in possession of southern Transjordan. Gilead was famous for various types of resins (Jer. 8. 22; 46. 11), and the caravan of Ishmaelites (or Midianites) that carried Joseph down to Egypt was on its way from Gilead via Dothan loaded with "gum, balm and myrrh" (Gen. 37. 25). The "sons of Sheth" appear in poetic parallelism with Moab (Num. 24. 17), and in like manner Cushan is parallel to Midian (Hab. 3. 7). Evidently these passages preserve the names of the ancient population in those regions.[28] Evidence from archaeology tends to confirm these textual references because Gilead, southern Transjordan and the Negeb were practically unoccupied in M.B. II and L.B. In contrast to the many towns located in most other sectors of the country (according to the later group of execration texts), these areas were still inhabited by the nomadic tribes of Sheth and Cush.

The degree of Egyptian control over Palestine in this period is not sufficiently clear. At present only one expedition to Retenu is known, and that from a single Egyptian source, viz. the tomb inscription of an Egyptian official named Khu-sebek, dating to the reign of Sen-Usert III (*c.* 1880–1840 B.C.).[29] This record, more or less contemporary with the later execration texts, refers to Egyptian penetration as far as Sekmem (*s-k-m-m*), which is evidently Shechem, "Then Sekmem fell, together with the wretched Retenu". This chance discovery strongly suggests that that was not the only military campaign in the land of Retenu. But it is surprising that the Egyptian army should go deep into the hill country. This is in harmony with the special prominence of Shechem and Jerusalem in the execration texts. Some Egyptian seal impressions found at Jericho testify to commercial relations with the country's interior during this period.[30] Connections with southern Palestine are also demonstrated by the Egyptian inscriptions from the mines in Sinai in which various workers from Retenu are mentioned, including some Asiatics from a place (written *ḥꜣmỉ*) which might possibly be identified with Hormah in southern Canaan. The same town may also be referred to in the first place in the later execration texts.[31]

Egyptian stelae and statues of Middle Kingdom date have been found at Ugarit, Byblos and Beirut on the Phoenician coast: at Nerab beside Aleppo; at Qaṭna and Tell Ḥizzin in the Lebanese Beqaʻ; and at Megiddo, Gezer and Tell el- ʻAjjul in Palestine.[32] Excavations at Megiddo brought to light the statuette base of Thut-hotep,[33] known to have been a high-ranking official during the nineteenth century. From the list of titles inscribed in his tomb we learn that he was in charge of the areas under the Egyptian rule in Asia. The erection of his statue at Megiddo is doubtless an indication that some form of Egyptian authority was exercised over that city. Therefore, the later execration texts may possibly be a true representation of Egypt's sphere of authority at the peak of its influence at the end of the nineteenth century when it was being threatened by dissolution. The absence of Megiddo from the execration texts may be an indication that it was not reckoned among the cursed rebels because it was still in Egyptian hands.[34] A few towns mentioned in the execration texts for which the rulers' names are not given may have been Egyptian bases or at least reckoned as Egyptian territory. This is clear as regarding Byblos and probably also with regard to Ullasa and Yarmut on the Phoenician coast, which are also known as Egyptian bases during the New Kingdom.[35]

IV. THE HYKSOS PERIOD

For information concerning Palestine during the eighteenth to fifteenth centuries B.C. we must again turn to archaeology, since we have no relevant Egyptian sources for this period. The disintegration of a central Egyptian authority under the Thirteenth Dynasty during the eighteenth century doubtless brought an end to Egyptian control over Palestine. In about 1720 Egypt itself was conquered by peoples coming down from the north who established the so-called "Hyksos rule". The word Hyksos is derived via Hellenistic sources from the standard Egyptian title "rulers of foreign lands" (*ḥqꜣ ḫꜣśwt*). It seems most likely that at least their earlier rulers had Amorite names.[36] It is also clear that the Hyksos kings of the Fifteenth Dynasty ruled over Egypt and Palestine-Syria simultaneously from their capital, Tanis (biblical Zoan), in the Nile delta. However, more detailed historical information is presently not available. We must depend, therefore, on archaeological research, supplemented by whatever conclusions we may derive from later sources about changes that took place in Palestine during this period.

The Hyksos' great military strength stems from a radical innovation in the art of warfare, introduction of the horse-drawn battle chariot. This highly effective weapon was expensive to maintain; originally its possession and operation seem to have been the sole prerogative of the *maryannū*,[37] a special class of noble chariot warriors. This gave rise to a form of government in the individual city-states supported mainly by the chariot force and the nobility who manned it. It was more or less feudal in structure, awarding lands and special privileges to the chariot nobles in exchange for their services to the local king, who was, in turn, a subject of the king dwelling in Tanis.

The Hyksos period also saw the extensive use of a fortification system consisting of a huge sloping ramp made of bricks and beaten earth and usually having a trench or moat at its foot, especially in level areas. It may have been used at first in constructing the Hyksos' large fortified centres and was later adopted in other towns.

Archaeological investigations have shown that in the Hyksos period (Middle Bronze II) civilization in the country attained a high state of development, especially in the same areas and cities mentioned previously in the execration texts. The remains of large towns with strong fortifications from this age have been discovered at Laish, Hazor, Jericho, Megiddo, Taanach, Dothan, Shechem, Bethel, Jerusalem, Beth-zur, Beth-shemesh, Gezer, Lachish, Tell Beit Mirsim, Tell Jerisheh (Gath-rimmon?), Joppa, Minat Rubin (H. Yavne Yam), Ashkelon, Tell en-Nejileh, Tell el-ʿAjjul (Beth-ʿeglaim) and Tell el-Farhʿah (Sharuhen), Tell el-Meshash (T. Masos), Tell el-Milḥ (T. Malḥata), *et al.* The Bible preserves the tradition that "Hebron was built seven years before Zoan in Egypt" (Num. 13. 22). It would seem that Hebron was one of the towns founded just prior to the Hyksos period which enjoyed great prosperity under their rule.

Hazor played a unique role under the Hyksos. On the north side of the ancient tell there was added now a huge rectangular area over half a mile in length. This whole enclosure, over 175 acres—ten times the size of the main tell, was surrounded by a high ramp, reinforced on two sides by an artificial moat. This is the largest Palestinian city ever built in the biblical period; in the Hyksos Age similar towns were built at Tell el-Yehudiyeh in Egypt, Qaṭna (Tell el-Mishrifeh) in Middle Syria, Carchemish on the Euphrates, and others.

Not enough excavation has been carried out on these tells to indicate the reason for such cities being founded. It remains to be seen whether they were originally settled towns or great military camps, perhaps centres for the concentration of chariot forces. Nevertheless, it is clear that Hazor was the military and political hub of Palestine in that period. This may explain the tradition about Hazor as the capital of Canaan.[38]

This agrees with the fact that it appears prominently in the Mari archives (though Laish is also mentioned once).[39] Mari also had close political contacts with Qaṭna, and Apum (the Damascene) is referred to as well as Byblos on the Phoenician coast. In a copy of the Babylonian "Dream Book", apparently derived from a source dating to this period, there is also a reference to *La-ba-an*. This is evidently Lebo(-hamath) in the Lebanese Beqa', the Labana of the Amarna tablets.[40] Hazor also appears in these texts as an important centre from which emissaries were sent to Babylon via Mari. The Mari letters contain references to emissaries from various cities in Mesopotamia who were on their way to Yamḫad (Aleppo), Qaṭna, Hazor and one other place whose name has been lost from the text, perhaps a more southern city or Egypt.[41] This same geographical order appears in the "Dream Book" which mentions the town of Mari, Emar, Aleppo, Qaṭna and Hazor. One document refers to gifts sent by the King of Hazor to Kaptara (Crete?) and Ugarit.

Therefore, the Mari tablets illuminate in a most interesting manner the important role of Hazor at that time. Its association with Amurru is especially prominent, and reference is made to migration by Yaminites ("sons of the south") from the Euphrates region to Yamḫad, Qaṭna and the land of Amurru, which stands here in place of Hazor. In another text we find allusions to emissaries from Hazor who are grouped with the emissaries of four Amorite kingdoms. The material is still insufficient to permit definite conclusions, but if Hazor was in the land of Amurru, then it was probably the capital. The biblical tradition about Hazor being "the head of all those kingdoms" may be founded on this situation in the Hyksos Age. The Alalaḫ tablets refer to horses delivered from Amurru, and the Mari tablets contain similar references concerning Qaṭna. Therefore, Qaṭna and Hazor were probably the main centres for chariotry and horses in Syria and Palestine at that time.

One may venture, therefore, to conjecture the development of Amurru as a geographical term. From a general name for Syria and Palestine in Akkadian documents towards the end of the third millennium B.C. Amurru became the political title for southern Palestine-Syria in the Hyksos Age. Later it was restricted to the small kingdom of Amurru, located in the Lebanon region during the Amarna Age; its kings were evidently striving to revive the ancient glories of Amurru in their small principality between Egypt and Hatti (cf. *supra,* p. 66). Hazor, the capital of Hyksos Amurru in Palestine, apparently supplies the connecting link that was missing between the ancient geographical term which was more general and the restricted political conception of the later period. In this way we can also understand how the name Amorite in the Bible became a parallel for Canaan, which was used when the interior, especially the hill country, was being emphasized[42] (cf. map 4, p. 71).

From later documents we learn that a considerable ruling class grew up in the various cities whose members bore Hurrian and Indo-European names. From an examination of the local rulers' names in the El Amarna inscriptions, the following picture emerges[43]: along the Phoenician coast from Byblos to Tyre only rulers with Semitic names were found; in the Beqa', the Damascus region, Bashan, the Jezreel Valley and the Plain of Acco the predominant names are Hurrian and Indo-European; in the regions farther south there is a considerable mixture. It would appear that this distribution of names gives some indication of the direction taken by the Hurrian penetration, viz. via the Beqa' to northern Transjordan and thence to the principal valleys of the country where the major centres of Hyksos domination are found. It has also become clear from excavations that the Hyksos Age was not a unified and continuous period; rather it was marked by numerous changes and destructions. Thus the Hyksos Age is usually divided, from an historical point of view, into two phases. This destruction is also quite noticeable at Hazor, because most of the buildings excavated thus far in the great lower town belong to the later Hyksos stratum; but below them were found remains proving that the great town was founded in a preceding period; this earlier town remains practically untouched by excavation. To this we may add the fact that the Egyptians called Palestine and Syria by the name Hurru (*ḫ-r*), i.e. the land of the Horites. The Egyptians certainly did not concoct such a name on their own; they must have encountered it in the country. Thus we can understand the appearance of Horites among the peoples of ancient Palestine.

V. THE RISE OF THE NEW EGYPTIAN EMPIRE

The Late Bronze Age is a direct continuation of the Hyksos period. The city-states in Palestine were not fundamentally changed; they simply transferred their allegiance from their former Hyksos masters to the pharaohs of the Egyptian New Kingdom. Though it continued to be a very important city, Hazor lost its position as the capital of Canaan; the Egyptian administration chose Gaza as its main base and the headquarters of its commissioner.[44] This latter place was doubtless chosen because it was an important centre on the southern branch of the great *Via Maris* and could be supervised efficiently from Egypt.

Except for the Egyptian administration there was now no factor which could unite the petty kingdoms of Canaan, and thus was developed the city-state regime so typical of the Late Bronze Age. The Egyptian authorities did not usually interfere in the cities' internal affairs; the local dynasties were permitted to remain in power so long as they submitted to the Egyptian yoke. The Egyptians had no desire to influence the occupants of Canaan culturally or religiously; they simply treated them as inferior subordinates. Their interest was confined to security of the highways, regular tribute for the Egyptian treasury and the fulfilment of certain responsibilities imposed upon various cities, e.g. supplying the Egyptian army or furnishing chariots and supporting troops. Egyptian bases were few, and except for Gaza, only Joppa, Megiddo and Beth-shean, Yarmut, Ullasa and Ṣumur are known to have served in this capacity, and not even these in all periods.[45] Sometimes small Egyptian garrisons were stationed in various cities alongside the local authorities, and it generally required only a token force to maintain control. Fidelity on the part of the Canaanite kings was also assured by the dispatch of their sons as hostages to Egypt. After these lads were educated at Pharaoh's court, they were enthroned over their home cities by the Egyptians. As a general rule the Egyptians did not interfere in minor conflicts between the petty Canaanite rulers; however, they would not tolerate any extensive alliances between city-states which were liable to threaten their own control over the country.

Neither did the population picture undergo any significant change. Settlement continued to exist in the same areas where it had flourished during the Middle Bronze Age, although a certain decline is observable, doubtless caused at least in part by the Egyptian policies of exploitation. This decadence is apparent in most of the towns and even more so in sparsely settled regions. For example, the excavations at Jericho and Beth-zur have shown that after their great prosperity in the Hyksos Age a sharp decline set in, as indicated by the very poor remains ascribable to L.B. The centres of Canaanite population came more and more to be concentrated along the main branches of the *Via Maris,* while the interior regions of the country were less heavily settled. Egyptian authority was mainly imposed upon the densely populated areas, but their influence was considerabley weaker in most of the hill regions and in Transjordan.

There seem to have been few unwalled villages on the plains; the population was mainly concentrated in the fortified towns. The Egyptian authorities encouraged the independence of these cities so that, although the number of royal Canaanite towns increased during L.B., each one controlled only a very limited area.[46] In the plain of Jezreel and the Valley of Beth-shean, for example, we have a considerable list of royal Canaanite cities: Jokneam, Megiddo, Taanach, Ibleam, Shimron (Shim 'on), Shunem, Anaharath, Beth-shean, Rehob and Hammath.

Only a few settlements were founded in L.B. Archaeological investigations have acquainted us with a few towns along the coast whose occupation began in this period: Tell Abu Huwam ([Shihor-]libnath ?) at the mouth of the Kishon, apparently Dor, Tell Abu Seleimeh (Laban ?) beside Sheikh Zuweid near the Egyptian frontier and perhaps Raphia. These were all stations along the *Via Maris,* doubtless founded primarily as seaports, perhaps with Egyptian help.

Since Palestine and Syria comprised an Egyptian province throughout the entire Late Bronze Age and since the Egyptians carried out many military campaigns to assure their control of these regions, we have an abundance of information about Palestine in that period from Egyptian sources.

The Expulsion of the Hyksos. Concerning the conquest of the land after the expulsion of the Hyksos from Egypt, we have only one tomb inscription from an Egyptian officer named Ah-mose, who served under Pharaoh Ah-mose I, founder of the Eighteenth Egyptian Dynasty, as well as Amen-hotep I and Thut-mose I during the second half of the fifteenth century B.C.[47] From this inscription it seems that, after the conquest of Tanis and the expulsion of the Hyksos from Egyptian soil, Pharaoh Ah-mose also marched into Palestine. For three years the Egyptian army besieged Sharuhen, evidently Tell el-Farh 'ah, a large tell in the western Negeb where strong Hyksos fortifications were discovered.[48] We do not know if additional battles were fought after the conquest of Sharuhen. Ah-mose's inscription then skips ahead to the reign of Thut-mose I (*c.* 1525–1508). Under that pharaoh Ah-mose participated in a campaign to Retenu and reached the border of Naharin, the Hurrian kingdom of Mitanni, in the region of the Khabur and the northern Euphrates Rivers. At that time Mitanni was Egypt's chief enemy in Asia. The annals of Thut-mose III indicate that his grandfather Thut-mose I had already set up a victory stele in Naharin on the eastern bank of the Euphrates,[49] thus it is possible that his sphere of influence included the southern and central Levant at least. The fact that Thut-mose I had been able to surprise his enemy in Naharin before the latter had had time to muster his forces, certainly indicates that the Egyptians had enjoyed the cooperation of the states in Palestine and perhaps in Syria.

VI. THE CAMPAIGNS OF THUT-MOSE III

A considerable amount of valuable information about the country can be derived from the inscriptions of Thut-mose III (*c.* 1468–1436), who carried out at least sixteen military expeditions to Palestine and Syria, even going as far as the Euphrates. The most detailed texts have to do with his first campaign when he went to war against an alliance of Canaanite kings in the Megiddo area; this was evidently one of the decisive victories in the New Kingdom's effort to retain control over Canaan (cf. map 9).

According to Thut-mose's inscriptions, more than 100 cities participated in the war.[50] They were led by the Kings of Kadesh on the Orontes and Megiddo, with assistance from the King of Mitanni. This was the greatest alliance of Canaanite kings ever to take a stand against Egyptian authority, and there is no doubt that the Mitannian kingdom was giving it full support in an attempt to challenge the Egyptian authority in Canaan.

The revolt encompassed the whole country "from Yurza (apparently Tell Jemmeh)[51] to the outer ends of the earth", from southern Palestine to the limits of Egyptian authority in Syria. An Egyptian garrison had been able to maintain its position at Sharuhen, the same southern stronghold that had formerly been a focal point in the Hyksos defence lines. From Sile, the chief frontier post on the Egyptian border, the army covered the 150 miles to Gaza in nine or ten days, a very rapid pace, which indicates that this southern portion of the *Via Maris* was firmly in Egyptian hands (cf. *supra,* p. 48). Gaza bears the title "That-which-the-ruler-seized", signifying its role as the chief Egyptian base in Canaan.

The next station mentioned in the annals is Yaḥam (Khirbet Yemma) in the Sharon. The 75 miles from Gaza to Yaḥam took them eleven or twelve days. The progress of the expedition was, therefore, considerably slower, doubtless because of opposition encountered from some of the settlements along the way. At Yaḥam a conference was called to decide which of the three routes leading from the Sharon to the Jezreel Valley should be taken. The general staff recommended either the southern route by way of Taanach or the northern which leaves the Sharon north of Zephath (Khirbet Sitt Leila)[52] and reaches the Jezreel Valley north of Megiddo. They warned Thut-mose against the danger of taking the narrow ʿAruna pass (Wadi ʿAra). In support of their advice they cited intelligence reports that the enemy was waiting at the mouth of this pass. However, when the Egyptian forces reached the Jezreel Valley, they found that the enemy had divided their troops and were actually waiting in ambush by the southern route.

Thut-mose did not countenance the advice of his generals; he decided to take the shortest route, through the ʿAruna pass. Thus he was able to take the enemy by surprise when his troops issued into the plain and assembled on the bank of the Brook Qina beside Megiddo while the allies were expecting him to come via either of the alternate routes. The

Canaanites evidently had based their plans on the use of chariotry and did not dare to make a stand against the Egyptian infantry, even under such convenient circumstances as offered by Wadi 'Ara. With a sudden chariot attack they may have planned to confound the Egyptian army as it marched in the Jezreel Plain.[53]

The decisive battle which took place in the vicinity of Megiddo was of brief duration and ended in complete Egyptian victory. The vast booty which they captured in the Canaanite camp outside the city walls included 924 chariots. The siege against the city itself lasted seven months[54]: "They measured [this] city, which was corralled with a moat and enclosed with fresh timbers of all their pleasant trees". With the fall of Megiddo most of the Canaanite Kings submitted to Egyptian authority: "Now the children of the princes and their brothers were brought to be *hostages* in Egypt. Now, whoever of these princes dies, his majesty was accustomed to make his son go to stand in his place."[55]

Evidently Thut-mose's authority in Palestine was permanently established after this victory. The rest of his campaigns were directed against Syria and Mitanni. On the fifth expedition he reached Ardat on the Phoenician coast. During the sixth he conquered Kadesh on the Orontes and then crossed over to the Phoenician coast (doubtless via the Eleutherus—Nahr el-Kebir), arriving at Ṣumur and Ardat. The seventh campaign was also directed against the Phoenician coast and culminated in the conquest of Ullasa. In his eighth campaign Thut-mose reached Naharin and set up his stele east of the Euphrates. On the way back he conquered the land of Ni in the vicinity of the northern Orontes.[56] From a tomb inscription belonging to one of his officers which seems to deal mainly with this campaign we find a reference to the Negeb as well as the conquest of Aleppo, Carchemish, a town called Meriu in the land of Taḫshi and Kadesh where a new wall had been built in the meantime.[57] Only general descriptions have been preserved concerning the remaining expeditions. In the last one, the sixteenth or seventeenth, Thut-mose conquered 'Arqat on the Phoenician coast, Tunip,[58] and three towns in the vicinity of Kadesh. We also have a legendary account describing the taking of Joppa by means of soldiers who hid in 200 baskets that were carried into the city on a ruse[59]—a story which doubtless contains a historical kernel about the conquest of the town and its conversion into an Egyptian base, evidently during the first campaign.

The topographical list of Thut-mose III provides the most detailed information available about the land of Canaan. Of his principal lists three copies have been preserved, two of them containing 119 names, which also appear on a third list which has, in addition, some 231 more, making about 350 all told.[60] The first of the two shorter lists contains towns in Palestine and southern Syria, while the second is concerned with middle and northern Syria as far as Naharin.[61]

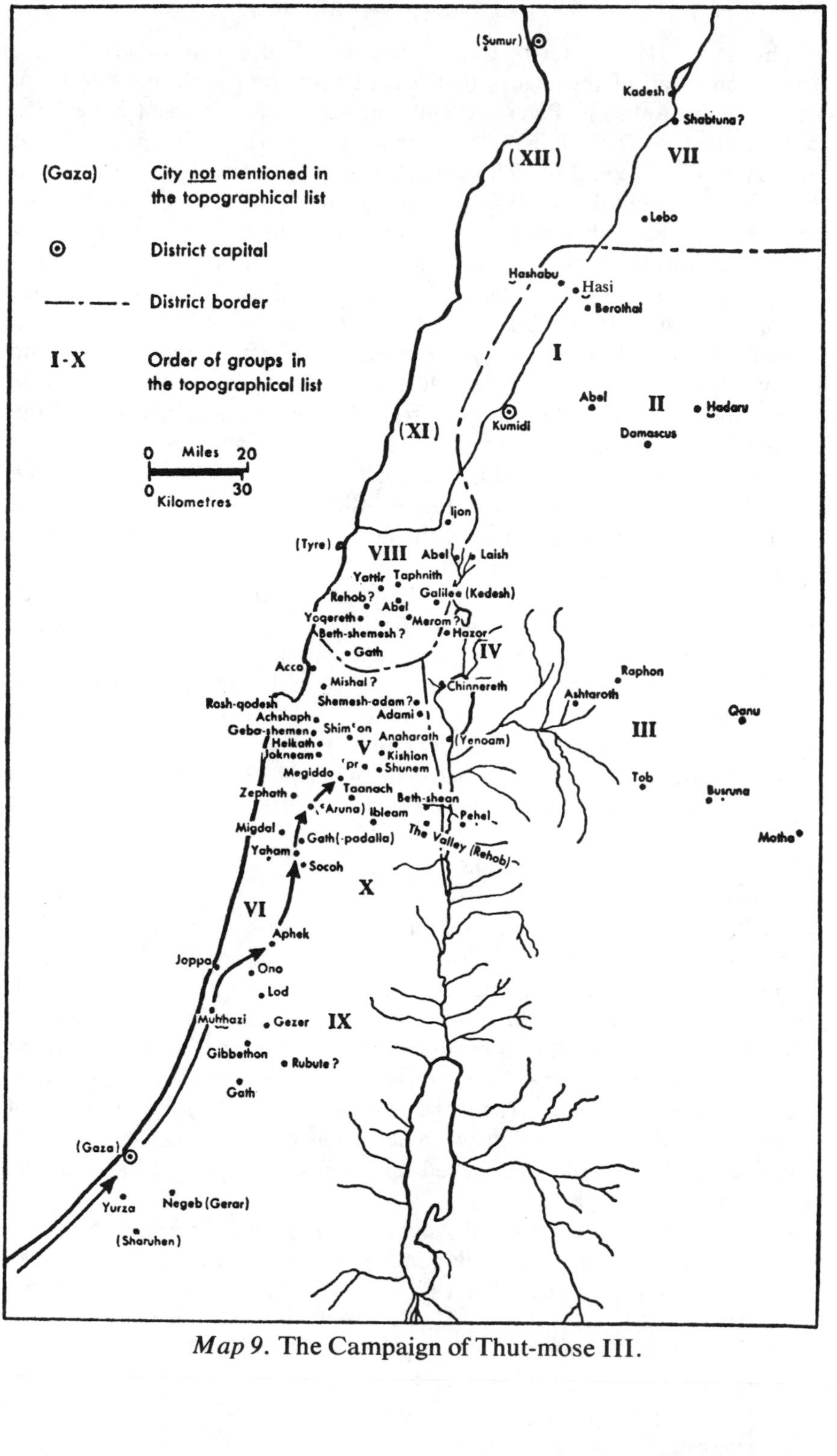

Map 9. The Campaign of Thut-mose III.

Thut-mose III's roster of Canaanite towns had a total of 119 names. Inasmuch as all of the places that can be identified with any degree of certainty are found in Palestine and southern Syria, it must have been composed after Thut-mose's first campaign which culminated in the victory beside Megiddo.[62] This assumption is supported by the fact that Kadesh and Megiddo stand at the very head of the list. Of course, the reference to Kadesh presents a certain difficulty; that city was only conquered on Thut-mose's sixth campaign. Generally there is a good reason for assuming that the list is a faithful representation of the historical reality; it is unlikely that towns were added which had not actually been subdued on that expedition. Some suppose that the original list referred to the Kedesh in Galilee, an important Canaanite town which is otherwise missing from this text; and since it had the same name as the famous town on the Orontes, it was mistaken for the northerly Kadesh and placed at the head of the list.[63] But it is possible that Kadesh on the Orontes is really intended here, it being included because it appeared at the head of the alliance crushed at Megiddo in the actual journal of the campaign.

Determination of the list's composition depends largely upon our approach to its structure, because the identification of many towns is contingent upon the order of their appearance in the list. A good illustration of this is the name *ʿ-r-n* (No. 27): although these consonants could stand for the ʿAruna mentioned in Thut-mose's annals, an identification is preferable with ʿAlunni in Bashan, the Ḫalunni from an Amarna letter (*EA,* 197. 14), because of its place in the list between *q-nw* (Kenath) and *ʿ-s-t-r-t* (Ashtaroth) in a group of towns from that region.

Two very important principles can be established which will guide us in analysing the list:

(1) The roster was composed on the basis of lists from the first expedition and contains only those towns conquered and subjugated during this campaign. This stands out clearly from a comparison with the annals. Sharuhen, which was still in Egyptian hands, does not appear on the list. On the other hand, the rebellious Yurza is included (No. 60). Most of the other towns referred to in the annals also appear in the roster, e.g. Yaḥam, Taanach, Zephath and Megiddo. Gaza and ʿAruna are absent, although we meet them in the narrative, but it is possible that they had not rebelled and are only mentioned as stations along the line of march.

(2) The towns are grouped geographically according to adjacent districts, which include the following regions: The southern Lebanese Beqaʿ and the Damascus district (Nos. 3–20); Bashan (Nos. 21–30); the northern Jordan Valley (Nos. 31–4); the Plains of Jezreel and Acco (Nos. 35–54); the southern coastal plain and the Sharon (Nos. 57–71);

the northern Lebanese Beqa' (Nos. 72–9 [84?]); Galilee (Nos. 80[85?]–102); the northern Shephelah (Nos. 103–6); the Beth-shean Valley (Nos. 107–10); the Carmel slopes (Nos. 111–17). The last two names are undecipherable. We have also skipped over Nos. 55–6, Ḫashabu and Tushulti, which are situated in the land of 'Amqi (southern Lebanese Beqa'),[64] and thus belong to the first group. Perhaps they were pushed out of their rightful place by the insertion of Kadesh and Megiddo, which were placed at the head of the list, though geographically they belong with the Jezreel Valley and the northern Beqa'.[65] A few names which seem to be nothing but geographical designations for particular regions present a special problem, e.g. Negeb (No. 57), "hill country" (*h-r*; No. 77), "the valley" ('*-m-q*; No. 107),[66] and perhaps Galilee(No. 80) and Sharon (No. 21). It is difficult to understand what place such general geographical designations would have in a list of cities. Therefore, the question arises as to whether these may represent principal cities dominating their respective regions and thus named after them. Following this suggestion, one may conjecture that Negeb is the title for Gerar, "valley" for Rehob (cf. Shishak's list, *infra,* p. 325), and possibly Galilee for Kedesh (cf. Josh. 20. 7; 21. 32, *et al.*). Each of these is the most important Canaanite town in its own district, and their absence from the list is surprising.[67]

Since Thut-mose's list is of such special importance, we are presenting it here in full,[68] with the conjectural Canaanite-Hebrew transcription and the corresponding form in the Bible and other sources (especially the El Amarna tablets) wherever possible (cf. the tables on pp. 159–163). Suggested identifications with presently known antiquity sites are also added (cf. map 9, p. 155).

There are still sharp differences of interpretation among scholars in all matters concerning the origin and nature of the list. In Noth's opinion the list reflects the line of march taken by Thut-mose's army starting with Nos. 53-119, the right-hand column, followed by Nos. 1-52, the left-hand column.[69] However, the towns are arranged in consecutive geographic order from south to north in only one small section (Nos. 57-71) consisting of towns situated along the *Via Maris* in the Sharon Plain. This section must, of course, represent the route followed by the expedition, but it is not followed by a logical geographic sequel. The next consecutive section may have been omitted from the annals, but it is also possible that the exact sequence was followed in regard to the southern region because the *Via Maris* was familiar to the Egyptian scribes in this standard form. Not only does the continuation of the text fail to present a reasonable order, but the towns of Nos. 53–119 cannot all be located in or south of the Jezreel Valley, which is Noth's basic assumption.[70] Comparison of these names with other sources removes all doubt that some of those towns were in the north, in Galilee and the Lebanese Beqa'. For this reason Helck has suggested that the original beginning of the list was the name Negeb (No. 57), which begins the section pertaining to the coastal route.[71] In his opinion this group was taken from the description of the military expedition to Megiddo while the other sections represent secondary thrusts in various directions by smaller units, some of which were transported by sea to the Phoenician coast from whence they marched southward into the Lebanese Beqaʿ. This theory attempts to explain a basic element in this list, viz. that it contains groups of towns in more or less consolidated regions. However, the order of cities within the framework of these regions cannot be reconciled with logical military operations, as Helck's own map clearly demonstrates.[72]

In the light of these consolidated geographical units represented in the roster, Yeivin's suggestion that the order of the list is based upon the administrative division of Canaan prior to Thut-mose's campaign is worthy of consideration.[73] Thus it is possible to assume that the section having to do with the *Via Maris* was taken from the expedition's list while the rest of the towns that participated in the rebellion were added according to a standard arrangement in the Egyptian administration.

The administrative theory stands up well under a scrupulous examination of the list, albeit in a form different from that suggested by Yeivin.[74] The only source from which we may derive information concerning the Egyptian organization of Canaan is the corpus of El Amarna letters; although they are nearly a century later, it is most likely that the administrative system was not fundamentally changed. In the El Amarna period we hear about three towns which served as headquarters for Egyptian commissioners (*rābiṣū*), viz. Gaza, Ṣumur and Kumidi. From this Helck deduced that the Egyptian province of Canaan was divided into three administrative districts: a southern one with its capital at Gaza; another in the north-west, which included Phoenicia and Amurru, with its capital at Ṣumur; and a third in the north-east comprised of the Lebanese Beqaʿ and Damascus with its capital at Kumidi.[75] The geographical regions of Thut-mose's list correspond nicely to this administrative division, and in fact, permit a more precise definition of it.

The first four regions belong to the district of Kumidi, including the southern Beqaʿ (Nos. 3–11 [12?] plus 55–56), the Damascene (Nos. 12[13?]-20),[76] Bashan (Nos. 21-30) and the northern Jordan Valley (Nos. 31–4). These are followed by two regions of the Gaza district consisting of the Plains of Jezreel and Acco (Nos. 35–54) and the Sharon (Nos. 57–71). Next we find two regions of the Ṣumur district, viz. the northern Beqaʿ (Nos. 72–9 [84?]) and Upper Galilee (80[85?]–102). These are the internal regions most naturally associated with the Lebanon range and the Phoenician coast. The watershed between the

+9

Group	No.	Transcription	Conjectural Canaanite-Hebrew Form	Biblical Form: English	Biblical Form: Hebrew	Other Sources (*Espec. EA*)	Identification
Leaders	1.	q-d-š	קדש	Kadesh	קדש	Qidša (*EA*)	Tell Nebi Mind
Leaders	2.	m-k-t	מגד	Megiddo	מגדו	Magidda (*EA*)	Tell el-Mutesellim
Upi	3.	ḫ-ṯ-y	חזי			Ḫasi (*EA*)	Tell Ḥizzin?
Upi	4.	k-t-ś-n	גדשן			Guddašuna (*EA*)	
Upi	5.	ʿ-n-š-w					
Upi	6.	d-b-ḫ	טבח	Tibhath *Tebah	טבח, טבחת 2 Sam. 8. 8	Ṭubiḫi	
Upi	7.	b-m-y					
Upi	8.	k-m-t	כמד			Kumidi (*EA*)	Kamid el-Loz
Upi	9.	t-t-y-n					
Upi	10.	r-b-n	לבן	Lebo(-hamath)?	לבוא (חמת)	Labana (*EA*)	Lebweh?
Upi	11.	q-r-t n-ḏ-n	קר(י)ת נצן			(Kiriath) nḏn (=Litani? Pap. Anast. I)	
Upi	12.	m-r-m	מרם				
Upi	13.	t-m-ś-q	דמשק	Damascus	דמשק	Dimašqa (*EA*)	esh-Sham
Upi	14.	i̓-t-r				Ḫadaru (Tiglath-pileser III)	
Upi	15.	i̓-b-r	אבל			Abila Lysaniae	Suq Wadi Barada
Upi	16.	ḥ-m-t	חמת				
Upi	17.	i̓-q-d-⟨w⟩					
Upi	18.	š-m-n					
Upi	19.	b-i̓-r-t	בארת	Berothai Berothah	ברתי ברתה		
Upi	20.	m-ḏ-n					
	21.	ś-r-n	שרן	(the pasture lands of) Sharon	(מגרשי) שרון		
	22.	t-b-y	טב	(the land of) Tob	טוב	Ṭubu (*EA*)	eṭ-Ṭaiyibeh

Region	No.	Transcription	Conjectural Canaanite-Hebrew Form	Biblical Form: English	Biblical Form: Hebrew	Other Sources (Espec. *EA*)	Identification
Bashan	23.	b-ḏ-n	בצ(ר)ן			Buṣruna (*EA*)	Buṣra Eski Sham
	24.	ỉ-m-š-n				Motha	Imtan
	25.	m-ś-ḫ				Mušiḫuna (*EA*)	
	26.	q-n̄w̄	קנ	Kenath	קנת	Qanū	Qanawat
	27.	ʿ-r-n	עלן			Ḫalunni (*EA*)	
	28.	ʿ-ś-t-r-t ʿ-s-t-r-t	עשתרת	Ashtaroth	עשתרת	Aštarti (*EA*)	Tell ʿAshtarah
	29.	n̄w̄-r-p-ỉ				ʿΡαφών (I Macc. 5. 37)	er-Rafeh
	30.	m-q-t	מקד			Μακέδ (I Macc. 5. 26)	
N. Jordan Valley	31.	r-w-ś	ליש	Laish	ליש		Tell el-Qaḍi
	32.	ḥ-ḏ-r	חצר	Hazor	חצור	Ḫaṣura (*EA*)	Tell el-Qedaḥ
	33.	p-ḥ-r	פחל			Piḫili(m) (*EA*)	Khirbet Faḥil
	34.	k-n-n-r-t	כנרת	Chinnereth	כנרת		Tell el-ʿOreimeh
Jezreel and Acco Plains	35.	š-m-(ʿ-)n	שמען	Shimron	שמרון	Šamḫuna (*EA*)	Khirbet Sammuniyeh
	36.	ỉ-t-m-m	אדמם	Adami-nekeb	אדמי (הנקב)		Khirbet et-Tell
	37.	q-ś-n	קשן	Kishion	קשיון		Khirbet Qasyun?
	38.	š-n-m	שנם	Shunem	שונם	Šunama (*EA*)	Solem
	39.	m-š-ỉ-r	משאל	Mishal	משאל		Tell Kisan?
	40.	ỉ-k-s-p	אכשף	Achshaph	אכשף	Akšapa (*EA*)	Tell Harbaj
	41.	k-b-ʿ ś-m-n	גבע־שמן				Tell ʿAmr
	42.	t-ʿ-n-k	תענך	Taanach	תענך	Taḫ[nuk]a (*EA*)	Tell Tiʿinnik
	43.	y-b-r-ʿ-m	יבלעם	Ibleam	יבלעם		Tell Belʿameh
	44.	k-n-t ỉ-ś-n	גת־אשן			Gintiašna (*EA*)	
	45.	r-t-m-r-k	(א)לתמלך	Allammelech	אלמלך		
	46.	ʿ-y-n	עין				
	47.	ʿ-k-ꜣ (ʿ-ꜣ-k)	עכ	Acco	עכו	Akka (*EA*)	Tell el-Fukhkhar

(Jezreel and Acco Plains)	48.	r-š q-d-š	ראש־קדש				Mount Carmel headland
	49.	k-r-y-m-n					
	50.	b-r	ב(א)ר				
	51.	š-m-š i̇̓-t-m	שמש־אדם	Adamah	אדמה		Qarn Ḥaṭṭin
	52.	i̇̓-n-ḫ-r-t	אנחרת	Anaharath	אנחרת		Tell el-Mukharkhash?
	53.	ᶜ-p-r wr	עפר־הגדולה (Great ᶜApr)	Ophrah?	עפרה		ᶜAffuleh?
	54.	ᶜ-p-r šr	עפר־הקטנה (Little ᶜApr)				
S. Beqaᶜ	55.	ḫ-š-b	חשב			Ḫašabu (*EA*)	Tell Ḥashbeh?
	56.	t-ś-r-t	תשלת			Tušulti (*EA*)	
Coastal Plain	57.	n-g-b	נגב	Negeb	נגב = Gerar?		Tell Abu Hureireh
	58.	i̇̓-š-š-ḫ-n	אשחן			Σεανα	
	59.	r-n-m	רמן?				
	60.	y-r-ḏ	ירז			Yurza (*EA*)	Tell Jemmeh
	61.	m-⟨i̇̓⟩-ḫ-ś	מחז			Muḫḫazi (*EA*)	Tell Abu Sulṭan?
	62.	y-p-⟨w⟩	יפו	Joppa	יפו	Yapū (*EA*)	Yafa
	63.	k-n-t k-n-ṯ	גת	Gath	גת	Cinti (*EA*)	Tell eṣ-Ṣafi
	64.	r-⟨w⟩-t-n	לדן	Lod	לוד		Ludd
	65.	i̇̓-nw	אנו	Ono	אונו		Kafr ᶜAna
	66.	i̇̓-p-q-n	אפקן	Aphek	אפק	Apqu (Esarhaddon)	Tell Ras el-ᶜAin
	67.	ś-⟨w⟩-k	שוכ	Socoh	שכה		Khirbet Shuweiket er-
	68.	y-ḥ-m	יחם				Khirbet Yemma [Ras
	69.	ḫ-b-ḏ-n					
	70.	k-n-ṯ	גת			Gitipadalla (*EA*)	Jett (in the Sharon)
	71.	m-k-t-r	מגדל				Tell edh-Dhurur?
	72.	i̇̓-p-t-n					
	73.	š-b-t-n				Shabtuna	South of Kadesh on the Orontes according to Ramses II

Region	No.	Transcription	Conjectural Canaanite-Hebrew Form	Biblical Form: English	Biblical Form: Hebrew	Other Sources (Espec. *EA*)	Identification
N. Beqaʿ	74.	t-y-ỉ					
	75.	n-w-n					
	76.	ḥ-d-⟨ỉ⟩-t					
	77.	h-r	הר				
	78.	y-š-p-ỉ-r	ישב־אל				
	79.	r-g-ḏ	רע׳ץ			Ruḫiṣṣi (*EA*)	
Upper Galilee	80.	k-r-r	גלל ?	Galilee	גליל=Kedesh ?		Tell Qades
	81.	h-r-ỉ-r	הראל				
	82.	r-b-ỉ	לבא	Lebo(-hamath)	לבוא	Labana (*EA*)	Lebweh
	83.	n-m-⟨ỉ⟩-n					
	84.	n-ᶜ-m-n	נעמן				
	85.	m-r-m-ỉ-m	מרמים	(Me-)Merom ("waters of Merom")	(מי)מרום	Marum (Tiglath-pileser III)	Tell el-Khirbeh ?
	86.	ᶜ-n-y	עין	En(-hazor ?)	עין (חצור)		ᶜAinitha ?
	87.	r-ḥ-b	רחב	Rehob (Josh. 19. 28)	רחב		Tell el-Balaṭ ?
	88.	ỉ-q-r	יקר(ת)			Yoqereth (יוקרת; Talmud)	Iqrit
	89.	h-y-k-r-y-m	היכלים	Beth-shemesh ?	בית שמש		Kh. Tell er-Ruweisi ?
	90.	ỉ-b-r	אבל				
	91.	ỉ-t-r-ᶜ	אדרע	Edrei (Josh. 19. 37)	אדרעי		
	92.	ỉ-b-r	אבל	Abel(-beth-maachah)	אבל		Abil el-Qamḥ
	93.	k-n-ṭ-ỉ-t	גת . . .				Jett (in Galilee)
	94.	m-q-r-p-t	מגרפ(ת) ?				

(Upper Galilee)	95.	ʿ-y-n	עין	Ijon	עיון		Tell ed-Dibbin
	96.	k-r-m-n					
	97.	b-t-ȝ-[?]					
	98.	t-p-n	תפן			Taphnith (תפנית; Talmud)	Tibnin
	99.	ỉ-b-r	אבל			En-bul (עין בול; Talmud)	ʿAin Ibl
	100.	y-r-t	? יתר			Yattir (יתיר: Talmud)?	Yaʿtir
	101.	ḥ-r-k-r					
	102.	y-ʿ-q-b-ỉ-r	יעקבאל				
Land of Gezer	103.	q-p-t	גבת	Gibbethon	גבתון		Tell Melat
	104.	q-ḏ-r	גזר	Gezer	גזר	Gazri (*EA*)	Tell Ạbu Shusheh
	105.	r-b-t	רבת	Rabbah	הרבה	Rubute (*EA*)	
	106.	m-q-r-t					
Land of Beth-shan	107.	ʿ-m-q	עמק	The valley	עמק = Rehob?		
	108.	ś-r-t					
	109.	b-ỉ-r-t	בארת				
	110.	b-t š-ỉ-r	בית־שאן	Beth-shean	בית־שאן	Bit-šani (*EA*)	Tell el-Ḥuṣn
Carmel Range and Foothills	111.	b-t b-n-t b-t ỉ-n-t					
	112.	ḥ-r-q-t	חלקת	Helkath	חלקת		Tell el-Qassis
	113.	ʿ-n q-n-ʿ-m	ע(י)ן (י)קנעם	Jokneam	יקנעם		Tell Qeimun
	114.	q-b-ʿ	גבע				Khirbet esh-Shuqqaq?
	115.	ḏ-r-r					Khirbet el-Khuḍeirah
	116.	ḏ-f-t	צפת				Khirbet Sitt Leila
	117.	b-r-q-n				Burquna (*EA*)	
	118.	h-⟨w⟩-m					
	119.	ỉ-k-t-m-ś					

Liṭani and the Orontes is the natural border between the northern and southern halves of the Beqaʿ, and Canaanite Upper Galilee was not associated with the Jezreel Plain because they were separated by a strip of forested and unoccupied territory. The campaign did not impinge upon the remaining regions of the Ṣumur district; thus the Phoenician coast and the land of Amurru are absent from the list. At the end of the roster there appear two additional regions belonging to the Gaza district, of which only the margins were touched: (*a*) the vicinity of Gezer (Nos. 103–6), that is, the fringes of the Judean hill country and the Shephelah, (*b*) the Beth-shean Valley (Nos. 107–10), and the Carmel slopes (Nos. 111-17), i.e. the outskirts of Mount Ephraim. To this last group Burquna (No. 117) must certainly belong. It was one of the towns demolished in the El Amarna period by Labʿayu, King of Shechem (*EA*, 250. 43). The last two names have not been identified, and we have also passed over Ḫashabu and Tushulti (Nos. 55 and 56) which belonged to the region of Ḫasi in the southern Lebanese Beqaʿ and were apparently substituted for Kadesh and Megiddo at the head of the list.

The roster is divided, therefore, into ten regions of which four belong to each of the districts of Kumidi and Gaza, with two from the Ṣumur district. We may assume that this latter district was also divided into four subsidiary units which provides the following organizational arrangement:

District	*Region*	*Nos. in Thut-mose III's List*
Kumidi	Southern Lebanese Beqaᶜ	3–11 (12?), 55–6
	Damascus and Vicinity	12 (13?)–20
	Bashan	21–30
	Northern Jordan Valley	31–4
Gaza	Plains of Jezreel and Acco	35–54, 2
	Coastal Plain and the Sharon	57–71
	Judean Hills and Shephelah	103–6
	Ephraimite Hill Country	107–17
Ṣumur	Northern Lebanese Beqaᶜ	72–9 (84?), 1
	Upper Galilee	80 (85?)–102
	Phoenician Coast	—
	Amurru	—

This administrative division not only seems probable from the geographical and historical standpoint, while conforming to the appearance of three commissioners' centres in the El Amarna letters, but it also accords well with the inter-city relationships and internal rivalries that find expression in that official archive. The kings of the various cities generally do not transgress the borders of their respective districts in their correspondence. Those in the Jezreel Valley and the Plain of

Acco interact with one another and refer to more southerly towns, but they do not mention the Phoenician coast or towns in the northern Jordan Valley. The kings of Peḥel and Hazor, on the other hand, are associated with Bashan and the north and make no reference to the nearby towns of the Jezreel Plain. A letter by Biryawaza (*EA*, 197) is most instructive in this regard: he refers to towns from Yeno' am in the northern Jordan Valley to Bashan and even as far as Damascus and Taḫshi, adding that he protects Kumidi, the city of the king. The Phoenician coast and Amurru are closely inter-related, and the commissioner of Ṣumur was responsible for them (*EA*, 155,. 66, *et passim*). In this light one may perhaps interpret the accusation by the King of Tyre against the King of Hazor that he has left his city and conquered royal lands with the help of the 'Apiru (*EA*, 148. 41 ff.). We may understand this as a serious charge, viz. that the King of Hazor had stepped out of the bounds of his district, thus removing himself from the sole jurisdiction of his commissioner.

The roster of Thut-mose III is also the first and most complete topographical list from which information can be derived concerning the important Canaanite centres, most of which were near the *Via Maris*. Only a very few additional names can be found in the later topographical texts from Amen-hotep II until Ramses III. Shishak's list, which does furnish some additions, already reflects the Israelite situation, and its composition is markedly different.[77] Texts other than that of Thut-mose supply such names as Raphia, Kiriath-anab (evidently a town in Bashan) and Beth-anath,[78] as well as Aphek and Beth-dagon which are too commonplace to be specifically identified. On the Phoenician coast we can add Usu, Tyre and Byblos, and in central Syria Qaṭna and Deper (*d-p-r*). Yeno' am is also missing from Thut-mose's lists, although it appears in the annals as one of the towns devoted to the temple of Amon.[79] The internal regions of the country are all missing from his topographical texts, e.g. the Shephelah, the Negeb, the hill country of Judah and Ephraim, Lower Galilee, the southern Jordan Valley, Gilead and southern Transjordan. Egyptian expeditions did not pass through these regions which seem to have had little importance for them.

A papyrus listing rations of grain and beer issued to *maryannū* from various cities in Canaan also belongs approximately to the reign of Thut-mose III.[80] This list includes the following eleven towns: Megiddo, Chinnereth, Achshaph, Shim' on, Taanach, Mishal, *t-n-n* (?), Sharon, Ashkelon, Hazor and *h-t-t-m* (?). Seven of these towns were in the northern valleys (nos. 31-53 in Thut-mose's list), viz. the northern Jordan Valley (Hazor, Chinnereth), the Valley of Jezreel (Megiddo, Taanach, Shim' on) and the Plain of Acco (Achshaph, Mishal). Besides Ashkelon, Sharon may also belong to the coastal plain; perhaps it represents one of the cities of Sharon such as Aphek or Joppa. So this list also gives a fair representation of the major Canaanite centres in the plains and valleys which were located along the *Via Maris* and served as centres of Egyptian authority in Canaan.

VII. THE CAMPAIGNS OF AMEN-HOTEP II

From the reign of Pharaoh Amen-hotep II (*c.* 1436-1410 B.C.), son of Thut-mose III, we have information concerning three military campaigns in the land of Canaan and in northern Syria (for the last two campaigns, cf. map 10).[81] The first of these expeditions was evidently begun while Amen-hotep was still coregent or crown prince. It was aimed at quelling a rebellion by seven rulers in the land of Takhsi; they were duly captured and executed. Thut-mose III apparently died while the crown prince was on his way back to Egypt.[82] In later editions of Amen-hotep's annals, the campaigns were renumbered and the real second campaign was now called the first and the real third was called the second. Thus, the so-called first campaign (actually the second) followed the *Via Maris* to the Lebanese Beqa', going from there as far as the land of Ni and perhaps to Ugarit. The first place mentioned is Shemesh-adam, evidently the Adamah of Naphtali, today Qarn Ḥaṭṭin.[83] After this Amen-hotep crossed the Orontes; he returned via the same route through the Beqa', and the inscription refers to Kadesh, the forest near Lebo(-hamath) where the King went hunting, Ḥashabu (in the land of 'Amqi) and finally the Sharon, where he captured an emissary from Naharin. A topographical list from the reign of Amen-hotep II[84] evidently pertains to this campaign; it preserves the following names: Retenu (apparently both Upper and Lower), Kadesh, Aleppo, Ni, *ś-ḏ-r* (Sinzar near Hamath ?), Tunip, Qaṭna and Hazor. The campaign had extended, therefore, to the very limit of Egypt's sphere of authority in Syria. The silence concerning events in the expedition north of Ni suggests that the objectives there were not achieved, and rebellion seems to have broken out even in southern Canaan. The capture of an emissary from Naharin in the Sharon Plain proves that the King of Mitanni was continuing his attempts to incite trouble in the Egyptian province.

His efforts bore fruit, as we learn from the so-called second(third) campaign of Amen-hotep II, which was directed only against the Sharon and Jezreel Plains. The Egyptian army advanced along the *Via Maris* in the eastern Sharon. Aphek, Socoh and Yaḥam are mentioned here. At this point the annals describe two raids made by Amen-hotep into the western Sharon; these produced considerable booty in the form of prisoners and cattle. Such a picture typifies that region, which still had a scattered and semi-nomadic population because of the many forests and swamps. The settlements referred to here at Mepesen (*m-p-ś-n*) and Khettjen (*ẖ-t-ṯ-n*) west of Socoh, with two others farther north, viz. Adorain (*i-t-r-n*) and Migdal-yene(t) (*m-k-t-r-ynt*). The name of this last

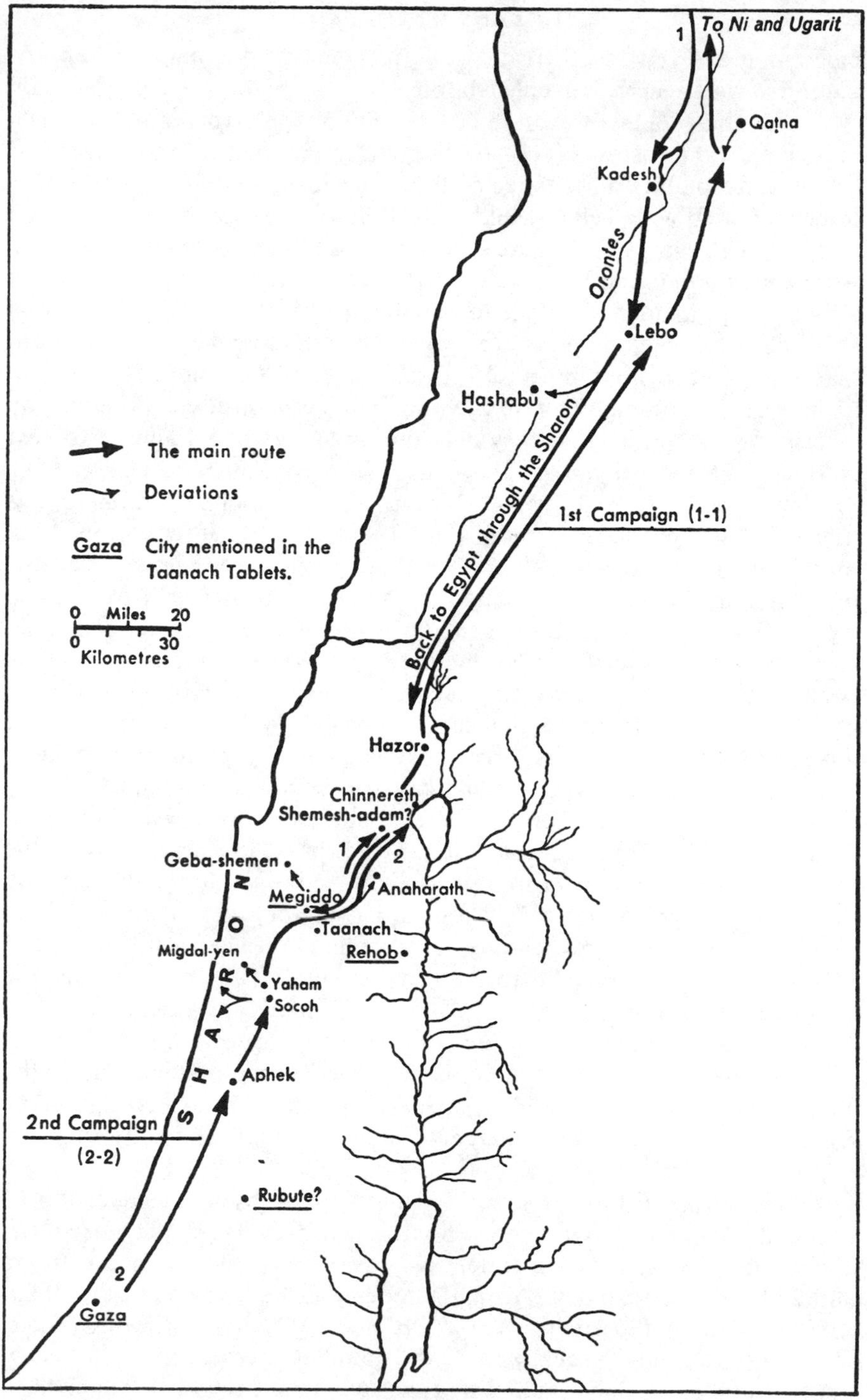

Map 10. The Campaigns of Amen-hotep II.

place is preserved in el-Mejdel and the ancient site may perhaps be identified with nearby Tell edh-Dhurur.[85]

The farthest objective on this expedition was Anaharath, a town known from the roster of Thut-mose III (No. 52, beside Adamah [*š-m-š i-t-m*]) and from the inheritance of Issachar (Josh. 19. 19). It is probably to be identified with Tell el-Mukharkhash five miles south-east of Mount Tabor.[86] This site is beside the highway, just like the other towns which were conquered in the Sharon, and as usual in a campaign description of Amen-hotep, incidental details are included which praise the heroism of Pharaoh, while major events are omitted, especially when the Egyptians failed to achieve their purpose. At Khirbet el- 'Oreimeh, the ancient Chinnereth, the fragment of an Egyptian stele was discovered bearing an inscription concerning a victory over the foreigners of Mitanni.[87] Its text is typical of the reigns of Thut-mose III and Amen-hotep II when Mitanni was Egypt's principal rival in Asia. Although Chinnereth is mentioned in Thut-mose's roster (No. 34), there is no information about any particular clash with Mitanni in that specific area. Therefore, it is possible that this stele was related to the last campaign of Amen-hotep when Mitanni had reached the peak of its greatness and expansion. That expedition was made in the month of November, that is, at the beginning of the rainy season. Such an unusual time for executing a military operation indicates that this was mainly a defensive manoeuvre aimed at repelling a serious threat posed against Egyptian supremacy in Canaan. Apparently Amen-hotep only succeeded in maintaining sway over the southern part of Canaan, about as far as the vicinity of Chinnereth. For this reason the annals pass in silence over the encounter with Mitannian forces in a region so far south, which certainly must not have culminated in a one-sided victory. From here Amen-hotep returned to the vicinity of Megiddo[88] where the King of Geba-somen was brought to him (apparently Tell el- 'Amr at the south-eastern end of the Jezreel Valley).[89] Evidently, there had been an Egyptian garrison at Megiddo ever since the victory of Thut-mose III. Information to this effect is also found in the Taanach tablets and in the El Amarna letters. Therefore, Amen-hotep was able to make his way from the Sharon to the Jezreel Valley without encountering any opposition.[90]

Amen-hotep's list of prisoners is illuminating as a cross-section of social classes in the population. The first group included 550 *maryannū,* 240 of their wives, 640 Canaanites, 232 royal sons,[91] 323 royal daughters and 270 royal concubines. A final summary lists: 127 rulers of Retenu, 179 brothers of the rulers, 3,600 *'apirū,* 15,200 living Shasu, 36,300 Ḫuru, 15,070 living Neges, and 30,652 families thereof. Since no entry appears twice, we may assume that the two lists should be combined to form one summary.

The groups having the smallest numbers represent the highest strata: the rulers; their brothers, i.e. members of the ruling class; the *maryannū,* the noble chariot warriors; and the Canaanites, wealthy citizens and merchants (cf. *supra,* p. 68). In the other passages the population as a whole was called Horite (Ḫuru); the Shasu were the Bedouin; the *'apirū* were gipsy-like wanderers, lacking permanent status, a type of sojourners. Neges apparently refers to people from Nuḫašši in northern Syria. Among the residents of Palestine the Horites account for 66 per cent, the Shasu 27.5 per cent and the *'apirū* 6.5 per cent. Though this is, of course, no population census list but a list of prisoners, these percentages may represent more or less the composition of the country's population in the fifteenth century. The *'apirū* and the Shasu became more and more numerous in the two centuries that followed.

The Taanach Tablets—a collection of unique epigraphic documents from the archives of the ruler at Taanach can be dated either to the latter part of Thut-mose III's reign or to that of Amen-hotep II. These few tablets were written in Akkadian cuneiform similar to that of the El Amarna texts and were brought to light by the earliest excavations at Taanach. They are addressed to its ruler. The sender of two of these epistles was an Egyptian named Amen-hotep, who commanded the ruler of Taanach to send men and various materials to Gaza and to Megiddo. We do not know if this Amen-hotep was one of the commissioners known to us from Egyptian sources or perhaps the Pharaoh Amen-hotep II, either before he took the throne or afterwards when he was on a campaign.[92] The absence of royal titles in the epistles and the apparent uncertainty expressed in them about the obedience of the ruler at Taanach suggest that the Amen-hotep who wrote two of these letters was indeed the son of Thut-mose III on his way to Takhsi, still acting as crown prince.[93] In any case, the content and style of the language dates him to this period. Gaza and Megiddo were Egyptian bases, and Taanach was one of the important towns in the Jezreel Valley, dominating practically the whole region. The other letters furnish a few more geographical references to towns having some connection with the ruler of Taanach: Rehob, apparently the one in the Beth-shean Valley (Tell eṣ-Ṣarem); possibly Gurra near Taanach (cf. "the ascent of Gur", 2 Kings 9, 27) though the reading is most uncertain and not supported by recent collation; another town mentioned is Rubute, evidently the biblical Rabbah in the northern Shephelah between Gezer and Jerusalem (cf. *infra,* pp. 174, 326).[94]

VIII. THE EL-AMARNA PERIOD

Towards the end of Amen-hotep II's reign Mitanni was weakening, apparently as a result of Hittite pressure, which led her to make overtures of peace to Egypt.[95] Thut-mose IV (*c.* 1410—1402) took advantage of this opportunity to retrieve for Egypt those Canaanite areas which had been lost during his father's reign. There is practically no information concerning his campaign against Mitanni (Naharin) described in a roster of sacrifices from Karnak.[96] Another inscription from the reign of Thut-mose IV alludes to captured residents (Ḫuru) from Gezer,[97] and from the El Amarna texts we know that this Pharaoh was at Sidon (*EA,* 85, 71).[98] However, it was during the course of his rule that a peace treaty was signed between Egypt and Mitanni,[99] and the strong ties between these two powers continued until the conquest of Mitanni by Suppiluliumas in the reign of Aḫ-en-aton (Amen-hotep IV, the famous heretic king).

Most illuminating information concerning the land of Canaan has been furnished by the royal Egyptian archive discovered at El Amarna, the famous Aḫet-aton, capital of Amen-hotep IV.[100] The archive included more than 350 letters dating to the reigns of Amen-hotep III (*c.* 1402–1364) and Amen-hotep IV (*c.* 1364–1347) written in cuneiform script on clay tablets. Their language was Akkadian, the *lingua franca* of that age, which was used for diplomatic correspondence. About half of these epistles come from the Kings of Canaan and the rest from other kingdoms of the Middle East, e.g. Hatti, Mitanni, Babylon, Alashia (Cyprus), while a few are letters from Pharaoh to those kings.

These texts reflect a certain weakening of Egyptian power, since the authorities were preoccupied with internal Egyptian affairs and give the impression that their interest in the land of Canaan had slackened. With the establishment of good relations between Egypt and Mitanni, there seems to have been no longer any need for sending military expeditions to Canaan (*EA,* 116. 61). As a result, the Egyptian authority became weakened in some regions.. Nevertheless, the situation should not be exaggerated to the point of seeing here an absolute collapse of the Egyptian government in Canaan. All of the epistles testify that the Egyptian authority remained unchanged; the Egyptians simply refused to entangle themselves in the political intrigues between the many Canaanite Kings so long as Egyptian interests were not in jeopardy. However, the moment those interests were endangered the Egyptians would step in and put down any rebellion. The hand of Egyptian authority was so strong that a token force of only ten Egyptian soldiers was able to maintain peace in a city and prevent any attack on its own position there (*EA,* 113. 16; 148. 14). Therefore, the El Amarna letters provide us with a representative picture of Egyptian power in Canaan, which had reduced the local kings to vassalage; the Eighteenth Dynasty Pharaohs were enjoying this heritage from their Hyksos predecessors. The archives thus shed some very welcome light on the main Canaanite cities and the regions of Egyptian influence in that period.

Only in the reign of Aḫ-en-aton was Egyptian authority seriously shaken in middle Syria along the border of the Hittite kingdom. In that region there now existed a kingdom called Amurru whose King, 'Abdu-Ashirta, and his son 'Aziru tried to expand their own territory by taking advantage of the rivalry between Egypt and the Hittites in that area. The Amarna letters inform us only about the areas of their encroachment, to the Lebanese Beqa' from the land of 'Amqi as far as Qaṭna, on the one hand, and to the Phoenician coast from Byblos to Arvad on the other.[101] Many of the letters deal with the intrigues between the Kings of Amurru and Byblos, Sidon and Tyre, along with other coastal towns. It is clear from them that Amurru had control over the town of Ṣumur. Judging from this, it would seem that their main centre must have been in the Lebanese mountains. From the Amarna letters and later documents as well we learn that the Kings of Amurru had been subservient to Egyptian authority at first, paying them lip service and even winning a certain encouragement from Pharaoh, who tried to gain their loyalty. However, as time went on, they went over to the side of the Hittites whose strength had greatly increased in that area and who may have raised their price for encouraging Amurru to desert the Egyptians.

The kingdom of Amurru was a unique phenomenon in the El Amarna period from the standpoint of its territorial limits. In contrast to the usual Canaanite city-states, Amurru was a more extensive kingdom whose capital city is still unknown. Perhaps this explains why its kings preserved the name Amurru, which had formerly been a broad geographical designation for all of Palestine and Syria and evidently served later as the name of the Hyksos kingdom in southern Syria and Palestine.

The picture obtained from the El Amarna tablets is not complete, because they comprised only a part of a larger archive, so the material preserved is strictly fortuitous. Nevertheless, the tablets that have been preserved provide a faithful cross-section of the land of Canaan in that period. The picture is fairly detailed with regard to the important Canaanite centres and their respective areas of influence (cf. map. 11).

The cities mentioned in the Amarna letters fall into the following regional groupings[102]:

The Syro-phoenician coast—*Ugarit, Arvad,* 'Arqat, Ardat, ULLASA, ṢUMUR, Batruna, *Byblos, Beirut,* YARIMUT, *Sidon, Tyre,* Usu, plus *Acco* and *Achshaph* on the Plain of Acco.

The Lebanese Beqa'—*Qatna, Kadesh, Lebo, Ṭubiḫi,* KUMIDI and various towns in the land of 'Amqi, e.g. Ḫasi, Ḫashabu, Tushulti, *et al.*

The Damascus region—the land of Upi, *Damascus* and the land of Taḫshi.

Bashan—*Ashtaroth, Buṣruna, Kenath, Ziri-bashan.*
The Jordan Valley—*Ḥazor,* Yenoʿam, BETH-SHEAN, *Peḥel,* and perhaps Zaphon.
The Jezreel Valley—*Megiddo, Taanach, Shimʿon,* Shunem, Gina[th] Japhia, plus Hannathon[103] in the Sahl el-Baṭṭof.
The coastal plain—Gath-padalla, Gath-rimmon, JOPPA, *Ashkelon,* GAZA, *Yurza.*
The Shephelah—*Gezer,* Rubute, Zorah, Aijalon, *Gath-carmel, Lachish,* Keilah, Mareshah.
The hill country—*Shechem, Jerusalem,* and apparently also Manahath and Beth-horon.

In contrast to the Egyptian topographical lists the texts from El Amarna include towns from the interior regions: the Shephelah, the hill country and the central Jordan Valley. Gilead, southern Transjordan and the Canaanite cities in the Negeb are missing, but this may be accidental. A town by the name of Ṣuḫru appears in two of the Amarna letters, once in association with Lachish (*EA,* 334, 335), and may be the biblical Zoar at the southern end of the Dead Sea. One may also conjecture that the ruler of Sharuna (*EA,* 241) actually dwelt at Aphek in the southern Sharon (cf. Josh. 12. 18; *infra,* pp. 187 n. 67 f.).

As headquarters cities of the Egyptian commissioners (*rābiṣū*) Gaza, Ṣumur and Kumidi are mentioned. Concerning the division of Canaan into three principal districts, each of which was evidently made up of four sub-districts, the evidence has already been discussed in connection with the topographical list of Thut-mose III (cf. *supra,* pp. 158, 164 f.).

A marked difference between the nature of the settlements in the plains and those in the hill country, which also finds expression in different political organizations, stands out in these inscriptions.[104] On the plain the royal Canaanite cities were not far from one another, and they were more numerous than in the hill regions. As a rule, each city in the lowland exercised authority over a more limited area. One might assume, on the basis of *EA* 365.[105] that Megiddo had control of Shunem and the northern part of the valley as far as the slopes of Lower Galilee (Japhia), but these were unusual circumstances brought about by the destruction of Shunem (*EA,* 250).[106] The King of Megiddo argued that not he alone but other kings as well were commanded to cultivate the lands in those areas. In another text we read that the Kings of Shimʿon and Acco had waylaid a Babylonian caravan at Hannathon in the Sahl el-Baṭṭof (*EA,* 8), but this highway robbery is no proof that they had permanent jurisdiction over that territory. The interests of each town were usually confined to its own limited sphere. The notice that the Kings of Acco and Achshaph had sent fifty chariots to assist the King of Jerusalem and Shuwardata (probably King of Gath, cf. *infra*) is a notable exception which in itself is an indication of the importance

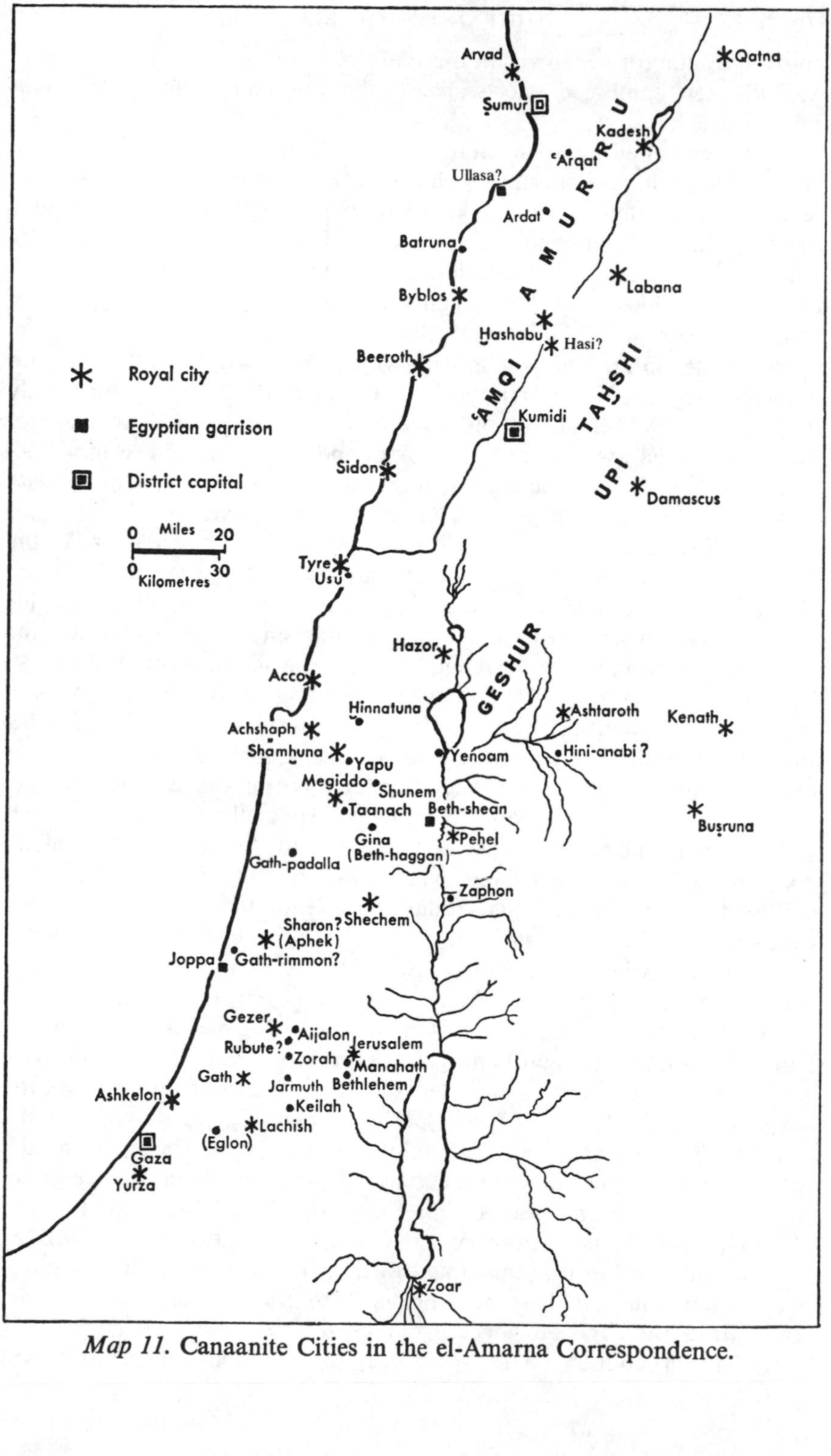

Map 11. Canaanite Cities in the el-Amarna Correspondence.

enjoyed by the former towns in the Plain of Acco, and apparently has to do with their combined efforts against the common enemy , Labʿayu, ruler of Shechem.

Areas controlled by towns in the Shephelah were evidently somewhat larger. Only three important political centres are mentioned in that region: Gezer, Lachish and the kingdom of Shuwardata, whose capital is not specifically mentioned. Albright is of the opinion that Shuwardata reigned at Hebron,[107] but one letter from the King of Jerusalem (*EA*, 290) makes it likely that his capital was Gath. In that text the King of Jerusalem accused Milkilu and Shuwardata of hiring soldiers from Gezer, Gath (Ginti) and Keilah with which they conquered the territory belonging to Rubute and another town called Bīt-NINIB (apparently Beth-horon).[108] Milkilu was the King of Gezer, and Keilah was one of the towns taken away from Shuwardata and later returned to him (*EA*, 279, 280). Would it not be logical, therefore, to assume that Shuwardata was none other than the King of Gath, which appears in this text after Gezer? In support of this it is worth remembering that at the end of the letter Milkilu, Shuwardata and Gath are evidently referred to again, although the text is broken. Nothing prevents the assumption that this was the Gath which, at a later time, became one of the five Philistine capitals. Furthermore, this strengthens its identification with Tell eṣ-Ṣafi (cf. *infra*, p. 271). It was one of the largest and most important tells in the Shephelah during the Late Bronze and Israelite periods, being situated about half-way between Gezer and Lachish. These were the most prominent royal cities in the Shephelah during the El Amarna Age; they were constantly seeking to expand, especially towards the east, which brought about a conflict of interest with the King of Jerusalem. As previously mentioned, Shuwardata, who already dominated Keilah, had seized Rubute (Rabbah, today Kh. Ḥamideh near Latrun) and Beth-horon while acting in league with the King of Gezer. This latter was ruler of Aijalon and Zorah (*EA*, 273) plus Manahath in the hill country (*EA*, 292). A tablet from the El Amarna period found at Tell el-Ḥesi (Eglon) testifies that the King of Lachish gave assistance to the King of Jarmuth. Albright is probably correct in assuming that Jarmuth had only just then become an independent royal city as the result of the decisiveness so typical of the period when Egypt dominated the country.[109] Another Akkadian tablet discovered at Gezer from the second half of the fifteenth century,[110] perhaps from the reign of Thut-mose IV,[111] was sent by an Egyptian official from the town of Gittim [. . .]. It is customary to identify this latter town with the biblical Gittaim, but it seems doubtful that this town had already come into existence in L.B. It is more probable that this letter was sent from Gath-Gimti, the city-state bordering on Gezer.[112]

In the hill country there were only a few political centres, and each of these ruled over a fairly extensive area. In all the hill country of Judah and Ephraim we hear only of Jerusalem and Shechem with possible allusions to Beth-horon and Manahath, towns within the realm of Jerusalem's king. The hill country was not nearly so densely populated; considerable areas were still forested and unoccupied. Nevertheless, a number of other towns besides these were also in existence, e.g. Dothan, Tirzah, Tappuah, Bethel, Hebron, Debir as well as the Gibeonite cities (Gibeon, Beeroth, Chephirah and Baalath). Since six letters have been preserved from the King of Jerusalem, one may not assume that the absence of these other towns from the Amarna archive is accidental. Apparently the kings of Jerusalem and Shechem dominated, to all practical purposes, the entire central hill country at that time.

The territory controlled by Lab' ayu, King of Shechem, was especially large in contrast to the small Canaanite principalities round about. Only one letter refers to Shechem itself, and we get the impression that this is not simply a royal Canaanite city but rather an extensive kingdom with Shechem as its capital. Lab' ayu was a serious contender with the kings of Jerusalem and Gezer. *EA*, 250 indicates that for some time he even dominated the entire Sharon, having conquered Gath-padalla (Jett in the central Sharon)[113] and Gath-rimmon (apparently the biblical town of this name, perhaps to be identified with Tell Jerisheh on the Yarkon).[114] Even in the north Lab' ayu was not content to possess only the hill country; he tried to penetrate into the Jezreel Valley, laying siege to Megiddo (*EA*, 244) and destroying Shunem and some other towns (*EA*, 250). This intrusion into the area of the *Via Maris* interfered with the interests of pharaoh, who lost patience with him. Lab' ayu was commanded to go to Egypt and render an accounting of his deeds, but he was murdered at Gina (biblical Beth-haggan, modern Jenin) as he tried to fleet (*EA*, 250) after escaping from his captors, the kings of Megiddo and Acco (*EA*, 245).

In the northern hill regions we find two important centres, viz. Ashtaroth and Hazor. Ashtaroth, the capital of Bashan at the time of the Israelite conquest, bordered on the kingdom of Hazor with whom it contended for the possession of three towns (*EA*, 364). The King of Ashtaroth also had hiṣ hand in affairs concerning Peḥel and the land of Gari (*Ga-*<*šu*>*-ri* for the biblical Geshur?) on the western slopes of Bashan (*EA*, 256).[115] Although Hazor was situated in the northern Jordan Valley beside an important branch of the *Via Maris*, its sphere of authority extended into the hill regions on both sides eastward towards Bashan and westward to Upper Galilee, as indicated by the clash between the kings of Hazor and Tyre (*EA*, 148).

The principalities in the hill country were therefore much larger than those on the plains, even encompassing a number of towns and a more varied population. These were the Amorite kings referred to in the Bible (Num. 13. 29; Deut. 3. 9; Josh. 5. 1; 11. 3). in juxtaposition to the Canaanite kings in the valleys.[116]

The presence of the *'apirū*[117] alongside the local populace is keenly felt in the Amarna correspondence. They are considered sworn enemies of Egypt, and various kings hurled accusations at one another about being in league with the *'apirū*, furnishing them weapons and supplies, and helping them to take over certain regions. Although the term *'apirū* is an ancient one referring principally to a special class of foreigners without property rights,[118] in this period it is associated with the wave of Semites just beginning to penetrate the lands of the Fertile Crescent, a movement which culminated in the arrival of the Hebrews and Arameans. The appearance of the *'apirū* in the El Amarna period apparently marks the beginning of the Hebrews in Palestine, and their numbers seem to have increased considerably over the previous century, e.g. in the reign of Amen-hotep II (cf. *supra*, p.168 f.). Doubtless it is not accidental that their presence is alluded to mainly with reference to the hill country. The King of Shechem and the rulers of the Shephelah are accused of aiding the *'apirū*, and Lab 'ayu even admits as much in one of his letters (*EA*, 254). The King of Hazor is also said to have given them assistance (*EA*, 148). The groups of *'apirū* which penetrated into the hill regions during that period must have been absorbed into the Israelite tribes when they arrived about a century later.

IX. THE CAMPAIGN OF SETI I

No information is available concerning Canaan during the second half of the fourteenth century B.C.; only with the rise of the Nineteenth Dynasty do stelae begin to reappear boasting of Egyptian conquests in Palestine.[119] The pharaohs of the Nineteenth Dynasty saw as their main objective the revival of the Egyptian empire, which had included Palestine and Syria. To this end they transferred their capital to the northern delta, to the same region and perhaps even the same place where Zoan, the Hyksos capital, had been located. From the days of Ramses II the new site was called Pa-Ramses, the biblical Ramses. The pharaos of the Nineteenth Dynasty also associated themselves with the Hyksos' religious tradition by worshipping their high god Seth, after whom two pharaohs were named Seti, "Seth's man". A unique document from this period is the "Stele of the Year 400" set up in Zoan-Ramses by Ramses II to commemorate the 400th year of reign by the god Seth, which anniversary had been celebrated at that place in *c.* 1320 by his father Seti before the dynasty was founded.[120] Without mentioning the Hyksos they were evidently commemorating the establishment of Hyksos rule in *c.* 1720, and the pharaohs of the Nineteenth Dynasty considered themselves the heirs and guardians of the Hyksos tradition.

The Nineteenth Dynasty kings strove energetically to reassert full Egyptian authority over the land of Canaan and to repel the Hittites who were challenging their position in Syria. A military campaign carried out by *Seti I* (*c*. 1303–1290) in the first year of his reign is known to us in some detail.[121] Annals concerning the expedition have not been preserved, but there are three types of sources that complement one another: victory stelae erected at the scene of various conquests; a series of reliefs depicting the victories of Seti in the temple of Amon at Karnak; topographical lists (cf. map 12).

1. The most important source concerning Seti's initial campaign is one of his stelae discovered in the excavations at Beth-shean bearing an inscription dated to the first year of his reign.[122] After the customary introduction events are narrated as follows: It is announced to Pharaoh that the King of Hammath has gathered a large force around himself and conquered Beth-shean. The King of Peḥel is in league with him, and together they have laid siege to Rehob. Pharaoh responded immediately by sending the first army of Amon to Hammath, the first army of Re to Beth-shean and the first army of Seth to Yeno'am. The insurrection was smashed in one day. This stele obviously represents the action in one phase of the campaign in accordance with developments in the Beth-shean region. Therefore, all of the places mentioned in the text must be located in the vicinity of Beth-shean: Hammath at Tell el-Ḥammeh, 9 miles south of Beth-shean, Rehob at Tell eṣ-Ṣarem, 3½ miles south of Beth-shean; Yeno'am at the tell of el-'Abeidiyeh, 13 miles north of Beth-shean. Yeno'am is the only town not mentioned at first as being among the rebellious cities of the region; so the reference to it probably indicates the direction in which the campaign continued. It is the first important town north of Beth-shean and commanded the highway junction south of the Sea of Galilee where the Jordan Valley road met the Darb el-Ḥawarnah as it crossed the rift on its way from Bashan through Lower Galilee to the Plain of Acco.

2. The Karnak reliefs[123] are separated by a gate into two groups. The eastern group concerns the first campaign and describes the following: (*a*) A battle with the Shasu, whose "tribal chiefs are gathered in one place, waiting on the mountain ranges of Ḫuru. They have taken to clamouring and quarrelling, one of them killing his fellow. They have no regard for the laws of the palace (i.e. of Egypt)." This scene is dated to Seti's first year. (*b*) Some Asiatics cutting down trees for the pharaoh, at "the town of Qeder in the land of Henem", whose rulers are "the great princes of Lebanon". (*c*) The conquest of Yeno'am portrayed as a town surrounded by a river and a heavy thicket. (*d*) Conquest of a town called "the town of the Canaan", with the caption "year 1 . . . . The desolation which the mighty arm of pharaoh . . . made among the foe belonging to the Shasu from the fortress of Sile to the Canaan." (*e*) A

picture of the forts and wells along the main road from Sile to Raphia (or Gaza); the southern sector of the *Via Maris* called "the way of the land of the Philistines" in the Bible (cf. *supra,* p. 46). (*f*) Pharaoh's return "from Upper Retenu, having extended the frontiers of Egypt. The plunder which his majesty carried off from these Shasu, whom his majesty himself captured in the year 1 . . . ."

3. In the topographical lists of Seti I a group of seventeen towns is repeated several times; the places included were all encountered on the first campaign and from them we can derive the following line of march[124]:

The Name in Seti's Lists	*The Canaanite-Hebrew Form*	*Suggested Identification*
1. p-ḫ-r	Peḥel (פחל)	Kh. Faḥil
2. ḥ-m-t	Hammath (חמת)	Tell el-Ḥammeh
3. b-t š-r	Beth-shean ([בית שאן [שאל)	Tell el-Ḥuṣn
4. y-n-⟨w⟩-ᶜ-m	Yenoᶜam (ינועם)	el-ᶜAbeidiyeh
5. [q]-m-h-m		
6. ᶜ-k-⟨ꜣ⟩	Acco (עכו)	Tell el-Fukhkhar
7. q-m-d	Gammad(im) ([גמד[ים)	Between Byblos and Arvad
8. ỉ-n̄r̄-ṯ	Ullasa (אלסה)	Between Byblos and Arvad
9. d̲-r	Tyre (צור)	eṣ-Ṣur
10. ỉ-ṯ-⟨w⟩	Usu (Hosah? חסה)	Tell Rashidiyeh
11. b-t ᶜ-n-t	Beth-anath (בית ענת)	Ṣafed el-Baṭṭikh? (Upper Galilee)
12. b?-r		
13. q-r-m-m	(גרמים, גרמון ?)	Near Beth-anath
14. q-d-[?]	Gedor? Kedesh? (גדר? קדש ?)	Tell Qades?
15. q-r-t ᶜ-n-b	Kiriath-anab=En-anab? (קרית ענב)	Tell esh-Shihab?
16. ḥ-d̲-⟨w⟩-r	Hazor (חצור)	Tell el-Qedaḥ
17. r-p-ḥ	Raphia (רפיח)	Tell Rafaḥ

These sources are sufficient for outlining the course followed by the expedition.[125] Like most Egyptian campaigns, it began at the southern end of the *Via Maris,* going from Sile via Raphia to Gaza, which is called here "the Canaan". The campaign was primarily directed against the Phoenician coast, and the Egyptian army marched via Acco, Usu and Tyre, reaching the area of *Gammad[im] (cf. Ezek. 27. 11, Heb) and Ullasa to the north of Byblos. Pharaoh's main objective was to renew the regular supply of Lebanese wood to Egypt. On the way the army, or certain units from it, turned inland to the Jezreel Valley, put an end to the insurrections in the Beth-shean area and then turned northward to Yeno ʿ am from whence it apparently continued northward via Hazor to Upper Galilee (Beth-anath and Kedesh ?) where the great battle with the Shasu may have taken place. The town preceding Hazor was called Kiriath-anab, which Papyrus-Anastasi I located in Bashan. This may be the En-anab (*Ḫi-ni-a-na-bi*) in the land of Gari (Ga-<šu>-ri, Geshur ?) from an El Amarna tablet (*EA*, 256. 26). A victory stele of Seti I was discovered at Tell esh-Shihab in the Yarmuk Valley about 24 miles east of Yeno' am.[126] The date was not preserved on it, so its connection with the first campaign is uncertain. However, since Kiriath-anab was located in the region, one may conjecture that it be equated with Tell esh-Shihab and that at least part of Seti's army had been there.

Information concerning Seti's subsequent campaigns, which were directed against more northerly regions, is insufficiently clear. In the Karnak reliefs on the other side of the gate battles with the Hittites and Libyans are portrayed; in the upper register only the reliefs depicting the conquest of Kadesh are preserved bearing the following caption: "The going up which pharaoh . . . made to desolate the land of Kadesh and the land of Amurru."[127] The fragment of another stele from Seti I was discovered at Kadesh on the Orontes,[128] so it is certain that he made an expedition against that town and the land of Amurru in the Lebanon. Here he had come into conflict with the Hittites. However, the Karnak relief portraying the conquest of Kadesh depicts the town as if it were located in a hilly region surrounded by a forest, and these details are incompatible with Kadesh in the Lebanese Beqa' .[129] Therefore, the relief in question may actually represent the conquest of Kedesh in Galilee, which doubtless was taken during the first campaign when the army was marching from Hazor to Upper Galilee. The vicinity of this latter town is certainly more like that described in the relief. Of course, this affects only the interpretation of one relief, without negating the assumption that Seti had reached Kadesh on the Orontes in some other campaign. His topographical lists also contain references to Qaṭna, Tunip and Taḫshi, which may have been conquered at the same time. One entry especially worthy of note is *ỉ-ś-r*,[130] which appears to be the earliest reference to the Israelite tribe of Asher.

A second stele of Seti I was discovered at Beth-shean,[131] for which the date is not preserved. Its inscription states that the *'apirū* from a Mount Yarumta with the Tayaru People had attacked the Asiatics ('Aamu) of Rehem. Pharaoh, angered that new disorders had broken out, immediately dispatched troops to the land of Djahi (Canaan). After two days his soldiers returned from Mount Yarumta crowned with victory. This stele is also concerned with events that took place in the vicinity of Beth-shean, apparently during a more extensive campaign. Mount Yarumta is doubtless to be associated with the Jarmuth-Remeth of Issachar (Josh. 19. 21; 21. 29; 1 Chron. 6. 73, Ramoth), i.e. in the elevated region north-west of Beth-shean. It is most interesting to learn

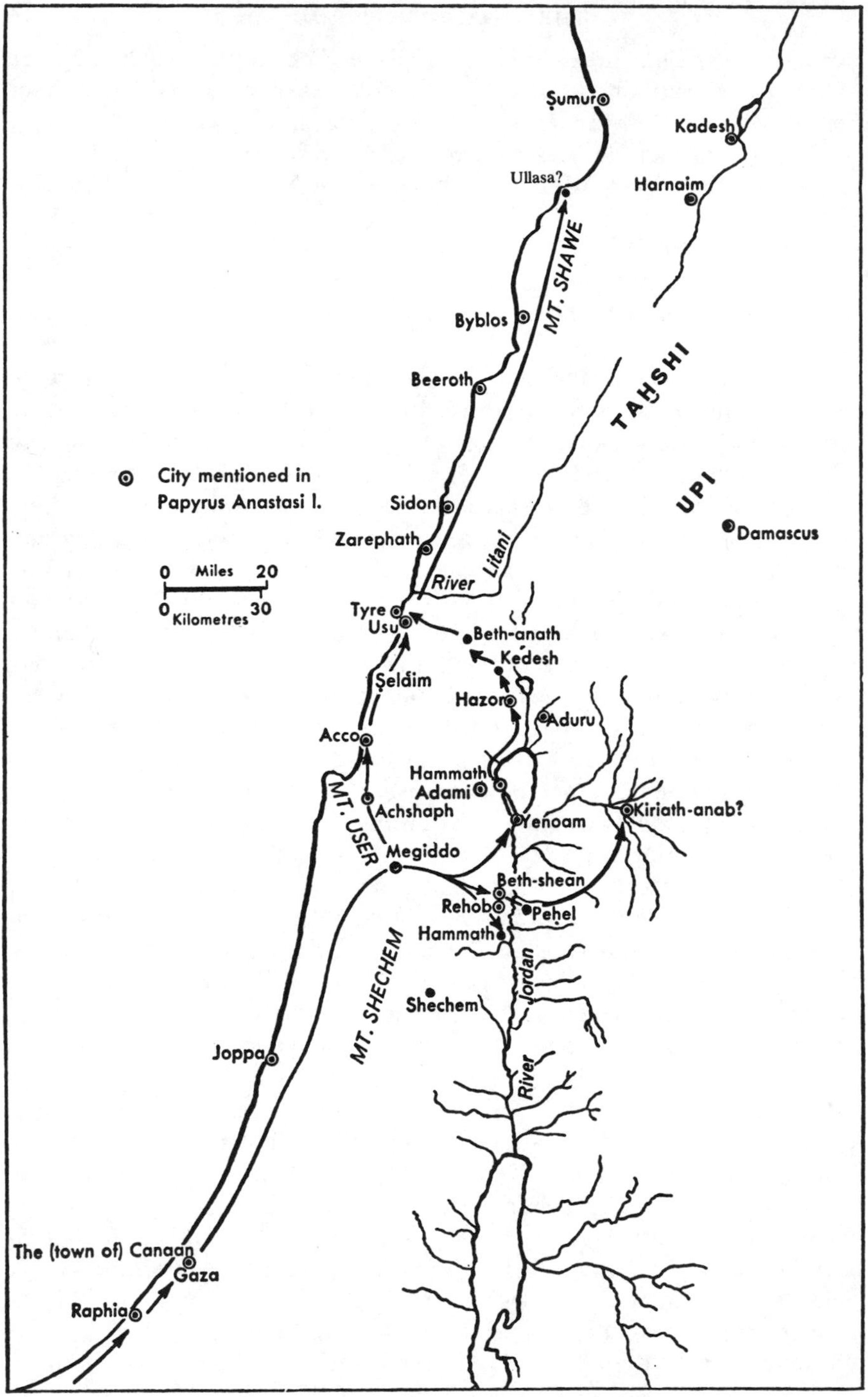

Map 12 The Campaign of Seti I.

that tribes of *'apirū* were already located in that region during the reign of Seti I (*c.* 1300).

X. THE REIGNS OF RAMSES II AND MERNEPTAH

The conflict with Hatti reached its climax during the reign of Ramses II (*c.* 1290–1224 B.C.). An inscription from his fourth year carved on the cliff near Nahr el-Kalb between Beirut and Byblos testifies to an expedition along the Phoenician coast in that year.[132] In *c.* 1286 his famous battle against Mutwatallis, King of the Hittites, took place at Kadesh on the Orontes. The reliefs and annals describing the encounter do not give detailed information about the army's march through Palestine. Only the customary starting point at Sile is mentioned, followed immediately by a town called Ramses in the Valley of Cedars located somewhere in Lebanon.[133] The text goes on to mention several places in the Lebanese Beqa' south of Kadesh: the towns of Lebo, Arnem, Shabtuna, near which the Egyptian army crossed the Orontes, and Timnah (the Taminta of Hittite sources).[134] The land of Amurru is also mentioned.

Although Ramses describes the battle of Kadesh as his greatest victory, it is clear that the contest ended in a draw, or perhaps even an Egyptian defeat. Ramses' main achievement was simply that he returned to Egypt alive after falling into an almost-fatal trap set for him by the Hittite army. Using tactics similar to those employed by the Canaanites at Megiddo during the reign of Thut-mose III, the Hittites staked everything upon a surprise attack by the chariotry, which threw the Egyptian formations into chaos.[135] Kadesh itself was not conquered, and from Hittite sources we learn about an invasion of the Damascus region (Upi) after this battle,[136] which shows that the Hittites had the upper hand.

Ramses conducted additional campaigns to Canaan in order to strengthen Egyptian authority, which had doubtless been weakened after the battle of Kadesh. However, details about these campaigns are quite scanty. One of his reliefs depicts the conquest of Ashkelon, specifying that the spirit of rebellion had penetrated even to the main centres of Egyptian power in southern Canaan.[137] A series of reliefs from Ramses' eighth year describe, among others, the capture of Kerep[na] (*k-r-p-*[*n*]) in the mountain of Beth-anāth, Kanah (*q-n*), and Merom (*m-r-m*), which are probably the Beth-anath of Naphtali, Kanah of Asher and Merom of the famous "waters of Merom"—all of them in Upper Galilee.[138] Reference is also made to Deper (*d-p-r*) in the land of Amurru, apparently in the Lebanon region near Kadesh, and finally a town named Shalem (*š-r-m*). Another relief depicts the conquest of Acco and a town whose name is written *q-ṯ-i̓-ś-r* which may be Gath-Asher, present-day Jett in western Galilee.[139]

A stele from the ninth year of Ramses II was discovered at Beth-shean.[140] Although the text is stereotyped and lacking in important details, it at least bears witness to a campaign in Canaan that year which must have passed Beth-shean. To one of these expeditions one must certainly associate his topographical list that was discovered in Amara,[141] which includes names in the Negeb, in Edom (Seir)[142] and in southern Canaan where we have the earliest recorded reference to the city of Dor on the route from the Sharon to the Plain of Acco.[143]

In recently discovered reliefs from Luxor the capture of two Transjordanian cities is mentioned: *B-<w>-t-r-t* in (the) Land of Moab (*m-w-i-b*) and Dibon (*t-b-n-i*).[144] This is the first mention of Moab and of Dibon, situated north of River Arnon. These Egyptian references to the hilly areas and to southern Transjordan in the thirteenth century are in agreement with the wave of dense settlement that had recently developed in these districts.

Evidently Ramses succeeded in stabilizing his authority over Palestine and southern Syria. In his twenty-first year (*c.* 1270) a peace treaty was made between Egypt and Hatti recognizing the status quo in the Levant. The text of this treaty, which has come down to us in both Egyptian and Hittite versions,[145] does not elaborate on the borders established by the agreement, but their main lines are fairly clear from other sources. Papyrus Anastasi III from the reign of Ramses II describes the extent of Canaan from Sile to Damascus (Upi), and a letter of Ramses II to Hattusilis III mentions the Egyptian commissioner in the land of Upi.[146] Certain passages from Papyrus Anastasi I, also contemporary with Ramses II, are of special interest in this regard.[147] This epistle, a letter from an Egyptian scribe to his rival, gives a description of the main roads in the Canaan of that day, describing them in terms of questions about the fate of a lonely and inexperienced traveller (cf. map 12). Indeed, the scribe does touch on roads leading to the land of the Hittites, to the Damascene, to Kadesh, *et al.* However, the description in consecutive order of the Phoenician towns begins in the north with "Ṣumur of Sessi (Ramses II)", i.e. the important harbour town at the mouth of the Eleutherus, where an Egyptian garrison was stationed by Ramses. Then follows the description of a dangerous journey into the Lebanon region, apparently to the treacherous land of Amurru. Reference is made to the mountain of Shawe (*š-w*), the Saue-Saua referred to by Tiglath-pileser III as a mountain bordering on Mount Lebanon, apparently Jebel ez-Zawiyah east of Tripolis.[148] A consecutive roster of Phoenician harbour towns from north to south follows: Byblos, Beirut, Sidon, Zarephath, Usu, Tyre, the River Liṭani (*n-ṯ-n*), Ṣelaim (*ḏ-r-ʿ-m*–צלעם, the "ladder of Tyre", today Ras en-Naqurah), Acco (*ʿ-k-n*) and Achshaph (misspelled *ʿ-k-sp*). The scribe goes on to discuss two mountain ranges: User, an Egyptian name meaning "strong" or "mighty", evidently a reference to Carmel: and Shechem, which probably means Mount Ephraim, an area dominated by the city of Shechem in that period.

Next we read about Hazor and its river, the nearby Jordan, followed by a description of the road south of Hammath (*ḥ-m-t*) on the Sea of Galilee and then to Yeno'am (*y-'-n*-[?]). Then we are told about the road to Adamim (*ỉ-d-m-m,* the biblical Adami-nekeb—Khirbet et-Tell above Khirbet ed-Damiyeh). In the following passage he treats various towns north of Damascus and in the Lebanese Beqa' as far as Kadesh: the land of Taḫshi, Timnat, Deper, Harnem (Arnem, cf. *supra,* p. 181) and Kadesh itself. The scribe then turns to Bashan and describes several towns: Kiriath-anab and Adurun (*ỉ-d-r-n*), evidently the *Ḫi-ni-a-na-bi* and Aduru in the land of Gari (*ga*<-*šu*>-*ri,* Geshur?; *EA,* 256. 24, 26); and a city named Ḫellez (*ḫ-n-r-ḏ*)on the border of Upi (Damascus). From there the scribe brings us back across the Jordan to Rehob and Beth-shean, the Brook Qina and Megiddo.[149] After this there follows an enlivened description of the passage through the narrow Wadi 'Ara. Reference is made incidentally to Qazaradi, chief of Asher (*ỉ-ś-r*). The use of this name to define a tribal group in Canaan at that time proves that it must be equated with the Israelite tribe of Asher.[150] The next stop is Joppa, where an amorous affair gets him into various troubles, including the loss of his chariot. But afterwards he is re-equipped by the Egyptian armoury and workshops there. Thus we have an interesting description of an Egyptian base in full operation. It would appear, however, that even Egyptians in Joppa were subject to the government and laws of the Canaanite population. Our geographical section closes with a description of the *Via Maris* between Sile and Gaza (cf. *supra,* pp. 46 ff.).

This papyrus gives us a general picture of Canaan as the Egyptians knew it during the reign of Ramses II. It extended from Ṣumur on the Phoenician coast to Egypt in the south and eastward to Kadesh in the Lebanese Beqa', plus the region of Damascus. Farther south of Damascus only the main highways, so essential to Egyptian control of Bashan, the northern Jordan Valley, the Valley of Jezreel, and the coastal plain are touched upon.

This is the land of Canaan as described in the biblical conquest narratives, and the detailed description of "the border of the land of Canaan" (Num. 34. 1–12) matches precisely the Egyptian province called Canaan in that period.[151]

Merneptah. Nothing is known about the situation in Canaan during the second half of Ramses II's long reign. However, it would appear that the *status quo* with the Hittites was maintained and that Egyptian rule in Palestine was more or less stable. The hold on Canaan may have been weakened again when Ramses died; in any case, his son

Merneptah (*c.* 1223–1211) set out for Palestine on a military expedition in his first years. This information is derived from the so-called "Israel Stele" dating to the fifth year of Merneptah's reign. Its text is mainly a song of victory composed after his triumph over the Libyans, but a passage was added at the end commemorating his previous victory in Canaan (*c.* 1220[152]:

> The princes are prostrate, saying: "Peace!"
>   Not one raises his head among the Nine Bows.[153]
> Desolation is for Tehenu (Libyans); Hatti is pacified;
> Plundered is the Canaan with every evil;
> Carried off is Ashkelon; seized upon is Gezer;
>   Yeno'am is made as that which does not exist;
> Israel is laid waste, his seed is not;
>   Hurru is become a widow for Egypt!
> All lands together, they are pacified;
>   Everyone who was restless, he has been bound
> by the king of Upper and Lower Egypt . . . Merneptah . . .

The few places mentioned in this text are located in different regions of the country: Ashkelon—the southern coastal plain, Gezer—the Shephelah, Yeno'am—the northern Jordan Valley. Thus it would seem that the expedition covered nearly the whole land, though we do not know how far north it went. Naturally the reference to an encounter with Israel is of the greatest significance. This is the only mention of Israel in Egyptian sources, and a most important piece of chronological information for fixing the date of the Israelite conquest.

A group of papyri from the reigns of Merneptah and his successor (the last quarter of the thirteenth century B.C.) that had served as practice texts for scribes[154] furnish information about the passage of travellers and emissaries from the border fortress at Sile to the land of Canaan. Gaza, Tyre and a fort of Merneptah in the vicinity of Sar-ram are mentioned as destinations for some of the couriers. Another passage describes the arrival of an officer from the "Wells of Merneptah", a place located on a mountain range. This could be a reference to the well of Me-nephtoah ("The Waters of Nephtoah"; Josh. 15. 9; 18. 15), the original form of which may have been the Well of Me(r)nephtoah,[155] located at Lifta three miles from Old Jerusalem. This is the first evidence for an Egyptian fort in the hill country of Canaan; it may have been erected because security was being threatened in those areas since the intrusion of the '*apirū,* as suggested by the Amarna correspondence. Papyrus Anastasi VI concerns permission that was granted to tribes of Shasu from Edom for passing over to the pools of Per-atum (the biblical Pithom) in order to preserve their cattle as well as their own lives. This is the earliest reference to Edom in Egyptian sources[156] and typifies the arrival of nomadic and semi-nomadic tribes which were now occupying Palestine, especially in the hill regions and Transjordan.

[1] For surveys of the material cultures of these periods cf. W. F. Albright, *The Archaeology of Palestine* (Pel. ed., 1949), pp. 49 ff.; K. M. Kenyon, *Archaeology in the Holy Land* (London, 1960), pp. 84 ff.; E. Anati, *Palestine Before the Hebrews* (New York, 1963).

[2] J. and J. B. E. Garstang, *The Story of Jericho* (London, 1940); K. M. Kenyon, *Digging up Jericho* (London, 1957).

[3] A. Gardiner, *Egypt of the Pharaohs* (Oxford, 1961) pp. 95 f.; *ANET*, pp. 227 f.

[4] This reading has been accepted instead of "the Gazelle's Nose", following E. Edel, *JNES*, 16 (1957), p. 70; however, the animal pictured in this hieroglyph may be of some other species.

[5] H. Goedicke (*Revista degli studi orientali*, 38 [1963], pp. 187–97) thinks that the eastern delta is meant. However, the term *ḥryw. š*'has a much broader meaning. Its definition in this document depends upon an evaluation of the historical situation.

[6] K. Sethe, *Urukunden des alten Reichs* (Leipzig, 1932), I, pp. 140-41, No. 29; M. Chehab apud W. A. Ward, ed., *The Role of the Phoenicians in the Interaction of Mediterranean Civilization* (Beirut, 1968), p. 3.

[7] For the statue of one ruler of Ebla, cf. G. Pettinato, *AAAS*, 20 (1970), pp. 19–22; P. Matthiae, *ibid.*, pp. 68–71, Fig. 8; also P. Matthiae and G. Pettinato, *Missione archaeologica Italiana in Siria*, IV (Roma, 1972), pp. 1–37, Tav. I—V. The great epigraphic discoveries from Ebla will undoubtedly illumine the third millennium B.C. when they are published; meanwhile cf. G. Pettinato, *BA*, 39 (1976). pp. 44–52; *idem*, *Reallexikon der Assyriologie und vorderasiatischen Archäologie*, V (Berlin, 1976), pp. 9-13. [Caution is in order with regard to direct connections with biblical studies, e.g. the personal names *Mika-ilu* and *Mika-ya* do not indicate the presence of Yahwism at Ebla. The *-ya* ending is simply a hypocoristicon, well known in cuneiform sources such as those from Ugarit. The forms *Mika-ilu* and *Mika-ya* correspond to Michael and Mickey in modern times. A.F.R.]

[8] Kenyon (*op. cit.*, note 1, pp. 135 ff.) emphasizes the particular aspect and culture of the first phase (the generally called Middle Bronze Age I) and proposes to define it as an intermediate phase, calling it "Intermediate Early Bronze-Middle Bronze period". This definition seems to be basically right, and we should perhaps see in these invaders a pre-Amorite group, whose affiliations and origins are unknown.

[9] N. Glueck, *AASOR*, 18–19 (1939), pp. 264 ff.

[10] N. Glueck, *BASOR*, 152 (1958), pp. 18 ff.; *idem*, *Rivers in the Desert* (New York, 1959), pp. 60 ff.

[11] B. Rothenberg, *God's Wilderness* (London, 1961), pp. 15 ff.; M. Kochavi, *BIES*, 27 (1963), pp. 284–292 (Hebrew).

[12] M. Evenari, Y. Aharoni, L. Shanan and N. H. Tadmor, *IEJ*, 8 (1958), pp. 249 f.; 10 (1960), pp. 110 f.

[13] Aharoni, *Settlement*, pp. 18 ff. (Hebrew).

[14] *Ibid.*, p. 24.

[15] M. Kokhavi, *The Settlement of the Negev in the Middle Bronze (Canaanite) I Age*, doctoral dissertation, Hebrew University, 1967, pp. 233–44 (Hebrew); *idem*, *Qadmoniot* 2 (1969), pp. 38–44 (Hebrew); W. G. Dever apud J. A. Sanders, ed. *Near Eastern Archaeology in the Twentieth Century* (New York, 1970), pp. 132–63, *idem*, *BASOR* 210 (April, 1973), pp. 37–63; E. D. Oren, *ibid.*, pp. 20–37.

[16] Ebeling-Meissner, *Reallexikon der Assyriologie*, I (Berlin, 1928), pp. 99 ff.

[17] A. F. Rainey, *IOS*, 2 (1972), pp. 388–94.

[18] For a discussion of the various opinions cf. H. H. Rowley, *From Joseph to Joshua* (London, 1950), pp. 61 ff., and cf. recently W. F. Albright, *BASOR*, 163 (1961), pp. 36–54.

[19] *ANET*, pp. 18 ff. For slightly different translations of this and the ensuing passages and for a detailed exposition of the social structure of the country where Sinuhe spent his years of exile, cf. Rainey, *IOS*, 2 (1972), pp. 369–408.

[20] This reading represents the most likely suggestion made thus far; the word is spelled iꜣꜣ and can certainly represent Araru: cf. *supra*, p. 114.

[21] B. Mazar, *EI*, 3 (1954), p. 21 (Hebrew).

[22] *Ḥqꜣ ḫꜣśwt*, "Rulers of foreign lands", the same title is ascribed at a later date to the foreign rulers who conquered Egypt; it has been preserved for us in the word Hyksos.

[23] *ANET*, pp. 328 f.; B. Maisler (Mazar), *Revue de l'histoire juive en Egypte*, 1 (1947), pp. 33 ff; *idem, EI*, 3(1954), pp. 18–32 (Hebrew); W. F. Albright, *BASOR*, 81 (1941), pp. 16–21; 83 (1941), pp. 30–36; A. Alt, *Zeitschr. ägypt. Spr. u. Altertumsk.*, 63 (1927), pp. 39-45; *ZDPV*, 64 (1941), pp. 21-39 (=*Kl. Schr.*, III, pp. 49-71).

[24] K. Sethe, *Die Ächtung feindlicher Fürsten, Völker und Dinge auf altägyptischen Tongefässscherben des Mittleren Reiches* (Berlin, 1926).

[25] G. Posener, *Princes et pays d'Asie et de Nubie* (Brussels, 1940).

[26] S. Yeivin, *ʿAtiqot*, 2 (1959), pp. 155 ff.

[27] *ANET*, p. 229; *ANEP*, No. 3.

[28] W. F. Albright, *BASOR*, 83 (1941), p. 34.

[29] *ANET*, pp. 230 f.

[30] Helck, *Beziehungen*², p.74.

[31] B. Mazar, *ibid.* (note 23), p. 22 (Hebrew).

[32] Helck, *Beziehungen*², pp. 69f.

[33] *Megiddo*, II, pl. 265; J. A. Wilson, *AJSL*, 58 (1941), pp. 225–31.

[34] B. Mazar, *ibid*, (note 23), pp. 30 f. (Hebrew).

[35] Helck, *Beziehungen*², pp. 63 f.

[36] This assumption is based upon several names of rulers who preceded the 15th Dynasty and who called themselves *ḥqꜣ ḫśwt* on scarabs, e.g. ʿAnath-har (*ʿnt-hr*), to which may be added other Semitic names such as Jacob-har (*yʿqb-hr*). However, it is possible that the Pharaohs having Semitic names preceded the Hyksos rule; or perhaps some of them were only subsidiary rulers. Manetho, in discussing the Hyksos conquerors, refers only to the Fifteenth Dynasty which ruled between *c.* 1680–1570. The names of six pharaohs from this dynasty are of uncertain origin, and it is not impossible that some of them are Hurrian, cf. Helck, *Beziehungen*², pp. 100-6. The dynasties of this intermediate period in Egypt, viz. the Fourteenth through the Seventeenth, evidently overlapped to a considerable extent; cf. D. B. Redford, *Orientalia* n.s. 39 (1970), pp. 1–51; R. de Vaux, *Histoire ancienne d'Israël*, I (Paris, 1971), pp. 78-84. [The term Hyksos is not an ethnic name. As explained above, it does not mean "Shepherd Kings." Furthermore, there is no mysterious people called Hyksos; they are simply the Asiatic rulers who invaded the delta. A.F.R.]

[37] This is an Indo-European word that first appears in our sources during the sixteenth century; it was apparently at this time that the battle chariot came into prominence, cf. A. Alt, *Die Herkunft der Hyksos in neuer Sicht* (Berlin, 1954), pp. 15f. (=*Kl. Schr.*, III, pp. 81 f.).

[38] A. Malamat, *JBL*, 79 (1960), pp. 12–19.

[39] For the main text references, cf. *ibid.*: for the more recently published allusion to Hazor and Laish, cf. *idem*, apud J. A. Sanders, ed. *Near Eastern Archaeology in the Twentieth Century* (New York, 1970), pp. 164–72; *idem, IEJ*, 21 (1971), pp. 31–38.

[40] Not Lebanon, because that is a mountain and/or a region, not a city.

[41] A. Alt, *ZDPV*, 70 (1954), pp. 130–34.

[42] Cf. Abel, *Géogr.*, II, pp. 30 ff.

[43] Helck, *Beziehungen*², pp. 478 ff.

[44] A. Alt, *ZDPV*, 67 (1944), pp. 9 ff. (=*Kl. Schr.*, I, pp. 222 ff.).

[45] A. Alt, *ZDPV*, 68 (1950), pp. 97–133 (=*Kl. Schr.*, III, pp. 107–40).

[46] W. F. Albright, *BASOR*, 87 (1942), pp. 37 f.

[47] *ANET*, pp. 233 f.

[48] W. M. Flinders Petrie, *Beth Pelet*, I (London, 1930); W. F. Albright, *BASOR*, 33 (1929), p. 7.

[49] *ANET*, p. 239.

[50] His topographical list for the towns conquered as a result of this campaign includes 119 names.

[51] B. Maisler (Mazar), *BIES*, 16 (1951), pp. 38–41 (Hebrew), *idem, PEQ*, 84 (1952), pp. 48–51; *idem, Cities and Districts in Eretz-Israel* (Jerusalem, 1975), pp. 141–46 (Hebrew).

[52] Y. Aharoni, *IEJ,* 9 (1959), pp. 110–16.

[53] S. Yeivin, *JNES,* 9 (1950), pp. 101-7. [However, the battle chariot was not a juggernaut but a light, mobile firing platform. Yeivin's conception of chariot strategy is therefore incorrect in that regard. A.F.R.]

[54] According to the Barkal Stele, cf. *ANET,* p. 238.

[55] From the "annals" of the sixth campaign, cf. *ANET,* p. 239.

[56] Gardiner, *Anc. Eg. On.,* I, pp. 158* ff., 166* ff.

[57] *ANET,* p. 240.

[58] The citizenry of Tunip refer to this conquest in *EA* 59.

[59] *ANET,* pp. 22 f.

[60] Simons, *Handbook,* pp. 27 ff., 109 ff.

[61] On the composition of the Syrian list, compiled apparently after the eighth campaign, cf. Helck, *Beziehungen*², pp. 142 ff.; M. Astour *JNES,* [22] (1963), pp. 220-41.

[62] Simons, *Handbook,* pp. 28 ff.

[63] Simons, *Handbook,* pp. 35 f.; Aharoni, *Settlement,* pp. 46 f. (Hebrew).

[64] Y. Aharoni, *IEJ,* 3 (1953), pp. 153–61.

[65] Aharoni, *Settlement,* p. 47.

[66] Compare Josh. 15: South (*Negeb*), valley *(Shephelah*), mountains (hill country, *Har*).

[67] One might think of Aphek in the Sharon (Josh. 12. 18), but that name is mentioned between Damascus and cities of Bashan and Aphek appears in another place (No. 66). [68] Simons, *Handbook,* pp. 115–19.

[69] M. Noth, *ZDPV,* 61 (1938), pp. 26–65. [Noth's resultant concept of Egyptian battle strategy, whereby small units were sent out from a larger base is founded on his faulty analysis of the Thut-mose list. A.F.R.]

[70] Aharoni, *Settlement,* pp. 40 ff.

[71] Helck, *Beziehungen*², pp. 121 ff.

[72] Helck, *Beziehungen*², p. 134. One may accept the basic picture as presented in Helck's map, although it is impossible to agree with all of his identifications. A prominent case of erroneous identification is Anaharath (No. 52). Helck's refusal to equate this place with Anaharath of Issachar is based entirely upon his assumption that it "has to be" in the Lebanese Beqa'.

[73] S. Yeivin, *JEA,* 34 (1950), pp. 51–62; *idem, EI,* 3 (1953), pp. 32–38 (Hebrew).

[74] We are especially unable to accept the "third district" (Nos. 31–49) which extends from Laish and Hazor as far as Acco, or the "fourth district" (Nos. 50–59) which included, in his opinion, the territory of Issachar to the north of the plain. Districts such as these are geographically improbable, and furthermore, they are based upon impossible identifications, e.g. the location of Ḫašabu and Tušulti in the region of Issachar and the equation of *n-g-b* with the biblical Ādami-*nekeb*; cf. Y. Aharoni, *Settlement,* pp. 42 ff. (Hebrew).

[75] Helck, *Beziehungen*², pp. 246 ff. It is difficult to accept Helck's opinion that these districts were called Canaan, Amurru, and Upi; however, the names are irrelevant to the delineation of the districts.

[76] Note the recent proposal to equate No. 20 with Muṣunnum from a Mari text; A. Malamat, *IEJ,* 21 (1971), pp. 34–35.

[77] Cf. the summary in *ANET,* pp. 242 f.

[78] Beth-anath may be listed in Thut-mose's roster as No. 97; *b-t-i-(ꜣ)-(?),* cf. Yeivin, *loc.cit.* (note 73), p. 36 (Hebrew); Aharoni, *Settlement,* p. 51 (Hebrew).

[79] *ANET,* p. 237.

[80] N. Golénischeff, *Les Papyrus hiératiques Nos. 1115, 1116A et 1116B de l'Hermitage Impériale à St. -Petersbourg,* 1913;n cf. recently Claire Epstein, *JEA,* 49 (1963), pp. 49–56; D. Amir, *BIES,* 27 (1963), pp. 276–83 (Hebrew).

[81] *ANET,* pp. 245–48; B. Maisler (Mazar), *Jerusalem,* 4 (1952), pp. 13–20 (Hebrew); *idem,* apud J. Liver, ed., *The Military History of the Land of Israel, in Biblical Times* (Jerusalem, 1964), pp. 33–39 (Hebrew); *idem, Canaan and Israel* (Jerusalem, 1974), pp. 84–92 (Hebrew); E. Edel, *ZDPV,* 69 (1953), pp. 97–176; A. Alt, *ZDPV,* 70 (1954), pp. 39–62; Y. Aharoni, *JNES,* 19 (1960), pp. 177–83; A. Malamat, *Scripta Hierosolymitana,* 8 (1961), pp. 218–31.

[82] A. Alt, *ZDPV,* 70 (1954), p. 40; D. B. Redford, *JEA,* 51 (1965), pp. 107–22; R. A.

Parker, apud *Studies in Honor of John A. Wilson* (Chicago, 1969), pp. 75–82; A. F. Rainey, *JARCE*, 10 (1973), pp. 71–75.

[83] Aharoni, *ibid*, pp. 117 ff.

[84] Simons, *Handbook*, pp. 129 ff.

[85] Y. Aharoni, *IEJ*, 9 (1959), pp. 121 f.; B. Mazar, *Canaan and Israel* (Jerusalem, 1974), p. 90, suggests that the Canaanite forces tried to stop Amen-hotep in the northern Sharon Plain instead of waiting to encounter him in the Jezreel Valley (unlike their tactics in the first campaign of Thut-mose III). [The theophany introduced in the text on the eve of the action in the northern Sharon supports Mazar's proposal; what followed the appearance of Amon to encourage Pharaoh was most likely the crucial battle of the campaign. A.F.R.]

[86] This is a large and lofty tell with remains from the Early, Middle and Late Bronze Ages and the Early Iron Age up to about the tenth century. It is the only site which fits the situation and importance of Anaharath in that region. At en-Na'urah and Tell el-'Ajjul nearby, two sites which have been suggested by various scholars, there are no suitable archaeological remains; Y. Aharoni, *JNES*, 26 (1967), pp. 212–15, P1. XXIII.

[87] W. F. Albright and A. Rowe, *JEA*, 14 (1928), pp. 281–87.

[88] Aharoni, *loc. cit.* (note 81), pp. 181 ff.

[89] S. Yeivin, *JEA*, 36 (1950), p. 57; B. Maisler (Mazar), *HUCA*, 24 (1953), p. 80 f.

[90] Aharoni, *loc. cit.* (note 81), pp. 182 f.

[91] The rulers of princes, i.e. the Canaanite kings, are called "great men" in the text.

[92] W. F. Albright, *JPOS*, 4 (1924), p. 140; *BASOR*, 94 (1944), p. 27; *JNES*, 5 (1946), p. 9; Malamat, *op. cit.* (note 81), pp. 218 ff.

[93] Rainey, *JARCE*, 10 (1973), 73–74.

[94] Y. Aharoni, *VT*, 9 (1959), pp. 229 f; *idem*, *VT*, 19 (1969), pp. 137–41, P1. I.

[95] Helck, *Beziehungen*², pp. 161, 163.

[96] R. Giveon, *JNES*, 28 (1969), pp. 54–59.

[97] W. Helck, *Urkunden der 18. Dynastie*, Heft 19 (Berlin, 19), p. 1554; *ANET*, p. 248; the text has only *q-ḏ*-[..], however the completion *qdr*=Gezer seems certain, Malamat, *op. cit*, (note 81) pp. 228 f considers the possibility, that the clay tablet from Gezer which has been sent from *kididm* [ ] (Gath, Gittaim?, cf. *infra*, p. 174) was sent during the campaign of Thut-mose IV.

[98] Helck, *Beziehungen*², p. 168.

[99] *EA*, 17; Helck, *Beziehungen*², pp. 163-64.

[100] J. A. Knudtzon, O. Weber und E. Ebeling, *Die El-Amarna Tafeln*, I–II (Leipzig, 1907–15); S. A. B. Mercer, *The Tell el-Amarna Tablets, I*–II (Toronto, 1939). A selection of the most biblically related letters may be found in *ANET*, pp. 483–90. For all texts not in Knudtzon's edition, cf. A. F. Rainey, *El Amarna Tablets 359–379* (*AOAT*, 8; Neukirchen-Vluyn, 1970, revised edition, 1978).

[101] Gardiner, *Anc. Eg. On.*, I, pp. 187* ff.

[102] Royal city-states are indicated by italics, Egyptian bases by capital letters.

[103] Ḫinnatuna, as compared with the masoretic vocalization Hannathon (Josh. 19. 14).

[104] A. Alt, *Die Landnahme der Israeliten in Palästina* (Leipzig, 1925), pp. 11 ff. (=*Kl. Schr.*, I pp. 89 ff).

[105] Numbered here according to Rainey, *op. cit.* (note 100 above); in *ANET*, p. 485, it is called *RA*, XIX, p. 97; in Mercer, *op. cit.* (note 100 above), it is *EA*, 248a.

[106] A. Alt, *PJb*, 20 (1924), pp. 34 ff. (=*Kl. Schr.*, III, pp. 169 ff.).

[107] W. F. Albright, *BASOR*, 87 (1942), p. 37.

[108] O. Schröder, *Orientalische Literaturzeitung*, 18 (1915), pp. 294 f.; contrary to the opinion of J. Lewy, *JBL*, 59 (1940), pp. 519–22.

[109] W. F. Albright, *BASOR*, 87 (1942), pp. 32–38.

[110] W. F. Albright, *BASOR*, 92 (1943), pp. 28–30.

[111] Malamat, *loc. cit.* (note 81); 228-31.

[112] An interesting problem arises concerning Tági, the father-in-law of Milkilu (*EA*, 249. 8). The King of Jerusalem accused him (*EA*, 289) of exactly the same deeds for which he had accused Shuwardata, viz. the conquest of Rubute in concert with Milkilu, threatening Jerusalem itself, and making a league with the men of Keilah. Tagi is from Gath-carmel (Ginti-kirmil) which is usually identified with Jett in the vicinity of the Carmel range. However, Gath in the Sharon Plain is quite far away from the Carmel and it is known as Gath-padalla in the El-Amarna correspondence (*EA*, 250. 13) as well as in the Shishak list

(No. 34). Since Carmel is a common name (cf. Carmel in Judah, Josh. 15. 55 *et al.*), it is not impossible that this is another designation for the Gath we are seeking. In another letter the King of Jerusalem wrote that hostile acts were carried out against him as far as the lands of *Še-e-ri* (Seir?) and as far as Gath-carmel (*EA*, 288; cf. Albright's translation, *ANET*, p. 488). Here it is certainly reasonable to interpret the passage as a refence to Gath (Tell eṣ-Ṣafi) on one hand and perhaps Zoar (Ṣuḫru) at the foot of Mount Seir on the other. Furthermore, it is worthy of note that Tagi writes in one of his letters about sending a caravan in his brother's charge which was almost wiped out (*EA*, 264); perhaps this brother was Shuwardata? Recently, F. M. Cross has read the name Gath-carmel on two Phoenician ostraca from Shikmonah, *IEJ*, 18 (1968), pp. 226 ff.; however, his readings of the place name do not stand up under close examination.

113 This identification is beyond doubt in view of its appearance on the Shishak list (no. 34, *ḏ-d-p-t-r*) between ʿAruna (No. 32) and Yaḥam (No. 35; cf. A. F. Rainey, *IEJ*, 18 (1968), pp. 1–14.

114 Cf. *Enc. Bibl.* (Hebrew), II, pp. 572–74; cf. also N. Avi-Gad, *EAEHL*, II (Jerusalem, 1976), pp. 575–78.

115 B. Mazar, *Zion*, 23–4 (1958–9), pp. 116 ff. (Hebrew); *idem*, *JBL*, 80 (1961), pp. 20–21; *idem*, *Cities and Districts in Eretz-Israel* (Jerusalem, 1975), pp. 193–95; *ANET*, p. 486.

116 Cf. A. Alt, *Die Landnahme der Israeliten in Palästina* (Leipzig, 1925), pp. 18 ff. (=*Kl. Schr.*, I, pp. 107 ff. = *idem*, *Essays on Old Testament History and Religion*, trans. by R. A. Wilson (Oxford, 1966), pp. 152 ff.

117 The correct form is **ʿapiru* as demonstrated by the Ugaritic and Egyptian consonantal spellings.

118 For a summary of the extensive literature on this subject, cf. Rowley, *Jos.-Josh.*, pp. 45 ff.; J. Bottéro *et al.*, *Le problème des Ḫabiru* (Paris, 1954); M. Greenberg, *The Ḫab/piru* (New Haven, 1955); R. Borger, *ZDPV*, 74 (1958), pp. 121-32; Helck, *Beziehungen*², p. 486.

119 For evidence suggesting a clash between Horemheb and Mursili, king of the Hittites, cf. A. F. Rainey, *UF*, 5 (1973), pp. 280–82; a hieroglyphic inscription on an alabaster bowl published recently by D. B. Redford, *BASOR*, 211 (1973), pp. 36 ff., would support this view but its formula has been called in question by several Egyptologists and there is good reason to suspect that this text is a modern forgery.

120 *ANET*, pp. 252 f.; with regard to this tradition and the association of Hyksos rule with the founding of Tanis, one may also understand the biblical tradition about the founding of Hebron seven years before Zoan (Tanis) in Egypt (Num. 13. 22).

121 M. Noth *ZDPV*, 60 (1937), pp. 210 ff.; R. O. Faulkner, *JEA*, 38 (1947), pp. 34 ff.

122 A. Rowe, *The Topography and History of Beth Shan*, I (Philadelphia, 1930), pp. 24–29; Pl. 41; *ANET*, pp. 253 f.; *ANEP*, No. 320.

123 Breasted, *AR*, III, p. 39, Fig. 1; Wreszinski, *Atlas*, II, Pls. 34–53a; *ANET*, pp. 254 f.; *ANET*, Nos. 322-31; R. Giveon, *Les bedouins shosu*, Les documents égyptiens (Leiden, 1971), pp. 39 ff.

124 Simons, *Handbook*, lists 13, 14, 15; Noth (*ZDPV*, 60 [1937], p. 213), had defined this group, but his identifications and interpretation of the passage are different from ours.

125 Aharoni, *Settlement*, pp. 55–64 (Hebrew).

126 G. A. Smith, *PEF QS*, 1901, pp. 344 ff.

127 *ANET*, p. 254.

128 M. Pézard, *Syria*, 3 (1922), pp. 108–10.

129 It is instructive to compare the picture of Kadesh-on-the-Orontes from the reign of Ramses II (cf. *ANEP*, No. 336) which depicts a deep moat all around the city.

130 Simons, *Handbook*, p. 147, list XVII, 4; Gardiner, *Anc. Eg. On.*, I, pp. 191* ff.

131 A. Rowe, *op. cit.* (note 122), pp. 29 f., Pls. 42-44; *ANET*², p. 255; Grdseloff, *Une Stèle Scythopolitaine du roi Séthos Ier* (Cairo, 1949); W. F. Albright, *BASOR*, 125 (1952), pp. 24–32.

132 *ANET*, p. 255.

133 Kumidi is perhaps intended, cf. Helck, *Beziehungen*², p. 198; Rainey, *UF, 5 (1973), p. 280.*

134 E. Edel, *Zeitschrift für Assyriologie*, NF 15 (1949), pp. 204 ff.

135 S. Yeivin, *JNES*, 9 (1950), pp. 101–7.

[136] *ANET*, p. 319.
[137] *ANET*, p. 256; *ANEP*, No. 334.
[138] Aharoni, *Settlement*, pp. 64 f. (Hebrew).
[139] *Ibid.*, p. 65; but this reading has been challenged, B. Oded, *AUSS*, 9 (1971), pp. 47–50.
[140] A. Rowe, *op. cit.* (note 122), pp. 33-36, Pl. 46; *ANET*, p. 255; J. Cerny, *EI*, 5 (1958), pp. 75*–82*.
[141] H. W. Fairman, *JEA*, 25 (1939), pp. 139 ff.
[142] B. Grdseloff, *Revue d'histoire juive en Égypte*, 1 (1947), pp. 69 ff.
[143] B. Mazar, *BIES*, 27 (1963), pp. 139-44 (Hebrew); *idem, Cities and Districts in Eretz-Israel* (Jerusalem 1975), pp. 154-59; cf. *supra*, p. 50.
[144] K. A. Kitchen, *JEA*, 50 (1964), pp. 47-50. Kitchen compares *b(w)trt* with Batora of the Tabula Peutingeriana, which has been located at el-Lajun in Central Moab. The reference to Dibon has been challenged, cf. Sh. Ahituv, *IEJ*, 22 (1972), pp. 141-42.
[145] *ANET*, pp. 199–203.
[146] A. Alt, *ZDPV*, 68 (1950), p. 98 (=*Kl. Schr.*, III, p. 107); *idem, Pedersen Vol.* (Kopenhagen, 1953), p. 4 (=*Kl. Schr.*, III, pp. 189 f.).
[147] *ANET*, pp. 476-78; Aharoni, *Settlement*, pp. 120-25 (Hebrew); Helck, *Beziehungen*[2] *pp. 328*–333.
[148] *ANET*, pp. 282–83; Aharoni, *Settlement*, p. 121.
[149] Concerning this sequence, cf. Aharoni, *Settlement*, p. 124, note 35.
[150] Contrary to the opinion expressed by Albright, *JAOS*, 74 (1954), pp. 222 ff.
[151] The only difference between Papyrus Anastasi I and the border description of the Land of Canaan in the Bible is that the former includes Ṣumur as an Egyptian base while the latter puts Byblos on the border of Canaan which extends to the boundary of the Amorites, i.e. Amurru (Josh. 13. 4–5; cf. *supra*, p. 73). Thus it appears that Papyrus Anastasi I must date from the beginning of Ramses II's reign while the biblical boundary belongs to his latter days after the treaty was established with Hatti, which removed Amurru from the Egyptian province of Canaan.
[152] A designation for the foreign countries.
[153] *ANET*, p. 378.
[154] Papyri Anastasi III, V, VI, cf. *ANET*, pp. 258 f.
[155] F. V. Calice, *Orientalistische Literaturzeitung*, 6 (1903), Sp. 224; W. Wolf, *Zeitschr. Äg. u. Altert.* 69 (1933), pp. 39 ff.
[156] B. Grdseloff, *loc. cit.* (note 142), pp. 69-99; for a reference to Moab in an inscription of Ramses II cf. *supra*, p. 182.

CHAPTER II

Israelite Conquest and Settlement

Today the various witnesses fix the Israelite beginnings on Palestinian soil in the thirteenth century B.C., but this was preceded by the penetration of the different Hebrew tribes.

I. FIRST STAGES OF PENETRATION

This period finds its biblical expression in the Patriarchal narratives. The idea expressed is that the Israelites are not coming to a new land but rather they are returning to the place where their forefathers had roamed during the Patriarchal Age. The Patriarchs made their livelihood as herdsmen, and only here and there did they engage in seasonal agriculture (Gen. 26. 12). They moved about only in the hilly and forested regions of the country and along the border. In the central hill country the Hebron vicinity (the Oaks of Mamre), Jerusalem and Migdal-eder, Bethel, Shechem and Dothan are mentioned; in Gilead—Mizpah, Mahanaim, Penuel and Succoth; in the Negeb—the region from Beer-sheba to Gerar, from whence the Patriarchs sometimes wandered as far as Kadesh (-barnea) and Shur (Egypt). In these regions they travelled about as sojourners, that is foreigners without real estate holdings, who acquired resident privileges from the local rulers at the price of various services. These relationships find their expression in the controversies of Abraham and Isaac with the lords of Hebron and Gerar. There were also occasional incidents of war and plunder such as Abraham's pursuit after the northern kings or Simeon and Levi's assault on Shechem. In every way their demeanour brings to mind that of the 'Apiru (Hebrews) in the El Amarna period, and therefore it is probable that a part of these 'Apiru are none other than Hebrew tribes that became united with the passage of time in the covenant of the Israelite tribes. It is perfectly feasible that the patriarchal narratives may preserve very ancient traditions, from the second millennium B.C. or even earlier. However, it has become evident that the stories connected with several localities in the country cannot have preceded the period of the Israelite conquest and settlement.[1] A definite case in point is Beer-sheba where excavations have proven the total absence of any

Bronze Age remains,[2] either at Tell es-Seba' or under the modern Beer Sheva' (formerly Bîr es-Seba').[3] At the tell itself, a unique well has been discovered which probably is the one that figures in the patriarchal narratives. It was evidently first sunk through the bed rock during the very earliest phase of the Israelite settlement, i.e., in the 13th century B.C.[4]

From the Egyptian sources we draw a certain amount of information concerning the penetration of these 'Apiru-Hebrews. The King of Shechem is working, so it is said, in league with the 'Apiru; and he even admits in one of his letters that a son of his has joined them (*EA*, 254). Against this background we can understand the tradition about intermarriage and strife with Shechem. For some reason this region is not mentioned in the conquest accounts, in spite of its having an Israelite population in the period of the Judges and its inclusion in the Manassite genealogy (although its internal population and government remained Canaanite until the days of Abimelech).

The King of Jerusalem complains in his letters that the 'Apiru are threatening the security of his city while various towns in the Shephelah, led by the kings of Gezer, Lachish and probably Gath, are helping them.

The penetration by Hebrew tribes into the northern approaches of the Jezreel Valley took another form. Here there were strong Canaanite cities, and the Egyptian government was very sensitive about this region. Therefore, Hebrew tribes were able to come in here only under the patronage of the Canaanite cities. A very instructive example of this was the ploughing of Shunem's lands by the King of Megiddo with the help of corvée labourers after its destruction by Lab'ayu (*EA*, 365; 250).[5] This reminds one of the manner in which the tribe of Issachar, whose name apparently means "man of hire, hireling"[6] settled in its territory, as hinted in Jacob's blessing: "Issachar is a strong ass, crouching between the sheepfolds; he saw that a resting place was good, and that the land was pleasant; so he bowed his shoulder to bear, and became a slave at forced labour (Gen. 49. 14–15)."[7] Likewise, we learn from Seti I's second stele at Beth-shean that in *c.* 1300 various 'Apiru tribes were settled in Mount *Yarumta* upon whom the Egyptians had imposed their yoke. This area in the hills of Lower Galilee north of the Jezreel Valley was also within the region of Issachar, and Mount *Yarumta* is certainly related to Remeth, i.e. Jarmuth of Issachar (cf. *supra,* p. 179).

About the penetration of 'Apiru into Galilee, we learn from the accusation of the King of Tyre that the King of Hazor had left his city and had united with the 'Apiru and that the land of the King had fallen into the hands of the 'Apiru (*EA,* 148). Seti made war on the Shasu in the "mountain ranges of Ḫuru", who had apparently assembled in the vicinity of Beth-anath in Upper Galilee. The tribe of Asher already appears in Egyptian sources of this period as does a city by the name of

Gath-asher in the days of Ramses II (cf. *supra*, p. 181). Since not one of the campaigns by the pharaohs of the New Kingdom was directed against the southern hill regions, it would appear that Asher was already settled in Galilee in this period, which would explain why it is mentioned in the lists of Seti I, who passed through Galilee on his first campaign.

In contrast to their previous appearance as migratory tribes during an extended period, one now notes a vital compulsion and a strong ambition to leave the semi-nomadic life, based mainly on cattle and pasturage, for that of the sedentary farmer, transferring more and more the centre of gravity of its economy to sedentary agriculture. This transition continued for several generations, passing through different stages and did not take place in all of the tribes at a uniform rate of development. Some tribes, especially those on the frontier, delayed their settlement; and a small part of them failed to take possession of their areas, usually due to objective causes, which made their transition to settled life difficult. However, all of the sources available to us testify to a general and energetic striving by the tribes to convert to agriculture and permanent habitation, and the main stage of settlement in the hill country was apparently completed in a relatively short time.

This fact stands out in the biblical descriptions, and is confirmed by archaeological research. In contrast to the descriptions of the Patriarchal period, where the main livelihood was from herds and flocks and dwellings were booths or tents, nearly all of the stories from the period of the Judges suggest farming and permanent habitation in towns or villages, with the exception of a few tribes which delayed the process of settlement, e.g. Dan, and Reuben. In the blessing of Jacob (Gen. 49. 1–27), which describes the tribal situation in the period of the Judges,[8] the typical economy is already agriculture and husbandry, such as olives and viticulture. The use of wine is now widespread, something that would be foreign to nomads and semi-nomads.[9]

Various settlements founded by the Israelite tribes have been excavated, especially in the tribal territories of Ephraim and Benjamin. Some of them were built in new locations, but others were founded anew on an ancient site after the destruction of the Canaanite town, frequently after a long occupational gap. At Bethel an Israelite settlement was built upon the ruins of the Canaanite city soon after its destruction. At Ai and at Mizpah (Tell en-Naṣbeh) an Israelite settlement was founded after a long period of abandonment. At Shiloh in the hill country of Ephraim Israelite occupation began after a long interval from MB II A (*c.* 19th century). Gibeah of Benjamin (Tell el-Ful) was founded by the Israelite tribe along with other places in the vicinity which have not yet been excavated, e.g. Ramah and Geba. In all of these places the remains and the pottery are of a uniform style and testify to the founding of these settlements within narrow chronological limits during the course of the thirteenth or the beginning of the twelfth century.

A similar picture is presented by the archaeological surveys in Transjordan and Galilee. In Gilead and in the southern regions of Transjordan hundreds of settlements from the beginning of the Iron Age were discovered during the survey by Nelson Glueck, some of which belong to the occupation by Edom, Moab and Ammon, and others to that of the Israelite tribes.[10] In the southern part of Upper Galilee between the Valley of Beth-haccerem and Naḥal Keziv (Wadi Qarn) a continuous chain of small settlements from the beginning of the Iron Age was discovered.[11] These are the first permanent settlements that were ever founded in that region, which is the highest section of Upper Galilee, apparently being forested in its entirety up until this time. They are small settlements, the biggest among them comprising an area no greater than about one acre. Some of them are built on hill-tops and some are situated on the slopes or in the valleys; the distances between them average no more than one to two miles and sometimes less. The deciding factor in the choice of a location for the settlement was a convenient approach to the small and scattered plots of land under difficult mountain conditions. Most of them were certainly unwalled settlements. This is a typical picture of families and clans at the beginning of the settling process. They inhabit small, adjacent settlements in rugged, forested, mountain regions.

According to the Patriarchal stories at least a part of the tribes were in the very same regions, i.e. in the hill country and in Gilead. Here they moved from place to place, mainly in accordance with the various seasons of pasturage, e.g. the wandering of Jacob's sons with their cattle from Hebron to Shechem and to the Valley of Dothan in the northern hill country of Ephraim (Gen. 37. 12 ff.). It is possible, therefore, that some of the tribes first reached these regions during the course of their natural migrations following seasonal changes in pasturage, as is the rule in semi-nomadic life.[12] The mountain regions, and the forest, served as ideal pasturage areas during the summertime with the deterioration of pasturage in the desert. The wandering of the Patriarchs from the Negeb and the eastern regions to the hill country of Palestine conforms well to the movement of semi-nomads with their herds and flocks according to the pasturage seasons, and the descent to Egypt in time of famine was certainly a movement of this type. This was usually done by agreement with the local residents who did not object, and who were unable to oppose the shepherds' passing over their land after the crop was harvested and before the new sowing in the winter, as is witnessed by the relations between the Patriarchs and various cities. At the same time it is impossible to accept the opinion of various scholars who see the whole process of settlement as a natural and slow transition of pasturage changes which led in the course of time to occupation of the summer meadows. This assumption is refuted by the biblical account, by the destruction levels which are found in various Canaanite cities and furthermore by the very fact of a swift and energetic occupation in a brief period of time. At least some of the Iraelite tribes forced their way into Transjordan and the Canaanite hill country, destroying various isolated towns as they went. The rapid and energetic transition to permanent settlement is understandable against the background of the period.

The invasion is not an isolated phenomenon; it is related to the great wave of expansion by Hebrew and Aramean tribes which exerted pressure in this period on all of the lands of the "Fertile Crescent" from the Euphrates to the Jordan. In about the same period the Ammonites, Moabites and Edomites settled in Transjordan; and the various Aramean tribes took extensive areas in Transjordan, Syria and the Euphrates region. The Israelite tribes belonged to this broad ethnic migration, coming from the eastern and southern wilds; and the pressure of this wave was doubtless the decisive factor which necessitated rapid settlement by the Israelite tribes when the opportune moment presented itself. The desert regions and frontier areas were seized rapidly by various tribes, and these cut off any alternative from the incoming tribes to return and utilize the winter pasturage in the desert and forced them to find their sustenance by vigorous occupation at any price. Their strength was insufficient to overpower strong Canaanite areas but was adequate to make a break-through so as to settle in the hill country and along the frontier.

II. THE EXODUS AND THE DESERT WANDERINGS

The Egyptian sources tend to indicate that at least one of the Israelite waves of conquest can be assigned to somewhere in the middle of the thirteen century B.C. (1)The mention of Ramses among the cities that were built by the Israelites in Egypt (Exod. 1. 11) points to the beginning of the reign of Ramses II when many forced labourers were employed in the building of his new capital at Tanis, which was called by his name, Pa-Ramses.[13] (2) According to the Merneptah Stele the people of Israel were in Canaan by c. 1220 (cf. *supra,* p.184).(3) Seir, Edom and Moab appear for the first time in Egyptian texts of the Nineteenth Dynasty. Therefore, the kingdoms of Edom, Moab and Ammon, which are mentioned in the conquest tradition, were evidently not in existence before the thirteenth century B.C. This also seems to match the evidence of the archaeological survey in Transjordan.[14]

It would seem, therefore, that the Exodus from Egypt took place early in the reign of Ramses II, and the penetration into Canaan happened during the middle of his reign or in the second half of his long rule, between 1260 and 1220.[15]

There is no reason to doubt the essential fact of the Exodus although we are unable to establish the names of the tribes that took part in it or the number of participants,[16] which was certainly not greater than a few thousands. Though the name of Israel or of one of the tribes has not yet been discovered in Egyptian records, we do have various contemporary documents which confirm the historical background of the period of enslavement and escape. In documents from the time of Ramses and Merneptah the employment of ᶜApiru is mentioned in relation to various building projects.[17] We have already mentioned papyri from border fortresses describing the careful watch kept on the passage of men through the net of forts along the desert border, the biblical "Wall (Shur) of Egypt", and the passage of nomadic tribes with their herds, e.g. nomads from Edom (c. *supra,* p. 184). The description of the pursuit after two fleeing slaves who slipped through the network of forts and escaped to the desert region north of Migdol[18] is also most instructive.

Only the beginning of the journey can be established with any degree of certainty, since only here do names occur which are also known from Egyptian sources (cf. map 13)[19] These are all located in the north-eastern part of the Nile delta. From Ramses the capital, the Israelites travelled to Succoth (Exod. 12. 37), which appears, perhaps, in Egyptian texts in the form *ṯ-k-w,* today Tell Maskhuṭah, a border fortress in the eastern portion of Wadi Ṭumilat (the biblical "land of Goshen"), west of the bitter lakes. From here they travelled through Etham on the edge of the desert (Exod. 13. 20), which is still unknown, to "Pi-hahiroth, between Migdol and the sea, in front of Baal-zephon" (Exod. 14. 2). It is possible that the name *pi-ha-ḥiroth* is connected with the root *ḥrt* (=to dig) and indicates a location on one of the canals of the Nile.[20] Baal-zephon is known from various sources as a temple for mariners located on the arm of land that embraces the Gulf of Serbonitis (Sabkhat Bardwil).[21] We have already mentioned Migdol which is well known as one of the Egyptian border fortresses north-east of Sile (today Tell el-Ḥeir, cf. *supra,* p. 48).

Therefore, it seems obvious that we have to look for the biblical "Reed Sea" in the same region. The reference here may be simply to one of the gulfs in the northern delta, since they contained sweet water in antiquity and papyrus reeds grew in their vicinity; perhaps it was the Gulf of Serbonitis, which separated Migdol from Baal-zephon. The biblical word used here for "Reed" (סוף) is an Egyptian term, and near Ramses the capital the existence of papyrus marshes by this name is known from Egyptian sources.[22]

The identification of the ensuing stations on the journey is a difficult problem. The only thing clear is the insistence that the Israelites did not follow the "way of the land of the Philistines, although that was near; for God said. 'Lest the people repent when they see war, and return to

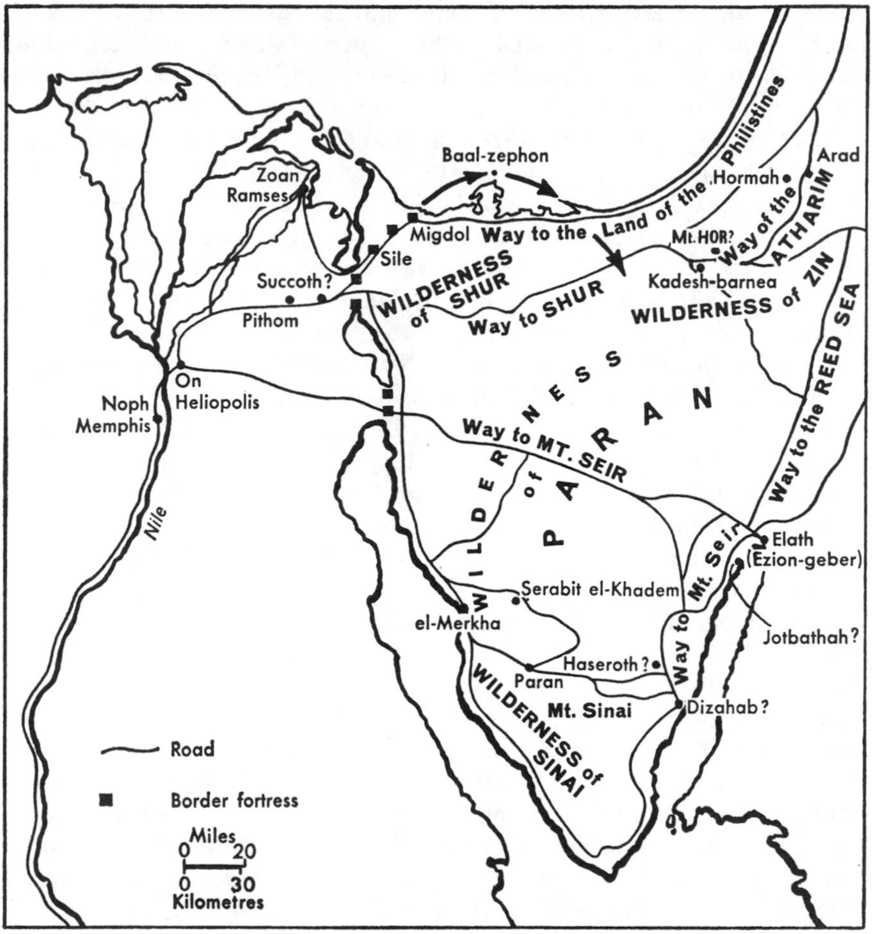

Map 13. The Exodus and the Desert Routes.

Egypt' " (Exod. 13. 17). The "way of the land of the Philistines" is an anachronistic designation for the southern portion of the important *Via Maris,* and it is no surprise that the nomadic tribes were unable to progress along this short and convenient route, because the network of Egyptian forts extended along its whole length (cf. *supra,* p. 48). Instead they went "by the way of the wilderness toward the Reed Sea" (Exod. 13. 18); one must assume that they moved southward quite rapidly to the desert interior, to areas that were outside of Egyptian control.

According to the continuation of the story, they went from the Reed Sea to the wilderness of Shur; and after a journey of three days in the wilderness they reached Marah, a place of central importance because "there the Lord made for them a statute and an ordinance, and there he proved them" (Exod. 15. 25). From here they went on to Elim, a place blessed with "twelve springs of water and seventy palm trees" (Exod. 15. 27). Thence they continued to the wilderness of Sin and Rephidim, and then to the wilderness of Sinai where they "encamped before the mountain" (Exod. 19. 2).

After the Sinai experience they marched on to the wilderness of Paran (Num. 10. 12) and made a three days' journey (*ibid.,* 10.33) to Taberah (*ibid.,* 11. 3). Going on, they reached Kibroth-hattaavah and Hazeroth, "After that the people set out from Hazeroth, and encamped in the wilderness of Paran" (*ibid,* 12. 16). In the continuation it is recounted that spies were sent to traverse the land, who set out "from the wilderness of Paran" and returned to "the wilderness of Paran at Kadesh" (*ibid.,* 13. 3, 26), that is, Kadesh-barnea, which is usually described as being in the wilderness of Zin (Num. 20. 1; 27. 14; 33. 36).

In addition to this literary tradition, there is preserved in the Bible a summary of the stations in the wilderness wanderings which lists forty-five stations and settlements on the way from Ramses to the "plains of Moab" (Num. 33), including many places which are not mentioned in the literary account of Exodus and Numbers. Opinions are divided as to whether this list is based upon ancient sources[23] or whether it is nothing but a sort of itinerary of desert roads from the Kingdom period[24]; but at any rate, it is clear that this is the most complete geographical list of the southern desert.

The first five names are taken from the stories of the Exodus from Egypt, and after mention of "the Sea" (the Reed Sea)[25] there is a series of twenty-five stations on the desert roads to Kadesh-barnea, among which the stations from the literary account also appear. At the end of the list there are ten stations from Kadesh-barnea to the plains of Moab.

In the large middle section containing twenty-five stations between "the Sea" and Ezion-geber, it is impossible to identify even one with certainty, and the accepted identifications are made mainly on the basis of the hypothetical line of march.[26] Some scholars assume that all of these stations are found in the southern Negeb in proximity to Kadesh-barnea, because of the central place which this oasis holds in the Wilderness period, and in the light of the first stations listed in the Exodus story which point in the same direction.

In conformity with this they seek Mount Sinai in the same region and have suggested Jebel Ḥalal, about 22 miles west of Kadesh-barnea.[27] Against this there are weighty considerations which tend to support the assumption that these stations were in a wider area extending even to the southern part of the Sinai peninsula where Mount Sinai should also be located.[28] These are the main arguments:

(1) Not one of the stations appears again in the Bible, either in the various stories or in the geographical lists. This applies as well to the large Negeb list of Shishak where it was permissible to expect the

presence of part of these names if they were in a more northerly region;

(2) Mount Sinai is also known by two synonymous designations, Mount Horeb and Mount Paran; and with reference to them, it is clear from the Bible that they are located in southern Sinai. Mount Horeb is far from Kadesh-barnea (Deut. 1. 2, 19; 1 Kings 19. 8), and Paran is evidently the general name for the southern deserts, today called the Sinai peninsula.[29] The wilderness of Paran does not appear in the list under discussion, in which the other portions of the wilderness are listed, apparently because there was no place for a general name in a detailed list. It is not compulsory to seek Mount Paran in the vicinity of Kadesh-barnea (Num. 13. 26), because the wilderness of Zin in which Kadesh-barnea is located (Num. 20. 1; 27. 14) is part of the great expanse known as the wilderness of Paran. Elath, too, was on the border of the wilderness of Paran according to Genesis 14. 6 "El(ath)-Paran on the border of the wilderness", i.e. Elath which borders on the Paran Desert. In spite of the fact that the wilderness of Paran is not mentioned in the summary (Num. 33), it does appear several times in the stories under discussion (Num. 10. 12; 12. 16). In contrast to the wilderness of Sinai which is referred to only in relation to the events at Mount Sinai, the wilderness of Paran is also mentioned in connection with other events in the south, e.g. in the story of Hagar's flight with Ishmael (Gen. 21. 21), in the escape of Hadad, King of Edom, from David (1 Kings, 11.18), and in David's fleeing from Saul (1 Sam. 25. 1; according to LXX "the wilderness of Maon"). Paran is also mentioned in the verse summarizing the sphere of Moses' activities at the beginning of Deuteronomy (1. 1). The main oasis in the south of the Sinai peninsula, Feiran, evidently preserves the ancient name of the wilderness of Paran. It is known from the Byzantine period and from Ptolemeos in the form Φαραν[30] and a tell has been found there with remains from the Iron Age (*c.* seventh century B.C.) up to the Arab period without any noticeable gap.[31]

Although the alternation of the names Sinai and Horeb raises a problem, it is clear that already in the biblical period they sought the mountain of God in the southern Sinai peninsula among the lofty granite mountains in the vicinity of Feiran-Paran;

(3) We should probably identify Jotbathah, the second station before Ezion-geber, with Ṭabeh, about seven miles south of Elath on the western shore of the Gulf of Aqabah.[32] In the Byzantine period an island in this region was known by the name Ἰωτάβη, which dominated the sea traffic to Elath. It was generally accepted to identify this island with Tiran at the southern end of the Gulf of Aqabah, especially in the light of the description by Procopius.[33] However, an archaeological investigation of Tiran proved that this island was never settled and that there is nothing on which to base its identification with Yotabe. In fact, there remains only the

small island Jezirat Far'un, about 10 miles south of Elath, in the vicinity of the oasis of Ṭabeh, which name resembles Jotbathah and Yotabe. On this island there are ancient remains of fortifications and a harbour.[34] We may presume a continuation of names from the biblical Jotbathah through the Byzantine Yotabe to the modern Ṭabeh, which strengthens the identification. Since Ṭabeh is situated to the south of Ezion-geber, this identification strongly suggests a southerly direction for the list of stations. Other possible identifications are: Hazeroth with 'Ain Khaḍra,[35] and Dizahab (Deut. 1. 1) with Dhahab,[36] both of which are in southern Sinai.

The identification of these stations and of Mount Sinai in the southern part of the Sinai penisula does seem at first glance to contradict the beginning of the journey in the northern Delta. However, if we remember that this is a summary of the various traditions concerning the period of the wanderings in the desert, a list based upon various stories and arranged systematically in geographic order, we will avoid difficulty. The long line of march according to Numbers 33 summarizes the extended period of wanderings in a geographical annotation, but one need not assume that it reflects a single and unified historical journey. A large number of men could not have existed in the southern deserts in one assembled group, but rather they were forced to scatter with their herds across the desert prairies over a wide area, just as the Bedouin are accustomed to doing today. At the same time they had sacred assembly places, and nothing prevents the assumption that one of them was in the southern peninsula, viz. Mount Sinai, in the region of the ancient turquoise and copper mines and of the lofty granite mountains which were sacred from time immemorial. The second was in the northern part of the peninsula at Kadesh-barnea on the border of the much-desired land of Canaan.

Kadesh-barnea is the largest oasis in the northern Sinai peninsula, and it served as a central assembly point for the Israelite tribes during the wilderness period.[37] Within its general vicinity were concentrated the burial traditions of the family of Moses and Aaron: here their sister Miriam died (Num. 20. 1), and Aaron himself died not far away at Mount Hor (Num. 20. 22-9; 33. 37-9). The biblical tradition stresses that at Kadesh-barnea the Israelites remained settled for a long time (Deut. 1. 46). It is possible that the first amphictyonic centre was located at this holy place around which the Israelite tribes united before their entry into the land of Canaan. In line with this, Kadesh appears in the tradition as the base for all attempts at penetration into Canaan. From here Moses sent the spies to survey the land; from here the tribes went up to fight with the King of Arad (Num. 21. 1-3; 33. 37 ff.); and from Kadesh they set out on their eastward journey to Transjordan (Num. 20. 16; cf. map 14).

III. THE CONQUEST OF TRANSJORDAN

The attempt at direct penetration from the Negeb into the hill country of Judah failed because of the strenuous opposition by the Canaanite cities situated along the stream beds of the northern Negeb: in the west Tell el- 'Ajjul (Beth-'eglaim), Tell Jemmeh (Yurza?) and Tell el-Far'ah (Sharuhen) on Wadi Ghazzeh (Besor); in the east Tell el-Milḥ (Arad) and Tell el-Meshash (Hormah) on the Wadi Milḥ; in the center Tell el-Khuweilifeh (Goshen?), Tell esh-Shari'ah (Ziklag?), Tell Abu-Hureireh (Gerar) and Tell Mughrabi on Wadi esh-Shari'ah. It would appear that the Beer-sheba Valley was not settled, and therefore the Patriarchs had already encamped there in close proximity to Canaanite Gerar.[38]

Coming from Kadesh-barnea the Israelite tribes encountered the King of Arad who dominated the eastern desert expanses and who smote them, according to the tradition, in neighbouring Hormah (Num. 14. 44-5; 21, 1; 33. 40; Deut. 1. 44). In the excavations at Tell 'Arad it became clear that the settlement on that place was founded only in the tenth century B.C., after an occupational gap of nearly 2,000 years; and therefore it cannot be considered the royal centre of the Canaanite King of Arad. Mazar suggested, as a solution for this dilemma, that Arad was no city in this period but rather a district, viz. "the Negeb of Arad" (Judg. 1. 16), and that the royal city was Hormah, which he identifies with Tell el-Milḥ.[39] However, the assumption seems more likely that Canaanite Arad was located at Tell el-Milḥ and that Hormah is neighbouring Tell el-Meshash. Both of these tells are situated beside rich water sources and were occupied in the Middle and Late Bronze Ages.[40] This idea is supported by Shishak's list which mentions two fortresses by the name of Arad: Great Arad, i.e. the main Arad; and the Arad of the House of Yeroham, which is probably the biblical Jerahmeel (cf. *infra,* p. 329). We may therefore conclude that Arad finally fell into the hands of the Jerahmeelites (cf. "the Negeb of the Jerahmeelites" and "the cities of the Jerahmeelites", 1 Sam. 27. 10; 30. 29), while the families of the Kenites settled north-east of the city in the Negeb of Arad, on the border of the wilderness of Judah (Judg. 1. 16). On the other hand, Hormah fell to Simeon, the centre of whose inheritance was in the vicinity of Beer-sheba (Josh. 19. 4; 1 Chron. 4. 30; Judg. 1. 17). It is noteworthy that popular etymology of the name Hormah (Hebrew *ḥrm* means "to devote to destruction") gave birth to a contrary tradition, viz. that at this place the Israelites conquered and utterly destroyed the Canaanites (Num. 21. 3).

The chain of fortified Canaanite cities in the northern Negeb forced the Israelites to turn eastward to Transjordan first. There exist two different traditions in the Bible concerning their route from Kadesh to Transjordan (cf. map 14). One of these finds clear expression in the summary of Numbers 33, which describes a direct line from Kadesh-barnea through the Arabah, Edom and Moab to the "plains of Moab" which are opposite Jericho. The sacred Mount Hor, where Aaron the priest died, is still not identified with certainty; one should look for this mountain on "the way of the Atharim" from Kadesh-barnea to the vicinity of Arad, because it is always mentioned on the line of this journey (Num. 20. 22–9; 21. 4; 33. 37–9; Deut. 32. 50). Therefore, there is no foundation for the various suggested identifications in the vicinity of the Arabah, e.g. Jebel Maḍrah in Nahal Zin (Wadi Fuqrah).[41]

A height named 'Imaret el-Khureisheh which towers over an important road junction about eight miles north of Kadesh-barnea deserves consideration; a wall and stone circles discovered on top of it testify to its sanctity.[42] Zalmonah has evidently been preserved in the name of a Roman fort in the Arabah (Calamona).[43] Punon is the great copper-mining centre of Feinan in Edom, at a distance of about 20 miles south-east of 'Ain Ḥuṣb. Ije-abarim on the border of Moab is at the ford of the Brook Zered, the border between Edom and Moab.[44] Dibon, today Dhiban, is the most important town on the road north of the Arnon which belonged, according to Joshua 13. 17, to Reuben, and according to Numbers 32. 34, to Gad. In the section under discussion it receives the anachronistic description Dibon-gad. The last two stations, Almon-diblathaim and the mountains of Abarim, are in the vicinity of Mount Nebo on the road from Dibon to the plains of Moab by the Jordan at Jericho.

The summary which was preserved in Numbers 33 denotes, therefore, a line of stations and settlements on the main road from Kadesh-barnea to Edom and Moab as far as the plains of Moab, which is one of the major branches of the King's Highway (cf. *supra*, p. 55). This line is contradictory to the tradition that the Israelites encountered the opposition of the kings of Edom (Num. 20. 14 ff.) and of Moab (Judg. 11. 17), who did not permit Israel to pass along the King's Highway, thus compelling them to travel "by the way of the Reed Sea" (Num. 21. 4; cf. Judg. 11. 18). From here they went up through the desert to the vicinity of Kedemoth east of the Arnon (Deut. 2. 26; 'Aleiyan?) and invaded the land of Sihon, the Amorite King of Heshbon (Num. 21. 21 ff.; Deut. 2. 26 ff.). This invasion took place under special historical circumstances: "For Heshbon was the city of Sihon, King of the Amorites, who had fought against the *former* (Hebrew text: 'the *first*') King of Moab and had taken all his land out of his hand, as far as the Arnon" (Num. 21. 26). Apparently, with the organization of the kingdom of Moab, the King of Heshbon took from its first king the table land (Hebrew: *ha-mishor*) between Heshbon and the Arnon, a district which the Moabites claimed for themselves throughout all their history. In Mazar's opinion the Amorite kingdom of Heshbon was founded after the failure of Ramses II at Kadesh as a consequence of which a Hittite invasion of Damascus took place, perhaps in co-operation with the King of Amurru.[45] However, it is difficult to associate them with colonization

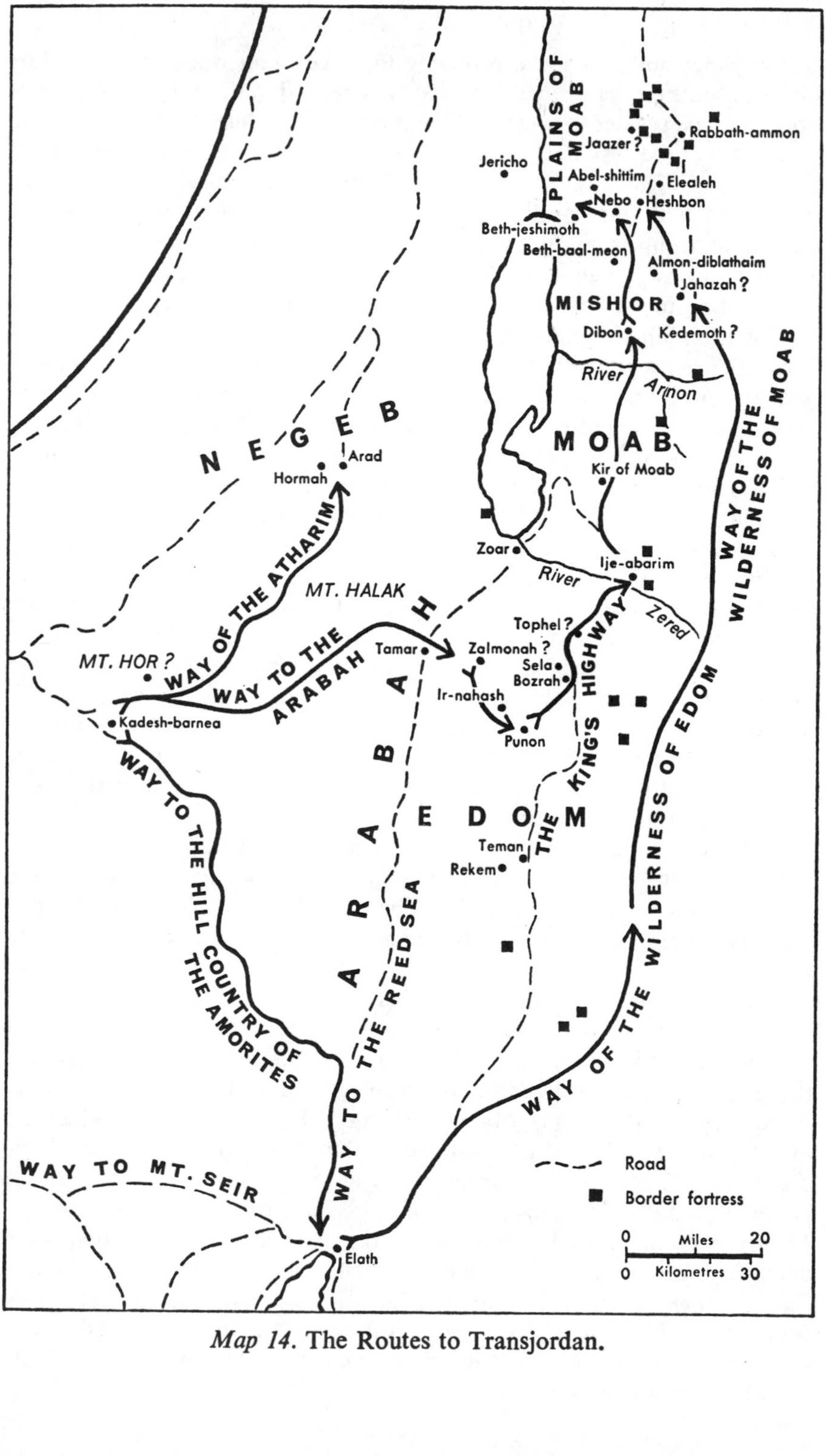

Map 14. The Routes to Transjordan.

of this type; and it is more probable that Heshbon was one of the few cities in southern Transjordan which was settled in the Late Bronze Age and that its residents were called Amorites in line with the biblical concept that the residents of the mountains and the interior regions were Amorites.[46] The expansion by the King of Heshbon was perhaps connected with the founding of the Moabite kingdom which seemed dangerous to him. In any case, these events served as a pretext for the Israelite tribes to penetrate into this area and to strike a decisive blow against the King of Heshbon at Jahaz (Khirbet el-Medeiyineh?).

This tradition, which is connected with particular historical events, is certainly trustworthy; but it is not reconcilable with the first tradition, which assumes that the route of the journey through Edom and Moab was a straight line from Kadesh to the plains of Moab without any opposition in these regions being encountered. In Noth's opinion this is not a historical tradition at all but rather an itinerary for the pilgrimage route to Mount Sinai in the Kingdom period which must be sought in the land of Midian, south of Mount Seir and east of the Gulf of Aqabah.[47] Against this view serious objections may be raised. In the literary account the same tradition is inserted, and several stations are mentioned within Edom: Oboth, Ije-abarim and the Brook Zered (Num. 21. 10 ff.); and the story of the brazen serpent which is mentioned before this is perhaps connected with Khirbet en-Naḥas (*naḥash*="serpent") in the vicinity of Punon, one of the important copper-mining centres in Edom.[48] In these traditions the route from Kadesh-barnea to Moab is described and not the road along the length of Transjordan or to Elath. This line can hardly be accepted as an important route in the period of the Israelite kingdom, during which a network of roads and forts in the Negeb and the Arabah was developed so that people need not go to Moab in order to reach Elath. This branch of the King's Highway was important only until the establishment of the Israelite kingdom which gained control over Elath and Kadesh-barnea. It is therefore difficult to cast doubt on the fact that we have before us an ancient tradition which has its historical background in the Conquest period.

In these two traditions entirely different conditions are envisaged and these have recently been considerably illumined by archaeological discoveries. In the area of Midian, south of Mt. Seir and east of the Gulf of ʿAqabah, a sophisticated culture of the Late Bronze Age has been discovered.[49] Its unique pottery is especially striking; it is almost completely different from the ceramics of Palestine in the same period. Most predominant is a bowl of simple form, but there are also juglets, all decorated with unique bi-chrome patterns including birds and human figures. The excavations in the small Egyptian temple at Wadi Meneʿiyeh (N. Timnaʿ) have shown that this pottery is to be dated to the thirteenth-twelfth centuries.[50] However, it seems clear that its beginnings in Midian are earlier.

Thus it is clear that a developed settlement, the centre of which was in Midian, preceded the Edomites in southern Transjordan. There is a biblical tradition to the effect that the autochthonous population in that area was Horite (Gen. 14. 6; 36. 20, etc.). Actually, there is a certain similarity between the pattern of decoration on the Midianite pottery and the Hurrian (i.e. Horite) pottery known mainly from Nuzi.[51] This resemblance may help to explain the biblical memory of Horites in the Midianite region.

But the most illuminating aspect of this discovery is the very existence of such a well developed culture prior to the arrival of the Edomites in the south having connections with the name of Midian. Two conflicting traditions regarding Midian are reflected in the Bible. One knows only about extremely hostile relations between Israel and Midian (Num. 25; 31). This encounter is associated with the Plains of Moab and nearby Baal-peor, i.e. the region to which a straight march through Edom and Moab had led. Furthermore, in the story about Balaam, which belongs with this strand of the tradition, the elders of Midian usually appear alongside the elders of Moab (Num. 22).

On the other hand, in the time of Moses, we find excellent relations between Israel and Midian. There Moses found asylum and married into a renowned priestly family. While in the service of Jethro he reaches Sinai and Jethro also instructs him about worship and judgement in the desert (Ex. 2. 15, etc.; 18).[52]

These contradictory strands are remarkably explained against the background of two waves of occupation that arrived at different times. The first belongs to the fourteenth century before an organized society had sprung up in Edom and Moab to block its path, so the tribes could pass through without encountering any resistance. As we shall see, this wave has to do with the arrival of the house of Joseph.

The second wave took place in the thirteenth century. Now the incoming tribes meet the organized settlement of Edom and Moab which prevented them from taking the King's Highway. In this period, there are no conflicting interests between Israel and Midian, which had been expelled from Mt. Seir and had lost its influence in southern Transjordan due to the new settlers. This is a remarkable correlation between archaeological finds, historical sources and a historical-geographical list.

It would seem, therefore, that there are preserved here memories of two different journeys, the first in the fourteenth century to the plains of Moab before the various kingdoms in this area became organized, and the second in the thirteenth century which led around Edom and Moab along the fringe of the desert and which ended in the conquest of Heshbon. These different routes constitute one of the conclusive evidences that the Israelite conquest was not carried out in one campaign or at one time but rather continued in several waves which were blended together in the tradition to a single campaign of conquest.[53]

It is natural that the southern portions of Transjordan served as the first objective for penetration by the various Hebrew tribes since the settlement of these regions was the sparsest and, in fact, was outside of Egypt's sphere of control. Against this background, one must understand the settlement by the Edomites, Moabites and Ammonites in the frontier regions of Transjordan a short time before the main Israelite wave of penetration in the thirteenth century. The Ammonites succeeded in gaining control of one of the few cities on the King's Highway in eastern Gilead which is henceforth called Rạbbath-(of the sons of)-ammon.[54] They settled around it along the fringe of the desert, but in the west their expansion seems to have been blocked by the Amorite Jaazer,[55] and at every opportunity they made an attempt to break through towards the west. The Edomites and Moabites settled in the southern regions of Transjordan, which were apparently not settled at all in this period, and the Brook Zered (Wadi el-Ḥesa) served as the boundary between them. The establishment of well organized kingdoms in these areas during the thirteenth century B.C. is more and more attested by archaeology. Recent excavations by B. Rothenberg in the copper-mining settlements of the southern Arabah have shown that their peak of activity was during the thirteenth to eleventh centuries. A special type of decorated "Edomite" pottery was found which gives evidence to the unique and high level of their material culture, reached already in this early period. The biblical traditions of "the border of Edom" (Num. 20. 14 ff.; 33. 37; Deut. 2 4 ff.) are thereby vividly illuminated.

As was mentioned previously, Moab encountered the territory of Amorite Heshbon on the north. It seems that in the first stage the Moabites succeeded in occupying the Mishor (table land) between Heshbon and the Arnon as well. But already during the reign of the first Moabite King, Sihon, the King of Heshbon, carried out a sweeping campaign and conquered all of the Mishor as far as the Arnon. Heshbon, which had managed to hold its own against Moabite pressure, finally fell before the stormy attack of the Israelite tribes who then assumed for themselves the privilege of taking over all of its land as far as the Arnon (cf. map 15). Henceforth, the Arnon was the traditional border for the Israelite tribes in eastern Transjordan. On the other hand, the Moabites considered this an encroachment upon their land. The pressure of their expansion was always directed northwards, and in different periods they succeeded in restoring this region to themselves as far as Medeba on the border of Heshbon and sometimes as far as the southern end of the eastern Jordan Valley, which was known even in Israelite tradition by the name "the plains of Moab".

We do not know if the early wave of Israelites brought about the first settlement in Gilead or whether these tribes remained nomadic until, with the passage of time, they crossed over in large measure to western Palestine. In the earlier traditions the land of Jaazer and the land of Gilead remained noteworthy cattle country (Num. 32. 1 ff.), a picture which did not change in its essentials even in the period of the Kingdom (1 Chron. 5. 9). Evidently Gad is related to the early wave, and took possession of the broad expanses in Gilead so that the names Gad and Gilead became almost synonymous. According to Numbers 32. 34 the cities of Gad were dispersed as far as the Arnon and included Dibon and Aroer. Dibon is called Dibon-gad (Num. 33. 45–6), and Mesha, the King of Moab, indicated on his stele that ". . . the men of Gad had always dwelt in the land of Ataroth" (line 10). In the north the inheritance of Gad extended as far as the Jabbok. Gilead north of the Jabbok was mostly covered with forests which were still partially in existence in the Kingdom period, e.g. the forest of Ephraim near Mahanaim (2 Sam. 18. 6), and remnants of them exist even today. The eastern Jordan Valley was nearly all reckoned as Gadite from Beth-haran and Beth-nimrah in the south through the Plain of Succoth and the city of Zaphon up to the shore of the Sea of Galilee (Josh. 13. 27). It seems that the Gadites infiltrated into this region, which was at least partially settled by Canaanites; and when the Israelite tribes gained sufficient strength these Caanite cities were added to the inheritance of Gad. A clear example is Zaphon (apparently Tell Saʿidiyeh, apparently known from the Amarna tablets,[56] which was now counted among the cities of Gad and its name associated with one of the chief Gadite clans (Num. 26. 15; Gen. 46. 16—Ziphion). Perhaps Jephthah, the Gileadite, was also connected with Zaphon ("the men of Ephraim were called to arms and they crossed to Zaphon", Judg. 12. 1; according to the LXX of Judg. 12. 7 he was buried at Zaphon). In the story of Jephthah a tradition is preserved that the Israelite settlement had been rooted in Gilead for a considerable period (300 years; Judg. 11. 26), but one may not build an exact chronology on this figure.

It is also worthy of note that Gad is the brother of Asher, both of them being sons of Zilpah the handmaiden of Leah. As we have seen, Asher certainly belonged to an early wave and this is evidently expressed in the genealogical scheme. An instructive example of this principle is the genealogy of the Aramean sons of Nahor who are also divided into eight tribes of the chief wife and four of the concubine (Gen. 22. 20–4), the names of these latter being known to us from Egyptian sources of the period preceding the Aramean settlement.[57]

By contrast, Reuben apparently belongs to a later wave which entered the region only in the thirteenth century. In the tradition he is the first-born of the tribes of Israel but he declined during the course of time. Therefore, it would seem that he had played an important role in the covenant of the tribes before their entry into Palestine. According to Numbers 32. 37–8 the Reubenites settled in Heshbon and its environs, and the conquest of this region is indeed connected with the migration of the later wave. Thus the Reubenites encountered serious difficulties in the process of their settlement, especially since other tribes had preceded them. They remained partially nomadic on the border of the desert (1 Chron. 5. 8–10), and various families evidently crossed over to western Palestine. There are clear witnesses to the connections between Reuben and Judah and Benjamin. On the border between Judah and Benjamin, west of Jericho, one finds "the stone of Bohan the son of Reuben" (Josh. 15. 6; 18. 17). On the boundary between Judah and Benjamin lay the Valley of Achor (Josh. 15. 7), where Achan the son of Carmi from the tribe of Judah was stoned (Josh. 7. 26), Carmi also being one of the leading clans of Reuben (Gen. 46. 9; Num. 26. 5–6; 1 Chron. 5. 3). The clan of Hezron is known among the clans of Reuben (Num. 26. 6) and Judah (Num. 26. 21), and the clan of Bela is shared by Reuben (1 Chron. 5. 8–10) and Benjamin (Gen. 46. 21; 1 Chron. 8. 1). The tradition is also interesting that at Migdal-eder, in the vicinity of Jerusalem, Reuben lay with Bilhah, his father's concubine (Gen. 35. 21), a deed which brought his father's curse upon his head.

As a consequence of the conquest of Heshbon, control over the Amorite Jaazer was apparently achieved as well (Num. 21. 32), which now remained isolated between the territories of Ammon and Gad. The biblical tradition goes on to tell about the conquest of the land of Og, the King of Bashan, who was defeated by the Israelites at Edrei. In the area of his former kingdom half of the tribe of Manasseh settled.

It is clear that the concept of half of the tribe of Manasseh in this region is related to the later phase of the period of the Judges, after Machir migrated thither from the hill country of Ephraim where he had still been dwelling at the time of the battle of Deborah (Judge. 5. 14). Nevertheless, the tradition about Og, the King of Bashan, is certainly old; and his sixty cities which were "fortified with high walls, gates and bars" (Deut. 3. 5; 1 Kings. 4. 13) correspond to the existence in this region of ancient Canaanite cities, at the head of which was Ashtaroth, in the Late Bronze Age. Information about the appearance of ʿApiru in this area is already found in the El Amarna tablets.

In that letter dealing with this region which mentions Yenoʿam, Ashtaroth, Buṣruna, Ḫalunni, Damascus and the land of Taḫshi, one of the rulers (Biridashwah) is accused of taking chariots from Ashtaroth and handing them over to the ʿApiru (*EA*, 197). It is possible that the tradition of the victory over Og belongs to about this period,[58] but one may not connect it with the Israelite conquest. The information about the iron bedstead of Og, which remained in Rabbath-ammon (Deut. 3.

11), bears witness that this tradition was also shared with the Ammonites, and it therefore belongs to the early stage of the penetration of Hebrew tribes into Transjordan.

The title half-tribe of Manasseh also includes other tribes whose origin is not clear and whose settlement seems to belong to the fourteenth to twelfth centuries. Prominent among them was Jair who is counted as a son of Manasseh (Num. 32. 41; Deut. 3. 14; 1 Kings 4. 13), and whose settlements are called Havvoth-jair ("encampments of Jair"). The Havvoth-jair were in northern Gilead (1 Kings 4. 13; 1 Chron. 2. 23) and on the border of Bashan (Deut. 3. 14; Josh. 13. 30), perhaps in the region of Ham, according to the amended text of Numbers 32. 41: "and Jair, the son of Manasseh, went and captured Havvoth-ham (for: *havvotheihem*—"their encampments") and he called them Havvoth-jair".[59] A local judge is also known in this area named Jair the Gileadite, who dominated twenty-three cities (cf. 1 Chron. 2. 22) which were called Havvoth-jair (Judg. 10. 3–5). It is possible that these sons of Jair are related to the great tribal federation that is known from Assyrian inscriptions in the Euphrates region beginning with the thirteenth century B.C. Adad-nirari I informs us that his fathers made war along the banks of the River Euphrates with encampments of Aḫlamu, Suti (Seth) and Yauri; Yari, or Yaḫiri are also mentioned in later Assyrian inscriptions.[60] It would seem that segments of them reached northern Gilead by about the thirteenth century and, in the course of time, became joined to the tribes of Israel, being considered "sons of Manasseh".

Another tribal organization which reached eastern Bashan was Nobah, who "went and took Kenath and its villages, and called it Nobah, after his own name" (Num. 32. 42). Kenath is probably Qanawat in eastern Bashan, but we have no additional information about Nobah, and even his connections with Manasseh are not clear.

It would appear, therefore, that in the first stages of settlement Israelite tribes took mainly the southern regions of Transjordan from the Arnon in the south to the Jabbok in the north. Into the northern Gilead and the districts of Bashan various related tribes penetrated at the same time, and only under the force of Machir's occupation at a later stage was this region transformed into an Israelite settlement and the various tribes made "sons of Machir and of Manasseh".

IV. THE HOUSE OF JOSEPH

Today we possess sufficient data to assign the occupation by the House of Joseph to the early wave during the fourteenth century B.C. The crossing of the Jordan from the Plain of Moab is associated with this early wave in Transjordan and with the "plague." Unfortunately, the text is incomplete at this point (Num. 25. 19), but it evidently has to do with a severe plague which left a deep impression on the national memory. It is not impossible that we have here an echo of the fatal plague which rampaged across the Near East for at least twenty years in the mid-fourteenth century, as evidenced by the Amarna letters and Hittite documents.[61]

The capture of Jericho (Josh. 6) also fits this dating. It is true that there was only a small fortress on the top of the mound at that time; the account about the falling of the walls is obviously a legendary embellishment. But the fortress was evidently taken during the third quarter of the fourteenth century.[62] That even may be the historical kernel around which the biblical story has developed.

On the other hand, the conquest of Ai (Josh. 7; 8) is a purely aetiological story lacking historical foundation.[63] It is a typical folk tale faithfully reflecting the situation during the period of the Judges when Israelite villages were being founded on the ancient mounds.[64] It is possible that those traditions had their origins at the shrines of Gilgal and Bethel which were important centres for the tribes during an early stage of the settlement process.[65]

The conquest of Bethel cannot be fixed with any degree of accuracy, either late in the fourteenth or during the thirteenth century,[66] but its capture is not really associated with the first stage of occupation (Judg. 1. 23–26). Nevertheless, we do have archaeological data for the foundation of tribal settlements already during the fourteenth century (cf. *supra,* p. 193).[67]

The concept "House of Joseph" probably included not only the two tribes of Ephraim and Manasseh, who were considered his sons, but also Benjamin, the younger brother of Joseph. It is likely that Ephraim and Benjamin are geographical names connected with their respective districts and do not ante-date the period of the settlement. Mount Ephraim is a geographical expression nearly always associated with all of the central mountain region (Josh. 17. 15; 20. 7; 21. 21; Judg. 7. 24; 1 Sam. 1. 1; 1. Kings 4. 8), and the sufformative *-aim* is a customary locative ending for geographical names. Possibly this name was first associated with the high mountainous district north of Bethel in which the Ephraimite inheritance was centred,[68] and with the increase of this tribe's importance the name was spread over a wider area.

Benjamin is a manifest geographical name meaning "son of the south", which is appropriate for the most southern tribe of the House of Joseph.[69]

Differences of origin did not, therefore, determine the names of the various tribes in the House of Joseph (including Benjamin), but rather the circumstances of their settlement, especially their differing relationships to the Canaanite (Amorite) residents of the hill country. The tribe of Manasseh, which was still called Machir in the days of the war of Deborah, was apparently made up mainly from Hebrew tribes which had entered the northern hill country of Ephraim already in the fourteenth century.[70] In the Bible we do not find any tradition about conquests or wars of Manasseh, in spite of the fact that Shechem appears as a central location in the tribal covenant (Josh. 24). The only warlike information bearing on this area is associated, surprisingly, with the southern tribes (Gen. 34; Judg. 1. 4 ff.), without any connection to occupation by the House of Joseph. It seems evident that Manasseh began by entering into amicable covenant relationships with the Canaanite cities that were in his area. We have already heard about covenant relationships between Shechem and the ʿApiru in the El Amarna period; and it seems that then the various Canaanite cities tried to utilize these unruly elements each to its own advantage. With the entrance of the House of Joseph the balance of power changed, and now the subdued cities joined the framework of the Israelite tribe which had become the dominant factor in the region. This situation is expressed in the genealogy by the inclusion of various Canaanite cities as sons and daughters of Manasseh, e.g. Shechem, Tirzah and Hepher (Num. 26. 31 ff.; 27. 1; Josh. 17. 2 ff.).

The history of Manasseh's settlement and expansion is characterized by the absorption of the Canaanite elements into the framework of the Israelite tribe. This development is dependent upon the nature of the region. In the hills of Judah and in the southern part of the hills of Ephraim the older settlement is mainly limited to the line of the watershed on which ran the main highway (cf. Judg. 20. 31; 21. 19). North of Shechem the hills decrease in height and the road forks out into two main branches, thus causing the settlement to branch out also. The fertile valleys gave rise to a stronger and more dense Canaanite settlement in this area. There were certainly considerable forested and uninhabitable regions here as well, which provided ample opportunity for the settlement by Israelite tribes, and in them they were able to settle alongside the already existing Canaanite cities.[71] On the other hand, the approach roads from the valleys to this region are more convenient than to the other parts of the hill country, thus helping to strengthen the ties between plain and hills.

Ephraim's form of settlement is entirely different from that of Manasseh. Its inheritance extended over the southern and highest part of the mountains of Ephraim. In this region there were only a few isolated Canaanite cities that were evidently conquered quickly and on whose ruins Israelite settlements were built. A special fate was ordained for Tappuah, a Canaanite city (Josh. 12. 17) on the border between Ephraim and Manasseh: "the land of Tappuah belonged to Manasseh, but the town of Tappuah on the boundary of Manasseh belonged to the sons of Ephraim'' (Josh. 17. 8), i.e. in spite of the fact that the Manassites possessed the lands of Tappuah, the city held out until it finally fell to the Ephraimites. The Ephraimite inheritance covered the mountain region only, but it constituted a continuous and uniform Israelite population. These circumstances caused the ascendance of this tribe to its dominant position in the Israelite tribal covenant during the period of the Judges.

Benjamin's region was evidently a focus of opposition between the Israelites and the Canaanite population in the hill country, thus contributing to the warlike nature of that tribe (Gen. 49. 27). Benjamin was compressed into a limited area between Bethel and Jerusalem where he encountered an additional factor—the four Hivite (or Hurrian according to LXX) cities of the Gibeonites: Gibeon (el-Jib), Chephirah (Khirbet el-Kefireh), Baalah=Kiriath-jearim (Deir el- 'Azar), Beeroth (Kh. el-Burj?). The tribe of Benjamin took possession of the land to the east of these cities, along the north-south highway and further east on the fringes of the wilderness. Two tells have been excavated here whose settlement began in the fourteenth to the thirteenth centuries and in whose earliest levels were found sherds typical of the beginning of Israelite settlement. These are: Gibeah (Gibeah of Benjamin, of Saul=Tell el-Ful) and Mizpah (Tell en-Naṣbeh).[72] The archaeological survey proved that between them a dense chain of small settlements was founded during this period, e.g. Ramah, Geba, Michmash, *et al.*

The strength of the Israelites overpowered the Gibeonite cities which submitted to domination by the tribe of Benjamin. Henceforth their area was also considered part of the Benjaminite inheritance (cf. especially 2 Sam. 4. 2), but the cities themselves were not incorporated into the tribal framework and were not reckoned as sons but rather were reduced to the status of lower-grade residents.

Establishment of a covenant of servitude with the Gibeonite cities was a pretence for the central conflict of the conquest, according to the account as preserved in the Bible (Josh. 10; cf. map 15). The Gibeonite cities are not known to us from Egyptian sources, and it seems evident that they were under the jurisdiction of the King of Jerusalem, (cf. *supra,* p. 175).

The King of Jerusalem rallied his allies from the hill country and the Shephelah: Hebron, Jarmuth (Khirbet el-Yarmuk), Lachish and Eglon. In comparing this covenant with the situation of the major cities in the El Amarna period, certain differences stand out. Jerusalem and Lachish appear as royal centres in that period also, and these two rivals now enter the ranks against the common enemy. Jarmuth only appears during the El Amarna period in the letter found at Tell el-Ḥesi (Eglon), in which Lachish is also mentioned (cf. *supra,* p. 174), and apparently this city has taken the place of Shuwardata, King of Gath, in the eastern

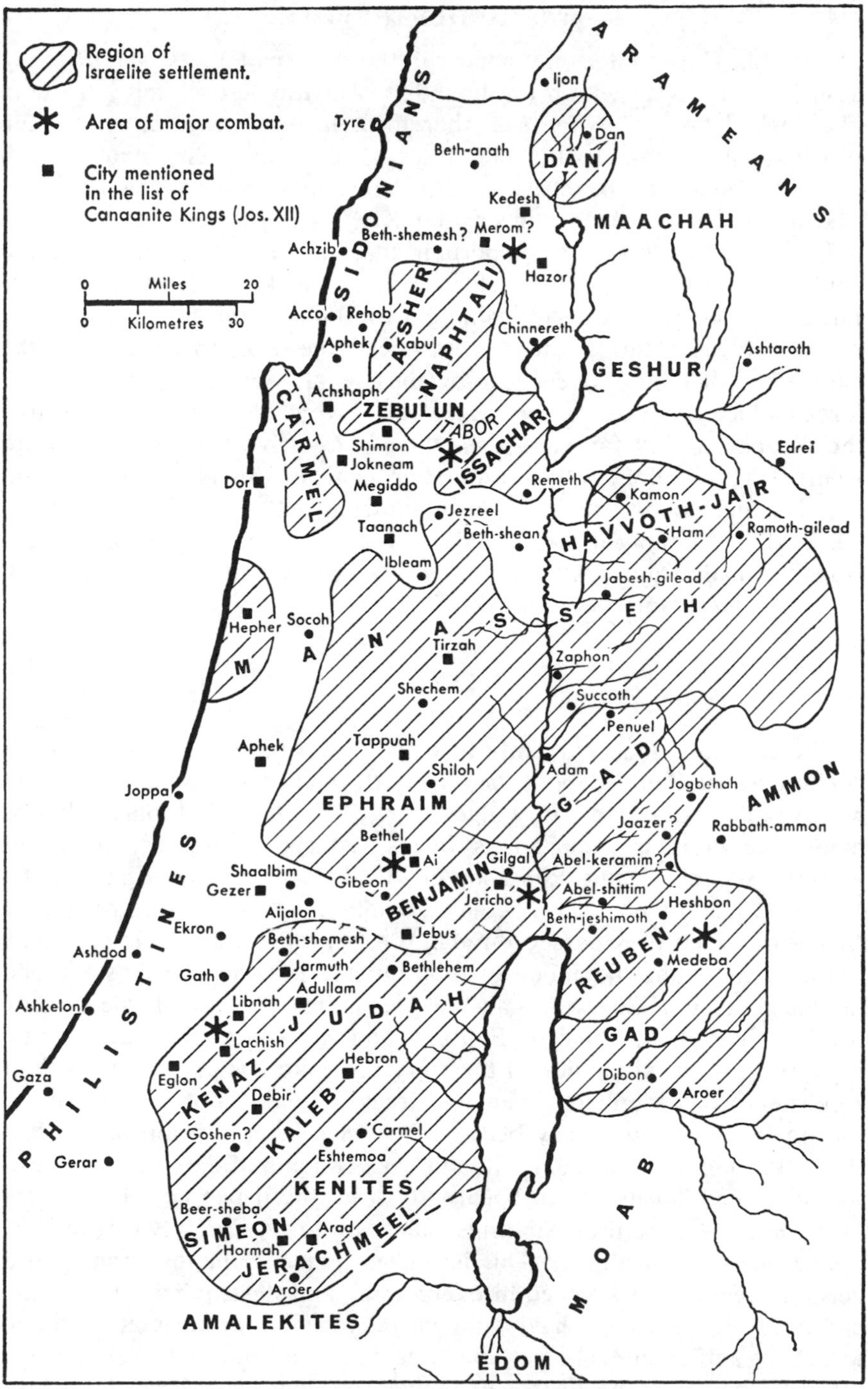

Map 15. The Conquest Narratives and the Regions of Early Israelite Settlement.

Shephelah. Hebron does not appear in the Amarna tablets, and one may assume that it was within the boundaries of the Jerusalemite kingdom like Debir. We are witnesses, therefore, to an intensification of the splitting up process in the old order of Canaanite city-states which evidently facilitated the intrusion of the tribes to the various regions.

Due to the increased danger, the King of Jerusalem succeeded in uniting around himself the important cities in the hill country and the southern and eastern Shephelah in order to make a stand against the Israelites who were steadily gaining a foothold in the territories to the north of Jerusalem. Joshua, from the House of Joseph, dealt the Canaanite alliance a decisive blow beside Gibeon and pursued their forces which were fleeing by way of the ascent of Beth-horon towards the Shephelah, as far as Azekah (Tell Zakariyeh in the Valley of Elah).[73] This victory left a resounding echo in the Israelite tradition, which found poetic expression in the ancient "Book of Jashar" (Josh. 10. 12–13). Probably it was mainly by virtue of this victory that Joshua was eventually transformed into the central personality around whom all of the conquest stories were woven.[74]

V. JUDAH

The tribe of Judah evidently belongs to the later wave of conquest which entered Canaan about the middle of the thirteenth century,[75] and his arrival is described in Judges 1. 1–20.[76] The first place that is mentioned in their campaign is Bezek (Khirbet Ibziq, in the north-eastern part of Mount Ephraim, cf. 1 Sam. 11. 8–11). That is, the Judahites destroyed one of the Canaanite cities in the region of Manasseh when they passed through the Ephraimite hill country. Some scholars doubt the likelihood of this, but the passing of tribes through the hill country of Ephraim is a widespread phenomenon (cf. the journey of Dan through the hills of Ephraim and its warlike conduct in that region). In the continuation of the story the conquest and destruction of Jerusalem are described. Even with regard to this notice there is no reason for doubt, precisely because it stands in opposition to the fact that Jerusalem remained Jebusite and was conquered only in the time of David. The Jebusites were apparently a northern people, Hurrians or Hittites (not Canaanites-Amorites), and we do not know when or how they came to Jerusalem.[77] This is not an unusual phenomenon, that a certain tribe should succeed in overcoming and destroying a Canaanite city in its region without having the means to settle it immediately due to a lack of sufficient technical and organizational ability to rebuild and refortify the town. As further examples, one may cite Hazor, Lachish and Tell Beit Mirsim.

Jerusalem evidently fell after a short time into the hands of the Jebusites who held it until the time of David. The Judahites took possession of the land of Jerusalem south of the city, and Bethlehem became their centre. The more southerly hills of Judah fell to other tribes who eventually became attached to Judah. The hill country from Hebron southward went to the Calebites, including the district of Debir (Kh. Rabud) which fell to their relatives the Kenazites.[78] The genealogical tables (1 Chron. 2; 4) also show us that the district of Hebron and the hill country south of it were occupied by Calebite families, e.g. Beth-zur, Ziph, Madmannah, *et al.* (cf. *infra,* p. 248). Still farther to the south were the areas of the Jerachmeelites and the Kenites. From Judges 1. 16 we learn that the vicinity of Arad was settled by Kenite families who immigrated thither from "the city of palm trees". Jericho, which is a great distance from here, is certainly not meant but rather Zoar at the southern end of the Dead Sea, which is also called "the city of palm trees" in the Talmud (Mishna *Yebamoth* 16. 7), or Tamar to the south of it.

It would seem that this route was the approach taken by the southern tribes—the Kenites, Jerachmeel, Kenaz and Caleb. Also the story of the spies, described as coming up from Kadesh to Hebron (Num. 13. 22), in which Caleb is the only one bringing an encouraging answer (vs. 30)—and likewise the many family connections with the inhabitants of Edom (cf. *infra,* p. 245)—imply the direct immigration of the southern tribes. By contrast, the various traditions teach that Judah and Simeon came from the north and invaded the hill countries of Ephraim and Judah via Transjordan in the same manner as the other Israelite tribes. Evidently, these two tribes were already connected with the tribal covenant; and therefore, in the final analysis, they are counted with the twelve tribes of Israel while the rest of the southern tribes are joined to them and recorded as their sons in the genealogical tables. Regarding the settlement by the Negeb tribes, we now possess archaeological data that indicate their association with the thirteenth century wave.

First of all, it has become clear that the tradition about the encounter of these tribes at the time of their arrival with the King of Arad, who dominated the eastern Negeb and who soundly defeated them at nearby Hormah (Num. 14. 44–45; 21. 1; 33. 40; Deut. 1. 44) is not well founded historically. The excavations at Arad have shown that settlement at the site occurred in the thirteenth-twelfth centuries after a gap of *c.* 1500 years.[79] Thus, there was no centre there for a Canaanite principality. Glueck has suggested that the King of Arad was a sort of bedouin sheikh,[80] while Fritz sees here an aetiological story like that about Ai.[81] Mazar believes that in this period Arad was not a city but only a region, i.e. the Negeb of Arad (Judg. 1. 16),[82] while the King of Arad resided at Hormah, which he identifies with Tel Milḥ (Malḥata).[83] But it seems more probable that Canaanite Arad was located at Tell Milh while Hormah was at neighbouring Kh. el-Meshash (T. Masos). Both these sites were occupied during Middle Bronze Age II and are located beside abundant wells. This idea receives support from the topographical list of Shishak,[84] which mentions two fortresses named Arad, viz. Great Arad and Arad of the house of *yrḥm* (Nos. 107–12), probably a clipped form of Jerahmeel. It is, therefore, most likely that the region of early Arad fell into the hands of the Jerahmeelites (cf. the Negeb of Jerahmeel and the cities of Jerahmeel, 1 Sam. 27. 10; 30. 29) while that north-eastern portion of the Negeb of Arad bordering on the Judean wilderness was occupied by families of the Kenites (Judg. 1. 16). Hormah, on the other hand, was settled by Simeon whose patrimony centred on the Beer-sheba region (Josh. 19. 4; 1 Chron. 4. 30; Judg. 1. 17). The name Hormah was explained now, not in terms of a Canaanite victory but just the opposite, as a memorial to the defeat and banishment of the Canaanites by the sons of Israel (Num. 21. 3).[85]

These proposed identifications conform well to the available data. At both Tell Milḥ and Kh. Meshash earthen ramparts of the Hyksos period were found, the only ones in that vicinity. That at Kh. Meshash was founded *c.* 1800 B.C. and existed for only a short period, but the enclosure at Tell Milḥ endured to the end of Middle Bronze Age II. As previously mentioned, Hormah seems to be mentioned in the execration texts and in a Sinai inscription from *c.* 1800 B.C. which would apply nicely to this southern site. At Kh. Meshash the largest unfortified, tribal settlement of the whole area has been found and this would be most suitable for the Hormah of Simeon. Even the strange allusion to the transfer of the name from Zephath to Hormah (Judge. 1. 17) may find its solution in this manner. At the beginning of the monarchy the Israelite settlement was transferred from Kh. Meshash to the nearby Kh. Gharrah (T. 'Ira) which dominates the whole region from its lofty perch. This latter place would suit remarkably well the name Zephath, "look out," and the tradition was transferred there from the true Hormah.

These identifications notwithstanding, no Late Bronze remains have been found either in the eastern or the western Negeb. With the arrival of the tribes, this area was void of Canaanite settlement. Therefore, the conquest tradition pertaining to it is not firmly anchored in history. Yet it is striking how well the traditions do reflect the geographical and occupational pattern when the two fortresses of Tell Milḥ and Kh. Meshash prevented the penetration of nomadic elements into the Negeb of Arad for a long period of time. This looks too authentic to be purely coincidental. Therefore, it would appear that we have a centuries old tradition taken over later by the Israelite tribes who finally came into possession of the area.

The Negeb, therefore, was one of those areas where the tribes encountered little or no resistance except the forces of nature. Their settlement became most intensive. At all the ancient ruined sites, they set up new settlements while other sites were founded for the first time, such as Beer-sheba.

Our clearest evidence concerning these settlements derives from Kh. Meshash. This is due not only to the vast extent of the new community, occupying an area of about 12 acres, but also because it was situated on a low, previously unoccupied hill, and was not destroyed by massive fortifications in the monarchial period. The various structures were easily uncovered by the excavations and several extensive quarters of the town have been laid bare.[86]

Three strata were discerned, the best preserved being the second because the upper was badly eroded and the first was reached only in limited areas. But it was clear that even the earliest stratum (III) had covered the entire site and it had also been preceded by an occupation phase represented only by pits and silos. The earliest pottery comes from the very end of the Late Bronze Age (thirteenth century B.C.) and an Egyptian scarab, apparently of the Nineteenth Dynasty, i.e. Seti II,[87] supports the assumption that the settlement was founded during the thirteenth century.

The pottery of stratum II also points in this direction since it contains Philistine (second half of the twelfth century)[88] and Midianite sherds (thirteenth-twelfth centuries).[89] Most of the buildings excavated belong to the type known as the "Four Unit House" with two rows of pillars down the long axis and a broad room at the back. Such houses are also well known from Israelite settlements in the north. Some fortified public buildings were also found. One of them was surrounded by a brick wall with salients in the style of Egyptian architecture. The wealth of small finds is surprising, including the pottery, especially a decorated bi-chrome ware known previously only from the northern coastal area, e.g. Tell Abu Huwam (IV) and Megiddo (VI), as well as luxury articles like an ivory lion's head carved in the best Canaanite tradition. All this testifies to the wealth of the settlement and to the open trade routes between the Mediterranean and the Gulf of ʻAqabah (Elath).

The picture that results from these excavations is most surprising.[90] This is not a primitive settlement as often supposed, but intensive occupation starting with the thirteenth century. If an unfortified settlement could exist during more than 200 years it becomes obvious that this was a relatively quiet period in which the Israelite settlements were not threatened by a dangerous rival. During the twelfth and eleventh centuries the Israelites even spread farther south. Along the routes through the southern wildnerness small settlements with the same pillared structures have been found, as well as a fortress at Beer-sheba from the first half of the eleventh century which may have served as the main centre for this southern network of forts and settlements.[91]

Therefore, one may now comprehend the southern zone, known as the Negeb, as one of the marginal areas of occupation like the hill country. In such zones as these the Israelite tribes were forced to make their new homes. This is the situation alluded to in the Bible, even with regard to the tribe of Simeon[92]: "They journeyed to the entrance of Gedor to the east side of the valley, to seek pasture for their flocks, where they found rich, good pasture, and the land was very broad, quiet, and peaceful; for the former inhabitants there belonged to Ham" (1 Chron. 4. 39–40). Though the Hebrew text refers to the enigmatic Gedor (Gerar according to LXX),[93] the date implied by the passage makes the description appropriate for the whole region. The memory of the autochthonous population is somewhat vague because sons of Ham could be Egyptians, Philistines or Canaanites (Gen. 10. 6–20).

In Judges 1. 18 we find the vague reference to a conquest of Gaza, Ashkelon and Ekron by Judah. It is difficult to conceive how Judah could have succeeded, during the initial period of settlement, in gaining control over these important cities along the *Via Maris,* which were centres of Egyptian authority and which became Philistine capitals in the middle of the twelfth century. Though it is true that an intermediate stratum was found at Ashdod between the Egyptian/Canaanite and the Philistine city,[94] the pottery in this stratum does not point to an occupation by the Israelites. Ekron was apparently founded by the Philistines, because in an exacting survey of its mound no earlier remains were found;[95] and it is difficult to conceive how Philistine Ekron could have been conquered by Judah at this early stage. It is plausible, therefore, that one should follow the LXX, "And Judah did *not* capture . . . " (in place of the Heb., "And Judah captured . . . "), and thus we more readily comprehend the meaning of the following passage: "And the Lord was with Judah, and he took possession of the hill country, but he could *not* drive out the inhabitants of the plain because they had chariots of iron" (Judg. 1. 19).

The conquest of the Canaanite cities in the hill country and in the Shephelah appears as a continuation of the Gibeonite war (Josh. 10. 16 ff.). First there is the aetiological story about the slaying of the five kings in a cave at Makkedah, which serves as a connecting link between the Gibeonite war and the conquest narrative concerning the various cities. Then, by way of continuation, the fall of Makkedah, Libnah, Lachish, Eglon, Hebron and Debir are recounted (cf. map 15). The uniform reiteration of city after city being conquered is only interrupted by the notice that the King of Gezer tried vainly to come to the aid of Lachish, and again we are reminded of the connections between Lachish and Gezer in the El Amarna period.

One must surely distinguish in essence between the Gibeonite war, which concerns the House of Joseph, and the conquest of the Shephelah, which has to do with the southern tribes, especially since the Canaanite members of the alliance and the cities which were conquered do not fully coincide. It is also necessary to distinguish between the conquest of the towns in the Shephelah and those in the hill country. The conquest of the latter, Hebron and Debir, is associated with Caleb and Kenaz as mentioned above. For this reason those towns come at the end of the narrative, and in the same order, and there is no point in searching for strategic factors that would determine the order of these conquests.[96]

In the narrative under discussion there remains, therefore, the conquest of four towns in the southern Shephelah: Lachish (Tell ed-Duweir), Eglon (Tell el-Ḥesi) and Makkedah, all three of which are included by Joshua 15. 39–41 in one district, and Libnah (Tell el-Bornaṭ?) a bit farther north. At this point the tradition is preserved about the conquest of several cities in the vicinity of Lachish. In this light it is possible to understand why the King of Gezer tried to aid Lachish, the central and largest of these towns.

In the excavations carried out at Lachish, Tell Beit Mirsim and Tell el-Ḥesi it was demonstrated that these cities suffered a total destruction at about the end of the Bronze Age. Lachish and Tell Beit Mirsim remained deserted for quite a while, which is typical of the cities conquered at an early stage of the Israelite settlement. The occupation of Tell el-Ḥesi was renewed, evidently after some passage of time, perhaps as a Philistine settlement; but it was limited to the small area of the ancient acropolis. This gap is the strongest argument that we are dealing here with traces of the Israelite conquest. It is still impossible to establish a more accurate date for these ventures. Imported Mycenean pottery of type III B (*c.* the end of the thirteenth century B.C.) was discovered in the destruction levels of all these sites. However, a date somewhat earlier or later cannot be excluded. The suggestion to fix a more precise date for the destruction of a Canaanite city was made with reference to Lachish on the basis of an Egyptian inscription on a bowl found in the city's destruction level; that text included a date in the fourth year of a pharaoh whose name is not given.[97] Albright insisted that the Pharaoh in question was most likely Merneptah,[98] but in more recent excavations another bowl has been found with an inscribed date of year 10 or more.[99] A scarab of Ramses III was also found, though out of stratigraphic context.

In any case, it is probable that the conquest of the cities in the Shephelah took place later than the beginning of settlement by the Judean tribes in the mid-thirteenth century. Therefore, we get the following picture: at first Judah took possession of the hill country around Bethlehem. From here, Judean clans spread out to the northern

Shephelah by nurturing friendly relationships with the Canaanite cities in this area, as we learn especially from the affair of Judah and Tamar (Gen. 38), in which Adullam, Kezib and Timnah are mentioned. At the same time the southern parts of the Judean hill country and the Negeb were seized by various tribes coming in, partly from the south (Caleb, Kenaz, Jerachmeel and the Kenites). At the end of the thirteenth century or, at the very latest, the beginning of the twelfth, the decisive battle was fought between the King of Lachish and the invading Judean tribes, as a consequence of which Lachish and its vicinity were conquered under the momentum of the Judean attack. Gezer's help did not save Lachish; however, Gezer and its neighbouring Amorite cities stood up to the Israelite pressure (Judg. 1. 29, 35, etc.). These conquests took place during the decline of the Nineteenth Egyptian Dynasty when the central authority in Canaan ceased, and conditions were ripe for the ultimate confrontation between Israel and Canaan.

VI. THE WARS IN THE NORTH

Galilee was occupied by four Israelite tribes: Issachar, Zebulun, Asher and Naphtali. Asher, who took western Galilee, is already mentioned in Egyptian inscriptions from the end of the fourteenth century. They settled down as neighbours to the strong Phoenician coastal cities, "among the Canaanites, the inhabitants of the land; for they did not drive them out" (Judg. 1. 32). Issachar occupied the eastern part of the Jezreel Valley and the hills north of it. The tribe was consolidated mainly from among the corvée workers, part of whom had already come to this area during the Amarna period.

These two tribes belong to an early wave. They had penetrated into the well-developed Canaanite area in the north but were only able to gain a foothold there by remaining subservient to the powerful cities.

We do not know the circumstances surrounding the occupation by the other two tribes. The inheritance of Zebulun extended over the central part of southern Galilee between the Jezreel Valley and the Valley of Beth Netophah (Sahl el-Baṭṭof). Naphtali took a wide area in eastern and central Galilee. From the active participation of these two tribes in the war of Deborah it is permissible to conclude that at this date they were already well established in their areas.

An archaeological survey in Galilee proved that the Israelite settlement took place in the interior parts of Lower and Upper Galilee, which were forested and unoccupied during the Bronze Age.[100] This is especially noticeable in the southern extremity of Upper Galilee which is the highest region of Galilee and the least convenient for settlement. Farther to the north a chain of Canaanite tells was discovered including, among others, Kedesh, Merom (Tell el-Khirbeh?), Jish (Gush-ḥalav = Gishala), Tell er-Ruweisi and Iqrit. In this area we probably must also look for Beth-shemesh and Beth-anath, the two Canaanite cities not conquered by Naphtali during the early stages of occupation (Judg. 1. 33). At the beginning of the Iron Age a dense Israelite population blossomed out precisely in the southern part where there are no Canaanite tells. This situation corresponds to the general picture of Israelite tribal penetration into the unsettled hill country not long after their arrival because of the superior strength of the Canaanite cities. From this it would appear that the Galilean tribes also began to occupy the forested hill regions of inner Galilee, and only at a later stage were they able to pit their strength against the Canaanite cities all around them in the valleys and in the table land of Upper Galilee.

The Bible preserves two descriptions of wars in the north: the battle at the waters of Merom (Josh. 11. 1–9) and the battle of Deborah (Judg. 4; 5; cf. map 16). The former is associated with Joshua and the latter with the period of the Judges. In both of them Jabin, King of Hazor, stands at the head of the Canaanite alliance, in spite of the fact that a tradition concerning the total destruction of Hazor is connected with the battle of Merom (Josh. 11. 10–13).

This difficulty has led some scholars to the conclusion that two different battles are confused in the tradition about Deborah. In their opinion Jabin did not originally belong to the Deborah story but only Sisera from Harosheth-ha-goiim, notably as Jabin's name is not mentioned in the Song of Deborah.[101] However, this reconstruction encounters serious obstacles. By comparison of the narrative chapter (Judg. 4) with the Song of Deborah (Judg. 5) it becomes clear that the prose passage does not depend upon the poem but furnishes various independent details which fit together to form a logical picture. On the other hand, the song, as is natural with poetry, jumps from one detail to another and by no means provides a complete reconstruction of the battle. In the middle it simply refers to the kings of Canaan without mentioning their names, and Sisera comes on the stage only with the description of the clash, his defeat and his death. How shall we explain the origin of that tradition which makes Sisera the commander of Jabin's army and which is also attested elsewhere (1 Sam. 12. 9; Ps. 83. 9 [Heb. vs. 10])? Sisera's flight towards "the oak of Zaanannim" (RSV, following the *Qeri*; Judg. 4. 11), which is known to be on the border of Naphtali's tribal inheritance in the vicinity of the Jabneel Valley (Josh. 19. 33), takes him away from the battle zone in the direction of Hazor.[102] It seems still more difficult to understand the rise of Harosheth-ha-goiim to the head of the Canaanite alliance, a place completely unknown in all other sources, both biblical and non-biblical.[103] It appears likely that Harosheth-ha-goiim is not a place name at all but refers rather to the forested regions of Galilee, i.e. "Galilee of the nations (Heb. ha-goiim)", in Isaiah's archaizing expression (Isa. 9. 1).[104] The LXX translates this expression in Judges 4. 16 as:

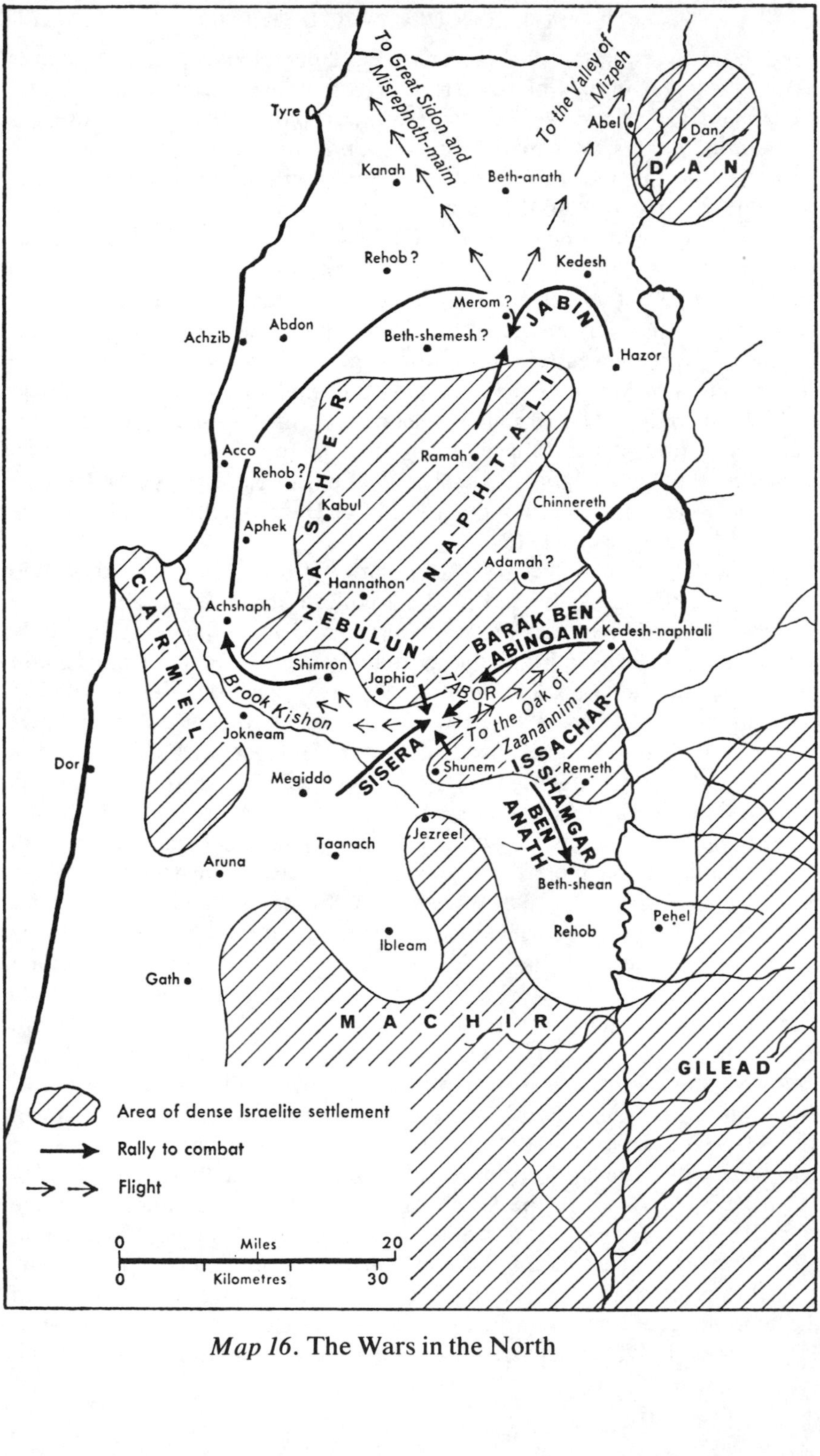

To Great Sidon and Misrephoth-maim
To the Valley of Mizpeh
Tyre
Abel
Dan
DAN
Kanah
Beth-anath
Rehob ?
Kedesh
Merom ?
JABIN
Achzib
Abdon
Beth-shemesh ?
Hazor
ASHER
NAPHTALI
Acco
Ramah
Rehob ?
Kabul
Chinnereth
Aphek
Adamah ?
CARMEL
Hannathon
Achshaph
ZEBULUN
BARAK BEN ABINOAM
Kedesh-naphtali
Shimron
Japhia
TABOR
Brook Kishon
To the Oak of Zaanannim
ISSACHAR
Jokneam
SISERA
Shunem
Remeth
Dor
Megiddo
SHAMGAR BEN ANATH
Jezreel
Taanach
Aruna
Beth-shean
Pehel
Ibleam
Rehob
Gath
MACHIR
GILEAD
Area of dense Israelite settlement
Rally to combat
Flight
0
Miles
20
0
Kilometres
30

Map 16. The Wars in the North

ἕως δρυμοῦ τῶν ἐθνῶν. . . ., showing that in the Hellenistic period it was already taken to mean "as far as the forest of the Gentiles". Therefore, a better solution to the difficulties is perhaps to accept the descriptions of the two battles as they are but to reverse the order of events.[105] According to this theory the two wars do not belong to the first stage of penetration but to a later period, and the battle of Merom was eventually associated with Joshua and all of Israel exactly as were the various battles in Judah. This assumption is supported by the results of the Galilee survey which show a stage of occupation that preceded the conquest of the Canaanite districts. It also conforms nicely to the internal logic of the event.

The battle of Deborah was preceded by a period of oppression of the Israelite communities by Sisera when the kings of the Canaanite cities apparently tried to impose their authority upon the tribes in Galilee (Judg. 4. 2–3; 5. 6). That Sisera "dwelt" (Heb. ישב) in Harosheth-ha-goiim, i.e. in the Galilee forests, means that he ruled that area as a governor and tyrant, just as Joab, the commander of David's army, "dwelt" (ישב) in Edom (1 Kings 11. 16) and Omri, King of Israel, "dwelt" in the Mishor of Moab (Mesha Stele, line 8).[106]

A considerable number of Canaanite kings participated in the alliance (Judg. 5. 19), having at their disposal 900 chariots of iron (Judg. 4. 3), a number which reminds one of the booty taken by Thut-mose III at the battle of Megiddo. It is possible that the list of defeated Canaanite kings (Josh. 12; cf. *infra*, p. 230) provides us with the major cities that participated in the battle as allies of Hazor, viz. Taanach and Megiddo (also mentioned in the Song of Deborah; Judg. 5. 19), Jokneam and Shimron (Shim 'on) in the Valley of Jezreel, Dor on the coast of Carmel, Achshaph in the Plain of Acco, Kedesh and apparently Merom (instead of Madon) in Upper Galilee—these cities are well known Canaanite centres in the northern valleys and in the Canaanite sectors of Upper Galilee. After them is mentioned "the King of Goiim in Galilee" (RSV following LXX; Heb. "Gilgal"; Josh. 12. 23) which may be a reference to "Galilee of the Gentiles (הגוים)". Apparently the list of Canaanite kings was made up from traditions about the wars of conquest more detailed than those preserved in the Bible, and the names of the northern kings were taken from stories about the battles in this region. We are not surprised that there is no city in the list by the name Harosheth-ha-goiim, but rather the ruler of "Goiim in Galilee" (cf. *infra*, p. 231).

At the head of the Israelite tribes that took part in the conflict stood Barak the son of Abinoam from Kedesh-naphtali, even though the initiative came from Deborah the prophetess whose home was "between Ramah and Bethel in the hill country of Ephraim".[107] It was generally accepted to identify the birthplace of Barak with Kedesh in Upper

Galilee (Tell Qades), which is mentioned as one of the Levitical cities and a city of refuge, counted among the fortified towns of Naphtali (Josh. 19. 37; 20. 7; 21. 32), viz. "Kedesh in Galilee in the hill country of Naphtali" (Josh. 20. 7). In reality this identification is absurd, because Kedesh was one of the great Canaanite cities in Upper Galilee which, according to Joshua 12, joined the ranks against the Israelites. From the narrative about the battle of Deborah it is clear that the Israelite Kedesh-naphtali was in the vicinity of the Jabneel Valley not far from Tabor. It was close to the oak of Zaanannim (Judg. 4. 11; cf. *supra*) on the southern border of Naphtali between Tabor and the Jordan (Josh. 19. 32); and since Barak assembled his troops there before the battle, it would have been ridiculous to march first to Upper Galilee, far away from the field of battle. East of the Valley of Jabneel, high on the slopes leading down to the Sea of Galilee, there is a large site from the Israelite period with many remains from the age of the Judges named Khirbet Qedish which fits the Kedesh-naphtali of Barak in every respect.[108]

The engagement itself took place at the foot of Mount Tabor (Judg. 4. 6, 12, 14).[109] The Israelite troops assembled on the sacred mount itself (Deut. 33. 19), at which the borders of Naphtali, Zebulun and Issachar came together. According to the narrative, Zebulun and Naphtali joined in the engagement (Judg. 4. 10); and according to the poem Issachar, Machir, Ephraim and Benjamin also participated (Judg. 5. 14–17). There is no need to see a contradiction here: Zebulun and Naphtali were two of the Galilean tribes that took an active part in the battle; this fact also stands out in the poem (Judg. 5. 18). The remaining tribes of the northern Israelite covenant came to their aid—Issachar in whose territory the battle took place and the three tribes from the Ephraimite hill country (the House of Joseph), viz. Machir [*sic!*], Ephraim and Benjamin. Other tribes failed to take part in the engagement for various reasons. Asher was unable to free himself from the pressure of the Phoenician cities in whose vicinity he was settled, and likewise Dan, who perhaps was already situated in the north by this time.[110] The Transjordanian tribes, viz. Reuben and Gilead [*sic!*], were outside of the land of Canaan and only somewhat loosely connected with the Israelite alliance. The southern tribes are not mentioned at all; it was inconceivable that they should participate in a northern engagement at this period.

The two topographical names mentioned in the description of the battle are Mount Tabor and the Brook Kishon (Judge. 4. 13; 5. 21). Therefore, it is probable that the actual fighting took place somewhere between them. The Kishon played an important role in the downfall of the Canaanite chariotry because its rising waters swept away the chariots as they retreated (Judg. 5. 21). Sisera's retreat in the direction of the Jabneel Valley (towards the oak of Zaa[na]nnim) also testifies that the fight took place near Mount Tabor. In the light of these facts it is possible to reconstruct the general course of the engagement as follows: the Canaanites put all their trust in the powerful chariotry at their disposal, just as they were accustomed to doing against the Egyptians (cf. Thut-mose III's conquest of Megiddo; cf. also *supra,* p. 154). Sisera was doubtless expecting that the appearance of the chariotry would suffice to terrify the tribal forces and cause them to scatter. He therefore made his brazen approach to Mount Tabor. To his great surprise the Israelite troops did not disperse when the chariots came on the scene. What is more, by choosing the moment of attack (Judg. 4. 14) Deborah deprived the chariots of their most potent sting, viz. the element of surprise. This was the first time that Israelite forces had dared to match blows with the mighty Canaanite chariotry and hence the deep impression made by this engagement which is so beautifully expressed in the biblical tradition. The Canaanite chariotry was routed; a sudden rising of the Brook Kishon,[111] which flowed across the plain between the Valley of Chesulloth and the Canaanite cities on the southern side of the plain, turned their reverse into a smashing defeat and prevented most of the chariots from returning to their bases.

The victory was not followed up by the conquest of the Canaanite cities, but the defeat of their chariotry on the plain brought an end to Canaanite hegemony in the north, and the dyke protecting the Canaanite territories collapsed before the pressure of Israelite tribes hungry for land: "so on that day God subdued Jabin, the King of Canaan, before the people of Israel. And the hand of the people of Israel bore harder and harder on Jabin, the King of Canaan, until they destroyed Jabin, King of Canaan" (Judg. 4. 23–4).

The battle of Merom took place in Upper Galilee. The "waters of Merom" must be the water source of the city Merom beside which the Canaanite forces assembled. Merom is known both from second-millennium Egyptian sources (from the reign of Ramses II and perhaps also Thut-mose III, cf. *supra,* p. 162) and from Tiglath-pileser III's account of his expedition to Galilee in 733–732 B.C. (*Marum*).[112] The description of the retreat provides further attestation that the encounter took place in the heart of Upper Galilee (Josh. 11. 8). One certainly cannot assume that this is an exact delineation of the line of march, because it corresponds too closely to the borders of the Canaanite lands unconquered by the Israelites (Josh. 13. 4–6; cf. *infra,* pp. 237). However, its importance is not diminished, because the fact remains that these lines of retreat can only be associated with Upper Galilee. It is generally accepted to identify Merom with Meirun at the foot of Jebel Jarmaq,[113] but in the absence of a suitable tell at this site,[114] an identification a bit farther north is preferable. Its name is possibly preserved in Jebel Marun and Marun er-Ras,[115] and we may consider its identification with Tell el-Khirbeh, one of the large Canaanite tells in the southern part of Canaanite Upper Galilee.[116] From Hazor both of the suggested identifications are about seven to eight miles as the crow flies.

In this conflict only three cities are mentioned on the side of Hazor: Achshaph on the Plain of Acco, Shimron (Shim ʿon) at the north-west edge of Jezreel and Madon. Madon is not mentioned in any other source and therefore it seems preferable to follow the LXX reading: Μαρρων—Maron, i.e. Merom where the battle took place (according to LXX, the "waters of Merom", ὕδωρ Μαρρων).[117] It is possible, however, that only the main cities in their respective regions were listed and that the alliance actually resembled in composition that in the battle of Deborah. The encounter took place not far from Hazor; according to the narrative the Israelites attacked the enemy forces concentrated at Merom to protect Canaanite interests in Upper Galilee. In the biblical account the Israelites capitalized on their victory by conquering the Canaanite cities, and the absolute devastation of Hazor is given special emphasis.

The Hazor excavations[118] have generally confirmed these assumptions, although various questions remain unsettled. Beginning with the Middle Bronze II period there was built on this site the largest Canaanite city in Palestine, having an area of about 200 acres, of which more than 175 acres comprised the great lower city founded early in the Hyksos period (cf. *supra,* p. 148 f).[119] Evidently the title "King of Canaan (Amurru?)" and the remark that "Hazor formerly was the head of all those kingdoms." (Josh. 11. 10) reflects the Hyksos period when a role of unprecedented importance in Palestine was enjoyed by this city (cf. *supra,* p. 148). Although a certain decline took place at Hazor in the course of the Late Bronze Age, a phenomenon common to most Canaanite cities, it maintained its expanded size until the thirteenth century, including both the upper and lower portions of the tell. It therefore continued to be one of the greatest, and perhaps the greatest, of the Canaanite cities.

The city suffered a total destruction at the end of the Late Bronze Age. No inscriptions were discovered by which one could fix an exact date for its devastation, but in the two latest Canaanite levels (XIV and XII) there were all of the pottery types typical of late strata from the Late Bronze Age, including Mycenaean III B imports which, according to all opinons, belong to the thirteenth century.

Before the total destruction of Hazor a sharp decline took place. This is especially noticeable in the lower city which evidently ceased to be fortified in the last stratum. Its temples were abandoned and apparently plundered, being rebuilt afterwards in a very poor and temporary form. This last town (stratum XIII), which was concentrated mainly on the high tell in an area of about 15 acres, suffered an utter devastation and burning, after which the Canaanite occupation was not renewed.

On the upper tell only traces were found of temporary buildings (stratum XII) erected on the ruins of the last Canaanite town. The pottery of this stratum resembles that of the Israelite settlements discovered in the archaeological survey of Upper Gaiilee.[120] It is clear, therefore, that this was an Israelite attempt at settlement which failed, because the city was soon abandoned and left in ruins until Solomon's time.[121] Some Galilean pþttery was found in the last Canaanite city, Stratum XIII.

The total destruction of Hazor and the attempted Israelite settlement conforms well to the biblical tradition that the city was demolished by the Israelites. It also seems likely that the sharp decline which preceded the final collapse (between strata XIV and XIII) came as a consequence of the war of Deborah. Not only was the city weakened by the collapse of its forces in the engagement but also the subsequent Israelite domination of the routes leading to Hazor, and perhaps of its villages and fields as well, caused a strangulation of the city that brought about its swift downfall. The battle of Merom was a last desperate attempt to defend the Canaanite "hinterland" of Hazor in Galilee, and it is clear that after this second defeat it could not maintain its existence. Hazor was no longer able to make a stand once all of the region was in Israelite hands; its strength waned and it doubtless fell quite rapidly.

Today we possess various data which permit us to fix a more exact date for those events, based on the correlation of archaeological evidence with the historical sources. We shall not base our argument on the reference to Shamgar son of Anath, who is credited with defeating the Philistines in the Song of Deborah (Judg. 5. 6). Many suggestions have been made about him; he is usually held to be a heroic leader of a band of Canaanite warriors—all this because of his name.[122] As for Jael, the wife of Heber the Kenite who "had separated from the Kenites, the descendants of Hobab the father-in-law of Moses, and had pitched his tent as far away as the oak in Zaananim, which is near Kedesh" (Judg. 1. 11), we now posses some new chronological data from the excavations at Arad. In the light of the high place and later sanctuary at the latter site, the Kenites, relatives of Moses, now appear as an honored priestly clan (Judg. 1. 15). Thus, we may assume that the oak in Zaananim was also a sacred site.[123]

Jael in her role as charismatic leader reminds us of Deborah and Jael with Shamgar appear as a pair of deliverers who preceded Deborah and Barak. As for the nature of the mighty deed which may have been ascribed to their joint leadership, one can only speculate. A date for that event as late as the Philistine occupation is out of the question. The only possibility here is an early arrival of one of the Sea Peoples. The only evidence pertaining to such a presence in the northern part of the country derives from Beth-shean. Some members of an Aegean ethnic group were evidently serving in that garrison as indicated by their anthropoidal coffins discovered there.[124] Of course, the older assumption that all anthropoid coffins are to be associated with the Sea Peoples has now been disproved by the discovery of such coffins in the burials of Egyptian dignitaries at Deir el-Balaḥ south of Gaza.[125] But at Beth-shean there are some sound indications that Aegean mercenaries were being buried in them. Some of the Beth-shean coffins have grotesque features and are adorned with head-dresses resembling those documented for the Philistines, the Danunians, the Sikels, etc., in the reliefs of Ramses III. In one of the burials a golden mouthpiece was found, a distinctly Aegean feature.[126]

Therefore, we interpret the deed of Shamgar as the capture of the Egyptian fortress at Beth-shean, an act which would appeal both to the Israelites and the Canaanites. Still, it is not possible to use the presence of the anthropoid coffins in fixing the date of Shamgar's deed since their relation to the stratigraphy is obscure.

The clearest date can be derived from the excavations at Megiddo and Taanach, the two cities mentioned in the Song of Deborah (Judg. 5. 19), which obviously existed as Canaanite cities in that period. The stratigraphy is clear at Megiddo: stratum VII A was destroyed during the third quarter of the 12th century, not later than *c.* 1125 B.C. This is obvious from the Egyptian inscriptions found there: an ivory box with the name of Ramses III from the treasure room of the stratum VII A palace and the base of a statue of Ramses VI found in a later stratum but evidently deriving from stratum VII A.

There is no doubt that Stratum VII A represents the last Canaanite city that could have played a role in the battle with Deborah. It is the last city with fortifications, a gate, a palace and the traditional Canaanite temple. The succeeding stratum, VI B, is an unfortified village lacking any public buildings. The 2000 year tradition of the sacred area is finally gone.

Everything points to the assumption that Stratum VI B is the first Israelite settlement. It suddenly contains a wealth of "collared rim" jars, and also pillared buildings, features typical of the Israelite settlements that sprang up in the hill country. The continuation of Canaanite pottery types alongside these new ones cannot be taken as an indication of the ethnic composition of the population, especially since such vessels have now been found at Kh. el-Meshash in the Negeb, where they have obviously been brought via the trade routes from the coast.

But this question is not pertinent for the date of Deborah's battle. It is sufficient to state that stratum VII A is the last Canaanite city that can be considered, and this is not disputed. This has been confirmed by Lapp's excavations at Taanach. The last Canaanite city there was destroyed at about the same time as Megiddo VII A and after its destruction the site was deserted until the beginning of the Monarchy.[127]

The third quarter of the 12th century is, therefore, the *terminus ad quem* for the battle of Deborah, but the historical-geographical sources point to an even earlier date. Taanach and Megiddo are mentioned in the list of unconquered Canaanite cities in the territory of Manasseh (Judg. 1. 27). The excavations at Taanach and Megiddo leave no doubt that this list, in its original form, cannot be later than the mid-12th century. The tribal situation in this roster is completely different from that in the Deborah chapters. Manasseh is now settled in northern Mt. Ephraim and Issachar remains unmentioned (just as it also lacks a border description of its own). During the time of Deborah, on the other hand, Issachar still plays an active role and Machir appears among the Mt. Ephraim tribes. But now Machir is the main tribe in Transjordan and also "in Issachar . . . Manasseh had . . . the inhabitants of Taanach and its villages and the inhabitants of Megiddo and its villages" (Josh. 17. 11). Between this situation, when Canaanite Taanach and Megiddo still existed beside Manasseh, which cannot be later than the mid-12th century, and the tribal situation in the days of Deborah and Barak, there occurred the fatal weakening of Issachar, the migration of Machir and the ascent and expansion of Manasseh. Though this does not provide an exact date, it indicates a process not of years but of generations.

To this we may add some more general historical considerations. Encounters of the scale of the battle of Deborah would hardly be tolerated by a strong Egyptian regime. Since a date during the decline of the 20th Dynasty is now out of the question, the only likely period is that of the weakening of the 19th Dynasty. A date late in the 13th century is thus the latest possible, but an even earlier date is not implausible. The later years of Ramses II's long reign was undoubtedly a time of relative weakness and the appearance of Israel as a people in the Mernephtah Stele may be the result of its crystallization and coalescence after the Deborah battle. The same text (i.e. Mernephtah's) reveals that the whole country was in revolt, from Ashkelon to Yeno'am.

This also agrees well with the evidence from Hazor, and there is no chronological argument in favour of excising the reference to Hazor in the Deborah text (Judg. 4. 2, 23-24). On the highest point of the tell a small high place was discovered (Stratum XI), later than the Israelite settlement of Stratum XII. The material remaining connected with it are all in the best Late Bronze tradition; thus it is clear that the unsuccessful Israelite settlement cannot be later than about the end of the 13th century.

These are revolutionary conclusions which will meet with much resistance from scholars used to a completely different view. However, the previous interpretations of some of these points have been shaken by more recent archaeological evidence.

VII. THE LIST OF CANAANITE KINGS

All of the cities mentioned in the conquest narratives are listed in a summary of the defeated Canaanite kings (Josh. 12. 7–24), roughly according to the order of their appearance in the various stories. The list includes some additional names as well, especially in the central and northern regions, and in this lies its main importance. It is clear that the author had before him additional descriptions more detailed than those which have been preserved. Therefore, the list supplements our knowledge to some degree, although in most cases we cannot know to which source a particular city belongs.

The list was evidently composed in a manner similar to that of the Egyptian topographical lists in which the kings of conquered towns are depicted as prisoners being led by the hand of Pharaoh. Long geographical lists were usually arranged in columns.[128] Accordingly, the list under discussion was also arranged in the form of a column, an ancient practice found at least as early as the Talmud.[129] This form put special emphasis upon the conquered kings who appear in this list, one after another. In the Egyptian lists the editor picked the names of cities from the military journal of the campaign being described. Thus, they appear according to the order in which they occur in the narrative, which does not always correspond to a simple geographic arrangement. This is also the case with our biblical list: the names of the towns were cited from the conquest narratives according to the order of their appearance in the stories. They were taken to represent a unified campaign in which "Joshua and the sons of Israel" smote the kings of the land (cf. map. 15, p. 213).

In the list being considered thirty-one cities are mentioned according to the traditional text. The LXX has only twenty-nine: Bethel is missing, and instead of "the King of Aphek, one; the King of Lasharon, one" (vs. 18) it has "the King of Aphek of the Sharon" (βασιλέα Αφεκ τῆς Σαρων). Perhaps Bethel was excised because of Judges 1. 22 ff., which states that the House of Joseph conquered Bethel "after the death of Joshua" (vs. 1). So we may suspect that this was an intentional excision from the original list. On the other hand, the LXX text is preferable in the second instance for the following reasons: (1) Aphek is situated in the Sharon; (2) there were many cities named Aphek, and therefore an additional geographical designation was required; (3) the phrase "of the Sharon" denotes a region, not a city, and corresponds to Jokneam *of* Carmel" (RSV, *in* Carmel) from our list (vs. 22); (4) there is also the possibility that the King of Aphek was called simply King of the Sharon in other sources (cf. *supra,* p. 172). It is possible that the original list included thirty names. This may have been intentional because thirty was a conventional number in the ancient Israelite period (cf. Judg. 10. 4; 12. 9, 14; 14. 12; 2 Sam. 23. 13, etc.), and it divides easily, permitting a symmetric arrangement.

The first part of the list parallels the narratives in Joshua 6–10, and the following cities are named therein: Jericho, Ai, Jerusalem, Hebron, Jarmuth, Lachish, Eglon, Gezer (Josh. 10. 33), Debir, Libnah, Makkedah. To this list was added Adullam. Genesis 38 tells about intermarriage between the clan of Judah and the residents of Adullam, but our list attests to a different tradition about war with them. Likewise a group of three other names was added: Geder, Hormah and Arad. Narratives are preserved concerning a war with Arad and the conquest of Hormah (Num. 21. 1; 33. 40; Deut. 1. 44; Judg. 1. 17); however, Geder is unknown as a Canaanite city. Towns named Geder, Gederah, Gederoth and Gederothaim are known to us in Judah; but it is doubtful that any one of these was a royal Canaanite centre. Perhaps we have here the usual confusion of Hebrew *daleth* and *resh*. The original reading therefore may be have been Gerar, the most important Canaanite city in the western Negeb[130]. Gerar occupies an important place in the Patriarchal tradition but is not mentioned at all in the biblical conquest narratives.

Next come four cities in the territory of the House of Joseph: Bethel and Tappuah in the hills of Ephraim, Aphek and Hepher in the Sharon. To this group must be added a fifth city, Tirzah from Manasseh's territory, which is at the end of the list. Only concerning the fall of Bethel was any information preserved (Judg. 1. 22 ff.). About the conquest of Tappuah by Ephraim, there is a hint in Joshua 17. 8, and there was doubtless a more detailed account of this event. With regard to the remaining three cities, no information was preserved in the Bible. Since they do not form a continuous topographical unit, there were probably separate stores about the opposition encountered at each one of them. There is no reason to postulate a narrative about a combined war against the cities in the Ephraimite hill country and the Sharon.

The last part of our list concerns the northern wars. In this section there are three variants in the LXX against the Massoretic text: (1) In place of Madon and Shimron-meron it reads "Shim'on and Maron (Μαρρων); (2) Kedesh comes before Taanach and Megiddo; (3) in place of the King of "Goiim in Gilgal", it reads "Goiim in Galilee", i.e. the King of the peoples in the region of Galilee ("*of* Galilee" just as "*of* Carmel", and "*of* Sharon"), and it is probably "Galilee of the Gentiles" that is meant (cf. Isa. 9. 1[Heb. 8. 23]). Therefore, according to LXX the following line-up is obtained: Hazor, Shimʿon, Maron, Achshaph, Kedesh, Taanach, Megiddo, Jokneam of the Carmel, Dor of Naphath-dor, Goiim in Galilee.

The first four cities belong to the battle of Merom. Thus, the Septuagint text which places Hazor at the head is preferable. Since a city named Madon is not mentioned in any other source, we have suggested that the reading of LXX, Maron, be accepted, referring to Merom near which the battle took place ("by the waters of Merom"; LXX ὕδωρ Μαρρων). There remain six names to which there is no narrative allusion in the Bible: one in Upper Galillee (Kedesh), three in the Plain of Jezreel (Taanach, Megiddo, Jokneam), one on the northern coast (Dor) and at the end a general term, the King of Galilee or "Galilee of the Gentiles" (LXX), since a Canaanite city named Gilgal is unknown,[131] and the archaic title "Goiim" evidently belongs to Galilee.

Taanach and Megiddo are mentioned in the Song of Deborah (Judg. 5. 19). Besides these two cities we hear from the biblical narrative only about Hazor and Sisera, the army commander from Harosheh-ha-goiim who headed the Canaanite alliance, plus a general reference to "the kings of Canaan" (Judg. 5. 19). Thus, it is probable that in our list are preserved the cities of the same Canaanite kings who took part in the battle of Deborah and who were known to the author from a more complete tradition than that preserved in the Bible. These are the most important cities in the north, and they correspond well to the battle's location between Tabor and the Kishon.

Because it does not include all of the important Canaanite cities in western Palestine, the list under discussion provides only a summary of the cities mentioned in narratives about the ancient wars. Cities in the Philistine region, the Plain of Acco (except Achshaph) and important places such as Beth-shean and Rehob to the south of it are missing since they are not mentioned in the war narratives. Generally speaking, however, the list gives a faithful picture of the important Canaanite cities—the same ones encountered by the Israelites in their efforts to occupy the various regions.

VIII. THE LIMITS OF ISRAELITE OCCUPATION

In the first stages of occupation the Israelite population was able to penetrate only into such regions as did not contain a strong and continuous Canaanite settlement, i.e. mainly in the mountain regions, the Negeb and the south-central portions of Transjordan. The biblical tradition continually stresses that the Israelite tribes were unable to try conclusions with the strong Canaanite cities in the plains because the latter had chariots of iron and mighty fortifications (Josh. 17. 18; Judg. 1. 19, *et al.*). The first districts of tribal occupation were far from the Egyptian administrative centres, and this explains the astonishing phenomenon that there is no mention in the Bible of the Egyptian presence in Palestine, in spite of the fact that during the time of Israelite penetration and conquest in the fourteenth and thirteenth centuries pharaohs of the New Kingdom still controlled the Egyptian province of Canaan.[132] For the same reason the Israelite penetration did not make a deep impression upon Egyptian sources, since the latter did not view them as a serious threat to peace or to their hegemony. Except for the Merneptah Stele from the final days of their rule, we have nothing but general information concerning ʿApiru and nomadic raiders in the hill country, part of whom were doubtless none other than the Israelite tribes. This finds a very illuminating expression in Papyrus Anastasi I from the early days of Ramses II. The moment that the lonely traveller reaches the hill country he is in serious danger; even on a main thoroughfare like Wadi ʿAra the marauders are depicted in frightening terms (cf. *supra,* p. 51).

Two documents are preserved in the Bible which define the unconquered regions of Canaan: the list of unconquered Canaanite towns and the description of "the land which remained" (cf. map 17).

1. The List of the Unconquered Canaanite Cities

This list serves to summarize and to describe the towns of western Palestine which were included in the respective tribal districts, enjoying some reciprocal relationships with them, but which were not actually conquered during the early stages of settlement. In outlook and content, therefore, there is an exact parallel between this list and the tribal borders as Alt has recognized.[133] Both accounts are based on the viewpoint that these cities were related to particular tribes, although they had not actually been conquered.

This connection was also obvious to the editors of the Bible. Thus, on the one hand, they included the list as a unit in Judges 1 and, on the other, they incorporated it, piece by piece, in the description of the various tribal inheritances in Joshua 15–19.

The list contains cities from the inheritances of six tribes: Benjamin, Manasseh, Ephraim, Zebulun, Asher and Naphtali. A seventh tribe is Dan, but the cities that exerted pressure on that tribe eventually came under the authority of the House of Joseph, i.e. they were assigned to Ephraim or Benjamin. The Transjordanian tribes are missing, as are the rest of the tribes from western Palestine: Issachar, Simeon and Judah. This combination conforms in its entirety to the tribal boundaries which included only the tribes in the hill country of Ephraim and Galilee, with the exception of Issachar (cf. *infra,* pp. 252 f.).

The only foreign city mentioned in Benjamin's district is Jebusite Jerusalem, although according to Joshua 15. 63 that city belonged to Judah. In conformity with our list, the description of the border between Judah and Benjamin emphasizes Jerusalem's belonging to Benjamin (Josh. 15. 8; 18. 16).

All of the unconquered cities within Manasseh's borders are in the northern part of his inheritance, in the Jezreel Plain (Beth-shean, Taanach, Ibleam, Megiddo) and in the northern Sharon (Dor). The same cities are mentioned in Joshua 17. 11–13. En-dor is added here,

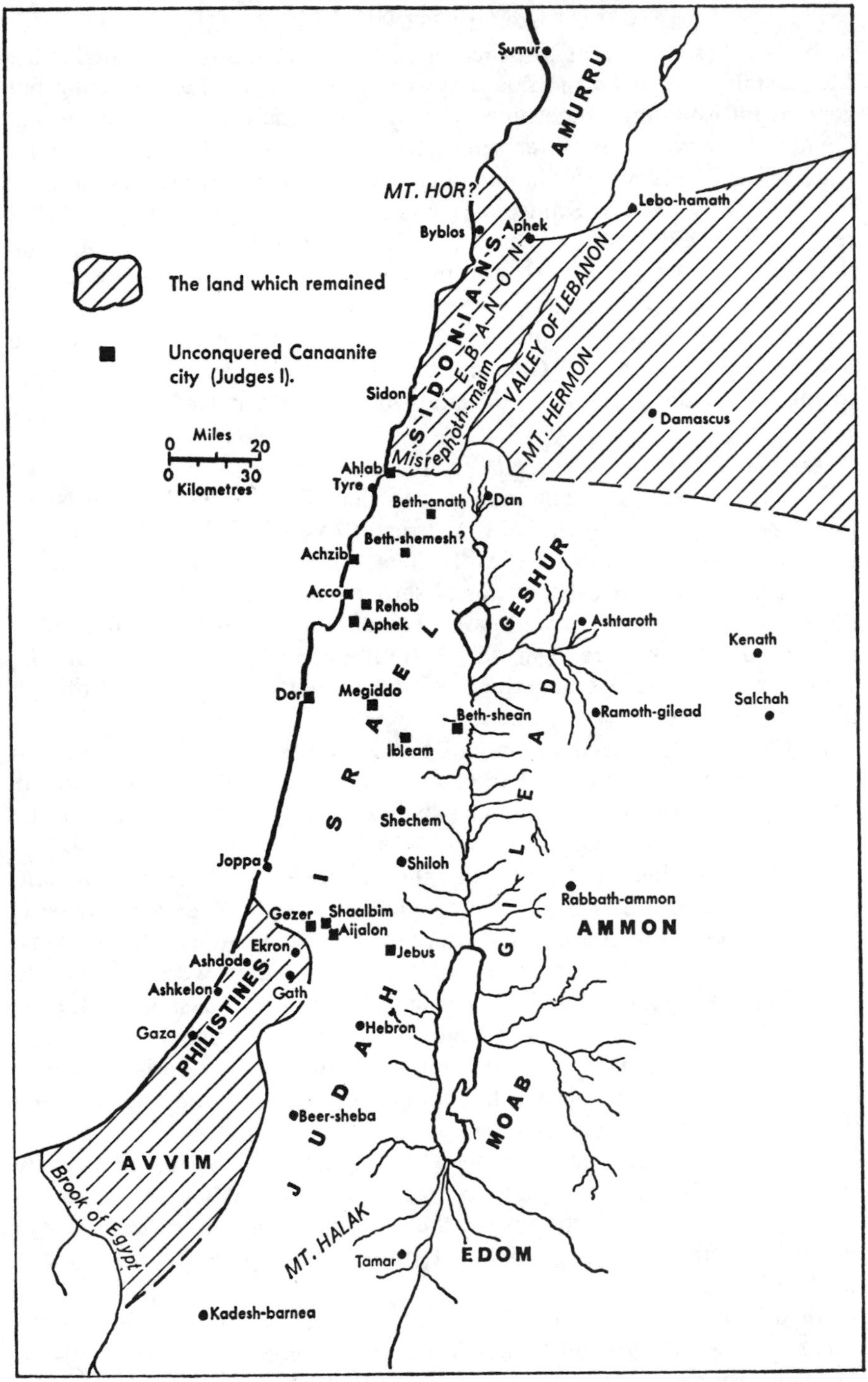

Map 17. The Land which remained and the Unconquered Canaanite Cities.

apparently because of its resemblance to Dor which precedes it, since there is no evidence that En-dor was a Canaanite centre. The introduction in Joshua 17. 11 "Also in Issachar and in Asher Manasseh had . . ." was inserted to stress the fact that these cities were not originally in his inheritance but rather in areas that were reckoned at first to the other two tribes.

In the inheritance of Ephraim only one town is mentioned, Gezer, which was on the south-western border. This is true of Judges 1. 29 and Joshua 16. 10 as well.

The two cities associated with Zebulun, Kitron and Nahalol, remain unidentified; they appear at the end of the description of Zebulun's inheritance in the form Kattath and Nahalal (Josh. 19. 15). It is difficult to accept the idea that their location is in the Plain of Acco outside of the borders of the tribe as defined in Joshua 19[134] because there is no evidence whatsoever to that effect; and everything seems to indicate, as mentioned above, that the two lists represent one historical phase. It is more likely that these cities were situated on the north-western edge of the Plain of Jezreel. They should each be identified with one of the tells in this area.

Several cities in the Plain of Acco are associated with Asher, viz. Acco itself, Achzib, Aphik (Aphek according to Josh. 19. 30) and Rehob.[135] Likewise, a Phoenician coastal city was reckoned to Asher, Ahlab-Helbah (Mehebel according to Josh. 19. 29), which is apparently Maḫalliba in the inscription of Sennacherib, today Khirbet el-Maḥalib, about four miles north of Tyre.[136] The mention of Sidon raises a special problem, since according to all of the sources, it was outside of the limits of Israelite occupation. Even the northern border of Asher's inheritance reaches "as far as Sidon the Great; then . . . to the fortified city of Tyre" (Josh. 19. 28-9; cf. also 2 Sam. 24. 6-7), i.e. as far as the border of Sidon the city, viz. the Liṭani which runs between the territories of Tyre and Sidon. The enumeration of the Canaanite cities at the end of Asher's list of towns in Joshua 19. 29–30 points to the same situation with slight textual variations, except that Sidon is missing. Therefore, we may interpret "the inhabitants of Sidon" as a more generalized annotation to "the inhabitants of Acco", since all of the inhabitants of the northern coastline, including the Plain of Acco, were reckoned as Sidonians in this period. It seems that the Phoenician coast as far as the border of the city of Sidon, including at least Tyre's coastal city (Usu, Palaityros), was reckoned theoretically as Asher's territory, even though the balance of power here was on the side of the Canaanites: "but the Asherites dwelt among the Canaanites, the inhabitants of the land; for they did not drive them out" (Judg. 1. 32).

Only two cities in this list are assigned to Naphtali's district: Beth-shemesh and Beth-anath. Concerning their location, there are many differences of opinion and the suggestions for their identification range from the Valley of Beit-netophah (Sahl el-Baṭṭof) in Lower Galilee to the northern extremity of Upper Galilee. In the light of the archaeological survey, it would seem today that cities in the northern part of Upper Galilee are intended since a strong and well-developed Canaanite settlement existed there up until the beginning of the Israelite period.[137]

Finally, there is also preserved in this list a tradition concerning the Amorite cities in the northern Shephelah that withstood the pressure of the tribe of Dan and forced its members to seek a new inheritance in the north. Of the three cities, the location of Aijalon and Shaalabbin in the Valley of Aijalon east of Gezer is clear. Har-heres is usually taken as a synonym for Beth-shemesh—Ir-shemesh which is farther south.[138] If this is correct, then it is a testimony to the early date of the Danite wandering, because Beth-shemesh is known as an Israelite town by the end of the period of the Judges (1 Sam. 6.9 ff.). It was also proved by excavation that the Canaanite city was destroyed in the early stages of the conquest.[139]

In its present form the list contains nineteen Canaanite cities in the different regions of western Palestine: in the northern Shephelah, in the northern Sharon, in the Plain of Jezreel, in the northern coastal plain, in Upper Galilee and one city in the central hills, Jerusalem. Only three cities are common to this list and that of the conquered Canaanite cities, viz. Gezer, Taanach and Megiddo, which appear in the war narratives, though they remained Canaanite during the first stages of settlement. From the standpoint of geography, therefore, this list complements that of the Canaanite cities. Regarding its date, we have seen above (p. 228) that in the light of the excavations at Megiddo and Taanach, it should come from the mid-12th century at the latest. Some of the towns included in the list fell into Israelite hands at about that time though others maintained their independence until the reign of David, e.g. Jerusalem, Gezer and probably Beth-shean. As for the remaining towns we lack evidence, but we may suppose that those in the Acco plain and Dor may have withstood Israelite pressure until David's rise to power.[140]

2. The Description of the Land which remains

This document is an account of the regions which actually "remained" foreign and which were still outside the limits of Israelite occupation, although they were included in the traditional borders of Canaan (Num. 34). In the framework of the biblical narrative, this description comes as an introduction to the division of the land by Joshua after the completion of the wars of conquest. It concludes by saying that Joshua must also divide "this land" between the various tribes (Josh. 13. 7). However, the document itself is based upon a different outlook. In spite of the fact that "the land that yet remains" belongs to Canaan, it is not in fact divided among the tribes. Alongside the tribal boundaries and the unconquered Canaanite cities included in those boundaries there is this "remaining" district of Canaan which actually stays outside the limits of Israelite conquest. This viewpoint is also expressed in other passages. Joshua 11. 17 states that Joshua conquered all of the land "from Mount Halak, it rises toward Seir, as far as Baal-gad in the Valley of Lebanon below Mount Hermon". In contrast to this "the land that yet remains" extends "from Baal-gad below Mount Hermon to Lebo-hamath" (Josh. 13. 5; cf. RSV "the entrance of Hamath").[141]

A more abbreviated description of the same unconquered districts is found also in Judges 3. 3, "the five lords of the Philistines, and all the Canaanites, and the Sidonians, and the Hivites who dwell on Mount Lebanon, from Mount Baal-hermon as far as Lebo-hamath".

The description of the land yet remaining is divided into areas south and north of the limits of Israelite occupation. Each one of them begins with the designation "all", after which follows a description of the border in the formula: "from . . . to . . . ", with additional details added here and there. This is the regular formula for the delineation of ancient boundaries; cf. e.g. the borders of "Aram in its entirety", on the Sfiré Stelae (cf. *supra,* p. 86). "All the regions of the Philistines" in the south, which are reckoned as part of the land of Canaan (cf. Gen. 10. 19), extended "from the Shihor, which is east of Egypt, northward to the boundary of Ekron" (Josh. 13. 3). They included the five Philistine territories from Gaza in the south to Ekron in the north, and that of the Avvim to the south of them. The Avvim are known as the autochthonous inhabitants of the southern frontier region who dwelled "in villages as far as Gaza" (Deut. 2. 23).[142] Therefore, one should certainly accept the versification in LXX which connects the word Avvim with the following phrase and reads "the Avvim in the south".

It is difficult to determine just what is meant by "all . . . of the Geshurites". In this passage they are associated with the southern districts; and they are also known to us in this same region from the sorties of David while at Ziklag (1 Sam. 27. 8). However, the northern Geshur, east of the Sea of Galilee, also remained outside the Israelite bounds (2 Sam. 13. 37). Perhaps both of them were mentioned in the original list and one was deleted by haplography.

The second portion of the land which remained is in the north, and it includes "all the land of the Canaanites" in the west and "all Lebanon" in the east. The boundaries of the Canaanite territory are " . . . Mearah which belongs to the Sidonians, to Aphek, to the boundary of the Amorites, and the land of the Gebalites" (Josh. 13. 4-5).

Unfortunately, the first word defining the southern boundary of the unconquered Canaanite territory is corrupted. In place of "Mearah" there must have been a designation "from [a certain place]", but every attempt to restore this name must remain purely conjectural. At the end of the description there is a general annotation, "all the inhabitants of the hill country from Lebanon to Misrephoth-maim, even all the Sidonians" (Josh. 13. 6). From a comparison with the description of the pursuit of the Canaanites after the battle of Merom (Josh. 11. 8), it appears that "Misrephoth-maim"[143] is a parallel expression for the southern boundary of Sidon. It has been proposed to equate Misrephoth-(maim) with Khirḅet Musheirefeh at the northern end of the Plain of Acco,[144] but the excavations carried out there did not support this identification because no remains from the end of the Late Bronze Age or the beginning of the Israelite period were discovered.[145] We have seen that Ahlab-Mahalab, situated south of the Liṭani is one of the Canaanite cities reckoned to Asher. From this it is probable that the boundary of the "land that remains" lies farther north. The question comes to mind whether "Misrephoth-maim" is not the river Liṭani whose name is not mentioned in the Bible.[146]

On the other hand, the northern boundary of the Canaanite territory is quite clear: it extended "to Aphek, to the boundary of the Amorites". The reference here is probably to Afqa near the sources of Nahr Ibrahim, south-east of Byblos. "The Amorite" here cannot have the general connotation usually found in the Bible. The kingdom of Amurru in the Lebanon region, well known to us from Egyptian and Hittite sources of the fourteenth and the thirteenth centuries B.C. is doubtless intended. This kingdom extended over the northern sector of the Lebanon. In the El Amarna period its kings reigned from Ṣumur near the mouth of the Eleutherus to Kadesh on the Orontes, and one of their chief enemies was the King of Byblos. Amurru was a disputed region on the border between the Hittite and Egyptian kingdoms. From Hittite treaties we know that it finally submitted to Hittite rule, and after the battle of Kadesh it remained in Hittite hands.[147] It is probable, therefore, that Aphek was on the southern border of Amurru which became the northern border of the Egyptian province of Canaan during the reign of Ramses II. This is the border of Canaan as the Israelite tribes found it (cf. *supra,* pp. 74 f.).

The second region is the eastern sector of the Lebanon (not the Anti-lebanon, the biblical name of which is Sirion-Senir), including the Valley of Lebanon (Beqa'),. The boundaries of this region extended from "Baal-gad below Mount Hermon to Lebo-hamath (RSV 'entrance of Hamath')". The northernmost point is the traditional boundary of Canaan, today Lebweh beside one of the sources of the Orontes. The exact identification of Baal-gad is not known. Judges 3. 3 substitutes for it "Mount Baal-hermon", evidently referring to the sacred southern peak of Hermon, i.e. the region above Dan, the traditional northern limit of the Israelite occupation. The population of this region was reckoned as Hivites, or Horites according to the LXX. "The land of Mizpah", or "the Valley of Mizpeh", located below Mount Hermon, where Hivites also dwelled (Josh. 11. 3, 8) is a parallel designation for the boundary of the Israelite occupation in the Hermon region. It is evidently to be equated with Marj ʿAyyun[148] or the valley of the Ḥeṣbani River.

This point also dovetails exactly with the viewpoint concerning "the land which remains", i.e. the unconquered sector of Canaan. According to the biblical tradition, Joshua's conquest extended from Mount Halak on the border of Seir in the Negeb to Baal-gad in the Lebanese Valley below Mount Hermon (Josh. 11. 17 and 12. 7). "The land that remains", on the other hand, extended from Baal-gad to Lebo-hamath, the well-known city on the northern border of Canaan.

IX. SETTLEMENT IN THE HILL COUNTRY

The density of the Israelite population in the hill regions necessitated the preparation of fresh land, mainly by cutting down the natural forest. This need is expressly stated in Josh. 17. 14–18:

> And the tribe of Joseph spoke to Joshua, saying "Why have you given me but one lot and one portion as an inheritance, although I am a numerous people, since hitherto the Lord has blessed me?" And Joshua said to them, "If you are a numerous people, go up to the forest, and there clear ground for yourselves (in the land of the Perizzites and the Rephaim)[149] since the hill country of Ephraim is too narrow for you". The tribe of Joseph said, "The hill country is not enough for us; yet all the Canaanites who dwell in the plain have chariots of iron, both those in Beth-shean and its villages and those in the Valley of Jezreel." Then Joshua said to the House of Joseph (to Ephraim and Manasseh),[150] "You are a numerous people, and have great power; you shall not have one lot only, but the hill country shall be yours, for though it is a forest, you shall clear it and possess it to its farthest borders . . . "

Opinions differ as to whether this description refers to the expansion by the House of Joseph eastward into Transjordan[151] or to settlement in the forested sectors of the Ephraimite hill country itself.[152] In any case, the general picture reflected here is one of inability to penetrate the Canaanite plains and the necessity to create sufficient room for occupation in the hilly regions by the cultivation of waste lands and the clearing of natural forest.

Extensive settlement of the hill country was facilitated by the tribal-patriarchal organization that was preserved in Israel during the period of the Judges, in spite of the changed circumstances. Defence of the population and its way of life was not founded on the strong fortifications and heavy armament of a unified settlement, as in the Canaanite cities. It was rather a sort of collective defence based upon tribal and clan organization. In the various stories from the period of the Judges there were very few instances of siege laid against an Israelite city by an enemy. But repeatedly we hear about enemy penetration into Israelite sectors and their repulsion by valiant warriors mobilized from the clan or tribe who attack the enemy at an opportune moment. Most of the Israelite settlements were small at the beginning, some being unfortified villages and a few having fortifications that were puny and makeshift compared to the mighty walls of Canaanite cities. This situation resulted from a lack of technical know-how during the early stages of settlement combined with a tribal rule that prevented the mobilization of manpower necessary for collective fortification building. Defence based on the tribal organization was better suited to a population dispersed through the widely scattered hill regions. Of course the difficult access routes also enhanced the security of the small, unfortified villages.

Settlement in the hill country was also furthered by the invention of the plastered cistern. In various excavations plastered and whitewashed water cisterns have been found in Late Bronze strata, especially in the later phases.[153] This invention freed the population from dependence upon a nearby well, which up to now had been a basic condition for permanent settlement. Henceforth it was possible to base a population's existence upon the collection and conservation of rain water in plastered cisterns throughout the year. This device was not original to the Israelites; it shows up in the Canaanite cities who had always spared no effort to assure an emergency water supply. But the newly arriving tribes took it over very quickly, and it helped them to found small independent settlements, widely dispersed and unrestricted by the limited number of wells (cf. *supra*, p. 107).

The narrow confines and heavy concentration of Israelite occupation left their impression in the special development of their society. Archaeological research has proved that the Israelites did not bring a consolidated tradition of material culture with them. Instead, they borrowed everything from the previous inhabitants. This is expressed in building construction, in weapons, in art objects and especially in pottery. The Israelite craftsman imitates the Canaanite product, and in the beginning creates more primitive vessels but in the same style. Along with this, unique vessels were soon developed in a characteristic and clearly definable style found only among the Israelite tribes. This phenomenon was quite apparent in the Galilee survey. When we compare the vessels found on the various Israelite settlements of

Galilee[154] and those from the earliest Israelite occupation at Hazor (stratum XII) with the Canaanite culture that preceded them (especially Hazor strata XIV–XIII), we see the similarity and the difference quite clearly. The cooking pot, for example, resembles the Canaanite cooking pot exactly *in form;* however, the rim is much longer and straight on the Israelite pot, while the rim of the Canaanite vessel turns outward; thus it is quite easy to distinguish between them. Not one short (triangular) rim was found in stratum XII or in the Israelite settlements of Galilee. The same holds true for the storage jar. Its general form is a clear imitation of the Canaanite pythos, of which many were found in Hazor XIII and XIV; but nevertheless it differs in fabric, in the shape of the rim and in the execution of plastic decoration. Most typical of the Israelite settlements are the "collared rim" jars, which have a ridge beneath the broad rim. The adoption of Canaanite culture coupled with rapid crystallization of independent forms is a theme which runs like a secondary thread through all phases of Israelite tribal life. Such a development is easily explained against the background of their settlement in closed, independent units working their lands and building their villages in the vicinity of the cities and the strong well-developed Canaanite district.

The unique nature of this occupation by Israelite tribes brought about the greatest habitational revolution that had ever taken place in the history of this country. Palestine is by nature a diversified land, being composed of the most divergent types of terrain located side by side. Until the Israelite period the population density varied a great deal between the different sectors. As previously mentioned, many of the hilly regions served as barriers which separated the fertile valleys from one another. It is not surprising that this brought about the development of independent urban settlement and the political fragmentation of the country. Only a strong imperial force from outside succeeded, bit by bit, in unifying the country under its authority; and it was aided by internal dissensions. The earlier waves of occupation changed the complexion of the population, but they always flowed into the same fertile sectors. By contrast, the Israelite occupation brought about a fundamental change. Now the hilly regions also became densely populated, and most of the spaces formerly left open between the various regions were filled. For the first time in the history of the country the centre of population actually moved into the hill country; and when the Israelite tribes grew in strength and completed their domination of the plains, the conditions necessary for uniting the land into one political and ethnic unit were established. In this unprecedented way the economic potential of Palestine was also increased by cultivation of extensive waste lands which had never been tilled before. These special features of the occupation caused the transformation of the land of Canaan into the land of Israel, not only in ethnic and political terms but also in a complete transformation of the population map. It is this factor which opened a new chapter in the history of Palestine and elevated it for the first time to the rank of a strong and influential country in the Middle East.

X. OCCUPATION AND MOVEMENT OF TRIBES AND CLANS

Settlement by the various tribes in their respective areas was a complex process not crowned by uniform success in every case. The picture presented in the Bible mainly reflects the results of this process in its later stages during the period of the Judges when the tribal framework had become crystallized and most of the tribes were firmly established. Supplementary information from certain narrative passages and the genealogical tables reveal that some reshuffling of the tribal inheritances had taken place. These movements were of two types: (1) a few tribes shifted to other regions after failing in their first efforts to take possession of their allotted territory; (2) certain clans transferred from one tribe to another according to the exigencies of their own situation. On occasion families of one clan became joined to different tribes with the result that the clan name is found in more than one tribe.

The only explicit narrative of a tribe's migrating after failure to occupy its assigned territory is that of the Danites (Judg. 17; 18). From this one should not assume that theirs was the last migration of this kind to take place (Machir's apparently occurred later). The Danite story was preserved due to its connection with the important temple founded by Moses' grandson (Judg. 18. 30),[155] whose priesthood continued to function until "the day of the captivity of the land", i.e. the invasion by Tiglath-pileser III. Therefore, this tradition fixes the Danite migration to a very early date, not long after the arrival of Judah, because the grandson of Moses came to Mount Ephraim from Bethlehem of Judah (Judg. 17. 7-8). There is no reason to doubt the truth of this tradition concerning the cause for their northward shift. The tribe was still mobile, camping temporarily and then travelling on with its cattle and baggage. Their attempts to occupy the Shephelah region around Zorah and Eshtaol encountered stiff opposition from the Amorite cities there (Judg. 1. 34–5). But there is no mention of the Philistine pressure which reached its peak in this area at a later date.[156] Dan's line of march must have taken him through the Ephraimite hill country from whence he continued northward via the Jordan Valley, a traditional route for tribal migrations (cf. Judah, Judg. 1. 1 ff.). Canaanite Laish was then overwhelmed by surprise attack. This may have taken place after the fall of Hazor early in the twelfth century, when Canaanite defences in the north had been seriously weakened.[157]

However, one should not assume that the entire tribe moved north. Some memories are preserved of a few Danite clans that remained in the south, eventually being absorbed into other tribes. The migration narrative itself only speaks of 600 members (Judg. 18. 11). The Danite clan of Hushim (Gen. 46. 23; Shuham according to Num. 26. 42) is elsewhere assigned to Benjamin (1 Chron. 8. 8). Samson was a Danite from Zorah (Judg. 13. 2), although the situation portrayed in his narratives belongs to the beginning of the eleventh century at the earliest, because the Philistines already dominated Judah. One certainly cannot date the Danite migration that late (cf. *supra*, pp. 236).

Various hints suggest that similar movements took place among other tribes, though the respective traditions have been lost. This is demonstrated primarily by the genealogical tables. The fact that Machir, the father of Gilead, is still counted among the tribes of Mount Ephraim in the Song of Deborah (Judg. 5. 14) provides some evidence concerning the migration of Manassite clans to Gilead. After that move the western tribe was called after Manasseh, who became its eponymous ancestor. In this manner the complicated genealogy of Manasseh was created in which Machir is the father of Gilead, i.e. a resident there, though certain districts of Mount Ephraim are also associated with him. The formative stages of this genealogy are still reflected in certain passages: Machir is the first-born of Manasseh, the father of Gilead, and the western clans, Abiezer, Helek, Asriel, Shechem, Hepher and Shemida, are called "the rest of the tribe of Manasseh" (Josh. 17. 1–2), being reckoned as sons of Manasseh and therefore brothers of Machir. But in the following verse a simpler family lineage is expressed: "Zelophehad the son of Hepher, son of Gilead, son of Machir, son of Manasseh" (vs. 3). The genealogical table in 1 Chronicles describes this development according to a different scheme[158]:

> The sons of Manasseh: Asriel, [Shechem, etc.], whom [his wife] bore; his Aramaean concubine bore Machir the father of Gilead . . . And Maachah the wife of Machir bore a son, and she called his name Peresh; and the name of his brother was Sheresh; and his sons were Ulam and Rekem. And the sons of Ulam: Bedan. [. . .] These were the sons of Gilead the son of Machir son of Manasseh (1 Chron. 7. 14–17).

According to this arrangement the western clans have descended from Manasseh's first wife while those in Transjordan are the progeny of his Aramaean concubine. The fact is therefore expressed that the population of Gilead was made up of different elements among which the Aramaean influence is notable.

A few references suggest that certain clans from the tribe of Issachar had affinities with the Ephraimite hill country. Among the judges that are enumerated after Gideon we find "Tola the son of Puah, son of Dodo, a man of Issachar; and he lived at Shamir in the hill country of Ephraim" (Judg. 10. 1). Puah is known as one of the main clans of

Issachar (1 Chron. 7. 1; Puvah—Gen. 46. 13; Num. 26. 23). Two other clan names in Issachar are reminiscent of the place names in Mount Ephraim: Shimron—Shemer, owner of the hill of Samaria (1 Kings 16. 24; cf. also the Shamir mentioned above); Jashub (Jashib in 1 Chron. 7. 1, but LXX Ιασουβ.)—Yashub, a place name from the Samaria ostraca.

In the genealogical table of Asher there are many hints concerning clan connections with the southern hill country of Ephraim (Gen. 46. 17 ff.; 1 Chron. 7. 30 ff.). Three Asherite clans are associated with the border districts of Benjamin and Ephraim: Japhlet—the Japhletite (Josh. 17. 3); Shual and Shilshah—the land of Shual (1 Sam. 13. 17); the land of Shalisha and also of Shaalim (1 Sam. 9. 4). Malchiel was the "father of Birzaith" (1 Chron. 7. 31), i.e. the clan had settled in Birzaith of which the LXX form (Βερζαιθ) strongly suggests an identification with the Βιρζηθω, Βαρζηθω mentioned by Josephus (*Antiq.* XII, xi, 1), today Khirbet Bir Zeit north of Beitin (Bethel). Two Asherite clans are also reckoned to the House of Joseph, Beriah in Ephraim and Benjamin (1 Chron. 7. 30; 8. 13) and Shemer in Benjamin (1 Chron. 8. 12 according to LXX). There might be some connection between Serah (1 Chron. 7. 30) and Timnath-serah, the town of Joshua in Mount Ephraim (Josh. 19. 50; 24. 30; called Timnath-heres in Judg. 2. 9) even though different Hebrew sibilants are involved (cf. Judg. 12. 6). These names indicate, therefore, that various Asherite clans and families had settled early in Mount Ephraim and eventually were incorporated into the southern part of Ephraim and in Benjamin.

Besides the Machir-Manasseh relationship and the Reubenite connections with Benjamin and Judah already mentioned (cf. *supra,* pp. 207 f.) there are additional reminiscences of ties between the western and the Transjordanian tribes. Various narratives indicate the special relationship between Benjamin and Jabesh-gilead (Judg. 21. 9–14; 1 Sam. 11. 1 ff.; 31. 11–13).[159] Information has also been preserved about the Judean clan of Hezron being associated with Machir and Gilead (1 Chron. 2. 21–3).

In the genealogies of Judah the southern tribes have prominent connections with the Arabah and Mount Seir. Of the four Calebite clans from Hebron (1 Chron. 2. 43) at least two are clearly of southern origin: Korah was an Edomite chief (Gen. 36. 16) and is associated with the Zoar region in the northern Arabah.[160] Rekem was a Midianite prince (Num. 31. 8; Josh. 13. 21) as well as being the ancient name of Petra. Shema also has affinities with that region. An inscription of Ramses II at Amara mentions "*š-m-ʿ-t* in the Bedouin country" together with Mount Seir.[161] The Shimeathites were a Kenite clan (1 Chron. 2. 55), and among the Simeonites one finds a clan named Shimei (1 Chron. 4. 26–7) for which the Negeb settlement Shema may have been named (Josh. 15. 26). Kenaz also appears as an Edomite chieftain (Gen. 36. 15).

Furthermore, there is some testimony to a relationship between the southern tribes and the ancient Horite families of Mount Seir. Among these latter one finds the clan of Shobal (Gen. 36. 20 ff.; 1 Chron. 1. 38 ff.), and a clan by this name settled at Kiriath-jearim, being associated with "Hur the first-born of Ephrathah" (1 Chron. 2. 50b-52). One family in the Shobal clan was Menuhoth (1 Chron. 2. 52) which seems to have some connection with Manahath south-west of Jerusalem, a town possibly mentioned in the El Amarna letters (*EA*, 292. 30). The Horite element is especially prominent among the sons of Jerahmeel (1 Chron. 2. 25 ff.): Onam, Jether and Oren are included among the Horite sons of Seir; and the descendants of Onam: Shesham, Ahlai, Peleth and Zaza (1 Chron. 2. 31–3) are apparently Hurrian names.[162]

The affinities of the Kenites, the venerable metal smiths, with Edom and the Arabah are beyond question.[163] And the Kenite "house of Rechab" (1 Chron. 2. 55) is connected with the clans of Caleb and Kenaz on the one hand and with the Edomite Ir-nahash ("Serpent City" [probably modified from "City of Copper"]) and Ge-harashim ("Valley of Craftsmen") on the other (1 Chron. 4. 12–14).[164] Likewise, there is some evidence for ties between the Kenites and the Amalakites from the southern wastelands (1 Sam. 15. 6; Judg. 1. 16 according to LXX).

Even in the genealogies of Judah and Simeon one finds associations with Mount Seir. Zerah of Judah is mentioned among the Simeonites (Num. 26. 13; 1 Chron. 4. 24) and also the Edomites (Gen. 36. 13, 17; 1 Chron. 1. 37). However, the Judean Zerah, which seems to have settled mainly in eastern districts near the Judean wilderness,[165] declined in importance as compared with Perez and the other Judean clans. It appears in the Simeonite genealogy only at the above-mentioned point, being absent from the lists in Genesis 46 and Exodus 6 where Zohar stands in its place. The Onan of Judah (Gen. 38. 4–10; 46. 12) might have some connection with the Jerahmeelite (and Horite) Onam.

The genealogical tables of the various tribes include information of great geographical value which can be classified under three headings:

(1) References to settlements interspersed among the genealogical records of the various tribes and clans in the early chapters of 1 Chronicles, which apparently belong to different periods. This includes the list of Simeon's towns (1 Chron. 4. 28–33) and Simeonite expansion towards Gedor (LXX: Gerar) and Mount Seir (1 Chron. 4. 39–43); the Reubenite settlements "in (from ?) Aroer, as far as Nebo and Baal-meon" and his eastward expansion "as far as the entrance of the desert this side of the Euphrates" (1 Chron. 5. 8–10); the border towns of Ephraim and Manasseh (1 Chron. 7. 28-9); the history of the Beriah clan which was associated with Gath, Aijalon and Beth-horon (1 Chron. 7. 21–4; 8. 13); the building of Ono and Lod by Benjaminite clans (1 Chron. 8. 12).

(2) References to geographical names (such as settlements and regions) within the genealogical framework, a phenomenon which we have already considered in relation to tribal migrations. The structure of these genealogies expressed the patriarchal viewpoint, viz. that all members of a tribe are the descendants of one venerable ancestor including towns and villages within the tribal inheritance. Some of these latter may have been founded by the tribesmen, e.g. Anathoth, Alemeth, Azmaveth and Mozah which appear among the sons of Benjamin (1 Chron. 7. 8; 8. 36); but others are ancient settlements that were absorbed into the Israelite tribal framework, e.g. Shechem, Hepher and Tirzah among the clans of Manasseh (Josh. 17. 2–3).

(3) In the genealogy of Judah (1 Chron. 2–4) the sons of various clans are mentioned along with the names of their respective settlements in such a way that a clansman becomes the father of the place occupied, e.g. "Laadah the father of Mareshah" (1 Chron. 4. 21), "Ezer the father of Hushah" (1 Chron. 4. 4), etc. It would appear that these passages originally belonged to a unique geographical list in which the clans and places were mentioned side by side (cf. map 19, p. 272).

By combining these various references one obtains an approximate reconstruction of the list somewhat as follows.[166]

1 Chronicles[167]

2. 3	The sons of Judah: (Er, Onan) and Shelah [and Perez].
4. 21	The sons of Shelah the son of Judah; Er the father of Lecah, Laadah the father of Mareshah, and the families of the house of linen workers at Beth-ashbea;
4.22	and Jokim, and the men of Cozeba, and Joash, and Saraph, who ruled in Moab.
4.23	and returned to [Beth]lehem (now the records are ancient). These were the potters and inhabitants of Netaim and Gederah; they dwelt there with the king for his work.
2. 19	[Hezron was the son of Perez son of Judah; Hezron] married Ephrath, who bore him Hur (cf. 2.24; 4. 4);
2. 50	The son[s] of Hur the first-born of Ephrathah: Shobal the father of Kiriath-jearim,
2. 51, 52	Salma, the father of Bethlehem, and Hareph the father of Beth-gader, Shobal the father of Kiriath-jearim had other sons: Reaiah (cf. 4. 2), half of the Menuhoth.
2. 53	And the families of Kiriath-jearim: the Ithrites; the Puthites, the Shumathites, and the Mishraites; from these came the Zorathites and the Eshtaolites.
4. 2	Reaiah the son of Shobal begat Jahath, and Jahath begat Ahumai and Lahad. These were the families of the Zorathites.
2. 54	The sons of Salma [the father of] Bethlehem: the

Netophathites, Atroth-beth-joab, and half of the Manahathites, (the Zorites).

2.55 The families also of the scribes that dwelt at Jabez: the Tirathites, the Shimeathites, and the Sucathites. These are the Kenites who came from Hammath, the father of Beth-rechab.

4.3 These were the [sons of Hareph? . . .], the father of Etam, Jezreel, Ishma, and Idbash <and Jehallelel>(cf. 4. 16), father of Gedor, and Ezer the father of Hushah.

4.16, 17 The sons of Jehallelel: Ziph, Ziphah, Tiria, and Asarel. The sons of Ezrah (Ezer); Jether, Mered, Epher. <And Jether begat> Miriam, Shammai, and Ishbah, the father of Eshtemoa.

4.18 [Mered married two wives: an Egyptian (?) and a Judean], and his <Egyptian> wife bore Jered the father of Gedor, Heber the father of Socho[h], and Jekuthiel the father of Zanoah. These are the sons of Bithiah, the daughter of Pharaoh, whom Mered married.

4.19 The sons of his <Judean> wife (the sister of) Naham, the father of Keilah the Garmite and . . . [the father of] Eshtemoa the Maacathite.

4.4 These are the sons of Hur the first-born of Ephrathah, (the father of Bethlehem).

2.24 After the death of Hezron, Caleb [went] to Ephrathah (and) the wife of Hezron <his father>, and she bore him Ashhur, the father of Tekoa.

4.5-7 Ashhur, the father of Tekoa, had two wives, Helah and Naarah; Naarah bore him Ahuzzam, Hepher, Temeni, and Haahashtari. These were the sons of Naarah. The sons of Helah: Zereth, <Zohar> (MT *Qeri*), and Ethnan . . .

4.11 Chelub, the <father> of Shuhah, begat Mehir, who was the father of Eshton. [And Mehir, father of] Eshton begat . . . [the father of] Beth-rapha, Paseah, and Tehinnah the father of Ir-nahash (these are the men of Recah).

2.42 The sons of Caleb (the brother of Jerahmeel): Mesha (LXX, Mareshah) his first-born, who was the father of Ziph, and <. . . .> (the sons of Mareshah) the father of Hebron.

2.43-45 And <. . . > [the father of] Hebron: Korah, Tappuah, Rekem, and Shema: Shema begat Raham, the father of Jorkeam; and Rekem begat Shammai. The son of Shammai: Maon; and Maon was the father of Beth-zur . . .

2.49 She also bore Shaaph the father of Madmannah, Sheva the father of Machbenah and <. . . > the father of Gibea. . . .

2.50 These were the descendants of Caleb.

Although this restoration and re-grouping is not absolutely certain it still may give us some idea of the Judean population's distribution. The genealogical list of Judah seems to consist of four major subdivisions:

(1) The sons of Shelah who are settled in Lecah (Lachish ?),

Mareshah, Beth-ashbea, Cozeba (?), Netaim and Gederah. Of these sites only Mareshah in the Shephelah is identified with certainty, but occupation of the Shephelah by Shelah seems to be suggested by Genesis 38.

(2) The sons of Hur (from the Hezron-Ephrath[ah] union), who dwelt in Kiriath-jearim, Bethlehem, Beth-gader, Manahath, Zorah, Eshtaol, Netophah, Ataroth, Jabez, Beth-rechab, Etam, Gedor, Hushah, Eshtemoa, Sochoh, Zanoah and Keilah. These towns are in the vicinity of Bethlehem and the north-eastern Shephelah around the Valley of Elah.

(3) The sons of Caleb and Ephrathah, who occupied Tekoa, Shuhah, Beth-rapha and Ir-nahash. Of these the only known location is that of Tekoa, which would seem to indicate that the region between Bethlehem and Hebron is intended.

(4) Caleb's other sons, who settled in Ziph, Hebron, Jorkeam, Beth-zur, Madmannah, Machbeneh and Gibea, i.e. in the Judean hills south of Beth-zur and Hebron.

XI THE TRIBAL LEAGUE AND ITS BORDER DESCRIPTION

During the period of the Judges the tribal framework became more or less consolidated, even though certain families and clans had not ceased their migrations and foreign elements were still being absorbed.

Descriptions of the tribal boundaries are preserved in the geographical chapters of the book of Joshua. For defining the tribal inheritances various sources were utilized; these have been brought together in chapters 13–19. Apart from the list of unconquered Canaanite cities, to which we have already referred (cf. *supra,* p. 233), one may discern two distinct sources, viz. boundary delineations and town lists.[168] Apparently these latter belong to administrative divisions of Judah and Israel; their utilization here is secondary, but a certain relationship was still felt between these districts and the traditional tribal territories. By contrast the boundary descriptions define the tribal inheritances by delineating precise boundaries between the various tribes. There is no reason to doubt that they reflect accurately the Israelite covenant that prevailed late in the period of the Judges (cf. map. 18).

The boundary delineation has been incorporated into a unified list, sections of which have been distributed among the descriptions of the various tribal inheritances (Josh. 15. 1–12; 16. 1–8; 17. 7–10; 18. 12–20; 19. 10–14, 25–9, 33–4). The original list from which they were taken apparently included only the names of border stations as Noth has demonstrated.[169] These places were lifted from their source and then linked together again by verbs. The probability of this suggestion is stregthened by a comparison of duplicate passages, especially those concerning the southern boundaries of Canaan and Judah in which most of the connecting verbs are different, although the place names are

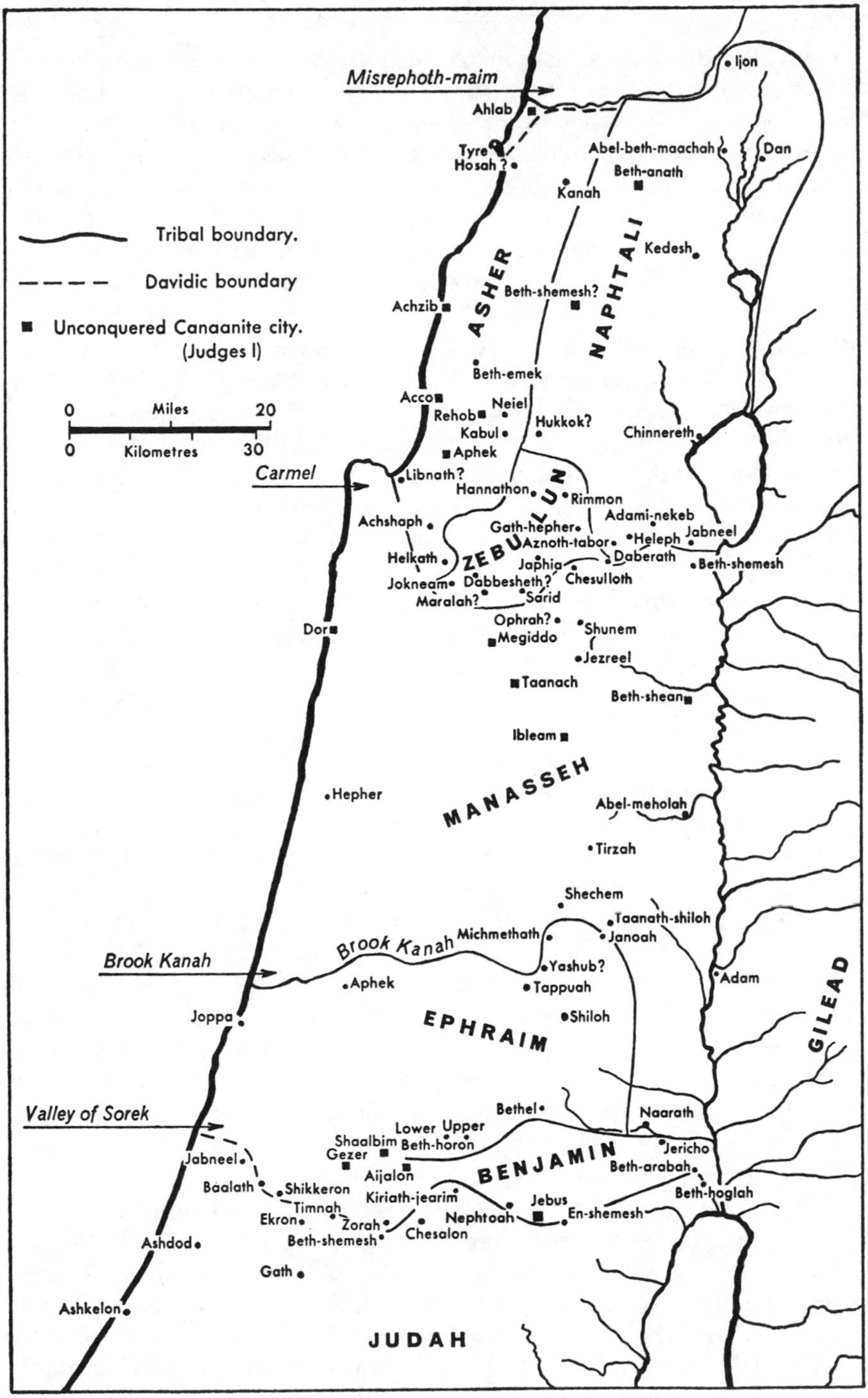

Map 18. The Tribal Boundaries.

practically identical. Collation of the passages concerning boundaries common to Judah and Benjamin (and between Benjamin and Ephraim) leads to the same conclusion. The order between the two texts is reversed, that of Judah going westward and that of Benjamin eastward. The sites are the essential element and the verbal forms only secondary.

At the same time, these verbs are the principal means for distinguishing between this document that describes the tribal boundaries and that comprising the town lists. The connecting verbs used here are somewhat unique, and at least one of them (ותאר, "and [it] turned") occurs only in this list. Evidently these were technical terms used especially for border delineation. One cannot agree with Noth that the lists made up of towns joined together by the conjunction were also border descriptions of more distant tribes with which the editors were simply not sufficiently acquainted. He thinks that for this reason they found it more difficult to insert the proper verb forms. Some of these are only general terms that do not demand special topographical knowledge, e.g. "(it) passed", "(it) turned", "(it) went out", and there is no reason why they could not have been used.[170] But the most decisive argument against his suggestion is that the order of towns in these lists, e.g. that of Issachar, does not produce a logical and continuous border line like one finds in the real boundary descriptions.[171]

The delineations of the borders vary considerably in the amount of detail they include. Some are very detailed, containing many geographical points at short distances from one another, while others are exceedingly brief. Were these lists really so different from one another, or have some of them been condensed in the description before us? The shortening process is especially prominent with regard to the northern territories where the descriptions do not repeat a boundary that is common to different tribes but simply indicate that it touched Zebulun and Asher, etc. Also it would appear that the cities included in the town lists were extracted from border descriptions or vice versa so as to prevent repetition.[172] Therefore, we may assume that all of the boundary delineations were basically quite detailed, being simplified and shortened in varying degrees for our present lists.

This assumption would explain the differences between the various passages describing borders. It also eliminates three difficulties:

(1) In parallel texts describing the same border not only do the connecting verbs differ but one also finds additional geographic features. For example, "to Debir from the Valley of Achor" and "Mount Ephron" on the boundary of Judah (Josh. 15. 7, 9) are missing from the border of Benjamin (Josh. 18. 15, 17); "the shoulder north of Jericho", "at the wilderness of Beth-aven", and "the mountain that lies south of Lower Beth-horon" appear only on the border of Benjamin (Josh. 18.

12–13) but are missing from that of the sons of Joseph (Josh. 16. 1–3). On the other hand, the Archites and the Japhletites are added in the latter text but are lacking in the Benjaminite list. In another parallel passage describing the southern border of Ephraim one finds Upper Beth-horon (Josh. 16. 5), which does not appear in either of the other two lists. These additions can be readily explained by the assumption that the editors made use of one detailed list, shortening it in various ways for the different passages. Therefore, we should take all of these geographical names into account and not reject some of them as spurious.

(2) The detailed description of the Benjamin-Judah boundary in the Jerusalem area requires careful scrutiny. Jerusalem rose to prominence only in the reign of David, and many take this as evidence for dating the list under discussion to that period.[173] But does it really seem likely that a king from the tribe of Judah would stress the capital's belonging to Benjamin? This difficulty can be removed by accepting our conclusion as stated above. The detailed account of Judah's border need not be considered something exceptional. It is simply a good example of an unabbreviated boundary description. We can assume that all of the borders were similarly defined, but that the editors were not concerned with preserving so much detail. The detailed description of the areas near Jerusalem is not, therefore, an argument for the date of the list, but only for that of its final edition and insertion in the book of Joshua.

(3) Most of the boundary delineations mention towns without specifying to which tribe they belong. One may surmise that not the city itself but its territory is meant; however, we are not told around which side of it the border should pass. We must suppose, therefore, that the original list recorded exact topographical features such as springs, hills, streams and such like but that the editors usually contented themselves with generalized references to the settlements and eliminated the rest. Only the local inhabitants would recognize the specific landmarks, and the general reader would not be interested in them. On the other hand, it is understandable that the border around Jerusalem, which is still referred to in the list as Jebus, should receive careful attention since all of those landmarks were well known.[174]

One could scarcely deny that the original text of such a detailed geographical list did represent a real geographical-historical situation. It could hardly have served any other purpose than that ascribed to it in the Bible, viz. the exact delineation of the tribal boundaries within the covenant framework. Use of the name Jebus in place of Jerusalem also points to its early date. The main argument against this view is that none of the evidence from the period of the Judges supports the existence of a large and effective tribal covenant to which the list could be related. Ties between the northern and southern tribes were especially weak as attested by the absence of Judah and Simeon from the Song of Deborah. The fact that they do not even come in for a rebuke indicates that no one expected their participation; they do not seem to have been included as members of the tribal covenant.[175]

However, these arguments may be refuted by a detailed examination of the sources involved. It is worth while to summarize the principal determining factors for understanding the nature and date of this list:

(1) The boundary descriptions conform to the tribal inheritances from the period of the Judges as expressed in all the sources available to us.

(2) They represent the land of Canaan in the real historical meaning of that term as defined in Numbers 34. The external tribal borders correspond to those of Canaan. The southern Judean and Canaanite borders are identical; the Mediterranean on the west and the Jordan on the east are both mentioned. Only in the north is there lack of conformity where the occupation limits of Naphtali and Asher fell far short of the northern Canaanite border. Apparently this is why Naphtali's northern boundary was not given and that of Asher on the north was only completed during the reign of David (cf. *infra,* p. 255).

It is most instructive to note that the descriptions of the Trans-jordanian tribes in Joshua 13 lack boundary delineations.[176] It seems, in fact, that the editors of the book of Joshua had at their disposal only two types of source material for this area, viz. town lists and border descriptions based on terminal reference points according to the formulation "from *X* to *Y*", completely different from the list under consideration. Note the case of Reuben: "So their territory was *from* Aroer, which is on the edge of the valley of the Arnon, and the city that is in the middle of the valley, and all the tableland *to* (by) Medeba" (Josh. 13. 16): and also Gad: "Their territory was Jaazer, and all the cities of Gilead, and half the land of the Ammonites, *to* Aroer, which is east of Rabbah, and *from* Heshbon *to* Ramath-mizpeh and Betonim and *from* Mahanaim *to* Lidebir (the territory of Debir)" (Josh. 13. 25–6). These are only descriptions of regions indicating the main population centres. To understand them as boundary lines consisting of reference points in a fixed order is certainly incorrect.

(3) The boundary descriptions divide up all of the land of Canaan without leaving any empty spaces between the various tribal inheri-tances. Even regions of foreign population were included within the respective tribal precincts; the same point of view is expressed by the list of Canaanite cities in Judges 1 (cf. *supra,* p 233). By the same token, one may not assume that this is a purely hypothetical viewpoint, as Alt suggests[177]; the tribes enjoyed reciprocal relationships with the foreign cities in their respective territories either subjugating them eventually or continuing to dwell "in the midst of the Canaanites".

(4) The boundary list does not include all of the tribes in western

Palestine. Alt had already noted the absence of three tribes: Issachar, Dan and Simeon.[178] In the description of their three tribal inheritances we find only town lists, and the use of the word "border" does not disguise this fact.[179] The absence of these tribes does not create any empty spaces in the list because their territories were included in the inheritances of neighbouring tribes which certainly must represent a historical reality. The original Danite territory is actually divided between Judah, Ephraim and Benjamin. The boundary of Judah extends from Kiriath-jearim past Chesalon and Beth-shemesh from whence it followed the Valley of Sorek to the sea. Ephraim's border ran from Beth-horon through Gezer to the coast (Josh. 16. 3). Evidently these two boundary lines also served as Benjamin's southern and northern borders respectively, because as a matter of fact, the western border of this tribe is missing. Between Beth-horon and Kiriath-jearim no boundary marker is mentioned (Josh. 18. 14). It is as though the western boundary of Benjamin was removed to make room for the Danite inheritance.[180] Issachar seems to have been included by the border lists in the territory of Manasseh[181] The northern boundary of Manasseh is missing, and in its place one finds the passage: "on the north Asher is reached, and on the east Issachar" (Josh. 17. 10); the text goes on to say that the various cities of the Jezreel Plain belong to Manasseh, although they were "also in Issachar and in Asher" (vs. 11). Manasseh's expansion into the territory of Issachar is also suggested by the story of Gideon.

However, the borders of Judah, too, are actually missing from the list under discussion. Not only are there no internal Judean boundaries even for the tribes that had become attached to Judah, e.g. Simeon, Caleb, Kenaz, etc., neither are there any external borders. The southern, eastern and western boundaries of Judah are identical with those of the land of Canaan, and that on the north corresponds to the southern boundary of Benjamin. The only section that appears nowhere else except in relation to the inheritance of Judah is the north-western portion from Kiriath-jearim to the sea. It is possible that even that part is really a continuation of the Benjaminite border which was shortened by the intrusion of Dan. But, as we shall see further on, it is more likely that the description of this section in its detailed form is later than the original boundary list in which segments passing through non-Israelite territory on the west were not described in detail. In any case, it is clear that we may not use this passage as proof that Judah was included in the boundary description, because even if we assume that this is an original tribal border, it had to serve not only as the northern boundary of Judah but also as the southern limit of its neighbour to the north.

A scrupulous analysis of the boundary list shows therefore that, apart from the boundaries of Canaan which provide a general framework, it includes only six tribes: Ephraim, Manasseh, Benjamin, Zebulun, Asher and Naphtali. As we have seen, the list of unconquered Canaanite towns in Judges 1 includes exactly these same tribes, and this correspondence is hardly coincidental. This combination shows clearly that the list originated from a covenant of the northern tribes, that is, Israel in the limited sense of the term.

The existence of such a covenant, whose boundaries and subdivisions were preserved in the list under discussion, is historically probable. With the rise of the Monarchy Israel and Judah appear as two consolidated units testifying to separate organizational frameworks that preceded the unification of the kingdom, and which even a centralized government was unable to nullify. During the period of the Judges the tribes of Mount Ephraim and Galilee participated together in concerted action; but there is no testimony about any war in which the Transjordanian and the southern tribes joined them. This situation prevailed as early as the battle of Deborah. Gideon called out Manasseh, Asher, Zebulun and Naphtali to fight (Judg. 6 35), and sent messengers to all of the Ephraimite hill country (Judg. 7. 24). It is certainly no accident that the same tribes are mentioned as those in the boundary list, while Issacher is missing, even though the conflict took place in his district. The same situation is reflected in the incident of the altar built by the Transjordanian tribes (Josh. 22). They dwell outside of Canaan and build their memorial "at the frontier of the land of Canaan, in the region about the Jordan, on the side that belongs to the people of Israel" (vs. 11). The ensuing negotiations are carried on with the "people of Israel", who have their centre at Shiloh in Mount Ephraim and are represented by the priest and the tribal chiefs. It is probable, therefore, that the boundary list belongs to this tribal alliance which considered itself the heir of Canaan whose borders it adopted when establishing its own inheritance. In the south this alliance took cognizance of Judah's existence, marking out two boundaries there: its own southern limits which corresponded to the northern border of Judah and the southern border of Canaan. The inclusion of Jebus (Jerusalem) in Benjamin suits well the assumption that this boundary is Israelite and not Judean. So the tradition that this description was written down and then confirmed "before the Lord in Shiloh" (Josh. 18. 8) is reliable.

Recognition of the tribal boundary list as an authentic source deriving from the northern Israelite alliance provides us with a factual documentary of this covenant and explains its historical role during the period of the Judges. These are the actual boundaries of the northern tribes which had become crystallized in that age. They do contain a certain hypothetical element in that the boundaries take in the whole land of Canaan without admitting that certain areas were still closed to Israelite settlement. But in such regions as these the borders are usually described in a brief and general fashion; we are simply told that the lines extend to the sea, e.g. on the southern boundaries of Ephraim and Manasseh (Josh. 16. 3, 8). Only two boundary lines are notable for detailed description of an area not settled right away by Israelite tribes, viz. the northern limits of Asher (Josh. 19. 28–9) and the western section of the border with Judah (Josh. 15. 10–12). Both of these are exterior boundaries: the first—with Phoenicia on the north; and the second—with Philistia on the south. From a comparison of Asher's boundary with the census by Joab (2 Sam. 24. 6–7) and the border of Judah with the list of Danite cities (Josh. 19. 43–4) it would seem that these boundaries originated during David's reign. Thus it becomes probable that these two sections did not belong to the original tribal boundaries,[182] but to a boundary delineation of David's kingdom. This was used by the editor as a supplementary source, similar to the utilization of the border of Canaan for the southern Judean boundary.

Apart from these segments the roster presents the actual borders between the Israelite tribes as fixed by the northern alliance. This source testifies that the tribal alliance was a real and authoritative framework whose functions were clearly defined. Alongside it there doubtless existed a Judean tribal covenant which probably included Judah, Simeon, Caleb, Kenaz, Jerahmeel and the Kenites with its centre at Hebron.[183] This explains the antagonism that grew up during the period of the Judges between Israel and Judah which even a united monarchy was unable to overcome.

The boundaries of the various tribes are defined as follows:

Benjamin (Josh. 15:5–11; 18:11–20)

As previously mentioned, the southern border is described in great detail in the passage concerning Judah's inheritance. It is defined in terms of the following reference points[184]: "The mouth of the Jordan"; Beth-hoglah—near 'Ain Ḥajlah (?); "north of Beth-arabah"—near 'Ain el-Gharabeh (?); "the stone of Bohan the son of Reuben"—unknown; "Debir from the Valley of Achor"—unknown; "Geliloth (instead of Gilgal, cf. Josh. 18. 17), which is opposite the ascent of Adummim, which is on the south side of the valley"—to be sought near Tal 'at ed-Damm south of the Wadi Qelṭ, which is "the valley" referred to here; "the waters of En-shemesh"—probably 'Ain el-Ḥoḍ, En-rogel—Bir Ayyub; "the valley of the son of Hinnom at the southern shoulder[185] of the Jebusite"—the slope south of Jerusalem; "the top of the mountain that lies over against the Valley of Hinnom, on the west, at the northern end of the Valley of Rephaim"—the ridge opposite the Old City of Jerusalem corresponding approximately to the present-day Jaffa Road; "the spring of the Waters of Nephtoah"—Lifta; "Baalah (that is, Kiriath-jearim)"—Tell Deir el-'Azar in Abu Ghosh; Chesalon—Kesla; this latter being identified with "the northern shoulder of Mount Jearim" which is associated with

Mount Seir and Mount Ephron[186]—probably hill tops in the forested regions between Jerusalem and Beth-shemesh, which were still virtually void of settlements; Beth-shemesh—Tell er-Rumeileh; Timnah—Tell Baṭashi[187]; "the shoulder of the hill north of Ekron"—the slope north of Khirbet el-Muqanna'; Shikkeron—apparently Tell el-Ful; Mount Baalah—probably the ridge of el-Mughar; Jabneel—Yebna. Thus the border turned north-west from the shore of the Dead Sea, passed south of Jericho and Wadi Qelṭ, and skirted the southern edge of Jerusalem, leaving the city in Benjaminite territory while its fields to the south were assigned to Judah. The border then continued past Kiriath-jearim whence it descended via the forested slopes of the Judean hills to Beth-shemesh, and from there it followed the Sorek Valley to the sea.

On the north Benjamin was contiguous to the House of Joseph, and this line is marked too by Ephraim's southern border (Josh. 16. 1—3, 5; 18. 11—13). On the basis of our assumption that these three parallel passages represent three shortened versions of the same list they can be combined to produce the following description:

The Jordan by Jericho, the waters of Jericho,
the shoulder north of Jericho, the hill country westward to Bethel,
the wilderness of Beth-aven, Luz,
the shoulder south of Luz (the same is Bethel),
the territory of the Archites, Ataroth-addar,
the territory of the Japhletites, Upper Beth-horon,
the mountain that lies to the south of Lower Beth-horon,
Gezer, the sea.

The line of demarcation is quite clear: from the Jordan to a spring east of Jericho (apparently 'Ain es-Sulṭan), thence to the mountain slope north of Jericho. It continued on north-westward towards Bethel to the wilderness of Beth-aven (Tell Maryam ?),[188] followed the ridge south of Bethel (Luz) and descended westward to Upper Beth-horon (Beit 'Ur el-Foqa) and to the hill south of Lower Beth-horon (Beit 'Ur et-Taḥta). Between these last two towns mention is made of Ataroth-addar (probably Kh. Raddana near Ramallah)[189] along with the territories of the Archites. In the passage concerning Benjamin the description stops at Beth-horon, but the parallel text about the House of Joseph preserved one more reference point between there and the sea, *viz.* Gezer.

Ephraim and Manasseh (Josh. 16: 1–8; 17: 7–9)

The southern border of the House of Joseph is described first; cf. the preceding section for a detailed outline. The rest of this passage pertains to the northern boundary of Ephraim which separated it from Manasseh.[190] The starting-point of this border was Michmethath (Khirbet Makhneh el-Foqa ?) near Shechem. From this central reference point the border is described in two segments, first the eastern and then the western. On the east are mentioned Taanath-shiloh (Khirbet Ta'na el-Foqa), Janoah (Khirbet el-Yanun), Ataroth, Naarah (Tell el-Jisr beside 'Ain Duq), Jericho and the Jordan. Towards the west the line followed Tappuah (Sheikh Abu Zarad), and the Brook Kanah (Wadi Qanah). Therefore, the border between Ephraim and Manasseh began just south of Shechem and descended on a sharp diagonal line in each direction, south-east to Jericho and westward along the Wadi Qanah which runs into the Yarkon. Between Jericho and the Jordan its line corresponded to the southern border of the House of Joseph, i.e. the northern border of Benjamin. The area of Ephraim's inheritance was thus limited to the hill region; the respective portions of the Jordan Valley and the Sharon Plain on either side were reckoned to Manasseh. The remaining boundaries of the House of Joseph are mentioned only in brief: on the west the sea, on the north the border of Asher, and on the east that of Issachar.

Zebulun (Josh. 19: 10–14)

The boundary description begins with *Sadud (instead of Sarid—Tell Shadud) at the south-eastern extremity of the tribal inheritance and turns westward from there to "the brook which is east of Jokneam" (Tell Qeimun), evidently Wadi Muṣrarah which joins the Kishon opposite Jokneam. Thus the boundary actually stretched along the Kishon, and the two places referred to on this line, viz Maralah and Dabbesheth, may be identified with Tell Thorah and Tell esh-Shammam respectively. The description then turns north-eastward from Sadud along the slopes of the Nazareth hills towards Lower Galilee to the Sahl el-Baṭṭof. On this line are mentioned Chisloth-Tabor (Iksal), Daberath (Daburiyeh), Japhia (Yafa), Gath-hepher (Khirbet ez-Zurra' beside Meshhed), Eth-kazin (?), Rimmon (Rummaneh). From here the boundary turns westward encompassing the western part of the Sahl el-Baṭṭof since it passes north of Hannathon (Tell el-Bedeiwiyeh), "and it ends at the Valley of Iphtahel" (evidently Wadi el-Malik). On the forested mountain slopes west of Bethlehem the boundary delineation is enclosed within the Valley of Iphtahel and the wadi opposite Jokneam. It should be noted that this is not only one of the most detailed descriptions of a tribal boundary in Galilee but also one of the most explicit of all.

Asher (Josh. 19: 24–29)

For this tribe we have the shortest boundary description, which has been combined with a list of towns.[191] If we ignore this latter document, we are left with more or less the following description:

> Their boundary included Helkath . . . on the west it touches Carmel and Shihor-libnath, then it turns eastward, it goes to Beth-dagon, and it touches Zebulun and the Valley of Iphtahel northward . . . ; then it continues in the north to Kabul . . . as far as Sidon the Great; then the boundary turns to Ramah, reaching to the fortified city of Tyre; then the boundary turns to Hosah, and it ends at the sea.

Thus the southern boundary evidently beginning with Helkath (Tell el-Qassis ?)[192] and ending at Shihor-libnath is described first. It is impossible to accept the opinion that Shihor-libnath is the swamp region of the rivers Nahr ed-Difleh and Nahr ez-Zerqa.[193] Dor is undoubtedly the town in Asher that belongs to Manasseh (Josh. 17. 11); but one should not use this as an argument for placing the border south of Dor. This section belongs to the list of unconquered Canaanite towns (Judg. 1. 27) which, as we have seen, has affinities with the border descriptions. Inasmuch as Beth-shean, Ibleam, *et al.* belonged to Manasseh in the territory of Issachar, this passage proves that Dor was within Manasseh's precincts according to the boundary delineation, even though it had formerly been under Asher's influence. There is therefore no doubt that the border ran along the Carmel, which is mentioned beside Shihor-libnath.[194] It is probable that this latter place is the mouth of the Kishon. Tell Abu Huwam was located here, and it is likely that Libnath was the ancient name of that harbour town.[195]

Next in order comes the eastern boundary which touches Zebulun and the Valley of Iphtahel (Wadi el-Malik) associated with it (Josh. 19. 14). Beth-dagon is mentioned first and should be sought somewhere between Helkath and the Valley of Iphtahel. Farther along Kabul (today the village of Kabul north-west of the Sahl el-Baṭṭof) is mentioned, but all the rest of the northern segment touching on Naphtali (Josh. 19. 34) is missing. Only the conclusion is preserved "as far as Sidon the Great", i.e. at the Sidonian border somewhere near the River Liṭani. Finally, the northern segment is given. Ramah is unknown.[196] The last two points at the western end are "the fortified city of Tyre" and Hosah. In LXX the former is translated "the spring of the fort of Tyre"; in Joab's census it is called "the fortress of Tyre" (2 Sam. 24. 7). Perhaps it may be identified with the coastal town opposite Tyre called Usu in the ancient non-biblical sources and Palaityros in Hellenistic texts, today Tell Rashidiyeh by the main watercourse of Tyre. Hosah may be the reflex of Usu since there is no other site between Tell Rashidiyeh and the seashore.[197] We have already noted the remarkable resemblance between this boundary delineation and the line followed by Joab during his census.

Naphtali (Josh. 19:32–34)

The description begins with the southern section from Mount Tabor to the Jordan.[198] Here are mentioned Heleph (apparently Khirbet ʿIrbadeh at the foot of Mount Tabor), the oak in Zaanannim, Adami-nekeb (Khirbet et-Tell above Khirbet ed-Damiyeh), Jabneel (Tell en-Naʿam) and Lakkum (Khirbet el-Manṣurah ?). Thus the boundary follows the line of Wadi Fajjas, somewhat south of it to be more exact, because the actual boundary reference points are missing between the oak of Zaanannim and Lakkum, two adjacent towns being inserted in their place. The western border is mentioned next beginning with Aznoth-tabor (Khirbet el-Jebeil at the foot of Mount Tabor) but then we are only told that it touched Zebulun on the south and Asher on the west (the reference to Hukkok is incomprehensible here since the borders of Naphtali and Zebulun already meet in the Tabor region). Finally, the Jordan is given as the eastern boundary[199] while Naphtali's northern border is entirely missing.

From the boundaries of the tribal inheritances it is possible to reach some conclusions concerning the nature of the settlement. In many of the boundary delineations the fact stands out that former Canaanite towns served as reference points. Frequently this did not mean the outer edge of the city's territory but the actual limits of the urban settlement itself, while its surrounding lands were assigned to another tribe.[200] On the border of Judah Jerusalem, Baalath (Kiriath-jearim) and Beth-shemesh are mentioned; but the fact is emphasized that the region south of Jerusalem belonged to Judah, although the town itself was within Benjamin's inheritance. The line between Benjamin and Ephraim passed by Bethel; that dividing Ephraim from Manasseh ran near Shechem and Tappuah; again it is stressed that Manasseh occupied the territory of Tappuah while Ephraim possessed the town (Josh. 17. 8). In the Valley of Jezreel we do not have accurate descriptions, but it is evident that the Canaanite cities in this region separated the tribes of the House of Joseph from those of Galilee. For instance, Jokneam appears on Zebulun's southern border and the Plain of Chesulloth on the eastern. The Valley of Jabneel serves as the southern boundary of Naphtali and towns are mentioned there that had formerly been Canaanite, e.g. Adami-nekeb (Adamim) and Jabneel. Farther west Hannathon, a city known from the El Amarna letters, appears on the northern border of Zebulun. The ancient trade route (Darb el-Ḥawarnah), which was lined with Canaanite settlements where it crossed Lower Galilee,[201] evidently served as the central dividing line between the Galilean tribes—Naphtali and Asher on the north, Issachar and Zebulun on the south.

From this we learn something about the nature of the Israelite occupation. If the initial penetration had begun with the conquest of

Canaanite cities in the various regions, these towns would have become tribal centres rather than border points. Note, for example, Laish which became the principal city of Dan after its conquest. Actually, the Canaanite population centres were on the periphery of the tribal districts. In other words, the tribes settled round about the Canaanite cities, and only at a later stage did the town itself fall into their hands, e.g. Bethel, which was taken by the House of Joseph, while the Benjaminite border was fixed to the south of it, or Tappuah, which fell to Ephraim so that the border was fixed north of it, though the fields originally belonged to Manasseh.

XII. THE CITIES OF SIMEON

In addition to the system of tribal boundaries there were also town lists of the various tribal entities. This is attested by the list of Simeon's cities (Josh. 19. 1—8; 1 Chron. 4. 28—33), the only text of its kind preserved in the Bible.[202] It is true that in the description of almost every tribal area, town lists are also integrated, but these were usually taken from district rosters of the monarchial period.[203] A distinct illustration is the list of Naphtali's towns which mentions Hazor (Josh. 19. 36) though that town was not occupied during the period of the Judges but was only resettled by Solomon. The editor evidently thought it legitimate to use the more complete and up-to-date lists from the monarchial period since it actually pertained to the same tribal area. On the other hand, he did not seem to have a later, monarchial, list for Simeon since that tribe's patrimony was no longer clearly defined (Josh. 19. 1, 9).

This has first of all been verified by archaeological research. The towns of Simeon flourished during the 13th–12th centuries and had suffered destruction by the time of the monarchy. Thus we read about them, "These were their cities until David reigned" (1 Chron. 4. 31). That statement, which had caused considerable bewilderment among scholars, can now be understood against the background of recent archaeological evidence.[204]

The Simeonite list contains 13 towns of which only the first, Beer-sheba, can be identified with certainty. Other plausible identifications are Hormah with Kh. Meshash,[205] 8 miles east of Beer-sheba, and Sharuhen, which Albright identified with the southern Tell el-Far 'ah,[206] *c*. 20 miles west of Beer-sheba. Ziklag was evidently on the western periphery of the patrimony so its identification with Tell esh-Shari 'ah is plausible.[207] The names of three of Simeon's towns have recently come to light on Hebrew ostraca from excavations in the Negeb. Hazar-susah has appeared on a text from Arad[208] while Tolad (=Eltolad; cf. 1 Chron. 4. 29) has been found at Beer-sheba[209] and Ezem at Tell esh-Shari 'ah.[210] One may perhaps assume that these ancient settlements were not far from the archaeological sites in which they receive mention. Finally, one may also consider the identification of Moladah with Kh. el-Waten, *c.* 5 1/2 miles east of Beer-sheba, though direct translations of the Hebrew name into Arabic are rare.

Most of Simeon's towns became incorporated later on into the Negeb of Judah, which covered a more extensive area (Josh. 15. 21–32). One of the four cities that are missing from the Judean list is Sharuhen. In its place we find Shilhim (Josh. 15. 32) or Shaaraim (1 Chron. 4. 31). This may not be accidental; the more westerly Sharuhen was possibly not included within the territory of the monarchy.

The composition of the later list leaves no doubt that the additions represent the various Negeb areas that were not originally within the area of Simeon, viz. the Negeb of Caleb, the Negeb of the Kenites and the Negeb of the Jerahmeelites. Among the Calebite clans we find Pelet and Madmannah (1 Chron. 2. 47, 49) which must have some relation to Beth-pelet and Madmannah of the enlarged list. Among the additions, Arad[211] also appears and it was originally Kenite (Judg. 1. 15). The name of Kinah, which is listed beside Arad, and which is now attested with Arad in an ostracon from Arad,[212] evidently reflects the clan name of the Kenites. Thus, these areas to the north and east were added to the original Simeonite nucleus in the monarchial period to form the Negeb district. The non-Simeonite areas were subsumed under the caption, "together with all the villages round about these cities as far as Baalath-beer, Ramath-negeb" (Josh. 19. 8; 1 Chron. 4. 33 has "as far as Baal"). This is now clear from the allusion to Ramath-negeb in the same Arad ostracon (where Arad and Kinah appear together); the context indicates that Ramath-negeb was the first outpost facing an Edomite threat and the commanders at Arad were ordered to reinforce its garrison.[213] Therefore, Ramath-negeb is probably to be sought to the south-east of Arad; its identification with Kh. Ghazzeh on the south-east edge of the Negeb, overlooking the road to Edom, is most probable.[214] This would place Ramath-negeb about on the border between the Kenite and the Jerahmeelite areas of the Negeb, those which were not originally Simeonite.

This northern enclave of Simeonite towns was later divided between the Shephelah and the Negeb districts in the monarchial division of Judah, which was based on geographical, rather than tribal, principles.

A further addition to the list of Simeonite towns is comprised of En-rimmon, Ether and Ashan according to Josh. 19. 7, and Etam, Ain, Rimmon, Tochen and Ashan according to 1 Chron. 4. 32. The entries for Ain and Rimmon in this latter passage are probably to be combined as one, En-rimmon (cf. Neh. 11. 29). Of the variants Ether and Tochan, the former is to be preferred. Ether and Ashan are mentioned together in the southeastern Shephelah district of Judah (Josh. 15. 42) and this indicates the direction in which we must look for their location.

En-rimmon probably should be identified with Tell el-Khuweilfeh while the ancient name is preserved in nearby Kh. Umm er-Ramamin.[215] The older tell is situated at the foot of the Judean hills overlooking the trough valley that extends northward along the eastern edge of the Shephelah. Tell Beit Mirsim is also located in the same valley, *c.* 6 miles north of Tell el-Khuweilfeh. About three miles north of Tell Beit Mirsim is Tell 'Aiṭun, which is no less impressive than the former in size and importance. There is a resemblance between its name and the Etam in our list. It would seem, therefore, that this enclave of towns extending from the Negeb into the southern Shephelah was also settled at one time by Simeonite clans. This assumption then permits the consideration of Tell Beit Mirsim with Ashan, one of the Levitical cities in Judah mentioned between Debir and Beth-shemesh (1 Chron. 6. 44). Its fortifications from the monarchial period and its general layout similar to Beth-shemesh make it suitable as a candidate for a Levitical town.

XIII. THE DEEDS OF THE JUDGES

The various wars described in the book of Judges are local affairs limited to particular regions and usually associated with only one tribe. In any case, they normally do not extend beyond the vicinity of one tribal inheritance. Battle narratives from different regions are built around the names of five judges. Othniel the son of Kenaz, the brother of Caleb, belonged to Judah and the Conquest tradition about Debir-Kiriath-sepher (Josh. 15. 15–19; Judg. 1. 11–15) is associated with him. His conflict with Cushan-rishathaim, King of Aram(-naharaim), is shrouded in mystery from the standpoint of historical geography.[216] Ehud the son of Gera led his own tribe of Benjamin in a successful campaign against the King of Moab, who had encroached upon Jericho.[217] This story demonstrates that the Moabite king had succeeded, at least for a time, in realizing his country's claim on the tableland between the Arnon and Heshbon. He evidently was not satisfied with controlling that area plus the plains of Moab opposite Jericho but even expanded his authority to include Jericho, thereby exerting pressure upon Benjamin. We do not have the means for fixing the exact date of these events nor for the length of time taken up by Moabite oppression. Neither do we know how long or to what degree the Moabites held their hegemony over the plateau and the plains of Moab. We do learn, however, that the Moabites were driven back across the Jordan and that Israelites "from the hill country of Ephraim" (Judg. 3. 27), apparently Benjamin and part of Ephraim, took part in the battle.

Gideon's war against the Midianites evidently occurred after the battle of Deborah. Incursions by desert nomads in search of plunder such as those carried out by the Midianites, the Amalekites and the people of the East (Judg. 6. 3) into the Jezreel Valley were possible only after the Canaanite cities in that region had been weakened by their defeat before Barak. The victory of Hadad the son of Bedad over "Midian in the country of Moab" (Gen. 36. 35) may have occurred at about this same time.[218] He was the fourth King of Edom, and four more rulers reigned after him up till the time of David. However, exact chronological determinations are precluded particularly as the list of Edomite kings may not be complete.

The battle of Gideon was carried out in the central Jezreel Valley (Judg. 6. 33) between the spring of Harod and the hill of Moreh (Judg. 7. 1), i.e. in the region of Israelite Jezreel. Although this district belonged to Issachar according to the tribal divisions, Gideon only sent for the other three Galilean tribes—Asher, Zebulun and Naphtali (Judg. 6. 35). In fact, it would seem that the only participants in this fight were members of his own clan, Abiezer of Manasseh. His home town of Ophrah is not identified with certainty, but it was probably located somewhere near the scene of the battle. The affinities of his clan with that region are also indicated by the information that his brothers were slain at Tabor (Judg. 8. 18 f.). Ophrah is usually identified with eṭ-Ṭaiyibeh north-east of the hill of Moreh,[219] but this is more likely the site of the Hapharaim belonging to Issachar (Josh. 19. 19). Therefore, an identification of Ophrah with ʿAffuleh in the centre of the Jezreel Valley south-west of the hill of Moreh is entirely possible. This latter place seems to correspond to the *ʿ-p-r* in the list of Thut-mose III (No. 53), and a tell containing occupational remains from the Bronze and Israelite periods has been discovered there.[220] This site is also suitable according to the testimony of Eusebius, who knows of a place called Αφραια. 6 miles north of Legio (Onom. 28. 25).[221] The Abiezer clan is also known from the Samaria ostraca to have been located in Mount Ephraim, but this does not negate the possibility that part of them had migrated northward to the Jezreel Valley. We have already noted the textual hint to Manassite expansion at the expense of Issachar (Josh. 17. 11); Manasseh's inheritance apparently bordered on Naphtali's. After Gideon's sudden defeat of the Midianite camp, evidently in the vicinity of En-dor north of the hill of Moreh (Ps. 83. 9–10), he was joined by men from Naphtali, Asher and "all Manasseh", i.e. the other Manassite clans from Mount Ephraim (Judg. 7. 23). These came out to join in the pursuit after Midian, obviously with an eye to the booty. The Midianites fled eastward[222] and suffered an additional trouncing at the hands of Ephraim who had blocked the Jordan fords (vs. 24). Here, as in the story of Jephthah, Ephraim's claim to primacy among the northern tribes is voiced.

Gideon did not stop there but continued in pursuit of the Midianites "by the caravan route" (Heb.: "the route of the tent camps", Judg. 8.

11) to Karkor (Qarqar in the Wadi Sirḥan).[223] On the way he was greeted by the men of Succoth and Penuel in a very unfriendly manner. Upon his return he punished the elders of Succoth quite severely and broke down the tower of Penuel. We do not know who the inhabitants of these towns were, but the reference to a tower at Penuel, which brings to mind the tower at Shechem, strongly suggests that it belonged to a Canaanite enclave in the Gad-Gilead region like the one at near-by Zaphon which had been absorbed by Gad.

In connection with Succoth, however, we hear only about the elders and their punishment. Nothing speaks therefore against their belonging to the Gadite settlers of the region.[224] It is no surprise that the residents of these towns looked with suspicion on Gideon's band, for they had already suffered enough at the hands of the Midianites.

The judges were charismatic personalities who came forward as saviours of the people under the influence of an inner compulsion to accomplish a particular task. However, when that job was done, it did not mean that their role was ended; they frequently stayed on as life-time rulers ("judges" in their respective tribes), occasionally exercising control over other tribes as well. Under Gideon's auspices Ophrah became a tribal cultic centre, and he is the only one known to us among the judges to be succeeded by his son, who made the first attempt at establishing an Israelite monarchy. In this premature venture Abimelech was dependent at first upon his mother's clan and the patricians of Shechem. Here he was crowned king after having hired a band of mercenaries with funds from Shechem's "house of Baal-berith" and having slain his brothers at Ophrah. It is clear from the ensuing events that the patricians at Shechem hoped to renew their city's rule over all of Mount Ephraim as in the days of Lab 'ayu. However, Abimelech had his own political aims, and in spite of his being crowned by the aid of the Shechemites, he considered himself an Israelite king. He established his residence not at Shechem but at Arumah (Judg. 9. 41; called Tormah in vs. 31), apparently Khirbet el-'Ormah on an elevated site five miles south-east of Shechem. The situation rapidly deteriorated into an open quarrel between him and the citizens of Shechem, resulting in Abimelech's siege of the town. He conquered and destroyed it and burned down its tower over the patricians trapped inside. A fortified temple, probably the "house of Baal-berith" or the tower of Shechem, built upon a high, artificial fill (evidently giving rise to the name "Beth-millo", Judg. 9. 6) was discovered during excavations at Shechem.[225] The latest investigations point to the destruction of this temple and the city during the first half of the twelfth century, but this date is based mainly on the absence of Philistine pottery, a fact that may not be relevant at a site located in the hill country.

Abimelech met his death during the siege of Thebez, also an ancient

Canaanite town as demonstrated by the presence of a mighty tower there (Judg. 9. 51). The accepted identification of Thebez with Tubas about nine miles north-east of Shechem[226] is doubtful. There is only a vague similarity between the names, and no suitable tell has been found on the site. The possibility suggests itself that Thebez is simply a corrupted spelling of Tirzah, the ancient Canaanite city identified with Tell el-Far'ah about six miles north-east of Shechem.[227] Tirzah and Shechem were strong Canaanite cities in Mount Ephraim that came to be included in the tribal framework of Manasseh (cf. *supra,* p. 211); evidently Abimelech wanted to win the allegiance of the Israelite population by annihilating the last Canaanite centres in the hill country.

Conflict in Transjordan is described in the story of Jephthah the Gileadite. On the one hand, some obvious legendary accretions have been assimilated to this narrative, e.g. the personification of his father Gilead and the story of his daughter. Neither is the historical debate between Jephthah and the Ammonite king a part of the original story, because it is actually an argument with Moab. On the other hand, it cannot be denied that there are clear historical elements in the account. The Israelite forces assembled at Mizpah (Judg. 10. 17), also called Mizpeh of Gilead (Judg. 11. 29), which was the site of a cultic centre (vs. 11), perhaps an ancient amphictyonic rallying point in Gilead. Its location has not been identified with certainty, but if it may be equated with the Ramath-mizpeh mentioned between Heshbon, Betonim and Mahanaim (Josh. 13. 26), then it must be sought in the area south of the Jabbok, perhaps near Jebel Jel 'ad and Khirbet Jel 'ad.[228] The towns referred to—Aroer, Minnith and Abel-keramim (Judg. 11. 33)—are unknown, but the district west of Rabbath-ammon is certainly meant. Finally, Jephthah's own place of residence is uncertain. Although it is stated that he had his home at Mizpah (Judg. 11. 34), there are also some indications that he resided at Zaphon to which the Ephraimites had assembled (Judg. 12. 1). Where the Hebrew text states that Jephthah was buried "in the cities of Gilead" (Judg. 12. 7) the LXX reads "in his city, Zaphon".

As in the passage about Deborah's war, Gilead is used exclusively in place of Gad. Perhaps this is an indication that the two conflicts were not widely separated chronologically. One also notes a parallel to the story of Gideon in the Ephraimites' special claims to leadership of the tribal alliance and their assertion that no one had authority to go to war without inviting their participation. But in contrast to Gideon, who shrewdly appeased them with smooth talk, Jephthah considered their actions as interference in something that was none of their business. He therefore dealt severely with them. The Ephraimite statement, "You are fugitives of Ephraim, you Gileadites, in the midst of Ephraim and Manasseh" (Judg. 12. 4), is difficult to understand. Perhaps these men of the House of Joseph looked upon the residents of Gilead as fugitives from Mount Ephraim, still subject to orders from their place of origin. The anecdote about Shibboleth—Sibboleth (Judg. 12. 6) bears witness to the existence of dialectical variations between different areas of the country.

The story of the concubine murdered at Gibeah (Judg. 19–21) serves as an illustration of controversies and blood feuds between the tribes during this period, although the historical details of the story are wrapped in legendary accretion. The geographical references are based on reality, e.g. the assembling of the Israelites at Mizpah and Bethel, "for the ark of the covenant of God was there in those days" (Judg. 20. 27), and the concentration of the Benjaminites at Gibeah (of Benjamin). The excavations have shown that the first stratum was actually destroyed during the 12th century and the site was then abandoned until the founding of Saul's fortress.[229] Though the story does contain an historical kernel, it is mostly legendary in nature and neither the exact course of events nor the date can be fixed with any certainty.

Beside the most famous saviour-judges there are also five "minor judges" who receive mention, although the traditions about their mighty deeds and battles are not preserved. It is only stated that they judged the people at a certain place, and sometimes their great wealth is emphasized (Judg. 10. 4; 12. 9, 14). Those mentioned are: Tola the son of Puah from Issachar, who resided in Mount Ephraim (Judg. 10. 1–2); Jair the Gileadite (vss. 3–5; is this a historical personage from Havvoth-jair or a personification of the tribal patriarch ?); Ibzan of Bethlehem (Judg. 12. 8–10), whether from Judah or Zebulun is impossible to determine; Elon the Zebulunite (vss. 11–12); and Abdon the son of Hillel from Pirathon in Mount Ephraim (vss. 13–15).

The office of judge may have enjoyed permanent status in the tribal framework, even though its authority was much more limited in peacetime. The leadership may have passed from one tribe to another in turn during this period, at least within the northern Israelite alliance.

The period of the Judges is depicted in the Bible as one of insecurity and recurrent wars under the incessant pressure of rivals against which the loosely organized tribal league was unable to act with efficiency: "And the people of Israel departed from there at that time, every man to his tribe and family, and they went out from there every man to his inheritance. In those days there was no king in Israel; every man did what was right in his own eyes" (Judg. 21. 24–25). This definition represents the polemic of the monarchy but the period of the Judges appears today in a completely different light. With the dating of the battle of Deborah in the second half of the 13th century, it becomes clear that this was a long period, extending over at least 300 years. Besides the major battles in the north we hear only of marginal invasions by

Moab, Ammon and Midian, which hardly posed a serious threat to the Israelite settlement. In a general way, this was a relatively peaceful period of intensive settlement, and until the expansion of the Philistines no serious rival endangered the growing Israelite population. The historical-geographical sources also seem to indicate that the tribal league was more organized and efficient than has been generally assumed.

XIV. THE PHILISTINES

The Philistines arrived in Canaan several generations after the Israelites. They belonged to the wave of "Sea Peoples" that migrated eastward from the islands of Greece and Asia Minor under pressure from the Dorian invasion of the Greek mainland.[230] Some of the Sea Peoples began appearing as mercenaries in the Egyptian army as early as the reigns of Ramses II and Merneptah, but the Philistines are mentioned for the first time in inscriptions of Ramses III. From the eighth year of his reign we have a detailed description of their eruption into Syria and Canaan and their subsequent attack upon Egypt.[231] In contrast to the Israelite penetration, the Sea Peoples carried out a mighty expedition of conquest which shook the kingdoms of the Middle East to their very foundations. According to Egyptian documents this took place in the eighth year of Ramses III, i.e. *c.* 1170, although they must have been exerting pressure on the Middle East before that time.

The Egyptian narrative tells us that these Peoples of the Sea approached simultaneously by land and by boat. The land contingent included wagons loaded with their wives, children and property. Altogether they consisted of five groups: *p-r-š-t* (Philistines), *ṯ-k-r* (Sikel ?), *š-k-r-š, d-n-n* and *w-š-š*. Ramses III tells us that they had already ravaged both Alashia and the Hittite kingdom, reaching even to Carchemish on the Euphrates before their advance was halted by his victory over them in Amurru.

Evidently these inscriptions of Ramses III correspond fairly well to the actual event. The Hittite kingdom had fallen, never to rise; the tempest of the Sea Peoples had lashed against the coast of Syria and Palestine, driving almost to the gates of Egypt. To win this victory the Egyptians exhausted their strength completely, and the period of Egyptian domination over the land of Canaan came to an end.

Ramses III seems to have put much effort into renewing the Egyptian control over Canaan that seems to have collapsed completely during the decline of the Nineteenth Dynasty and the inner confusion in Egypt (*c.* 1210–1175). Inscriptions of Ramses III from Beth-shean show that during his reign the Egyptian base was re-established there and the temples rebuilt (level VI). Burials in "anthropoid" coffins whose occupants were evidently Philistines have been found at Beth-shean.

Perhaps some of these date to that period and belonged to Philistine mercenaries in service to the Egyptians there.[232] A list of cities belonging to the priests of Amon dating to the reign of Ramses III mentions nine towns in Ḫuru,[233] and these may have served as both cultic and administrative centres at that time just as the Levitical cities did later.[234] Among them a "City in the Canaan" is named, probably Gaza. Three plaques from a collection of ivories found at Megiddo mention by name a singer of the god Ptah from Ashkelon.[235] In this same group was discovered a box with an inscription including the name of Ramses III. From this it would appear that a temple to the Egyptian god Ptah existed at Ashkelon during his reign.[236]

Not long after the victories of Ramses III we find the Philistines established as the rulers of the southern coastal region of Canaan. Gaza was one of their chief cities, the city that had been the regional capital for centuries under the Egyptians. The assumption is widely accepted that they were settled there after the war to serve as garrison troops for the Egyptians,[237] a view that is based on the following summary of the deeds of Ramses III as given in Papyrus Harris I:

> I extended all the frontiers of Egypt and overthrew those who had attacked them from their lands. I slew the Denyen in their islands, while the Tjeker and the Philistines were made ashes. The Sherden and the Weshesh of the Sea were made nonexistent, captured all together and brought in captivity to Egypt like the sands of the shore. I settled them in strongholds, bound in my name. Their military classes were as numerous as hundred-thousands. I assigned portions for them all with clothing and provisions from the treasuries and granaries every year.[238]

Thus Ramses is boasting that after his victory he settled them in Egyptian forts as garrison troops paid out of treasury funds. This was done in various places, e.g. Upper Egypt, so it is assumed that the same held true for the Egyptian administrative centres in Canaan.

Today there is no doubt that this assumption is basically wrong. A burned level was found at Ashkelon between the last Canaanite city and the Philistine city that followed it.[239] At Ashdod there was even an intermediate level between the destruction of the last Canaanite city and the foundation of the Philistine city.[240] Yet the deciding factor is the Philistine pottery. This unique ware which appears with their arrival from the Aegean does not belong to the last phase of the classic Myceneaen pottery (Myc. IIIB) which was used until *c.* 1200, but rather to the *second* phase of the sub-Mycenaean pottery (Myc. IIIC$_2$).[241] There is, therefore, a definite span between the beginning of the 12th century, i.e. the time of the battles with Ramses III, and the settlement of the Philistines. Their arrival cannot precede approximately the mid-12th century, when the Egyptian rule in Canaan came to an end.

Historical records about their actual arrival are lacking. It was doubtless due to a military invasion, perhaps mainly by ship from Cyprus where Philistine pottery has been discovered.

A special source for illuminating the situation in Canaan at the beginning of the eleventh century is the story of Wenamon.[242] This narrative concerns an excursion by an Egyptian named Wenamon, priest in the temple of Amon at Karnak, who was sent to Byblos with orders to acquire trees for constructing a sacred barque. Throughout the whole affair there is never a mention of Egyptian rule in Canaan or on the Phoenician coast. The Egyptian emissary encounters indifference and callousness on the part of the local rulers who feel no obligation towards him and are only prepared to sell him their merchandise for cash on the line. The first station in his journey is Dor, which is now in possession of the *ṯ-k-r*. Here Wenamon was robbed of his money by one of his own sailors who jumped ship. He requests the King of Dor to try and catch the thief, but the ruler denied that it was his responsibility. After becoming exasperated with the procrastinating King of Dor, Wenamon continued on his journey and somewhere, perhaps at Tyre, he was able to seize a boat belonging to the *ṯ-k-r* from which he recouped part of his loss. As a result, eleven ships of the *ṯ-k-r* followed him to Byblos. He managed to elude them and sailed for Cyprus; after a few lines describing his arrival the text is broken off.

From this account we not only learn about the new political situation that had arisen after the collapse of Egyptian rule but we also gain some important geopolitical details: (1) This is the only indication that Dor was occupied by one of the Sea Peoples who came with the Philistines, viz. the *ṯ-k-r* . Since there is no hint of this in the Bible, it is probable that they had become subsumed under the title of Philistines to whose domination they may have submitted with the passage of time. Philistine authority extended as far as the Valley of Jezreel during Saul's reign. (2) We are told about a fleet manned by the *ṯ-k-r,* and this is the only explicit reference to maritime activities on the part of the one of the Sea Peoples after their arrival on the Canaanite coast. This leaves room for the assumption that the coastal towns, Gaza, Ashkelon, Ashdod and Jaffa, continued to engage in sea trade (cf. *supra,* p. 17). It also explains the special importance of Dor in the framework of the Israelite Monarchy as a harbour town with a maritime tradition. Thus it became one of Solomon's twelve district capitals and was governed by the King's son-in-law.

The Philistines occupied the coastal region of Palestine from the Yarkon southward. One sees this not only in the Bible; it is also attested by the "Philistine" pottery so typical of that region.[243] This type of ware shows a strong influence from forms typical of the late Mycenaean culture, but Egyptian and Canaanite characteristics are also noticeable.

The Aegean features were doubtless brought by them from their homeland, but local influences soon made themselves felt. The Egyptian traits in this pottery may reflect some degree of Egyptian hegemony during the first stages of Philistine onslaught. Not only the styles of these vessels but also their distribution leaves no room for doubt that this is real Philistine ware; therefore, they provide an important evidence for the centres of Philistine occupation. Of course, such pottery is found to some degree in more distant areas, but it becomes more and more scarce the farther we recede from the main Philistine concentration.

The Philistines were organized in a sort of confederation comprising five cities ruled over by "tyrants".[244] Three of their towns were located near the coast on the *Via Maris:* Gaza, Ashkelon and Ashdod. The other two were farther east in the Shephelah: Gath and Ekron (cf. map 19).

The three western cities were ancient Canaanite centres which came under Philistine domination. Gaza and Ashkelon are known from many Egyptian sources; it has been noted that they were important centres of Egyptian rule in Canaan. Ashdod is now known from texts found at Ugarit as a seaport from which wool, fabrics, fish and other products were exported (cf. *supra,* p. 17). Among Egyptian documents it is only known from the "Onomasticon of Amenope" from the end of the twelfth century. This document, which is a sort of encyclopaedic list of terms, mentions the western Philistine centres and the Sea Peoples one after another[245]: Ashkelon, Ashdod, Gaza (262–4); *š̌-r-d-n, ṯ-k-r, p-r-š̌-t* (268–70). Between them we find *ỉ-s-r* (265), apparently the tribe of Asher which is also on the coast, though north of the others. The list seems to represent the actual situation at the end of Egyptian rule in Canaan. Therefore, it is quite possible that the Sherdanu people had settled in a certain area, although we have no other information to this effect.

The other two Philistine capitals were located more to the east on the edge of the Shephelah. Ekron is now identified with considerable certainty as Khirbet el-Muqanna', about three and a half miles west of Tell Baṭashi (Timnah) south of Wadi Ṣarar (the Sorek).[246] This site corresponds well to the northern boundary description of Judah which describes a line following the Sorek from Beth-shemesh past Timnah to "the shoulder of the hill north of Ekron" (Josh. 15. 11), i.e. to the steep incline north of the town.[247] At Tell el-Muqanna' a fortified city has been discovered dating to the Iron Age, which comprised an area of about 40 acres. It was obviously the largest and most important town in the area, and an abundance of Philistine ware was found there. Although archaeological excavations have yet to be carried out on this site, it has been subjected to an intensive survey which revealed no evidence for settlement prior to the Israelite period except for a small amount of Early Bronze sherds. It would seem, therefore, that Ekron was founded by the Philistines.

The location of Gath is still much debated. The suggestion to equate it with Tell Sheikh el- 'Areini beside 'Araq el-Menshiyeh[248] has been discredited by excavations carried out on the site. It was shown that the Iron Age town was built only on the high tell, no more than three or four acres in area.[249] A more recent suggestion to identify Gath with Tell en-Nejileh,[250] about seven and a half miles farther south, has also been disproved archaeologically. In spite of the intensive survey carried out there, no Philistine ware has been found. Excavations have now shown that it was an important town in the Hyksos period but has very few remains from the Late Bronze or Iron Ages. Tell el-Ḥesi, about four miles north-west of this on the same wadi, was also a large city in the Canaanite period; but the Iron Age settlement is restricted to the rather small higher mound. This accords well with its usual identification as Eglon but is not congenial to an identification with Gath. The same is true for Tell esh-Shari 'ah, a relatively small site that may have had a maximum area of *c.* 5 acres.[251]

Since there remains no suitable tell in this more southerly region, we should reconsider an earlier proposal to equate Gath with Tell eṣ-Ṣafi.[252] This is a large and outstanding site with a contemporary lower city spread out at its feet in which an abundance of Philistine pottery was discovered.[253] Its position at the point where the Wadi es-Sanṭ (the Valley of Elah) enters the western Shephelah corresponds nicely with the account of David's victory over Goliath the Gittite. Their fight took place farther east between Sochoh and Azekah (1 Sam. 17. 1), and afterwards the Israelites pursued the Philistines "as far as Gath (LXX; cf. MT which reads *gai,* 'valley') and the gates of Ekron, so that the wounded Philistines fell on the way from Shaaraim as far as Gath and Ekron" (vs. 52). The other biblical references to Gath do not provide any precise topographical information, but neither do they contradict an equation with Tell eṣ-Ṣafi. We cannot always be certain as to whether a particular passage is discussing Gath of the Philistines or some other Gath, e.g. Gath-Gittaim near Gezer.[254] If the Gath conquered by Hazael, the King of Syria, is Gath of the Philistines (2 Kings 12. 17), then the reference tends to support an identification with Tell eṣ-Ṣafi, which is located on one of the important passes leading to Jerusalem.[255]

The equation of Gimti, the city of Shuwardata in the El Amarna period, with the Philistine Gath provides additional corroboration (cf. *supra,* p. 174). It also helps to explain the one difficulty encountered by this identification, viz. the nearness of Tell eṣ-Ṣafi and Khirbet el-Muqanna ' (Ekron), which are only about five miles apart as the crow flies. During the El Amarna period we noted three principal royal cities in the Shephelah: Gezer, Gath and Lachish. The Amorite residents of Gezer and its vicinity held their own throughout the period of the

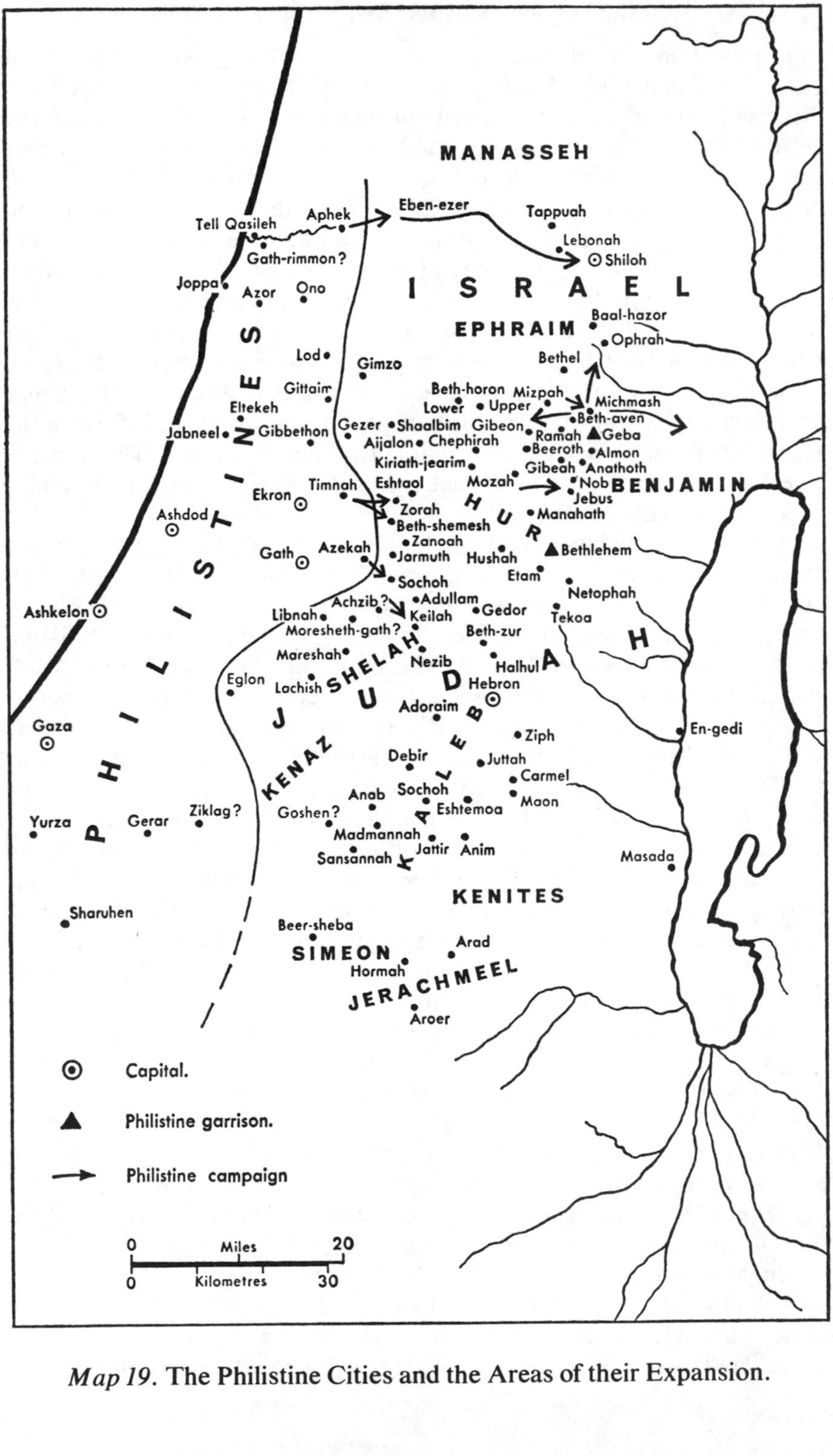
MANASSEH
ISRAEL
EPHRAIM
BENJAMIN
PHILISTINES
JUDAH
SHELAH
HUR
KALEB
KENAZ
KENITES
SIMEON
JERACHMEEL
Tell Qasileh
Aphek
Eben-ezer
Tappuah
Lebonah
Shiloh
Gath-rimmon?
Joppa
Azor
Ono
Baal-hazor
Ophrah
Lod
Gimzo
Bethel
Gittaim
Beth-horon
Lower
Upper
Mizpah
Michmash
Beth-aven
Eltekeh
Jabneel
Gibbethon
Gezer
Shaalbim
Gibeon
Ramah
Geba
Aijalon
Chephirah
Beeroth
Almon
Kiriath-jearim
Gibeah
Anathoth
Timnah
Eshtaol
Mozah
Nob
Jebus
Ekron
Zorah
Manahath
Ashdod
Beth-shemesh
Zanoah
Gath
Azekah
Jarmuth
Hushah
Bethlehem
Etam
Sochoh
Netophah
Ashkelon
Achzib?
Adullam
Gedor
Libnah
Keilah
Tekoa
Moresheth-gath?
Beth-zur
Mareshah
Nezib
Halhul
Eglon
Lachish
Hebron
Adoraim
Gaza
Ziph
En-gedi
Debir
Juttah
Carmel
Anab
Sochoh
Maon
Eshtemoa
Yurza
Gerar
Ziklag?
Goshen?
Madmannah
Jattir
Anim
Sansannah
Masada
Sharuhen
Beer-sheba
Arad
Hormah
Aroer
Capital.
Philistine garrison.
Philistine campaign
0
Miles
20
0
Kilometres
30

Map 19. The Philistine Cities and the Areas of their Expansion.

Judges. The Lachish area, on the other hand, was conquered by Israelite tribes before the Philistines arrived (cf. *supra,* p. 220). Therefore, the Philistines only gained a foothold in the central Shephelah around Canaanite Gath, and in this area they developed two eastern settlements, the ancient Gath and Ekron which they founded themselves. The two cities rivalled each other during the periods of their existence, and the region was dominated first by Gath and later by Ekron.

Except for the names of the five Philistine capitals very little else is known about their settlements. Evidently, they seized control over the whole southern coastal region and enforced their rule upon the local Canaanite populace. Most of the Canaanite towns continued to exist, though under a new leadership, and part of their residents doubtless were absorbed by the Philistines with the passage of time. However, the example of Ekron demonstrates that the Philistines did found some settlements of their own. Such was also the case with Tell Qasileh on the northern bank of the Yarkon. Excavations there have shown that it was a small harbour town founded by the Philistines (levels XI–XII).[256] This also proves that Philistine settlements reached at least as far as this area, although it is also possible that other groups from among the Sea Peoples had occupied this more northerly coastal region. Aphek at the sources of the Yarkon seems to have become the northern border town of the Philistines, because there they usually assembled in preparation for military campaigns farther north or north-west (1 Sam. 4. 1; 29. 1). Their influence also reached the eastern Shephelah and was felt in the Israelite settlements there. Beth-shemesh, for example, was Israelite at the end of the period of Judges as seen quite clearly from the story of the ark's return from Ekron (1 Sam. 6. 9 ff.). Nevertheless, excavations on that tell found an abundance of Philistine pottery (in level III), just as in a Philistine town.

However, the cultural impact of the Philistines was only felt for a few generations. By the middle of the eleventh century their unique ware had already begun to disappear.[257] Evidently, they themselves became completely assimilated to Canaanite culture as time went by. Their fate was like that of many invading waves that have passed over the country, each in its turn enjoying a position of dominance for a while only to be absorbed rather quickly into the life of Canaan without adding much to its local colouring.

For about 150 years the Philistines were the dominant factor in the life of Palestine. This was due to their excellent military organization within the framework of their five-city-state alliance, their well-perfected fighting methods and the superior equipment of their forces, as illustrated on Egyptian reliefs (cf. also the description of Goliath's armour; 1 Sam. 17. 4–7). The Philistine soldiers carried sophisticated weapons. The common assumption that they brought the art of smelting iron with them (perhaps having obtained it from the Hittites), and succeeded in maintaining their monopoly over this industry throughout the period of the Judges (1 Sam. 13. 19–22) is doubtful. The passage does not mention iron and the archaeological evidence is negative. At that time there was no enemy strong enough to contest their supremacy. Egyptian strength had been seriously weakened so that they were unable to interfere in Palestinian affairs. The Canaanite population was weak and divided, its main centres having been smitten first by the Israelites and then by the Philistines. The Israelites themselves and the neighbouring Aramean tribes as well were in a transitional stage between a migratory and a settled mode of life. Thus they had yet to organize themselves into larger and more effective groups that could compete with the Philistines.

For about 100 years, until the mid-eleventh century, the Philistines contented themselves with governing the area of their own settlement; we do not hear of larger attempts on their part to subjugate other regions. Their control may have extended all along the *Via Maris,* even reaching the Valley of Jezreel where we meet them during the reign of Saul, but our information is most uncertain on this point. It would seem that the decisive struggle between the Israelite tribes and the Philistines was encompassed within the span of two or three generations, in the second half of the eleventh century. There is no evidence that the Philistines tried to impose their rule on the hill country before that time. Philistine expansion evidently began precisely at the time when the Israelites were becoming firmly established and asserting their independence. It was probably then that the Philistines began to feel the presence of a serious opponent who posed a threat to their security. Thus they tried to smash this new force while it was still in a formative stage

The Samson narratives reflect the beginning of this conflict in the Shephelah. He has no connection with the Danite migration. Although Samson himself comes from the tribe of Dan, it is seen from these stories that Zorah and its territory already belonged to Judah (cf. 1 Chron. 2. 53; 4. 2), and the Philistine pressure was being exerted on this latter tribe (Judge. 15. 9 ff.). The border between Judah and Philistia at that time ran between Israelite Zorah and Philistine Timnah (Tell el-Baṭashi). Ekron doubtless had control over Timnah, though it does not appear in these narratives. The boundary between Ekron, and Beth-shemesh which is reflected in the passage about the wanderings of the ark, seems to indicate the same situation, because the line certainly lay between Timnah, a subsidiary of Ekron, and Beth-shemesh which is located just below Zorah.

The struggle for control of the Shephelah finally came to a head in the decisive battle between the Philistines and the Israelite tribes led by the

House of Eli. This clash took place between Aphek and Ebenezer (1 Sam. 4). It ended in complete victory for the Philistines, who destroyed Shiloh, the contemporary centre for the northern Israelite amphictyony. Though the town's devastation is not mentioned in this text, it is alluded to in the Psalms and the prophecies of Jeremiah (Ps. 78. 60; Jer. 7. 12, 14; 26. 6, 9) and proven by archaeological excavations.[258] Therefore, as a consequence of this battle, the Philistines not only penetrated into the heart of the Israelite region to destroy their covenant centre, they also tried to impose their own control over the tribes. At the beginning of Saul's reign we find Philistine garrisons stationed at Geba =Gibeath-elohim (1 Sam. 10. 5; 13. 3); and as previously mentioned, they prevented the processing of iron in Israel (1 Sam. 13. 19–22).

It is evident that the Philistines succeeded in dominating the Israelite hill country during this period. On the other hand, the Bible also preserves a contradictory piece of information about Samuel's victory over the Philistines at Mizpah, as a result of which it is said: "The cities which the Philistines had taken from Israel were restored to Israel, from Ekron to Gath; and Israel rescued their territory from the hand of the Philistines. There was peace also between Israel and the Amorites" (1 Sam. 7. 14). The territory of Gath and mainly Ekron had evidently been expanded considerably at the expense of the neighbouring Shephelah settlements, Israelite and Amorite, who then banded together in opposition to the Philistines. This must have been a time of continuous action and reaction between the opposing sides; the destruction of level XI at Tell Qasileh may perhaps be assigned to that period. This correlation would suit the demographic situation in the central area where the territory of Gath and especially Ekron was expanded at the expense of the Israelite and Amorite population in the Shephelah who were forced to join hands against the Philistines. We have no firm dating on which to base a more precise historical interpretation. However, it is clear from the situation at the beginning of Saul's reign that the Philistines eventually regained the upper hand and made a concerted effort to establish their permanent rule over the Israelite regions.[259]

The Philistine menace was the great challenge that forced Israel to face up to the question of its existence and continued development. This marks the end of the period of the Judges and the beginning of the United Israelite Monarchy which transformed Israel into the dominant force of Palestine and broadened the concept of "the land of Israel" to include the entire country.

[1] A recent expression of this viewpoint may be found in B. Mazar, *JNES,* 28 (1969), pp. 73–83; *idem, Canaan and Israel* (Jerusalem, 1975), pp. 131–43 (Hebrew); similarly, T. L. Thompson, *The Historicity of the Patriarchal Narratives* (*ZAW* Beiheft, 113 1974); the patriarchal narratives are assigned to a post-exilic context by J. van Seters, *Abraham in History and Tradition* (New Haven, 1975).

[2] Y. Aharoni, *Tel Aviv,* 2 (1975), pp. 148–51; *idem, BA,* 39 (1976), pp. 55–76. *idem, Beer-sheba I* (Jerusalem, 1973), p. 4.

[3] R. Gophna and Y. Yisraeli, apud Y. Aharoni, ed., *Beer-sheba I,* pp. 115–18.

[4] Aharoni, *Tel Aviv,* 2 (1975), p. 151.

[5] A. Alt, *PJb,* 20 (1924), pp. 34 ff. (=*Kl. Schr.,* III, pp. 169 ff.); A. F. Rainey, *IEJ,* 20 (1970), pp. 194 f.

[6] W. Gesenius and F. Buhl, *Handwörterbuch über das Alte Testament*[17] (Leipzig, 1921), p. 322; L. Koehler and W. Baumgartner, *Hebräisches und aramäisches Lexicon zum Alten Testament,* I (3rd ed. revised by W. Baumgartner, B. Hartmann and E. Y. Kutscher; Leiden, 1967), pp. 442f.

[7] Y. Aharoni, apud *The Beth Shean Valley* (Jerusalem, 1962), pp. 31 ff. (Hebrew).

[8] Cf. J. Coppens, *VT Suppl.,* 4 (1957), pp. 97–115.

[9] Abraham, for example, serves his guests milk and not wine (Gen. 18. 8), and Jael the wife of Heber does the same, being a tent dweller still (Judges 4. 19; 5. 25).

[10] N. Glueck, "Explorations in Eastern Palestine I–IV", *AASOR,* 14 (1934); 15 (1935); 18–19 (1939); 25–28 (1951).

[11] Aharoni, *Settlement,* pp. 17 ff.

[12] A. Alt, *PJb,* 35 (1939), pp. 24 ff. (=*Kl. Schr.,* I, pp. 139 ff.); Noth, *Geschichte*[3] pp. 67 ff.; *idem, The History of Israel*[2] (trans. by P. R. Ackroyd; London, 1960), pp. 68 ff.

[13] P. Montet, *RB,* 39 (1930), pp. 5–28; *Syria,* 17 (1936). pp. 200–2; W. F. Albright *BASOR,* 109 (1948), p. 15.

[14] Cf. Glueck, *loc. cit.* (note 10).

[15] It is possible that the failure of Ramses at Kadesh, *c.* 1286, caused a ferment that made possible the escape of the forced labourers.

These dates cannot be reconciled with the biblical chronology: viz. the counting of 480 years from the Exodus to the founding of Solomon's temple (1 Kings 6. 1). That event took place about 965 and according to this reckoning the date of the Exodus would be about 1445, i.e. in the time of Thut-mose III. It is possible to explain this number by assuming that the tradition had twelve generations, and according to the reckoning of forty years per generation, which is a hypothetical reckoning (e.g. the generation in the wilderness), they arrived at the figure of 480. If one takes twenty-five years as an actual generation we arrive at the date 1265, which is close to our estimate (Bright, *History*[2], p. 121).

However, the date of 430 years which is given in the biblical chronology for the Israelites' remaining in Egypt (Exod. 12. 40–41) is also very far off; and therefore we cannot take these figures into account. Only by general historical considerations is it possible to fix the time of the entry into Egypt. The author is inclined to place it in the El Amarna period, 2–3 generations before the Exodus, and not in the Hyksos period, according to the view of various scholars, cf. the discussion in Rowley, *Jos.-Josh.,* pp. 24 ff.

[16] The total number of about 600,000 which is given in the biblical tradition (Num. 1. 46; 26. 51) is unreasonable. Attempts have been made to interpret this as meaning about 600 families on the assumption that the Hebrew word *eleph* actually means "family" rather than "thousand" (G. E. Mendenhall, *JBL,* 77 [1958] pp. 52–66), or that this number is taken from a much later historical situation, e.g. from the census by Joab that was carried out in David's time (W. F. Albright, *JPOS,* 5 [1925], pp. 20–25). For another explanation, cf. A. Malamat, *Biblica,* 51 (1970), pp. 9–10; also B. Mazar, *World History of the Jewish People,* III (Jerusalem, 1971), pp. 70–71.

[17] *ANET,* p. 259.

[18] *ANET,* p. 259.

[19] For a detailed exposition of the Exodus from another viewpoint, cf. K. A. Kitchen apud M. C. Tenney, ed., *Zondervan Pictorial Encyclopedia of the Bible* (Grand Rapids, 1975), pp. 428–36.

[20] W. F. Albright, *BASOR,* 109 (1948), p. 16.

[21] O. Eissfeldt, *Baal Zafon, Zeus Cassios und der Durchzug der Israeliten durch das Meer* (Halle, 1932); N. Aime-Giron, *Annales du service des antiqu. de l'Eg.,* 40 (1941), pp. 433–36; M. Noth, *Eissfeldt Vol.* (Halle, 1947), pp. 181–90; W. F. Albright, *BASOR,* 109 (1948); pp. 15 f.

[22] Gardiner, *Anc. Eg. On.,* II, pp. 201* f. The exact translation of Hebrew *yam suph* is "Reed Sea" and not "Red Sea".

[23] M.-J. Lagrange, *RB*, 9 (1900), pp. 63–86, 273–87; R. Weil, *Le séjour des Israélites au désert* (Paris, 1909); H. Cazelles, *RB*, 62 (1955), pp. 321–64.

[24] M. Noth, *PJb*, 36 (1940), pp. 5–28.

[25] It is interesting that the list under discussion does not use the name "Reed Sea", but simply says "the Sea" (Num. 33. 8). The Reed Sea appears only after passing three more stations (vs. 10). The reason for this is clear: in the Kingdom period the Gulf of Aqabah was known by the name "Reed Sea" (Exod. 23. 31; 1 Kings 9. 26 *et al.*), which is beyond doubt though we do not have an explanation for the transfer of the name.

[26] Abel, *Géogr.*, II, pp. 210 ff.

[27] C. S. Jarvis, *PEQ* (1938), pp. 25–40; J. Gray, *VT*, 4 (1954), pp. 148–54.

[28] Of the many studies about this problem cf. especially M.-J. Lagrange, *RB*, 8 (1899), pp. 369–92; Abel, *Géogr.*, I, pp. 391–96; M. Noth, *Ueberlieferungsgeschichte des Pentateuchs* (Stuttgart, 1948), pp. 63–67; *idem, Geschichte*³ (Göttingen, 1956), pp. 120 ff.; G. Hölscher, *Bultmann Vol.* (Stuttgart, 1949), pp. 127–32; Bright, History, pp. 113 ff.; Y. Aharoni apud B. Rothenberg, *God's Wilderness* (London, 1961), pp. 115 ff.

[29] Aharoni, *ibid.*, pp. 167–69.

[30] It is possible that this is only a part of the name which defined its general region, like El(ath)-Paran.

[31] Aharoni, *op. cit.* (note 28), pp. 166 f.

[32] Its identification with *'Ain Ghaḍyan* is based on the similarity of the name to the nearby *Sabkhat Ṭabeh* and does not represent a careful analysis of the sources.

[33] Procopius, *De Bell. Pers.*, 1, 19 (ed. Haury, pp. 100 f.); Abel, *Géogr.*, II, p. 201.

[34] B. Rothenberg, Y. Aharoni and A. Hashimshoni, *op. cit.* (note 28), pp. 86 ff., 162 ff., 183 ff.

[35] Abel, *Géogr.*, II, p. 214.

[36] Abel, *Géogr.*, II, p. 307; Aharoni, *op. cit.* (note 28), pp. 144 161.

[37] C. L. Woolley and T. E. Lawrence, *PEF An.*, 3 (1914), pp. 55 ff.; N. Glueck, *AASOR*, 15 (1935), pp. 118 ff.; R. De Vaux and R. Savignac, *RB* (1938), pp. 88 ff.; Rothenberg and Aharoni *op. cit.* (note 28), pp. 33 ff., 121 ff.

[38] Tell es-Seba' (Beer-sheba) no pottery was found earlier than the Israelite period. The notion that Gerar was Philistine in this period is an anachronism.

[39] B. Mazar, *JNES*, 24 (1965), pp. 297–303.

[40] Y Aharoni, *Yediot*, 28 (1964), pp. 172–75 (Hebrew); *idem*, BA, 31 (1968), pp. 30–32; *idem, Tel Aviv*, 2 (1975), pp. 114 ff.

[41] H. C. Trumbell, *Kadesh-Barnea* (London, 1884), pp. 132 ff.; G. L. Robinson, *The Sarcophagus of an Ancient Civilization* (New York, 1930), pp. 263 ff.

[42] Aharoni, *op. cit.* (note 28), pp. 139–41.

[43] A. Alt, *ZDPV*, 58 (1935), p. 26; M. Avi-Yonah, *Historical Geography*, p. 165 (Hebrew).

[44] Abel, *Géogr.*, II, pp. 216 f.; N. Glueck, *AASOR* 18–19 (1939), pp. 68 f.

[45] *Enc. Bib.* (Hebrew) I, col. 694 f.

[46] It is possible that some of the Amorite cities of Transjordan were founded in the Late Bronze Age with the expulsion of the Hyksos from Canaan, e.g. Tell Deir 'Alla (Succoth) which was founded in the Late Bronze Age according to excavations carried out on the site (H. J. Franken, *VT*, II [1961], pp. 361–72).

[47] Noth, *loc. cit.* (note 24).

[48] N. Glueck, *AASOR*, 15 (1935), pp. 26–28.

[49] P. J. Parr, G. L. Harding and J. E. Dayton, *Bulletin of the Institute of Archaeology*, 8–9 (London, 1970), pp. 193–242; J. E. Dayton (London, 1972), pp. 25–33.

[50] B. Rothenberg, *Timna* (London, 1972), pp. 63–207.

[51] Cf. S. M. Cecchini, *La ceramica di Nuzi, Studi semitici*, 15 (Rome, 1965).

[52] W. F. Albright, *BA*, 36 (1973), pp. 56 ff.

[53] Cf. Rowley, *Jos.-Josh.*, pp. 3 ff.

[54] At this site the ruins of a temple from the Late Bronze Age have been discovered which testify to a sedentary occupation (cf. L. Harding, *PEQ*, 1958, pp. 10 ff.), it seems that its earlier name was Rabbah (cf. Josh. 13, 25). Cf. now J. B. Hennessy, *PEQ*, 1966, pp. 155 ff.; G. H. R. Wright, *ZDPV*, 84 (1968), p. 9; V. Hankey, *Levant*, 6 (1974), pp. 131 ff. [The fanciful interpretation of this shrine as a cultic centre for a tribal league, E. F.

Campbell and G. E. Wright, *BA*, 32 (1969), pp. 104 ff., is based on two misconceptions: (1) that Glueck's survey precludes any urban centres in Transjordan in the Late Bronze Age; (2) that there was no settlement near the Amman temple. The remains of the settlement are to be found under the control tower of the Amman airport (personal communication, B. Hennessey). A.F.R.]

[55] Jaazer has not yet been identified with certainty. Various scholars incline to identify it with Khirbet eṣ-Ṣar, about seven miles west of Rabbath-ammon, and in any case, one must look for it in approximately that vicinity; cf. the most recent summary of the various opinions in M. Noth, *ZDPV*, 75 (1959), pp. 62 ff.

[56] W. F. Albright, *BASOR*, 89 (1943), pp. 7 ff.

[57] M. Noth, *ZDPV*, 68 (1951), pp. 19 ff.

[58] A. Bergman (Biran), *JPOS*, 16 (1936), pp. 224–54.

[59] A. Bergman, *JAOS*, 54, (1934), p. 176.

[60] Luckenbill, *AR*, I, §73; B. Mazar, *Enc. Bib*, (Hebrew), III, col. 415 f.

[61] *ANET*, pp. 394–95; Helck, *Beziehungen*² p. 183.

[62] K. M. Kenyon, *Digging up Jericho* (London, 1957), pp. 256 ff.; *idem, EAEHL*, II (Jerusalem, 1976), pp. 563–4.

[63] Rowley, *Jos.-Josh.*, pp. 19 f.; M. Noth, *Aufsätze*, I pp. 8f., 12, 23f., 43–45, 210 f., 214–28. Albright's attempt to explain the account by transferring the story from Ai to Bethel, *The Biblical Period from Abraham to Ezra: An Historical Survey* (rev. and enlarged, New York, 1963), pp. 29 f., is unconvincing.

[64] J. A. Callaway, *JBL*, 87 (1968), pp. 312–20; Z. Kallai, apud M. Kochavi, ed., *Judaea, Samaria and the Golan* (Jerusalem, 1972), pp. 154 f. (Hebrew).

[65] A. Alt, *ZAW* Beiheft, 66 (1936), pp. 20 f. (=*Kl. Schr.*, I, pp. 183 f.); H. J. Kraus, *VT*, 1 (1951), pp. 184 f.

[66] W. F. Albright, *BASOR*, 29 (1928), pp. 9 ff.; 35 (1929), p. 5; 55 (1934), pp. 23 ff.; 56 (1934), pp. 2 ff.; 57 (1935), pp. 27 ff.; 58 (1935), p. 13; 74 (1939), pp. 17 f.; J. L. Kelso, *BASOR*, 151 (1958), pp. 3 ff.; *idem, AASOR*, 39 (1968), pp. 31 f., 48.

[67] Concerning the early date of the inscription at Kh. Raddana, cf. Y. Aharoni, *IEJ*, 21 (1971), pp. 130–35.

[68] There are some who assume that there existed a place named Ephraim, relying especially on 2 Sam. 13. 23 (cf. W. F. Albright, *JPOS*, 3 [1923], pp. 36 ff.; *idem, AASOR*, 4 [1924], pp. 127 ff.; A. Alt, *PJb*, 24 [1928], pp 35 ff.; Noth, *Geschichte*³, p. 60), but there is insufficient proof for this.

[69] In the Mari tablets from the eighteenth century B.C. a strong tribal union is known by the name "sons of Yamin" (*mārū Yamīn*) in contrast to the tribes of the "sons of Sim'al" (*mārū Sim'āl*), i.e. sons of the south and sons of the north. Because of the clear geographical significance of this name one should not seek to associate them with the biblical Benjaminites, particularly since they are separated by a period of about 500 years. Assyriologists have long recognised that DUMU. MEŠ-*yamina* cannot be read *Banū-Yamīna* or *Binū-Yamīna;* G. Dossin, *RA*, 52 (1958), pp. 60 ff.; H. Tadmor, *JNES*, 17 (1958), p. 130 n. 12 (citing B. Landesberger), I. Gelb, *JCS*, 15 (1961), pp. 37 f. In fact, the biblical *Yemīnī* can take any one of several construct elements, *bēn, bᵉnē, 'iš, 'ereṣ;* cf. A. Malamat, *XVe Rencontre assyriologique* (Liège, 1967), p. 137 n. 1.

[70] Y. Aharoni, apud *Eretz Shomron* (Jerusalem, 1973), pp. 38–46.

[71] Cf. especially the surveys in the Samaria region: R. Bach, *ZDPV*, 74 (1958), pp. 41–54. R. Gophna and Y. Porat, apud M. Kochavi, ed. *Judaea, Samaria and the Golan* (Jerusalem, 1972), pp. 198 f.

[72] W. F. Albright, *AASOR*, 4 (1924); *idem, BASOR*, 52 (1933), pp. 6 ff.; L. A. Sinclair, *AASOR*, 34–35 (1960), pp. 5 ff.; W. F. Bade, C. C. McCown and J. C. Wampler, *Excavations at Tell en-Naṣbeh*, I–II (Berkeley and New-Haven, 1947).

[73] Makkedah, which has to be located somewhere in the Lachish region (Josh. 15. 41) is evidently an addition and its name is missing in vs. 11.

[74] A. Alt, Josua, *ZAW* Beiheft, 66 (1936), pp. 13–29 (=*Kl. Schr.*, I, pp. 176–192).

[75] B. Mazar, *Enc. Bib.* (Hebrew), I, col. 694 ff.; W. F. Albright, *BASOR*, 58 (1953), pp. 10–18, for further bibliography cf. Rowley, *Jos.-Josh.*, pp. 4 ff.

[76] There is no doubt that the brief notices collected in Judges 1 are among the most

trustworthy, and there is no reason to suspect their historicity, precisely because they do not always measure up to the later historical outlook, which describes the conquest as one single campaign; contrary to the opinion of G. E. Wright, *JNES*, 5 (1946), pp. 105–14.

[77] B. Maisler (Mazar), *JPOS*, 10 (1930), pp. 189–91.

[78] It is interesting to note the way in which a biblical tradition is consolidated, still preserving the information that Hebron and Debir were conquered by Caleb and Kenaz (Josh. 15. 13–19; Judg. 1. 12–15). But in the course of time, these conquests were associated with Judah (Judges 1. 10–11), and finally, with all of Israel under the leadership of Joshua (Josh. 10. 36–9). The location of Debir at Kh. Rabud in the hill country has finally made sense out of the passages pertaining to that area, of M. Kochavi, *Tel Aviv*, 1 (1974), pp. 2 ff.

[79] Y. Aharoni, *EAEHL*, I (Jerusalem, 1975), p. 82.

[80] N. Glueck, *Rivers in the Desert*² (New York, 1968), pp. 114 f.

[81] V. Fritz, *ZDPV*, 82 (1966), pp. 340 ff.

[82] B. Mazar, *JNES*, 24 (1965), pp. 299 ff. (=*Canaan and Israel* [Jerusalem, 1974], pp. 124 ff.; Hebrew).

[83] *Idem, EI*, 3 (1954), p. 22 (=*Canaan and Israel*, pp. 22 f.; Hebrew).

[84] Simons, *Handbook*, pp. 89 ff, 178 ff.

[85] The ensuing discussion is based on Y. Aharoni, *Tel Aviv*, 2 (1975), pp. 114–24.

[86] Cf. most recently, Y. Aharoni, V. Fritz, and A. Kempinski, *Tel Aviv*, 2 (1975), pp. 97 ff.

[87] R. Giveon, *Tel Aviv*, 1 (1974), pp. 75f.

[88] Y. Aharoni, V. Fritz and A. Kempinski, *ZDPV*, 89 (1973), pp. 203 ff.; *idem, Tel Aviv*, 1 (1974), Pl. 15. 4–7.

[89] V. Fritz, *Tel Aviv*, 2 (1975), p. 109, Pl. 23. 3.

[90] Aharoni, *Tel Aviv*, 2 (1975), pp. 118 ff.

[91] Aharoni, *IEJ*, 25 (1975), pp. 169 f., Pl. 17.A.

[92] Aharoni, *IEJ*, 6 (1956), p. 27.

[93] *Ibid*, n. 1.

[94] M. Dothan, *Ashdod II–III* (= *'Atiqot*, Eng. ser. IX–X; Jerusalem, 1971), pp 19–20, 26, 156, 185.

[95] J. Naveh, *IEJ*, 8 (1958), pp. 87 ff., 165 ff.; *idem, Enc. Bib.* (Hebrew), VI, cols. 339–43.

[96] Against the theory of G. E. Wright, *JNES*, 51 (1946), pp. 109 ff.

[97] Olga Tufnell, *Lachish*, III (London, 1953), pp. 51 f.; *idem, Lachish*, IV (London, 1958), pp 36 ff., 49 f.

[98] W. F. Albright, *BASOR*, 58 (1935), pp. 10–18; 68 (1937), pp. 22–26; 74 (1939), pp. 20 ff.

[99] M. Gilula, *Tel Aviv*, 3 (1976), pp. 107–8.

[100] Aharoni, *Settlement*, pp. 17 ff. (Hebrew).

[101] W. F. Albright, *JPOS*, 1 (1921), pp. 54 ff.; A. Alt, *ZAW NF*, 19 (1944), pp. 67 ff. (=*Kl. Schr.*, I, pp. 256 ff.).

[102] Aharoni, *Settlement*, pp. 99 ff. (Hebrew).

[103] There is no basis for its identification in the vicinity of el-Ḥarithiyeh (Abel, *Géogr.*, II, p. 343 f.; W. F. Albright, *JPOS*, 2 [1922], pp. 284 ff.; Garstang, *Jos. Judg.*, pp. 380 f.). The assumption that this city was founded by the Sea Peoples, and that Sisera was one of its princes is an attempt to remove this difficulty (cf. Alt, *loc. cit.* note 101), but there is no evidence for this. The text deals with a war of the kings of Canaan and not of the Philistines or some similar people. And what was the fate of Harosheh-ha-goiim after this?

[104] B. Maisler (Mazar), *BJPES*, 11 (1945), pp. 38–41 (Hebrew) = *BIES Reader B* (Jerusalem, 1965), pp. 57–60 (Hebrew) = *Cities and Districts in Eretz-Israel* (Jerusalem, 1975), pp. 115–20 (Hebrew); *idem, HUCA*, 24 (1952–3), pp. 80–4.

[105] Maisler (Mazar), *HUCA*, 24 (1952–3), pp. 83 f.; Aharoni, *Settlement*, pp. 103 ff. (Hebrew).

[106] However, the story goes on to tell about a pursuit "as far as Harosheth-ha-goiim" (vs. 16). It seems, therefore, that the original meaning of the name was quickly forgotten and it was taken for a place name.

[107] There are some who assume that Deborah was from Issachar (Judges 5. 15), her name being connected with Daberath on the border of Issachar, and that her place of

origin was mistaken because of Deborah the nurse of Rebecca (Gen. 35. 8), cf. C. F. Burney, *Judges* (London, 1920), pp. 78 f.

[108] J. Press, *BJPES*, 1, 3 (1933–4), pp. 26 ff. (Hebrew); Aharoni, *Settlement*, pp. 100 f.; M. Kochavi, *Yediot*, 27 (1963), pp. 165–72 (Hebrew).

[109] Some scholars latch on to the words of the poem "at Taanach by the waters of Megiddo", and assume that the engagement was in the vicinity of those cities, in the south-western sector of the plain; but the battle was certainly not fought beside the water sources of Megiddo, and besides, why does the poem assign such a decisive role to the Brook Kishon in this engagement? It is simpler to assume that here the poet is merely pointing out the two great Canaanite bases which are near the field of battle. It is worth remembering that in the El Amarna period Megiddo already dominated Shunem and Japhia on the northern edge of the plain (cf. *supra*, p. 172); and perhaps the Canaanite chariot camp was near Megiddo as in the narrative about the wars of Thut-mose III and Amen-hotep II. Therefore, it is difficult to agree with Albright that in this period the waters of Megiddo were within the boundaries of Taanach because Megiddo itself was destroyed (*BASOR*, 62 [1936], p. 29; 68 [1937], p. 25).

[110] For bibliography of the different opinions cf. Rowley, *Jos.-Josh.*, pp. 18 ff.

[111] From the Elijah narrative it is clear that the Kishon flowed westward at the foot of Mount Carmel (1 Kings 18. 40); and therefore the attempt to indentify it with Wadi Bireh, that flows from Tabor to the Jordan, because of the town Kishion in that region, must be rejected (an opinion that is already found with Ashtori ha-Parḥi).

[112] *ANET*, p. 283

[113] Abel, *Géogr.*, II, p. 385

[114] Aharoni, *Settlement*, p. 96 (Hebrew).

[115] Garstang, *Jos-Judg.*, pp. 191 ff.

[116] Aharoni, *Settlement*, pp. 95–97.

[117] Aharoni, *Settlement*, pp. 91 f. There is no basis whatsoever for the accepted identification of Madon with Qarn Ḥaṭṭin because of Khirbet Madin on its northern flank. This identification is based entirely upon the similarity of the name which is doubtful in itself.

[118] Y. Yadin, *et al.*, *Hazor* I–IV (Jerusalem, 1958–61).

[119] This is an area ten times larger than other main cities, cf. e.g. Megiddo—about 15 acres, Lachish and Gezer—about 20 acres.

[120] Aharoni, *Settlement*, pp. 20 ff. It is possible that they are a bit later. This stands out especially with comparison of the store-jar from Khirbet et-Tuleil (*ibid.*, Fig. 4. 4) which is closer to the Canaanite pythos (*Hazor* I, P1. CXXXIV. 8), than to the regular store-jar from stratum XII at Hazor, which apparently represents a slightly later development.

[121] Except for isolated buildings, e.g. a small shrine which was found on the top of the tell (stratum XI).

[122] For discussion of this and various ensuing details, cf. Y. Aharoni apud J. A. Sanders, ed., *Near Eastern Archaeology in the Twentieth Century* (Garden City, 1970), pp. 254 ff.

[123] B. Mazar, *JNES*, 24 (1965), pp. 297–303 = *Canaan and Israel*, pp. 121 ff. (Hebrew).

[124] T. Dothan, *EI*, 5 (1958), pp. 55 ff. (Hebrew); *idem*, *The Philistines and their Material Culture* (Jerusalem, 1967), pp. 211 ff. (Hebrew).

[125] T. Dothan, *IEJ*, 22 (1972), pp. 65–72, Pls. 9–13; *idem*, *IEJ*, 23 (1973), pp. 129–46, *idem*, and Y. Bet-Arieh, *Qadmoniot*, 5 (1972), p. 26 (Hebrew).

[126] E. D. Oren, *The Northern Cemetery at Beth-Shan* (Leyden, 1973).

[127] P. Lapp, *BASOR*, 173 (1964): p. 8; 185 (1967), pp. 3, 25 f.; 195 (1969), pp 2–49; *idem*, *BA*, 30 (1967), pp. 8 f.

[128] Aharoni, *Biram Vol.* (Jerusalem, 1956), pp. 29–36 (Hebrew) (cf. *supra.*, p. 94).

[129] "Brick upon brick and block upon block", *Jeru.* Megillah 3, 8 etc. Cf. S. Klein, *BJPES*, 2, 2 (1934), p. 39 (Hebrew).

[130] Y. Aharoni, *IEJ*, 6 (1956), p. 27.

[131] There is no foundation to Albright's suggestion to identify this Gilgal with Jiljulieh in the Sharon, cf. W. F. Albright, *BASOR*, 11 (1923), pp. 7–9.

[132] This matter is, of course, also related to the origin of the biblical stories which deal primarily with events related to specific sites, so that the overall background is missing.

133 A. Alt. *Sellin Vol.* (Leipzig, 1927), pp. 17 ff. (=*Kl. Schr.*, I, pp. 197 ff.).

134 W. F. Albright, *AASOR*, 2–3 (1923), p. 26.

135 Rehob is mentioned beside Dor in a list of Ramses II from Amara and therefore it seems necessary to locate it in the southern plain of Acco, cf. B. Mazar, *Yediot*, 27 (1963), pp. 139–44 (Hebrew).

136 In the LXX Dor is also added. Is this a reflection of the tradition that Dor was first reckoned to Asher?

137 Aharoni, *Settlement*, pp. 70–75 (Hebrew).

138 Abel, *Géogr.*, II, pp. 282, 343.

139 E. Grant and G. E. Wright, *Ain Shems Excavations*, V (Haverford, 1939), pp. 11 f.

140 Rainey, *IEJ*, 20 (1970), pp. 197–99.

141 For a different view cf. Maisler, *Untersuchungen*, pp. 59 ff.

142 For a conjecture concerning their origin cf. E. Speiser, *AASOR*, 13 (1933), p. 30, note 67.

143 It is possible that the name is simply Misrephoth in which case the second part might be vocalized *miyyam*, i.e. "on the west", cf. Noth, *Josua*,[2] pp. 68 f.

144 Maisler, *Untersuchungen*, pp. 67 f.; Garstang, *Jos.-Judg.*, p. 396.

145 Miriam Tadmor and M. Prausnitz, *Atiqot*, 2 (1959), pp. 72–88.

146 The only mention of the Liṭani is in Papyrus Anastasi I in the form "the river *n-ṯ-n*" (cf. *supra*, p. 182), and note Kiriath (=city of) *n-ḏ-n* in Thut-mose's list (No. 11).

147 *ANET*, pp. 203–5.

148 Maisler, *Untersuchungen*, p. 75; Aharoni, *Settlement*, p. 95 (Hebrew).

149 Missing in LXX.

150 Missing in LXX.

151 K. Budde, *ZAW*, 7 (1887), pp 123 f.; C. E. Burney, *Israel's Settlement in Canaan (London, 1919), pp. 20 ff.*

152 *Ed. Meyer, Die Isr. u. i. Nachb.*, pp. 512 ff.; it is possible that Noth's view is correct, viz. that two parallel sources have been mixed in this passage (*Josua*[2], pp 106 f.); the second, which is the oldest, referred to the forested regions of the hill country of Ephraim, but it is preceded here by a later tradition associated with the Transjordanian settlement. It is clear that "the land of Rephaim" is a typical expression for Transjordan (cf. Gen. 14. 5; Deut. 2. 11, 20; Josh. 12. 4 etc); but these words are missing in the LXX.

153 A. Barrois, *Manuel d'archéologie biblique*, I (Paris, 1939), p. 226; Albright, *APB.*, p. 132; *idem, SAC.*, p. 212; cf. also the deep water cistern from Hazor, stratum XIV, from the thirteenth century B.C.

154 Aharoni, *Settlement*, Figs. 4–5 (Hebrew).

155 The Massoretic text reads "Manasseh" (*mⁿšh*), with *nūn suspensa;* the original reading, "Moses" (*mšh*) is preserved in some MSS of LXX, Vulgate, and the Talmud (*Baba Bathra* 109), cf. C. F. Burney, *The Book of Judges*[2] (London, 1920), pp. 434 f.

156 Concerning the prevalent opinion which associates this migration with the expansion of the Philistines cf. bibliography in Rowley, *Jos.-Josh.*, p. 84, note 2. Some would even amend the text of Judges 1. 34 to read "Philistines", instead of "Amorites", cf. F. Schmidtke, *Die Einwanderung Israels in Kanaan* (Breslau, 1933), p. 181; according to Noth (*Geschichte*,[3] p. 67, note 1), "Amorites" in this passage are to be taken in a general sense as the pre-Israelite population, which also included the Philistines.

157 In this regard the decisive factor is the interpretation of a difficult verse in the Song of Deborah: "And Dan, why did he abide with the ships?" (Judg. 5. 17a); cf. the various opinions listed by Rowley, *ibid.*, pp 8[1] ff. Dan's association with ships and seafaring is as difficult to understand in the south as in the north. His original tribal inheritance never did reach the sea-coast, because the Canaanite cities of the Shephelah stood in the way, and they were not engaged in marine activity. The description of Dan's original territory cannot be utilized here because it reflects a different and much later situation (cf. *infra*, pp. 298–99). The question arises as to whether this passage is an allusion to Dan's dependence upon Phoenician ships like the Canaanite Laish had been formerly (Judg. 18. 7, 28), but even this interpretation is forced. Perhaps the text is corrupt, but any correction is by nature hypothetical. The author is presently inclined to view the movement of the Danites as a consequence of Hazor's downfall, assuming the relatively earlier date for that city's destruction.

[158] The text is partly corrupted, however its basic meaning is clear, cf. W. Rudolph, *Chronikbücher* (Tübingen, 1955), pp. 68–71.

[159] E. Z. Melamed, "Benjamin and Gilead" *Tarbiz,* 5 (1933), pp. 121–25 (Hebrew).

[160] S. Klein, *Eretz Yehudah* (Tel Aviv, 1939), p. 140 (Hebrew); B. Maisler (Mazar), *Dinaburg Vol.* (Jerusalem, 1949), p. 322 (Hebrew).

[161] Mazar, *ibid.,* p. 323 (Hebrew); Helck, *Beziehungen*², p. 238, (cf. *supra,* p. 182).

[162] Ginsberg-Maisler, *JPOS,* 14 (1934), pp. 262 ff.

[163] N. Glueck, *PEQ* (1940), pp. 22–24; R. J. Forbes, *Studies in Ancient Technology* (Leiden), VII (1963), p. 130; VIII (1964), pp. 91 ff.; S. Abramski, *EI,* 3 (1954), pp. 116 ff. (Hebrew).

[164] "These are the men of Recah", must probably be amended according to LXX ". . . Rechab".

[165] Ed. Meyer, *Die Isr. u. i. Nachb.,* pp. 433 ff.

[166] Following the study of Noth (*ZDPV,* 55 [1932], pp. 97–124); he inclines to date this list to the ninth century B.C., but for this there is insufficient evidence.

[167] Emendations to the Massoretic text have been indicated as follows: ()=later additions to the text: []=restorations: <>=corrections.

[168] A. Alt, *PJb,* 21 (1925), pp. 100 ff. (=*Kl. Schr.,* II, pp 276 ff.); *idem., Sellin Vol.* (Leipzig, 1927), pp. 13 ff. (=*Kl. Schr.,* I, pp. 193 ff.).

[169] M. Noth, *ZDPV,* 58 (1935), pp 185–255; in his terminology "Grenzfixpunkte".

[170] The general meaning of these verbs is clear, but it is not always possible to distinguish the narrow shades of meaning expressed by them. The expressions "and it goes up" and "and it goes down" are related to the topography; "and it returns" is generally used when the boundary description comes back to a point, from whence it had started, to another direction; "and it passes" or "and it touches" seems to indicate that the line touches a certain point in passing; "and it turns", "and it bends" indicate a turning or change of direction: "and it goes out to" generally indicates a goal towards which the line was directed; "and its goings out were" usually summarizes the description of several segments in the border and is principally used in boundary descriptions.

[171] We may assume that the connecting verbs belong to the primary editor, who utilized this source material.

[172] A. Alt, *ZAW,* NF 4 (1927), pp. 61 ff.

[173] W. F. Albright, Archaeology and the Religion of Israel (Baltimore, 1942), pp. 123f.; Z. Kallai, *The Northern Boundaries of Judah* (Jerusalem, 1960), pp. 9 ff. (Hebrew).

[174] Here and there points such as these are preserved in other descriptions which confirm our assumption. ". . . the mountain that lies south of Lower Beth-horon" (Josh. 18. 13) is shortened in Josh. 16. 3 to "Lower Beth-horon". In place of "the waters east of Jericho" (Josh. 16. 1) we find in 18. 12 "the shoulder north of Jericho". These variations are readily explained if we assume that the original list contained many topographical points, in this instance, a well to the east of Jericho and a ridge to the north of it which were used selectively by the editor(s). Elsewhere it was deemed sufficient to include only the name of the town (Josh. 16. 7).

[175] Cf. especially S. Mowinckel, *Zur Frage nach dokumentarischen Quellen in Josua 13–19* (Oslo, 1946), pp. 20 ff.; on the basis of the Song of Deborah he concludes that the Israelite tribal covenant included ten tribes.

[176] Contrary to the opinion of Noth *loc. cit.* [note 169], pp 230 ff.), who posits some very strange boundary lines from which he makes some unlikely historical deductions.

[177] A. Alt, *Sellin Vol.* (Leipzig, 1927), pp. 17 ff. (=*Kl. Schr.,* I, pp. 197 ff.).

[178] Alt, *ibid.,* pp. 13 ff. (=*Kl. Schr.,* I, pp. 193 ff.).

[179] The Hebrew word "*gebul*" (גבול) *not only means "border" but also "territory".*

[180] *Noth, loc. cit.* (Note 169), pp. 135 ff.

[181] Alt. *loc. cit.* (note 172), pp. 67.

[182] The expression "to the sea", which occurs after Kiriath-jearim both in the description of Judah's boundary (Josh. 15. 10) and that of Benjamin (Josh. 18. 15—MT), is perhaps a remnant of the ancient boundary description for this segment, which contained only this general designation. In two instances general geographical features are used for the description of the western sections of the boundaries, viz. the Carmel range (Josh. 19. 26) and the Brook of Kanah (Josh. 16. 8; 17. 9). We may assume that similar general

descriptions were used in the two sections under discussion, perhaps Misrephoth-maim the border of "Great Sidon" in the north (cf. Josh. 11. 8; 19. 28; 2 Sam. 24. 6) and another river bed (the valley of Sorek ?) in the south.

[183] Cf. M. Noth, *Geschichte,*[3] p. 167; concerning unions of six tribes cf. *ibid.*, pp. 85 ff.

[184] For the boundary of Benjamin, cf. Kallai, *op. cit.* (note 173).

[185] The meaning of the word "shoulder" as a sloping hillside has been confirmed by the tomb inscription from Silwan village, which is carved in the slope opposite the site of ancient Jerusalem and reads: "(Tomb-)chamber on the slope of the rock (or mountain) . . .", cf. N. Avigad, *IEJ,* 5 (1955), pp. 163 ff.

[186] The Massoretic text reads "the cities of the mountain of Ephron", but "cities" in the plural cannot designate a point along a boundary; the word for "cities" is missing in LXX.

[187] Concerning this segment of the border, cf. Y. Aharoni, *PEQ* (1958), pp. 27–31.

[188] Concerning this segment of the border, cf. Z. Kallai, *EI,* 2 (1953), pp. 108 ff. (Hebrew).

[189] J. A. Callaway and R. E. Cooley, *BASOR,* 201 (1971), pp. 9–19; F. M. Cross and D. N. Freedman, *BASOR,* 201 (1971), pp. 19–22; Y. Aharoni, *IEJ,* 21 (1971), pp. 130–35

[190] Concerning this segment of the border, cf. W. J. Phythian-Adams, *PEQ* (1929), pp. 228 ff.; K. Elliger, *ZDPV,* 53 (1930), pp. 265 ff.; *idem, PJb,* 33 (1937), pp 7 ff.; S. Klein, *ZDPV,* 57 (1934), pp. 7ff.; M. Noth, *ZDPV,* 58 (1935), pp. 201 ff.; F. M. Abel, *RB* (1936), pp. 103 ff.; G. Wallis, *ZDPV,* 77 (1961), pp. 38 ff.

[191] A. Alt, *ZAW,* NF. 4 (1927), pp. 68 ff.

[192] Y. Aharoni, *IEJ,* 9 (1959), p. 119f.

[193] Alt. *loc. cit.* p. 69; Noth, *Josua,*[2] p. 117.

[194] Perhaps it could be the *r-b-n-t* mentioned in the list of Ramses III alongside Beth-dagon; cf. Simons, *Handbook,* lists XXVII, 71, XXIX, 9.

[195] Mazar has suggested to identify it with the later Zalmonah; cf. *BASOR,* 124 (1951), pp. 21–25.

[196] The Lower Galilean Ramah in the Valley of Beth-haccerem is the Ramah of Naphtali (Josh. 19. 36) and could not possibly be associated with this border description.

[197] It is possible to restore the text accordingly: "Then the boundary turns to Ramah, reaching to the fortified city of Tyre [which is] Hosah, and it ends at the sea."

[198] Contrary to the opinion of Noth, who considers this section to be the northern border of Naphtali, cf. *ZDPV,* 58 (1935), p. 225 f.; *idem, Josua,*[2] pp. 120 f. On this border cf. A. Alt, *loc. cit.* (note 191, above), pp. 69 ff.; *idem, PJb,* 23 (1927), p. 42; Saarisalo, *Boundary,* pp. 96 ff.; J. Press, *BIES,* 1, No. 3 (1933–4), pp. 26 ff. (Hebrew); R. de Vaux, *BIES,* 11 1944), pp. 33 ff. (Hebrew); Aharoni, *Settlement,* pp. 77 ff. (Hebrew).

[199] The beginning of this section is apparently corrupted; the words in the Massoretic text: "and in Judah", are obscure.

[200] A. Alt, *PJb,* 35 (1939), pp. 14 ff. (=*Kl. Schr.,* I, pp. 131 ff.).

[201] Saarisalo, *Boundary, passim.*

[202] W. F. Albright, *JPOS,* 4 (1924), pp. 149 ff.; Noth, *Josua,* pp. 113–14; Y. Aharoni, *IEJ,* 8 (1958), pp. 26–38; S. Talmon, *IEJ,* 15 (1965)), pp. 235–41.

[203] Cf. the discussion of the respective tribes in the preceding section.

[204] Y. Aharoni, *Bible et Terre Sainte,* 174 (1975), pp. 8–12; *idem, BA,* 37 (1974), pp. 2–6.

[205] Y. Aharoni, *Tel Aviv,* 2 (1974), pp. 114–24.

[206] W. F. Albright, *BASOR,* 33 (1929), p. 7.

[207] Y. Aharoni, *Enc. Bib.* (Hebrew), VI (1971), cols. 764–765; E. Oren, *IEJ,* 22 (1972), pp. 167–69; *idem, IEJ,* 23 (1973), pp. 251–54; *idem,* and E. Netzer, Qadmoniot, 6 (1973), pp. 53–56 (Hebrew); S. Groll, *ibid.*, pp. 56–57 (Hebrew).

[208] Y. Aharoni, *Arad Inscriptions* (Jerusalem, 1975), Text No. 32, p. 62, [Hazar]-susah.

[209] Y. Aharoni, *Beer-sheba I,* pp. 71–73.

[210] *Hadashot Arkheologiot,* 53 (1975), p. 27.

[211] The MT has *ʿEder* while LXX reads Αρα (B) or Εδραι.

[212] Aharoni, *Arad Inscriptions,* Text No. 24. 12, p. 50.

[213] *Ibid.*, p. 50; Aharoni, *BASOR,* 197 (1970), pp. 16 ff.

[214] *Ibid.*, pp. 24–25; Y. Aharoni, *IEJ,* 8 (1958), pp. 33–35; *idem, IEJ,* 17 (1967), p. 3.

[215] A. Alt, *PJb,* 29 (1933), pp. 14 f.

216 For the various suggestions cf. M. F. Unger, *Israel and the Arameans of Damascus* (London, 1957), p. 40 f.; A. Malamat, *JNES*, 13 (1954), pp. 231 ff.

217 This is evidently what is meant by the "city of palm trees", though also Zoar at the southern end of the Dead Sea is called by this name, cf. *supra*, p. 215.

218 Ed. Meyer, *Die Isr. u. i. Nachb.*, pp. 355 ff.; A. Malamat, apud B. Mazar, *World History of the Jewish People*, III (Jerusalem, 1971), p. 153.

219 Abel, *Géogr.*, II, pp. 402.

220 M. Dothan, *ʿAtiqot I*, 1 (1955), pp. 19–70.

221 As noted by Z. Kallai, *The Tribes of Israel* (Jerusalem, 1967), p. 355 n. 197.

222 The description of the flight is difficult and Judg. 7. 22 may be interpreted in the following way: and the host fled to Beth-hashittah in the direction of Zarethan (instead of Zeredah), and to the border of Abel-meholah in the direction of Tabbath, i.e. to two places situated near fords of the Jordan, Beth-hashitah and Abel-meholah (Khirbet Tell el-Ḥilu ?), in order to pass the Jordan and to reach Zarethan (Tell Umm Ḥamad ?) and Tabbath (Ras Abu Ṭabat ?).

223 Garstang, *Josh.-Judg.*, p. 390.

224 In the recent excavations at Tell Deir ʿAlla, apparently Succoth, no fortified city was discovered but mainly a sanctuary surrounded by dwellings and stores (H. J. Franken, *VT*, 10 [1960], pp. 386–93; 11 1961], pp. 361–72; 12 [1962], pp. 378–82; 14 [1964], pp. 417–22). It flourished during the Late Bronze Age and its sanctuary was finally destroyed in the first decades of the twlefth century, as indicated by a cartouche from the very end of the Nineteenth Dynasty (Jean Yoyotte, *VT*, 12 [1962], pp. 464–69).

Franken casts doubt on the identification of this tell with Succoth in the light of his investigations, and inclines to place Succoth at Tell el-Ekhṣaṣ located near by (cf. Abel, *Géogr.*, II, p. 470). However, Tell Deir ʿAlla is the largest and most prominent tell in the Succoth Valley, and its identification with Succoth remains most probable. The elders of the Gideon story may well have belonged to this kind of central sanctuary. We may even accept the destruction of the sanctuary as the date of Gideon's battle, which harmonizes well with the assumption that it took place in the first half of the twelfth century, somewhat after the battle of Deborah. However, the next phase of occupation with its new semi-nomadic settlers can also be taken into consideration.

225 E. Sellin, *ZDPV*, 49 (1926), pp. 229 ff.; 50 (1927), pp. 205 ff.; 51 (1928), pp. 119 ff.; 64 (1941), pp. 1 ff.; G. E. Wright, *BASOR*, 148 (1957), pp. 11 ff.; R. J. Bull, *BA*, 23 (1960), pp. 110 ff.; *BASOR*, 161 (1961), pp. 28 ff.; G. E. Wright, *Shechem* (New York, 1965), pp. 80 ff.

226 Abel, *Géogr.*, *II*, p. 477.

227 As suggested by A. Malamat, *op. cit.* (cf. n. 218 above), p. 320 n. 61.

228 There is no basis whatever for identifying it with Ramoth-gilead.

229 P. W. Lapp, "The Conquest of Palestine in the Light of Archaeology," *Concordia Theological Monthly*, 38 (1967), p. 291.

230 Of the large bibliography about the Philistines and their origins cf. especially R. A. S. Macalister, *The Philistines* (London, 1914); W. J. Phytian-Adams, *BBSAJ*, 3 (1923), pp. 20–27; J. Hempel, *PJb*, 23 (1927), pp. 52–92; A. R. Burn, *Minoans, Philistines and Greeks B.C. 1400–900* (London, 1930); G. A. Wainwright, *PEQ* (1931), pp 203–16: O. Eissfeldt, *Philister und Phönizier (Leipzig, 1936);* E. Grant *JBL*, 55 (1936), pp. 175–9; W. F. Albright, *AJA*, 54 (1950), pp 162–76; G. A. Wainwright, *VT*, 6 (1956), pp. 199 ff.; Helck, *Beziehungen*[2] pp. 240 ff.

231 *ANET*, pp. 262 f.; *ANEP*, No. 341.

232 L. H. Vincent, *RB* (1923), pp. 435 ff.; Trude Dothan, *Antiquity and Survival*, 2 (1957), pp. 154 ff.; however, cf. *supra*, p. 228 concerning the possibility of an earlier date.

233 *ANET*, p. 261.

234 B. Mazar, *VT Suppl.*, 7 (1959), p. 205; A. Malamat, apud B. Mazar, ed., *The World History of the Jewish People*, III (Jerusalem, 1971), p. 36 n. 54.

235 *ANET*, p. 263.

236 A. Alt, *ZDPV*, 67 (1944) pp. 1 ff. (=*Kl, Schr.*, I, pp. 216 ff.).

237 Alt, *ibid.*

238 *ANET*, p. 262.

239 M. Avi-Yonah and Y. Eph'al, *EAEHL*, II, 121–25.

[240] M. Dothan, *EAEHL*, II, p. 108.

[241] A. Furumark, *The Mycenaean Pottery* (Stockholm, 1941), p. 575; *idem, The Chronology of Mycenaean Pottery* (Stockholm, 1941), pp. 115–28; *idem, Opuscula archaeologica*, 3 (1944), pp. 260–65.

[242] *ANET*, pp. 25–29.

[243]For a discussion of the Philistine pottery, cf. T. Dothan, *Antiquity and Survival*, 2, (1957), pp. 151–54,; *idem, The Philistines and their Material Culture (Jerusalem, 1967), pp. 71*–208 (Hebrew).

[244] Hebrew: *srn*; the origin of this word is apparently connected with the Greek *Tyrannos*.

[245] Gardiner, *Anc. Eng. On.*, 1, pp. 190* ff.

[246] J. Naveh, *IEJ*, 8 (1958), pp. 87–100, 165–70.

[247] Y. Aharoni, *PEQ* (1958), p. 27–31.

[248] W. F. Albright, *AASOR*, 2–3 (1923), pp. 11 ff.

[249] S. Yeivin, *First Preliminary Report on the Excavations at Tel 'Gat'* (Jerusalem, 1961), pp. 9 f.

[250] S. Bülow and R. A. Mitchel, *IEJ*, 11 (1961), pp. 101–10.

[251] This site was proposed by G. E. Wright, *BA*, 29 (1966), pp. 70–86; *idem, HTR*, 64 (1971), pp. 437–48 H *BA*, 34 (1971), pp. 76–86.

[252] K. Elliger, *ZDPV*, 57 (1934), pp. 148–52.

[253] F. J. Bliss and R. A. S. Macalister, *Excavations in Palestine* (London, 1902), P1. 44.

[254] B. Mazar, *IEJ*, 4 (1954), pp. 227–35.

[255] For a summary of the written sources dealing with the identification of Gath, cf. A. F. Rainey, *EI*, 12 (1975), pp. 63*–76*

[256] B. Mazar, *IEJ*, 1 (1950–1), pp. 61 ff.

[257] *Ibid.*, pp. 128 ff.

[258] H. Kjaer, *JPOS*, 10 (1930), pp. 97 ff.

[259] It is likely that this chain-reaction also caused changes in the political structure of the Philistines; however, our sources are extremely meagre. I owe to Prof. Mazar the suggestion that Gath was raised in this period to supremacy over the other Philistine cities. It appears now as the main enemy of Israel, and in David's elegy after Saul's and Jonathan's death Gath and the market (harbour) of Ashkelon are singled out as the representatives of Philistia (2 Sam. 1. 20). Also the identification of Achish with Abimelech King of the Philistines (Ps. 34. 1; cf. Gen. 26. 8) is notable. This fits well the central location of Gath at Tel eṣ-Ṣafi with its large domains as far as the Negeb.

CHAPTER III

The United Monarchy

The Philistine threat aroused the tribes of Israel to concerted action, which led to the founding of the Israelite Monarchy. Thus was opened a new chapter in the history of Palestine.

I. SAUL

The first Israelite king was Saul the son of Kish from the tribe of Benjamin. He belonged apparently to a prominent family of Gibeah of Benjamin (Tell el-Ful), which dominated the highroad from Judah to Mount Ephraim at the border of the two tribal confederations (cf. especially Judg. 19. 12 ff.). With the establishment of the monarchy Gibeah became the first capital of Israel and was henceforth known as Gibeah of Saul (1 Sam. 11. 4).[1] His birthplace may have been at Zela (Ha-eleph) where he was buried (2 Sam. 21. 14; cf. Josh. 18. 28); according to 1 Chron. 8. 29–30 his family was related to Gibeon.

The small but centrally located tribe of Benjamin was enduring heavy pressure from the Philistines, who had established a garrison at Geba (Jeba') of Benjamin, also known as Gibeath-elohim because of its highplace (1 Sam. 10. 5).[2] Since these two names are so similar and the confusion between them is increased by the LXX renderings, the identification of this site is much debated.[3] It seems safe to say today that the fort discovered at Tell el-Ful, built after a long period of abandonment at the site, was not constructed by the Philistines.[4] All the finds, especially the pottery, belong to the common hill country repertoire and no influence from the coastal region can be detected. Furthermore, we now have another such fort of similar date at Beer-sheba.[5]

There remain, therefore, the alternatives of Geba or Gibeon. The first is bolstered by the fact that this was the site where the Israelite forces assembled against the Philistines, and its importance as a border city of Benjamin is demonstrated by its being fortified by Asa (1 Kings 15. 22) and by its being mentioned as being on the border of Judah in the days of Josiah (2 Kings 23. 8).

Saul's first military action was not against the Philistines but rather the deliverance of Jabesh-gilead from the Ammonites. Some residents from Jabesh-gilead already had affinities with the tribe of Benjamin

(Judg. 21. 8 ff.). As Saul marched through the Israelite hill country he was doubtless joined by other tribes, and from Bezek (Khirbet Ibziq) in the northern hills of Ephraim he made a surprise attack on the besiegers of Jabesh-gilead.

We do not know whether this action was carried out unbeknown to the Philistines or whether the Philistine garrison considered Saul a trusted vassal and did not object to his Transjordanian expedition. But after the battle Saul did not disband the troops that had gathered around him. His son Jonathan took Geba by surprise "and all Israel heard it said that Saul had defeated the garrison of the Philistines, and also that Israel had become odious to the Philistines. And the people were called out to join Saul at Gilgal" (1 Sam. 13. 4). The establishment of a monarchy and the rebellion against Philistine domination were closely related to one another.

The Philistines responded at once. They came up and encamped at Michmash from whence they launched three retaliatory raiding parties to the north, west and east. Evidently they intended to create consternation among the Israelite tribes and to scatter Saul's forces before the decisive battle. Saul acted quickly, and Jonathan made a daring attack by crossing the deep Wadi Suweiniṭ, separating Geba (Jeba') from Michmash. The Philistine camp was overrun, and its troops fled via Beth-horon to their home bases.

The struggle against the Philistines continued throughout Saul's reign in the Shephelah (1 Sam. 14. 52), but until his death the Philistines were kept out of the Israelite hill country. Saul's manner of rule is summarized in one brief text:

> When Saul had taken the kingship over Israel, he fought against all his enemies on every side, against Moab, against the Ammonites, against Edom, against the kings of Zobah, and against the Philistines; wherever he turned he wrought deliverance [according to LXX; MT "he made it worse"]. And he did valiantly and smote the Amalekites, and delivered Israel out of the hands of those who plundered them (1 Sam. 14. 47–8).

We have no details about Saul's Transjordanian wars. It appears that he attacked the various peoples there who were adjacent to the area of Israelite settlement. He dealt a decisive blow to the nomads of the southern desert and pursued them into the Sinai peninsula as far as "the city of Amalek"[6] and "from Havilah as far as Shur"(1 Sam.15. 5–7).

There are only a few bits of information about his conflicts with the Philistines. The duel between David and Goliath took place in the Valley of Elah, between Sochoh and Azekah, where the border between Saul's kingdom and Gath of the Philistines was probably located. In the Davidic narratives we find an incident when the Philistines fought against Keilah and were robbing the threshing floors (1 Sam. 23. 1).

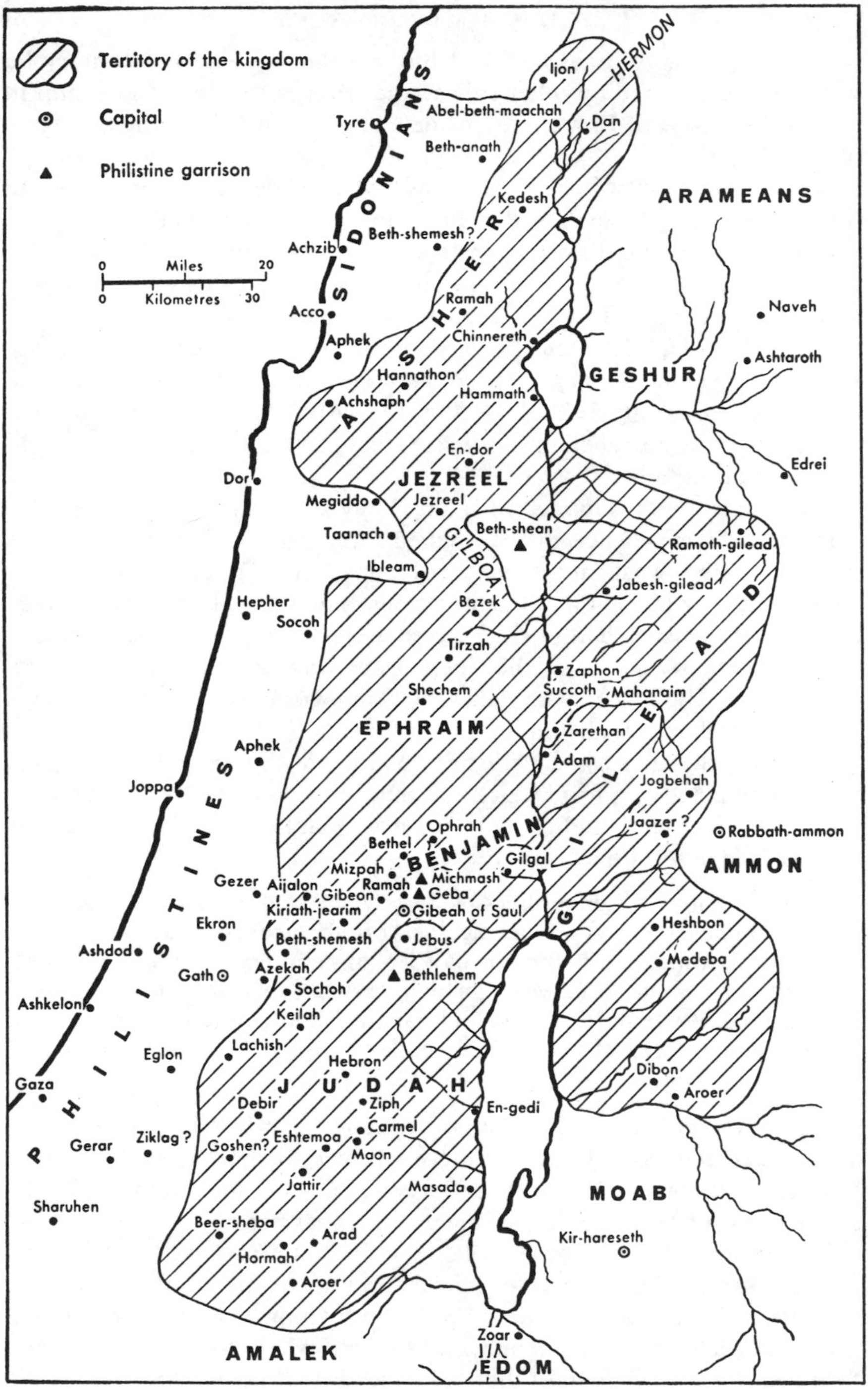

Map 20. The Kingdom of Saul

These seem to have been limited border skirmishes and plundering raids; David's troops sought to strike back at these Philistines in order to gain the loyalty of Judah.

From the passage describing the kingdom of Ish-bosheth (Eshbaal according to 1 Chron. 8. 33; 9. 39; but Ishvi in 1 Sam. 14. 49), Saul's son, we learn something about the districts and probably also the administration of that time:

> Now Abner the son of Ner, commander of Saul's army, had taken Ishbosheth the son of Saul, and brought him over to Mahanaim; and he made him king over Gilead and the Asherites (in place of Ashurites, i.e. Assyrians) and Jezreel and Ephraim and Benjamin and all Israel (2 Sam. 2. 8–9).

Besides these areas called "all Israel" Saul's authority was also extended over Judah, which broke away from the kingdom after his death and crowned David to rule them separately. Thus Saul's original kingdom included six districts: Gilead, Galilee, that part of the Jezreel Valley under Israelite control,[7] Mount Ephraim, Benjamin and Judah[8] (cf. map 20).

The definition of five districts in Saul's kingdom as "all Israel" to the exclusion of Judah is certainly not accidental. This reflects the form of his administrative organization, based upon the traditional tribal inheritances. Three of the districts are named after tribes (Asher, Ephraim, Benjamin), but each one actually included two tribes. Although it is essentially a geographical term, Gilead was used as a tribal name during the period of the Judges, being synonymous with Gad. The only town named is Jezreel, an Israelite centre in the Jezreel Valley, which was still largely Canaanite in Saul's day. The town had been assigned to Issachar (Josh. 19. 18), but we have already noted that this tribe was not included in the boundary delineations. In this instance the monarchial organization differed from that of the tribal alliance, so that the district is named after its most prominent city, doubtless the regional capital. We will note a similar organizational pattern during Solomon's reign.

Although the cleavage between Judah and Israel had been very deep during the time of the Judges, it appears that Saul's authority was accepted without serious objection even in Judah. The Philistine threat which brought about his rise to power also achieved the postponement of the old feuds, and the danger from without remained throughout Saul's reign. Furthermore, Saul had won the hearts of the Judean patricians by repulsing the Amalekites and driving them deep into the southern wilderness. After this campaign he erected a victory stele at Carmel, a town south-east of Hebron (1 Sam. 15. 12). Saul's firm grip on Judah is also proved by the experiences of David as a renegade. Early in his flight he tried to find refuge with Achish, King of Gath; but after encountering hatred and suspicion there, he returned to Judah and assembled a band of warriors. For a while he was able to hide in a cave near Adullam, but he soon fled from there to Moab where he left his parents in safe keeping (1 Sam. 22. 1–4). The most direct route to Moab led through the wilderness of Judah, down the passes of Wadi Saiyal, and crossed the Dead Sea in the shallow area opposite the Lisan. Masada is situated opposite this ford and may have been the fortress used by David as his base in the wilderness (1 Sam. 22. 4–5; 23. 14; 24. 1).[9]

From his stronghold in the desolate Judean wastes David made incursions from time to time into the adjacent Judean territory. In particular we find him going to Ziph, Carmel and Maon, all of them south-east of Hebron (1 Sam. 23. 15; 25. 2; 26. 1) and bordering on the wilderness that surrounds En-gedi and Masada. We also hear about a daring expedition to Keilah in the Shephelah in order to deliver it from attacks by the Philistines who were robbing the threshing floors (1 Sam. 23. 1–6). However, he was soon forced to retreat again to the wilderness because, in spite of his assistance by which he had expected to gain the loyalty of the patricians at Keilah, it became apparent that they might turn him over to Saul. But even in the Judean wilderness David was not completely safe from Saul's power. He was finally compelled to escape to Achish, the King of Gath (1 Sam. 27. 1 ff.).

Therefore, it is clear that Saul exercised complete authority over all areas of the Israelite occupation, including Judah. Yet he evidently did not try to expand his rule to take in the foreign population, either in Transjordan or among the Canaanites and Philistines. When David escaped to Gath, Saul did not try to pursue him further (1 Sam. 27. 4). Although Saul's capital was at Gibeah of Benjamin, there is no intimation that Jebusite Jerusalem caused him any trouble, and the presence of that enclave did not prevent his complete control over Judah. As a rule, it appears that Saul maintained normal relations with the neighbouring foreign population, as long as they did not bother the Israelites. The "land of Israel" in Saul's day was still confined to the precincts of the Israelite settlements, i.e. it was still a limited term (cf. 1 Sam. 13. 19). The Philistines must have finally become reconciled to this situation, that is, until the balance of power in the Jezreel Valley was broken. When Saul gained control over the central part of the Jezreel Valley, it was tantamount to closing off the *Via Maris* against the Philistines in that area.

The narrative of this war has been truncated to some degree by the insertion of the story about David. But one can still follow its general line. The Philistine rulers assembled their forces at Aphek at the sources of the Yarkon (1 Sam. 29. 1) preparatory to marching on Jezreel (vs. 11). Saul's troops "were encamped by the fountain which is in Jezreel" (vs.

1); on the eve of the battle they ranged themselves on Mount Gilboa. The Philistines made camp across from them at Shunem (1 Sam. 28. 4). The conflict ended in Philistine victory, while Saul and his three sons fell during the retreat at Gilboa. After this the Philistines may have penetrated once again into the hill country, thus forcing Abner to establish Eshbaal's new capital at Mahanaim in Transjordan. However, this is far from certain. At least it is clear that the balance had shifted temporarily in favour of the Philistines. But, after the United Monarchy was re-established under David, Israel's hour of greatness had arrived when it would dominate the whole country.

II. THE CAMPAIGNS OF DAVID

During the last year or two of Saul's reign David had dwelt at Ziklag,[10] one of the many distant towns subject to the King of Gath (1 Sam. 27. 5–6). Even though David governed there as a vassal of the King of Gath, he was able to exercise a great deal of independence in his own region. Henceforth Ziklag belonged to the Judean kings and was included among the cities of Simeon (Josh. 19. 5; 1 Sam. 27. 6). The town was located on the fringe of the Negeb; from there David carried out raids against the nomads of the southern desert: "The Geshurites, the Girzites, and the Amalekites; for these were the inhabitants of the land from *of old* (according to LXX Telem, cf. Josh. 15. 24; 1 Sam. 15. 4), as far as Shur, to the land of Egypt" (1 Sam. 27. 8). But, according to the narrator, he told Achish that he had been raiding the territories of Judah, e.g. the Negeb of Judah, the Negeb of the Jerahmeelites and the Negeb of the Kenites. Therefore, Ziklag was on the border of the Negeb near the Israelite districts in that region. It was also supported by a considerable territory of its own; it was a small vassaldom in the kingdom of Gath. For this reason it seems much more likely to identify it with Tell esh-Shari 'ah, a prominent mound, though not exceedingly large, located on the Wadi esh-Shari 'ah east of Gerar (Tell Abu Hureireh) and north-west of Beer-sheba.[11] If Gath was really located at Tell eṣ-Ṣafi, then the distance between them is considerable (about 23 miles). This would testify to the great expansion and subsequent dominance of Gath at this time; it became the main Philistine capital in the Shephelah while Ekron was somewhat overshadowed. Hence also David's prominent status as a vassal enjoying great political independence. His activities at Ziklag demonstrate that he actually ruled over an extensive district in the Negeb besides his own town. This region probably corresponds to the first group of Simeonite towns (Josh. 19. 2–6; 1 Chron. 4. 28–31) which bears the explicit date "until David reigned" (1 Chron. 4. 31). The division of Simeon's cities into two groups is therefore rendered intelligible, and one can understand how this Simeonite region came to be called the Negeb of Judah in Davidic sources (1 Sam. 27. 10; 30. 14; 2 Sam. 24. 7.).

David succeeded by these activities in gaining the loyalty of the Judean populace, in spite of his being under Philistine patronage. By his raids into the southern desert he delivered the residents of the Negeb from the pressure of marauders. After his devastating attack upon the camp of the Amalekites who had plundered Ziklag in his absence, he wisely sent gifts from the booty to the elders of Judah (1 Sam. 30. 26–31). In the list of towns to whom these gifts were sent, some Negeb settlements are included, e.g. Bethel, Ramoth of the Negeb, Aroer, Hormah, the cities of the Jerahmeelites and of the Kenites and towns in the southern Judean hill country, e.g. Jattir, Eshtemoa and Hebron. These are all in regions settled by the southern tribes that had been joined to greater Judah, e.g. Caleb, Kenaz, the Kenite and the Jerahmeelite. David was trying to win over those tribes who felt no great affinity with the Israelite alliance and the House of Saul.

His efforts bore fruit. After Saul's death David went up to Hebron and established a monarchy over Judah alone while Eshbaal (disgraced to Ish-bosheth) the son of Saul continued to reign over "all of Israel" from his temporary Transjordanian capital at Mahanaim (2 Sam. 2. 8–9). Thus David began by arousing the ancient animosity between Judah and Israel in order to take over the kingdom by stages. It is clear that David had not created this feud which was an ancient legacy from the days of the occupation and settlement, coupled with the special circumstances of the period of the Judges. Nevertheless, he intensified it and, for the first time, established it as an element in the structure of the kingdom. This development was fraught with dire consequences for the future.

There is no mention of any Philistine interference during this stage of David's rise to power. Achish probably still thought of him as a loyal vassal, and the Philistines doubtless encouraged the rift between Judah and Israel.

After the death of Abner and Eshbaal there was no serious opponent who could stand up to David, so all the tribes of Israel submitted to his rule. One of his first acts was the conquest of Jebusite Jerusalem and its establishment as the new capital of the newly united Judah and Israel. The Jebusite fortress of Zion became henceforth the city of David, the exclusive possession of his dynasty. Only when Jerusalem became his capital in his eighth year[12] did his rule over all Israel and Judah become an accomplished fact, something that was impossible during his seven-year reign at Hebron (2 Sam. 5. 5). In this manner David founded a capital that was neutral in relation to all of the quarrelling tribes, since it was entirely his by right of conquest. At the same time this move announced the new line of development to be taken by his kingdom: a bursting forth from the confines of the limited Israelite area and the absorption of all alien territories remaining in the land.

Only now did the Philistines realize the great danger which David's kingdom represented. But their interference was already too late. Twice they tried to reach Jerusalem, and twice they suffered a serious defeat at the hands of David in the Valley of Rephaim south-west of the city. The stronghold to which David went down when the Philistines invaded is certainly the fortress of Zion and not the one dating back to his renegade days which was way off in the desert. The tale of David's three heroes who forced their way through to the well (cistern) at the gate of Bethlehem while "David was then in the stronghold; and the garrison of the Philistines was then at Bethlehem" (2 Sam. 23. 13–17; 1 Chron. 11. 15–19) may belong to this period. If so, it means that the Philistines had succeeded at first in gaining control of Bethlehem. When they were routed the second time David pursued them along the road to Beth-horon from Gibeon as far as Gezer (2 Sam. 5. 25; 1 Chron. 14. 16).

In the years that followed, David smote his enemies round about one by one and established a greatly expanded kingdom. At that time there was no strong exterior force that could interfere in the affairs of Palestine. When the Israelite tribes united into a well-organized kingdom, their king was able to overcome with relative ease the small peoples that had distressed the individual tribes during the period of the Judges, e.g. the remaining Canaanite cities, the Philistines, the Ammonites, the Moabites, the Edomites and the Bedouin of the Negeb. There were only two serious opponents vying with him for supremacy in Syria and Palestine: the Arameans in northern Transjordan and Syria and the Phoenicians on the Lebanese coast. The Arameans, who were dominated at that time by the kingdom of Aram-zobah (Zoba) in the Lebanese Beqa', were defeated by David and their territory annexed to his kingdom.

David's principal conquests are probably preserved for us in the parallel sections of Psalms 60 and 108.[13]

> God has spoken in his sanctuary:
> "With exultation I will divide up
> Shechem
> and portion the Vale of Succoth;
> Gilead is mine; Manasseh is mine;
> Ephraim is my helmet;
> Judah is my sceptre.
> Moab is my washbasin;
> upon Edom I cast my shoe;
> over Philistia I shout in triumph."
> Who will bring me to the *fortified city*
> (*'îr māṣôr*; Psalms 108. 10, *'îr mibṣār*)?
> Who will lead me to Edom? (Psalms 60. 8–11;
> 108.7–10).

These are the conquests of David as they came in chronological order in accordance with other sources: first his domination over Judah and Israel and then his external conquests. Only one emendation is necessary; Edom appears twice while Aram is absent. The interchange between these two names is a common mistake in the Massoretic text[14] since their spelling is graphically very similar both in ancient Hebrew and later Aramaic scripts. Thus, the first appearance of Edom should probably be corrected to read Aram since it is known that the conquest of Edom was last (Psalms 60: superscription). The "fortified city" is most probably the mainland city of Tyre, known as Usu, the conquest of which is clear from the description of the census conducted by Joab (2 Sam. 24. 7; cf. Josh. 19. 29). Both the emendation of Edom to Aram and the interpretation of the "fortified city" as belonging to Tyre are supported by the Aramaic Targum.

It is obvious, therefore, that David was able to put strong pressure on Tyre, which was now dependent upon him for a great deal. However, he chose to treat her with magnanimity as a partner in the development of the major trade routes. Henceforth, Tyre's efforts were directed westward and she eventually became the principal sea power in the Mediterranean.

Although we do not have detailed information about David's wars, the general picture is clear. Concerning the subjugation of Philistia, only a laconic statement is recorded: "After this David defeated the Philistines and subdued them, and David took Methegh-ammah out of the hand of the Philistines" (2 Sam. 8. 1). The parallel passage in 1 Chronicles 18. 1 substitutes "Gath and its villages" for Methegh-ammah. That the Chronicles passage is more correct seems doubtful, because Achish, the King of Gath, was still an independent ruler during the reign of Solomon (1 Kings 2. 39). Neither would the conquest of Gath-Gittaim west of Gezer exhaust David's achievements in that area. In view of the list pertaining to Levitical cities which must be dated to David's reign (cf. *infra.*, pp. 301—4), it would seem that David took all the northern Shephelah away from the Philistines, i.e. what had in fact been the land of Ekron. Therefore, it is probable that our passage defines his complete victory over the Philistines in general terms. He took those areas away from them which were essential to forming a bridge between Jerusalem and Joppa and the Sharon, thus assuring his supremacy in this region.[15]

One of David's first moves was logically to conquer the Canaanite cities still in existence on the plains. We have no explicit information about this except the fact that these regions are Israelite under Solomon's reign. His district list includes the *Via Maris* in the Sharon and the main cities in the Jezreel Valley (1 Kings 4. 10–12). From Joab's itinerary during the census we learn that these conquests also included

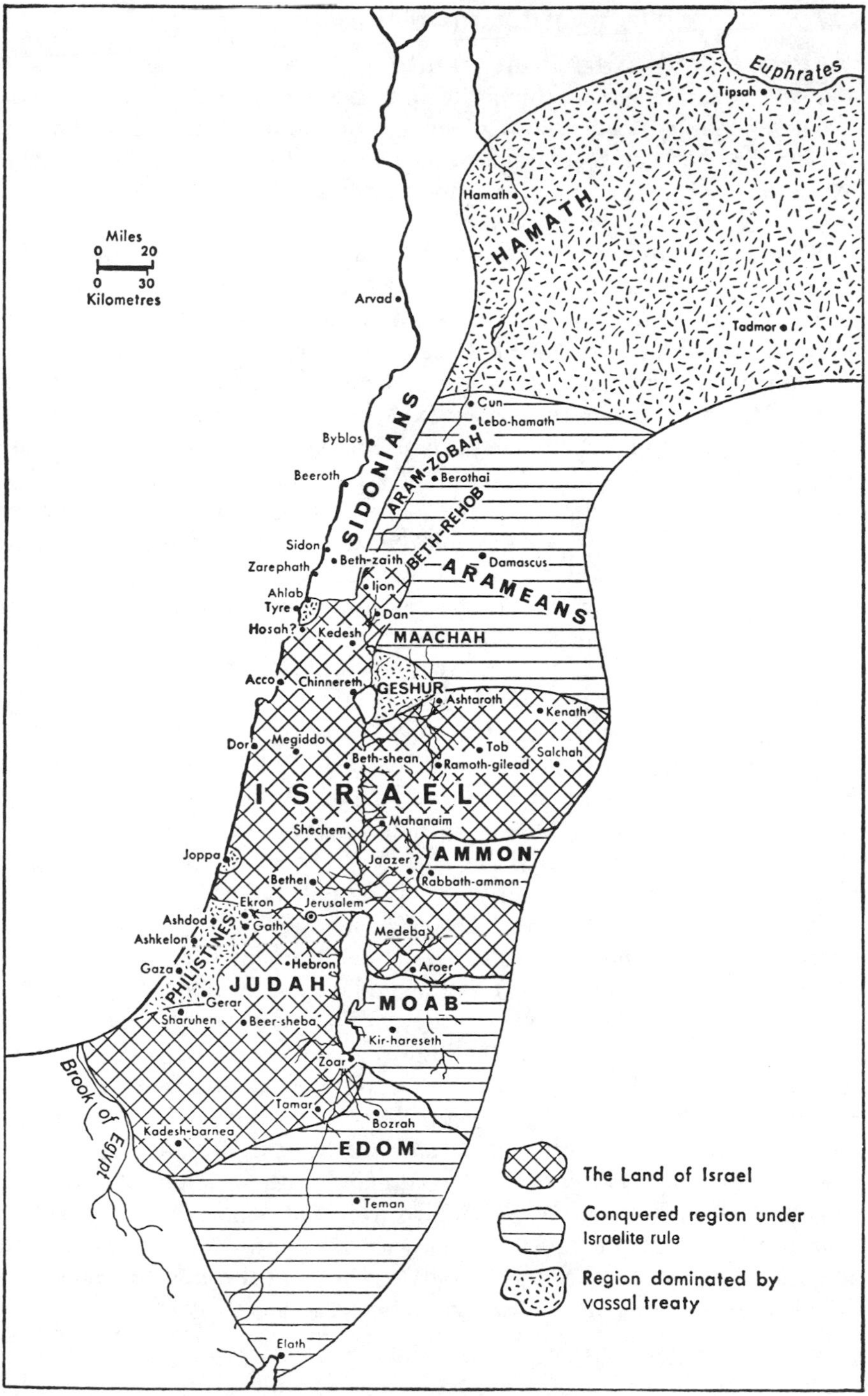
Euphrates
Tipsah
Hamath
HAMATH
Tadmor
Miles
0 20
0 30
Kilometres
Arvad
Cun
Lebo-hamath
SIDONIANS
Byblos
ARAM-ZOBAH
Beeroth
Berothai
BETH-REHOB
Sidon
Zarephath
Beth-zaith
Damascus
ARAMEANS
Ijon
Ahlab
Tyre
Dan
Hosah?
Kedesh
MAACHAH
Acco
Chinnereth
GESHUR
Ashtaroth
Kenath
Dor
Megiddo
Tob
Salchah
Beth-shean
Ramoth-gilead
ISRAEL
Mahanaim
Shechem
Joppa
Jaazer?
AMMON
Bethel
Rabbath-ammon
Ekron
Jerusalem
Ashdod
Gath
Ashkelon
PHILISTINES
Medeba
Gaza
Hebron
Aroer
JUDAH
Gerar
MOAB
Sharuhen
Beer-sheba
Kir-hareseth
Zoar
Brook of Egypt
Tamar
Bozrah
Kadesh-barnea
EDOM
Teman
Elath
The Land of Israel
Conquered region under Israelite rule
Region dominated by vassal treaty

Map 21. The Kingdom of David.

the Plain of Acco as far as the "fortress of Tyre" (cf. *infra,* pp. 297 f.). Those Canaanite areas which had long been reckoned as part of the tribal inheritances were now added to the Israelite kingdom. Thus a political and territorial continuity was achieved from Dan to Beer-sheba, including the coastal region from the "fortress of Tyre" (2 Sam. 24. 7) to the border of Ekron (Josh. 13. 3).

Now David turned to Transjordan, and here he met a powerful opponent, Aram-zobah. According to the narrative, Hadadezer, the King of Aram-zobah, came to the aid of Ammon. From 1 Chronicles 19. 7 we learn that the first clash between their respective forces took place at Medeba, an important city on the King's Highway at the northern edge of the Moabite plateau. It would appear, therefore, that this was a struggle for control over that important Transjordanian route connecting Damascus with Elath.[16] David emerged the victor, thereby supplementing his domination over the *Via Maris* with similar mastery over the King's Highway. He conquered Moab and enslaved its territories and smote the Aramean alliance which had come to their help under the leadership of the king of Aram-zobah three times in succession: at Medeba, beside Rabbath-ammon, and at Helam in northern Transjordan (2 Sam. 10; 1 Chron. 19). Subsequent to these victories, he also conquered Rabbath-ammon (2 Sam. 11; 12; 1 Chron. 20. 1–3), Damascus and the Beqa‘ as far as the border of Hamath (2 Sam. 8. 3 ff.). Finally, he smote Edom[17] in the Valley of Salt south of the Dead Sea; he also subjugated it and placed garrisons throughout the country (2 Sam. 8. 2, 13–14; 1 Kings 11. 15–16; 1 Chron. 18. 2, 12–13).

Among the towns of the Beqa‘ a few are mentioned from which David took a great deal of bronze, viz. Betah (Tibhath), Berothai and Cun (2 Sam. 8. 8; 1 Chron. 18. 8). David gained control over the kingdoms of Transjordan plus the Aramean principalities that had been subservient to Aram-zobah; in all these places he established garrisons. From the situation that prevailed early in Solomon's reign we know that his rule extended to Tadmor, the important desert oasis on the route to Mesopotamia, and Tiphsah on the Euphrates (1 Kings 4. 24). It is obvious, therefore, that David controlled the entire King's Highway from Edom to Damascus and the Euphrates. References to the development of Ezion-geber and commerce with southern Arabia (the kingdom of Sheba) during Solomon's reign (1 Kings 9. 26–10. 22; 2 Chron. 8. 17–9. 21) demonstrate that Israel was now a major power and that she dominated all of these routes. She held the key to trade with South Arabia, which unlocked stores of wealth to its owners.[18]

III. THE KINGDOM AT THE HEIGHT OF ITS EXPANSION

David's realm extended from Lebo-hamath and the Lebanese border in the north to the Egyptian border in the south, from the desert on the east to the Great Sea (the Mediterranean) on the west. In the north it included Damascus and the Sirion region (Anti-Lebanon) plus the important trade routes to Tadmor and Tiphsah. During the first half of the tenth century there was no serious competitor to this kingdom. In the north it bordered on the Neo-Hittite Hamath and with the Phoenician Tyre and Sidon, which wisely maintained good relations with David throughout his reign. In the south the Philistines seem to have preserved some degree of independence, but their territory was restricted and their striking power neutralized so that David could impose his will on them. All of those states must have recognized David's political supremacy, although the explicit statement to this effect refers to the beginning of Solomon's reign (1 Kings 4. 21–4). They were probably dominated by a kind of a vassal treaty. This is indicated by the presents from Hamath (2 Sam. 8. 9–10; 1 Chron. 18. 9–10) and Tyre (2 Sam. 5. 11), by David's marriage with a princess of Geshur (2 Sam. 3. 3), by the services of Joppa's harbour (2 Chron. 2. 16) and by the delivery of escaped slaves from Philistine Gath (1 Kings 2. 39–40). Among the peoples whom David conquered Edom (instead of Aram), Moab, Ammon, Philistia, Amalek and (Aram-)Zobah (2 Sam. 8. 11–12) are mentioned.

1. The Davidic Census

Within the framework of the kingdom one must distinguish between the conquered regions in Transjordan now governed by commissioners or vassal princes—Edom, Moab, Ammon and the various Aramean states—and the "land of Israel", which had come to include Israel, Judah and the assimilated Canaanite territories (cf. map 21). The internal make-up of the kingdom is revealed in the description of the census carried out by Joab under David's orders (2 Sam. 24. 5–6) which furnishes us a segment of the Israelite boundary delineation during David's reign. The census included all of the Hivite and Canaanite towns (vs. 7) which were now an integral part of Israel, but the areas of foreign conquest were excluded.

The description begins in Transjordan on the southern border. The first reference point was south of Aroer beside the Arnon, the traditional boundary of Moab. Next three Transjordanian districts are mentioned: Gad (a general designation for southern Transjordan including Reuben), Jaazer and Gilead. The next reference, "the land of Tahtim-hodshi" is evidently the result of textual corruption. From the context one would expect some area in northern Transjordan.[19]

Next on the list is Dan, followed by a brief passage describing the northern border: "and they came to Dan-jaan and (they went ?) around to Sidon, and came to the fortress of Tyre" (2 Sam. 24. 6–7). Jaan is probably Ijon to the north of Dan (cf. 1 Kings 15. 20). The line ran along the Sidonian territorial boundary, coinciding more or less with the Liṭani; and it reached the coastal fortress of Tyre, Usu of the Egyptian and Assyrian sources, the Hellenistic Palaityros (Tell Rashidiyeh). A comparison of this passage with the border delineations of Asher is most illuminating (Josh. 19. 28–9).

At the end one reference point in the Negeb is given, namely, Beer-sheba, which was the administrative centre of the Judean Negeb province during that period (cf. 1 Sam. 8. 2; 27. 10).

Since Joab's census took in Judah, Israel and the Canaanite cities, it would appear that David was trying to organize his kingdom into a stable unit within the framwork of "all Israel" according to the wider meaning of that term. It is hardly incidental that the same term is used in its narrower sense, defining the northern tribes only, before and after the days of David. Along with this there appears the idea of the twelve Israelite tribes organized around Jerusalem and its temple, an idea which found no place in the reality preceding the monarchy. We may assume therefore that this was a revival of an ancient tradition, which was meant to overcome the inner frictions of the kingdom.[20] We have no explicit information to this effect; but there are two documents evidently related to David's reign which support the same conclusion, viz. the lists of the tribal chieftains and the Levitical cities.

Chapter 27 of 1 Chronicles contains the names of the chief administrative officers—military, civilian and royal—of David's reign. Among these we find the commanders of thousands, the tribal chieftains, the ministers in charge of royal stores and finally the members of the highest ranking officialdom. There is no basis for doubting the integrity of this list, which shows that David based the internal administration of his kingdom upon the traditional Israelite tribes, both of Judah and of Israel. Twelve chieftains are included in the list, providing we ignore Zadok, senior official of the House of Aaron, who certainly did not belong to the original list. On the other hand, two other tribes are absent—Dan and Asher.[21] This is hardly accidental since those tribes were the ones most weakened during the period of the Judges, Dan by its migration and Asher by the pressure of its assimilation to the Canaanite coastal society. With their exclusion place was created for a second chieftain of Manasseh in Transjordan and for a chieftain from the tribe of Levi. This latter was associated with the special task assigned to the Levitical families during David's reign.

2. The City Lists of Simeon and Dan

The town lists used by the editor of the book of Joshua for describing the tribal inheritances were taken from the regional division of the kingdom (cf. *supra,* p. 88). The lists of Simeon and Dan (Josh. 19. 1–6, 40–6; 1 Chron. 4. 28–31), which do not belong to the districts of Judah, are apparently from David's reign. They were given for the purpose of defining the territories of those tribes which were not represented in the traditional boundary descriptions. The towns of Simeon comprise only a part of the later Negeb district of Judea (Josh. 15 21–32), that section which had its centre at Beer-sheba and was called "the Negeb of Judah" in the Davidic period.[22] But this list includes other towns not referred to in Joshua 15, viz. Beth-Marcaboth, Hazar-susah and Sharuhen. Of these three only one is known to us, viz. Sharuhen, which was identified by Albright with Tell el-Far 'ah,[23] one of the most important fortified cities on the Philistine border. Its inclusion in Israelite territory indicates the climax of western expansion. The city was destroyed in Shishak's campaign, and excavations have demonstrated that it did not recover from this disaster.[24]

Analysis of the Danite city list also points to its origin in the Davidic reign.[25] It takes in the coastal region from the Wadi Sorek, i.e. from the territory of Ekron and Eltekeh (Tell esh-Shallaf) to the Yarkon opposite Joppa. This region was not conquered before David, and after his death it must have broken away again within a very short period of time. After the division of the kingdom we hear about Gibbethon as the border town between Israel and Philistia. The parallel between this list and that of the Levitical cities in the same area is complete; this latter document probably belongs to David's reign (cf. *infra,* p. 302). Evidently Solomon's second administrative district, which included part of this area (1 Kings 4. 9), was somewhat smaller, taking in only its eastern part, since by this time Gezer had already become a border town between Israel and Philistia as a result of Egyptian intervention (cf. *infra,* p. 305).

The reign of David was marked by a strong Israelite pressure on the neighbouring region. Concerning the conquest of the "Danite region" at about this time, we have evidence from the contemporary destruction level at Tell Qasileh.[26] Only the inclusion of Ekron among the Danite cities (Josh. 19. 43) is difficult. It is most likely that we should read here "Timnah of Ekron" (for discussion cf. *infra,* p. 312).

With this slight emendation the list of Danite cities corresponds to the boundary of Judah as described in Joshua 15. 10–11 which ran from Beth-shemesh to Timnah and then passed slightly north of Ekron ("to the shoulder of the hill north of Ekron"). Likewise, we have seen that the northern boundary of Asher (Josh. 19. 28–9) is identical to that of Israel in David's reign as demonstrated by Joab's census (2 Sam. 24. 6–7). Since David depended upon the traditional tribal boundaries for his administrative division, it would appear that he made use of the border descriptions from the northern tribal alliance to which were added town lists from other tribes (Simeon, Dan, Issachar and those in Trans-jordan).[27]

All of the available evidence indicates that David organized the Israelite nucleus of his kingdom according to the traditional pattern of twelve tribes, embracing Israel, Judah and the Transjordanians. This

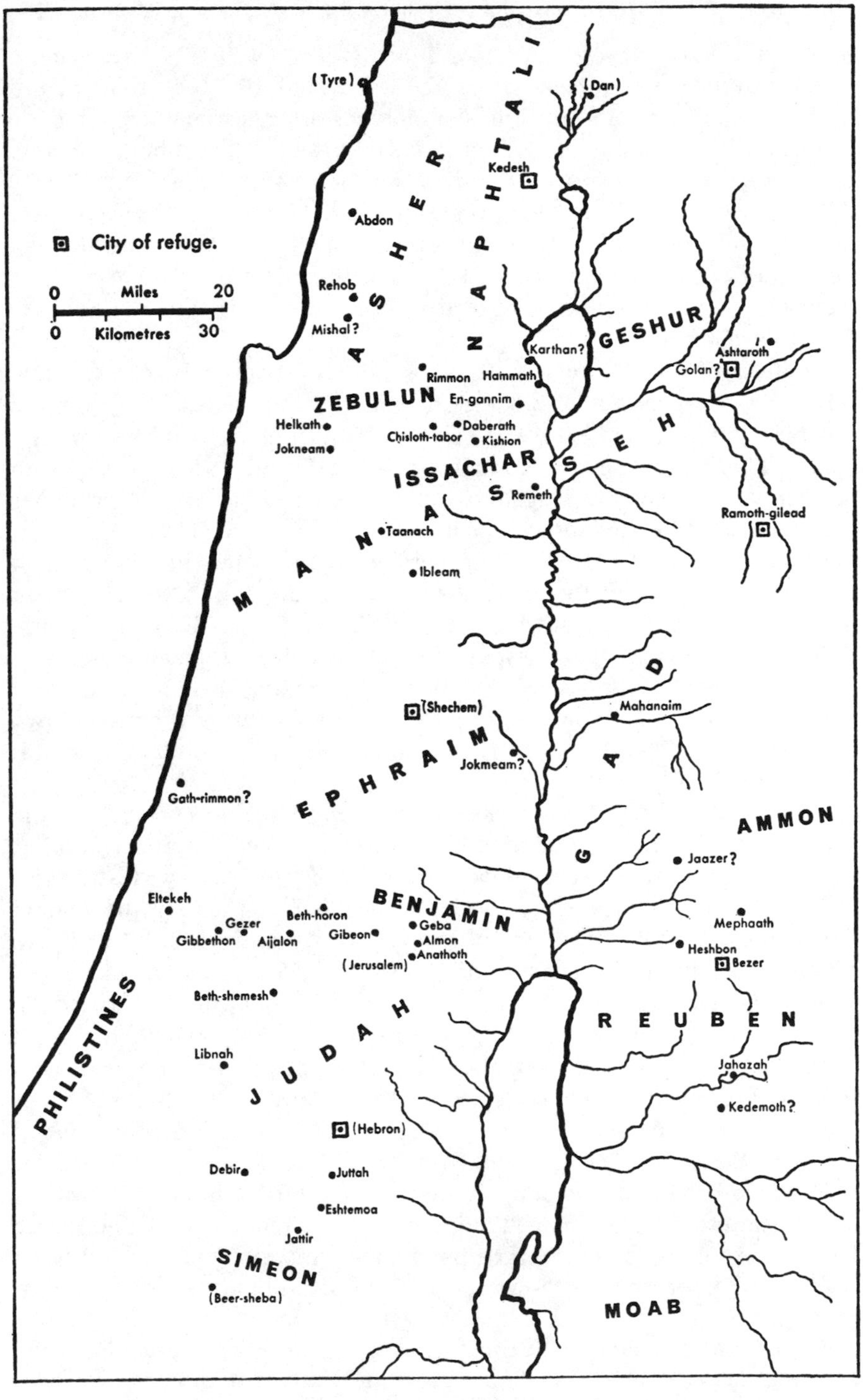

Map 22. The Levitical Cities.

system had no basis in the situation prevailing before the rise of the monarchy, which consisted of two separate alliances in Israel and Judah, granting some special status to the tribes in Transjordan. David was probably trying to revive an ancient tradition dating back to a period before the settlement, or at least to its early stages. In this manner he must have hoped to overcome the internal rivalry between Judah and Israel. The constitution of Jerusalem as a monarchial centre to which the ark of the covenant was transferred and where the main shrine was established was done to make it the new amphictyonic centre of the traditional twelve tribes. It was not the rivalry between the various tribes but the antagonism between the two tribal alliances and their institutions which endangered the kingdom. The united monarchy saw itself as heir to the ancient tribal alliance, which embraced Judah as well as Ephraim.

This tradition has become predominant in the biblical narratives, since it continues to exist in the organizational institutions of the Jerusalem temple.[28] However, it could not adapt itself to the realities of the monarchy and was soon replaced as an administrative system.

IV THE LEVITICAL CITIES

This is a unique roster listing towns located in all of the Israelite tribal territories where Levites were settled.[29] Two versions of the text have been preserved with minor divergences from one another, the first in Joshua 21 and the second in 1 Chronicles 6. Albright was evidently correct in saying that the two passages originate in one list that contained forty-eight towns, four for each tribe.[30] On the basis of this assumption one can reconstruct the roster in accordance with the table on pages 303—4 (cf. map 22).

Klein and Albright have proven that the content of the list evidences a date in the period of the United Monarchy. Only then were all of these towns in Israelite possession. Those in the coastal region, e.g. Gibbethon, Eltekeh, Gath-rimmon and Gezer, had not been conquered heretofore; and towns such as Gibbethon and Ramoth-gilead were detached from Israel a short time later. To date the list any earlier one must introduce utopian features.[31] However, there is no justification for interpreting a geographical list in the Bible as utopian when it is possible to associate it with a real situation in some particular period. This is especially true with regard to the text under discussion, which does not include many of the known cultic centres and whose towns are not evenly distributed throughout the country. It was Alt who first pointed out that most of these towns are located either in frontier regions or in areas that had formerly been Canaanite, while there are no Levitical cities in central Judah or in Mount Ephraim. The areas envisioned by the list were mostly conquered in David's reign and must have contained extensive royal lands which were assigned to the Levites. This would also be the case in Benjamin where David had doubtless inherited the property of Saul.

Mazar has defined the special function of the Levitical cities as cultic and royal centres under the United Monarchy. Such a role is suggested by the genealogical table of Levitical clans which states that various branches were appointed ". . . to outside duties for Israel, as officers and judges . . . the oversight of Israel westward of the Jordan for all of the work of the Lord and for the service of the king. . . . In the fortieth year of David's reign a search was made and men of great ability among them were found at Jaazer in Gilead. King David appointed (them) to have the oversight of the Reubenites, the Gadites and the half-tribe of the Manassites for everything pertaining to God and for the affairs of the king" (1 Chron. 26. 29–32). It is evident that the Levitical cities were related to the monarchial organization during David's reign, since he settled in them Levitical clans from Judah that were loyal to the royal house "for all of the work of the Lord and for the service of the king". This explains why they were not evenly distributed throughout the various regions of the country.[37] For such an organization, based on royal centres with cultic significance, there is evidence in Egyptian sources,[38] especially the list of towns belonging to the priesthood of Amon from the reign of Ramses III.[39]

The organization of the Levitical cities must certainly belong to the reign of David, who sought to base the internal administration of his kingdom upon the traditional tribal alliance, appointing chiefs for the respective tribes, including one for the Levites.[40] In David's fortieth year Levites were living at Jaazer (1 Chron. 26. 31), i.e. in the period of transition when Solomon was taking over. Nothing prevents the assumption that they had lived there prior to this. The Levitical cities in Asher are Mishal, Abdon, Helkath and Rehob. Abdon is the only one identified with any degree of certainty (Khirbet ʻAbdeh, three and three-quarter miles east of Achzib). However, Rehob is mentioned among the Canaanite cities that Asher had not conquered (Judg. 1. 31). Since this list includes towns in the Plain of Acco and on the Phoenician coast, one must assume that at least Rehob and probably also Abdon were among the twenty towns which Solomon returned to Hiram, the King of Tyre, in the middle of his reign (1 Kings 9. 10–13). The date of the Levitical cities must therefore be earlier than the second half of the Solomonic era.

At first sight the inclusion of Gezer among the Levitical cities seems irreconcilable with a date in the Davidic reign, because Solomon received this town from the Egyptians as a dowry when he married Pharaoh's daughter (1 Kings 9. 16). However, this supposition is a dubious over-simplification. It is hard to imagine that Gezer, which dominated the route to Jerusalem could have successfully resisted David

THE LIST OF THE LEVITICAL CITIES

Josh. 21	*1 Chron. 6*	*Supposed original list and number*	
Judah and Simeon	*Judah*	*Judah and Simeon*	
Hebron	Hebron	——[32]	
Libnah	Libnah	Libnah	(1)
Jattir	Jattir	Jattir	(2)
Eshtemoa	Eshtemoa	Eshtemoa	(3)
Holon	Hilen	Holon (Hilen ?)	(4)
Debir	Debir	Debir	(5)
Ain	Ashan	Ain (Ashan ?)	(6)
Juttah	——	Juttah	(7)
Beth-shemesh	Beth-shemesh	Beth-shemesh	(8)
Benjamin	*Benjamin*	*Benjamin*	
Gibeon	——	Gibeon	(9)
Geba	Geba	Geba	(10)
Anathoth	Anathoth	Anathoth	(11)
Almon	Alemeth	Almon, Alemeth	(12)
Ephraim	*Ephraim*	*Ephraim*	
Shechem	Shechem	——[32]	
Gezer	Gezer	Gezer	(13)
Kibzaim	——	Kibzaim	(14)
——	Jokmeam	Jokmeam	(15)
Beth-horon	Beth-horon	Beth-horon	(16)
Dan		*Dan*	
Eltekeh	——	Eltekeh	(17)
Gibbethon	——	Gibbethon	(18)
Aijalon	Aijalon	Aijalon	(19)
Gath-rimmon	Gath-rimmon	Gath-rimmon	(20)
Manasseh	*Manasseh*	*Manasseh*	
Taanach	Aner[33]	Taanach	(21)
Gath-rimmon[34]	Bileam	Ibleam	(22)
Golan	Golan	Golan	(23)
Be-eshterah	Ashtaroth	Ashtaroth	(24)
Issachar	*Issachar*	*Issachar*	
Kishion	Kedesh	Kishion	(25)
Daberath	Daberath	Daberath	(26)
Jarmuth	Ramoth	Jarmuth, Ramoth	(27)
En-gannim	Anem	En-gannim	(28)
Asher	*Asher*	*Asher*	
Mishal	Mashal	Mishal	(29)
Abdon	Abdon	Abdon	(30)

Josh. 21	*1 Chron. 6*	*Supposed original list and number*	
Helkath	Hukok	Helkath	(31)
Rehob	Rehob	Rehob	(32)
Naphtali	*Naphtali*	*Naphtali*	
Kedesh	Kedesh	Kedesh	(33)
Hammoth-dor	Hammon	Hammath	(34)
——	——	Dor (?)	(35)
Kartan	Kiriathaim	Kartan (Kiriathaim)	(36)
Zebulun	*Zebulun*	*Zebulun*	
Jokneam	——	Jokneam	(37)
Kartah[35]	Tabor	(Chisloth ?)- tabor	(38)
Dimnah	Rimmono	Rimmon(ah)	(39)
Nahalal	——	Nahalal	(40)
Reuben[36]	*Reuben*	*Reuben*	
Bezer	Bezer	Bezer	(41)
Jahazah	Jahazah	Jahazah	(42)
Kedemoth	Kedemoth	Kedemoth	(43)
Mephaath	Mephaath	Mephaath	(44)
Gad	*Gad*	*Gad*	
Ramoth in Gilead	Ramoth in Gilead	Ramoth-gilead	(45)
Mahanaim	Mahanaim	Mahanaim	(46)
Heshbon	Heshbon	Heshbon	(47)
Jaazer	Jaazer	Jaazer	(48)

when he conquered all of the Canaanite cities in the land and pushed as far as the Lebanese Beqa‘ and Damascus. On the other hand, why should the Egyptians have carried out such a deed for Israel at the beginning of Solomon's reign; wouldn't they have considered him rather as an opponent who should be weakened? And isn't the strength displayed in a campaign across Philistia in order to conquer Gezer contradictory to the weakness usually ascribed to the Egyptians in the Solomonic period?[41]

In fact, the Bible only states that Pharaoh had captured Gezer and slain its Canaanite inhabitants. We know that it was not David's policy to slay the residents of the Canaanite towns but rather to absorb them into the kingdom. Therefore, nothing prevents the assumption that Gezer had submitted to David like most of the other Canaanite centres and had been forced to accept a colony of Levites. Pharaoh's campaign at the beginning of Solomon's reign was mainly intended to restore Egyptian authority in Philistia, and the destruction of Gezer was clearly a threat to Israel. However, the Egyptians were not yet strong enough to continue their penetration on into the centres of the Solomonic kingdom. For this reason they preferred to make a peace treaty with

Israel. With this agreement, strengthened by a royal marriage,[42] Egypt relinquished Gezer which became a border town of the Israelite kingdom, and only this detail is recounted in the Bible. Thus Solomon fortified it soon after, just as he did at Hazor and Megiddo (1 Kings 9. 15), which were not Levitical cities. That Gezer marked the boundary of Israelite authority is seen in the itinerary of Shishak's campaign carried out shortly after Solomon's death; Gezer is the first town he mentions after leaving Gaza.[43]

The network of Levitical cities serving the administrative needs of the crown corresponds with David's political policy of organizing the realm on the basis of the traditional twelve tribes. Solomon abandoned this framework in his redistribution of administrative districts. Nevertheless, the Levitical cities must have continued to fulfil their function in Solomon's reign, and this institution was banished only with the division of the kingdom. Since the Levitical cities continued to exist in Solomon's reign alongside his regular administrative framework, it is clear that there is no exact correspondence between them. The Levitical cities were established probably principally as royal Israelite centres near the borders intended for strengthening the kingdom's authority by promulgating Yahwistic worship, national solidarity, and loyalty to the Davidic dynasty at Jerusalem, besides their administrative functions. There is no need to assume that the tribal chieftains resided in these cities. Rulers of the northern Israelite kingdom were certainly not interested in the Levitical clans whose sympathies were with Judah and the House of David. Evidence for this is the passage from the reign of Rehoboam: ". . . the Levites left their common lands and their holdings and came to Judah and Jerusalem, because Jeroboam and his sons cast them out" (2 Chron. 11. 14).

V. GROWTH AND DEVELOPMENT OF THE SOLOMONIC KINGDOM

The reigns of David and Solomon were the most prosperous and flourishing period that the land of Israel had ever known. The kingdom of Israel dominated both the *Via Maris* and the King's Highway, thus maintaining absolute control over the important trade routes in the Middle East. A sudden rise in the standard of living and perfection in every kind of product is noticeable in archaeological excavations. The pottery forms now reach a new standard of technical perfection, while imports from Phoenicia and Cyprus reappear. Monumental constructions and well-perfected fortificiations are found in which strong Syrian influence is felt. The typical Israelite dwelling takes the more or less fixed form of "the four-room house" with a row of columns on one or both sides of the court.[44] Beginning with David's reign one finds the perfected use of hewn stone in construction, and the palace entrances are ornamented with proto-aeolic capitals.[45] Casemate walls constructed in this period have been found in various cities, e.g. Hazor, Beth-shemesh and Tell Beit Mirsim; on the other hand, solid walls were also used at such places as Megiddo and Beer-sheba. In Solomon's three main fortified cities—Hazor, Megiddo and Gezer (1 Kings 9. 15)—there was a special type of gate with four piers on each side which rank among the most perfectly constructed structures of their kind in Palestine.[46] Various towns such as Beth-shemesh and Tell Beit Mirsim contained store houses for the collection of agricultural produce from their respective areas.

Great progress is also seen in the Negeb, resulting from the development of the trade routes. Instead of the forts along "the way of Atharim" (cf. *supra,* p. 58),[47] strong fortified cities were built at Beer-sheba, Arad, Tell el-Milḥ, Kh. Gharrah, *et al.* Ezion-geber was established on the Gulf of Aqabah near Elath (1 Kings 9. 26, *et al.*) as revealed by the excavations of Nelson Glueck at Tell el-Kheleifeh.[48] This was a very strong fort surrounded by a casemate wall which was later replaced by a solid wall.[49] Large store-rooms were constructed inside[50] which served the needs of commercial caravans and the maritime trade on the Gulf of Aqabah. This was a key point dominating the routes to South Arabia. It is no accident that the Bible should mention the riches brought in by ships operating from this port (1 Kings 10. 11, 22, *et al.*). and the trade in precious spices and perfumes with Sheba.[51]

No appreciable changes took place in David's great kingdom during the latter part of his reign. The only shocks it suffered were from internal revolts. Absalom's rebellion shook the foundations of the kingdom and served as a turning point in the organization of David's realm. It would appear that Absalom had succeeded in gaining the sympathy of the most influential people in both Judah and Israel by restoring the tribal institutions that David had abandoned, e.g. the elders of Israel (2 Sam. 17. 4) and "the men of Israel" (2 Sam. 15. 13; 17. 4).[52] Evidently David had tried to do away with the independent institutions of Judah and Israel in his effort to ground the organization of the realm on the traditional twelve tribes, and Absalom gathered his support by making concessions to their former independence. David found refuge at Mahanaim in Transjordan, just as Eshbaal had done. The Trans-jordanian tribes were actually neutral with respect to the quarrel between Judah and Israel; they were interested in seeing a strong centralized government because Israelite Gilead was always the first to suffer when the kingdom was weak. With David's return from Manahaim after his victory we see a clear example of the animosity between Judah and Israel; David was forced to accept the situation and to depend henceforth mainly on his kinsmen in Judah (2 Sam. 19. 15, 40–3). He gave up his attempts to unite Judah and Israel into one monarchial organization and contented himself with their separate internal organizations, accompanied by a preference for Judah.

This action caused the immediate revolt of Sheba the son of Bichri from Benjamin. His rebellion bears the clear stamp of Israelite uprising against Judean authority; for the first time the slogan is heard: "We have no portion in David, and we have no inheritance in the son of Jesse; every man to his tents, O Israel!" (2 Sam. 20. 1). As a result ". . . all the men of Israel withdrew from David, and followed Sheba the son of Bichri, but the men of Judah followed their king steadfastly from the Jordan to Jerusalem" (vs. 2). Joab quickly stamped out the revolt, using the elite corps of loyal knights and mercenaries, but henceforth the internal division between Judah and Israel was an acknowledged fact.

The kingdom's territory began to shrink remarkably during Solomon's reign. The Egyptians, who had supported David's enemies against him whenever they could, now took advantage of every opportunity to cause trouble for the monarchy under Solomon. Hadad, the Edomite, who had found asylum in Egypt during David's reign returned to Edom during Solomon's reign and apparently succeeded in leading large portions of his country in revolt (1 Kings 11. 14–22), even though Solomon maintained his control over the Arabah, Ezion-geber and Elath. The conquest of Gezer at the beginning of Solomon's reign (1 Kings 9. 16) testifies to an Egyptian campaign in Philistia, apparently under Pharaoh Siamun.[53] Although this expedition culminated in the establishment of a treaty with Israel, which was strengthened by a marriage between the royal houses and the return of Gezer to Solomon, it would seem that the supremacy over Philistia was retrieved by Egypt after an intermission of nearly two centuries. The conquest and handing over of Gezer seems to indicate an innovation that was not in Israel's favour. The territory of Ekron and the coastal region as far as the Yarkon was taken out of Israelite hands so that Gezer became a frontier fortress of the kingdom.

Neither did Solomon succeed in maintaining the northern boundaries of the Davidic kingdom. Damascus revolted and Rezon son of Eliada established the new Aram-Damascus Monarchy there. This kingdom became the heir of Aram-zobah as the leader of the Aramean states, eventually becoming a first-rate power in Syria, and Israel's strongest enemy. It is not known whether Solomon lost control over the Lebanese Beqa‘ at the same time. The reference to his fortifying Tadmor (2 Chron. 8. 4) might be an indication that Solomon tried to establish strong bases on the desert route to the Euphrates region even after he lost Damascus.[54]

The border with Phoenicia changed in the middle of Solomon's reign when he was compelled to relinquish twenty Galilean towns to Hiram, King of Tyre (1 Kings 9. 10–13). This transfer of territory was apparently caused by a deficit in the balance of trade with Tyre, but it

Map 23. The Solomonic Districts.

also indicates a gradual change that was taking place in their relative strength. Tyre was undoubtedly interested in its coastal *hinterland* which had been an Israelite possession since the time of David. The surrender of this district was a bitter pill for Israel to swallow. During Joab's census it had been reckoned as native Israelite, unlike Damascus or Edom which were simply conquered regions. This is apparently the reason that the transaction is explained in opposite terms by 2 Chronicles 8. 1–2, while even 1 Kings 9. 12–13 represents an attempt to gloss over the loss. The name Kabul does not mean it was a poor district, as hinted in the biblical description; besides the name "land of Kabul" could not fit the Phoenician coast and the Plain of Acco where many important cities were located. It would appear, therefore, that Kabul (the village by this name is nine miles south-east of Acco) became a new reference point on the border between Israel and Phoenicia, a border that continued its existence in later times as the line between Jewish Galilee and Hellenistic Acco (Josephus, *Wars,* III, iii, 1; *Life,* 43). Evidently the popular interpretation of the name Kabul did not encompass the whole region but only the new boundary strip which in itself was certainly not very important to Tyre.[55]

VI. SOLOMON'S ADMINISTRATIVE DISTRICTS.[56]

The list of Solomon's district governors (1 Kings 4. 7–19) is the only avowedly administrative division preserved in the Bible about which we have explicit information. It is, therefore, of special importance not only for the understanding of Solomon's realm, but also for these types of geographical texts, which are generally used by the biblical compilers for the description of other matters.

The basic analysis of the list was made by Alt[57] and it still stands today in spite of all attempts to refute it. We follow his two basic principles, which will guide us in the understanding of the list and its details:

(1) The Solomonic districts include only northern Israel in the limited meaning of that term. They do not include Judah and nothing can be learned from this document about the situation there, whether it was subject to a similar division in this period or not. Benjamin was obviously part of Israel until the division of the kingdom and, thus, is the southermost region included in the list.

(2) The list contains two fundamentally distinct types of districts: those which virtually comprise one of the old tribal areas, and which usually are defined by their tribal names, and those which do not fit the tribal areas and are defined, instead, by the names of cities located in them. The latter districts are found mainly in the valleys, and most of the cities mentioned were previously Canaanite towns that came into Israelite possession only at a later date. These districts appear together

in one block (Districts II–V) comprising the northern Shephelah, the Sharon and the northern valleys.

There is no basis whatever for the attempts by various scholars to discredit the second assumption by questioning the identification of Hepher.[58] Alt is right that out of these cities mentioned in the third district, only Socoh can be identified with confidence, viz. with Shuweiket er-Râs, 3 km. north of Tul Karm. Regarding the two other cities we possess no further data and the information that Hepher was originally a Canaanite city again fits Alt's assumption, but does not help in its identification. The same is true for the mention of Hepher in the genealogical lists of Manasseh (Num. 26. 32–33; 27. 1; Josh. 17. 2–3). Families of Manasseh spread out into the Sharon and Jezreel valleys, thus taking in Canaanite cities which were then integrated into the tribal organization. The genealogical list itself is based on historical development, without any consistent geographical order. This is very clear in the lists of Manasseh.[59] With the migration of Manasseh into Transjordan, he became the "father" of Gilead. Thus was created the genealogical tree, "Hepher son of Gilead, son of Machir, son of Manasseh" (Num. 27. 1; Josh. 17. 3). If we locate Hepher in northern Mount Ephraim because of these lists, we may by the same logic locate it in Transjordan, or we may place Gilead on Mount Ephraim. If there exists any datum at all regarding the location of Hepher, it is only its appearance beside Socoh in the Solomonic list of districts. To base an obtuse interpretation of the list on a speculative identification of Hepher is methodologically out of the question. We remain true to Alt's basic conception that all the cities of Districts II–V which can be identified are on the plains.

For understanding specific details we must be guided by another line of reasoning which we have emphasized regarding all the geographical lists and descriptions in the Bible: the editor's method of selection and abbretiation. Actually, we only possess a complete list of the officers' names.[60] To them has been added just the briefest description of each commissioner's territory. We should not expect that this was the full original description of the districts. The original was doubtless much more detailed; but the editor, as usual, limited himself to a selection of what in his view, was most important. He only intended to furnish us with a general geographic orientation.

This is clear, first of all, with regard to those districts that are defined solely by tribal names, among which in some cases two neighbouring tribes were united in one district. These are comprised of Ephraim and Manasseh in Mount Ephraim, Naphtali, Asher and Zebulun (!), Issachar and Benjamin. Town lists, which evidently were the basic means of defining all districts, also existed for the tribal districts, but the editor felt that it was sufficient to note that this district is actually identical with the old tribal area. These lists were used by the editor of Joshua for the descriptions of the various tribal areas. We have seen this most distinctly in the city list of Naphtali, which included Hazor, rebuilt only in the days of Solomon. It is, therefore, our duty to use these lists for the more detailed definition of the districts. On the other hand, the town lists in the non-tribal districts are also hardly complete. Even here the editor was selective as usual, as we shall see clearly in the analysis of the various districts.

In the light of these three fundamental conceptions, the basic geographical analysis of each district leaves no serious doubts, though not all details are equally clear, of course.

I. The first district included all Mount Ephraim, excluding Manasseh. Definitions like Ephraim or Manasseh would be vague, since their tribal areas included more than just the mountain region. The geographical term Mount Ephraim, on the other hand, is clear.

II. The second district if defined by the names of three or four cities, only two of which can be identified with confidence: Beth-shemesh and Shaalbim (Selbît) in the Aijalon Valley. Beth-shemesh was included in the days of David among the Levitical cities of Judah, but this was a border town the tribal connections of which were evidently doubtful. Its inclusion in the Israelite district list is, therefore, hardly disturbing.[61]

Regarding Elon-beth-hanan, we cannot prove whether the allusion is to Aijalon in the neighbourhood of Shaalbim, or to another city defined here by the family attributed to Elon of the Hanan family. Makaz is completely unknown.

On the ground of the identification of two cities out of four, it is completely conjectural to assume that this district included only the eastern Shephelah and that there remained a gap between it and the third district.[62] This is refuted by the detailed list of cities that was used for the description of Dan (Josh. 19. 41–46). As we shall see, this list can only derive from the Solomonic district list.[63]

It is true that regarding the origin of this list, opinions are sharply divided. The most extreme suggestion is that the city list of Dan is only a literary creation, without any realistic background of its own, compiled with the help of the border description, plus the addition of the Levitical cities.[64] Today, this extreme view must be unequivocally rejected. First, there is not a single example of this kind in the Bible, but there is also no basis whatever in this case. Besides the two possible sources indicated, also given only in part, there is no known source which could furnish the hinterland of Joppa that appears in the list. Its appearance in the list provides ample evidence for its origin in a real situation, which is only suitable for our period.

Mazar[65] has shown that the Danite city list only fits the background of the United Monarchy, though we cannot accept his restriction of it to the reign of David. The coastal region between Jabneh and the Yarkon River did not become Israelite before the days of David, who had to put pressure on the "border of Joppa" through which timber for Solomon's royal building was later transported (2 Chr. 2. 15 MT; 2. 16 Eng.).

The conquest of this area finds an illuminating parallel in Josiah's days, as is now evident from his fortress at Meṣad Ḥashavyahu built between Jabneh and Ashdod.[66] On the other hand, at least part of that area had become Philistine a short time after Solomon's death as attested by the conflicts over Gibbethon (1 Kings. 15. 27; 16. 15).

It is true that one difficulty remains, viz. that of Ekron (Josh. 19. 43). There is no evidence for its being conquered, and the seizure of some of its territory is insufficient to explain its inclusion in an administrative list of cities incorporated into the Israelite kingdom. Ekron is preceded in this list by Timnah (Timnatha), which suggests that perhaps the original text read "Timnath-Ekron." When a town bears a very common name, the addition of a second element for the sake of clarity is not at all unusual. Thus a place name may be defined more precisely by the indication of its region, territory or population, e.g. Ramoth-gilead, Kadesh-barnea, Kedesh-naphtali, Bethlehem-judah, *et. al.* In this very same list we have Gath-rimmon, so written in order to distinguish it from other places named Gath, e.g. the biblical Gath of the Philistines and Gath-hepher and the non-biblical Gath-asher, Gath-padalla, *et al.* Timnah is a rather common place name; therefore, Joshua's town is called Timnath-serah (or Timnath-heres) by way of more precise definition (Josh. 19. 50; 24. 30; Judg. 2. 9). Even in Judah there were at least two other places named Timnah, one south-east of Hebron (Josh. 15. 57) and another near the Valley of Elah at Khirbet Tibneh/ Tibbâneh/Tabbâna[67], about 10 miles from the Timmah on our list, the latter being located at Tell el-Baṭâshī.[68] Furthermore, Timnah was certainly a Philistine town in the territory of Ekron until David's reign, as we learn from the Samson narrative (Judg. 14. 1 ff.) and the story of the ark's being sent from the land of Ekron to Israelite territory near Beth-shemesh, which was not far from Timnah (1 Sam. 6. 9 ff.). Therefore, if one wanted to distinguish this Timnah from its many namesakes, the most appropriate definition would be "Timnah of the Philistines," or to be more precise, "Timnah of Ekron," i.e. Timnath-ekron.

The list used by the biblical editor(s) for the description of the Danite territory thus defines the second Solomonic district more precisely. It includes the area between the Sorek and Aijalon Valleys, which is clear also from the abbreviated version of the list, including Beth(=Ir) -shemesh and Shaalbim. Both Aijalon and an unknown city, Elon, are mentioned. In the continuation (Josh. 19. 44) comes the description of the western area between Jabneh (Eltekeh, Gibbethon and Baalath; Jabneh is not mentioned) and the Yarkon River. Then the cities in the hinterland of Joppa (Josh. 19. 45) are listed (Jehud [LXX Azor], Bene-berak and Gath-rimmon). The same region (Beth-dagon, Joppa, Bene-berak, Azor) appears later in the Sennacherib inscription as a dominion of Ashkelon.[69] Most illuminating is the ending "with the territory over against Joppa" (Josh. 19. 46), excluding the city and its harbour from the jurisdiction of the district. David was interested in good relations with the sailors of Joppa and their continued service, and therefore, he was careful not to harm the city proper. He behaved in the same way with Tyre (cf. *supra,* p. 294).

III. As mentioned above, out of three cities of the third district only Socoh can be identified in the centre of the Sharon. That district extended, therefore, from the Yarkon River to the border of the fourth district which also cannot be defined explicitly.

IV. The fourth district is denoted only by the important harbour town, Dor, situated on the Carmel coast. The definition Naphath– appears only with that city. It has been proposed to derive this term from the language of one of the Sea Peoples (the Tjeker, Sikel) and its suggested cognate in archaic Greek means "wooded country," which is a semantic equivalent to Sharon.[70] Naphath-Dor would thus mean, "Dor of the Sharon," like Aphek of the Sharon according to LXX Josh. 12. 18.

V. This district includes the northern valleys with the previously Canaanite Taanach, Megiddo and Beth-shean. The editor furnished us with additional information in order to clarify two matters.

(1) Jezreel and its vicinity, the main city of Issachar, was not included in the fifth district. The order of the description has to be emended: "and all Beth-shean below Jezreel".[71]

(2) That district also included part of the Jordan valley south of Beth-shean: "and from Beth-shean to Abel-meholah as far as the other side of (including) Jokmeam which is beside Zarethan".[72] Abel-meholah has now been identified with much confidence with Tell Abū Ṣûṣ on the bank of the Jordan, 15 km. south of Beth-shean.[73] Jokmeam was one of the Levitical cities of Ephraim (1 Chr. 6. 53 MT; 6. 68 Eng.) and therefore cannot be far from the Ephraim-Manasseh border (possibly Tell el-Mazar).[74] Its location was specified by relating it to Zarethan (apparently Tell Umm Ḥamad),[75] the well-known city in the vicinity of the Adam ford across the Jordan, which is also used in Josh. 3. 16 for the definition of a lesser-known site in this region. The large district included, therefore, most of the central valley from the Great Plain down to Beth-shean and the western Jordan Valley to the vicinity of Wâdı Far'ah. There is no foundation for the assumption that it also included part of the eastern Jordan Valley.[76]

VI. The sixth district was complemented by an unusual literary addition, "sixty great cities with walls and bronze bars," which obviously is an explanatory gloss by the editor taken from the traditional biblical description of the Bashan cities. There remain, thus, the city of Ramoth-gilead, viz. Tell er-Rumeith in northern Gilead, the villages of Jair in northern Gilead and the region of Argob in Bashan, evidently the rich and fertile region north of the Yarmuk River.

VII. For that district the editor left only one city, Mahanaim, today western Tell edh-Dhahab, north of the Jabbok. This evidently was its chief city, which we remember as the temporary capital of Israel in the days of Ish-baal son of Saul (2 Sam. 2. 8), and also during the Absalom revolt (2 Sam. 17. 24). The district extended, therefore, to the north and to the south, but for details, we must also examine the last, twelfth district, and the city lists of the Transjordanian tribes.

If we have recognized a literary addition in the sixth district, all that remains of the description of the twelfth is a notation of this kind: "This country of Sihon king of the Amorites and Og king of Bashan." It is obvious that this is a troublesome gloss, because the Bashan is already included in the sixth district. We may assume that the list before the editor contained Heshbon and all that is left is its literary explanation. In other words, for the southern district of Transjordan he probably had only the name of one central city, Heshbon, which was situated at the northern border of the Moabite tableland, the Mishor. The expression, "in the land of Gilead," is not particularly informative; it is only a general term for Israelite Transjordan in that period. The interpretation of LXX, which reads, "the land of Gad," is impossible. Heshbon is a city of Reuben (Num. 32. 37; Josh. 13. 17) and Mahanaim is a city of Gad (Josh. 13. 26).

For details, we may again have recourse to the city lists, this time of Reuben (Josh. 13. 15–23) and Gad (Josh. 13. 24–28). They contain no systematic boundary description, but only town lists prefaced by a border delineation according to the formula, "from . . . to," probably based on the town lists. Accordingly, the area of Reuben took in territory from the Arnon to Heshbon, including all of the Mishor to (instead of "by") Medeba and in the north to Heshbon itself. The area of Gad extended from the border of the territory of Heshbon to the vicinity of Mahanaim, including Jaazer. All the eastern Jordan Valley is attributed to Gad, from Beth-haram and Beth-nimrah to the Succoth Valley, "having the Jordan as boundary, to the lower end of the Sea of Chinnereth, eastward beyond the Jordan" (Josh. 13. 27).

The geographical division of the three Transjordanian districts is thus clear: the southern extended over all the Mishor from the Arnon to Heshbon; the central from Jaazer to Mahanaim, including all the eastern Jordan Valley; and the northern from Ramoth-gilead to the Argob district in the Bashan.

VIII. Naphtali occupied eastern Galilee, from Tabor and the Jezreel Valley on the south, through upper Galilee to the river Liṭani on the north, plus the northern Jordan Valley, including the western shore of the Sea of Galilee (Chinnereth) and the vicinity of Hazor. We have no data for its western limits, north of Tabor.[77]

IX. This district included what was left of Asher after the transfer (1 Kings 9. 12–13) of almost all of the Acco Plain to Tyre, and also the tribal area of Zebulun, since Bealoth is most likely a textual corruption of Zebulun.[78] The district extended from the north-western edge of the central valley (the Great Plain) and included western Galilee bordering on Naphtali. Its western border was along the eastern edge of the Plain of Acco, from Mount Carmel and Beth-emek (Tell Mımas) in the south to Cabul and to Abdon, the original form of misspelled Ebron[79] in the north.

X. The district of Issachar (Josh. 18. 17–23) included the central part of the Jezreel Valley with the town of Jezreel. It extended eastward to the Jordan between Beth-shean and the Sea of Galilee, northward to the Jabneel Valley and westward to Mount Tabor.[80]

XI. The Benjamin district (cf. Josh. 18. 12–27) included the area north of Jerusalem.[81] It is true that Jebus also appears in the Benjaminite city list (Josh. 19. 27 LXX), but this is an archaic allusion, clearly taken from the list of unconquered Canaanite cities (Judg. 1. 21) usually appended at the end of most tribal descriptions. Eastward, the district included Jericho and northward, Mount Bethel with Bethel itself, Zemaraim, Ophrah and the northern Geba at Khirbet et-Tell.[82]

The Benjaminite town list is divided into two groups, and the reason for this is obvious. The border between Judah and Israel after the division of the Kingdom went between Mizpeh and Zemaraim—Bethel.[83] Most of the Israelite Benjamin district was now part of Judah (Josh. 18. 26–28) while only the northern section remained in Israel (Josh. 18. 21–25). It is probable that the editor used a still more up-to-date list of Judah's districts and added only the missing Benjaminite cities out of the Solomonic district list.

XII. We have already dealt with the last district in southern Transjordan in the analysis of the seventh district, above.

Examination of the various districts reveals that no effort was made to equalize the area of the districts and their economic potential.[84] The attempt to prove the opposite either ignores the geographical analysis of the list or distorts the district borders to suit the hypothetical assumption, and even then no real semblance of equality is achieved.

Beside large and rich districts like Mount Ephraim, the northern valleys and northern Transjordan, we have some economically quite limited districts like Benjamin, Issachar and Dor. The attempt to compare these districts as equal regarding their economic potential and production stands in complete contradiction to the analysis of the list.

Even so, we read at the head of the list: "Solomon had twelve officers over all Israel, who provided food for the king and his household; each man had to make provision for one month in the year'' (1 Kings 4. 7). The central function of the officers evidently was the taxation in kind and the levying of labour forces (*mas 'ôbēd* and *sēbel*) according to fixed duties of the various families and classes.[85]

Was it Solomon's intention to punish or reward different tribes by imposing on them an equal yearly taxation in spite of their different potentials? This seems very improbable. This list is based on administrative reality by creating homogeneous geographical districts while at the same time preserving as far as possible the traditional tribal entities. Wherever it was feasible to preserve the tribal unit, this was done. That decision was evidently well received by the tribal population, who saw in it a certain recognition of their distinctiveness, even within the framework of the monarchy. The deep-rooted existence of the family and clan structure is attested in the Samaria ostraca. Obviously, no attempt was made to amend tribal borders in order to create economic equality.

This analysis leaves no doubt that one should not accept the heading as an indication of the total duty laid on each district. The heading deals only with annual dues to the royal court and this was only a certain part of the total burden imposed on the respective districts, probably according to the size and to the number and potential of their settlements and populace. The monthly duty was some kind of care of the central sanctuary during one month of the year.[86] That is a very early tradition in the Ancient East; we find it already in the period of the Sumerian Third Dynasty of Ur in the latter part of the 3rd millennium B.C.[87] There also, the care of the central sanctuary, one month annually, did not constitute the whole tax burden borne by each district. Contrary to the opinion of various scholars, there is no reason to doubt the Solomonic date of our present biblical text. Nothing contradicts a Solomonic date, and it even seems justified to fix a more precise date not before the middle of his reign. This is clear from the list of officers. Two of them are sons-in-law of the king (1 Kings 4. 11, 15), which would hardly have been possible at an earlier date. It is also clear from the absence of the cities in the Plain of Acco, which were transferred to Tyre in the middle of Solomon's reign (1 Kings 9. 10).

The detailed analysis of this important document gives us first of all a clear definition of the Israelite territory in its limited sense, during the latter half of Solomon's reign. It included the northern Shephelah from the Sorek Valley and Jabneh, excluding the city of Joppa. Thus, the return of Gezer to Solomon (1 Kings 9. 16–17) also included this area, through which the Egyptian army undoubtedly had had to pass. In the north, ''Israel'' included all of Galilee, excluding the Plain of Acco and in the east all of Transjordan from the Bashan to the Arnon, excluding of course, the territory of Ammon which was limited to a moderate area around their capital at Rabbah. The division into districts is based primarily on administrative and geographical considerations. Usually the division between hill country and plain is followed, similar to the geographical division which was also the basic principle of the later Judaean districts. However, this principle is violated in three instances: (1) The Jordan Valley was combined with central Gilead, and Mahanaim on the Jabbok was their connecting link. To leave this narrow and elongated region of the Jordan Valley as a separate district evidently was deemed unwise, but one must note that the Valley itself was not divided. (2) In the Naphtali district the northern Jordan Valley was added to eastern Galilee. (3) In the Benjamin district the region of Jericho was combined with the central mountain area. In the two latter instances, this was evidently done out of respect for the historical associations between these regions within their respective tribal areas.

No attempt was made to interfere with the traditional tribal areas. Wherever it was possible to preserve the tribal entity, this was done,[88] and only when administrative considerations outweighed it was the principle violated. The single tribe did not endanger the United Monarchy. The real threat was from the deep-seated antagonism between the two principal entities, Israel and Judah, the inheritance of the respective amphictyonic leagues. Our list of Solomon's districts proves that he had bowed to the prevailing circumstances, evidently following the example of his father.

That remains, of course, the most striking conclusion from the analysis of this document. Hereby, the antipathy between Judah and Israel was officially recognized in the administration of the kingdom. This was one of David and Solomon's most fatal mistakes; it was a decisive factor in the rapid distintegration of the United Monarchy.

[1] For a description of the excavations at T. el-Ful, see W. F. Albright, *AASOR*, 4 (1924); L. A. Sinclair, *AASOR*, 34–35 (1960), pp. 1–52.

[2] Gibeath-elohim is sometimes identified with Gibeah of Benjamin (Saul), however, in 1 Sam. 13. 2 f. we hear explicitly that the Philistine garrison resided at Geba, while Jonathan was still at Gibeah of Benjamin and Saul with his troops in Michmas (Michmash) and the region of Bethel. This also explains why the Philistines set up their camp at Michmash opposite Geba, to which Saul now retreated; cf. also *infra*, p. 404.

[3] For a recent discussion, cf. A. Demsky, *BASOR*, 202 (1971), pp. 16 ff.; *idem*, *BASOR*, 212 (1973), pp. 25 ff. These most important studies will have considerable bearing on the solutions to the problems involved.

[4] L. A. Sinclair, *EAEHL*, II, pp. 444–46.

[5] Y. Aharoni, *IEJ*, 25 (1975), pp. 169–70, dealing with the 1975 season; further information on this fort came to light in 1976.

[6] The place and its location are unknown; the same is true of Telaim, where he assembled his forces (1 Sam. 15. 4), perhaps it is the Telem of Josh. 15.24.

[7] In the previous chapter, it was indicated that Megiddo and probably other Canaanite towns in the Valley had become Israelite in the twelfth century B.C.

[8] Y. Aharoni, "The Districts of Israel and Judah", in "*The Kingdoms of Israel and Judah*" (Jerusalem, 1961), pp. 114 f. (Hebrew).

[9] Iron Age sherds found at Masada indicate that even in the Israelite period this natural fortress had been in use.

[10] The MT indicates "a year and four months" (1 Sam. 27. 7); according to LXX it was only four months.

[11] Tell el-Khuweilifeh is much too far to the east; like Tell Beit Mirsim, it was reckoned as part of the Judean hill country. If David had been making his sorties from here, he would have had to pass through the area of Israelite settlement in the south; from Tell esh-Shari 'ah he could march southward across the Negeb plains without intruding upon the Israelite settlement in the Negeb.

[12] A. Alt, *ZDMG NF,* 4 (1925), pp. 13 ff.; *idem,* Die Staatenbildung der Israeliten in Palästina (Leipzig, 1930), pp. 55 ff. (=*Kl. Schr.*, II, pp. 45 ff.).

It is hard to believe that David waited such a long time after becoming King of Israel before taking action to conquer Jerusalem. David may have counted the years of his reign from some time before his being crowned at Hebron, at least from the time that he became a vassal ruler of Ziklag and the Negeb of Judah. Mazar has offered the conjecture that David may have conquered Jerusalem immediately after becoming King at Hebron over the northern tribes too, but that he did not transfer the capital to it until it had been rebuilt as a royal city, which may have taken some years. Another possibility is that the two-year reign of Eshbaal son of Saul (2 Sam. 2. 10) is an error (cf. 2 Sam. 3. 1).

[13] Y. Aharoni, apud *Bible and the History of Israel,* Studies in Honor of Yaakov Liver (Jerusalem, 1972), pp. 13–17.

[14] Cf. the remarks by H. L. Ginsberg, apud *Alexander Marx Jubilee Volume* (New York, 1950), pp. 348 n. 4, 356 n. 31.

[15] On the problem of Gezer cf. *infra,* p. 302 ff.

[16] B. Mazar, *BA,* 25 (1962), pp. 102 f.; it is more natural from a geographical standpoint to think that the battle of Medeba was associated with the conquest of Moab and that the Aramean forces had come to her aid.

[17] It is interesting that the text of 2 Sam. 8. 13 has Aram instead of Edom; this may be an error, but it is also possible that the King of Aram had rushed to the assistance of Edom just as he had sought to block David's expansion into Ammon and Moab.

[18] On the trade with South Arabia cf. G. S. van Beek, *JAOS,* 78 (1958), pp. 141 ff. ; *idem, BA,* 23 (1960), pp. 70 ff.

[19] *RSV* accepts the dubious reading of the Lucianic recensions of LXX, εἰς γῆν Χεττιειμ Καδης;"Kadesh in the land of the Hittites". The Vaticanus reads εἰς γῆν θαβασων, ἥ ἐστιν 'Αδασαι.i.e. apparently "to the land of Bashan which is *Hodshi*". We may perhaps suppose a corruption from "The Land under Mount Hermon" which is spelled quite similarly in Hebrew.

[20] Y. Aharoni, *op. cit.* (note 8), pp. 110 ff.; contrary to Alt's hypothesis cf. especially A. Alt, *Die Staatenbildung der Israeliten in Palästina* (Leipzig, 1930) (=*Kl. Schr.*, II, pp 1–65.).

[21] Cf. 1 Chron. 2. 2 where Gad and Asher appear at the end of the list of tribes.

[22] Y. Aharoni, *IEJ,* 8 (1958), pp. 26–38.

[23] W. A. Albright, *BASOR,* 33 (1929), p. 7.

[24] Abel, *Géogr.*, II, p. 89; Cross and Wright, *JBL,* 75 (1956), p. 214.

[25] During the reign of Solomon, in the opinion of Mazar who emphasizes the factors that would date it to the United Monarchy, cf. B. Mazar, *IEJ,* 10 (1960), pp. 65–77.

[26] B. Mazar, *IEJ,* 1 (1950–1), pp. 136 ff.

[27] As previously noted, Judah was not represented in that alliance either, but its territory was defined by the border of Benjamin.

[28] It was Prof. Mazar who pointed out to me the principal role of the temple in that tradition.

[29] S. Klein, *Mazie vol.* (Jerusalem, 1934), pp. 81–107 (Hebrew); J. Kaufmann, *The Biblical Account of the Conquest of Palestine,* (Jerusalem, 1953), pp. 40–46, M. Haran, *Tarbiz,* 27 (1958), pp. 421–39 (Hebrew); W. F. Albright, *L. Ginzberg Vol.* (New York, 1945), pp. 49–73; A. Alt, *Festungen und Levitenorte im Lande Juda* (1952), *Kl. Schlr.*, II, pp. 306–5; B. Mazar, *VT Suppl.*, 7 (1960), pp. 193–205.

[30] Compare Num. 35. 7.

[31] Cf. Kaumann, *op. cit.* (note 29).

[32] Added from the list of cities of refuge.

[33] An error for Taanach.

[34] A repeat of this town from Dan.

[35] A repeat of Kartan from Naphtali.

[36] Preserved only in LXX.

[37] Alt, *op. cit.* (note 29).

[38] Mazar, *loc. cit.* (note 29).

[39] *ANET*, pp. 260 f.

[40] Contrary to the opinion of Mazar, *loc. cit.* (note 29) who assigns the list to the second half of Solomon's reign.

[41] A. Malamat, *JNES*, 22 (1963), pp. 10–17.

[42] It should not be assumed that Solomon actually married a daughter of Pharaoh, which was contrary to Egyptian practice, but that he took a wife from among the palace royalty (cf. 1 Chron. 4. 18).

[43] B. Mazar, *VT Suppl.*, 4 (1957), pp. 57 ff.

[44] W. F. Albright, *AASOR*, 21–22 (1943), pp. 49 ff.

[45] W. F. Albright, *The Archaeology of Palestine* (Pel. ed., 1949), pp. 125 ff.

[46] Y. Yadin, *IEJ*, 8 (1958), pp. 80–86.

[47] *IEJ*, 10 (1960), pp. 23–36, 97–111.

[48] N. Glueck, *BASOR*, 71 (1938), pp. 3–17; 75 (1939), pp. 8–22; 79 (1940), pp. 2–18; 80 (1940), pp. 3–10; 82 (1941), pp. 3–11.

[49] Z. Meshel, *BIES*, 25 (1961), pp. 157–59 (Hebrew).

[50] Glueck has now abandoned his earlier assumption that this was a copper refinery (*BA*, 28 [1965], pp. 70–87); the refining processes were carried out near the mining sites. The finds and the ground plans from Tell el-Kheleifeh bear witness to the existence there of a strong fortress and storehouses, cf. Rothenberg *infra*. Just as they did at Arad, the residents must have engaged in certain crafts, including metal work.

[51] It has been assumed that the copper mines in Wadi Mene 'iyeh and the immediate vicinity were mainly exploited during this period (cf. B. Rothenberg, *PEQ* [1962], pp. 5 ff.). However, recent excavations by Rothenberg have shown that the mines are earlier and belonged to the Edomites, cf. *supra*, p. 206.

[52] H. Tadmor, in a forthcoming study.

[53] J. Goldwasser, *BIES*, 14 (1948), pp. 82–84 (Hebrew); A. Malamat, *JNES*, 22 (1963), pp. 10 ff.

[54] However, in the parallel text of 1 Kings 9. 18 it is "Tamar in the wilderness, in the land", and the problem is not at all simple. Solomon's conquests in "Hamath-zobah" and the storehouses that he built in Hamath (2 Chron. 8. 3–4) are surprising, especially since Hamath was the enemy of Aram-zobah (2 Sam. 8. 10). "Hamath-zobah" is doubtless an error; perhaps we should follow the LXX, which has Βαισωβα, "Be(th)-zobah", and understand that Solomon fortified his positions in the Lebanese Beqaʿ and Tadmor in response to the loss of Damascus.

[55] Y. Aharoni, "The Land of Kabul", in *Western Galilee* (Haifa, 1961), p. 171–78 (Hebrew). Perhaps we may understand the information about the land of Kabul in a manner similar to that of Gezer, on the assumption that only the final events have been reported to us describing a certain concession in Israel's favour, i.e. that the transaction ended in Hiram's conceding Kabul to Israel since he had received all of the Plain of Acco, and that Solomon constructed fortifications along the newly formed border as was his practice elsewhere.

[56] Y. Aharoni, Tel Aviv, 3 (1973), pp. 5–15, fig. 1.

[57] A. Alt, "Israels Gaue unter Salomo," apud *Alttestamentliche Studien Rudolf Kittel zum 60. Geburtstag dargebracht, BZAW*, 13 (Leipzig, 1913), pp. 1–19 (=*Kl. Schr.*, II, pp. 76–89).

[58] W. F. Albright, *JPOS*, 5 (1925)., pp. 28–31; *idem, JPOS*, 11 (1931), pp. 248–51; G. E. Wright, *EI*, 8 (1967), pp. 61*–64*; Z. Kallai, *The Tribes of Israel* (Jerusalem, 1967), pp. 43–52 (Hebrew).

[59] Y. Aharoni, apud J. Aviram, ed., *Eretz Shomron* (Jerusalem, 1973), pp. 38–46 (Hebrew).

[60] A. Alt, *Archiv Orientalni,* 18 (1950), pp. 9–24 (=*Kl, Schr.*, III, pp. 198–213).

[61] Cf. most recently Y. Tsafrir, *EI,* 12 (1975), pp. 44–45 (Hebrew).

[62] B. Mazar, *IEJ,* 10 (1960), pp. 67–69 (=*Cities and Districts in Eretz-Israel* [Jerusalem, 1975], pp. 94–96, Hebrew).

[63] Wright, *op. cit,* pp. 64*–65*.

[64] F. M. Cross and G. E. Wright, *JBL,* 75 (1956), pp. 209–11.

[65] Mazar, *op. cit.*, p. 71.

[66] J. Naveh, *EAEHL* (Hebrew), II, pp. 373–75.

[67] M. Avi-Yonah, *Historical Geography of Palestine from the End of the Babylonian Exile up to the Arab Conquest* (Jerusalem, 1962), p. 113; *idem, The Holy Land* (Grand Rapids, 1966), pp. 53 f.

[68] Y. Aharoni, *PEQ,* 90 (1958), pp. 28 f.

[69] *ANET,* p. 287.

[70] M. Ben-Dov, *Tel Aviv,* 3 (1976), pp. 70–73.

[71] Y. Aharoni, apud *The Beth Shean Valley* (Jerusalem, 1962), pp. 36–38.

[72] Aharoni, apud A. Malamat, ed., *The Kingdoms of Israel and Judah* (Jerusalem, 1961), p. 111 n. 8; contrast W. F. Albright, *JPOS,* 5 (1925), pp. 32 ff.

[73] N. Zori, *BIES,* 31 (1967), pp. 132–35 (Hebrew).

[74] B. Mazar, *VT Suppl.,* 7 (1960), p. 198 (=*Canaan and Israel* [Jerusalem, 1974] pp. 225–26, Hebrew).

[75] B. Mazar, *EI,* 3 (1954), p. 26 (Hebrew) (=*Canaan and Israel,*p. 33).

[76] Wright, *op. cit.*, p. 66*.

[77] Z. Kallai, *op. cit.*, pp. 191, 203.

[78] Alt, *op. cit.* (*supra,* n. 57), p. 14; Wright, *op. cit.*, p. 59*, Fig. 1 and n. 8.

[79] W. Ewing, apud J. Hastings, ed., *Dictionary of the Bible,* I (New York, 1901), p. 637; Y. Aharoni, *Enc. Bib.* (Hebrew), VI, p. 24.

[80] Ahroni, apud *The Beth Shean Valley,* pp. 31–44 (Hebrew); Kallai, *op. cit.*, pp. 355–60.

[81] Kallai, *op. cit.*, pp. 107–16.

[82] B. Maisler (Mazar), *BIES,* 8 (1941), pp. 35–37 (Hebrew) (= *Cities and Districts in Eretz Israel,* pp. 84–87).

[83] Aharoni, *VT,* 9 (1959), pp. 232–34.

[84] *Contra* Wright, *op. cit.*, p. 59*.

[85] A. F. Rainey, *IEJ,* 20 (1970), pp. 191–202; R. de Vaux, *Ancient Israel* (New York, 1961), pp. 135, 141f.

[86] M. Noth, *Das System der zwölf Stämme Israels* (Stuttgart, 1930).

[87] W. W. Hallo, *JCS,* 14 (1960), pp. 88–96.

[88] *Contra* W. F. Albright, *Archaeology and the Religion of Israel*[3] (Baltimore, 1953), p. 140.

CHAPTER IV

The Kingdoms of Israel and Judah

After the death of Solomon the kingdom broke up into its two internal divisions, Judah and Israel. Jeroboam the son of Nebat from Zeredah in Mount Ephraim had rebelled while Solomon was still alive. As a consequence he was forced to flee to Egypt where he found asylum with Shishak, founder of the Twenty-second Egyptian Dynasty (1 Kings 11. 26–40). When Solomon died, his son Rehoboam went to Shechem where he expected to have his rule acknowledged by "all Israel", having first been enthroned over Judah (at Hebron ?). The tribal sheikdoms made their submission conditional: "Your father made our yoke heavy. Now therefore lighten the hard service of your father and his heavy yoke upon us, and we will serve you" (1 Kings 12. 4). When he refused to yield to their request, they revolted against him and crowned Jeroboam as King over Israel.

I. THE HOUSE OF JEROBOAM AND BAASHA[1]
(*c.* 928–882 B.C.)

The kingdom of Israel now included all of the northern tribes: the House of Joseph, the tribes of Galilee and those of Transjordan. The southern tribes—Judah, Simeon and also Benjamin—comprised the Judean kingdom. This division served to give a monarchial form to tribal-geographical entities which had existed before the rise of the United Monarchy and had maintained their separate identities as administrative units during Solomon's reign. The only change concerned Benjamin, which now identified itself with Judah (1 Kings 12. 21) because of its association with Jerusalem. Transjordan became an integral part of the northern kingdom. The recurrent notices about siege operations on the part of Israelite kings against "Gibbethon, which belongs to the Philistines" (1 Kings 15. 27; 16. 15–17), apparently Tell Melaṭ west of Gezer, prove that the boundaries of Israel, Philistia and Judah met in that vicinity during this period.

The ensuing civil war weakened both kingdoms and caused them to lose their dominion over the areas conquered under the United Monarchy. We have no certain information about the control of Transjordan where the northern kingdom considered itself the heir to the domination of Ammon and Moab; neither are we informed about the

Judean control over Edom. At least part of Edom had been lost during Solomon's reign. According to the Mesha Stele, it would seem that Moab had also gained independence from Judah and Israel, to be subjugated again at a later date by Omri. Evidently the two kingdoms resulting from the United Monarchy did not have the strength necessary for holding the conquered territories.

It was only after a conflict lasting several generations that the boundary between the two kingdoms was fixed.[2] The dispute was mainly concerned with the territory of Benjamin which was claimed by both sides. At first the boundary ran south of Bethel, where a royal sanctuary was established like the one at Dan in the north. On the east the border passed south of Jericho (cf. 1 Kings 16. 34, *et al.*), thus approximating the traditional borders between Judah and Benjamin. On the west Aijalon was on the Judean side (2 Chron. 11. 10; 28. 18). Therefore, the line here must have corresponded roughly to the original boundary between Benjamin and Ephraim.

During the reigns of Rehoboam and Jeroboam there was unceasing war over the disputed portions of Benjamin (1 Kings 14. 30). Towards the end of Jeroboam's reign Abijah son of Rehoboam gained the upper hand: "And Abijah pursued Jeroboam, and took cities from him, Bethel with all its villages and Jeshanah with its villages and Ephrain (Ophrah) with its villages" (2 Chron. 13. 19). Thus Abijah seized the hill country around Bethel, a region belonging to Ephraim according to the tribal boundary descriptions, though it appears in the list of towns belonging to Benjamin (Josh. 18. 21–4). However, during the reign of Baasha, King of Israel, the balance of power shifted. He overpowered Asa, the King of Judah, and not only returned to Israel the Bethel district but he also drove southward and fortified Ramah of Benjamin, only five and a half miles from Jerusalem (1 Kings 15. 16 ff.). In his hour of distress Asa turned to Ben-hadad, King of Aram-Damascus, who gladly took advantage of the opportunity to invade Israel while it was engaged in conflict with Judah. Thus Asa succeeded in regaining the Benjaminite area for Judah, though Bethel and its environs remained Israelite. Asa fortified Geba of Benjamin (not Gibeah of Benjamin)[3] and Mizpah on the main roads to Jerusalem. Both places dominated the border; on the latter site (Tell en-Naṣbeh) a solid, thick city wall was uncovered built with salients and recesses, which apparently belonged to Asa's fortification.[4] Henceforth the boundary between Judah and Israel remained fixed in this region between Mizpah and Bethel. When relations between the two kingdoms improved during the Omride Dynasty no further attempts were made to change it. It remained unchanged until the fall of the northern kingdom at which time it became the boundary for the Assyrian province of Samaria. The towns of Benjamin are also divided into two geographical groups according to this boundary line, which evidently reflect separate Benjaminite districts during the Divided Monarchy (Josh. 18. 21–4, 25–8 respectively).[5]

Only in the reign of Josiah was this boundary changed. At that time it was moved northward at the expense of the Assyrian province called Samaria. Bethel was then included in Judah (2 Kings 23. 4),[6] and his stand against Pharaoh Necho near Megiddo (2 Kings 23. 29–30; 2 Chron. 35. 20–4) was possible only after the complete annexation of Samaria. In fact, it is probable that Josiah controlled the whole of the Megiddo province, i.e. Galilee. However, it is likely that Josiah also changed the interior boundary between Judah and Samaria within the administrative framework of his kingdom, by incorporation of the Bethel region into Judah. This is indicated by the fact that Bethel was part of Judah in the Post-exile period; one must assume, therefore, that the Persians simply left things as they found them.[7]

Jeroboam established his first capital at Shechem, which had been the ancient capital of the Mount Ephraim district. He also built the two royal sanctuaries as competitors to Jerusalem, one at Bethel on his southern border and the other at Dan in the northernmost extremity of his kingdom. The discovery of such a royal sanctuary at Arad, founded apparently during Solomon's reign, proves that the establishment of small temples on the borders was an accepted practice designed to represent the kingdom's sovereignty in those regions. A short time later he went out from Shechem "and built Penuel" (1 Kings 12. 25). The action hints at a time of emergency, just as in the reign of Eshbaal the son of Saul or of David during Absalom's rebellion, both of whom moved their provisional capitals to Mahanaim beside Penuel. Jeroboam's move was probably made during the early years of his reign, perhaps to escape from the heavy pressure being exerted by Rehoboam prior to Shishak's invasion.

II. SHISHAK'S CAMPAIGN

The military expedition carried out by Shishak in Palestine took place in the fifth year of Rehoboam the son of Solomon (*c.* 924 B.C.). The Bible preserves only a brief notice to the effect that Shishak, the King of Egypt, came up against Jerusalem and took plunder from the treasures of the house of the Lord and from the king's house (1 Kings 14. 25–8). 2 Chronicles preserves the same information (12. 1–12), adding that Shishak captured the fortified cities of Judah and came as far as Jerusalem where, rather than conquering the city, he was satisfied to accept a heavy tribute.

The inscription of Shishak containing a long topographical list preserved in the Amon temple in Karnak not only confirms the brief biblical notices but also provides us with many other details about the campaign.[8] It is clear from the Egyptian text that the main objectives of the expedition were not the towns of Judah and Jerusalem but rather the

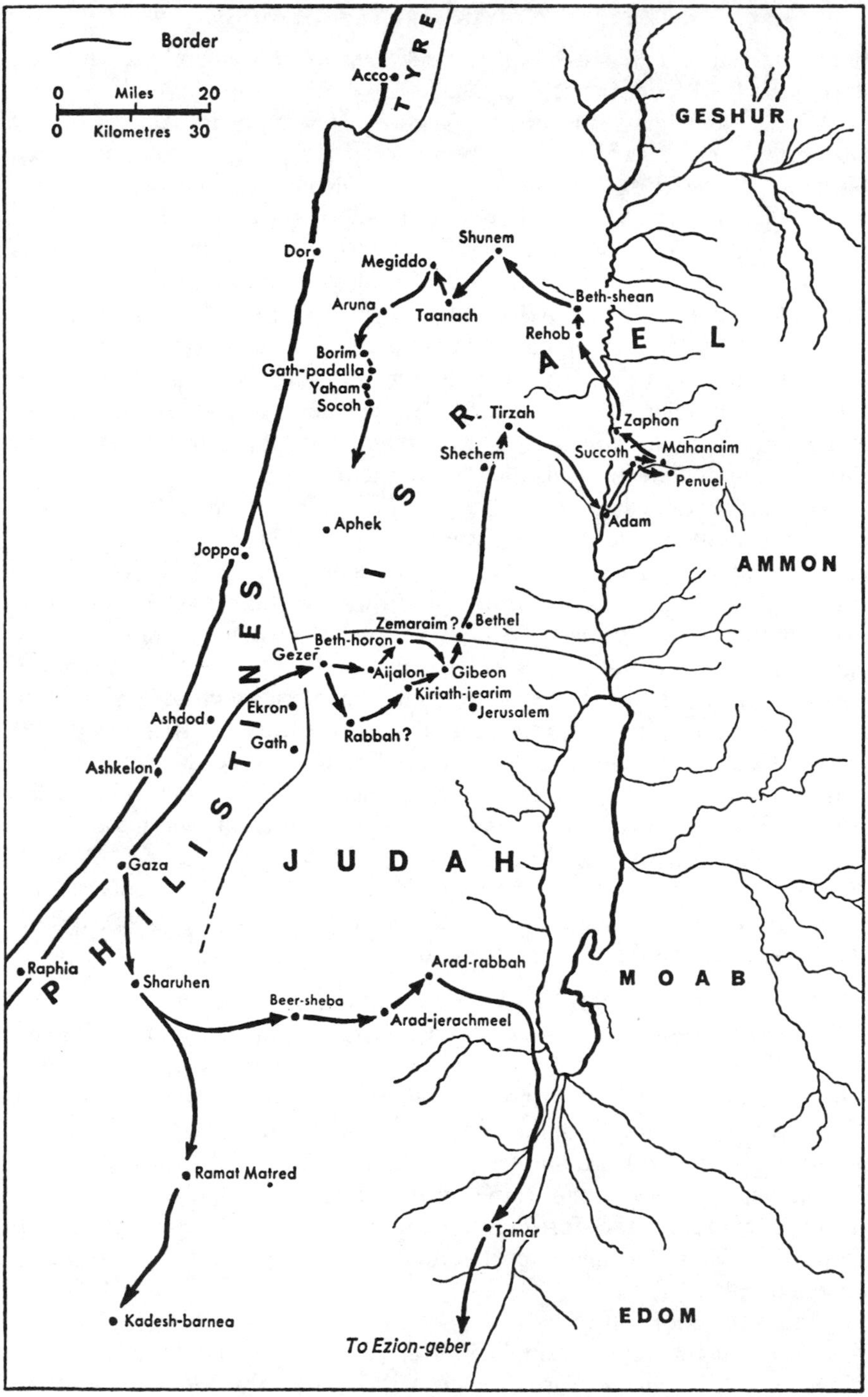

Map 24. The Campaign of Shishak.

kingdom of Israel on one hand and the Negeb of Judah on the other (cf. map 24).

From the standpoint of lay-out and content Shishak's inscription is divided into three sections: (1) Nos. 1–65, towns in central Palestine (of these Nos. 1–10 are the usual "Northern Countries"); (2) Nos. 66–150, settlements of the Negeb; (3) the third group contained about thirty names of which only the last five are preserved, these being towns in the southern coastal region.

1. Towns in Central Palestine

When one reads the first lines of this inscription in boustrophedon order, the names fall into a logical geographical sequence. In other words, one must go contrary to the normal practice in Egyptian inscriptions and read every other line into the figures' backs instead of into their faces. If we adopt this method for reading the inscription and add the towns from line five in their proper geographical position, we obtain the following list[9]:

1 (11). Gaza
2 (12). Gezer
3 (13). Rubute
4 (26). Aijalon
5 (25). Kiriathaim
6 (24). Beth-horon
7 (23). Gibeon
8 (57). Zemaraim
9 (64). [Go]phnah?
10–13 (60–63). Missing
14 (59). [Ti]rzah?
15 (58). Migdal
16 (56). Adam
17 (55). Succoth
18 (54). Kedesh
19 (53). Penuel
20 (22). Mahanaim
21 (21). *š-w-t*
22 (20). Zaphon
23 (19). Adoraim
24 (18). Hapharaim
25 (65). The Valley (*p. ʿ-m-q*)
26 (17). Rehob
27 (16). Beth-shean
28 (15). Shunem
29 (14). Taanach
30 (27). Megiddo
31 (28) Adar
32 (29). Yad-hammelech ("Hand [or stele] of the King")
33 (30). Missing
34 (31). Honim
35 (32). ʿAruna
36 (33). Borim
37 (34). Gath-padalla
38 (35). Yaḥam (*y-ḥ-m*)
39 (36). Beth-olam (or Beth-arim ?)
40 (37). *k-q-r-w*
41 (38). Socoh
42 (39). Beth-tappuah

This line-up of towns gives us a logical and continuous route, thus making it possible to reconstruct the expedition's line of march. The first town is Gaza, the only place in Philistia mentioned in this list. Gaza, as the ancient capital of Canaan and Philistia, evidently marked the conquest of the entire Philistine region, where the Egyptians do not seem to have met any resistance since their domination had been established over this territory early in Solomon's reign (cf. *supra*, pp. 304–5). The second town on the list is Gezer, one of Solomon's main fortified towns on the border with Philistia. From there Shishak ascended via Aijalon and Beth-horon (also fortified by Solomon) to Gibeon, which is north-west of Jerusalem. Therefore, Shishak entered the hill country by the ancient and well-known "ascent of Beth-horon", the northern route to Jerusalem made famous by many battles. This road followed approximately the new boundary between the kingdoms of Israel and Judah. Gibeon was one of the important Judean towns north of Jerusalem, and Aijalon was also on the Judean side, according to the list of Rehoboam's forts (2 Chron. 11. 10).

We have no information about the political status of Beth-horon and Gezer in this period. They were both assigned to the House of Joseph according to the traditional boundary description, but one could hardly think that Shishak's line of march passed alternatively from Israelite to Judean territory and back. Therefore, it would appear that all of these towns were Judean at that time. It is clear that Gezer belonged to Judah at a later date; during the reign of Ahaz, Gimzo, which is north of Gezer, belonged to Judah (2 Chron. 28. 18). Gezer belonged to Judah in the days of Hezekiah—as evidenced by the royal Judean seal impressions found there.[10] The excavations indicate that Gezer suffered a destruction at about the time of Shishak's campaign which caused a decline in its greatness from which it recovered only very slowly. The passage "And he took the fortified cities of Judah and came as far as Jerusalem" (2 Chron. 12. 4) must refer to this part of the campaign from Gezer to Gibeon.

Between Gezer and Aijalon a town is mentioned by the name *r-b-t* which also was listed beside Gezer in the list of Thut-mose III (No. 105) and appears in the Amarna letters as Rubute with regard to disputes between the kings of Gezer and Jerusalem (*EA*, 289, 29). The roster of Judean towns mentions Rabbah (Josh. 15. 60) with Kiriath-baal = Kiriath-jearim.

If the reading Kiriathaim (No. 5 [25]) is correct,[11] then this town which appears in the list between Aijalon and Beth-horon ought to be Kiriath-jearim—Baalath. It would seem, then, that Shishak's army captured all of the fortified towns on the main roads to Jerusalem between Gezer and Gibeon. It is not by coincidence that we have references to these towns being fortified during the reigns of David and Solomon: Aijalon and Beth-horon appear in the list of Levitical cities; Gezer, Beth-horon and Baalath (Kiriath-jearim ?) are among Solomon's forts.

The negotiations with Rehoboam described in the Bible must have taken place at Gibeon, and after receiving the heavy tribute from Jerusalem, Pharaoh's army turned northward towards the kingdom of Israel. At Zemaraim, which must be sought in the vicinity of Ramallah and el-Bireh on the Judean border (2 Chron. 13. 4; Josh. 18. 22), Shishak invaded the Israelite kingdom along the principal mountain highway (cf. Judg. 21. 19). At this point there seems to be a gap in the list that can be supplied by the names in line five. It is possible that the next town conquered was Gophnah, four miles north of Ramallah, which is otherwise known to us only from later sources.[12] If the restoration of Tirzah is correct, then we may deduce that Shishak penetrated into the heart of the Ephraimite hill country. Shechem may have been one of the names obliterated in this section. Tirzah became the capital of Israel, perhaps as early as the reign of Jeroboam (1 Kings 14. 17), but at least by the time of Baasha (1 Kings 15. 21 ff.). Therefore, one should not suppose that it had suffered too drastically from Shishak's attack.

At Tirzah the Egyptians turned eastward towards the Jordan Valley. The first reference there is to Adamah (Adam), which dominated the Jordan fords south of the Jabbok. Next they came to Succoth and continued eastward up the valley of the Jabbok to Penuel and Mahanaim. This line of march can be explained in the light of the fact mentioned above, viz. that Jeroboam had moved his capital to Penuel. Therefore, Shishak conquered all of Israel's chief cities in order to overpower Jeroboam.

From Mahanaim Shishak returned to the Plain of Succoth where he turned northward following the eastern side of the Jordan Valley to Zaphon and the Valley of Beth-shean. The next two towns, Adoraim and Hapharaim, are unknown. The reference to "the plain" (*p.ʿ-m-q*) probably alludes to the Valley of Beth-shean, as indicated by the references to Rehob and Beth-shean. There Shishak turned westward into the Valley of Jezreel where he conquered Shunem, Taanach and Megiddo. The absence of Jezreel from this list is notable; it would appear that its rise to prominence occurred later under the House of Omri. The fragment of a stele belonging to Shishak was discovered at Megiddo,[13] thus confirming his conquest of the city and indicating that this important place remained under Egyptian control at least for a time. The Megiddo of Solomon (level IVB) with its great gate and elaborate buildings was destroyed at this time according to the excavations.[14]

Upon leaving Megiddo Shishak returned via Wadi ʿAra to the Sharon; and from Borim (Khirbet Burin) he followed the *Via Maris* southward, conquering a chain of towns well known from other Egyptian sources: Gath-padalla, Yaḥam (*y-ḥ-m*) and Socoh. At this point the text is broken off.

2. .Negeb Settlements

The list of towns in the Negeb, the second group, is the largest segment of Shishak's list. It includes 85 name plates, but since there are at least 14 compound names requiring two plates each, we are left with about 70 place names. This list is of special importance as being the only detailed roster of towns in the Negeb among all our sources, both biblical and Egyptian. In spite of the fact that only a small percentage of these towns have been identified to date, it is certain that not only they but the others are located in the Negeb because the term "Negeb" itself comprises one element in several of the compound names.

It is possible, with some degree of accuracy, to identify the following names: Yurza (133) and Sharuhen (apparently 125, *š-r-ḥ-m*) in the western Negeb and perhaps also *f-t-y-š* which resembles the later Photis (Khirbet Fuṭeis)[15]; Arad in the eastern Negeb, Ezem, known as a town of Simeon and perhaps (Ezion-)geber[16] on the Gulf of Aqabah. These names prove that Shishak penetrated into the heart of the Negeb from the west to the east and via the southern towns of Simeon to the farthest point within Judean control, viz. Ezion-geber. It is surprising how few parallels there are to the biblical lists of towns in the Negeb. This is probably to be explained by the fact that the biblical lists pertain mostly to towns in the northern Negeb, while Shishak concentrated his activities in the southern Negeb from which we have practically no other written sources.

On the other hand, there are additional parallels to clan names from southern tribes preserved in the Bible, especially in 1 Chronicles, chapters 2 and 4. Two out of the three names that have the additional element "the Negeb" (*p.n-g-b*) resemble biblical clan names, viz. *p.n-g-b ʿ-ḏ-n-t* (84–5), apparently the Negeb of the Eznites, a clan which produced one of David's heroes—Adino the Eznite (2 Sam. 23. 8, MT supported by LXX; the RSV following Luther and most modern commentators adopts the parallel expression in 1 Chron. 11, 11 "he lifted up his spear"); *p.n-g-b ꜣ-š-ḥ-t* (92–3), i.e. the Negeb of the Shuhathites, which looks like the clan name Shuhah (1 Chron. 4. 11).[17] Several regional names from the Negeb mentioned in the Bible with reference to David's reign and called after tribal or ethnic groups are phrased like some of the names of Shishak's Negeb list: the Negeb of Judah, Caleb, the Jerahmeelites, the Kenites and the Cherethites (1 Sam. 27. 10; 30. 14; cf. *supra*, p. 291 f.).

By adopting this method, it is possible to identify the following clans: Jahallel (*ꜣ-r-h-r-r*, 70; 1 Chron. 4. 16); Tappuah (82; 1 Chron. 2. 43); Hanan (94), and Tilon (101; cf. Ben-hanan and Tilon, 1 Chron. 4. 20); Yeroham (112, 139; cf. Jerahmeel, 1 Chron. 2. 9); Peleth (*p-r-t-m*, 121; 1 Chron. 2. 33); Onan (140; cf. Onam, 1 Chron. 2. 26); and Maachah (145; cf. the wife of Caleb, 1 Chron. 2. 48).

Nine place names on this list are compounded with the element *p.ḥ-q-r*, *"the fort"*: *p.ḥ-q-r f-t-y-š* (68–9), *p.ḥ-q-r ꜣ-b-rm* (71–2), *p.ḥ-q-r n-ʿ-ḏ-t* (77–8), *p.ḥ-q-r š-n-t* (or *š-n-m*, 87–8), *p.ḥ-q-r ḥ -n-n* (94–5), *p.ḥ-q-r ꜣ -l-g-d* (96–7), *p.ḥ-q-r t-r-n* (101–2) and *ḥ-q-r-m ʿ-r-d r-b-t ʿ-r-d n b-t y-r-ḥ-m*(107–12). This latter may be rendered: "(The) forts (of) Great Arad (and of) Arad of the House of Yeroham". The interpretation of *ḥ-q-r* as "fort" from the Semitic root חגר, "to encompass with a belt, to fortify", is supported by the Mishnaic form חגרא, referring to the southern border fortifications of the Roman period, the *Limes Palaestinae*.[18]

Of these fortresses it is possible to identify only Great Arad, which is Tell ʿArad, and the Arad of Beth-yeroham (the Jerahmeelite ?) with Tell el-Milḥ, the site of Canaanite Arad. A special system of fortification by means of earthen ramparts and glacis was found to exist at the major Negeb sites constructed during the United Monarchy. Perhaps this type of construction is that reflected in the term **ḥagar*.[19] Two of these were Arad and Tell el-Milḥ (Tel Malḥata), which we would equate with the forts (*ḥ-q-r-m*) of Great Arad and Arad of the House of Jerahm(eel). Another very important rampart and glacis fortification was found at Tell es-Sebaʿ. We would suggest that this royal citadel was the *p.-ḥ-q-r 3-b-r-m* No. 71–2), i.e. the "Ḥagar of Abra(ha) m."[20] on the basis of the sacred traditions attaching to the site. Examples of similar citadels with special names are perhaps the City of David in Jerusalem and Mamre at Hebron.

At all three of these heavily fortified Iron Age sites Roman forts were also discovered.[21] The *Limes* had thus occupied the same line and its early name is evidently preserved in the later Talmudic term *ḥagrā̄*.[22]

We have already noted that in the third and final group only the last five names are preserved. Two of these are identifiable: Raphia and Laban, both of them towns on the southern coast north of the Brook of Egypt. Laban is also associated with that brook in Assyrian sources[23] and was apparently situated to the south of Raphia, perhaps at Tell Abu Seleimeh beside Sheikh Zuweid.[24] Since at least some of the towns in the Shephelah were destroyed at about this time as indicated by excavations, e.g. Lachish Stratum V and Tell Beit Mirsim B_3, it is possible that the missing section had included the cities in the Shephelah of Judah.

On the basis of Shishak's list it is therefore possible to reconstruct the objectives of his expedition and his conquests, thus supplementing our biblical information. His campaign was directed against both Judah and Israel for the purpose of strengthening the Egyptian domination of Philistia, while gaining control of the important trade routes that pass across Palestine. First Shishak went up against Jerusalem via Beth-horon; but after accepting a heavy tribute from Rehoboam, he turned northward and invaded the kingdom of Israel. After conquering Tirzah and Penuel, Jeroboam's new capital, he moved northward up the Jordan Valley until he reached Beth-shean. From there he turned west to the Valley of Jezreel and made his way back to the Sharon via Megiddo. Then he headed south along the *Via Maris*. This part of the campaign was aimed at seizing control over the *Via Maris* in the Jezreel Valley and the Sharon, while weakening the two kingdoms of Israel and Judah.

At the same time his battalions marched deep into the expanses of the Judean Negeb and apparently reached even to Ezion-geber. The international commerce with South Arabia via Elath and the Negeb which had developed during Solomon's reign was doubtless a thorn in Pharaoh's flesh. The Negeb invasion was intended first and foremost to cut off these trade routes. Apparently this goal was achieved, at least for a while, and the last remnants of control over Edom were snatched from Judean hands. The excavations at Ezion-geber prove that the Solomonic fort had been destroyed and over it a new fortification was built in the ninth century, evidently during the reign of Asa or Jehoshaphat.[25]

III. REHOBOAM'S FORTRESSES

It would appear that Rehoboam's list of fortresses preserved in 2 Chronicles 11. 5–12 is to be dated after Shishak's campaign, although the Bible does not assign a date to it and the passage appears in the text prior to the Shishak expedition. Rehoboam's list includes fifteen towns distributed among the most strategic points in Judah (cf. map 25). Hebron, Beth-zur and Bethlehem are on the main highway down the ridge of the Judean hills. Etam, Tekoa and Ziph protected the approaches from the wilderness of Judah. Adoraim, Adullam and Socoh guarded the various routes to the Shephelah and Philistia. A continuous line of forts was built along the western boundary with Philistia: Lachish, Mareshah and Gath in the south; Azekah, Zorah and Aijalon in the north.[26] Of these only Gath is doubtful as to identification. One can hardly agree with the widely accepted opinion that Gath of the Philistines is meant, because wherever we look for that town, whether at Tell eṣ-Ṣafi or elsewhere, it is bound to be west of Rehoboam's line of forts in the Shephelah. Likewise, it is clear that Gath was still a Philistine city during Solomon's reign (1 Kings 2. 39): not only are we without any hint about its being conquered, but the words of Amos about the destruction of Philistine Gath (Amos 6. 2) contradict the assumption that this town had become an Israelite fort as early as the tenth century. On the other hand, the absence from Rehoboam's list of Tell el-Judeideh would be remarkable, since it is a lofty mound situated at a strategic point on the roads between Lachish and Mareshah in the south and Azekah in the north. This site is probably to be identified with Moresheth-gath[27]; so it is most likely that this is the Gath referred to.[28]

Therefore, the fortifications of Rehoboam form a logical and continuous line for the defence of his kingdom from the west, the south and the east, with additional forts located at the important road junctions. There were no forts in the north on the boundary with Israel, evidently because of Rehoboam's constant desire to expand in that direction. The Shephelah defence line is pulled back quite a way towards the east, probably as a result of Shishak's campaign. The Pharaoh had probably expanded his sphere of influence in Philistia at the expense of Judah.

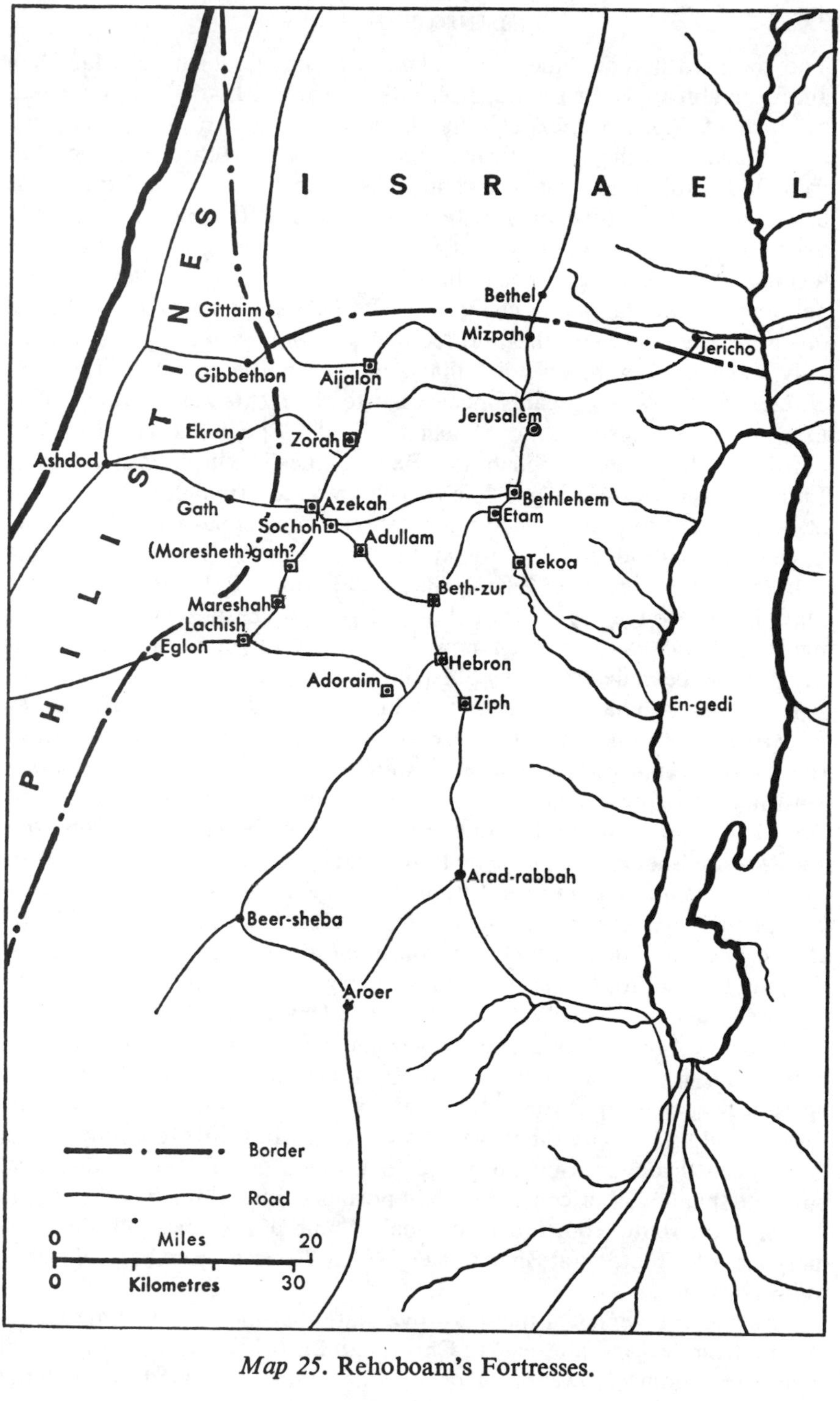

Map 25. Rehoboam's Fortresses.

The southern defence line which extended from Lachish via Mareshah and Adoraim to Hebron and Ziph is surprising. Must we assume that because of Shishak's expedition all of the southern Shephelah, the Negeb and even the southern hill regions as far as Hebron were cut off from Judah for some time ? Perhaps it is permissible to supplement the list of forts by adding the Levitical cities in Judah which had already been fortified during the reigns of David and Solomon; most of them are located in the southern Judean hills.[29] If this be so, then the southern defence line would run from Debir to Jattir, Eshtemoa and Juttah, i.e. on the border between the hill country and the Negeb. Aijalon is the only town in Rehoboam's list that appears on the roster of Levitical cities,[30] and it was probably necessary to renew its fortifications after they had been destroyed by Shishak. In the Shephelah the Levitical cities included *Ashan,* Libnah and Beth-shemesh. The identification of Libnah is uncertain; it is possible that this was a fort slightly to the west at Tell Bornaṭ, but its absence from Rehoboam's list suggests that it may have been lost to Judah through the activities of Shishak (cf. what happened at a later time; 2 Kings 8. 22; 2 Chron. 21. 10). Beth-shemesh may have been a connecting link between Azekah and Zorah, or perhaps Zorah was fortified now because Beth-shemesh, which was nearby, had been destroyed by Shishak.

Rehoboam's chain of forts served the kingdom of Judah as an effective defence line for at least two or three generations, even though the country enlarged its borders again later, especially in the south. Information is preserved in 2 Chronicles about two invasions during the first half of the ninth century B.C. which were repulsed from this fortification line, although the historical background of them is not clear: (1) the invasion of Zerah the Ethiopian, who was defeated at Mareshah and pursued by Asa (*c*. 908–868) as far as Gerar (2 Chron. 14. 8–14); (2) that of the Moabites, Ammonites and their allies from across the Dead Sea via En-gedi to the heart of Judea during the reign of Jehoshaphat (*c*. 867–852), which was halted near Tekoa (2 Chron. 20. 1–28). This latter invasion was both daring and dangerous, but the precise geographical references leave no room for doubt that the narrative has a real historical background. En-gedi is the most important desert oasis in the Judean wilderness, and the forts dating to the Judean Monarchy which have been discovered on the route to En-gedi and in the Wadi Saiyal indicate that a trail of considerable importance passed this way; this was the shortest route from Judah to Moab. Some of the forts guarding this passage, e.g. the one at Shakarat en-Najjar,[32] were probably built after this invasion.

The opening verses of this narrative state that the enemy came "from Aram, from beyond the sea" (2 Chron. 20. 2). It is customary to correct Aram to Edom. However, Moab is the country located beyond the

Dead Sea and not Edom. The reading "Aram" is apparently correct, this being a reference to Aram-Damascus which became Israel and Judah's most dangerous enemy during the ninth century B.C. and which expanded its authority to include the King's Highway on the Transjordanian heights.[33] Therefore, it is not impossible that Aram-Damascus was in control of this region until the reconquest of Moab by the Omrides, which probably took place some time after this attack on Judah.[34]

The Aramean domination of Transjordan and certain regions in the north was evidently established by the campaign of Ben-hadad I who took advantage of the strife between Israel and Judah to invade the kingdom of Israel in c. 885 B.C. The Bible describes the conquest of part of Galilee ("the land of Naphtali")[35] and the region around Chinneroth (the Sea of Galilee; 1 Kings 15. 17–22). Only three border towns are mentioned in this text: Ijon, Dan and Abel-beth-maacah.[36] However, the excavations at Hazor proved that it was also destroyed in that period when its Solomonic fortification wall was breached and laid in ruins.[37] As a consequence of this campaign, it is probable that the remaining areas of Israelite authority in Transjordan were lost. There is probably also an allusion to the results of Ben-hadad's campaign in the passage: "But Geshur and Aram took from them Havvoth-jair, Kenath and its villages, sixty towns" (1 Chron. 2. 23).

The kingdom of Israel itself was considerably weakened by the reduction of its northern territory. It would seem that the Israelite dynasty of Baasha may have met its downfall as the result of this catastrophe, because Baasha died a short time later and his son Elah was murdered after ruling only a few days.

IV. THE OMRIDE DYNASTY (*c.* 878–842 B.C.)

The establishment of the Omride Dynasty brought about significant changes in Israel's political policy towards Judah and the other neighbouring kingdoms. One of Omri's first acts was to move the capital of his kingdom away from Tirzah, which had recently been devastated. Tirzah may have had special associations with the House of Baasha and, furthermore, its location at the eastern extremity of Mount Ephraim was inconvenient for an efficient handling of government affairs. However, Omri did not choose one of the former urban centres of Mount Ephraim such as Shechem. Instead he founded a new capital at Samaria, about seven miles north-west of Shechem, on a strategic site dominating the western approaches to the hill country. This resembled David's action in choosing for his capital a place like Jerusalem, which was strictly the possession of the royal house and had no associations with older tribal traditions. Omri's chosen site was apparently the possession of a man named Shemer, who may have been related to the Shimron clan of Issachar (cf. *supra,* p. *244*).[38] Omri himself may have come from the tribe of Issachar, like his immediate predecessors on the throne (1 Kings 15. 27); this would explain the choice of Jezreel, the former capital of Issachar, as the secondary capital of the new dynasty. At this latter site was located the royal winter house, while the summer house was at Samaria (Amos 3. 15). The choice of Samaria was most propitious because of its excellent strategic position on a high and isolated hill in Mount Ephraim. Samaria became the chief rival of Jerusalem, and its name soon attached itself to the whole region, thus displacing the former term, Mount Ephraim.

The principal enemy threatening the kingdom of Israel was Aram. Therefore, Omri wisely put an end to the disputes with Judah and strengthened the alliance with his southern neighbour by marrying his daughter (or grand-daughter),[39] Athaliah, to Jehoram son of Jehoshaphat, King of Judah. He likewise established a strong covenant relationship with Tyre, which was reinforced by the marriage of his son Ahab to Jezebel daughter of Ethbaal, King of the Sidonians. So, in his foreign policy as well, Omri was following in the footsteps of David and Solomon. Tyre was the mightiest sea power on the Mediterranean in that period.[40] Its colonies were spread as far as Spain and Africa; its rich and extensive trade with Israel and other countries is ably depicted in Ezekiel's lament. The products that Israel sold to Tyre were mainly agricultural surpluses such as grain, fruits and spices (Ezek. 27. 17), while Tyre supplied her with wood and finely manufactured wares. The alliance with Israel and Judah opened up for Tyre the trade route to Arabia, and the ties between these countries were doubtless strengthened because of Aramean pressure on both parties.

This intelligent policy strengthened both Israel and Judah, permitting their economic growth and the expansion of their borders. Large, flourishing cities dating to this period were discovered not only at Samaria but also at Megiddo and Hazor. At Hazor (level VIII) the town was doubled in size and fortified by a thick wall like that at Megiddo; at a peak of the tell a magnificent palace was built and at its centre a royal storehouse was established. Most of Transjordan, including Moab, was reconquered, as we learn from the Mesha Stele.[41] Judah re-established its authority over Edom, where a deputy of the king was appointed (1 Kings 22. 47); under Jehoshaphat an attempt was made to renew the commercial shipping from Ezion-geber (1 Kings 22. 48–9; 2 Chron. 20. 35–7). The contemporary fortifications uncovered at Ezion-geber prove that the fort was surrounded at that time by a thick wall and a triple gate of the order of that at Megiddo (IVA).[42] Some of the "fortresses and store cities" built by Jehoshaphat were in the Negeb (2 Chron. 17. 12). Beer-sheba was rebuilt and refortified with a new casemate wall in the mid-9th century (Stratum III).[43]

V. WARS WITH ARAM AND ASSYRIA

During the reign of Ahab, the contemporary of Jehoshaphat, the kingdom of Israel achieved considerable power and expansion. Its chief opponent was Ben-hadad, King of Damascus, who threatened the very existence of Israel for a time. Ben-hadad was the title of the Aramean kings and not a personal name. This is clearly demonstrated by the inscription of Shalmaneser where the same king is called Hadadezer. It would appear that the battles described in the Bible took place near the end of Ahab's reign, although there is no precise chronological data available. At one stage Ben-hadad laid siege to Samaria itself, but when he failed to conquer it, his retreat was turned into a rout (1 Kings 20. 1–21).

In the following year the armies of Israel and Aram met once again near Aphek, which may possibly be identified with the Iron Age site at 'En-Gev on the eastern shore of the Sea of Galilee,[44] while the ancient name has been preserved at Fiq just east of the Sea of Galilee.[45] This time Ben-hadad was dealt a decisive blow, being captured himself at Aphek. Ahab set him free but imposed severe conditions of submission: "And Ben-hadad said to him, 'The cities which my father took from your father I will restore; and you may establish bazaars for yourself in Damascus, as my father did in Samaria' " (1 Kings 20. 34). The cities referred to here were doubtless in the disputed area of Transjordan, northern Gilead, Bashan and the Ramoth-gilead district, which was now returned to Israel with the addition of privileges for establishing a commercial monopoly in Damascus.

At the siege of Samaria there were thirty-two subordinate kings with Ben-hadad, and the Bible associates this military disaster with a reorganization of the Aramean kingdom: "Remove the kings, each from his post, and put commanders in their places" (1 Kings 20. 24). Henceforth the various Aramean kingdoms were probably united into one state under the leadership of Damascus, a development that not only made itself felt in a stronger Aramean army but also in every phase of the Aramean material and spiritual culture—religion, language, art, economy, etc.[46] This unification is evidently reflected in the inscriptions of Shalmaneser III.

Those extensive organizational changes in the Aramean kingdom evidently took place under the shadow of the Assyrian menace which had appeared on the horizon. The alliance between Ahab and Ben-hadad which was renounced by prophetic circles, was probably made for the same reason. In 858 B.C. Shalmaneser III assumed power in Assyria; with his reign the great period of Assyrian imperialistic expansion begins. In his very first year he carried out a campaign of conquest in the West, crossing the Euphrates and the Orontes, he reached the Amanus mountains and even the Mediterranean.[47] In his sixth year (853

B.C.) his chronicles tell about his mighty battle against an alliance of kings who opposed him at Qarqar on the Orontes. At the head of this alliance of 12 kings stood Hadadezer (Adad-idri) of Damascus. He was accompanied by Irḫuleni, King of Hamath, as well as "Ahab, the Israelite" (*A-ḫa-ab-bu* ^{māt}*Sir-'i-la-a-a*). Other units were furnished by various kings of Syria and Phoenicia; supporting troops from Egypt, Arabia and Baasha son of Rehob from Ammon were also in the ranks.[48]

Ahab stood alongside the kings of Damascus and Hamath at the head of this mighty force and furnished, according to the inscription of Shalmaneser, more than half of the war chariots in the battle (2,000 out of 3,940). [However, it has recently been pointed out that the figure of 2,000 is far too high. The Assyrian empire at the height of its power only mustered about 2,000 chariots![49] Therefore, it is more reasonable to assume that Ahab had 20 chariots which would compare favorably with the following entries in the same passage. A. F. R.] It is surprising that Jehoshaphat, the King of Judah, Ahab's close ally, is not mentioned in Shalmaneser's list; perhaps his troops are included with those of Ahab. We also learn from this inscription that Ammon was still maintaining the independence that it had apparently achieved when the Israelite kingdom was split.

Although Shalmaneser boasts of a victory, it appears that the alliance achieved its goal, at least temporarily. The Assyrian advance was blocked and only in his tenth year (849 B.C.) did Shalmaneser return to Syria. The battle of Qarqar took place about two years before Ahab's death; though it is not mentioned in the Bible, there is one apparent reference to an alliance between Israel and Aram in time of emergency: "For three years Syria and Israel continued without war" (1 Kings 22. 1). But when the Assyrian danger had slackened, the old feud broke out once again. In the third year Ahab and Jehoshaphat went out together against Ben-hadad to recoup Ramoth-gilead for Israel. Either Ben-hadad had not fulfilled the promises made after his defeat at Aphek or else he had broken the agreement and recaptured the disputed territory at some opportune moment. This time the Israelite expedition did not achieve its objective; Ahab himself was slain on the field of battle.

VI. THE REBELLION OF MOAB UNDER MESHA

The wars with Aram towards the end of Ahab's reign and the resultant loss of territory in Transjordan led to the rebellion of Moab. Concerning this country's liberation from the Israelite yoke, we have evidence in the Bible (2 Kings 1. 1; 3. 4–27) and also the stele of Mesha, King of Moab.[50]

The Mesha Stone which was discovered in 1868 at Dibon is the only victory stele of its kind from a Palestinian king of the Israelite period. In addition to its historical content, it contains many topographical details about the Mishor (tableland) north of the Arnon, the oft-disputed region between Moab and Israel (cf. map 27). According to the stele's inscription the revolt had broken out during Ahab's reign. Mesha and his father, *Chemosh-yatti,[51] reigned at Dibon in the southern part of the Mishor, but Moab was subservient to Israel during the reign of Omri and "half the days of his son". From this it would seem that when Moab became independent after the death of Solomon it had also gained control over the southern portion of the Mishor, about as far as the Wadi el-Wala. A little farther north at Ataroth the population was Israelite, while at Kerioth (cf. Jer. 48. 24) it was Moabite (lines 10–13). When the kingdom of Israel regained its strength under Omri, Moab was reconquered, though Dibon continued to be the residence of its subject kings. Thus it is clear that the line of demarcation between Israel and Moab remained north of Dibon, and the Israelite kings contented themselves with the annual payment of tribute mentioned in the Bible (2 Kings 3. 4). This tax was paid in kind from produce of the cattle and flocks, the branch of agriculture so typical of Transjordan; the "flocks of the land" are also mentioned in the Mesha Stele (line 31).

Evidently Mesha took advantage of an opportune moment during the Aramean wars towards the end of Ahab's reign in order to throw off Israel's yoke. He did not stop with liberating Moab itself but succeeded in expanding the limits of his dominion by conquering the entire Mishor. The main events seem to be recounted in the inscription according to their proper sequence. The building activities in these areas are interspersed among the descriptions of battles. In the first stage Mesha gained control over Medeba, thus advancing along the King's Highway to the northern part of the Mishor (cf. Josh. 13. 16, "From Aroer . . . all the tableland *as far as* [instead of 'by'] Medeba"). In this region he built two cities, Baal-meon (biblical Beth-baal-meon, today Ma'in south-west of Medeba) and Kiriaten (biblical Kiriathaim).[52] As his second step Mesha relates the conquest of Ataroth, where "the men of Gad had always dwelt". Therefore, Ataroth, apparently Khirbet 'Aṭṭarus eight miles north-west of Dibon, was settled by the Gadites in conformity with the biblical statement (Num. 32 34). Ataroth had been built by the King of Israel, evidently as a fortified town on the border with Moab; after its conquest by Mesha, men of Sharon and Maḥarith, settlements or districts of Moab unknown from other sources, were settled therein. Mesha also mentions a special object (the אראל דודה, "altar of David"?) which he dragged before Chemosh, the Moabite deity in Kerioth. This is the biblical Kerioth (Jer. 48. 24; Amos 2. 2; today el-Qereiyat south of Ataroth) where a temple to Chemosh was probably located.

Mesha's next military move was the conquest of Nebo, the Israelite town near Mount Nebo (Jebel Neba) north-west of Medeba. This town, which was located at the northern end of the Mishor close to Heshbon

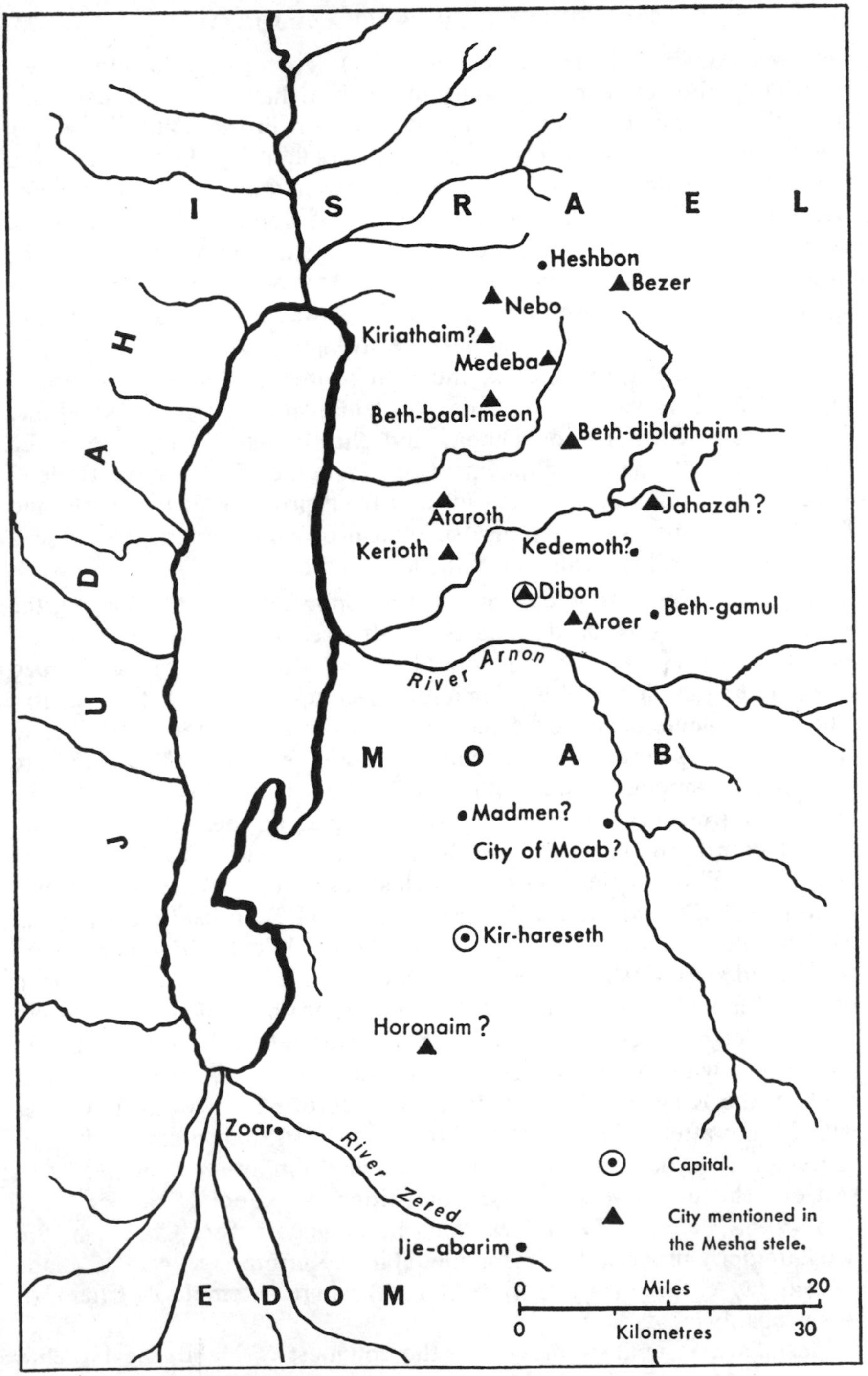

Map 26. Moab according to the Mesha Stele.

(cf. "Aroer, as far as Nebo", 1 Chron. 5. 8), was the northernmost town to be conquered by Mesha. After a night march he conquered the place by an onslaught that lasted "from the break of dawn until noon", and annihilated its 7,000 inhabitants. From the statement that he "took from these the [implements ?] of Yahweh, dragging them before Chemosh" (lines 17–18), we learn that Nebo was the site of an Israelite cult place destroyed by Mesha.

Mesha's last military action on the Moabite plateau was the conquest of Jahaz (Jahazah), the well-known fortified town on the fringe of the desert (Khirbet el-Medeiyineh ?). In this connection, we learn that "the King of Israel had built Jahaz, and he dwelt there while he was fighting against me" (lines 18–19). Ahab must have carried out a campaign of reprisal against Mesha, which was at least partially successful and resulted in the fortification of Jahazah. This latter place was known as a Levitical city, the royal administrative centre in that region during David's reign (Josh. 21. 36; 1 Chron. 6. 78).

Mesha goes on to tell about the royal building activities which he carried out in the newly conquered territories as well as in the vicinity of Dibon. At Dibon he built the Qarḥoh (the royal citadel ?), the wall of the forests (cf. the arsenal in Jerusalem called "the house of the forests", Isa. 22. 8), the wall of the Ophel (cf. the Ophel in Jerusalem, 2 Chron. 27. 3, *et al.*), gates, towers and the King's house. He lays special emphasis upon the reservoir(s), cisterns and similar installations (perhaps tunnels ?) which were constructed, partly with Israelite captives, in order to assure the water supply. Next he mentions the building of Aroer and that portion of the King's Highway that passed over the Arnon close to Aroer ("I made the highway in the Arnon", line 26; cf. Jer. 48. 19). The other cities which he built were farther north in the Moabite plateau: Beth-bamoth (apparently the biblical Bamoth-baal, cf. Num. 22. 41; Josh. 13. 17); Bezer, the city of refuge "in the wilderness on the tableland" (Josh. 20. 8; present-day Umm el- 'Amad); Medeba, Beth-diblathen (the biblical Almon-diblathaim; Num. 33. 46–7) and Beth-baal-meon (mentioned already above). The concluding passage of the inscription is broken off; enough is preserved to show that Mesha went down to fight against Ḥauronen, the biblical Horonaim. This final passage probably concerns the Israelite campaign described in the Bible.

According to the biblical account the King of Moab rebelled when Ahab died (2 Kings 1. 1; 3. 5). Comparison with the Mesha Stele seems to indicate that this is not a reference to the beginning of his rebellion, which dates back to Ahab's reign, but rather to its later stages. This was probably a renewal of the revolt which may have been partially checked by Ahab as hinted in the stele's reference to Jahaz. At least two or three years must have passed between the death of Ahab and the organization of the Israelite expedition against Moab. The King of Israel (Joram) in league with the King of Judah (Jehoshaphat) and the King of Edom, evidently a royal commissioner ruling in Edom as a vassal of Judah (cf. 1 Kings 22. 47), set out to attack Mesha.[53] They chose the "way of Edom" (2 Kings 3. 20), i.e. the road descending from Arad to the southern end of the Dead Sea (cf. *supra,* p. 58), apparently in order to by-pass the strong forts that Mesha had built on the northern border of his kingdom. The important road that went up from Zoar to Moab is called "the road to Horonaim" (Isa. 15. 5) or "the descent of Horonaim" (Jer. 48. 5); therefore, it is possible to assume that the Israelite campaign was carried out along this route and that the concluding passage of the Mesha Stele is concerned with this event. According to the biblical account the Israelites succeeded at first against the Moabite forces, thus conquering many towns, but the siege of Kir-hareseth (Kir of Moab, Isa. 15. 1; el-Kerak) failed, and as usual in such cases, the retreat apparently became a rout.

The boastful words of Mesha were not without foundation, for not only did Moab throw off the Israelite yoke but henceforth the entire Mishor became Moabite. In the prophecies of Isaiah (15–16) and Jeremiah (48) reference is made to many of the towns that appear in the Mesha Stele as belonging to Moab. Even Heshbon, Elealeh, Sibmah and Jaazer belonged to Moab according to these prophecies, which shows that its kingdom had expanded even farther to the north, thus exceeding the bounds of Mesha's expansion by imposing its rule on southern Gilead.

A short time after Mesha's revolt Edom also fell away from Judah. Jehoram, King of Judah, tried to quell this rebellion without success. The battle with Edom took place in the vicinity of Zoar (eṣ-Ṣafi) south of the Dead Sea, the district through which the kings of Judah and Israel had marched, accompanied by Edomite forces, when they went up to fight against Moab (2 Kings 8. 20–22; 2 Chron. 21. 8–10). The revolt of Libnah, which also gained its independence from Judah, is mentioned incidentally in this passage. Evidently there were changes to Judah's disadvantage on the border with Philistia at this time.

VII. THE HOUSE OF JEHU AND THE LAST DAYS OF THE ISRAELITE KINGDOM

The rise of the House of Jehu in Israel put an end to the foreign policies of Omri and Ahab. Israel's relations with Tyre and Judah were worsened after the murder of Jezebel and Ahaziah; the balance of strength between Israel and Damascus gradually inclined in favour of the latter. Hazael had come into power at Damascus some time before, and he was able to hold his own against the Assyrian attacks. Shalmaneser boasts in his inscriptions that in his eighteenth year (841 B.C.)

he besieged Damascus and destroyed the gardens around it, but he did not conquer the city itself.[54]

In the course of this expedition the Assyrian army passed through Israelite territory for the first time. From Damascus Shalmaneser continued southward as far as Mount Hauran, destroying towns without number. This is probably a reference to the Aramean sectors in northern Transjordan, the many towns of Bashan. This campaign is evidently that referred to by Hosea: "as Shalman destroyed Beth-arbel on the day of battle" (Hos. 10. 14). From here Shalmaneser marched to a mountain by the name of Ba' li-ra' si on the seacoast; there he set up a royal stele and received the tribute of Tyre and Israel. It is usually assumed that this is a reference to Nahr el-Kalb, the Lykos of Hellenistic sources, about six miles north of Beirut, because several Egyptian and Assyrian victory inscriptions have been found there. However, it is difficult to imagine that the Assyrian army would have reached the Phoenician coast from Bashan via any other route except the Valley of Jezreel. Therefore, scholars have long since conjectured that Ba' li-ra' si was actually the Carmel headland.[55] This supposition has received confirmation from another edition of the annals discovered not long ago which contains additional details on the campaign with which we are concerned.[56]

> I went to Mount Ba' li-ra' -si which is by (over against) the sea and by (over against) the land of Tyre. I set up my royal image therein. I received the tribute of Ba' li-ma-AN-zer, the Tyrian, and of Jehu the son of Omri. On my way back I went up to Mount Lebanon, and I set up my royal image beside the image of Tiglath-pileser, the great king, my predecessor.

This description leaves no doubt that Ba' li-ra' si is Mount Carmel, designated here as "Baal of the headland", which was on the border between Israel and Tyre at this time.[57] From here Shalmaneser turned and followed the line of the Phoenician coast to the mouth of Nahr el-Kalb in the Lebanon region where he had another relief inscribed. On the way to Mount Carmel he passed through Israelite territory; to this campaign one may assign the destruction of level VIII at Hazor. There he received the tribute of Tyre and Israel, referring to the King of Israel as "Jehu the son of Omri" after the dynasty that had been in power when he first encountered the kingdom of Israel.[58]

Throughout the rest of Shalmaneser III's and Shamshi-Adad V's reigns Asshur was preoccupied with other affairs; for nearly forty years Assyrian pressure on Syria and Palestine was relaxed. In the unavoidable contest between Aram and Israel that ensued, it was the Arameans who held the upper hand. In the latter part of Jehu's reign and that of his son Jehoahaz, Israel suffered an unprecedented decline, its territory actually being reduced to the confines of Mount Ephraim. At the time of Jehu's revolt the kings of Israel and Judah had still been fighting with the Arameans in the Ramoth-gilead region, and Ramoth-gilead itself was apparently in Israelite hands (2 Kings 8. 28 ff.). In the days of Jehu "the Lord began to cut off parts of Israel. Hazael defeated them throughout the territory of Israel: from the Jordan eastward, all the land of Gilead, the Gadites, and the Reubenites, and the Manassites, from Aroer, which is by the Valley of Arnon, that is, Gilead and Bashan" (2 Kings 10. 32–3; cf. Amos. 1. 3). Therefore, Hazael had gained control over all of Israelite Transjordan; in his desire to control the King's Highway and the commerce with South Arabia he probably asserted his authority over Moab and Edom as well. This may be inferred from the inscription of Adad-nirari concerning his campaign in Syria and Palestine in which he refers to tribute from Israel (the House of Omri!), Edom and Damascus.[59] Evidently these three principalities were all controlled by the ruling dynasty at Damascus and were required to pay tribute along with their masters. During his own campaign of 815–14 Hazael went as far as Gath (Gath of the Philistines or Gath-Gittaim?)[60] and was only dissuaded from invading Judah by the heavy tribute he received from Jehoash, its king (2 Kings 12. 17–18). Level VII at Hazor was evidently destroyed at this time; most of Galilee and the important valleys were taken over by the Arameans. According to an addition of the LXX to 2 Kings 13. 22, Hazael took all of Philistia from the sea to Aphek. Aram-Damascus had now reached the apogee of its greatness, while the kingdoms of Israel and Judah were reduced to small dependencies. The Israelite chariotry was limited to fifty horsemen and ten chariots (2 Kings 13. 7).

At the end of the ninth century Israel and Judah were liberated from the Aramean yoke by the revival of Assyria which renewed its heavy pressure upon Damascus: "The Lord gave Israel a saviour so that they escaped from the hand of the Arameans; and the people of Israel dwelt in their homes as formerly" (2 Kings 13. 5). This saviour came to Israel in the form of Adad-nirari III, King of Assyria, who renewed the expansionist policies of Shalmaneser III. In 806 B.C. he took stern disciplinary action against Damascus, breaking its power and levying a heavy tribute on it.[61] Though tribute was also required of Israel, Edom and Philistia,[62] at least those kingdoms gained some relief from the heavy Syrian yoke. They were fortunate that Adad-nirari's invasions ceased for a while at least until the last days of his reign.

A chronological synchronization is now provided by the appearance of ^{I}*Ia-<ú>-'a-su* ^{kur}*Sa-me-ri-na-a,* "Joash the Samarian," in a recently discovered stele from Tell Rimah in Northern Mesopotamia. Joash is mentioned there as rendering tribute to Adad-nirari III.[63] It would appear that this is an allusion to the events in 796 rather than in

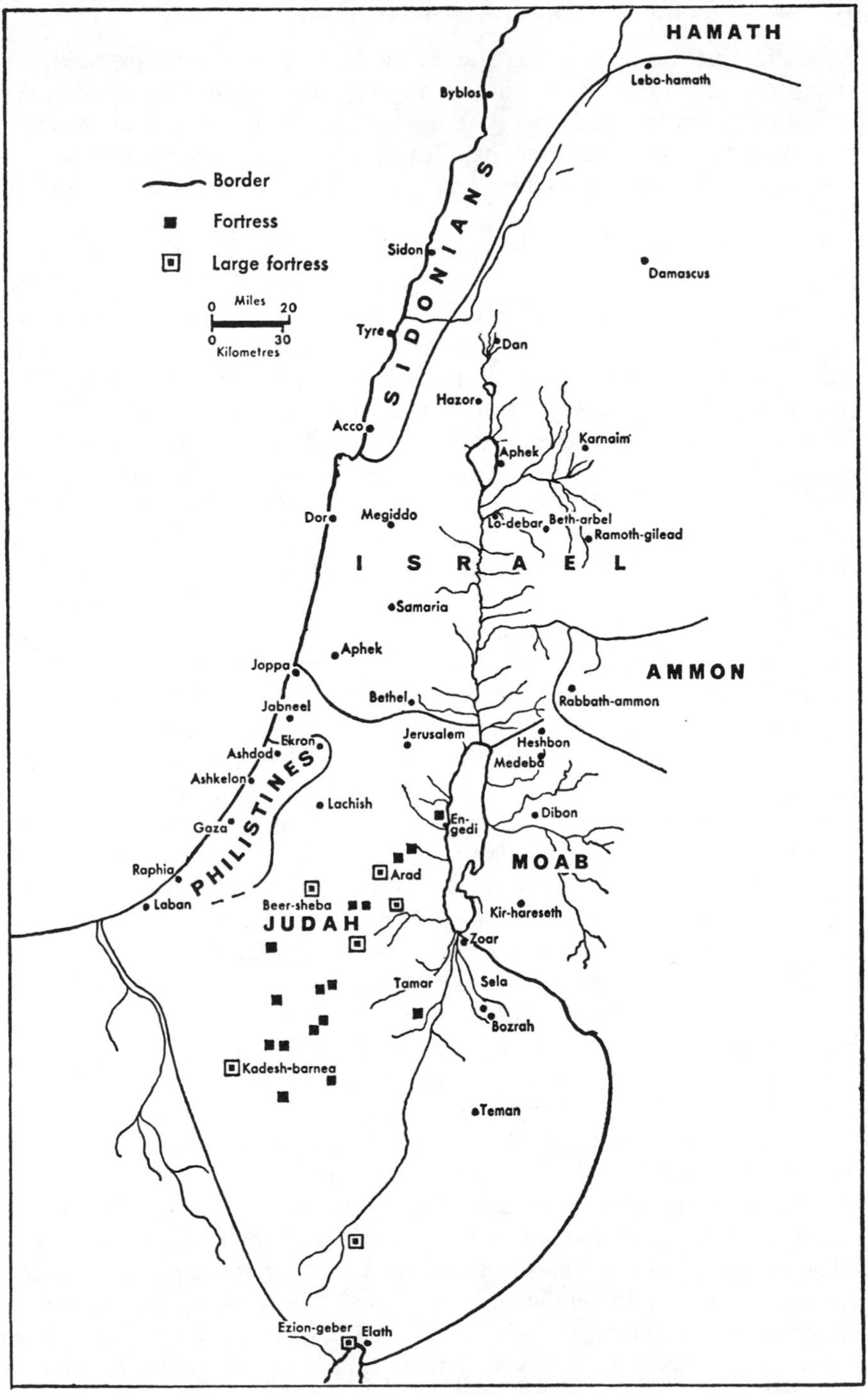

Map 27. Israel and Judah in the days of Jeroboam II and Uzziah.

806/5. During the reign of his successor Assyria was again preoccupied with internal affairs and the fierce struggle against her northern neighbour Urartu. This was the last breathing spell that Assyria permitted to the kingdoms of Syria and Palestine; during the first half of the eighth century B.C. Israel and Judah enjoyed their last period of greatness.

The diminishing strength of Damascus disintegrated completely in its desperate struggle against its northern neighbour, Hamath, as we learn from the inscription of Zakir, King of Hamath.[64] Joash son of Jehoahaz, King of Israel, took advantage of this opportunity to throw off the Aramean yoke: "Then Jehoash the son of Jehoahaz took again from Ben-hadad the son of Hazael the cities which he had taken from Jehoahaz his father in war. Three times Joash defeated him and recovered the cities of Israel" (2 Kings 13. 25). Again the decisive battle was fought beside Aphek (2 Kings 13. 17), which apparently resulted in the destruction of level II in the tell at 'En Gev.[65] In his days and those of his son Jeroboam II the power of Aram-Damascus was broken, and even though we lack details about the various battles, it is clear from the text that during Jeroboam's reign the borders of the Israelite kingdom were extended northward and eastward until they included almost the same territories as under David. Amos alludes to two decisive Israelite victories in northern Transjordan, the first at Lo-debar (Umm ed-Dabar ?), and the second at Karnaim which had inherited the place of Ashtaroth as capital of Bashan (Amos 6. 13). Jeroboam "restored the border of Israel from Lebo-hamath as far as the Sea of the Arabah" (2 Kings 14. 25),[66] i.e. he controlled the region formerly belonging to Aram-Damascus from Lebo (Lebweh) in the Lebanese Beqa' on the border of the kingdom of Hamath to the Dead Sea region in the south. His authority was also imposed upon Damascus itself (2 Kings 14. 28); and if the Wadi Arabah is identical with the "Brook of the Willows" ('^{a}*rābîm;* Isa. 15. 7), then he probably had subjugated Moab as well. This would mean that he dominated the entire length of the King's Highway in Transjordan, from the border of Edom to that of Hamath (cf. map 27).

Judah also availed itself of this opportunity to extend the limits of its power southward and westward once more. Amaziah, King of Judah, smote the Edomites in the Valley of Salt, the perennial battlefield south of the Dead Sea, and gained control over Sela and northern Edom (2 Kings 14. 7). These conquests were evidently achieved by the help of the King of Israel, probably with the aim of dominating the southern portion of the King's Highway. However, this joint effort ended in a sharp disagreement between Judah and Israel (2 Kings 14. 7–14; 2 Chron. 25. 5–24). Amaziah, King of Judah, and Joash, King of Isrrael, clashed at Beth-shemesh in Judah. After a decisive victory for Israel, Beth-shemesh was captured, and Amaziah was taken prisoner; the Israelite army went up against the now-defenceless Jerusalem, plundered it and broke down part of its walls.

The defeat carried with it no serious or long-lasting consequences for Judah. Uzziah (Azariah) the son of Amaziah continued his father's policy with great success and extended the Judean borders to their greatest limits. We do not know to what extent he capitalized on the conquest of Edom by Amaziah but he did rebuild Elath as a fortified harbour town and way-station on the important trade route to South Arabia (2 Kings 14. 22; 2 Chron. 26. 2). This is doubtless a reference to the refortification of Ezion-geber (Tell el-Kheleifeh) near Elath; in the excavations there a seal was found bearing the inscription "(belonging) to Jotham", perhaps Jotham the son of Uzziah, who ruled as co-regent with his father during the latter's illness (2 Kings 15. 5; 2 Chron. 26. 21).[67] Uzziah reduced the extent of Philistine territory to an unprecedented degree, conquering Gath,[68] Jabneh and Ashdod. Besides building towns in those areas, he also smote the Arabs and the Meunites[69] in the south (2 Chron. 26. 6–7). The great expansion into the Negeb regions was accompanied by the erection of many forts and settlements and the development of agriculture even in semi-arid regions. Development of frontier areas, the Negeb, the desert and the caravan routes passing through them apparently reached new heights never before achieved (2 Chron. 26. 10; cf. map 27). Evidently this period was marked by the construction on the borders and at the main highway junctions of large forts surrounded by a casemate wall and defended by eight towers, one on each corner and at the mid-way point on each side. Thus far forts of this type have been discovered at Kadesh-barnea [70] (at the border of the Negeb on the "way of Shur"), at Tell 'Arad, at Khirbet Ghazzeh[71] five miles south-east of Tell 'Arad (near the starting point of the "way of Edom"), and on the road between Azekah and Tell el-Judeideh.[72] The pottery found at these forts indicates that they were not founded before the eighth century; the fortress atop the tell of Azekah was probably also built at about this time.[73] Furthermore, it may be that the northern portion of the Judean wilderness saw the founding of certain settlements in this period, as shown by the presence of a few *lmlk* jar handles in recent excavations in the *Buqei'ah* valley.[74] At the same time, Uzziah increased the Judean military forces and strengthened the fortifications of Jerusalem (2 Chron. 26. 11–15).

It seems most likely that good relations between Israel and Judah were restored during the reigns of Jeroboam II and Uzziah. The two sister kingdoms were the strongest powers in Palestine and Syria during that period, and together they ruled an area about as great as the kingdom of David. Uzziah's varied activities strengthened Judah and raised it in the second half of his long reign (fifty-two years) to its greatest level of power. Although Uzziah succumbed to leprosy in the middle of his reign (probably in his twenty-ninth year, *c*. 758 B.C.) and was forced to dwell in a "separate house", he evidently continued to hold the reins of power through the entire co-regency of his son Jotham (*c*. 758–42) and even during

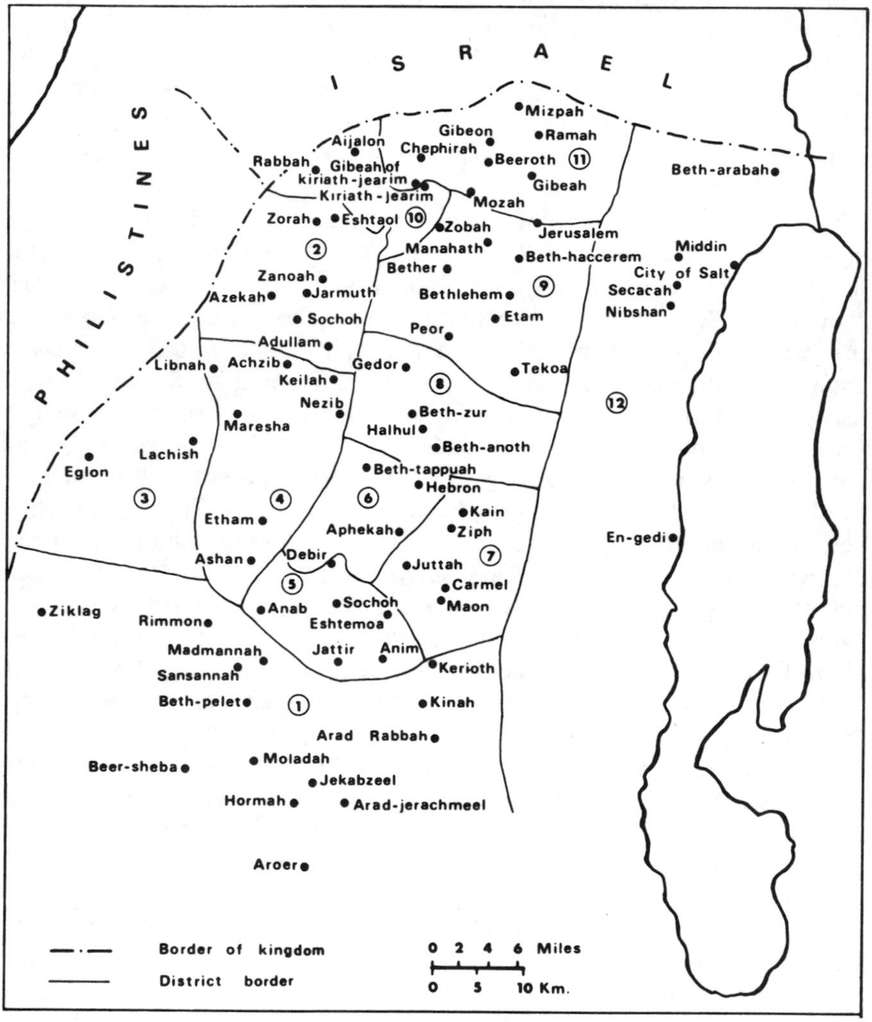

Map 28. The Districts of Judah.

the first years of his grandson Ahaz's reign (until *c.* 735).

After the death of Jeroboam II and the murder of his son Zechariah (*c.* 748), the kingdom of Israel saw a sharp decline during the reigns of the various kings who competed in replacing one another in the short period that followed.[75] This is perhaps the period when Judah succeeded in gaining control over part of the Israelite-dominated territory in Transjordan as indicated by Jotham's victory over the Ammonites and the heavy tribute which they paid to him for three years (2 Chron. 27. 5). On the other hand, the assumption that Uzziah's preeminence is also demonstrated by his leading a coalition of western states in taking a stand against Tiglath-pileser III in 738 B.C. has now been refuted.[76]

VIII. THE DISTRICTS OF JUDAH

Today there is practically no disagreement with the original suggestion of Alt[77] that the town list used by the editor of Joshua to represent the patrimony of Judah in Josh. 15. 21-62 is based on an administrative document in force during the Judean monarchy. Present controversies are usually limited to details concerning the make-up of the various districts and the date of the roster as a whole.

The list is divided by appropriate subtitles into sections corresponding to the four standard geographical divisions of Judah: the Negeb (one district), the Shephelah (three districts), the hill country (seven districts including Benjamin) and the wilderness (one district).[78] A numerical summary is appended to each group of towns. There are ten such groups in the Hebrew text, but the LXX preserves the 11th (vs. 59b) which had been lost from MT. Bethlehem was included in this latter district. By adding the Benjaminite towns that belong to the kingdom of Judah, we obtain a list of districts totalling twelve, the traditional number of tribal and administrative organization as reflected in the Solomonic districts (1 Kings 4. 7). Therefore, the structure of this roster leaves no doubt that the origin of the original document is in the district division of the Judean kingdom.

Opinions are divided mainly with regard to the general composition of the list, which determines the extent of Judah during its own period and thereby its date. Alt's basic assumption was that all the town lists preserved in the description of the southern tribes were taken from one original document which he differentiated from a second list of Galilean towns. In the descriptions of Ephraim and Manasseh no city rosters are preserved and Alt assumed that no list from the central part of the country was available to the editors of Joshua. He therefore concluded that the cities of Dan and Benjamin belonged to the southern document. For the northern towns he made the dubious suggestion that they derived from a document of the Assyrian province of Megiddo.

As another proof of his view that the Danite and Benajminite lists must be combined with the southern document Alt pointed to the double appearance of some towns: Eshtaol and Zorah in the northern Shephelah district of Judah (Josh. 15. 33) and in the Danite city list (Josh. 19. 41), Kiriath-jearim in the northern hill country district (Josh. 15. 60) and in one of the Benjaminite districts (Josh. 18. 27 LXX), and Beth-arabah in the Judean wilderness (Josh. 15. 61) and in the other Benjaminite group (Josh. 18. 22). In Alt's opinion the editor behaved in a careless manner when he divided the towns between the tribal territories by leaving some settlements in more than one tribe. The double names also serve him as a guideline for the original composition of the respective districts but not in a consistent manner. He combined the two Benjaminite districts with the relevant Judean districts, the wilderness because of Beth-arabah and the northern hill district because of Kiriath-jearim. On the other hand, he left the cities of Dan as a special district, a fourth division of the Shephelah, and this in spite of the double appearance of Eshtaol and Zorah. The reason for this inconsistent method is obvious. Alt saw the need to reach a total of twelve districts so he achieved that number by the addition of Dan. He justified its assumed position at the northern flank of the Shephelah by reference to Josh. 15. 45–47 which appears in the chapter between the Shephelah and the Hill Country districts: "Ekron, with its towns and its villages; from Ekron to the sea, all that were by the side of Ashdod, with their villages. Ashdod, its towns and its villages; Gaza, its towns and its villages; to the Brook of Egypt, and the Great Sea with its coast-line." But this is only a continuation of Alt's inconsistency; this section differs from the regular town lists in form, e.g. it includes an expansive geographic description but lacks the usual subtotals. Furthermore, the inclusion of Ekron, Ashdod and Gaza in a district list of Judah is unrealistic. Without going into the question of its origin, one may say with certainty that this passage does not represent a part of the original administrative roster under discussion.

On the basis of the list's general composition Alt fixed its date in the reign of Josiah. Only in the days of that king did Judah expand to the west and north. It is true that Josiah ruled a much larger area, but the Judean topographical list in Josh. 15 seems to be dealing with the traditional, internal territory of Judah. There are good reasons to assume that Bethel and its surrounding hill region was added by Josiah to the integral body of Judean territory. This was an old ambition of Judean kings and truly, in the post-exilic period that same district belonged not to Samaria but to the Yehud Province (Ezra 2. 28; Neh. 7. 32). With regard to the northern part of Philistia, we have proof today that it was annexed by Josiah, viz. the Hebrew ostracon from Meẕad Ḥashavyahu between Jabneh and Ashdod on the shore, a text which reflects Judean rule in the area during the late seventh century B.C.[79]

Alt's interpretation gave the impression of being well founded and was accepted almost universally. However, it suffers from several weaknesses which led Alt into some inconsistences in method and in his conclusions. His assumption about the alleged carelessness of the original editor of Joshua is most unconvincing. The appearance of identifical towns in different lists must be taken as an indication of diverse origin and not *vice versa.* Even in this matter Alt shows his inconsistency by using the presence of double names in different ways to suit his purposes.

Moreover, his basic assumption that there were only two original documents, a Galilean and a southern, lacks conviction. All of the city lists of the northern tribes fit very well into the framework of the Solomonic districts, including the cities of Dan and of northern Benjamin. That document must have been at the disposal of the editor from the royal archives in Jerusalem; for the cities of Judah he was able to rely on a more up-to-date list. There remains, of course, the question of the absence of the cities of Ephraim and Manasseh. Though we do not always understand the editor's method in selecting his materials, a plausible explanation may be suggested for this instance. Since the division of the kingdom, the antagonism had grown between Jerusalem and Samaria and the Judean editor had little interest in the latter. His attitude also shows up in his description of the tribal boundaries. He has given us only the border description between Ephraim and Manasseh while the rest of Manasseh's borders are missing. Rather than falling prey to complex theorizing, it would seem the simplest course to assume that the Ephraimite and Manassite towns have been omitted through the editor's selectivity. All of the town lists at our disposal, including that of Simeon, most probably derive from two major documents, the Solomonic districts and the administrative division of Judah.

Cross and Wright were the first to criticize the hypothesis of Alt. Their main objection was that there is no valid reason to add the Danite list to that of Judah.[80] However, they were unable to offer a better suggestion and fell back on the assumption that the Danite text was purely a literary composition, a view that lacks all justification. But since they adhered to Alt's basic method, they were deprived of Dan's district for completing the twelve districts assumed for Judah. At this point they erred with the same inconsistency as Alt; they combined the southern Benjaminite district with the Kiriath-jearim district of Judah on the grounds that two towns were insufficient to comprise an independent district. Then they left the northern Benjaminite district intact as the twelfth of Judah, and this in spite of the double appearance of Beth-arabah. Such a district contradicts the general tenor of the document by combining the Jericho region with the hill country of Bethel.

Such an hypothesis creates an even greater difficulty. The borders of

Judah thus posited would include the hill country of Bethel but exclude the northern Shephelah. There is only one short interval when such a border would have been in effect, viz. the brief reign of Abijah after his conquests (2 Chron. 13. 19) and the early days of Asa. Cross and Wright do not suggest such a date for the list; they maintain that the same geographical situation endured until the reign of Jehoshaphat to whom an administrative division is attributed: "he placed forces in all the fortified cities of Judah and set garrisons (better: commissioners) in the land of Judah, and in the cities of Ephraim which Asa his father had taken" (2 Chron. 17. 2). They hold that these cities of Ephraim are from the conquests of Abijah, ignoring the well known events that occurred in between. Not only did Baasha recapture the hill country of Bethel, he advanced the border of Benjamin south to Ramah. Only with the help of a diversionary attack by Ben-hadad did Asa manage to repulse Baasha's thrust and to recapture part of Benjamin up to Mizpah and Geba (1 Kings 15. 17–22). These are the towns which Asa took and it is obvious that the Bethel region was not part of Judah during the reign of Jehoshaphat (cf. Amos 7. 10 ff.).[81]

At least in this point Kallai is more consistent in relating the Benjaminite town lists to the reign of Abijah, assuming also that another, third group of Benjaminite towns is missing.[82] The towns of Judah, on the other hand, are attributed by him to the reign of Hezekiah because of the absence of Beth-shemesh that had been captured by the Philistines in the reign of Ahaz (2 Chron. 28. 18). But two of the towns taken at that time also appear in the Judean roster, viz. Socoh and Gederoth (Josh. 15. 35, 41). Under Hezekiah the geopolitical situation changed radically; given the heavy pressure that he exerted on Ekron, it is impossible to assume that Beth-shemesh had remained in Philistine hands. But Kallai's hypothesis suffers from an even more basic weakness. When he separates the town lists of Benjamin from those of Judah, he is left with two (in his opinion three) of Benjamin and eleven of Judah and he is without an explanation of their origin. The fundamental assumption of Alt that the city lists derive from the provincial division has not been refuted and any new suggestion must take it into account.

One should be consistent. The double appearance of cities in different lists must be taken as evidence that they derive from divergent sources. Thus those with duplicate towns cannot belong to the Judean roster. That holds true for the tribal list of Dan and of northern Benjamin. It also seems very unlikely that the correspondence between the division of Benjamin into two groups and the border that separated Judah and Israel throughout most of the monarchial period can be coincidental.

However, the double mention of Kiriath-jearim may be only apparent. "Kiriath-baal (that is Kiriath-jearim)" (Josh 15. 60) appears among the towns of Judah in contrast to "Gibeath (the hill of) Kiriath-<je>arim"

(Josh. 18. 28). The difference is hardly incidental. Gibeah ("the Hill") at Kiriath-jearim is known to us from the narratives about the return of the Ark (1 Sam. 7. 1; 2 Sam. 6. 3–4). That Gibeah was evidently near Kiriath-jearim, "a city belonging to the tribe of Judah" (Josh. 18. 14), and it is mentioned among the towns of Benjamin. This means that there is not really a duplication of names between Benjamin and Judah with regard to Kirath-jearim. But that does not preclude the possibility that the two groups of names could be combined into one district though there is no real evidence for it. The two districts are very different in size and there were various divisive historical factors. It is also not necessary to assume that the Kiriath-jearim district had only two towns.[83] There is also the possibility that other towns have been dropped accidentally (as in a neighbouring verse, Josh. 15. 59) or intentionally by the editor. As we shall see, this district did include some additional cities known to us from this region, such as Aijalon.

A roster obtained by taking the eleven districts of Judah plus the southern district of Benjamin gives a geographical result that matches the known borders of the Judean kingdom in most periods. There is, therefore, no internal evidence in the document's composition to aid in fixing its date.

For dating the text one has to rely on archaeological data and historical considerations pertaining to particular cities. Unfortunately, the available information is quite meagre and has to do with only two towns: Beth-haccerem and Beth-shemesh. Cross and Wright also tried to utilize the archaeological researches in the Buqei ʻah of the Judean Desert by identifying some of the discovered sites with towns in the Wilderness District.[84] But not only are their identifications of doubtful value, their ninth century dating is highly questionable and an eighth century date is equally possible. Mazar has suggested a date for the Judean topographical list in the reign of Josiah because of the results of his excavations at Tell el-Jurn (Tel Goren) in En-gedi where the Iron Age settlement starts in the seventh century B.C.[85] However, such a late date is only relevant for Tell el-Jurn; the burials in the En-gedi vicinity show quite clearly that there was an earlier Iron Age settlement at the En-gedi oasis.

The identification of Beth-haccerem with Kh. Ṣaliḥ at Ramat Rahel has been made very probable as a result of the archaeological excavations.[86] Beth-haccerem appears as Karem in the Bethlehem district of Judah as preserved in the LXX of Josh. 15. 59b. The earliest ceramic evidence discovered there (in the light of the stratigraphical excavations at Arad)[87] comes from the eighth century B.C. Thus, the inclusion in the Judean town list of a place founded in the eighth century may furnish a *terminus a quo* for its date.

At Beth-shemesh three strata have been distinguished during the monarchial period (IIa, IIb and IIc) extending over the tenth to the eighth centuries. There is no basis for the assumption that a substantial gap existed between Strata IIa and IIb.[88] The ninth century is represented in the pottery no less than the others; the three strata belong roughly to the tenth, ninth and eighth centuries. From a purely archaeological point of view there is no explanation for the absence of Beth-shemesh from the Judean town list until the end of the eighth century.

A historical consideration may be of some assistance here. We know about a major event pertaining to Beth-shemesh, viz. the clash between Joash and Amaziah that took place near the city (2 Kings 14. 11–13). Amaziah was captured and Joash came up to Jerusalem and destroyed part of its walls. It would be contrary to the general rule if Beth-shemesh was not looted and burned at the same time (if for no other reason, to reward the victorious troops). Stratum IIb is the last fortified city and Stratum IIc is only an unfortified village, evidently constructed some time after the last destruction. If there was really a gap in habitation at Beth-shemesh, Amaziah's short reign and the early days of Uzziah would be the most plausible time for it. This would suggest a date commensurate with that indicated by the founding of Beth-haccerem.

Uzziah was one of the activist rulers who reorganized the kingdom and the army (2 Chron. 26. 11–14) and the suggestion that the Judean topographical document derives from his rejuvenated administration is quite plausible. This does not mean that the original provincial division of Judah was carried out during his reign. There is no reason to doubt that Jehoshaphat had appointed commissioners throughout the country (2 Chron. 17. 2).[89] This was evidently done after the stabilization of relations between Judah and Israel with the concomitant acceptance of the Davidic dynasty's limitation to Judah only (cf. 1 Kings 22. 44). It must have been necessary from time to time to bring the district list up to date with the foundation or abandonment of towns, especially during the reigns of dynamic rulers like Uzziah. The editor of Joshua used the most up-to-date roster available to him. As we shall see further on, this system was cancelled during the reign of Hezekiah, who streamlined the network into four districts; this in itself required the conclusion that the system of twelve units was earlier.

The list may be analysed according to its districts as follows (we have designated most of them by the name of the conjectured capital of each district, which does not always come at the head of the towns in its group, cf. map 28).

The Negeb

1. The Negeb district: there is only one district for the Negeb, but it includes thirty towns.[90] This large administrative unit took in the various

regions of the Negeb that were still designated during David's reign by the clans that occupied them, e.g. the Negeb of Judah, the Negeb of Caleb, the Negeb of the Jerahmeelite and the Negeb of the Kenite (cf. *supra,* p. 328). The towns in this administrative district were dispersed over an area between Ziklag (Tell esh-Shari 'ah) on the west to Arad (instead of Eder) in the east, and Aroer (Adadah) about 10½ miles south-east of Beer-sheba. It is doubtful that Kedesh (Josh. 15. 23) could be Kadesh-barnea, because this list does not seem to include the network of southern forts and stockades. The capital of this extensive district was evidently Beer-sheba. However, its largest, most impressive fortified city was located in the centre of the alluvial basin comprising the eastern portion of the Negeb at Kh. Gharrah (Tel ' Ira), which exceeds all its neighbouring settlements in size and strength; it probably inherited the name of neighbouring Hormah.[91] In the north the Negeb district extended up to the slopes of the Judean hill country; here we can identify Madmannah (Kh. Tatrit),[92] Sansannah (Kh. esh-Shamsaniyat).

The Shephelah

2. The Socoh district: this, the northernmost district of the Shephelah, included thirteen to fifteen towns and extended from the Sorek Valley to just south of the Valley of Elah. We have chosen Socoh as its hypothetical capital because it is located in the middle (Azekah, for instance, is close to the border with Philistia). Socoh's special role in the administration is clearly seen from the royal seal impressions dating to the period of Hezekiah (cf. *infra,* p. 394). The Socoh district extended northwards to Zorah and Eshtaol. In addition to them, one may identify the following towns: Zanoah (Kh. Zanu'), Jarmuth (Kh. el-Yarmuk), Adullam (esh-Sheikh Madhkur beside Kh. ' Id el-Ma) and Azekah (Tell Zakariyeh).

3. The Lachish district: the southern Shephelah, which was broader, was divided into two parallel districts. The Lachish district is the westernmost, on the Philistine border. Of its sixteen towns it is possible to identify only Lachish (Tell ed-Duweir) and Eglon (Tell el-Ḥesi), which must have been very close to the western border. In the south this district bordered on the Negeb, but its northern boundary depends upon the area determined for district four.

4. The Mareshah district: this district, which included nine towns, lay in the eastern Shephelah between Nezib (Khirbet Beit Neṣib) and Keilah (Khirbet Qila) in the east to Mareshah (Tell Ṣandaḥannah) in the south-west. The location of Libnah (Tell Bornaṭ ?) determines its western boundary. The fourth district includes two towns that are also mentioned among the settlements of Simeon, viz. Ether and Ashan (Josh. 15. 42; cf. Josh. 19. 7). As we saw there are reasons for locating these sites on the edge of the south-eastern Shephelah in the valley which extends from Tell el-Khuweilfeh (En-Rimmon) towards Tell

'Aiṭun (Etam). As previously stated, the appearance of Ashan in the Simeonite enclave and also among the Levitical cities suggests that it should be identified with Tell Beit Mirsim, which was rebuilt and fortified in the tenth century. That furnishes us with the south-eastern border of this district which is contiguous to the Negeb between Tell Beit Mirsim and Tell el-Khuweilfeh.

The Hill Country

5. The Eshtemoa district: this is the first and also the southernmost district in the hill country; it included eleven towns. The extent of this district, which had up to now been distorted by the erroneous identification of Debir with Tell Beit Mirsim, has now been clarified by Debir's very plausible identification with Kh. Rabud, about 7½ miles SW of Hebron. Tell Beit Mirsim is not located in the hill country and its inclusion in the Eshtemoa district violated the geographical principle on which the entire list is based. All identified sites in the "trough" separating the hill country from the Shephelah (Adullam, Keilah, Nezib) belong to the latter and never to the hill districts. All the data indicate that Debir was an important Canaanite and Israelite city in the hill country south of Hebron. Albright had also looked for it here but failed to find the proper site; this led him to seek Debir at a suitable tell with the proper archaeological features for such a city. Most European scholars never accepted his identification with Tell Beit Mirsim because that site is not in the hills; they remained faithful to the biblical evidence.

The long sought after site has now been found at Kh. Rabud, a large tell of *c.* 15 acres with the remains of fortified cities from the Late Bronze and Iron Ages. Its location among the towns already identified in the same southern hill country district makes its equation with Debir most plausible.[93] Among the remaining cities in this district it is possible to identify Jattir (Kh. 'Attir), Socoh (Kh. Shuweikeh), Anab (Kh. 'Unnab eṣ-Ṣaghir)[94] and Anim (Kh. Ghuwein). In the immediate vicinity there are two sites called Kh. Guwein et-Taḥta and Kh. Guwein el-Foqa. Iron Age pottery was found at both. Now it has become clear from one of the Arad Ostraca (No. 25) that both neighbouring settlements were in existence and bore the names Lower Anim (*'nm tḥtnm*) and Upper Anim (*'nm 'lynm*). Evidently, they are both to be subsumed under the name Anim in our list.

6. The Hebron district: its chief city, Hebron, was the former capital of Judah. The district contained nine towns, including Beth-Tappuah (Taffuḥ) and Dumah (Khirbet Domeh ed-Deir).

7. The Ziph district: the ten towns of this district were concentrated in an area just east of Hebron bordering on the wilderness of Judah. The following identifications are possible: Maon (Khirbet Ma'in), Carmel (Khirbet el-Kirmil), Juttah (Yaṭṭa) and perhaps Kain (en-Nebi Yaqin).

One may assume that the capital was Ziph (Tell Zif), which was one of Rehoboam's fortresses. Its appearance on the royal seal impressions shows that it ranked with Hebron and Socoh as an administrative centre.

8. The Beth-zur district: this district lay north of the first two, and of its six towns these are identifiable: Halhul (Ḥalḥul), Gedor (Khirbet Jedur) and Beth-anoth (Khirbet Beit ʿAnun)—all of them in the vicinity of Beth-zur (Khirbet eṭ-Ṭubeiqeh).

9. The Bethlehem district: only LXX preserves this district (Josh. 15 59a). The passage reads:

> Tekoa (**Θεκω**) and Ephrathah which is Bethlehem (***Εφραθα, αὕτη ἐστὶν Βηθλεεμ***) and Peor (*Φαγωρ*), and Etam (*Αιταμ*), and Koulon (?, *Κουλον*), and Tatam (?, *Ταταμ*), and Zobah (? B—*Σωρης*, or A—*Εωβης*), and Karem (***Καρεμ***), and Gallim (*Γαλλιμ*), and Bether (*Βαιθηρ*), and Manahath (***Μανοχω***): 11 cities with their villages.

Therefore, this district was located between Beth-zur and Jerusalem in the territory around Bethlehem. The following towns may be identified: Tekoa (Khirbet Tequʿ), Peor (Khirbet Faghur), Etam (Khirbet el-Khokh), Bether (Khirbet el-Yehud) and Manahath (el-Malḥah). If Zobah is the correct reading, assuming that Σωβης was the original Greek text, then this may be a reference to the birthplace of one of David's heroes (2 Sam. 23. 36), which can be equated with modern Ṣuba. Karem (Beth-haccerem) is apparently the tell at Ramat Raḥel.

10. The Kiriath-jearim district: here the list only includes two towns, "Kiriath-baal (that is, Kiriath-jearim), and Rabbah". Since this district extended north of Zorah and Eshtaol and may have included the Aijalon Valley beside which we have found a site (Kh. Ḥamideh) that we propose to identify with Rabbah/Rubute,[95] it would seem likely that it included some other towns such as Aijalon and Gamzu. The former was fortified by Rehoboam (2 Chron. 11. 10) and both of them are said to have belonged to Ahaz (2 Chron. 28. 18).

This would mean that the district, listed among the hill country districts, was partly in the Shephelah. Thus interpreted, the district would violate the geographic principle upon which the entire list is founded.[96] However, given the identifications of Kiriath-baal (Kiriath-jearim) and Rabbah, this conclusion is inescapable. The factor at work seems to be the organization of the approaches to Jerusalem into one district, as in the division of the Solomonic districts. These approaches were always of major importance from the military, political and economic standpoint.

11. The Benjamin district: by this we mean the southern group of Benjaminite cities preserved in Joshua 18. 25–8 which included about fourteen towns. One may suggest the following as the original text:

"The Jebusite (that is, Jerusalem), and Gibeah . . . and Gibeath-kiriath-jearim, fourteen cities with their villages" (Josh. 18. 28). Kallai has noted the absence of some eastern Benjaminite towns but there is no reason to assume that a third group is missing. The subtotal points to some defect in the list, however, perhaps due to haplography between Gibeah and Gibeath. The district took in most of the important towns of Benjamin, e.g. Gibeon (el-Jib), Ramah (er-Ram), Beeroth (Kh. el-Burj beside Nebi Samwil and Kh. el-Biyar), Mizpeh (Tell en-Naṣbeh), Chephirah (Tell Kefireh), Mozah (Qalunyah?), and the Gibeah of Kiriath-jearim. According to the subtotal, there should be at least one more town in this group, e.g. Geba or Michmash (for Geba in Josh. 18. 24, cf. *infra,* p. 404).

12. The Wilderness district: the last six towns of the roster are included in this district, from Beth-arabah in the north to En-gedi in the south. The City of Salt could perhaps be identified with Kh. Qumran near the shore of the Dead Sea in view its mention in the Copper Scroll.[97] The identification of Middin, Secacah and Nibshan has been proposed with the three sites discovered in the Buqei'ah region, viz. Kh. Abu Ṭabaq, Kh. es-Samrah, Kh. el-Maqari.[98] However, some further candidates for these identifications have been found along the shore between 'Ain Feshkha and En-gedi.[99] Meanwhile, all the various suggestions to equate the towns in this district with any of the known antiquity sites in the region must remain doubtful. The very useful archaeological researches in the area have yet to produce any conclusive data for making geographical identifications. Therefore, the topographical logic of the entry for this district is still shrouded in mystery.

IX. THE SAMARIA OSTRACA

Important topographical information about Mount Ephraim in the days of the Jehu Dynasty is derived from a collection of unique inscriptions found in the excavations at Samaria—the Samaria Ostraca.[100] In a storehouse of the citadel at Samaria sixty-three ostraca were discovered bearing inscriptions concerning the dispatch of wine and oil. The texts include a date, place and clan name, personal names and sometimes the commodity—a jar[101] of old wine or fine oil.

The inscriptions fall into two categories according to their different formulations: one formula is used in texts dating to the years 9 and 10; the other to year 15.[102] We present here examples from the two collections:

The text on a few ostraca differs from this pattern. On Nos. 1 and 2 there are several personal names followed by numerals. No. 1 reads as follows:

In the tenth year. To Shamaryau from Poraim, a jar of old wine.

Pega (son of) Elisha	2
Uzza (son of) Kabesh (?)	1
Eliba	1
Baala (son of) Elisha	2
Yedayau	1.

Two ostraca from the tenth year (Nos. 3, 13) also contain references to clans (Shemida and Abiezer respectively), which normally are only found in texts from year 15. The information from all of these texts is arranged schematically in the following table (proper names are given in their biblical form if such exists; non-biblical names and those which differ slightly from known biblical forms are marked with an [*] and spelled in accordance with the generally accepted practice for biblical names in English, with the exception of *y* which has *not* been transcribed by *j*);

TABLE A

Ostraca No.	Date	Place	Recipient	Commodity
4–6	In the Ninth Year	from *Kozoh (מקצה)	to *Gaddiyau (לגדיו)	jar of old wine
9–10	In the Ninth Year	from *Yazith (מיצת)	to Ahinoam (לאחנעם)	jar of old wine
12	In the Ninth Year	from *Siphtan (משפתן)	to *Baalzemer (לבעלזמר)	jar of old wine
16	In the Tenth Year	from Sepher (מספר)[103]	to *Gaddiyau	jar of fine oil
18	In the Tenth Year	from Hazeroth (מחצרת)	to *Gaddiyau	jar of fine oil

TABLE B

Ostraca No.	Date	Clan	Recipient	Sender	Place
22–3	In Year ךΛ	from Helek (מחלק)	to *Aśa (son of) Ahimelech (לאשא·אחמלך)	Helez (חלץ)	from Hazeroth
24	In Year ךΛ	from Helek	to *Aśa (son of) Ahimelech	Rapha (son of) *Anmes (רפא·ענמש)	from Hazeroth
28	In Year ךΛ	from Abiezer (מאבעזר)	to *Aśa (son of) Ahimelech	*Baala (בעלא)	from *Elmattan (מאלמתן)
29	In Year ךΛ	from Shemida (משמידע)	to *Aśa (son of) Ahimelech	Kedar (קדר)	from *Sepher
30	In Year ךΛ	from Shemida	to Helez (son of) Gaddiyau	Gera (son of) *Hanniab (גרא·חנאב)	?

No.	*Year*	*Place*	*Clan*	*Recipient(s)*	*Sender(s)*	*Commodity*
1.	10	from *Poraim (מפארים)		to *Shamaryau (לשמריו)	*Pega (son of) Elisha (רגע·אלישע)	2 jars of old [wine]
					Uzza (son of) *Kabesh (?) (עזא·קבש)	1
					*Eliba (אלבא)	1
					*Baala (son of) Elisha	2
					*Yedayau	1
2.	10	from *Azzah (מאזה)		to *Gaddiyau	*Abibaal (אבבעל)	2
					Ahaz (אחז)	2
					Sheba (שבע)	1
					Meribaal (מרבעל)	1
3.	10		from Shemida	to [. . .]a (ל . . . א)		jar of [ol]d wine
				to *Baala A[. . .] (לבעלא ע . . .)		
4.	9	from *Kozoh		to *Gaddiyau		jar [of old wine]
5.	9	from *Kozoh		to [*Gaddi]yau		jar of old wine
6.	9	from *Kozoh		to *Gaddiyau		jar of old wine
7.	?	?		to *Gaddi[yau]		[jar of o]ld [wine]
8.	9	from Geb[a] (מגב[ע])		[to Ahino]am		jar of [ol]d [wine]
9.	9	from *Yazith		to Ahinoam		[j]ar of old wi[ne]
10.	9	from *Yazith		to Ahinoam		jar of old wine
11.				[to Ahi]noam		[j]ar of wine
12.	9	from *Siphtan (משפתן)		to *Baalzemer		jar of old wine

13.	10	from Abiezer from *Tetel (? מתתל)		to *Shamaryau to *Aś[a?]		jar of old wine [?]
14.	9	from A[zn]oth-*Par'an (מא[זנ]ת פראן)		to *Shamaryau		jar of old wine
15.		from Hazeroth		to [. . .]		jar [of . . .]
16.	10	from Sepher		to *Gaddiyau		jar of fine oil
17.	10	from *Azzah		to *Gaddiyau		jar of fine oil
18.	10	from Hazeroth		to *Gaddiyau		jar of fine oil
19.	10	from Yazith		to Ahinoam		jar of fine oil
20.	10	from *Cherem-hatte[l] (מכרם הת[ל])				[jar of] fine oil
21.	10	from *Tetel (?)		to *Shamaryau		jar of fine oil
22.	15	from Hazeroth	from Helek	to *Aśa (son of) Ahimelech	Helez	
23.	15	from Hazeroth	from Helek	to *Aśa (son of) Ahimelech	Helez	
24.	15	from [Ha]zeroth	[from He]lek	to *Aś[a] (son of) Ahime[lech]	Rapha (son of) *Anmes	
25.		from Hazeroth	*from Hele*[k]	[to *Aśa (son of) A]himele[ch]	Ahazai	
26.		from Ha[zeroth]	[from Hele]k	to *Aśa (son of) [Ahimelech]	[Hele]z (son of) H[. ? .]n	
27.	15	Baal-meon (בעלמעני)	from Helek	to *Aśa (son of) Ahimelech	*Baala (the) Baalmeonite	
28.	15	from *Elmattan	from Abiezer	to *Aśa (son of) Ahimelech	*Baala	
29.	15	from Sepher	from She[mida]	[to] *Aśa (son of) Ahimelech	*Ke*dar	

No.	Year	Place	Clan	Recipient(s)	Sender(s)	Commodity
30.	15		from Shemida	to Helez (son of) Gaddiyau	Gera (son of) *Hanniab	
31.	15		from Shemida	to Helez (son of) *Aphzech (לחלץ אפצח)	*Baala (son of) Zecher (בעלא זכר)	
32.	15		from She⟨m⟩ida	to Helez	*Ahima (אחמא)	
33.	[1]5		from Shemi[da]	[to He]lez (son of) *Gaddiyau	. . . ? (מֹנת . . .)	
34.	15		from [Shem]i[da]	[to Helez (son of) *Ga]ddiyau	. . . ? (. . . צ)	
35.	15		from She[mida]	to Helez (son of) *Gaddiyau		
36.			[from] Shemid[a]		[Ge]ra	[o]ld wine
37.	15		from Shemida	to *Ahima	*Aśa (son of) *Baalzecher (אשא בעלזכר)	
38.	15		from Shemida	to *Ahima	*Ullah (son of) Ela (עלה אלא)	
39.	15		from Shemida	[to] *Ahima	[*Aś]a (son of) [Baalzecher?]	
40.			[from] Shemida	to? (. . . לע)		
41.					.?.sha (son of) *Egliyau (. . . שע עגליו)	
42.	15	from *As(h)ereth (מעשרת)	from ⟨A⟩srie[l] משרא[ל]	to *Yedayau (לידעיו)	*Meronyau (son of) Gaddiya[u]	
43.	(h ?)			[to] Hannan . . . (. . . חנג)	El . . . (. . . אל)	
44.	15		from Shechem (משכם)	(. . . הפ·ר)	(. . . ה)	wine
45.	15	from *Yaz[ith]	from Hogla[h]	to Hanan (son of) Ba[ar]a	[*Meron]yau (son of) Nathan ([מרנ]יו נתן)	

46.	15			to Hanan (son of) Ba[ara] (לחנן ב[ערא])	(. . . א)	
47.		from *Yazith	[from] Hoglah (מחגלה)	to Hanan (son of) Baara	? (. . . מ)	
48.	15	from *Yashub (מישב)	from ⟨A⟩srie[l]	to *Yedayau (son of) Ahimelech	Joshua (ישע)	
49.			[from Shemid]a	to He[lez (son of) *Gaddiyau]	? (מזׄ כסׄר)	
50.	15		from Noah (מנעה)	to Gomer (לגמר)	*Obadyau to *Uriyau (עבדיו לאריו)	
51.	10				*Aha the Judea[n] (אחא היהד[י])	
52.	15				*Abiyau	
53.	10	*Cherem-hattel				wine, in a jar of fine oil
54.	10	*Cherem-hattel				wine jar of fine oil
55.	10	*Cherem-Yeḥo-eli (כרם יחועלי)				jar of fine oil
56.	15	*from* *Hatt[el]		to Nimsh[i] (לנמש[י])?	(דל . . . ׳עׄדׄ)	
57.			Shem⟨i⟩da	Abda	? (יו . ״ . . נא . . . יו)	
58.	15	*Cherem-hattel		to **Be*deyau (לבׄדיו)		
59.						jar of f[in]e oil
60.		*Cherem-Yeho-el[i]				
61.	15	*Cherem-hattel				
62.			Shemid[a]			wine
63.	17	(?)	from Shemid[a]			
3892.	10	*Cherem-hattel				wine, in a jar of fine oil
3893.	(10)	*Chere[m-hattel]				wine, [in a jar of fine] oil

The ostraca include, therefore, sixteen place names plus seven names known as clans from the tribal genealogy of Manasseh (Num. 26. 30–3; Josh. 17. 2–3; 1 Chron. 7. 14–19), viz. Shemida, Abiezer, Helek, [A]sriel[104] Shechem, Hoglah and Noah. For the understanding and topographical interpretation of these inscriptions the connection of place names with clan designations and with the different persons is of fundamental importance:

1. Distribution of places according to clans: Abiezer—Tetel, Elmattan; Shemida—Sepher; Helek—Hazeroth, Baal-meon; Hoglah—Yazith; [A]sriel—As(h)ereth, Yashub.

2. Men who received the disbursements from different places: Shamaryau—Poraim, Tetel, A[zn]oth-par'an (Abiezer); Gaddiyau—Azzah, Kozoh, Sepher, Hazeroth (Shemida, Helek); Ahinoam—Geba, Yazith (Hoglah); As(h)a (son of) Ahimelech—Hazeroth, Baal-meon, Elmattan, Sepher (Helek, Abiezer, Shemida); Yedayau (son of) Ahimelech—As(h)ereth, Yashub ([A]sriel).

There is hardly room for doubt that the men whose names appear in combination with the preposition "to" (*l*) were the recipients of the commodity. They may have been tax collectors, government officials in charge of certain areas, or high-ranking courtiers and ministers to whom the income from particular places was allotted in conjunction with their office or rank. This latter interpretation was suggested by Rainey on the basis of comparisons with texts from Ugarit.[105]

[Recent comments by F. M. Cross[106] make it advisable to present a more detailed discussion of why the land-grant explanation is the only satisfactory one. First of all, we must settle the question of the nature of the texts. They can hardly be "tax receipts" as assumed by Cross; such receipts would not have been left in the storehouse and, besides, there is no proof that such documents were ever issued to those paying taxes. On the other hand, there is plenty of evidence, especially in the cuneiform world, for the use of "scratch-pad notations" (on small lumps of clay in Mesopotamia) which were later summarized in a ledger. This is obviously the nature of the Samaria ostraca; it also explains why they had been discarded. The final ledger was most likely of papyrus.

However, there are several points on which we can readily agree with Cross. He notes that the men denoted by *lamed,* the "*l*-men," appear repeatedly in the texts and receive commodities from more than one place. Thus, they could hardly be tax officials since an overlapping of responsibilities would mean chaos in the administration.

Furthermore, Cross has noted that the "non-*l*-men," whose names are not governed by a preposition, are more carefully specified, often with patronymic, gentilic or town of origin. Each one only appears with the same "*l*-man". But several "non-*l*-men" can give to the same "*l*-man", as e.g., in text No. 1. These factors will be seen to conform amazingly well with the land-grant interpretation.

We can also agree with Cross that the small commodities, a jar or two of wine or oil, does not represent the entire produce of an estate. On the other hand, we must disagree with him on the following points: Rations being sent to nobles and/or functionaries for their personal use in the capital would not have to be larger amounts. It is not known whether the "*l*-men" were permanently located in Samaria or whether they were serving a "tour of duty" there. Even if they had fixed residences in the capital, the shipments need only have been for limited needs. The main storehouses for a landowner would be located in his own district; there would not be room in the city of Samaria for *all* the produce belonging to individual citizens living there. In addition, there is no reason to assume that every shipment to the recipients would be delivered directly to them instead of being channelled through the royal storehouse, especially if the recipients in question ate "at the king's table" (cf. 2 Sam. 9. 10, 13).[107]

Kaufman, taking a cue from Yadin, has pointed to texts Nos. 20, 53, 54, 55, 61 (and perhaps 63), 3892 and 3893 which have no "*l*-man" (and no "non-*l*-men," either). Those texts have been cited as an argument against the land-grant theory. However, they are an even stronger argument against the "tax receipt" explanation. They are simply "scratch-pad notations" of shipments from royal vineyards.[108] All of these ostraca record shipments from *Cherem-hattel except No. 55 which deals with a shipment from *Cherem-Yeḥo-eli; No. 60, also from the latter place, may belong in this same category. Since the recipient was the crown, there was no need to record the fact. Thus, there is no contradiction here to the land-grant interpretation of the remaining ostraca.

That the "*l*-men" were recipients of wine and oil from their own estates is highly probable for the folowing reasons: Estates were acquired by various means. The basic holding would be the man's patrimony inherited from his father; other parcels of land (and even whole towns) could be granted to a person by the king. This system was recognized in 1 Sam 8. 14–15.[109] The estates, fields, orchards, etc. available to the crown for such awards may have been confiscated from traitors[110] or other wrongdoers, or else from estates where debts or illness had reduced the legal owner to desperate straits.[111]

As we have previously pointed out,[112] the case of Meribaal (Mephibosheth) is illustrative of the way an estate owner living at the capital would enjoy the produce of his patrimony or land grant. The "house of Saul," the family estate in Benjamin, was assigned to Meribaal by David (2 Sam. 9. 7) but the recipient himself was to eat at the king's table. But this did not mean that he would be eating at the king's expense; Ziba, the steward of Saul's estate was explicitly ordered to "bring in the produce, that your master's son may have bread to eat"

(2 Sam. 9. 10). An entry jotted down in the royal stores at Jerusalem would have noted the year of David's reign, "from Gibeah," "to Meribaal" (*l-mrbʿl*), the commodity, and "Ziba, steward (*nʿr*) of Saul" would appear as the "non-*l*-man."

Therefore, from a sociological point of view, the land-grant interpretation fits all the data. A person serving in the capital would receive from his family estate and might also get shipments from other land holdings that he had acquired as grants from the crown. Very important officials and nobles were also in a position to acquire the property of oppressed citizens by crooked and illegal means, and such behaviour was notorious precisely in the eighth century when the shipments recorded on the Samaria ostraca were being made (cf. Amos 2. 6–7, 5. 10–12, 8. 4–6; Micah 2. 1–2, 9; Isa. 3. 13–15, 5. 8).

Finally, we may add the grammatical argument. It is simply inconceivable that an ancient Hebrew scribe would indicate the *sender* or *donor* of a shipment by the *lamed* preposition. Though the phrase *l* + PN may indicate ownership,[113] ownership is *not* used to identify the sender. The *lamed* preposition used in juxtaposition to *mi(n)* could hardly have indicated anything else but "to" in contrast to "from." That *lamed* indicates the recipient in ancient Hebrew, in both verbal and non-verbal clauses, has been abundantly demonstrated.[114] When a sender or donor is indicated, the scribe used the compound preposition *mēʾēt*,[115] or else he placed the donor's name in the genitive after the commodity which is in the construct.[116] It is the latter practice which led to the listing of the stewards as "non-*l*-men" in the Samaria Ostraca. A.F.R.]

Although the names of the men on the ostraca from years 9 to 10 differ from those from the year 15, the relationship of the various places to specific individuals does not seem to have changed. Among the places whose deliveries went to Gaddiyau in the tenth year Hazeroth and Sepher are mentioned; in the fifteenth year the deliveries from these two places are again designated for the same recipient, Aśa (son of) Ahimelech. From this we can conclude that Aśa (son of) Ahimelech had taken over Gaddiyau's position. From the combination of place names it seems probable that they received deliveries from at least six places (Azzah, Kozoh, Sepher, Hazeroth, Baal-meon and Elmattan), which were divided among three clan districts (Helek, Abiezer and Shemida).

Attempts to explain these texts and to establish their date have encountered two main difficulties:

1. There is no correlation between the clans and the recipients. The deliveries from one clan go to different men, and one man receives commodities from different clans. If the clan areas actually served in this period as administrative units and if the deliveries represent taxes, then why was the tax assessment not regulated in accordance with these

units ? For this reason Noth, on the basis of Egyptian analogies, suggested that the ostraca record deliveries coming in from royal vineyards. A few vinyeards are mentioned among the geographical names (Cherem-hattel, Cherem-Yeḥo-eli), but it is precisely these texts which lack any reference to clans. Furthermore, why did the formal pattern of the inscriptions change between those of the ninth and tenth years and those of year 15 with the clan names appearing almost exclusively in the latter ? Noth concludes that this change is evidence of an administrative reform which he thinks was carried out during the tenth year, because clan names are mentioned in Nos. 3 and 13. However, the question arises as to why the clan names were included at all if they had no relevance to the deliveries of wine and oil in question.

2. .All of the personal names on ostraca from the ninth and tenth years differ from those belonging to year 15, even though some of the place names appear in both groups.[117] If these were royal officials, tax collectors, land-owners or what have you, it is necessary to explain how all of them could have been replaced within the space of five years.

A solution to this latter question may help us in dating the ostraca. Scholars all begin with the assumption that this is a question of one king who ruled at least fifteen or seventeen years.[118] Palaeographical and archaeological considerations limit the choice of kings to those who ruled during the second half of the ninth or the first half of the eighth century B.C.[119] Therefore, only three kings are eligible for consideration: Jehu, Jehoahaz,[120] or Jeroboam II. However, the problems which we listed can be solved if we assume that the ostraca belong to the reigns of two different kings, those of years 9 and 10 to one king and those of year 15 (plus the one from year 17) belong to another king, most probably to his son. On the basis of this assumption a generation passed between the two groups of ostraca, which helps to explain the dissimilarity of personal names and presents less difficulty in explaining the changed formulation. Furthermore, certain palaeographical differences are notable between the two groups of texts.[121]

In the light of this conclusion it is possible to establish a date for the ostraca with greater certainty. If it is correct that we have to do here with two successive kings, the second of whom ruled at least seventeen years, then the most likely candidates are Joash, who reigned fifteen or sixteen years (*c.* 800–785 B.C. and Jeroboam II, his son (*c.* 785–49). Explicit information is preserved in the Bible about a census of the Israelite population carried out by Jeroboam II (1 Chron. 5. 17); perhaps this explains the inclusion of clan names on the ostraca from his reign. These are not administrative districts but clan territories that were recorded by the census in different parts of Mount Ephraim. All of the deliveries are, of course, from the same administrative region, viz. Mount Ephraim (cf. 1 Kings 4. 8) and the various places are apportioned among the officials, whether they be tax collectors or privileged recipients. On the ostraca from the years 9 and 10 the place name is recorded first (after the date), which is an indication that they were filed in geographical order. With the census of clans carried out in Jeroboam's reign, the tax burden was distributed according to the clans so that these become listed first in the formula of the later ostraca. Nevertheless, changes were not introduced in the apportionment of the places themselves within the framework of the administrative regions. On the other hand, deliveries from royal vineyards such as Cherem-hattel and Cherem-Yeḥo-eli are listed without reference to a clan. Of course the clans themselves were not created during Jeroboam's reign, so it is not surprising that we find an occasional reference to them in the ostraca from year 10 (Nos. 3, 13). However, the formula used in these cases differs from that of the year 15: in both texts two personal names appear in combination with the preposition "to". Therefore, the purpose here is not to credit a certain delivery to a particular clan as on the ostraca from year 15; this may be, rather, an instance of one jar of old wine delivered from Abiezer in addition to a delivery from Tetel and another from Shemida together with some other place. Even if we cannot interpret these entries with absolute certainty, it is clear that the formulation is quite different from the recording of clan and place names on the texts from the fifteenth year.

If this explanation of the Samaria ostraca is correct, then they are evidence for the population census in Jeroboam's reign which was made to expedite the collection of taxes according to a more equitable apportionment. They also indicate the scrupulous and well-ordered administration in his reign as well as that of his father Joash. The most interesting fact is that all of the clan names appear in the Bible as children of Manasseh, which is illuminating evidence for the existence of the ancient clan divisions that had maintained their integrity even late in the Monarchial period. This, in turn, shows that the agrarian social structure had continued to prevail. All of the places mentioned on the ostraca are in the northern part of Mount Ephraim, the ancient territory of Manasseh, which may have become an administrative district in the kingdom with Samaria as its capital. The district of Mount Ephraim was much larger in the Solomonic administrative framework, but it probably lost considerable territory in the south with the expansion of the Benjamin district, which had largely gone over to the Judean kingdom.

The geographical names from the Samaria ostraca are a most welcome addition to our hitherto scanty knowledge of that region. Because additional sources about the northern portion of Mount Ephraim are so scarce, most of the identifications are based on preservation of the ancient name in that vicinity. Acceptable identifications have been proposed for the following places (cf. map 29):

Azzah—Zawata, 3 miles south-east of Samaria;
Elmattan—Immatin, 6 miles south of Samaria;
Geba—Jeba ʿ, 4 miles north of Samaria;
Hazeroth— ʿAṣireh esh-Shamaliyeh, 5 miles south-east of Samaria;
Yazith—Yaṣid, 5½ miles east-north-east of Samaria;
Yashub—Yasuf, nearly 12 miles south of Samaria[122]:
Sepher—Sefarin 4½ miles west of Samaria;
Kozoh—Khirbet Quṣin, 2½ miles south of Samaria;
Shechem—Tell Balaṭah, 7 miles south-east of Samaria;
Siphtan—Shufah, 6 miles west of Samaria.

In the light of these identifications it is possible to determine the location of the Manassite clan territories in Mount Ephraim: Asriel in the south (Yashub); Abiezer in the south-west (Elmattan, Tetel); Helek in the east (Hazeroth, and perhaps Azzah); Shechem in the south-east; Shemida in the south-west (Sepher and Kozoh near by); Hoglah in the north-east (Yazith and apparently also Geba). Five of these clan names correspond to sons of Manasseh, according to the genealogies, and all of them are located in the hill country. Only one of Manasseh's six sons is missing, viz. Hepher, which was evidently in the Sharon (cf. 1 Kings 4. 10).

Two of the clans are by tradition daughters of Zelophehad, the son of Hepher, viz. Noah and Hoglah. Since the Hoglah clan was situated north-east of Shechem, and Tirzah (also a daughter of Zelophehad) is identified at Tell el-Far ʿah to the east of it, it is probable that Noah was in the area north-west of Samaria. Thus it would seem that their arrangement in the genealogy of Manasseh reflects a certain geographical order: the sons of Manasseh (except Hepher) dwell in the central part of Mount Ephraim, the southern half of Manasseh's inheritance, while the daughters are found in the northern part of Mount Ephraim. This order was probably brought about by the historical circumstances of the settlement process, reflecting a gradual movement northward from the heart of the hill country.

From the Samaria ostraca we obtain a considerable number of geographical names belonging to ancient settlements in central Mount Ephraim which are not preserved in the Bible or any other source. To some degree they make up the deficiency pertaining to Mount Ephraim in the biblical town list and present an illuminating picture of the dense agricultural population in the Samaria region at the time of the Israelite Monarchy.

X. TIGLATH-PILESER III'S CAMPAIGNS AND THE FALL OF ISRAEL

The death of Jeroboam II and the murder of his son Zechariah in *c.* 748 B.C. brought an end to the Jehu Dynasty which had ruled Israel for nearly a century. A period of decline set in for the kingdom of Israel

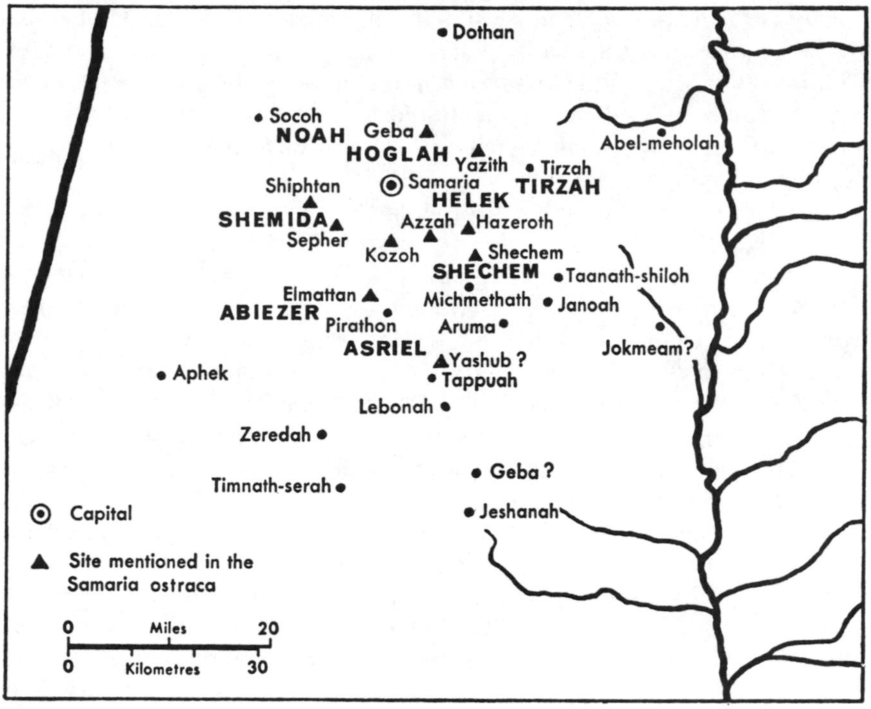

Map 29. Mount Ephraim in the Light of the Samaria Ostraca

which assumed disastrous proportions in the days of Tiglath-pileser III, King of Assyria (745–27 B.C.).[123]

This monarch renewed the expansionist ambitions of Assyria, becoming the father of the great Assyrian empire which eventually swallowed up all of the small kingdoms of Syria and Palestine. Not being satisfied with campaigns of plunder and the extortion of tribute from the various principalities, he began the permanent absorption of their territories by converting them into provinces. Over these provinces he appointed Assyrian governors, at the same time transferring most of the population's upper strata to another region, while replacing them by similar deportees from elsewhere.

His first encounter with the states in the West led to the establishment of Assyrian hegemony. The inscription of Tiglath-pileser does not explain how this war broke out, but after an Assyrian victory he gained the mastery over northern Syria as far as the Lebanon and Amanus ranges, establishing provinces in the kingdom of Hamath.[124] The list of rulers who subsequently rendered tribute to Assyria includes the kings of Byblos, Tyre, Damascus (Rezon), Samaria (Menahem) and even the queen of Arabia.[125] Menahem collected the sum required by means of a heavy tax levied on all land owners in his kingdom (2 Kings 15. 19—20) which impoverished the nation, so weakening the royal house that it fell within a few years' time. Assyrian domination of the Phoenician coast was made secure and can be illustrated from the correspondence of the commissioner, Qurdi-asshur-lamur,[126] who forbade the Sidonians to sell lumber to Egypt or to Philistia.

Soon afterwards the political order in Palestine changed completely. Uzziah died in *c.* 735 B.C., and his grandson Ahaz became the sole ruler of Judah. In the same year Pekahiah the son of Menahem, King of Israel, was murdered by Pekah the son of Remaliah. Pekah apparently rose to power on the wave of bitterness caused by the complete submission to Assyria, and with his rise a new alliance against Assyria was formed, headed by Pekah and Rezin, King of Damascus. Only in this light can we understand their joint operation against Judah, carried out with the intention of removing the rival Davidic king and replacing him with the son of Tabeel (Isa. 7. 5 ff.). This man was evidently the scion of an illustrious family that enjoyed close ties with Judah, perhaps even with the royal house.[127] They seemed to have dominated the central Gilead region and their hegemony may even date to the reigns of Uzziah-Jotham (1 Chron. 5. 17; 2 Chron. 26. 8). In another epistle from the Nimrud excavations the same Assyrian commissioner, Qurdi-asshur-lamur, reports that a letter has been brought by an emissary from Ayanur the Tabeelite (*IdAia-nu-ri kurṬa-ab-i-la-aia*) containing information about people from the land of Geder (*kurGi-di-ra-aia*) who had conducted hostilities against the population of a Moabite town.[128] This Geder is most probably the Γαδαρα/Γαδωρα/Gedor, the capital of the Peraea district in the Second Temple period,[129] today Tell 'Ain Jedur near eṣ-Ṣalṭ in central Gilead. The Tabeel family were probably the forefathers of the prominent Tobiads who dominated central Gilead during the Second Commonwealth. Tobiah the Ammonite slave (Neh. 2. 19) probably came from the same family and the same may be true of the Tobiyahu in the Lachish letters, who bore the title "servant of the king."[130] They undoubtedly exercised considerable influence in the royal Judean house at the end of the First Temple Period. The son of Tabeel whom Rezin and Pekah sought to place on the throne in Jerusalem was probably exiled to Assyria by Tiglath-pileser III and "the sons of Pahath-moab" (Ezra 2. 6; 8. 4; Neh. 7. 11) who returned after the exile may be the descendants of his and other venerable families from the Transjordan area.

The house of Tabeel/Tobiah was not the only Judean family gaining prominence in Gilead during the monarchial period. Beerah, the Reubenite chieftain exiled by Tiglath-pileser (1 Chron. 5. 6) must have also belonged to such a noble family maintaining ties with Judah. His family probably held a position in the Mishor of Moab comparable to that of the Tabeelites/Tobiads in Gilead.

Ahaz had evidently refused to join the coalition proposed by Rezin and Pekah, so the kings of Israel and Aram were anxious to set up a king of their own choice in Jerusalem who would agree to their anti-Assyrian plans. Judah's other neighbours also took this opportunity to break their ties with her. The Judean hold over Edom was broken, apparently with the help of Rezin, King of Aram, and Elath returned once more to Edomite hands (2 Kings 16. 6; 2 Chron. 28. 17). The excavations at Ezion-geber prove that the site saw an Edomite occupation in that period. The Philistines also chose this moment to expand their own sphere of rule in the Shephelah and the Negeb; especially damaging to Judah was the capture of a number of towns controlling the passes to Jerusalem: Gimzo and Aijalon in the north, Timnah and Beth-shemesh in the Sorek Valley, Socoh and apparently also Gederoth in the Valley of Elah (2 Chron. 28. 18). The changes that took place in this period with regard to the political and territorial positions of the kingdoms in Palestine and Syria are surprising: three or four years after the appearance of Uzziah at the head of all of these kingdoms the boundaries of Judah were markedly reduced.

In this time of trouble Ahaz turned to Assyria for help, against the advice of Isaiah who understood that the Assyrian danger was immeasurably greater than the internal quarrels of the Levantine states. He saw that expansion by Assyria was endangering the very existence of these smaller kingdoms.

Tiglath-pileser's action was swift and forceful and doubtless would have been taken even without a specific invitation from Judah (cf. Map 30). His first expedition to Palestine in 734 was directed against Philistia.[131] The Assyrian army advanced southward along the Levantine coast, reaching Gaza and continuing on to the Brook of Egypt (Wadi el- 'Arish), the traditional boundary between Palestine and Egypt. Although Tiglath-pileser crossed Israelite territory in the Sharon, his campaign did not touch heavily upon Israel; the fateful blows against Israel and Damascus were levelled in the two years that followed (733–2 B.C.).

Concerning Tiglath-pileser's campaigns in 733–2[132] we have one brief passage in the Bible and a few references from his own inscriptions.[133] According to the Bible, Tiglath-pileser "captured Ijon, Abel-beth-maacah, Janoah, Kedesh, Hazor, Gilead and Galilee, all the land of Naphtali; and he carried the people captive to Assyria" (2 Kings 15. 29). In this expedition Tiglath-pileser marched southward through the Lebanese Beqa' and entered the territory of Naphtali, breaking the chain of fortified towns at the northern end of the Jordan Valley (Ijon, Abel-beth-maacah and Hazor). This enabled him to conquer all of Galilee, including Kedesh and Janoah, and Gilead, i.e. Israelite Transjordan.

Further details about this expedition may be gleaned from the passage in Tiglath-pileser's own inscriptions.[134] One fragmentary text provides a summary of his campaigns, listing various towns conquered in northern Syria and on the Phoenician coast. It goes on to include the conquest of Galʾaza (Gilead) and Abil<ma>akka (Abel-[beth]-maacah) on the borderland of "the land of Beth-Omri" (Israel) and Beth-Hazael[135] (Aram-Damascus), over which Assyrian governors were appointed. Then the capture of Gaza is mentioned. Next we are told that the men of Beth-Omri rebelled against their king, Pekah (*Pa-qa-ḫa*), whom Tiglath-pileser replaced with Hoshea (*A-ú-si-ʾ a*); as a consequence the Israelites were also required to pay a heavy tribute. Large emoluments paid to the Assyrians by various countries of Arabia are also listed.

Apparently Tiglath-pileser's strategy was to isolate Aram from her southern allies first before turning the full might of Assyria against Damascus itself. Therefore, the most likely reconstruction of his three campaigns is as follows:

> *Year 734*—an expedition against Philistia, the conquest of Gaza and seizure of the Brook of Egypt in order to prevent any attempted interference on Egypt's part.
>
> *Year 733*—expedition against Israel, conquest of Galilee, Gilead and the coastal region, which were reorganized into Assyrian provinces.
>
> *Year 732*—the conquest of Damascus and the land of Aram, the exile of part of its population (2 Kings 16. 9) and reorganization of its kingdom into an Assyrian province. To this expedition doubtless belongs the relief describing the exile of people from Ashtaroth by Tiglath-pileser's army.[136]

More details about Tiglath-pileser's Palestinian conquests are preserved in another passage[137]:

> In my former campaigns I had reckoned all of the towns of [. . . as . . .]. its [. . .]I had taken as spoil. Only the town of Samaria did I lea[ve, and Pekah (?)] their king [. . . like a] fog [. . .]. The provinces of the land of Beth-[Omri (?) I to]ok (?). [. . . prisoners of] the town [. . .] barā ([. . .]-*ba-ra-a*), 625 prisoners of the town [. . .' . . . prisoners of the town] Hannathon (*Ḫi-na-tu-na*), 650 prisoners of the town Kanath (*Qa-na*), [. . . prisoners of the town Jo]tbah ([*Ia*]-*aṭ-bi-te*), 650 prisoners of the town Ir[runa (?), all these] people with their possessions [I took as booty . . .] The town of Rumah (*A-ru-ma*) and the town of Merom (*Ma-ru-um*) . . . .

All of the towns in this passage that can be identified with any degree of certainty were located in Galilee: Merom (Tell el-Khirbeh ?) and Yiron (Ir[runa], modern Yarun) in Upper Galilee; Hannathon (Tell el-Bedeiwiyeh), Kanah (Khirbet Qana), and Jotbah (Khirbet Jefat perched above Sahl el-Baṭṭof) in Lower Galilee. Therefore, the Assyrian

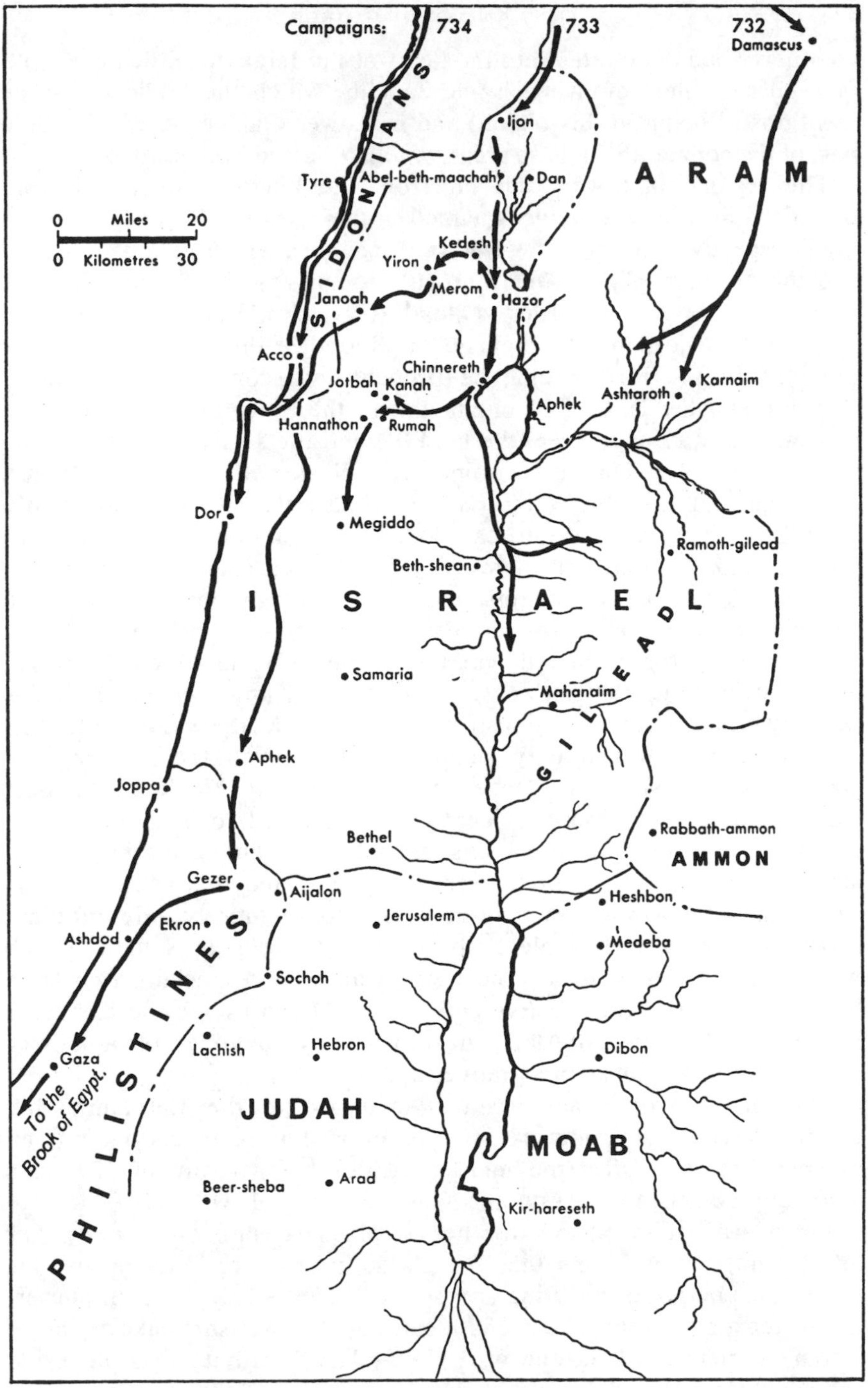

Map 30. The Campaigns of Tiglath-pileser III.

conqueror had penetrated into the heart of the Israelite settlement, both in Upper Galilee (cf. Kedesh and Janoah, which the biblical passage mentions as being in this region) and in Lower Galilee. A considerable part of the population in these areas was also carried away into exile.

The regions that were cut off from the kingdom of Israel were organized into three provinces named in the Assyrian lists according to their respective capitals[138]: Megiddo (Magiddu), which included Galilee and the northern plains; Dor (Du'ru), comprising the Sharon Plain as far as the Philistine border; Gilead (Gal'aza),[139] corresponding to Israelite Transjordan. These events are doubtless the subject of Isaiah's oracle: "In the former time he brought into contempt the land of Zebulun and the land of Naphtali, but in the latter time he will make glorious the way of the sea, the land beyond the Jordan, Galilee of the nations" (9. 1). This is certainly an allusion to Tighlath-pileser's campaign and the three Assyrian provinces that were subsequently established: "the way of the sea" (Dor); "the land beyond the Jordan" (Gilead) and "Galilee of the nations" (Megiddo: cf. map 31).

This situation is clearly reflected in the excavations at Hazor and Megiddo. Hazor was completely destroyed in this period, the buildings and the fort on top of the tell were burned (level V), and the town which arose on its ruins (level IV) was only a poor, unwalled village. This actually brings to an end the history of Hazor as a city; shortly after this it was abandoned and only small citadels existed there during the Babylonian, Persian and Hellenistic periods. At Megiddo the destruction of level IV must evidently be attributed to Tiglath-pileser's campaign.[140] The entire town was laid waste, including the large royal structures such as the storehouses, the palace and the gate. Over the ruins a new town was now built according to an entirely different plan. Streets laid out at right angles were lined with dwellings, some of which were built according to a typical Assyrian plan, especially two large buildings near the gate.[141] Evidently level III represents the capital of the Assyrian province of Magiddu, occupied by the governor, a military garrison and the local administrative staff.

The kingdom of Israel was now confined to the Ephraimite hill country. Even that limited region was only allowed to continue as an independent state after the murder of Pekah by virtue of Hoshea's complete submission to Assyria (2 Kings 15. 30; 17. 1–3).

Judah was relieved of the heavy pressure put on her by her neighbours, but it seems that Ahaz's submission to Assyria and his request for help did not bring any special favours from Tiglath-pileser. Edom remained independent of Judean control. Kaushmalaku, King of Edom, is mentioned on one of Tiglath-pileser's tribute lists alongside Jehoahaz (*Ia-ú-ḫa-zi*), King of Judah.[142] Kings of Edom also appear in the inscriptions of Sargon II, Esarhaddon and Ashurbanipal.[143] Hence-

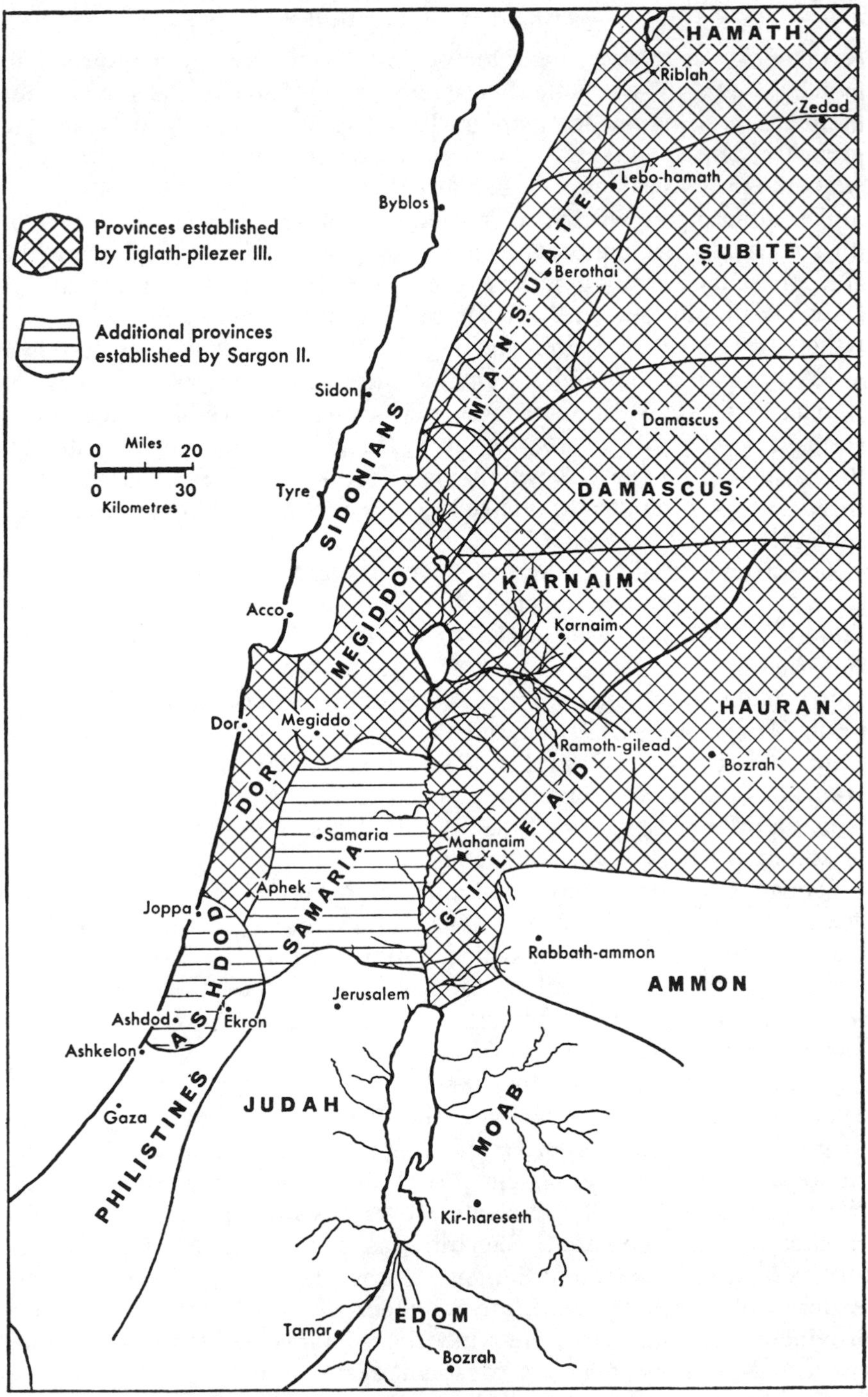

Map 31. The Assyrian Provinces in Palestine.

forth, Ezion-geber was an Edomite fort and never again returned to Judean control. The wealth of Assyrian pottery found at the site testifies to the firm Assyrian domination. That can also be deduced from the presence of the Assyrian fortress discovered at Bozrah (Buṣeirah) similar to the "Residency" at Lachish.[144]

We do not know whether or not Tiglath-pileser returned the towns of the Shephelah that had been taken away by the Philistines to Judah. In 2 Chronicles the narrative of these events (28. 18 ff.) concludes by saying: "So Tiglath-pilneser [*sic!*], King of Assyria, came against him, and afflicted him instead of strengthening him", which seems to indicate that the Assyrian monarch did not enlarge Judah's borders. Nevertheless, it is clear that at least some of these towns eventually returned to Judean control, because Socoh was Judean in Hezekiah's reign as indicated by the royal seal impressions with its name (cf. *infra*, p. 394), and Azekah, which is west of Socoh, is referred to as a Judean town in an inscription from the reign of Sennacherib.[145]

The sixteen districts of Aram-Damascus were reorganized into four or five Assyrian provinces, viz. Damascus, Karnaim, Hauran, Zobah (Ṣubite) and perhaps Manṣuate.[146] Thus was laid the foundation for the Assyrian provincial organization of Palestine and Syria which changed only slightly during the period of Assyrian domination and was inherited by the kingdoms of Babylon and Persia. A few of these provinces are mentioned by Ezekiel in his description of the country's borders: Hamath, Damascus, Hauran and Gilead (chap. 47. 17–18). Only Samaria (Mount Ephraim), Judah, the Philistine cities and the kingdoms of southern Transjordan continued to exist as vassal kingdoms during the reign of Tiglath-pileser. In lists of tribute that he received he mentions, among others, the kings of Ammon, Moab, Edom and Gaza.[147] With the Assyrians' domination over Damascus and Transjordan and their control of the King's Highway, the roads to Arabia were open before them; henceforth special gifts from these kingdoms are regularly mentioned in Assyrian inscriptions.

The process of transforming the various kingdoms of Palestine and Syria into Assyrian provinces and the deportation of their populations was largely completed during the reign of Tiglath-pileser III's successors. Hoshea rebelled against the Assyrian authority when Tiglath-pileser died, and in 724 B.C. Shalmaneser V came up against Samaria. Hoshea himself submitted, Samaria was conquered, after a siege of three years, in 722–21, and Sargon II, who had meanwhile risen to the Assyrian throne, converted the kingdom of Israel into an Assyrian province called Samerina. He exiled many Samarian nobles to various cities in Media and northern Mesopotamia (2 Kings 17.6).[148] As time passed the Assyrians replaced these citizens with exiles from Babylon and vicinity, and from Hamath in Syria, who left their imprint upon the local population mixture (2 Kings 17. 24 ff.). Apparently the new province of Samaria also included the former province of Dor, since Aphek in the southern Sharon belonged to the Samarian province during the reign of Esarhaddon.[149] It is true that Dor is mentioned in a list of Assyrian cities composed mainly of the provincial capitals, but a governor of Dor is not mentioned in the Assyrian Eponym Lists, though the names for governors of Samaria and Megiddo do occur. Therefore, the testimony of Esarhaddon seems decisive in this regard. The formation of a province along the coast ("the way of the sea", Isa. 9. 1) was justified only so long as Assyrian provincial control was limited to this region. But when Samaria was added to their provinces, the Assyrians probably renewed the administrative connection between the Sharon and Mount Ephraim. Naphath-dor must have continued to exist as a secondary administrative district within the province, which would explain its appearance in the list of Assyrian towns.

Sargon II advanced southward to Raphia, conquered Gaza, smote the Egyptians who had come to help the rebelling kingdoms and received tribute from the Egyptians and the Arabs. While in this region he also subdued the prince of the town called Laban, which is also listed beside Raphia in Shishak's list,[150] apparently to be identified with Tell Abu Seleimeh near Sheikh Zuweid, excavated by Petrie.[151] Another rebellion broke out in 720 B.C. in which Samaria again participated. Sargon devastated Hamath and turned it into an Assyrian province. He also marched as far as Gaza and Raphia, which he destroyed and whose population he exiled.[152] In the years 713 and 712 the Assyrian armies returned to Palestine in order to quell a new rebellion. This time the offenders were led by Ashdod, which had the support of Shabako, founder of the Twenty-fifth (Ethiopian) Dynasty in Egypt (Isa. 18; 20).[153] According to Sargon's inscription, Judah, Edom and Moab also participated in the revolt, but they evidently surrendered in the nick of time. The Assyrian blow was mainly levelled at Ashdod, which was then reorganized as an Assyrian province. In 712 B.C. Gath,[154] Gibbethon and Ekron[155] were captured as well as Ashdod and its harbour town, Ashdod-yam (Asdudimmu).

In spite of all the military activity there was an increase in commerce and Hezekiah was able to have a share in it. Sargon's conquest of the southern coastal area opened the trade route to Egypt: "I reorganized these cities (and) settled therein people from the [regions] of the East which I had conquered personally. I installed an officer of mine over them and declared them Assyrian citizens and they pulled the straps (of my yoke). The king of Ethiopia who [lives] in [a distant country], in an inapproachable region, the road [to which is . . .], whose fathers never—from remote days until now—had sent messengers to inquire after the health of my royal forefathers, he did hear, even (that) far away, of the might of Ashur, Nebo, Marduk." "From Pir'u, the king of Muṣru, Samsi, the queen of Arabia, It'amra, the Sabaean,—these are the kings of the seashore and from the desert—I received as their presents, gold in the form of dust, precious stones, ivory, ebony seeds, all kinds of aromatic substances, horses (and) camels."[156] This situation is reflected in the Egyptian oracle of Isaiah: "In that day there will be a highway from Egypt and Assyria, and the Assyrian will come into Egypt, and the Egyptian into Assyria, and the Egyptians will serve the Assyrians" (Isa. 19. 23).

The same oracle is illuminating from still another aspect. The prophet describes an apocalyptic age when Egypt will behave like Judah and thus, he actually describes the situation in Judah of his own times: "In that day there will be *five cities* in the land of Egypt which speak the language of Canaan and swear allegiance to the Lord of Hosts. One of these will be called the City of the Sun. In that day there will be an altar to the Lord in the midst of the land of Egypt, and a pillar to the Lord at its border" (Isa. 19. 18–19). Isaiah speaks of five cities in which the holy tongue will be spoken, i.e. in which Yawistic temples would stand, one probably being the ancient capital of Heliopolis. Only in the central one was there to be an altar. Those along the borders would have stelae (*maṣṣebot*). That was precisely the situation in Judah during the reign of Hezekiah as indicated by archaeological discoveries and biblical allusions. As mentioned previously, a temple was discovered at Arad, erected in the United Monarchy and rebuilt several times along with its citadel after each destruction. Yet in the days of Hezekiah (Stratum VIII) the altar was not repaired and worship found expression only in drink offerings and incense before *maṣṣebot* erected in the Holy of Holies.[157] The temple was finally put completely out of commission near the end of the seventh century.

The situation was similar at Beer-sheba. A large horned altar was discovered there, it having been dismantled in the reign of Hezekiah and its temple completely destroyed.[158] Even though the fortified city was not rebuilt after the disaster during Sennacherib's campaign, the sanctity of the site was not forgotten and in the Hellenistic period a new temple was built on the open high place on top of the mound.[159]

At Lachish two temples were also discovered from the Persian and Hellenistic periods respectively; they were similar in plan to the Arad and Beer-sheba temples.[160] It was also shown that they were preceded on that spot by an earlier tradition of cultic practice. In the Sennacherib reliefs depicting Lachish, two soldiers are carrying as a major part of the booty two decorated incense burners.

During the reign of Hezekiah, there existed, therefore, cultic buildings in at least three places: Arad, Beer-sheba and Lachish. All three were royal cities dominating border regions, Arad facing Edom, Beer-sheba facing towards Egypt and Lachish towards Philistia. It is hardly accidental that the two places in Israel where Jeroboam erected his own temples have the same function, viz. Bethel near the border facing Judah and Dan facing Aram. Their royal character is expressed by Amaziah the priest of Bethel: ". . . it is the king's sanctuary, and it is a temple of the kingdom" (Amos 7. 13).

What we seem to have here is a royal institution of temples dominating border areas, in addition to the central sanctuary in the capital. They symbolized the deity's rule over his people and his country (cf. Judg. 11. 24; 1 Sam. 6. 9; 27. 19, etc.) and his presence as their defence and the sustainer of their independence.

Amos was the first to denounce them (Amos 5. 5; 8. 14), seeing in them an obstacle to pure monotheism in which the rule of God is supposed to know no boundaries. Hezekiah was the first monarch to limit their function by centralizing the offering of sacrifices in Jerusalem (2 Kings 18. 4 and especially the words of the Rabshakeh, 18. 22). Josiah completed that reform by completely abolishing all the local cult places outside Jerusalem and transferring their priests "from Geba to Beer-sheba" to the vicinity of Jerusalem (2 Kings 23.8). One of his main ambitions had been the abolition of the Bethel temple which sanctified the border separating Israel from Judah.

This seems to be the situation depicted in the prophecy of Isaiah about Egypt: a centrally located temple with a sacrificial altar at the capital and four border sanctuaries having only stelae (*maṣṣebot*) on the borders of the kingdom. In Judah the site of a fourth sanctuary is not certain; there probably was one facing Israel in the north. The most probable sites would be either Geba (note the above mentioned passage from the reign of Josiah) or Mizpah with its old cultic tradition.

[1] Since only in Israel was there a series of dynastic changes (in contrast to Judah where the House of David was firmly established), we have used the Israelite kings to denote the subdivisions of this period; these dynasties also correspond to the principal phases of Judah's history.

[2] For the changes of the borders cf. Z. Kallai, *The Northern Boundaries of Judah* (Jerusalem, 1960) (Hebrew).

[3] Cf. 2 Chron. 16. 6; Geba rules the pass of Wadi Suweiniṭ (cf. *supra,* p. 287) and a description of a campaign along this route is preserved with Isa. 10. 28 ff.

The assumption that Asa built Gibeah of Benjamin (Tell el-Ful) as a second stronghold on the central road to Jerusalem is improbable also in the light of the excavations at the place, cf. L. A. Sinclair, *AASOR,* 34–5 (1960), pp 7 f.

[4] C. C. McCown, *Tell en-Naṣbeh,* I (Berkeley, 1947), p. 202.

[5] Y. Aharoni, *VT,* 9 (1959), pp. 232 ff. and cf. *infra,* p. 347 ff.

[6] For the special Judaean border definition in his days, "from Geba to Beer-sheba" (2 Kings 23. 8), cf. *infra,* p. 404.

[7] Cf. A. Alt, *PJb,* 21 (1925), pp. 108 ff. (=*Kl. Schr.,* II, pp. 281 ff.); Z. Kallai, *The Northern Boundaries of Judah* (Jerusalem, 1960), pp. 74 f. (Hebrew).

[8] Chicago Epigraphic Survey, *Reliefs and Inscriptions at Karnak,* III, *The Babastite Portal* (Chicago, 1954); Simons, *Handbook,* pp. 89 ff., 178 ff.; M. Noth, *ZDPV,* 61 (1938),

pp. 277–304 (=*Aufsätze* II, pp. 73–93); for up-to-date discussion and bibliography cf. K. Kitchen, *The Third Intermediate Period in Egypt* (Warminster, 1973), pp. 432–47.

[9] B. Mazar, *VT Suppl.*, 4 (1957), pp. 57–66 (=*Canaan and Israel*, Jerusalem, 1974, pp. 234–44, plus excellent photographs by B. Grdseloff, Pls. 10–11). When in Chicago in 1954, Mazar conferred closely with the scholars of the Epigraphic Survey with regard to the various readings. We have followed Mazar's arrangement of this list with the exception of line 5 which we have inserted differently. Since it is agreed that these towns are not in their original order, it seemed more likely to us that Shishak went from Zemaraim to Tirzah and descended to Adam via the Wadi Far'ah, rather than going first to the Valley of Succoth and returning thence to Tirzah.

[10] On the date of the royal seal impressions cf. Y. Aharoni, *Excavations at Ramat Raḥel, Seasons 1959 and 1960* (Rome, 1962), pp. 51 ff. It is possible that after the city was destroyed by Shishak the territory of Gezer was temporarily included in the kingdom of Israel; this is suggested by the wars of the Israelite kings against Philistia and Gibbethon; cf. also. Z. Kallai, *op. cit.* (note 2), pp. 55–56.

[11] This reading was suggested by Grdesloff and Mazar as a correction of *q-ḏ-t-m* on the assumption that the sculptor of this inscription was reading from a hieratic copy. In hieroglyphs the *r* (a mouth) is clearly distinguishable from the *d* (a hand), but in hieratic the two signs are quite similar. However, this similarity has nothing to do with the confusion of *resh* and *daleth* so common in West Semitic scripts.

[12] Abel, *Géogr.*, II, p. 339.

[13] R. S. Lamon and G. M. Shipton, *Megiddo* (Chicago, 1939), I, pp. 60 f.

[14] G. E. Wright, *BA*, 13 (1950), pp. 39 ff.; Y. Yadin, *BA*, 23 (1960), pp. 62 ff.

[15] Tell el-'Uṣeifer, where Iron Age remains have been found, is a likely possibility for the site of the ancient town.

[16] The text reads: *š-b-r-t / n g-b-r,* i.e. "the *Shibboleth* (ear of grain ?) belonging to Geber".

[17] Or perhaps the Sucathites, 1 Chron. 2. 55.

[18] M. Noth, *ZDPV*, 61 (1938), pp. 294–300 (=*Aufsätze*, II, pp. 86–90); B. Mazar, *VT Suppl.*, 4 (1957), p. 64; *idem*, *Epstein Vol.* (Jerusalem, 1950), pp. 316–19.

[19] Y. Aharoni, *BA*, 39 (1976), pp. 55 ff., especially pp. 68–69; *idem* and R. Amiran, *Archaeology*, 17 (1964), pp 43–53; *idem*, *IEJ*, 14 (1964), pp. 131–47.

[20] Y. Aharoni, *BA*, 35 (1972), pp. 114–15.

[21] Y. Aharoni, *IEJ*, 17 (1967), pp. 1–17.

[22] Noth, *loc. cit.* (note 18).

[23] ANET, p. 286; A. Alt, *ZDPV*, 67 (1945), pp. 29 ff. (=*Kl. Schr.*, II, pp. 226 ff.).

[24] Excavations were carried out there by Sir Flinders Petrie, which were published under the title *Anthedon*. Remains dating from the Late Bronze Age through the Early Roman period were discovered.

[25] N. Glueck, *The Other Side of the Jordan* (New Haven, 1945), pp. 99 ff.

[26] Concerning the structure of this roster, cf. especially G. Beyer, *ZDPV*, 54 (1931), pp. 113–34; A. Alt, "Festungen und Levitenorte im Lande Juda" (1952), *Kl. Schr.*, II, pp. 306–15; Z. Kallai, *EI*, 10 (1971), pp. 245–54.

[27] Abel, *Géogr.*, II, p. 392.

[28] The original text may have been: "Adullam, Moresheth-gath, Mareshah etc.", from which "Moresheth" accidentally fell out due to its similarity to "Mareshah" near by.

[29] Concerning the relationship between these two lists, cf. Alt. *loc. cit.* (note 26).

[30] Hebron apparently did not belong to the original list of Levitical towns, cf. *supra*, pp. 303 n.32.

[31] Some hold the opinion that Zerah is Osorkon I (*c.* 914–874 B.C.). the successor of Shishak, an assumption which is supported by the information that his army contained Ethiopians and Libyans (2 Chron. 16. 8).

[32] Y. Aharoni, *BIES*, 22 (1958), pp. 30–32 (Hebrew).

[33] B. Mazar, "The Aramean Empire and its Relations with Israel", *BA*, 25 (1962), pp. 98 ff.

[34] Cf. *infra*, pp. 336 ff.

[35] According to 2 Chron. 16. 4, "and all the store cities of Naphtali".

[36] According to 2 Chron. 16. 4; "Abel-maim".

[37] Y. Yadin *et al.*, *Hazor,* I (Jerusalem, 1958), I, pp. 10, 22 f.; Y. Yadin, *et al.*, *Hazor,* II (Jerusalem, 1959), pp. 4 f.

[38] Contrary to the excavators' opinion, it seems likely that there were remains from the tenth and perhaps also the eleventh centuries B.C.; cf. W. F. Albright, *BASOR,* 150 (1958), pp. 22 f.; Y. Aharoni and Ruth Amiran, *IEJ,* 8 (1958), pp. 178 ff.; G. E. Wright, *BASOR,* 155 (1959), pp. 20 ff.

[39] H. J. Katzenstein, *IEJ,* 5 (1955), pp. 194–97.

[40] W. F. Albright, *Leland Vol.* (Menasha, 1942), pp. 11 ff. (=*The Bible and the Ancient Near-East,* ed. G. E. Wright [New York, 1961], pp. 328 ff).

[41] *ANET,* p. 320 f.; cf. *infra,* pp. 336 ff.

[42] Z. Meshel, *BIES,* 25 (1961), pp. 157–59 (Hebrew). N. Gleuck, *BA,* 28 (1965), pp. 70–87; *idem,* apud. D. W. Thomas, *AOTS,* 1967, pp. 428–53; *idem, Rivers in the Desert,* revd. ed., 1968, pp. 158–68. V. R. Gold apud C. F. Pfeiffer, ed., *The Biblical World* (Grand Rapids, 1966), pp. 233–37.

[43] Y. Aharoni and M. Aharoni, *BASOR,* 224 (1976), pp. 73–90.

[44] B. Mazar, A. Biran, M. Dothan, I. Dunayevsky, *IEJ,* 14 (1969), pp. 1–49.

[45] In the trial excavation carried out by B. Mazar, A. Biran and M. Dothan on the tell of ʿEn-Gev on the eastern shore of the Sea of Galilee a large fortified town was discovered which was in existence during the tenth through the eighth centuries B.C. This town preceded Hippos (Susita), which was built above it; it was apparently a Geshurite-Aramean stronghold dominating the eastern shore of the Sea of Galilee. This tell is just three and a half miles down the slope from Fiq, and it is difficult to imagine that two fortified towns existed so close to one another during the same period. If the battle took place in the Yarmuk Valley, then the tell of ʿEn-Gev is more suitable for the biblical Aphek than any other site. Perhaps it may have been a "lower city" corresponding to "Upper Aphek" on the order of other double-sited towns during the biblical period, e.g. Upper and Lower Beth-horon.

[46] Mazar, *loc. cit.* (note 33), pp. 109 ff.

[47] *ANET,* pp. 277 f.

[48] *ANET,* pp. 278 f.

[49] N. Na'aman, *Tel Aviv,* 3 (1976), pp. 89–106, demonstrates both the logistic impossibility of such a large Israelite chariot force and the general untrustworthiness of the provincial scribe who composed the text in question. He argues for an Israelite force of 200 chariots, but even this seems much too high.

[50] About the Mesha stone and the campaigns cf. *ANET,* pp. 320 f.; M. Noth, *ZAW N.F.,* 4 (1944), pp. 42 ff.; A. H. van Zyl, *The Moabites* (Leiden, 1960), pp. 139 ff., 161 ff.; B. Mazar, *Enc. Bibl* (Hebrew), IV, col. 921–26; J. Liver, *PEQ,* 99 (1967), pp. 14–31; M. Miller, *PEQ,* 106 (1974), pp. 9–18, especially pp. 17–18.

[51] This is evidently the full name of Mesha's father, according to the recently discovered fragment of another stele from Kerak, cf. W. L. Reed and F. V. Winnet, *BASOR,* 172 (1963), pp. 1–9. The vocalization adopted above is that suggested by H. L. Ginzberg (*ibid.*, p. 8, note 20a), as a variant for *Kemoš-yattin,* "(it is) Chemosh (who) gives". Reed and Winnet think that the stele belonged to Mesha's father, but its close resemblance to the inscription from Dibon makes it more likely that the new stele was also erected by Mesha himself. If so, then the first line may be completed: "[I am Mesha the son of Che]mosh-yatti, King of Moab, the [Dibonite]"; cf. D. N. Freedman, *BASOR,* 175 (1964), pp. 50 f.

[52] A recent suggestion would locate it at Khirbet el-Qureiyeh about six miles north-west of Medeba, cf. A. Kuschke, *ZDPV,* 77 (1961), pp. 24 ff.; 78 (1962), pp. 139 f.; but this place seems to lie too far north. Qaryat el-Mekhaiyet about three miles west-north-west of Medeba would be a better location.

[53] This was evidently during the time when Jehoram served as coregent to Jehoshaphat his father, about 850 B.C.

[54] *ANET,* p. 280.

[55] A. T. Olmsteadt, *History of Assyria* (New York, 1923), p. 139.

[56] F. Safar, *Sumer,* 7 (1951), pp. 11 ff.; E. Michel, *Die Welt des Orients* (1954), p. 39.

[57] Y. Aharoni, in *Western Galilee and the Coast of Galilee* (Jerusalem, 1965), pp. 56–62 (Hebrew).

[58] [The attempt by P. Kyle McCarter to disprove this synchronization, *BASOR*, 216 (1974), pp. 5–7, involves so many impossibilities, linguistic, sociological (that someone might be called Yaw!) and chronological, as to be hardly worthy of notice. A.F.R.]

[59] Mazar, *loc. cit* (note 33), p. 114; Luckenbill, *AR*, I, § 739.

[60] B. Mazar, *IEJ*, 4 (1954), pp. 227–35; perhaps Amos 6. 2 is an allusion to this destruction.

[61] *ANET*, pp. 281 f.; note that recent discoveries prove that Adad-nirari III did not campaign in Philistia, H. Tadmor, *IEJ*, 19 (1969), pp. 46–48.

[62] The Nimrud Slab, *ANET*, p. 281; D. J. Wiseman apud D. Winton Thomas, ed., *Documents from Old Testament Times* (Edinburgh, 1958), pp. 51–52. renders the passage correctly by Philistia and not "Palestine", which is wholly unrealistic for this period.

[63] S. Page, *Iraq*, 30 (1968), pp. 139–53; A. R. Millard and H. Tadmor, *Iraq*, 35 (1973), pp. 57–64; H. Tadmor, *ibid.*, pp. 141–50. The spelling of the Israelite king's name is obviously defective, cf. M. C. Astour, *IBD Supplement* (Nashville, 1976), p. 479; the reading proposed by A. Malamat, *BASOR*, 204 (1971), pp. 37–39, has nothing to commend it.

[64] *ANET*², pp. 501 f.

[65] Cf. *IEJ*, 11 (1961), p. 193.

[66] Cf. Amos 6. 14, "From Lebo-hamath to the Brook of the Arabah".

[67] N. Glueck, *BASOR*, 79 (1940), pp. 13 f.; N. Avigad, *BASOR*, 163 (1961), pp. 18–22.

[68] In Mazar's opinion (*loc. cit.*, note 60), Gath-Gittaim (Ras Abu Ḥumeid), but a great deal depends upon the identification of Gath of the Philistines. Royal Judean seal impressions found at Tell eṣ-Ṣafi indicate that the place was within the bounds of Judah at the end of the eighth century B.C.therefore, if Gath of the Philistines may be identified with that site, then it, too, comes in for consideration: cf. A. F. Rainey, *EI*, 12 (Jerusalem, 1975), pp. 73*

[69] Concerning the problem of the Meunites and their possible identification with one of the Arabian peoples known in Hellenistic literature as the **Μιναιοι**, cf. F. V. Winnet, *BASOR*, 73 (1939), pp. 3 ff.; M. Noth, *ZDPV*, 67 (1944), pp. 48 ff.

[70] C. L. Woolley and T. E. Lawrence, *PEF An.*, 3 (1914), pp. 64 ff.

[71] Y. Aharoni, *IEJ*, 8 (1958), pp. 33–35.

[72] In Khirbet Rasm eḍ-Ḍab' (Map ref. 1433 1172), cf L. Y. Rahmani, *Yediot*, 28 (1964), pp. 209–14 (Hebrew).

[73] R. A. S. Macalister and J. F. Bliss, *Excavations in Palestine* (London, 1902), pp. 12 ff. The fortress of this type found in the excavations at Arad (cf. *supra*, p. 329) was built in the latter part of the eighth century B.C. and lasted till the end of the Judean Monarchy. The earlier fortresses on this site had been constructed according to a different plan.

[74] Nevertheless, the pottery found *in situ* in those small fortified settlements was largely seventh century; L. E. Stager, "Ancient Irrigation Agriculture in the Buqê' ah Valley", unpublished Ph.D. dissertation, Harvard University, 1972.

[75] From the murder of Zechariah in 748 until the conquest of Samaria in 722/1 five kings ruled in Israel; Shallum, Menahem, Pekahia, Pekah and Hoshea.

[76] N. Na'aman, *BASOR*, 214 (1974), pp. 25–39; the text in question has been proven to belong to the reign of Hezekiah and pertains to Sennacherib's campaign in 701 B.C.

[77] A. Alt, *PJb*, 21 (1925), pp. 100–16 (=*Kl. Schr.*, II, pp. 276–88); F. M. Cross and G. E. Wright, *JBL*, 75 (1956), pp. 202–26; Z. Kallai-Kleinmann, *VT*, 8 (1958), pp. 134–60; Y. Aharoni, *VT*, 9 (1959), pp. 225–40.

[78] Y. Yadin, *BASOR*, 163 (1961), pp. 6–12, is of the opinon that this geographical division is connected with the military organization which did not correspond to the regular administrative division of the kingdom. This is difficult to accept because one cannot assume that in that period the civilian and military administrations were separated, since they were so closely intertwined. One fails to see a sound military reason for having one district that included all of the hill country of Judah and Benjamin alongside another in the sparsely settled wilderness of Judah, especially since there was never any serious danger in this area. Its capital, Ziph, according to Yadin, is a town in the hill country not far from Hebron which was the capital of its own district. It is natural that an administrative-regional division should be made according to clear-cut geographical areas, but, of course, each area would be subdivided in accordance with its own special nature.

[79] J. Naveh, *IEJ*, 10 (1960), pp. 129–39, and 14 (1964), pp. 158–59.

[80] *JBL*, 75 (1956), pp. 209–11.

[81] Y. Aharoni, *VT*, 9 (1959), pp. 232–34; cf. *infra*, pp. 347 ff.

[82] Z. Kallai, *The Tribes of Israel* (Jerusalem, 1967), pp. 107–16; also Z. Kallai-Kleinmann, *VT*, 8 (1958), pp. 134–60.

[83] [Nevertheless, the very existence of a two-town district in the text argues against its artificiality; an editor would hardly have invented such an oddity, A.F.R.]

[84] *JBL*, 75 (1956), pp. 223–24.

[85] B. Mazar apud D. W. Thomas, ed., *Archaeology and Old Testament Study* (Oxford, 1967), pp. 222–30.

[86] Y. Aharoni apud D. W. Thomas, *ibid.*, pp. 171–84.

[87] Y. Aharoni and M. Aharoni, *BASOR*, 224 (1976), pp. 73–90.

[88] Cross and Wright, *op. cit.*, pp. 216, 226.

[89] The first to date the administrative organization reflected in Josh. 15 to the reign of Jehoshaphat was B. Mazar, *Enc., Bibl.* (Hebrew), I, col. 718; III, col. 566; he was followed by Cross and Wright, *loc. cit.*

[90] The numerical subtotal is twenty-nine, but it is difficult to determine whether some names refer to one town or more, e.g. "Kerioth-hezron (that is, Hazor)", in Jos. 15 25.

[91] *Y. Aharoni, Tel Aviv*, 2 (1975), pp. 114–18; *idem, BA*, 39 (1976), pp. 66–70, 73.

[92] M. Kochavi, *Judea, Samaria and the Golan, Archaeological Survey* 1967–1968 (Jerusalem, 1972), pp. 80–31 (Hebrew); A. F. Rainey, *IBD Supplement*, (Nashville, 1976), p. 561.

[93] M. Kochavi, *Tel Aviv*, 1 (1974), pp. 2–33: *idem*, *IDB Supplement*, p. 222.

[94] M. Kochavi, *op. cit.* (*supra*. n. 92), pp. 21, 76, 78; A. F. Rainey, *IDB Supplement*, p. 25.

[95] On the basis of the Egyptian sources; Y. Aharoni, *VT*, 19 (1969), pp. 137–45.

[96] [For this reason, the identification of Rabbah/Rubute with Kh. Ḥamideh is suspect; the hills of Judah come to an abrupt halt at Bab el-Wad while the ridge beside Kh. Ḥamideh is in the Shephelah. A.F.R.]

[97] J. M. Allegro, *The Treasure of the Copper Scroll* (London, 1960), pp. 32 ff., 68–74, 144 ff., 172, 186; Z. Kallai, *The Tribes of Israel* (Jerusalem, 1967), p. 333 (Hebrew); *idem, Enc. Bibl.* (Hebrew), V, cols. 1044–5.

[98] F. M. Cross and J. T. Milik, *BASOR*, 142 (1956), pp. 5–17.

[99] P. Bar-Adon, *RB*, 77 (1970), pp. 398–400.

[100] Reisner-Fisher, *Harvard Excavations at Samaria*, I (Cambridge, Mass. 1924), pp. 227 ff.; D. Diringer, *Le iscrizioni antico-ebraiche Palestinesi* (Florence, 1934). To the problems of their date, purpose and the location of the sites mentioned in them, cf. F. M. Abel, *RB* (1911), pp. 290 ff.; W. F. Albright, *JPOS*, 5 (1925), pp. 38 ff.; 11 (1931), pp. 241 ff.; B. Maisler (Mazar), *JPOS*, 14 (1934), pp. 96 ff.; 21 (1948), pp. 117–33; M. Noth, *ZDPV*, 50 (1927), pp. 219 ff. (=*Aufsätze*, I, pp. 157–82); S. A. Birnbaum, *PEQ*, 74 (1942), pp. 107 f.; Y. Yadin, *Scripta Hierosolymitana*, 8 (1960), pp. 1–17; *IEJ*, 12 (1962), pp. 64–66, F. M. Cross, *BASOR*, 163 (1961), pp. 12 ff.; A. F. Rainey, *IEJ*, 12 (1962), pp. 62 f.; Y. Aharoni, *IEJ*, 12 (1962), pp. 67–69; Rainey, *PEQ*, 99 (1967), pp. 32–51; *idem*, 102 (1970), pp. 45–51; F. M. Cross, *AUSS*, 13 (1975), pp. 7–10. The most recent detailed study is I. T. Kaufman, *The Samaria Ostraca, A Study in Ancient Hebrew Palaeography*, Th.D. Dissertation, Harvard Divinity School, Cambridge, Mass., 1966; by use of infra-red photographs, Kaufman was able to read the text on two of the hitherto unpublished sherds thus adding two more to the corpus, Nos. 3892 and 3893.

[101] The Hebrew word used here (*nebel*) can mean a leather bottle, but it is also a standard biblical term for a pottery jar, cf. J. L. Kelso, *BASOR, Suppl. St.*, 5–6 (1948), pp. 25 f.

[102] Yadin proposed to interpret the sign 7Λ as the number 9 because the sign 7 resembles the symbol for "4" on shekel weights. However, the representation of 9 by a combination of 4 + 5 is completely without precedent; furthermore, it fails to explain the number on ostracon No. 63 (IItΛ). Noth has shown that this sign represents the cipher 15 (Λ=10, 7=5) in Egyptian hieratic writing. Meanwhile it has become clear from the Arad ostraca that in the Israelite administration the Egyptian hieratic numerals were indeed used. The hieratic signs for 5, 10, 20 and 30, used with this value in official Hebrew documents, stood for different units on the weights which were equal to 4, 8, 16 and 24 shekels respectively.

[103] This reading in place of the previously accepted *sq* was proposed independently by H. Michaud, *Sur la pierre et l'argile* (Nuechatel, 1958), p. 58, and by Cross, *loc. cit.* (note 100).

[104] This reading, first suggested by Albright, is now proposed again by Cross instead of *srq*.

[105] *IEJ,* 12 (1962), pp. 62–63.

[106] F. M. Cross, *AUSS,* 13 (1975), pp. 7–10.

[107] Cf. Also UT 1098 which records items received from various places and recorded in the palace ledgers of Ugarit. Alongside the regular shipments to the crown, some allotments sent to specific recipients are also listed. This shows that such payments could certainly be channelled through the royal storehouse; A. F. Rainey, *PEQ,* 99 (1967), pp. 36–38; *idem,* apud *Proceedings of the International Conference on Semitic Studies held in Jerusalem, 19–23 July 1965* (Jerusalem, 1969), pp. 205–11.

[108] At least with regard to these entries, M. Noth was correct, *op. cit.* (*supra,* n. 100).

[109] As first seen by I. Mendelsohn, *BASOR,* 143 (1956), pp. 17–22; though he misunderstood a few of the Akkadian passages in question, his initial observation was a brilliant insight.

[110] Such was ostensibly the excuse for taking Naboth's vineyard, 1 Kings 21. 10, 13.

[111] Widows and orphans were especially vulnerable, cf. 2 Kings 4. 1 ff.

[112] Rainey, *PEQ,* 99 (1967), p. 39.

[113] Rainey, *IEJ,* 16 (1966), pp. 187–90.

[114] Rainey, *PEQ,* 102 (1970), pp. 45–51.

[115] Exod. 29. 28; Num. 7. 84; 18. 28; Deut. 18. 3; also Arad texts 5. 2, 6. 2, 9. 2 in Y. Aharoni, *Arad Inscriptions* (Jerusalem, 1975).

[116] Num. 7. 17, 23, 29, *et passim.*

[117] *ʾḥmʾ* on ostracon No. 3 from the year ten is simply a restoration based upon Nos. 37–39; actually only the last letter is preserved.

[118] According to Yadin's system it was only ten years; therefore he proposed Menahem.

[119] One must remember that we do not have any cursive inscriptions from this period; therefore, it is difficult to arrive at a precise date on palaeographical considerations only. The excavators indicate that the ostraca were found in several rooms of the building, "in the lowest part of debris of occupation" (Reisner-Fischer, *op. cit.* [note 100], p. 227), together with an alabaster vessel bearing the name of Osorkon II. In another place (p. 62) they state: "This floor was 10–40 cm. thick, an accumulation of fine, black debris such as is laid down by the occupation of earthfloored courtyards, representing, perhaps, a considerable period of time." According to the investigation by Crowfoot and Kenyon (*Samaria-Sebaste,* III, p. 469) most of the ostraca belong to period IV which, in their opinion, must date to the first half of the eighth century.

[120] It is doubtful if Jehoahaz reigned seventeen years, cf. Y. Aharoni, *Tarbiz,* 21 (1950), pp. 92 f. (Hebrew).

[121] Since photographs of the ostraca are not given in the publication, it is difficult to arrive at sure palaeographic conclusions. Nevertheless, we may point out a difference with regard to at least one letter: *q*—Cross has already pointed out that two types of *qof* are found in the Samaria ostraca. "One has a head drawn in a circular motion clockwise . . . The other *qof* is made with two semicircular strokes, much like the *ʿayn* . . . ostraca Nos. 4, 5, 6, have type one; 22–24; 26–27 the second type" (*BASOR,* 165 [1962], p. 41). The first type, the older, is found therefore on ostraca from the years 9 and 10, while the second type appears in year 15. This is an obvious palaeographic development which would be astonishing in a period of only five years.

[122] The accepted identification for Yashub is Khirbet Kafr Sibb on the Sharon Plain beside Shuweikeh, 10½ miles north-west of Samaria; but this would be the only place outside of Mount Ephraim, and its identification depended upon the reading *srq,* Yashub's clan district. With the alternative reading (A)sriel for this district the identification with Yasuf in the hill country near Tappuah seems more probable. This place is called Yasub in Jewish midrashic literature and the Samaritan Chronicle (cf. S. Klein, *ZDPV,* 57 [1934], pp. 7 ff.). It is possible that "the inhabitants of En-tappuah on the border of Manasseh" (Josh. 17.7) should be read "Yashub and En-tappuah", which is supported by LXX (cf. F. M. Abel, *RB* [1936], pp. 103 ff.). Jashub was also a clan of Issachar that may have had some association with this place (cf. *supra,* p. 244).

[123] Cf. H. Tadmor, *Introductory Remarks to a New Edition of the Annals of Tiglath-Pileser III, Proceedings of the Israel Academy of Sciences and Humanities,* Vol. II, No. 9 (Jerusalem, 1967).

[124] *ANET*, pp. 282 f.

[125] *ANET*, p. 282

[126] H. W. F. Saggs, *Iraq,* 17 (1955), No. XII, pp. 127 ff., also No. XIII, pp. 130 f. Though Saggs dates these letters to the reign of Tiglath-pileser III, H. J. Katzenstein, *The History of Tyre* (Jerusalem, 1973), pp. 232–38, would place them in the early part of the reign of Sargon II; since the same commissioner seems to have dealt with affairs in Transjordan (cf. *infra*), it is unlikely that he had his headquarters at Ṣimirra (the Ṣumer of the Late Bronze Age) as suggested by Katzenstein.

[127] For the history of the Tabeelites/Tobiads from the First to the Second Temple periods, cf. B. Mazar, *IEJ,* 7 (1957), pp. 137–45, 229–38 (=*Canaan and Israel,* Jerusalem, 1974, pp. 270–90, Hebrew).

[128] Saggs, *Iraq,* 17 (1955), Text No. XIV (ND 2773), pp. 131–32.

[129] Jos. *War,* IV, 7. 3 (413); Ptolm. V, 14. 4; Mishnah *Arakhin,* 9.6.

[130] Lachish Letter 3. 9; *ANET*, p. 322.

[131] D. J. Wiseman, *Iraq,* 13 (1951), pp. 21 ff.; A. Alt. "Tiglathpilesers III. erster Feldzug nach Palästina" (1951), *Kl. Schr.*, II, pp. 150–62; H. Tadmor, *BA,* 29 (1966), pp. 86–102.

[132] There is some doubt regarding the different events during both years.

[133] On this campaign cf. especially B. Maisler (Mazar), *BIES,* 1, 1 (1933–4), pp. 1–6 (Hebrew); Aharoni, *Settlement,* pp. 129–32 (Hebrew); H. Tadmor, *IEJ,* 12 (1962), pp. 114–22; E. Vogt, *Biblica,* 45 (1964), pp. 348–54.

[134] *ANET*, pp. 283 f.; Tadmor, *ibid.*

[135] This reading is now established on the basis of a new inscription, cf. D. J. Wiseman, *Iraq,* 18 (1956), pp. 117 ff.

[136] *ANEP,* No. 336; the relief depicting the conquest of Gazri (*ANEP,* No. 369) is probably to be associated with the campaign in 734 or 733 and there is no reason to doubt its identification with Gezer in Palestine.

[137] *ANET*, p. 283.

[138] E. Forrer, *Die Provinzeinteilung des assyrischen Reiches* (Leipzig, 1920), pp. 52 ff.; A. Alt. *ZDPV,* 52 (1929), pp. 220–42 (=*Kl. Schr.*, II, pp. 188–205).

[139] The name of its capital is not certain. Apparently (Ramoth-) gilead is meant (cf. Hos. 6. 8). However, a town by the name of Hammath which is mentioned in Assyrian lists also comes in for consideration; it is identified with Tell 'Ammata north of Tell Deir 'Alla. cf. Alt. *ibid.*, p. 241 (=*Kl. Schr.*, II, p. 204) cf. most recently B. Oded, *JNES,* 29 (1970), pp. 177–86.

[140] K. M. Kenyon, *Archaeology in the Holy Land* (London, 1960), pp. 282, 286; Y. Aharoni, *IEJ,* 11 (1961), p. 90.

[141] R. B. K. Amiran and I. Dunayevsky, *BASOR,* 149 (1958), pp. 25 ff.

[142] *ANET*, p. 282.

[143] *ANET*, pp. 287, 291, 294.

[144] C. M. Bennet, *Levant,* 5 (1973), pp. 1–11; 5 (1974), pp. 1–24; 6 (1975), pp. 1–15.

[145] N. Na'aman, *BASOR* 214 (1974), pp. 25–39.

[146] On the provinces cf. *ANET*, p. 283; Forrer, *op. cit.* (note 138).

[147] *ANET*, p. 282.

[148] *ANET*, p. 284; H. Tadmor, *JCS,* 12 (1958), pp. 22–41, 77–101.

[149] *ANET*, p. 292.

[150] *ANET*, p. 286; Simons, *Handbook,* p. 186, No. 3bis.

[151] W. M. Flinders Petrie, *Anthedon* (London, 1937).

[152] *ANET*, p. 285.

[153] *ANET*, pp. 286 f.

[154] In Mazar's opinion, *loc. cit.* (note 60), Gath-Gittaim (Ras Abu Ḥamid), but in view of the proposed identification for Gath of the Philistines with Tell eṣ-Ṣafi (cf. *supra,* p. 271) it is probable that this latter city is meant here. It is worthy of note that in the excavation of Tell eṣ-Ṣafi fragments were found from an Assyrian stele, cf. F. J. Bliss and R. A. S. Macalister *Excavations in Palestine* (London, 1902), p. 41.

[In fact, the inscription of Sargon only makes good topographical sense if Gath at Tell eṣ-Ṣafi is meant; Rainey, *EI*, 12 (1975), pp. 73*–74*.]

155 Tadmor, *loc. cit.* (note 148), p. 83.

156 *ANET*, p. 286b and a respectively.

157 Y. Aharoni, *BA*, 31 (1968), pp. 18–32.

158 Y. Aharoni, *BA*, 35 (1972), pp. 123–27; *idem*, *BA*, 37 (1974), pp. 2–6.

159 Y. Aharoni, *Tel Aviv*, 2 (1975), pp. 158–65.

160 Y. Aharoni, *Lachish V*, pp. 7–11.

CHAPTER V

The Latter Days of the Judean Kingdom

The last phase in the history of the Judean Monarchy was marked by a continual struggle for survival in the face of Assyrian and later of Babylonian imperialism with periodic attempts by Egypt to sway the small Palestinian states from their allegiance to the northern empires.

I. SENNACHERIB'S CAMPAIGN

The death of Sargon and the succession of Sennacherib in 705 B.C. occasioned a series of new rebellions throughout the empire. In Palestine it was Hezekiah, King of Judah, who led the conspiracy. The arrival in Jerusalem of envoys from Merodach-baladan, King of Babylon (2 Kings 20. 12–19), was evidently related to this revolt which, as usual, was also supported by Egypt (Isa. 30. 1–5; 31. 1–3). Among the Philistine cities it was Ashkelon who now raised the banner of insurrection, and the citizenry of Ekron joined the rebels after deposing their king, Padi, and handing him over in fetters to Hezekiah.[1] Evidently Hezekiah hoped to restore his kingdom to the position of influence that it had enjoyed under Uzziah. He even tried to expand his influence over the Assyrian provinces which now comprised the former kingdom of Israel; his cultic innovations were probably related to this programme (2 Chron. 30. 1–12).

Apparently Hezekiah understood well the risk that he was taking upon himself, as witnessed by his meticulous preparations for the ensuing conflict. His most famous project was the Siloam tunnel in Jerusalem, which was dug for the purpose of diverting the waters from the Gihon spring to within the city walls (2 Kings 20. 20; 2 Chron. 32. 30). The walls of Jerusalem were hastily strengthened by using stones from the buildings near by (Isa. 22. 8–11). The stables which he built (2 Chron. 32. 28) doubtless reflect a reinforcement of the chariotry. We also hear about the building of storehouses "for the yield of grain, wine, and oil" (*loc. cit.*). It would seem that the construction of these new store cities reflects the reorganization of his tax-collecting system. Furthermore, the census carried out during Hezekiah's reign, which even took in the great Negeb expanses (1 Chron. 4. 38 ff.), must date to this period. It was doubtless carried out to increase the efficiency of conscription and tax gathering. Hezekiah also expanded the borders of Judah at the expense of the Philistine cities. He evidently was putting special pressure on those towns which had refused to participate in the revolt, e.g. Gaza (2 Kings 18. 8). His expansion in the western Negeb to the approaches of Gerar (according to LXX; MT reads Gedor) is most probably connected with this antagonism to Gaza. Even the invasion of Mount Seir referred to in the same passage (1 Chron. 4. 42–3) may be interpreted as an attempt to restore Judah's control over Edom at this same time.[2]

Sennacherib's campaign to Palestine was carried out in 701 B.C. after he had quelled the various rebellions in Mesopotamia and the East. Many details are preserved about this event, both in the Bible (2 Kings 18. 13–19. 35; Isa. 36. 1–37. 36; 2 Chron. 32. 9–21) and in Assyrian inscriptions[3] (cf. map 32). There are some apparent discrepancies between the biblical sources and the Assyrian annals but by a careful analysis they can be reconciled. Besides the minor details such as the amounts of tribute, 300 shekels in the Bible (2 Kings 18. 14) and 800 talents in the annals, the main divergence pertains to the timing of the Egyptian intervention. Sennacherib's text brings in the clash with the Egyptians very early, just after the account of the conquest of Joppa. On the other hand, the biblical record has Tirhakah (Taharka) arriving on the scene only after the fall of Lachish; Jerusalem is already under siege and the conquest of the Shephelah is continuing:

> The Rabshakeh returned, and found the king of Assyria fighting against Libnah; for he heard that the king had left Lachish. And when the king heard concerning Tirhakah king of Ethiopia, "Behold, he has set out to fight against you," . . . (2 Kings 19. 8–9).

There can be no doubt that the biblical sequence is the more accurate.

The Sennacherib annal is more of a summary than a chronological account. For example, it is obvious that Sennacherib could not have exiled Ṣidqia, king of Ashkelon, before he arrived in Philistia. But the account of Ṣidqia's stubbornness is introduced very early, just after the submission of the other rulers from Amurru. The point being made is that these others hastened to pay their tribute and thus avoided disaster while Ṣidqia did not. Then the text goes on to recount how Sennacherib's army moved on to conquer Joppa and its immediate hinterland, territory subservient to Ṣidqia. Furthermore, the return of Padi to his throne would hardly have been accomplished right after the conquest of Ekron; it must have taken place after Hezekiah had already seen the handwriting on the wall and decided to placate the invader. Thus, the biblical chronology will give us an intelligible sequence to which the annals may be harmonized.

According to the annals of Sennacherib the Assyrian army proceeded southward along the Phoenician coast. He lists a series of towns from Sidon to Acco, all of them said to be fortified cities of the King of Sidon: Great Sidon, Little Sidon, Beth-zaith (Bīt-zitti), Zarephath (Ṣariptu), Mahalab (Maḫalliba; cf. Josh. 19. 29; Judg. 1. 31), Usu (the mainland suburb of Tyre, classical Palaityros), Achzib and Acco.

At this point Sennacherib refers to the tribute paid by the kings of Amurru as a sign of their submission, e.g. the rulers of Sidon, Arvad, Byblos, Ashdod,[4] Ammon (Bīt-Ammana), Moab and Edom.[5]

Next Sennacherib describes the conquest of Beth-dagon, Joppa, Bene-berak and Azor, cities belonging to Ṣidqa, King of Ashkelon. It is doubtful whether we may deduce from this passage that Joppa and its dependencies had belonged to Ashkelon in other periods, because Sennacherib himself explains the chain of events leading up to the expansion of Ashkelon and Judah. The citizens of Ekron had rebelled against Padi, their king, who was loyal to Assyria. Then they had handed him over to Hezekiah, the acknowledged leader of the Palestinian revolt. One would naturally expect that the rebellious principalities would seize control over as much territory as possible belonging to the states loyal to Assyria that were interfering with their plans. Judah exerted intensive pressure on Ekron in the north and Gaza in the south; it is therefore probable that Ashkelon also annexed various districts belonging to Ashdod and Ekron.

From Joppa the Assyrian army continued southward in a move directed against Eltekeh (Tell esh-Shallaf, two miles north of Jabneh),[6] Timnah (Tell el-Baṭashi) and Ekron (Khirbet el-Muqanna'), punishing the latter town severely for its insurrection. Now the full might of the Assyrian expeditionary force could be turned against Judah which was left standing alone.

> As for Hezekiah, the Judean, he did not submit to my yoke. Forty-six of his strong cities, fortresses, and countless small towns in the vicinity, I besieged and conquered by building earthworks, by bringing up siege engines, with the help of assault troops, by breaches in the walls, by mines under the ramparts and onslaughts with the battering ram. I deported from among them and counted as spoil 200,150 persons, young and old, men and women, and horses, mules, asses, camels, sheep, and cattle, in countless numbers. Himself, I imprisoned in Jerusalem, his residence, like a bird in its cage.[7]

Sennacherib unfortunately gives us no more than a very general description of his attack on Judah. It would have been most illuminating if the scribe had given the names of the conquered towns and the order in which they were taken.

The Judean towns conquered by Sennacherib were handed over to the kings of Ashdod, Ekron and Gaza. Although Judah's area was thus considerably diminished, the sum of its annual tribute was increased.

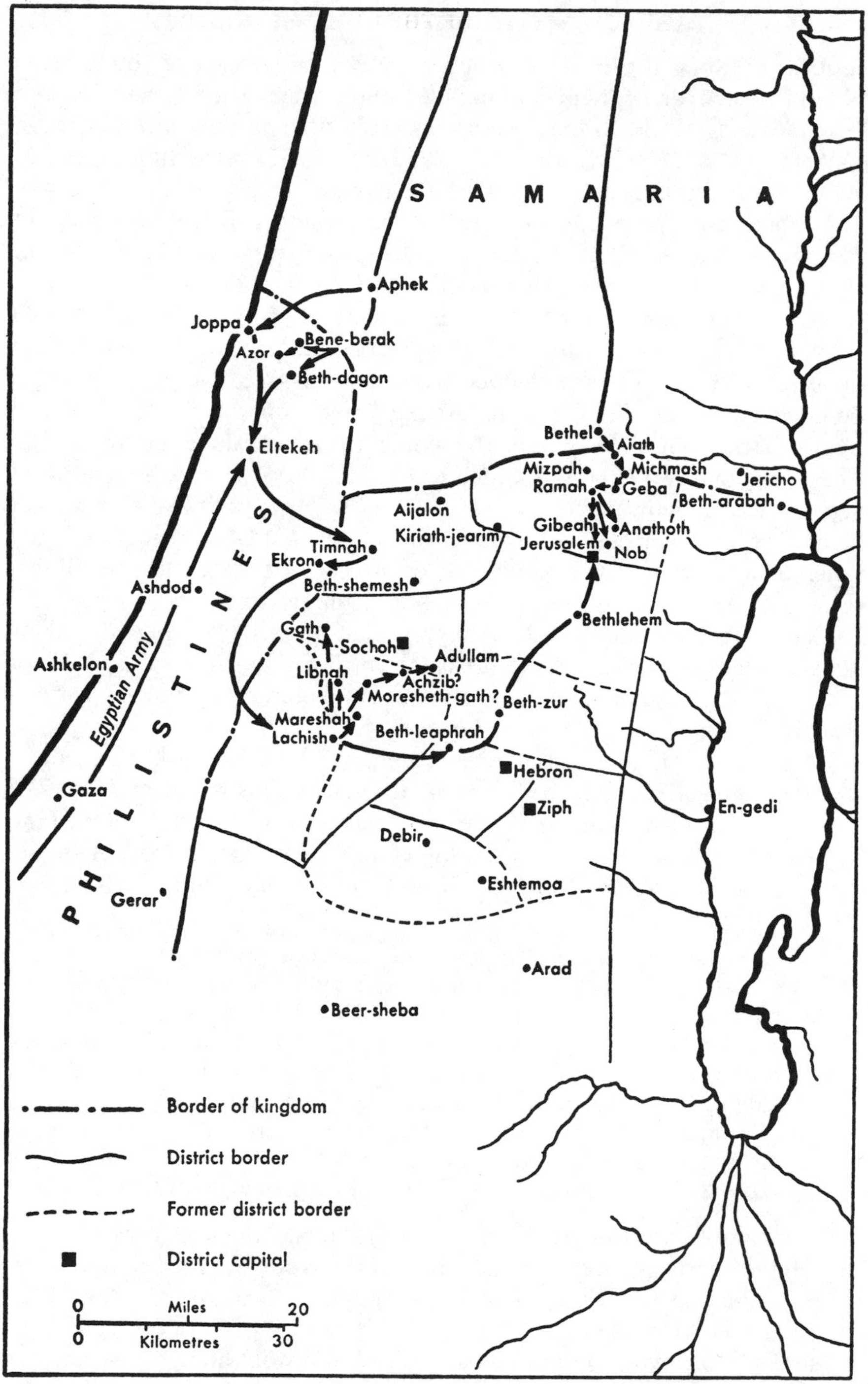

Map 32. The Districts of Hezekiah and the Campaign of Sennacherib.

The text records a payment to the sum of 30 talents of gold, 800 talents of silver and other precious items.[8]

Recently it has been shown that another inscription, formerly thought to belong to previous rulers, actually reports Sennacherib's activities during this campaign.[9] The text is comprised of two fragments, one published originally as part of Tiglath-pileser's annals[10] and the other interpreted as a report by Sargon.[11] The resultant passage is as follows:

(1) . . . .
(2) . . . .
(3) [. . . . . Anshar, my lord, encourag] ed me and against the land of Ju[dah I marched. In] the course of my campaign, the tribute of the k[ngs of Philistia? I received . . . . .
(4) [. . . . with the mig]ht? of Anshar, my lord, the province of [Hezek]iah of Judah like [. . . . .
(5) [. . . . .] the city of Azekah, his stronghold, which is between my [bo]rder and the land of Judah [. . . .
(6) [like the nest of the eagle?] located on a mountain ridge, like pointed iron? daggers without number reaching high to heaven [. . . .
(7) [its walls] were strong and rivaled the highest mountains, to the (mere) sight, as if from the sky [appears its head? . . . . .
(8) [by means of beaten (earth) ra]mps, mighty? battering rams brought near, with the attack by foot soldiers (using) mi[nes, breeches . . . . .
(9) [. . . . .] they had seen [the approach of my cav]alry and they had heard the roar of the mighty troops of the god Anshar and [their hea]rts became afraid [. . . . .
(10) [the city Azekah I besieged,] I captured, I carried off its spoil, I destroyed, I devastated, [I burned with fire . . . . .
(11) [the city of Gath?] a royal [city] of the Philistines, which H[ezek]iah had captured and strengthened for himself [. . . . .
(12) [. . . . .] like a tree [standing out on a ridge? . . . . .
(13) [. . . . .] surrounded with great [to]wers and exceedingly difficult [its ascent? . . . . .
(14) [. . . . .] palace like a mountain was barred in front of them and high is [its top? . . . . .
(15) [. . . . .] it was dark and the sun never shone on it, its waters were situated in darkness and [its?] overflow [. . . .
(16) [. . . . .] its [mou]th was cut with axes and a moat was dug around it [. . . .
(17) [. . . . . warriors] skillful in battle he caused to enter into it, their weapons he bound (on them) to [offer battle . . . . .
(18) [. . . . . I caused the warriors of Amurru, all of them, to carry earth [. . . . .
(19) [. . . . .] against them. In the seventh time his [. . . . .] the great like a pot [of clay? I smashed? . . . . .

(20) [. . . . . cattle and she]ep I carried out from its midst [and counted as] spo[il . . . . .

(21) . . . . .[12]

[It looks as though the Assyrians may have used a systematic tactic in isolating the main inland cities of Philistia from Judah before attacking them. Timnah had been seized, thus blocking the Valley of Sorek; the rebellious Ekronites would have no chance of getting help from Hezekiah. When moving farther south, the valley of Elah was blocked by the conquest of Azekah. This left the field open for the siege of a major Philistine city which had previously been taken over by Hezekiah. Na'aman suggests with a high degree of plausability that this latter city, the name of which is not preserved, was none other than Gath, located at Tell eṣ-Ṣafi.[13] A.F.R.]

As Na'aman has also noted, the excavations at Tell eṣ-Ṣafi produced jar handles bearing the *lmlk* seal impressions. These date from the reign of Hezekiah and strengthen the argument for the identification of the important Philistine city in this text with Gath; in turn, the new inscription supports the equation of Gath with Tell eṣ-Ṣafi.[14]

In addition to the annals, reliefs have been discovered at Nineveh from Sennacherib's reign which portray the conquest of Lachish. That city's double walls and heavily fortified gate are clearly depicted. A battering ram has been brought to bear on the gate defences by means of a siege ramp.[15]

The general order of events may be derived from the biblical sources (2 Kings 18–19; Isa. 36–37; 2 Chron. 32. 9–28). Sennacherib's most important step was the conquest of Lachish, the most prominent city in the Shephelah. From here [probably near the end of Lachish's resistance, A.F.R.] he initiated negotiations with Hezekiah during the course of which he received heavy tribute from the latter. But he was not satisfied with this and demanded the complete capitulation of Jerusalem. After the fall of Lachish, he busied himself with the further conquest of the Shephelah. Micah's lament over the destruction of cities in the Shephelah evidently pertains to this phase of the campaign. In that connection the prophet refers to the following towns: Gath (Tell eṣ-Ṣafi ?), Beth-leaphrah (eṭ-Ṭaiyibeh), Shaphir, Zaanan, Beth-ezel, Maroth (these four places as yet unidentified), Lachish, Moresheth-gath (Tell el-Judeideh ?), Achzib (Tell el-Beiḍa ?), Mareshah and Adullam (Micah 1. 10–15). While Sennacherib was engaged in the siege of Libnah, he heard that the Egyptians were on their way. [They evidently managed to penetrate Philistia by marching along the coastal route in an effort to cut off the Assyrians' lines of supply leading north. A.F.R.] Sennacherib met them on the Plain of Eltekeh and claims a stunning victory. However, it is at this point that the biblical sources credit the deliverance of Jerusalem. [According to the very attenuated, legendary account preserved by Herodotus,[16] the Assyrians suffered a defeat because rats had eaten their leather accoutrements. A.F.R.] Therefore, it may very well be that the Assyrian version is a cover up for the true disaster.

There is another passage, viz. Isa. 10. 28–32, which is often ascribed to the Sennacherib campaign. However, one finds no confirmation in other sources that an Assyrian army ever marched on Jerusalem from this direction. Nevertheless, given the fact that Samaria was now an Assyrian province, the possibility existed that they might use this route to strike at Hezekiah's capital. In the prophet's vision an army is depicted as marching on Jerusalem from the north via the province of Samaria, conquering a series of towns as it passed through the district of Benjamin (Isa. 10. 28–32). This attack began on the eastern branch of the principal mountain thoroughfare, evidently so as to by-pass Mizpah (Tell en-Naṣbeh) which was strongly fortified; first the Assyrians attacked Aiath (Khirbet Ḥaiyan) and Michmash (Mukhmas). Next they crossed the steep pass of Wadi Suweiniṭ (cf. 1 Sam. 14. 4 ff.) and arrived at Geba (Jeba'). From here they turned towards Ramah (er-Ram) from whence they followed the main thoroughfare to Gibeah of Saul (Tell el-Ful). Finally several places to the north or north-east of Jerusalem are mentioned (including Gallim, Laishah, Madmenah, Gebim) of which it is possible to identify only Anathoth (Ras el-Kharrubeh beside 'Anata) and Nob ('Isawiyeh ?). We may probably accept Sennacherib's figure of forty-six conquered towns with their surrounding villages; it doubtless includes most of the Shephelah towns of Judah[17] plus some others in the hill country, perhaps mainly in Benjamin.

Jerusalem itself was not conquered. Sennacherib might have contented himself with the heavy tribute that he had exacted; but there seem to have been other reasons for his sudden return to Assyria, because the deliverance of Jerusalem left such a deep impression on contemporary writers. From Assyrian records it is clear that Sennacherib was assassinated in 681 B.C., but for the intervening period of twenty years our sources are practically nil.[18]

In spite of the deliverance of Jerusalem, the Shephelah, and probably most of the kingdom, suffered terribly. This has been amply illustrated by archaeological excavations. All the investigated sites reveal heavy destruction by fire, e.g. Lachish (Stratum III), the key site in establishing the chronological sequence for Judean ceramic and palaeographic typology, Tell Beit Mirsim (Stratum A_2), Beth-shemesh (Stratum II_C), Beer-sheba (Stratum II) and Arad (Stratum VIII). Some of them were never rebuilt as fortified cities, e.g. Beer-sheba and Beth-shemesh. Others saw only a partial recovery, on a less impressive scale, e.g. Lachish (Stratum II) and Tell Beit Mirsim (Stratum A_3). Arad, farther to the east and thus more remote from the border with Philistia, may have been rebuilt much more quickly. This would seem to reflect the situation depicted in Sennacherib's annals whereby he took the western territories away from Hezekiah and gave them to the Philistines.[19] At Lachish a magnificent palace in the Assyrian style was built, the "Residency," where an Assyrian governor may have made his headquarters in order to supervise this border zone.[20]

Today there is no longer even the slightest support for the "two campaign theory" so popular in certain circles as a solution to the apparent discrepancies in the sources for Sennacherib's campaign.[21] The Assyrian records, though admittedly scanty, give no credance to a second campaign by Sennacherib in the west. By following the biblical sequence of events as we have done herein, the main problems can be resolved. Even the Egyptian texts, so often cited by Albright and others in support of a two campaign interpretation, have usually been viewed by Egyptologists as contrary to the meaning Albright sought.[22] There can be no doubt that the Kawa Inscriptions, when subjected to the proper syntactic analysis, preclude a ço-regency between Taharqa and Shebitku while confirming that the former was indeed able to march at the head of an Egyptian army in 701 B.C.[23]

II. THE ROYAL SEAL IMPRESSIONS AND THEIR GEOGRAPHICAL-ADMINISTRATIVE SIGNIFICANCE

Royal seal impressions stamped on storage jars which have been found in large quantities on various Judean tells give evidence for a new administrative division of the Judean kingdom during Hezekiah's reign.[24] In the centre of the impressions stands one of the following symbols: either a four-winged scarab or a double-winged sun disk.[25] Both of these different designs are accompanied by the same type of inscriptions: above the central figure there appears the phrase "To the King" ‹למלך› and below it is written one of four place names, viz. Hebron, Socoh, Ziph or the enigmatic *mmšt*. Various opinions have been expressed concerning the significance of these seal impressions. For instance, some have thought that the jars represented a standard measure used in collecting taxes and that they were manufactured at the royal potteries in the four towns mentioned. Others have held the view that these four places were royal estates whose products were stored in the jars. Finally there is the suggestion that the four geographical names represent administrative centres or store cities for taxes collected in kind. The seal impressions can only be properly interpreted in the light of their date which has now been fixed by archaeological finds at several sites to the years just preceding Sennacherib's campaign.

Date of the Seal Impressions

The following data serve to establish a date for the royal seal impressions:

(1) *Ramat Raḥel.* Impressions from every type have been found in

the fill below the floor of the fortress at Ramat Raḥel.[26] This citadel, probably to be identified with Beth-haccerem, was in existence until the fall of the first temple, evidently having been erected in the reign of Jehoiakim (Jer. 22. 13–19).[27] From this it is obvious that the royal seals were in use before this structure was built; it is most unlikely that they continued to be used until the fall of the Judean kingdom.

(2) *Lachish.* 310 seal impressions were discovered in the excavations at Lachish, more than at any other site; most of them were of the four-winged type. Nearly all of these seals were found in rooms from level III in context with numerous sherds and handles from these jars. Impressions of the double-winged type are relatively fewer and in the British excavations they came from loci of which the stratification was poorly defined.[28] However, the recent excavations there have produced some whole vessels bearing the two-winged seal impressions found in a clear Stratum III context.[29]

Not all scholars have agreed that the destruction of level III dates to the campaign of Sennacherib in 701 B.C.; some of the opinion that it resulted from the first expedition by Nebuchadnezzar in 597.[30] However, there is really no room for doubt.[31] The resemblance between pottery fragments from levels III and II does not prove that they are necessarily close chronologically. It has been clearly demonstrated from other excavations that very few changes took place in Judean pottery styles between the end of the eighth and the beginning of the sixth centuries.[32] On the other hand, there are certain differences between these two levels that could hardly be explained on the assumption that they are separated by a period of only ten to eleven years. Furthermore, it has been pointed out that Sennacherib's reliefs depicting the siege of Lachish bear an amazing resemblance to the structure of that town as it existed in level III.[33] It is a well-known axiom in archaeological excavations that every stratum contains vessels mainly from the latter years of its existence, especially if it was devastated by fire. Since nearly every room of level III contained jar fragments and seal impressions of the four-winged type, and several of the two-winged type, one cannot escape the conclusion that this kind of seal was in use up to the destruction of that level.

Therefore, the evidence from Lachish proves that both the four- and two-winged insignia were used until that city was destroyed by Sennacherib in 701.

(3) *Palaeographic evidence.* The letters on these seal impressions resemble in form those of the Siloam inscription from the reign of Hezekiah.[34] On the other hand, attempts to distinguish palaeographic differences between the two types of seals do not stand up under criticism.[35]

Additional palaeographic material has been discovered in the excavation of the great pool at Gibeon where royal seal impressions, mainly of the double-winged style were found along with other inscriptions.[36] There appears in these texts a special kind of *aleph* known also from a burial inscription found at Siloam village dating to *c.* 700 B.C.[37] One may also add the recent testimony of a newly found seal bearing the inscription: "Belonging to Yehozaraḥ, son of Ḥilqiyahu (Hilkiah), servant of Hezekiah."[38] Palaeographically it shows affinities with other private seals, the *lmlk* inscriptions and also the Siloam and Silwan inscriptions.[39] Such seals carry the title of the seal owner (and not his father; note how many seals give a rank without patronymic!) so we have a dated sample of palaeography on a seal.

Thus the palaeographic evidence is also consistent with a date in the reign of Hezekiah, although it does not help us to obtain further chronological precision.

(4) *The number of seals.* For establishing the length of time during which these designs were in official use great importance should be attached to the number of seals actually used to make the various seal impressions. Although no actual seal of this type has been discovered, it is usually possible from the impressions themselves to determine whether a particular group was made from one seal or from several exemplars. Comparison of the seal impressions has demonstrated the surprising fact that all of the many examples discovered so far were stamped from only twenty-one to twenty-four seals.[40]

All of these seal impressions can be classed in one of three generally accepted categories according to the design of the insignia (Type I—four-winged, realistic; Type II—four-winged, stylized; Type III—double-winged. According to this classification the number of seals from which the different impressions were made is as follows:

Type	*Hebron*	*Ziph*	*Socoh*	*mmšt*
I	2	1	—	1
II	2	1	1	1
III	4	1–3	3	4

This limited distribution points to the chronological conclusion that these seals were used during a very limited time only. All of the impressions from Ziph, Socoh and *mmšt* from types I and II discovered thus far were made from one seal for each type, while those from Hebron of the same types were stamped from only two different seals. Since these jars were manufactured in great quantities (at Lachish alone, 260 four-winged impressions were found!), it is hard to believe that the ancient potters could have used one seal over a period of many years, and we cannot escape the conclusion that the four-winged insignia was in vogue for only a few years. The double-winged impressions were made from three or four seals to each town, which would seem to indicate that they were in use for a longer period, though hardly more than twenty or thirty years.

If we have already established in the light of the archaeological findings at Lachish that both types were being used until 701 B.C., then we can also assume, on the basis of the average number of seals, that these impressions were officially adopted only a few years previously. In other words, they were mainly in vogue for only a short time prior to Sennacherib's campaign.

(5) *Distribution of seal impression types according to sites.* The percentage of seal impressions from the different types varies considerably at each archaeological site. Furthermore, these differences can be explained in the light of chronological and historical considerations. Of the 310 impressions discovered at Lachish 265, i.e. 85 per cent, were four-winged (most of them Type II) while only 45 bore the double-winged insignia. This picture is in sharp contrast to that of tells in the hill country where the double-winged impressions predominate, e.g. 82 per cent at Tell en-Naṣbeh (Mizpah), 85 per cent at Gibeon and 88 per cent at Ramat Raḥel. The large number of double-winged impressions at sites in the hill country is explicable in terms of the fact that they were used longer. But how shall we explain the opposite situation at Lachish, which can hardly be accidental in view of the many seal impressions discovered there? The small number of double-winged impressions found at Lachish can be explained on the assumption that Hezekiah inaugurated the use of four-winged impressions shortly before Sennacherib's invasions. The great destruction suffered by Lachish at this time would account for the relative absence of the later insignia. It seems clear now that the symbol was changed during the reign of Hezekiah but the possibility still remains that the jars continued in use for some time after his reign.

(6) *Geographical distribution.* Jar handles with these impressions have been discovered only on Judean tells; not one has appeared outside of Judah's territory, e.g. at one of the northern Israelite cities. The northern limit is Tell en-Naṣbeh (Mizpah), the eastern—Jericho, the southern—Kh. Gharreh and Arad in the Negeb where four-winged impressions have been found,[41] the western—as far as Gezer and Tell eṣ-Ṣafi. Such a distribution confined to the limits of the Judean kingdom tallies with their use during a limited period of time. On the other hand, this situation would be hard to explain in terms of an extended period of usage such as the reign of Josiah, who ruled over a much larger kingdom. For example, in all of the extensive excavations at Megiddo and also at Bethel, not one such seal impression was discovered, although Josiah's sphere of authority doubtless included these cities (2

Kings 23. 29; 2 Chron. 35. 22). One much larger jar was found in the burned gate of Beer-sheba bearing a four-winged impression, also dated to the Sennacherib destruction.

The Purpose

The fixing of a date for these impressions has a decisive bearing on the interpretation of their function. If the assumption is correct that they came into use a short time before Sennacherib's campaign, then they must represent one aspect of Hezekiah's activity in reorganizing and strengthening Judah to face the impending war with Assyria and the intention was probably to bring more efficiency to the collection of government taxes in kind. It logically follows that the four geographical names appearing on them represent new administrative centres where the tribute was to be concentrated, in biblical terminology: store cities. Therefore, one of Hezekiah's most important activities in the years prior to the invasion was a reorganization of the tax-collecting procedures and concentration of tribute in kind at four main store cities—a move for which allusions are also found in the Bible (2 Chron. 32. 27–9).

To understand the establishment of these four new store cities we must begin with the administrative division of Judah into districts that preceded Hezekiah's activity, apparently dating to the reign of Jehoshaphat (cf. *supra,* pp. 347–356). Territorial divisions are usually not made sight-unseen, and every such reorganization is generally based on the system that preceded it. If we compare the three identifiable geographical names from the royal seals with the twelve former districts, the relationship between them becomes apparent.[42] Three of the former districts are united around each of the main store cities (cf. maps 28, 32); Socoh—the three Shephelah districts (II, III, IV); Ziph—the Negeb district plus the two southernmost districts in the Judean hill country (I, V, VII); Hebron—the three central mountain districts (VI, VIII, IX). Except for Hebron, which was formerly the capital of Judah, these towns are not centrally located in their districts; but they were all three important, having been fortified already under Rehoboam (2 Chron. 11. 7–10), and they were situated on roads leading to Jerusalem. These factors explain why those towns were selected.

The three remaining districts must have been assigned, therefore, to the mysterious *mmšt,* viz. those of Jerusalem, Benjamin and the wilderness. In view of the other towns chosen it is probable that Jerusalem itself was the tax-collecting centre for these latter districts, all of which are adjacent to it. Inasmuch as a town named *mmšt* is otherwise unknown, it is difficult to avoid the conclusion that this is none other than Jerusalem in its role as store city for the northern districts. It may have been thought improper for the name Jerusalem to appear alongside other provincial towns on the royal seals, so *mmšt* served as a designation for the city in its administrative function.

Ginsberg had already suggested that *mmšt* was simply an abbreviated form of the Hebrew word for "government".[43] In support of his suggestion one may point to the biblical usage of the term for "government"(ממשלה-ממשלת),precisely during the reign of Hezekiah, in the narrative about a visit of Babylonian envoys to Jerusalem. When describing Hezekiah's pride in showing them his wealth the text concludes with these words: "there was nothing in his house or in all *his government* (ממשלתו)that Hezekiah did not show them" (2 Kings 20. 13; Isa. 39. 2). Since this text is concerned with the king's riches in Jerusalem, it would appear that a distinction is being made between the treasures in the royal house and those "in his government", i.e. in the storehouses of the provincial administration. The visit of these ambassadors from Merodach-baladan was connected with preparations for the war, so Hezekiah was probably showing them one of the storehouses built for that very purpose.

Centralization of the royal administration around four main store cities instead of the elaborate division into twelve districts, which was only a vestige of time-honoured tradition, seems much more practical for a small state like Judah. The Assyrians also organized the various conquered kingdoms into larger units under their own provincial administrators. In Israel they established three or four provinces in place of the twelve former districts, in Aram four or five instead of sixteen,[44] etc.

The situation may be summarized as follows: The royal seal impressions were adopted by Hezekiah a few years before Sennacherib's invasion to facilitate the reorganization of his kingdom's administration around four store cities. First, the four-winged insignia was stamped on the storage jars, but sometime before 701 B.C., it was replaced by the double-winged symbol with the frequent addition of the personal seal impression of an official [probably to confirm that he had checked the jar for its size or manufacture, A.F.R.]. The new district division apparently continued in use through the ensuing reigns to the end of the Judean monarchy. This seems to be indicated by the text of an ostracon from Arad dating to the end of the seventh century B.C. It records shipments of taxes in kind from several places; it reads:

> "[From . . .] *ḥqt* (an Egyptian measure) 10 of barley (symbol); [from] Anim the Lower, 30 *ḥqt* of barley; from the Upper, *ḥqt* 60 (of barley); from Maon, *ḥqt* 10 (of barley)."[45]

Thus, it preserves the names of three places which are easily located. Lower and Upper Anim are Kh. Ghuwein et-Taḥta and el-Foqa, respectively, seven miles north of Arad and about one mile apart. At both sites Iron Age pottery has been collected from the surface.[46] Eusebius also knew of two sites in this area called Αναια, one a settlement of Jews, the other of Christians (Onom. 26. 9, 13). The new Arad text proves that the two neighbouring towns were called Upper and Lower Anim (cf. Upper and Lower Beth-horon and the Upper and Lower springs near Debir, Josh. 15. 19). Maon is Kh. Maʿ in, less than seven miles northeast of Anim and about ten miles from Arad.

Of particular interest here is the presence of payments to one fort (Arad) in the Negeb from three places in the hill country. The latter are not even from the same hill country district: Anim is in the southern mountain district (Josh. 15. 50) and Maon is in the southeastern (Josh. 15. 55),[47] i.e. the district shared with Ziph. Arad (corrupted in the text to Eder) is in the Negeb (Josh. 15. 21). These three districts were evidently combined to form the southern district in Hezekiah's reform as indicated by the royal seal impressions.

However, the use of the seal impressions with geographical names seems to have been terminated, at least a short time after 701 B.C. The rosetta design may have been authorized instead. The rosetta seal impressions have been found on jar handles similar to those bearing the winged insignia discussed above. A considerable number of these rosettas have been discovered at Ramat Raḥel on or above the floor of the fortress; therefore, they must have been in use during the latter days of its existence. They apparently served as royal Judean insignia in that period as they had in Hittite Asia Minor.[48]

It must be assumed that these jars served for storing tribute in kind at the four main store cities. Their dispersal throughout the towns of Judah evidently took place after their initial usage. Either the government used them for shipping supplies to garrisons and local administrative units or else they had finally come into private use.[49]

III. THE LAST KINGS OF JUDAH

The campaign of Sennacherib stablized the political situation in Palestine for a considerable period of time. During the latter days of Hezekiah and throughout all of Manasseh's long reign there is no reference to any changes whatsoever. Judah was left as one of the isolated principalities of Palestine, but it was in complete subjection to Assyria whose empire reached its peak of greatness and expansion under Esarhaddon (681–69) and Ashurbanipal (668–33). Esarhaddon realized the ancient dream of Assyria by conquering Egypt. It was apparently only on the Phoenician coast that he was forced to quell a rebellion led by Tyre and Sidon, whom he conquered and punished severely.[50] Palestine was evidently quiet during his reign; and he mentions the name of Manasseh (*Me-na-si-i*), King of Judah (*Ia-ú-di*), in a list recording the heavy tribute which he collected from the kings of Tyre, Edom, Moab, Gaza, Ashkelon, Ekron, Byblos, Arvad, Samsimuruna, Beth-Ammon and Ashdod.[51] In the south he conquered

Arza-Arzani near the Brook of Egypt and deported its king. Arza is apparently the Yurza of Egyptian sources which has been tentatively identified with Tell Jemmeh (cf. *supra,* pp. 161), and in this period its ruler evidently dominated the western Negeb. At the site an Assyrian palace has been discovered.[52] Esarhaddon also made war on the Arabs and collected a heavy tribute from them.

On his tenth campaign in 671 B.C. Esarhaddon conquered Egypt.[53] He tells us that on the way he conquered Tyre, Aphek in the land of Samaria[54] and Raphia which was near the Brook of Egypt. Then he traversed the difficult road to Egypt. His son Ashurbanipal (669–33) also passed through Palestine on his expeditions to Egypt; he evidently encountered opposition only in Phoenicia, for he mentions the submission of Tyre and Arvad.[55] In his ninth year he carried out a campaign against the Arabs in which he passed through Transjordan. In this connection he mentions Edom, Beth-Ammon, Moab and the districts of Hauran and Zobah.[56] On the way back he had to punish the Phoenicians; he reports the conquest of Ushu (Usu) and Acco.[57]

The reign of Ashurbanipal comprised the last days of Assyrian greatness. The mighty empire fell apart rapidly after his death (633 B.C.). Egypt had broken away while Ashurbanipal was still alive; Psamtik I had founded the Twenty-sixth Egyptian Dynasty in about 655. In 626 Babylon gained its independence under Nabopolassar, founder of the Neo-Babylonian (Chaldean) kingdom. Henceforth Assyria was sorely pressed by Babylonia and Media, which caused it to decline rapidly. Asshur fell in 614 and Nineveh was conquered two years later (612). A final attempt by Ashur-uballit II to recapture Haran with the remnant of the Assyrian army failed in 609. After this Babylon began to annex and reorganize the remaining portions of the Assyrian empire.

The 24 years from the death of Ashurbanipal to the destruction of the last remnants of the Assyrian army at Haran comprised a period of final resurgence for Judah. Josiah (640–609), who ascended the throne as a youngster eight years of age, sought, on reaching maturity, to expand Judean authority over all of Palestine, and in large measure he succeeded (cf. map 33).

Judah's expansion was closely connected with the disintegration of Assyrian authority. Throwing off the Assyrian yoke had a profound religious effect, the stages of which are described by the biblical writers in considerable detail.[58] He began his independent activity in his eighth year (2 Chron. 34. 3) which coincided with the death of Ashurbanipal (633). Evidently it was then that the first steps were taken towards renouncing Assyrian supremacy and removing the foreign cults associated with it. The second stage took place in his twelfth year (629), apparently at the death of Ashur-etil-ilani son of Ashurbanipal, who was succeeded by his brother Sinsharishkun on the Assyrian throne. The

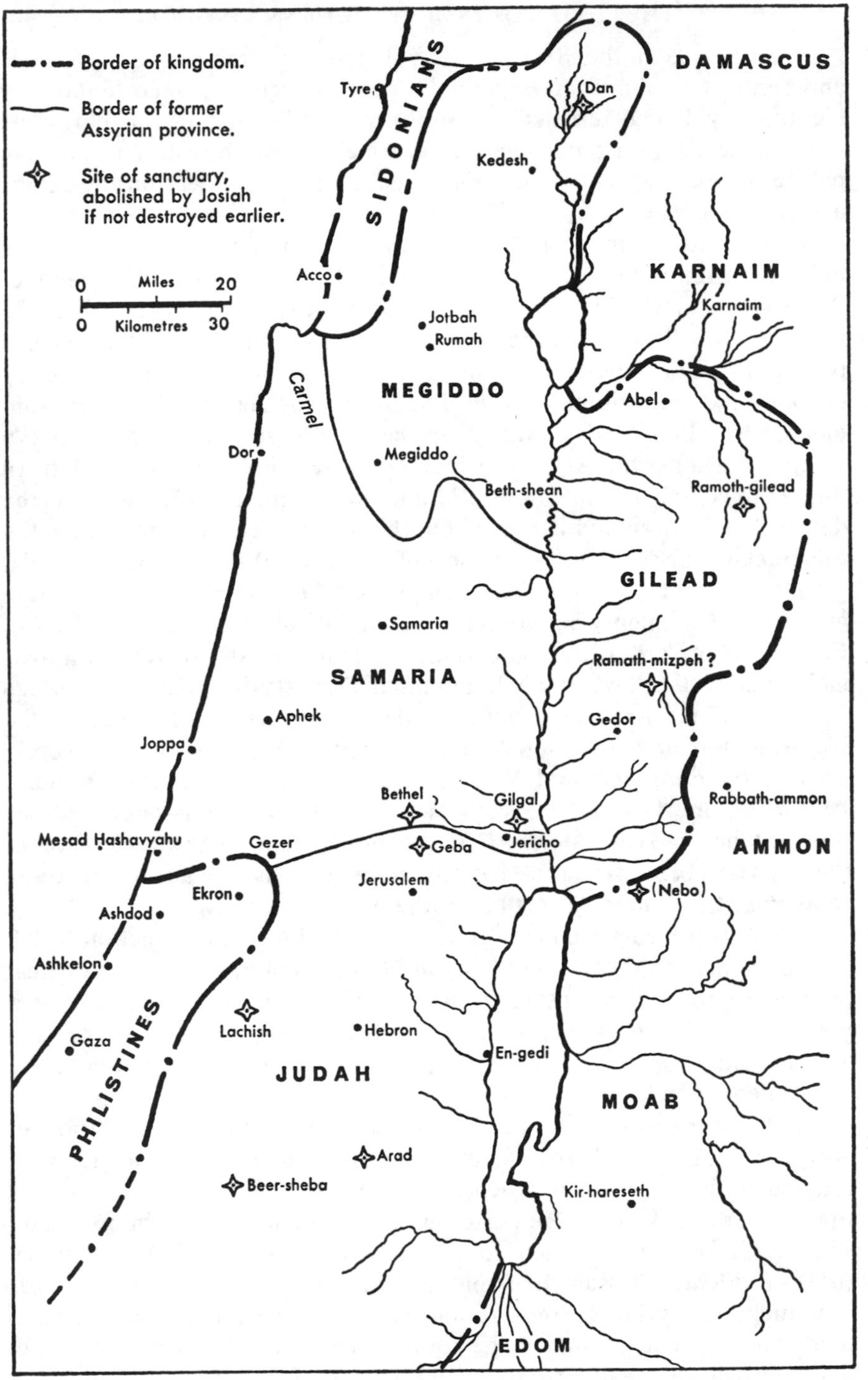

Border of kingdom.
Border of former Assyrian province.
Site of sanctuary, abolished by Josiah if not destroyed earlier.
0 Miles 20
0 Kilometres 30
DAMASCUS
SIDONIANS
Tyre
Dan
Kedesh
Acco
KARNAIM
Karnaim
Jotbah
Rumah
Carmel
MEGIDDO
Abel
Dor
Megiddo
Beth-shean
Ramoth-gilead
GILEAD
Samaria
Ramath-mizpeh ?
SAMARIA
Aphek
Gedor
Joppa
Bethel
Gilgal
Rabbath-ammon
Mesad Hashavyahu
Gezer
Geba
Jericho
AMMON
Jerusalem
(Nebo)
Ekron
Ashdod
Ashkelon
PHILISTINES
Lachish
Hebron
Gaza
En-gedi
JUDAH
MOAB
Arad
Beer-sheba
Kir-hareseth
EDOM

Map 33. The Kingdom of Josiah.

ritual purification which Josiah carried out in that year was concerned not only with Judah and Jerusalem but also "in the cities of Manasseh, Ephraim, and Simeon, and as far as Naphtali . . . throughout all the land of Israel" (2 Chron. 34. 6–7). Since the very fact of Josiah's having dominion over these areas is beyond all doubt, there is really no reason to question the chronological notations concerning it in the book of Chronicles.[59] Josiah had as his aim the renewal of the Davidic rule over all of Palestine, and he doubtless took advantage of the first opportunity that presented itself for realizing his ambition.

Only a modicum of detail has been preserved about the size of Josiah's kingdom. 2 Kings indicates that he controlled Bethel (23. 4, 15), which was formerly on the border of the Israelite kingdom and later on the boundary of the Samarian province when it was first established (2 Kings 17. 28). It is also clear that he had established his authority at Megiddo (2 Kings 23. 29; 2 Chron. 35. 22), and he evidently had managed to build the large fortress of level II at Megiddo that was constructed over the earlier palace in level IV.[60] The ostracon discovered at Meṣad Ḥashavyahu on the seashore about one mile south of Minat Rubin proves that that fort was in Judean hands during Josiah's reign.[61] From all this it seems clear that Josiah had annexed the provinces of Samaria and Megiddo to his kingdom and had taken over a certain area in northern Philistia to the detriment of Ekron and Ashdod. Ties with the various regions of the kingdom were strengthened by marriages with important families in border districts. The mother of Josiah's sons Jehoahaz and Zedekiah was from Libnah, a city on the border with Philistia (Tell Bornaṭ ?) that had rebelled against Judah in the reign of Jehoram (2 Kings 8. 22). The mother of Jehoiakim, another of Josiah's sons, was from Rumah, evidently Khirbet er-Rumeh in Sahl el-Baṭṭof, which is called Aruma in the annals of Tiglath-pileser III.[62] Similarly, one of the wives of Manasseh was from Jotbah (2 Kings 21. 19), the Jotapata of the Roman period (Khirbet Jefat),[63] on a hill above Sahl el-Baṭṭ of which also appears in Tiglath-pileser's text ([*Ia*]-*aṭ-bi-te*).[64] This shows us that the dense Israelite population was not removed completely by Tiglath-pileser; evidently it revived quite rapidly after the calamities and deportations that it had suffered.

Regarding the question of just how successful Josiah really was in reuniting the Assyrian provinces formed from Israelite territory, we have a very suggestive piece of evidence. It is a fragmentary ostracon from Arad containing parts of three lines:

> I have become king in k[. . .]
> Make military preparations and [. . .]
> the king of Egypt to [. . . .][65]

In spite of the disconnected nature of the preserved text, the main thrust seems clear. The king of Judah is informing the commander at Arad of his own assumption of power; he demands urgent military preparations, evidently because of something to do with the king of Egypt. The most suitable context for such a message would be 609 B.C. with the enthronement of Jehoahaz upon the death of his father Josiah (2 Kings 23. 30–33; 2 Chron. 36. 1–3). He evidently stayed on the throne only so long as Pharaoh Necho was preoccupied at Carchemish. So Jehoahaz would have enjoyed the realm of his father for only a short time. Unfortunately, only the first letter of the expression designating the place or sphere of rule in our new ostracon has been preserved. But the only plausible restoration of the text is *k*[*l*] for Hebrew *kōl,* "all," which would give the reading, "in a[ll the land]," or "in a[ll the land of Israel]" (cf. 2 Chron. 34. 6–7).[66] This strengthens the impression that Josiah had succeeded in expanding his sway to include an entity that would justify the title, "all of (the land of) Israel." It is at least suggestive that he had gained control of the whole contry, including Gilead.

We have almost no information about the inner organization and administration of Josiah's kingdom. From the fact that Bethel was part of Judah in the Post-exilic period (Ezra. 2. 28; Neh. 7. 32) we may deduce that this change took place during the reign of Josiah, because the Babylonians and Persians probably left the borders between Judah and Samaria as they found them.[67] This would mean that Josiah accepted the framework in which Judah, Samaria and Megiddo, and perhaps Gilead were administrative units, however he expanded the territory of Judah at Samaria's expense. The newly annexed territory had always been in dispute; it had fallen into Judean hands once before during the reign of Abijah (2 Chron. 13. 19). Now Josiah was able to make this administrative change within the framework of his enlarged kingdom.

With regard to the religious reforms of Josiah, we are told that he "defiled the high places where the priests had burned incense, from Geba to Beer-sheba" (2 Kings 23. 8). Some scholars have seen in this passage a delineation of Josiah's kingdom at a certain stage of his reign,[68] but it is really just a definition of the original kingdom of Judah. His method of dealing with Judah was to discontinue the worship at the local high places and to bring their priests to Jerusalem. On the other hand, he slew the priests of the northern kingdom and defiled the altars by burning human bones on them (2 Kings 23. 15–20). The Geba which is juxtaposed to Beer-sheba in 2 Kings 23. 8 is surely the same as that in 1 Kings 15. 22, viz. the one located at modern Jebaʿ. There is no need to seek another Geba farther north.[69] Just as Beer-sheba was not right on the southern border, we need not expect Geba to be on the northern. These were royal centres dominating the border regions at the two extremities of the country.[70]

This last age of Judean greatness was short-lived. It was possible only so long as the Assyrian empire was in its death throes, creating a political vacuum in Palestine that Josiah utilized to the best of his ability. With the final downfall of Assyria a contest of strength was inaugurated between Babylon and Egypt to determine who would inherit the Assyrian hegemony in Syria and Palestine. During this struggle Judah was finally annihilated.

For a few years before Assyria's final collapse Egypt sided with the Assyrians in order to stop the Babylonian advance and to seize control of the Levant. As early as 616 B.C. an Egyptian army made its appearance in Mesopotamia; it must have passed, of necessity, through Palestine. In 609 Pharaoh Necho II (609–593) marched again to Carchemish in order to assist Ashur-uballit in his attempt at reconquering Haran. Josiah attempted to stop Necho in the vicinity of Megiddo, the most strategically located pass on the *Via Maris*; he evidently hoped to block the Egyptians' passage (2 Kings 23. 29–30; 2 Chron. 35. 20–4). We do not know whether Josiah was acting in league with Babylon as Hezekiah had done before him; his main objective was doubtless to prevent the Egyptian domination of Palestine. His attempt failed. Josiah fell during the battle which took place in the Megiddo Valley, and his death marked the end of Judah's brief period of independence. The Egyptian defeat at Haran did not keep them from holding sway over Palestine and Syria for the next four years. A fragmentary stele of Necho was found at Sidon.[71]

Even though Jehoahaz son of Josiah submitted to Egyptian authority by going to Riblah in Hamath to appear before Necho, who was returning from the Euphrates region, pharaoh made a display of his superiority by enthroning Jehoiakim over Judah in his stead (2 Kings 23. 33–5). Judah's borders in this period are not defined for us; however, it is possible that Necho reduced its territory to about its former size before Josiah's expansion. Bethel and its surrounding hills may have been left to Judah, nevertheless, because that town was within the sphere of the Yehud province during the post-exilic period. At the same time, Necho exacted a heavy tribute from Judah[72], which was collected by Jehoiakim from all the free citizens of Judah. Jehoiakim, not realizing the seriousness of the hour, wasted his kingdom's depleted resources in building a new palace for which project he employed forced labour from Judah (Jer. 22. 13–19).[73]

In Jehoiakim's fourth year (605 B.C.) Nebuchadnezzar soundly defeated the Egyptian army at Carchemish on the Euphrates (Jer. 46. 2) and followed up with another victory over them at Hamath.[74] [By 604 B.C. Nebuchadnezzar had gained the mastery over nearly all of the Levant. Ashkelon was apparently captured in this year and many of its residents deported to Babylon.[75] An Aramaic papyrus discovered in

Egypt appears to relate something of these events. The writer, perhaps the King of Ashkelon (or Ashdod or Gaza),[76] requests help from Egypt against the Babylonian army which has already reached Aphek; he does not say, at least not in the preserved part of the text, that the Babylonians have taken Aphek.

In 603 B.C., the army of Nebuchadnezzar conquered another Levantine city, evidently after much effort. The name of that town is not preserved and the entire passage is badly broken. However, it seems most logical to assume that the victim was Gaza.[77] The following year, his troops made a show of force and collected tribute. Jehoiakim had already become subservient in 604 and paid his own tribute for three years (2 Kings 24. 1). However, in 601, Nebuchadnezzar tried his mettle against the Egyptians and suffered heavy losses. This must have encouraged Jehoiakim to stop his payments. While he was replenishing his military might, "bands of the Chaldeans, and bands of the Edomites,[78] and bands of the Moabites and bands of the Ammonites" were sent against Judah (2 Kings 24. 2). This harassment may account for the destruction of the smaller Judean outposts, such as En-gedi and Arad, but even from the biblical text it is clear that no major campaign was as yet undertaken. A.F.R.] It was only in 598–7 that the full force of the Babylonian army finally carried out a campaign of reprisal against Judah. Before they reached Jerusalem King Jehoiakim had died (perhaps having been assassinated ?; cf. Jer. 22. 18–19) and was succeeded by his son Jehioachin, who surrendered and was deported to Babylon with many residents of Jerusalem, especially from the royal family, the courtiers, the upper classes and the craftsmen (2 Kings 24. 12–16). [The Babylonian and biblical texts do not permit the assumption that a major campaign was waged at this time against other great cities of Judah such as Lachish?[79] A.F.R.]

Jehoiachin's submission saved Judah from total destruction once more; Nebuchadnezzar appointed Jekoiakim's brother Zedekiah as king. Judah's territory was evidently diminished, all of the Negeb and part of the Shephelah probably being taken away from her (Jer. 13. 19; cf. discussion concerning "the other towns" listed in Neh. 11; *infra,* p. 409 f.). The Edomites probably took this occasion to occupy some of the towns in the Negeb. Evidence of an Edomite threat to Ramoth-negeb at about this time is found in an ostraca from Arad.[80] Troops from Kinah (perhaps Kh. Ṭaiyib, *c.* 3.4 miles NNE of Arad)[81] and Arad were to be rushed to Ramoth-negeb, "lest Edom should come there." Ramoth-negeb is evidently the Judean fortress closest to the Edomite border, which suggests Kh. Ghazzeh, *c.* 5.6 miles SE of Arad.[82] It is possible, of course, that the defence of Ramoth-negeb commanded in this text pertains to the events of 594 B.C., the fourth year of King Zedekiah (cf. Jer. 51. 59). One might even suggest that the date on an Arad jar, "in the third (year)'' is an indication that Arad fell at about that time.[83] The loss of these important Judean territories and the severe Babylonian oppression rekindled the fires of revolt in Judah which finally broke out towards the end of 589 B.C. in concert with other Palestinian states and under Egyptian encouragement. Babylonian counter measures were not long in coming, and Judah suddenly found herself standing alone against the might of Babylonia. Tyre and Ammon may have given some resistance but they were quickly crushed and duly punished (Ezek. 21. 18–32; Jer. 40. 13–41. 15). Edom apparently took this opportunity to avenge herself on Judah (Obad. 10–14; Lam. 4. 21–2; Ps. 137. 7).

The Babylonian army conquered the towns of Judah one after another and laid siege to Jerusalem (2 Kings 25. 1; Jer. 52. 4). Only a brief reference is made to this campaign: ". . . the army of the king of Babylon was fighting against Jerusalem and against all the cities of Judah that were left, Lachish and Azekah; for these were the only fortified cities of Judah that remained'' (Jer. 34. 7). This mention of siege operations against the last two fortresses in Judah, Lachish and Azekah, received surprising confirmation in one of the Lachish letters. Twenty-one inscribed ostraca were discovered in one of the guard rooms built into the city gate at Lachish among the charred remains of the last destruction level. No. 4 of this collection contains the following passage: " . . . we are watching for the signals of Lachish, according to all the indications which my lord hath given, for we cannot see Azekah''.[84] Furthermore, excavations in various Judean sites have proved that all of them suffered total destruction at this time except some of the towns in Benjamin, principally Mizpeh where the Babylonian appointed governor was to have his headquarters (2 Kings 25. 23).

Jerusalem itself was conquered in the summer of 587 B.C. Zedekiah, who tried to escape to Transjordan, was captured beside Jericho and brought before Nebuchadnezzar at Riblah. In the month that followed, the Babylonians burned the city to the ground, tore down its walls and deported the rest of the population, leaving only "some of the poorest of the land to be vinedressers and ploughmen'' who remained in the villages (2 Kings 25. 1–21; Jer. 52. 4–27).

Twenty-two years after the death of Josiah the last traces of Judean-Israelite independence were erased, and Judah was added to the Babylonian provincial organization.

IV. EXILE AND RESTORATION

This last phase of Old Testament history has to do not with a Judean kingdom but with a Judean province. Although there was no more room in Palestine for independent political entities, some of the ethnic groups from the previous era were able to maintain their identity. It is this struggle on the part of the surviving Judeans, whom we can now call

Jews, which laid the foundations for the Judaism of a later age. In order to understand the cultural processes at work here, one must recognize the geopolitical factors involved.

1. The Babylonian Kingdom

Our information about Palestine is very scanty for the period of Babylonian rule from the destruction of Jerusalem in 587 to the fall of Babylon in 539 B.C. It would seem that the Babylonians generally did not introduce changes in the provincial organization which they inherited from Assyria. Ezekiel in his description of the promised land (Chaps. 47–8; cf. *supra,* pp. 73 f.) mentions the provinces of Hamath, Damascus, Hauran and Gilead, known to us already from the Assyrian period. When the Judean Monarchy fell Syria and Palestine became a region completely made up of Babylonian provinces, with the exception of a few Phoenician cities (Tyre, Byblos and Arvad). It is doubtful whether one may assume a certain degree of independence for some Philistine cities on the basis of references to the kings of Gaza and Ashdod in a document from Nebuchadnezzar's court, because Jehoiachin, King of Judah, also appears on a similar document from Babylon.[85] The fate of the southern Transjordanian kingdoms remains uncertain. At the time of Judah's devastation the kingdoms of Moab, Ammon and Edom still enjoyed a modicum of independence. Refugees from the Judean disaster found a haven in those kingdoms (Jer. 40. 11). The assassins of Gedaliah son of Ahikam were sent by Baalis, King of the Ammonites, and escaped to Ammon after the murder (Jer. 40. 14; 41. 10, 15). According to Josephus (*Antiq.,* X, IX, 7) Nebuchadnezzar terminated the monarchies in Ammon and Moab during his expedition to Syria in his twenty-third year (582 B.C.) when he also carried out further deportations from Judah (Jer. 52. 30). Nebuchadnezzar's inscription at Nahr el-Kalb concerning an expedition in the Lebanon region[86] is probably related to this campaign. The kingdom of Edom evidently collapsed under pressure from the Nabataeans who had penetrated the southern regions of Transjordan. Many of the Edomite residents from Mount Seir migrated to the southern hill country of Judah which was now sparsely inhabited. When they returned from exile the Jews encountered a strong Edomite population settled in the region from Hebron southward; in Hellenistic times this area became known as Idumaea.[87]

In 585 B.C. Nebuchadnezzar laid siege to Tyre (Ezek. 26–8), but the town was able to hold out in its island fortress for thirteen years, aided by its fleet as well as the determination of its inhabitants. Nebuchadnezzar was forced to concede its limited independence (Ezek. 29. 17–20).[88] In 568 Nebuchadnezzar invaded Egypt,[89] putting an end to Egyptian interference in Palestinian affairs. There is no further reference to additional campaigns by Nebuchadnezzar or his successors in Syria and Palestine except for an expedition by Nabonidus to Syria in 553,[90] for which no explicit details are available. Apparently there were no real changes in the political situation of Syria and Palestine until the end of Babylonian domination, because most of the small states in that area had been prostrated and impoverished by the many wars so recently inflicted upon them.

Judah was probably annexed to the Samarian province, although there is no clear proof of this. After the destruction of Jerusalem the Babylonians appointed Gedaliah son of Ahikam as governor over Judah and established his headquarters at Mizpah (Tell en-Naṣbeh; 2 Kings 25. 22–6; Jer. 40–1). Gedaliah was from a highly honoured family in Jerusalem, and a seal impression discovered at Lachish indicates that he held the exalted rank of "(Steward) over the (royal) house",[91] doubtless during the reign of Zedekiah. In his new role as governor we do not know the extent of his authority, but it is logical to assume that he was under the Babylonian governor of Samaria. Neither is it too clear why he established residence at Mizpah. Perhaps because it was the closest major town to Samaria,[92] or simply that all the other large centres in Judah were in ruins. A short time later Gedaliah and the entire Babylonian garrison there were murdered; after that the Babylonians probably put an end to the last small measure of Judean independence.

In the wake of the utter devastation suffered by Judah a population vacuum was left behind which existed for some time. The Babylonians did not bring in deportees from other countries, which made possible the return of part of the exiles in the Persian period without their encountering a foreign population. The poor folk of the land did take immediate possession of the ruined settlements and their adjacent fields (Jer. 40. 10), and the anger which this action aroused among the Babylonian exiles found fierce expression in the words of Ezekiel:

> In the twelfth year of our exile . . . a man who had escaped from Jerusalem came to me and said, "The city has fallen." . . . the word of the Lord came to me: "Son of man, the inhabitants of these waste places in the land of Israel keep saying, 'Abraham was only one man, yet he got possession of the land; but we are many; the land is surely given to us to possess.' Therefore, say unto them . . .: You eat flesh with the blood, and lift up your eyes to your idols, and shed blood; shall you then possess the land? . . . As I live, surely those who are in the waste places shall fall by the sword; and him that is in the open field I will give to the beast to be devoured and those who are in strongholds and in caves shall die by pestilence . . ." (Ezek. 33. 21–27).

Surprisingly, some populous Judean settlements were apparently able to hold their own in the border regions of Judea, viz. in the Negeb, the

Shephelah and the district of Benjamin, as may be deduced from the list of towns representing "the rest of Israel" preserved in Nehemiah 11. 25–35.

The distribution of Judean towns in that list does not tally with its concluding summary, "from Beer-sheba to the Valley of Hinnom", because with the exception of Kiriath-arba no settlements are mentioned in the Judean hill country. On the other hand, the passage contains a long list of towns in the Negeb and the Shephelah that were outside the limits of Post-exilic Judea. In the Negeb are mentioned Dibon (Dimonah ?; cf. Josh. 15. 22), Jekabzeel, Jeshua (Tell es-Sa'weh ?), Moladah (Khereibet el-Waṭen), Beth-pelet (Tell es-Saqaṭi ?), Hazar-shual, Beer-sheba (Tell es-Seba'), Ziklag (Tell esh-Shari'ah ?), Meconah and En-rimmon (Tell Khuweilifeh). All of these were towns in the Negeb district of Judah (Josh. 15. 21–32). To them are added some towns in the northern Shephelah, viz. Zorah, Jarmuth (Khirbet Yarmuk), Zanoah (Khirbet Zanu'), Adullam (Tell esh-Sheikh Madhkur) and Azekah (Tell ez-Zakariyeh), all of them in the northern Shephelah district of Judah (Josh. 15. 33–6). Lachish is the only town in the southern Shephelah mentioned.

Since all of these setttlements were outside the limits of Post-exilic Judea, it would appear that a permanent Judean population had avoided deportation in the Babylonian period and had remained in the land.[93] The Negeb district was probably detached from Judah as early as 597 B.C. (cf. Jer. 13. 19). In any case, it is unlikely that such thorough deportations were made from the border areas as from the hill country of Judah.

The Benjaminite towns in the list under discussion also fall into two distinct groups. Nine of them were situated between Jerusalem and Bethel in the central and eastern portions of Benjamin's inheritance, viz. Geba (Jeba'), Michmas (Mukhmas), Aija (Khirbet Ḥaiyan), Bethel (Beitin), Anathoth (Ras el-Kharrubeh beside 'Anata), Nob ('Isawiyeh ?), Ananiah (Bethany; el-'Azariyeh ?), Hazor (Baal-hazor, Tell 'Aṣur north of Bethel ?) and Ramah (er-Ram). That region may also have been conquered somewhat earlier than Jerusalem so that the Babylonians may not have carried out mass deportations from there. This might also explain why Mizpah was selected to be the headquarters of Gedaliah; but after his murder Mizpah was probably laid waste and therefore does not appear in our list. Six towns in the northern Shephelah are also added, viz. Gittaim (Ras Abu Ḥumeid), Hadid (el-Ḥaditheh), Zeboim, Neballat (Beit Nabala), Lod and Ono (Khirbet Kafr 'Ana). Evidently this means that there was also a Judean population in this area that managed to survive the downfall of Jerusalem.

Groups of Israelites doubtless remained in other parts of the country, especially in Galilee and Gilead where foreign deportees were not settled by the Assyrians. The large numbers of Jews in those areas during the Maccabaean period certainly did not spring up overnight, but we have no evidence about them from the Babylonian period.

2. The Period of Persian Rule

Babylon fell in 539 B.C. to Cyrus, King of Persia, who established the greatest and most extensive empire in the history of the Ancient East, extending from the Iranian highlands to the border of Egypt, which was also conquered and annexed by Cambyses, son and successor to Cyrus (in 525). There is no record of battles being fought in Palestine during their reign; Syria and Palestine probably fell automatically to Cyrus with the conquest of Babylon. Palestine remained under Persian rule until it was conquered by Alexander the Great in 332 B.C. For these 200 years of Persian domination we are left with only a few meagre sources. As a general rule the Persian authorities evidently accepted the administrative division in the respective parts of their empire as they found it, i.e. as it had been established in the Assyrian and Babylonian periods. Nevertheless, they practised a certain measure of liberality concerning internal freedom and religious and ethnic autonomy throughout the empire. The realm was divided into satrapies, each governed by a Persian commissioner (satrap, the biblical *Aḥašdarpan,* Dan. 3. 2–3, 27; 6. 2–7). These large satrapies were in turn subdivided into smaller units called "provinces" in the Bible (מדינה), each of which was under the supervision of a governor.[94] Within the Persian governmental framework considerable autonomy was allowed to the various provinces, and many of the governors were descendants of the local nobility.

Palestine belonged to the satrapy "Beyond the River", meaning the region west of the Euphrates.[95] This was a general geographical term that included Syria, Phoenicia and Palestine which originated in the Assyrian period (*eber nāri;* cf. *supra,* p. 78). During the days of Cyrus we hear of only a single governor in charge of "Babylon and the land Beyond the River", i.e. probably over all the territories formerly belonging to the Neo-Babylonian kingdom.

According to Herodotus[96] a reorganization of the Persian empire into twenty satrapies took place at the beginning of the reign of Darius I (522–486 B.C.). However, in his days we still hear about a single governor for "Babylon and the land Beyond the River", and Tattenai, the governor of "Beyond the River", was his subordinate.[97] Darius probably created only a sub-province "Beyond the River" and the administrative set-up reflected in Herodotus' list was apparently that of the historian's own days (*c.* 450 B.C.).[98] Babylon lost its provincial status after its rebellion in 482 B.C., and the separation of "Beyond the River" from Mesopotamia was probably carried out at this time.[99]

According to the description in Herodotus, "Beyond the River" was the Fifth Satrapy, which extended from Poseidion in Cilicia (today Basiṭ in north Syria) to the border of Egypt, omitting Arabian territory south of Gaza which was free of tax. Phoenicia, Syria and Palestine (Παλαιστίνη), and Cyprus were all included. This is the earliest evidence of the use of the term Palestine as a general designation for the whole country; formerly it had only stood for Philistia, the Philistine territory in the limited sense. The Greek and Hellenistic writers first came in touch with the coastal regions of Syria and Palestine; therefore, they extended the range of the terms that they encountered there to include the whole of the country.

We have very little information about any historical events within the satrapy "Beyond the River" during the Persian period. From the various campaigns against Egypt we learn, mainly indirectly, about the passage of the Persian army through Palestine. Though in their route they hardly penetrated the hilly region it seems plausible that various events in Judah known from the Bible are connected with them.

Cambyses passed Palestine on his way to Egypt in 525 B.C., and, according to Strabo XVI, 758, he mustered his forces at Acco. In his passage through the desert he was assisted by the Arabian king (probably of Kedar, cf. *infra,* p. 414), who provided the water supply with the help of camels. In return the coastal strip between Gaza and Ienysos (?) on the Egyptian border, which was under the control of the Arabs, was exempted from taxes.[100]

The tension between Judah and her neighbours concerning the rebuilding of the temple in Jerusalem (Ezra 4. 1–5; 5. 3–17; Hag. 1) was probably connected with the series of uprisings in Babylon and other places (522–20 B.C.) that accompanied Darius I's rise to power. The favourable decision of the Persian authorities and the consequent completion of the temple indicate that Judah took no part in the troubles. Darius passed through Palestine on his way to Egypt in the winter of 519/518 B.C.[101] The fate of Zerubabel is unknown, and his conjectured rebellion and execution lacks basic evidence.[102]

Egypt rebelled again with the death of Darius I (486 B.C.) and to this situation belong the new accusations against the inhabitants of Judah and Jerusalem (Ezra 4. 6). This was evidently a time of great disturbances in Palestine[103]; however, little is known about them. Matters were again under the control of the Persian authorities after the passage of Xerxes I through Palestine and the subjugation of Egypt in 483 B.C. In its invasion of Greece the Persian army was formidably assisted by a Phoenician fleet.[104]

The mission of Ezra, which took place probably in 458 B.C.,[105] was perhaps connected with the rebellion of Egypt in 459 B.C. with the assistance of an Athenian fleet.[106] Megabyzus, the satrap of "Beyond the River", succeeded in quelling the rebellion (456–454 B.C.) with the help of a Phoenician fleet, but afterwards he himself revolted in 448 B.C. These troubles apparently left their traces also in Jerusalem (Ezra 4. 23; Neh. 1. 3). They were counteracted through the appointment of Nehemiah as governor of the Yehud province in the year 445 B.C.

With the death of Darius II in 404 B.C. Egypt revolted again, this time succeeding in gaining its independence for about 60 years. The struggle with his brother which accompanied the accession of Artaxerxes II Mnemon brought for the first time a large hired Greek army into northern Syria. Various discoveries of Egyptian objects point even to a certain Egyptian influence in the Palestinian coastal area. At Gezer have been found a stone slab and a scaraboid with the name of Nepherites, who founded the twenty-ninth dynasty in 398 B.C.[107] Inscriptions with the name of Achoris (393–80 B.C.) have been found in the Eshmunezer temple north of Sidon,[108] and at Acco.[109] He succeeded in repelling a new Persian invasion with the help of the King of Cyprus, who invaded Phoenicia and captured Tyre. Cyprus was reconquered during the years 381–79 B.C.; however, a renewed attack on Egypt in 373 B.C. failed.[110] The Persian forces and its fleet mustered once again at Acco.

The "Revolt of the satraps" (*c.* 368–60 B.C.), which shook the Persian empire to its very foundations, was assisted by the Phoenician cities of Arvad, Sidon and Tyre. Pharao Tachos (Teos) invaded Palestine in 359 B.C. with the help of 10,000 Greek mercenaries; however, inner disturbances forced him to surrender to Ochus (Artaxerxes III) at Sidon.

In 351 B.C. Artaxerxes III undertook another unsuccessful invasion of Egypt, which was followed by a major revolt of Phoenicia. After its initial success it was oppressed by Artaxerxes personally and Sidon was captured and destroyed (345 B.C.).[111]

Only in 343 B.C. did Artaxerxes finally succeed in conquering Egypt and stabilizing the Persian domination of the adjacent regions. However, with his assassination in 338 B.C. the Persian empire hastened towards its final dissolution.

Our information about the provincial organization of Palestine stems mainly from the Bible. It is likely that the Persians left the internal political structure very much as they had inherited it from the Babylonians and Assyrians. Within Palestine there is recorded a change in Judah's fortune; it was granted the status of a province. Cyrus in his first year as emperor (538 B.C.) reacted favourably to the requests of the Babylonian exiles and permitted their return to the land of Judah. The royal decree defined both the political and religious autonomy of Judah as well as arranging for the temple to be reconstructed (Ezra 1. 2–4; 6. 3–5). The newly appointed governor for Judah was Sheshbazzar (Ezra. 5. 14), who also bore the local title "Prince of Judah" (Ezra 1. 8). He is evidently to be identified with the Shenazzar who was a son of

Jehoiachin (1 Chron. 3. 17–18). He was succeeded in the rank of governor by his nephew Zerubbabel, son of Shealtiel[112] (Ezra 3. 2; Neh. 12. 1; Hag. 1. 1, *et al.*). Thus it is clear that Judah was granted the status of a province under a Judean governor who was, at least at the beginning, a descendant of the royal family.

From the various historical sources the names of several other governors who ruled in Judah during the fifth and fourth centuries B.C. are known. Most if not all of them were Jewish, although they are no longer connected with the Davidic Dynasty.

In the Bible we have Nehemiah (Neh. 5. 14; *c.* 445–25). The Elephantine papryi contain references to a Judean governor named Bagohi who, because of his typical Persian name (Bagoas in Greek sources), is usually thought to be a Persian. However, among the returnees from exile there was a family named Bigvai (containing the same Iranian element, *baga* meaning "god"; Ezra 2. 2; Neh. 7. 7, *et al.*), so the aforementioned governor may just as well have been Jewish. The names of two additional rulers are known from seal impressions discovered at Ramat Raḥel (Beth-haccerem), viz. Jehoezer (*yhw ʻzr*) and Ahzai (*ʼḥzy*) who bear the title of governor (*pḥwʼ*).[113] A coin, several examples of which were found at Beth-zur and Tell Jemmeh, bears the inscription, "Hezekiah, the governor (*hpḥh* = *hap-peḥāh*) of Judah,"[114] who is evidently Ezekias, a high priest in the early Hellenstic period mentioned by Josephus (*Contra Apionem* I, 187–9). Apparently the latter three, Jehoezer, Ahzai and Hezekiah, held the office of governor and high priest at the same time, since the priesthood was now the most prominent element in the State. This would indicate that throughout the Persian period Judah remained an autonomous province, usually (and perhaps always) under Jewish governors originally from the House of David and later from the priestly families.

The Bible also refers to Judah's neighbouring provinces (Neh. 2. 19; 4. 1–8, *et al.*) whose governors were adversaries of Nehemiah: Sanballat of Samaria, Tobiah the Ammonite, Geshem the Arab and the Ashdodites (the name of Ashdod's governor is not given). The descendants of Sanballat, who inherited his office, are known now from the newly discovered Samaria Papyri.[115] Tobiah was the son of an influential Jewish family with connections in Jerusalem. His capital was the Tyre (Ṣor) which apparently was called "the Tyre of the House of Tobiah" in Gilead. He was evidently the Persian-appointed governor of Ammon which had been joined to the province of Gilead.[116] Geshem was undoubtedly the governor of the Arabian district which Herodotus included in the southern part of his Fifth Satrapy (cf. *supra,* p. 411 f.). From the discovery of his name on a silver bowl from a temple at Tell el-Maskhuṭah in the eastern Delta region we know that he was King of Kedar.[117] The influence of this Arab kingdom is felt in the eastern Delta area, where they had been permitted to establish colonies at least as early as the days of Darius I.[118] In its possession also was the coastal area south of Gaza, as attested by Herodotus. The remarkable amount of Attic pottery discovered at Tell el-Kheleifeh (Ezion-geber) testifies to the extensive trade with the west, which was in the hands of Geshem.[119] His domain probably included Edom, where the Nabataeans were in the first stages of settlement, and perhaps the southern Judean hill country now occupied by the Edomites. The hill region south of Hebron was not included in the province of Judah; in Hellenistic sources it is referred to as Idumaea. Since Geshem the Arab was interfering in the affairs of Judah along with the governors of Samaria, Ammon and Ashdod, it is probable that Idumaea, which borders on Judah, was within his sphere of authority.[120] If so, then we have evidence for four provinces that bordered on Judah: Samaria in the north, Ammon-Gilead in the east, Arabia-Idumaea in the south and Ashdod in the west. In contrast to the preceding period, the provinces of Ammon and Arabia are new; however, the campaigns of the Assyrians and Babylonians in these regions make it probable that those provinces were created either in the Assyrian or the Babylonian period. In the north the province of Megiddo must have continued to exist, although we cannot be sure that its capital remained at Megiddo, inasmuch as the Persian stratum I was the last in the history of that city. However, there is no basis for Alt's assumption that the capital of that province had been transferred to Acco.[121] The various harbour towns on the Palestinian coast were placed by the Persians under the authority of the southern Phoenician cities Tyre and Sidon. These harbours were indispensable to the Phoenician mariners as way stations where they could find a haven for their ships at night or during a storm. The Persian government was profoundly interested in expanding Phoenician maritime activity as competition for the Greeks. The inscription of Eshmunezer informs us that he had received from the Persian king ("the Lord of Kings") the territory of "Dor and Joppa, the mighty lands of Dagon, which are in the Plain of Sharon".[122] An important source in this regard is a Greek composition which describes the Palestinian coast in the fourth century, though it is ascribed to the Greek mariner Skylax who lived in the fifth century (Pseudo-Skylax). After Tyre he lists the following cities:

> The city [Achzib ?] and a river; the city Acco; outside of the bay [Shikmonah or Haifa ?], a city of the Tyrians; . . . a mountain and a temple to Zeus (on Mount Carmel); Adaroth (corrected from Arados, perhaps ʿAthlit ?) a city of the Sidonians; Dor, city of the Sidonians; the city [Crocodilonpolis ?] and a river . . . the Tyrians; [Joppa, city of the Sidonians]; Ashkelon, city of the Tyrians and palace of the king.[123]

Therefore, the towns south of Acco were alternately colonies of either Tyre or Sidon: Haifa, Crocodilonpolis (?) and Ashkelon were Tyrian;

Adaroth ('Athlit ?), Dor and Joppa were Sidonian. On the future site of Caesarea a fortress was established called the "Tower of Straton". It was evidently founded in the fourth century by Straton ('Abd- 'ashtart), King of Sidon, to serve as an additional Sidonian stop-over between Dor and Joppa. There were also Phoenician colonies in the interior, e.g. at Shechem and Mareshah. The southernmost seaport in Palestine was Gaza, which had always served as a major terminal for relationships with Egypt and an export centre for goods from Arabia. In the highest stratum (Persian) at Ezion-geber an abundance of Attic sherds were discovered, testifying to the extensive commerce that developed in that period between South Arabia and the West, part of which traversed the Negeb routes from Gaza to the Gulf of Aqabah.

The territory of Judah was seriously diminished by the exclusion of the southern Judean hill country. The boundary passed between Beth-zur and Hebron whose precincts had become Edomite. On the other hand, the northern boundary conformed to its Pre-exilic line north of Mizpah and Bethel and included Jericho on the east. On the west the Judean province took in part of the Shephelah as far as Keilah in the south. Lod, Hadid and Ono in the northern Shephelah are mentioned in the list of returnees (Ezra 2. 33; Neh. 7. 37), but it is doubtful whether that region was actually part of Judea during the Persian period.[124] We have also noted that Jews were living in various Negeb settlements as well, where the population was evidently not deported by the Babylonians, but these settlements were obviously not reckoned as part of the Judean province. Concerning the limits of the Jewish population in the Persian period, it is also possible to derive some information from the diffusion of storage jars bearing seal impressions inscribed "Yehud" (with certain spelling variations), and "Jerusalem". Thus far these impressions have been discovered at Jerusalem, Ramat Raḥel, Bethany, Jericho, En-gedi, Mizpah, Azekah and Gezer. Apparently Gezer was outside of the Judean province at first, and from the cuneiform tablets discovered there it would seem that towards the end of the First Temple period the population was mainly Assyrian.[125] In the Persian period the Judean element must have prevailed again (cf. map 34).

Many of the Judean settlements in this period are known to us from the roster of "the people of the province who came up out of the captivity" (Ezra 2. 1–35; Neh. 7. 6–38). The majority are in the former Benjaminite region north of Jerusalem: Nob (instead of Nebo), Anathoth, (Beth-)azmaveth, Ramah, Geba, Michmas, Ai (apparently Aiath-Aijah; Khirbet Ḥaiyan), Bethel and the four Gibeonite towns: Gibeon, Chephirah, Ḳiriath-jearim and Beeroth. South of Jerusalem only two towns are mentioned, Bethlehem and Netophah, and on the east Jericho. The north-western Shephelah is represented by Lod, Hadid and Ono.

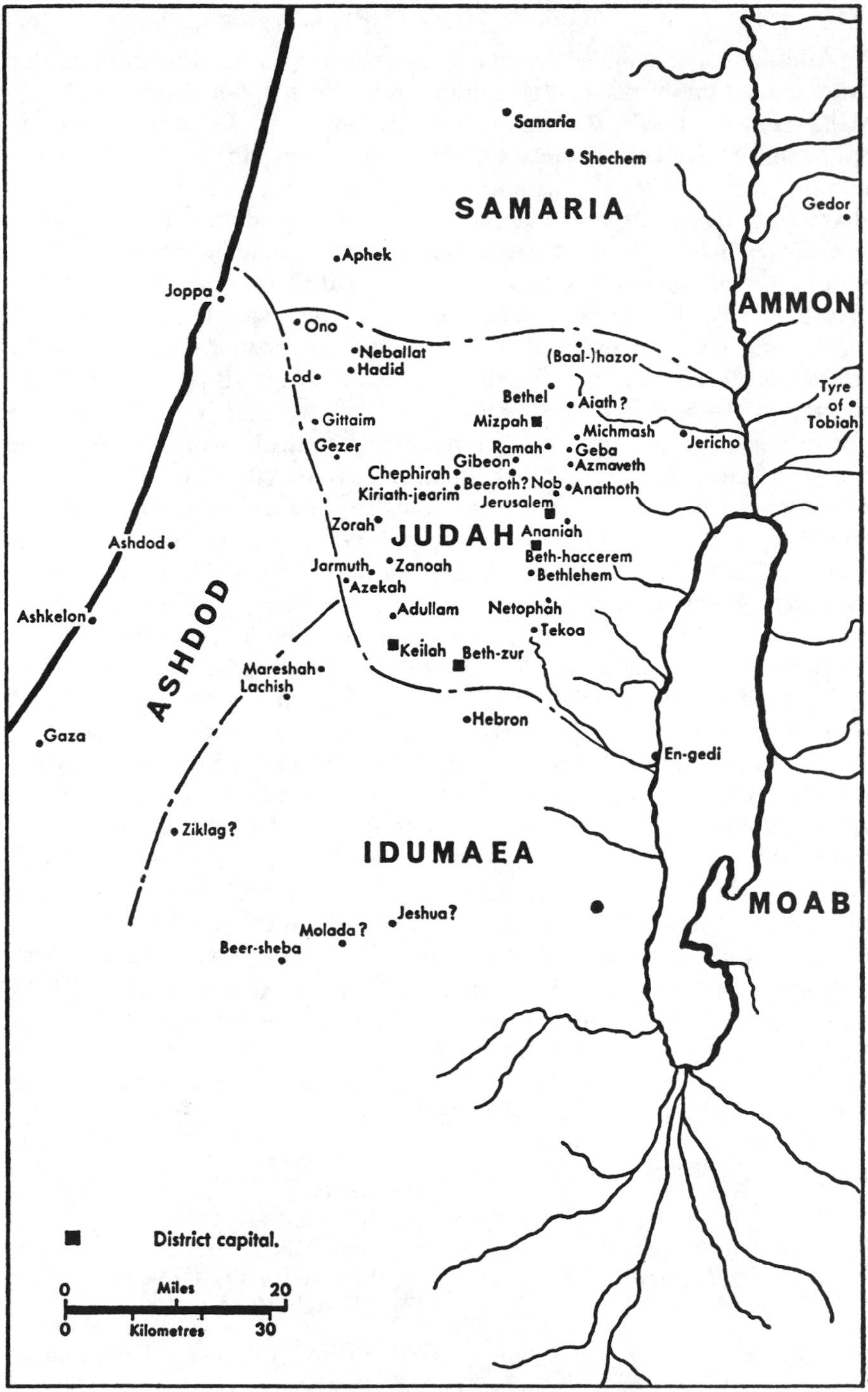

Map 34. Judah in the Post-exilic Period.

Additional place names appear on the roster of those who participated in building the walls of Jerusalem under Nehemiah (Neh. 3. 1–32): Mizpah in the north; Beth-haccerem, Beth-zur and Tekoa in the south; Zanoah and Keilah on the west. It is interesting to note that this list contains only two settlements that also appear in the record of returnees, viz. Gibeon and Jericho. Besides Jerusalem itself four towns are referred to as district headquarters, viz. Mizpah, Beth-haccerem, Beth-zur and Keilah. This would suggest that the roster of builders was made up according to the administrative centres of Judah. At least some of these places were evidently established in towns that had survived the Babylonian destruction; Mizpah is a case in point since it had already served as the seat of Babylonian authority under Gedaliah. Others were located in isolated strongholds not associated with towns, such as the Persian fortress at Ramat Raḥel, apparently Beth-haccerem.[126]

Thus, from this list we are able to deduce something of the administrative organization within the Judean province of the Persian period. The district headquarters proved that this division preserved the former framework of four districts (excluding Jerusalem) as established in the reign of Hezekiah. However, these new districts conformed to the depleted territory of Judah: Keilah in the Shephelah (in place of Socoh), Mizpah in the north (instead of *mmšt*-Jerusalem), Beth-haccerem and Beth-zur representing the southern hill region (replacing Hebron and Ziph). Except for Beth-haccerem, which included the Bethlehem region, each district was subdivided into two sub-districts because our roster contains two sub-district commissioners from Keilah, Beth-zur, and Jerusalem and two officers from Mizpah. The four other towns appearing in the list possibly also served as administrative centres for the district commissioners, viz. Zanoah in the Shephelah beside Keilah; Tekoa in the south-east with Beth-zur; Gibeon, north-west of Jerusalem; Jericho in the Jordan Valley, which certainly must have comprised the eastern sub-district under the officer at Mizpah, including the wilderness of Judah. The nine towns mentioned in the list of builders were therefore the administrative centres of the Judean province. This organization can be represented by the following table:

Districts	*Sub-Districts*
Keilah	(1) Zanoah, (2) Keilah
Beth-zur	(3) Beth-zur (4) Tekoa
Beth-haccerem	(5) Beth-haccerem
Jerusalem	(6) Jerusalem, (7) Gibeon
Mizpah	(8) Mizpah, (9) Jericho

The area of Judah was quite restricted and the Judean population developed very slowly because of interference from the outside and tensions within the community between those who had remained and those who had returned from exile. No further information is available concerning developments in Judah during the latter part of the Persian period, but the emergence of a well-established Jewish population in the Hellenistic period indicates that progress was steady, albeit gradual. The three main forces that became consolidated in Palestine at this time were the coastal towns with their mixed population; the Samaritans in Mount Ephraim, comprised of the Israelite population intermingled with the foreign settlers brought in by the Assyrians from Hamath and Babylonia; and Judea, which though limited in territory enjoyed strong ties with a considerable Jewish population outside of its borders, including the two regions where the Israelite population had remained more or less undisturbed by deportations, viz. Gilead (Peraea) and Galilee. These are the three "lands of the Jews" in the Mishnah: Judah, Transjordan and Galilee (*Shebiith* 9.2) where centres of Jewish culture flourished during the period of the Second Temple.

[1] *ANET*, p. 287.

[2] B. Maisler (Mazar), *EI*, 2 (1953), p. 171 (Hebrew).

[3] *ANET*, pp. 287 f.

[4] Ashdod's provincial status under Sargon II was only temporary; concerning the reappearance of a local king there cf. A. Alt, *ZDPV*, 67 (1945), pp. 138 ff. (=*Kl. Schr.*, II, pp. 234 ff.).

[5] [Perhaps this treachery, abandoning the league with Judah and going over to the side of the Assyrians, was "the great evil" committed by Edom according to an ostracon from Stratum VIII at Arad; Y. Aharoni, *Arad Inscriptions* (Jerusalem, 1975), No. 40. 15, pp. 72, 76. A.F.R.]

[6] B. Mazar, *IEJ*, 10 (1960), pp. 72 ff.

[7] Translation following L. H. Grollenberg, *Atlas of the Bible* (London, 1957), p. 89, with only slight changes; cf. also *ANET*, p. 288.

[8] According to 2 Kings 18. 14, "three hundred talents of silver and thirty talents of gold."

[9] N. Na'aman, *BASOR*, 214 (1974), pp. 25–39.

[10] K 6505; G. Smith, *The Cuneiform Inscriptions of Western Asia*, Vol. III (London, 1870), pl. 9, No. 2; P. Rost, *Die Keilschrifttexte Tiglat-Pilesers III* (Leipzig, 1893), pp. 18–20, lines 103–19.

[11] H. Winckler, *Altorientalische Forschungen*, Vol. II (Leipzig, 1898), pp. 570–74; H. Tadmor, *JCS*, 12 (1958), pp. 80–84.

[12] Na'aman, *op. cit., pp. 26–28.*

[13] *Ibid.*, pp. 34–35; [thus we remove the difficulties seen by Na'aman in the mention of Azekah before the Philistine city. A.F.R.]

[14] Rainey, *EI*, 12 (1975), pp. 73*–75*.

[15] *ANEP*, pp. 129–32; R. D. Barnett, *IEJ*, 8 (1958), pp. 165–70; recent excavations have confirmed that Sennacherib's conquest is represented by the destruction of Stratum III at Lachish.

[16] Bk. II, 141.

[17] The Shephelah districts contained thirty-nine towns according to Joshua 15. 33–44.

[18] There is insufficient evidence to support the opinion that there were two campaigns by Sennacherib as has been suggested in order to explain the payment of tribute alongside the miraculous deliverance of Jerusalem; cf. W. W. Hallo, *BA*, 23 (1960), pp. 57–59.

[19] Cf. A. Alt, *PJb*, 25 (1929), pp. 80–88 (=*Kl. Schr.*, II, pp. 242–49) for a far-reaching hypothesis.

[20] Aharoni, *Lachish V*, pp. 33–40; also M. Eilat, apud *Lachish V*, pp. 68–69.

[21] For the most up-to-date summary of the "two campaign theory" with complete bibliography, cf. J. Bright, *A History of Israel*[2] (Philadelphia, 1972), pp. 296–308.

[22] Most recently, K. A. Kitchen, *JANES*, 5 (1973), pp. 225–33; *idem, The Third Intermediate Period in Egypt* (Warminster, 1973), pp. 154–61. Unfortunately, Kitchen's mastery of the Egyptian historial sources is not matched by a similar control of biblical topography; his sketch maps on p. 384 of the latter work are valueless. He would posit two Egyptian interventions, a solution that is very difficult though perhaps not impossible.

[23] In fact he was in some sense marching at the head of an army when he came from Nubia to join his brother in Egypt; for a syntactical discussion and translation of the relevant Kawa passages, cf. now. A. F. Rainey, *Tel Aviv*, 3 (1976), pp. 38–41.

[24] A. H. Sayce, *PEQ* (1893), pp. 240–42; W. F. Albright, *JPOS*, 5 (1925), pp. 45–54; *idem, AASOR*, 21–22 (1943), pp. 74–75; C. Watzinger, *Denkmäler Palästinas*, I (Leipzig, 1933), pp. 116–17; D. Diringer, *Le iscrizioni antico-ebraiche Palestinesi* (Florence, 1934), pp. 145–57; *idem, PEQ* (1941), pp. 91–101; *idem, BA*, 12 (1949), pp. 70–86; *idem*, apud O. Tufnell, *Lachish*, III (London, 1953), pp. 342–47; E. L. Sukenik, *Qedem*, 1 (1942), pp. 32–36 (Hebrew); H. L. Ginzberg, *BASOR*, 109 (1948), pp. 20–22; G. E. Wright, *BA*, 12 (1949),pp. 91–92; S. Moscati, *L'epigrafia ebraica antica, 1935–1950* (Rome, 1951)pp. 83–99; J. B. Pritchard, *Hebrew Inscriptions and Stamps from Gibeon* (Philadelphia, 1959), pp. 18–26; P. W. Lapp, *BASOR*, 158 (1960), pp. 11–22; Y. Yadin, *BASOR*, 163 (1961), pp. 6–12; Y. Aharoni, *Excavations at Ramat Raḥel, Seasons 1959 and 1960* (Rome, 1962)pp. 51–56; A. F. Rainey, *BASOR*, 179 (1965), pp. 34–36; *idem, IEJ*, 16 (1966), pp. 187–90; P. Welten, *Die Königs-Stempel* (Weisbaden, 1969); F. M. Cross, *EI*, 9 (1969), pp. 24 ff.; H. D. Lance, *HTR*, 64 (1971), pp. 316–32; A. D. Tushingham, *BASOR*, 200 (1970), pp. 71–78; 201 (1971), pp. 23–35. D. Ussishkin, *BASOR*, 223 (1976), pp. 1–13.

[25] This interpretation seems most likely in the light of comparison with Assyrian and Hittite designs, cf. Watzinger, *ibid*; Lapp, *ibid.*, p. 12; there certainly is no basis for the recently proposed derivation of one of the symbols from the royal insignia of northern Israel, A. D. Tushingham, *ibid.*

[26] Y. Aharoni, *ibid.*, pp. 20, 40 f., 51.

[27] *Ibid.*, pp. 59 f.

[28] Olga Tufnell, *Lachish*, III (London, 1953), p. 340.

[29] Ussishkin, *op. cit.*, pp. 1 ff.; the presence of private seals on handles of the self-same jars with the double winged symbols indicates that all the handles with private seal impressions belong to the same administrative system, cf. Ussishkin's remarks, pp. 11–13. The formulae on the royal and private impressions represent two different semantic fields; the former designate the commodity as royal property, probably rendered as taxes; the latter indicates only that the seal belongs to the person named on it; the *lamed* preposition in neither case indicates that the king or the person is the donor or sender; A. F. Rainey, *BASOR*, 179 (1965), pp. 34–36, *idem, IEJ*, 16 (1966), pp. 187–90.

[30] B. W. Buchanan, *AJA*, 58 (1954), pp. 335–39; G. E. Wright, *VT*, 5 (1955), pp. 97–105.

[31] The excavations in 1976 have shown that the only stratum that is a candidate for equation with Sennacherib's campaign is Stratum III: D. Ussishkin, *Tel Aviv*, 4 (1977), pp. 28–60.

[32] Y. Aharoni and M. Aharoni, *BASOR*, 224 (1976), pp. 73–90.

[33] R. D. Barnett, *IEJ*, 8 (1958), pp. 161–64

[34] D. Diringer, *BA*, 13 (1949), pp. 85 f.

[35] Lapp, *loc. cit.* (note 24), pp. 19–21.

[36] J. B. Pritchard, *Hebrew Inscriptions and Stamps from Gibeon* (Philadelphia, 1959), p. 18.

[37] N. Avigad, *IEJ*, 9 (1959), p. 132.

[38] R. Hestrin and M. Dayagi, *IEJ*, 24 (1974), pp. 27–29.

[39] Cf. the observations of A. R. Millard, apud J. R. Bartlett, *PEQ*, 108 (1976), p. 61 n. 18.

[40] Lapp, *loc. cit.* (note 24); Aharoni, *op. cit.* (note 24).

[41] Y. Aharoni, *IEJ*, 8 (1958), p. 36, Pl. 16D.

[42] Aharoni, *op. cit.* (note 24), pp. 51–56, Fig. 32.

[43] H. L. Ginsberg, *BASOR*, 109 (1948), pp. 20 f.

[44] *ANET*, p. 283.

[45] Y. Aharoni, *Arad Inscriptions* (Jerusalem, 1975), pp. 52–53.

[46] M. Kochavi, *Judaea, Samaria and the Golan, Archaeological Survey, 1967–1968* (Jerusalem, 1972), pp. 81–82, Nos. 248, 250.

[47] These districts were organized according to the local wadi systems with a watershed separating each of them; M. Kochavi, *Tel Aviv,* 1 (1974), pp. 26–33, especially Fig. 12 on p. 29.

[48] W. F. Albright, *BASOR,* 80 (1940),, p. 21, note 51.

[49] The circles carved on many jar handles bearing royal seal impressions are probably connected with this phenomenon. Unlike the impressions which were stamped at the pottery before the jar was fired in the kiln, these circles were engraved by use of a special compass at a later time. They may have meant that the vessel was officially disqualified and now available for private use.

[50] *ANET,* pp. 290 f.

[51] *ANET,* p. 291; the same list is also preserved in a text dating to the reign of Ashurbanipal, *ANET,* p. 294.

[52] G. van Beek, *IEJ,* 22 (1972), pp. 245–46, 24 (1974), pp. 138–39, 274–75.

[53] *ANET,* pp. 292 f.

[54] Concerning the conclusions about the Assyrian provinces derived from Aphek's belonging to Samaria, cf. *supra,* p. 377.

[55] *ANET,* pp. 295 f.

[56] *ANET,* pp. 297 f.

[57] *ANET,* p. 300; cf. H. J. Katzenstein, *The History of Tyre* (Jerusalem, 1973), pp. 293–94.

[58] F. M. Cross and D. N. Freedman, "Josiah's Revolt against Assyria", *JNES,* 12 (1953); pp. 56–58; H. Tadmor, *JNES,* 15 (1956), pp. 226–60.

[59] For a different view, cf. W. Rudolph, *Chronikbücher* (Tübingen, 1955), p. 320.

[60] M. Avi-Yonah and S. Yeivin, *The Antiquities of Israel* (Tel Aviv, 1955), p. 313 (Hebrew); A. Malamat, *JANES,* 5 (1973), pp. 267–79.

[61] J. Naveh, *IEJ,* 10 (1960), pp. 129–39.

[62] *ANET,* p. 283.

[63] W. F. Albright, *JBL,* 58 (1939), pp. 184 f.

[64] Cf. *supra,* p. 372.

[65] Y. Aharoni, *Arad Inscriptions* (Jerusalem, 1975), No. 88, pp. 103–4. [For the idiom, *malakti b-,* cf. Gen. 36. 31, 32; 2 Sam. 3. 21; 1 Kings 11. 37; 14. 20; 1 Chron. 1. 43; 16. 31. A.F.R.].

[66] [There is nothing to commend the interpretation by Y. Yadin to the effect that this text is an announcement by Asshur-uballit that he was ruling "in Ca[rchemish]," *IEJ,* 26 (1976), pp. 9–14. First of all, Asshur-uballit had already become king at Harran; cf. *ANET,* p. 305 and now A. J. Grayson, *Assyrian and Babylonian Chronicles* (Locust Valley, 1975), pp. 94–95, lines 49, 60–61. Secondly, no Assyrian king would use the wording of that Arad ostracon to describe his establishing headquarters at a provisional capital at Carchemish. A.F.R.]

[67] Cf. A. Alt, *PJb,* 21 (1925), pp. 108 ff. (=*Kl. Schr.,* II, pp. 281 ff.); Z. Kallai, *The Northern Boundaries of Judah* (Jerusalem, 1960), pp. 74 f. (Hebrew); cf. *supra,* p. 323.

[68] B. Mazar, *Enc. Bib.* (Hebrew), II, col. 412.

[69] *Ibid.*; Mazar equated the Geba in question with the Γηβα of Eusebius, *Onom.,* 74. 2, which is located at et-Tell, M. Avi-Yonah, *The Holy Land*² (Grand Rapids, 1977), pp. 154, 156 and Map 14 on p. 152.

[70] [It is obvious that 2 Kings 23. 8 cannot refer to the beautiful ashlar altar discovered at Beer-sheba; this latter was dismantled in the reign of Hezekiah; cf. Z. Herzog, A. F. Rainey and Sh. Moshkovitz, *BASOR,* 225 (1977), pp. 49–58, *contra* Y. Yadin, *BASOR,* 222 (1976), pp. 5–17. A.F.R.]

[71] F. Ll. Griffith, *PSBA,* 16 (1894), p. 91.

[72] It is possible that Arad ostracon No. 34, a listing of commodities in hieratic script, was part of the inventory of the supplies at Arad, taken in connection with Necho's imposition of Egyptian control over Judah; Y. Aharoni, *Arad Inscriptions,* pp. 64–66.

[73] Apparently this is the palace discovered at Ramat Raḥel of which the ancient name was Beth-haccerem; cf. Y. Aharoni, *BA,* 24 (1961), p. 118; *idem, op. cit.* (note 24), pp. 59 f.

[74] Concerning the wars in this period and up to the destruction of Jerusalem in the light of previously unknown fragments from the Babylonian chronicle published by D. J. Wiseman (*Chronicles of Chaldean Kings* [625–556] *etc.* [London, 1956]); cf. W. F.

Albright, *BASOR*, 143 (1956), pp. 28–33; D. N. Freedman, *BA*, 19 (1956), pp. 50–60; J. P. Hyatt, *JBL*, 75 (1956), pp. 227–84; E. Vogt, *VT Suppl.*, 4 (1956), pp. 67–96; A. Malamat, *IEJ*, 6 (1956), pp. 246–56; *idem, IEJ*, 18 (1968), pp. 137–56; *idem, VT Suppl.*, 28 (1975), pp. 123–45; A. F. Rainey, apud *Lachish V*, pp. 45–60. For the principal text, cf. D. J. Wiseman, *Chronicles of Chaldean Kings*, pp. 66–73; *ANET*³, pp. 563 f.; A. K. Grayson, *op. cit.*, pp.99–102.

[75] [The name of the city conquered in this year is written uru x-x-(x)-*il-lu-nu*, Grayson, *op. cit.*, p. 100, line 18 and Commentary; Wiseman had read uru *IŠ*(?)-*qi*(?)-*il-lu-nu*, *op. cit.*, pp. 28, 85. It still seems to be the most logical assumption that Ashkelon was the object of this year's campaign. A.F.R.]

[76] A. Dupont-Sommer, *Semitica*, 1 (1948), pp. 43–68; H. L. Ginsberg, *BASOR*, 111 (1948), pp. 24–27; J. Bright, *BA*, 12 (1949), pp. 46–52; A. Malamat, *BIES*, 15 (1950), pp. 33–39 (Hebrew); *idem, IEJ*, 18 (1968), pp. 142–43; S. H. Horn, *AUSS*, 6 (1968), pp. 29–45; J. A. Fitzmeyer, *Biblica*, 46 (1965), p. 44.

[77] A. F. Rainey apud *Lachish V*, pp. 55–56. [The suggestion by W. H. Shea, *BASOR*, 223 (1976), pp. 61–63, that Aphek was Nebuchadnezzar's objective in 603 B.C. is negated on two counts: (1) as we see from Esarhaddon's inscription, Aphek was not an independent state in the seventh century B.C. so there is hardly any reason for it to be involved in resistance to the Babylonians; (2) Nebuchadnezzar's progress from year to year was steadily southwards—it seems most unlikely that he would have conquered Ashkelon in 604 and Aphek only in 603. A.F.R.]

[78] H. L. Ginsberg, *Alexander Marx Jubilee Volume* (New York, 1950), p. 356 n. 1; J. Lindsey, *PEQ*, 108 (1976), p. 24.

[79] Rainey, *op. cit.* (*supra*, n. 74).

[80] Y. Aharoni, *Arad Inscriptions*, no. 24, pp. 48–51; *idem, BASOR*, 197 (1970), pp. 16–28.

[81] Y. Aharoni, *Arad Inscriptions*, pp. 746–47.

[82] *Ibid.*, p. 151.

[83] *Ibid.*, p. 151, regarding No. 20, pp. 42–43.

[84] H. Torczyner, *The Lachish Letters (Lachish I)* (London, 1938), p. 79; *ANET*, pp. 321 f.

[85] *ANET*, p. 308.

[86] *ANET*, p. 307.

[87] Abel, *Géogr.*, II, p. 135.

[88] Compare Jos., *Contra Apionem*, I, 156.

[89] *ANET*, p. 308.

[90] *ANET*, p. 305.

[91] S. Moscati, *L'epigraphia ebraica antica, 1935–1950* (Rome, 1951), p. 61.

[92] The special function of Mizpah in the provincial framework of the Fifth Satrapy may be alluded to in Neh. 3. 7; however, this verse is difficult of interpetation. Cf. W. Rudolph, *Esra und Nehemia* (Tübingen, 1949), p. 116; Z. Kallai, *The Northern Boundaries of Judah* (Jerusalem, 1960), pp. 89–90 (Hebrew).

[93] A. Malamat, *JNES*, 9 (1950), pp. 226 f.

[94] Cf. "to the king's satraps and to the governors over all the provinces" (Esther 3. 12); "to the king's satraps and to the governors of the province Beyond the River" (Ezra 8.36) *et al.*

[95] A. F. Rainey, AJBA, 1 (1969), pp. 51–78.

[96] *Historiae*, III, 86.

[97] A. T. Olmstead, *JNES*, 3 (1944), p. 46; his name appears as Tattanu in cuneiform sources.

[98] O. Leuze, *Die Satrapieeinteilung in Syrien und im Zweistromlande von 520–320* (Halle [Saale], 1935), pp. 237–42; A. T. Olmstead, *History of the Persian Empire* (Chicago, 1948), pp. 236 ff., 243, 293.

[99] Olmstead, *ibid.* pp. 112, 115.

[100] Herodotus, *Historiae*, III, 4–9.

[101] R. A. Parker, *AJSL*, 58 (1941), pp. 373–77; C. G. Cameron, *JNES*, 2 (1943), pp. 307–13.

[102] Olmstead, *op. cit.* (note 98), p. 142.

[103] J. Morgenstern, *HUCA*, 27 (1956), pp. 101–79; 28 (1957), pp. 15–47; 31 (1960), pp. 1–29; G. E. Wright, *Shechem* (New York, 1965), pp. 167–69.

[104] Herodotus, *Historiae*, VII, 89; VIII, 67.

[105] [Though many scholars have preferred a later date in the reign of Artaxerxes II, (cf. J. Bright, *A History of Israel*² (Philadelphia, 1972), pp. 392–403), F. M. Cross has now demonstrated conclusively the correctness of the traditional order of events, *JBL*, 94 (1975), pp. 5–18. A.F.R.]

[106] J. B. Bury, *A History of Greece* (London, 1955), pp. 354 f., 357 f.

[107] R. A. S. Macalister, *The Excavations of Gezer*, II (London, 1912), p. 313, Fig. 452; A. Rowe, *A Catalogue of Egyptian Scarabs* (Cairo, 1936), pp. 230–31.

[108] W. F. von Landau, *Mitteilungen der vorderasiatischen Gesellschaft*, 5 (1904), pp. 342–47.

[109] A. Rowe, *op. cit.* pp. 295 f.

[110] Isaeus, *Nicostrat.*, 7.

[111] Olmstead, *op. cit.* (note 98), pp. 436 f.

[112] According to I Chron. 3. 19 he was the son of Pedaiah, a brother of Shealtiel.

[113] Y. Aharoni, *Excavations at Ramat Raḥel, Seasons 1959 and 1960* (Rome, 1962), pp. 56–59. The reading *'ḥzy* suggested by F. M. Cross seems preferable to my *'ḥyw*, assuming that an Aramaic Yodh was used. Professor Cross suggests also the reading *pḥr'*, i.e. the potter; however, it is improbable that a potter impressed his name on jars with a prefixed *lamed* (i.e. belonging to) and the reading *pḥw'* seems preferable on part of the stamps. Now the reading *pḥw'* has been thoroughly vindicated by the discovery of some bullae of the Persian period with an unequivocal spelling; N. Avi-gad, *Bullae and Seals from a Post-Exilic Judean Archive* (*Qedem*, 4, Jerusalem, 1976), pp. 6–7.

[114] C. R. Sellers. *The Citadel of Beth-Zur* (Philadelphia, 1933), pp. 73–74; E. L. Sukenik, *JPOS*, 14 (1934), pp. 178 ff.; 15 (1935), pp. 341 ff.; L. Y. Rahami, *IEJ*, 21 (1971), pp. 158 ff.

[115] F. M. Cross, *BA*, 26 (1963), pp. 120 f.

[116] B. Mazar, *IEJ*, 7 (1957), pp. 137–45, 229–38.

[117] F. M. Cross, *BA*, 18 (1955), pp. 46 f.; I. Rabinowitz, *JNES*, 15 (1956), p. 2. The inscription reads: "That which Qainū bar Geshem, King of Qedar, offered to han-'Ilat". On the kingdom of Kedar cf. W. F. Albright, "Dedan", in *Geschichte und Altes Testament* (Tübingen, 1953), pp. 4, 6; cf. the useful monograph by W. J. Dumbrell, *BASOR*, 203 (1971), pp. 33 ff. There is no excuse, however, to take the Persian residency and (so-called solar) shrine at Lachish as evidence for Kedarite occupation as Dumbrell does, *ibid.*, p. 43. That temple is not a solar shrine nor is it Persian in date; furthermore, Lachish had a recognized Jewish population (Neh. 11. 30).

[118] Rabinowitz, *ibid.*, pp. 6 ff. The biblical land of Goshen is rendered in Gen. 45. 10 by the Septuagint as "the land of Geshem the Arabian".

[119] N. Glueck, *Rivers in the Desert* (New York, 1959), p. 172.

[120] A. Alt, *PJb*, 27 (1931), pp. 66 ff. (=*Kl. Schr.*, II, pp. 338 ff.).

[121] A. Alt., *PJb*, 33 (1937), pp. 65 ff. (=*Kl. Schr.*, II, pp. 374 ff.).

[122] *ANET*² p. 505.

[123] Müller, *Geographi graeci minores*, I, pp. 78 ff.; K. Galling, *ZDPV*, 61 (1938), pp. 66–87 (=*Studien zur Geschichte Israels im persischen Zeitalter* [Tübingen, 1964], pp. 185–209).

[124] M. Avi-Yonah, *The Holy Land*² (Grand Rapids, 1977), pp. 28–31.

[125] K. Galling, *PJb*, 31 (1935), pp. 75–93.

[126] Aharoni, *op. cit.* (note 113), pp. 49 ff.; other examples outside the Judean province are the Persian fortresses at Lachish and Hazor, built at a time when towns no longer existed on these sites.

APPENDIX 1

Chronological Table*

Date	*Palestine* archaeological	/ historical division	*Egypt*	*Syria, Anatolia, Mesopotamia*
5000	Neolithic	Beginning of agriculture and permanent settlement	Fayum A	Jarmo
				Nineveh I–II
				Halaf
4000	Chalcolithic	Widespread rural settlement	Badarian	Obeid
			Amratian	
				Uruk
3150	Early Bronze I	Urbanization	Gerzean	
2850	Early Bronze II	Huge fortifications	*Old Kingdom*	Jemdet Nasr
			I–II Dyn.	
				Sumer, 2800–2360
2600	Early Bronze III	Beth-yerah culture intrusion	III–V Dyn. (Age of the Pyramids)	
				Dyn. of Akkad, 2360–2180
2300	Early Bronze IV	Continuation of local culture	VI Dyn. 2315–2175	Sargon I, 2360–2305
			Pepi I, 2315	
				Naram-Sin, 2280–2244
			Pepi II, 2270	Gudea of Lagash
				Gutians
2150	Middle Bronze I	Nomadic intrusion	First Intermediate	III Dyn. of Ur, 2060–1950

		Amorite wave	*Middle Kingdom*	
2000	Middle Bronze IIA	Foundation of new cities	XII Dyn., 1991–1786	
			Amenemhet I, 1991	
			Sen-Usert I, 1971	Dyn. of Asshur, Isin, Larsa
			Amenemhet II, 1929	
			Sen-Usert II, 1897	
			Sen-Usert III, 1878	
			Amenemhet III, 1842	I (Amorite) Dyn. of Babylon, 1830–1531
			XIII Dyn., 1785–1720	
1750	Middle Bronze IIB	Hyksos period		Mari archives
			Second Intermediate	
				Hammurapi, 1728–1686
			XV (Hyksos) Dyn. 1678–1570	
1550	Late Bronze I	Egyptian rule	*New Kingdom*	Early Hittite Kingdom
			XVIII Dyn.	
			Ahmose, 1570	
			Amenhotep I, 1545	Mitanni
			Tuthmose I, 1525	Cossean Dyn. in Babylon
			Tuthmose II, 1508	
			(Hatshepsut, 1484)	
			Tuthmose III (21th year), 1469	
			Amenhotep II, 1436	
			Tuthmose IV, 1410	

Date	*Palestine* *archaeological*	/ *historical division*		*Egypt*	*Syria, Anatolia, Mesopotamia*
1400	Late Bronze IIA			Amenhotep III, 1402	*New Hittite Kingdom*
		El Amarna period		Amenhotep IV (Akhnaton), 1364	Suppiluliuma,
				Tutankhamun, 1346	
				Ay, 1337	
				Haremhab, 1333	Mursil II
1300	Late Bronze IIB			XIX Dyn.	Muwattili
				Seti I, 1303	Urhi-Teshub
		Israelite invasion		Ramses II, 1290	Hattusili III
				Mernephtah, 1223	Tudhaliya IV
1200	Iron Age IA				
				XX Dyn.	
				Ramses III, 1175	Aramean invasion
1150	Iron Age IB	Philistine invasion			
				Ramses IV–IX, 1144–1090	
					Tiglath-pileser I, 1116–1078
				XXI Dyn. 1065–935	
		Saul, 1025			Hadadezer (Aram-zobah)
1000	Iron Age IIA	David, 1006			Hiram I (Tyre)
		Solomon, 968		Siamun	
		Judah	*Israel*	XXII Dyn.	
		Rehoboam, 928	Jeroboam, 928	Shishak	
		Abijah, 911			
		Asa, 908	Nadab, 907	Osorkon I	

900	Iron Age IIB		Baasha, 906		*Aram-Damascus*
			Elah, 883		Ben-hadad I–II, 890–842
			Tibni-Omri, 882		*Assyrian Empire*
		Jehoshaphat, 867	Ahab, 871		Shalmaneser III, 859
		Jehoram, 851	Ahaziah, 851		
		Ahaziah, 843	Joram, 850		
		Athaliah, 842	Jehu, 842	Osorkon II	Hazael, 842–806
		Jehoash, 836	Joahaz, 814		Shamshi-Adad V, 824
800	Iron Age IIC	Amaziah, 799	Joash, 800		Ben-hadad III
					Adad-nirari III, 811
		Uzziah, 786	Jeroboam II, 785		Shalmaneser IV, 783
		(Jotham), 758	Zechariah, 749	XXV Dyn., 751–656	Asshur-dan III, 773
			Shallum-Menahem, 745		Asshur-nirari V, 775
		Ahaz, 742	Pekahiah, 737		Rezin, 740–732
					Tiglath-pileser III, 745
			Pekah, 735		Shalmaneser V, 727
			Hoshea, 731		Sargon II, 722
		Hezekiah, 726	Fall of Samaria, 722/1		
			Assyrian rule	Shabako, 710–696	Sennacherib, 705
		Manasseh, 697		Tirhaka, 685–663	Esarhaddon, 681
				Assyrian conquest, 671	
		Amon, 642			Ashurbanipal, 669
		Josiah, 640		XXVI Dyn., 663–525	Fall of Nineveh, 612
		Jehoahaz, 609		Necho II, 609–594	*Chaldean Dyn. of Babylon*
		Jehoiakim, 608	Babylonian rule		Nabopolassar, 626
		Jehoiachin, 598		Psammetichus II, 593–588	Nebuchadnezzar II, 605–562
		Zedekiah, 597			
		Fall of Jerusalem, 587			

Date	Palestine: archaeological	Palestine: historical division	Egypt	Syria, Anatolia, Mesopotamia
587	Persian period	Babylonian rule		
				Nabonidus, 555–539
		Persian rule, 539–332		Cyrus conquers Babylon, 539
		Edict of Cyrus, 538	Psammetichus III, 526–525	Cambyses, 530
			Persian conquest	Darius I, 522
				Xerxes I, 486
		Ezra, 457(?)		Artaxerxes I, 464
		Nehemiah, 445–425		Darius II, 423
				Artaxerxes II, 404
				Artaxerxes III, 359
				Arses, 338
				Darius III, 335
332	Hellenistic period	CONQUEST OF ALEXANDER THE GREAT		

* For the chronology of the earlier periods we have followed mainly the summaries of E. G. Wright and E. F. Campbell, in *The Bible and the Ancient Near East* (*Albright Volume*), New York 1961. The chronology of the Israelite and Judean monarchies is my own, cf. *Tarbitz* 21 (1946), pp. 92–100 (Hebrew). Most dates have a certain degree of uncertainty: a century and more in the earlier periods; ten to twenty years in the second half of the second millennium, and not more than a few years in the first millennium.

All dates are B.C. If only one date is given the beginning of the period is indicated.

APPENDIX 2

List of Site Identifications

Ancient names in *italics* are not in the Hebrew Bible. Arabic place names have generally been transcribed according to the system followed in publications by the American Schools of Oriental Research (cf. W.F. Albright, *BASOR*, 76 (1939), p. 15 n.) Modern Hebrew names are spelled in accordance with current Israeli maps; linguists should take note that in this system Semitic ḥ is represented by ẖ and ṣ by ẓ. Besides the number of maps in the book we have added the map reference corresponding to the Palestine-Syrian grid of coordinates. This will enable the reader to locate a site accurately on any modern map. The list does not include sites outside of Palestine and Syria, which appear mainly on maps 1 and 13. Modern names, mainly in maps 5 and 6, are included in the general index.

T. = Tell (Arabic), Tel (Hebrew). Kh. = Khirbet (Arabic). H̱. = H̱orvat (Hebrew).

Ancient Name	*Modern Arab Name*	*Modern Hebrew Name*	*Map Reference*	*Numbers of Maps*
Abdon	Kh. ʿAbdeh	T. ʿAvdon	165272	16, 22–3
Abel (Damascus)	Suq Wâdī Baradā		254337	9
— (Galilee)	ʿAin Ibl		188279	9
— (Gilead)	T. Abil		231231	33
Abel-beth-maachah, Abel	Abil el-Qamḥ	T. Avel Bet Maakha	204296	8, 9, 16, 18, 20, 23, 30
Abel-keramim	Naʿûr?		228142	15
Abel-meholah	T. Abû Sûs		203197	18, 23, 29
Abel-shittim	T. el-Ḥammâm		214138	14, 15
Acco	T. el-Fukhkhâr	T. ʿAkko	158258	2–4, 6, 8–9, 11–12, 15–18, 20–21, 23–4, 27, 30–1, 33
Achshaph	Kh. el-Harbaj?	T. Regev	158240	8–9, 11–12, 15–16, 18, 20, 23
Achzib (Asher)	ez-Zîb	T. Akhziv	159272	5, 15–18, 20, 23
— (Judah)	Kh. T. el-Beiḍā?	H̱. Lavnin	145116	19, 28, 32
Adadah	*see* Aroer (Negeb)			
Adam	T. ed-Dâmiyeh		201167	4, 15, 18, 20, 23, 24
Adamah, *Shemesh-adam*	Qarn Ḥaṭṭîn?	H̱. Qarne Ḥiṭṭim	193245	16, 23
Adami-nekeb	Kh. et-Tell (ed-Dâmiyeh)	T. Adami	193239	9, 12, 18, 23
Adoraim	Dûrā		152101	19, 25
Adullam	esh-Sheikh Madhkûr	H̱. ʿAdullam	150117	15, 19, 25, 28, 32, 34
Aduru	ed-Dûrā		212266	12

Ancient Name	Modern Arab Name	Modern Hebrew Name	Map Reference	Numbers of Maps
Ahlab	Kh. el-Maḥâlib		172303	17–18, 21
Ai	Kh. et-Tell		174147	5–6, 15
Aiath	Kh. Ḥaiyân?		175145	32, 34
Aijalon	Yâlō •		152138	11, 15, 17–20, 22–5, 28, 30, 32
Ain	Kh. ʿAyyûn?		212235	3
Alemeth	*see* Almon			
Almon	Kh. ʿAlmît		176136	19, 22
Almon-diblathaim, Beth-diblathaim	Kh. Deleilât esh-Sherqîyeh?		228116	14
Anab	Kh. ʿAnâb eṣ-Ṣeghîreh		145091	19, 28
Anaharath	T. el-Mukharkhash?	T. Rekhesh	194228	9–10, 23
Ananiah	el-ʿAzarîyeh		174131	34
Anathoth	Râs el-Kharrûbeh		174135	19, 22, 32, 34
Anim	Kh. Ghuwein et-Taḥtā	Ḫ. ʿAnim	156084	19, 28
Aphek (Lebanon)	Afqā		231382	3, 17
— (Asher)	T. Kurdâneh	T. Afeq	160250	15–18, 20, 23
— (Transjordan)	Kh. el-ʿÂsheq?	ʿEn Gev	210243	23, 27, 30
— (Sharon)	Râs el-ʿAin	T. Afeq	143168	4–6, 8–11, 15, 18–20, 23–4, 27 29–34
Apum	*see* Damascus			8
Arad (Canaanite city)	T. el-Milḥ	T. Malḫata	152069	13–15, 19–20, 24, 28
— (Israelite citadel)	T. ʿArâd	T. ʿArad	162076	5, 24, 28, 30, 32–3
Ardat	Ardât		237424	11
Aroer (Reuben)	ʿArâʿir		228097	15, 20–1, 23, 26
— (Negeb)	Kh. ʿArʿarah	Ḫ. ʿAroʿer	148062	15, 19–20, 25, 28
ʿ*Arqat* (Arkath)	T. ʿArqā		250436	8, 11
Arumah (Ephraim)	Kh. el-ʿOrmah		180172	29

Aruma (Galilee)	*see* Rumah			
ᶜ*Aruna*	Kh. ᶜÂrā		157212	9, 16, 24
Arvad	er-Ruâd		229473	1, 11, 21
Ashdod	Esdûd	T. Ashdod	117129	5, 15, 17–21, 23–5, 27, 30–4
Ashkelon	ᶜAsqalân	T. Ashqelon	107118	5–6, 8, 11, 15, 17, 19–21, 24, 27, 31–4
Ashtaroth	T. ᶜAshtarah		243244	2–4, 6–7, 9, 11, 15, 17, 20–3, 30
Ataroth (Reuben)	Kh. ᶜAṭṭārûs		213109	23, 26
Azekah	Kh. T. Zakarîyeh	T. ᶜAzeqa	144123	5, 19–20, 25, 28, 34
Azmaveth	Ḥizmeh		175138	34
Azmon	ᶜAin Muweiliḥ?		085010	3
Aznoth-tabor	Kh. el-Jebeil?	T. Aznot Tavor	186237	18
Azor	Yāzûr	Azor	131159	5, 19, 32
Azzah (Samaria)	Zawâtā?		171183	29
Baalah	*see* Kiriath-jearim			
Baalath (Dan)	el-Mughâr?		129138	18, 23
Baal-hazor	T. ᶜAṣûr		177153	19, 34
Batruna	Batrûn		212409	11
Beeroth (Phoenicia)	Beirût		195367	11, 12, 21
Beeroth (Benjamin)	Kh. el Burj		167137	19, 28, 34
Beer-sheba	T. es-Sebaᶜ	T. Beer Shevaᶜ	134072	2–5, 17, 19–22, 25, 27, 28, 30, 32–4
Bene-berak	Kheirîyeh (Ibn Ibrâq)	Ḫ. Bene-beraq	133160	23, 32
Berothah, Berothai	Bereitân		257372	9, 21, 31
Beten	Kh. Ibṭîn?	Ḫ. Ivṭan	160241	23
Beth-anath	Ṣafed el-Baṭṭîkh?		190289	12, 15–18, 20, 23
Beth-anoth	Kh. Beit ᶜAnûn		162107	28
Beth-arabah	ᶜAin el-Gharabeh		197139	18, 23, 28, 32
Beth-arbel	Irbid		229218	27
Beth-aven (**Beth-on*)	T. Maryam?		175141	19
Beth-azmaveth	*see* Azmaveth			
Beth-baal-meon	Māᶜîn		219120	14, 23, 26

Ancient Name	Modern Arab Name	Modern Hebrew Name	Map Reference	Numbers of Maps
Beth-dagon	Beit Dajan	Bet Dagan	134156	32
Beth-diblathaim	*see* Almon-diblathaim			26
Beth-ʿeglaim	T. el-ʿAjjûl		093097	7
Bethel	Beitîn		172148	5, 15, 18–21, 23–5, 28, 30. 32–4
Beth-emek	T. Mīmâs	T. Bet Ha-ʿEmeq	164263	18, 23
Bether	Kh. el-Yehûd		162126	28
Beth-gamul	Kh. el-Jumeil		235099	26
Beth-haccerem	Kh. Ṣâliḥ	Ramat Raẖel	170127	28, 34
Beth-haggan, *Gina*	Jenîn		178207	11
Beth-haram, Beth-haran	T. Iktanû		214136	8, 23
Beth-hoglah	Deir Ḥajlah		197136	18
Beth-horon Lower	Beit ʿÛr et-Taḥtā		158144	18–19, 22–4
Beth-horon Upper	Beit ʿÛr el-Fôqā		160143	18–19, 23
Beth-jeshimoth	T. el-ʿAẓeimeh		208132	14–15, 23
Beth-leaphrah	eṭ-Ṭaiyibeh?		153107	32
Bethlehem (Zebulun)	Beit Laḥm	Bet Leẖem Hagelilit	168238	23
— (Judah)	Beit Laḥm		169123	11, 15, 19–20, 23, 25, 28, 32, 34
Beth-nimrah	T. el-Bleibil		210146	23
Beth-shan, Beth-shean	T. el-Ḥuṣn	T. Bet Shean	197212	3, 5, 11–12, 15–18, 20–1, 23–4, 30, 33
Beth-shemesh (Naphtali)	Kh. T. er-Ruweisī?	T. Rosh	181271	8–9, 15–18, 20, 23
— (Issachar)	Kh. Sheikh esh-Shamsâwī?	H̱. Shemesh	199232	18, 23
— (Judah), Rabbah(?)	T. er-Rumeileh	T. Bet Shemesh	147128	5, 15, 18–20, 22–3, 32
Beth-tappuah	Taffûḥ		154105	28
Beth-yeraḥ	Kh. el-Kerak	T. Bet Yeraḥ	204235	5, 6
Beth-zaith	Zeitā		188323	21

Beth-zur	Kh. eṭ-Ṭubeiqeh		159110	5, 19, 25, 28, 32, 34
Betonim	Kh. Baṭneh		217154	23
Bezek	Kh. Ibzîq		187197	20
Bezer (Reuben)	Umm el-ᶜAmad?		235132	22, 26
Borim	Kh. Būrîn	Ḫ. Borin	153203	24
Bozrah (Bashan), ***Buṣruna***	Buṣra Eski-Shâm		289214	4, 8, 31
Bozrah (Edom)	Buṣeirah		208016	4, 14, 21, 27, 31
Buṣruna	*see Bozrah* (Bashan)			9, 11
Byblos, Gebal	Jebeil		210391	1–2, 8, 11–12, 17, 21, 27, 31
Carmel (Judah)	Kh. el-Kirmil		162092	15, 19–20, 28
Chephirah	Kh. el-Kefîreh		160137	19, 28, 34
Chesalon	Keslā	Kesalon	154132	18
Chesulloth, Chisloth-tabor	Iksâl		180232	18, 23
Chinnereth, Chinneroth	Kh. el-ᶜOreimeh	T. Kinrot	200252	9–10, 15–16, 18, 20–1, 23, 30
Chisloth-tabor	*see* Chesulloth			22
City of Moab	Kh. el-Medeiyineh?		232076	26
City of Salt	Kh. Qumrân?		193127	28
Cun	Râs Baᶜalbek?		283406	21
Dabbesheth	T. esh-Shammâm?	T. Shem	164230	18
Daberath	Dabûriyeh		185233	18, 22
Damascus	esh-Shâm (Dimasq)		272324	1–4, 7–9, 11–12, 17, 21, 27, 30–1
Dan, Laish	T. el-Qâḍī	T. Dan	211294	2–3, 7, 15–18, 20–3, 27, 30, 33
Debir	Kh. Rabûd		151093	15, 19, 20, 22, 28, 32
Dibon	Dhibân		224101	5, 14–15, 20, 23, 26–7, 30
Dizahab	Dhahab?		104769	13
Dor	Kh. el-Burj	T. Dor	142224	2, 4, 15–18, 20–1, 23–4, 27, 30–1, 33
Dothan	T. Dôthān		172202	5–6, 23, 29
Dumah (Judah)	Kh. ed-Deir Dômeh		148093	28
Edrei (Bashan)	Derᶜā		253224	3, 15, 20

Ancient Name	*Modern Arab Name*	*Modern Hebrew Name*	*Map Reference*	*Numbers of Maps*
Eglon	T. el-Ḥesī	T. Hasi	124106	8, 11, 15, 19–20, 25, 28
Ekron	Kh. el-Muqannaʿ	T. Miqne	136131	15, 17–21, 23–5, 27, 30–3
Elath, Eloth, El-paran	ʿAqabah		150882	1, 4, 13, 14, 21, 27
Elealeh	el-ʿÂl		228136	14
Elmattan	Immātîn		165177	29
Eltekeh	T. esh-Shallâf?	T. Shalaf	128144	19, 22–3, 32
El-paran	*see* Elath			7
En-dor	Kh. Ṣafṣâfeh	H. Zafzafot	187227	20
En-gannim	Kh. Beit Jann?		196235	22
En-gedi	ʿAin Jidī (T. Jurn)	ʿEn Gedi (T. Goren)	187097	4–5, 19–20, 25, 27, 28, 32–4
En-haddah	el-Ḥadatheh	T. ʿEn Hadda	196232	23
En-rimmon	Kh. Khuweilfeh	T. Halif	137087	
En-shemesh	ʿAin Ḥôḍ		175131	18
Eshtaol	Ishwaʿ	Eshtaol	151132	19, 28
Eshtemoa	es-Semûʿ		156089	15, 19, 22, 28, 32
Etam	Kh. el-Khôkh		166121	19, 25, 28
Ether	Kh. el-ʿAter	T. ʿEter	138113	28
Ezion-geber	T. el-Kheleifeh		147884	5, 13, 24, 27
Gath (Asher)	Jett		172264	9
— (Sharon)	Jett		154200	16
Gath (Philistine)	T. eṣ-Ṣâfi	T. Zafit	135123	9, 11, 15, 17–21, 23–5, 32
Gath-hepher	Kh. ez-Zurraʿ	T. Gat Hefer	180238	18
Gath-padalla	*see Gath*(Sharon)			9, 11, 24
Gath-rimmon	T. Jerîsheh?	T. Gerisa	132166	11, 19, 22–3
Gaza	Ghazzeh		099101	1–4, 9–12, 15, 17, 19–21, 23–4, 27, 30–4
Geba (Samaria)	Jebaʿ		171192	29
Geba (North Benjamin)	Kh. et-Tell?		174158	28, 29

— (Benjamin)	Jebaʿ		175140	19–20, 22–3, 32–4
Geba-somen	T. el-ʿAmr	T. Meʿamer	159237	9–10
Gebal	*see* Byblos			8
Gedor (Gilead)	*T. ʿAin-Jedû*r		220160	33–4
Gedor (Judah)	Kh. Jedûr		158115	19, 28
Gerar	T. Abū Hureireh	T. Haror	112087	9, 15, 19, 21, 32
Gezer	T. Jezer (Abū Shûsheh)	T. Gezer	142140	5–6, 9, 11, 15, 17–20, 22–4, 30, 33, 34
Gibbethon	T. Melât	T. Malot	137140	9, 19, 22–3, 25
Gibeah				
(of Benjamin, of Saul)	T. el-Fûl		172136	19–20, 23, 28, 32
Gibeah of Kiriath-jearim	Abū Ghôsh?		160134	28
Gibeon	el-Jîb		167139	5, 15, 19–20, 22–4, 28, 34
Gilgal	Kh. el-Mefjer?		193143	15–20, 33
Gimzo	Jimzū	Gimzo	145148	19
Gina	*see* Beth-haggan			11
Gittaim	Râs Abū Ḥumeid		140145	19, 25, 34
Golan	Saḥm el-Jōlân?		238243	22
Ḫadaru	Kh. Ḥader		292336	9
Hadid	el-Ḥadîtheh	T. H̱adid	145152	34
Halhul	Ḥalḥûl		160109	19, 28
Hali	Kh. Râs ʿÂlī	T. ʿAlil	164241	23
Ham	Hâm		226213	7, 15
Hamath	Ḥamā		312503	1, 21
Hammath (Naphtali)	Ḥammâm Ṭabarîyeh	H̱ame Ṭeveriya	201241	12, 20, 22, 23
Hammath (Beth-shan)	T. el-Ḥammeh		197197	12
Hammon (Asher)	Umm elʿAwāmîd		164281	23
Hannathon, *Ḫinnatuna*	T. el-Bedeiwîyeh	T. H̱annaton	174243	16, 18, 20, 23, 30
Hapharaim	eṭ-Ṭaiyibeh		192223	23
Harnem	Hermel		281423	12
Ḫashabu	T. Ḥashbeh		249382	9–11

Ancient Name	Modern Arab Name	Modern Hebrew Name	Map Reference	Numbers of Maps
Hazar-addar	ʿAin Qedeis?		100999	3
Hazar-enan	Qaryatein		360402	3
Hazeroth (Samaria)	ʿAṣîreh esh-Shamālîyeh?		175184	29
Haseroth (Sinai)	ʿAin Khaḏrā?		096814	13
Hazezon-tamar	*see* Tamar			
Ḫasi	T. Ḥizzîn?		255377	9, 11
Hazor	T. el-Qedaḥ	T. H̲az̲or	203269	1, 3–5, 8–12, 15–16, 23, 27, 30
Hebron	el-Khalîl		160103	7, 15, 17, 19–23, 25, 28, 30, 32–4
Heleph	Kh. ʿIrbâdeh?	H̲. ʿArpad	189236	18
Helkath	T. el-Qassîs?	T. Qashish	160232	9, 18, 22
Hepher	el-Ifshâr?	T. H̲efer	141197	15, 18, 20, 23
Heshbon	Ḥesbân		226134	14–15, 20, 22–3, 26–7, 30
Ḫini-anabi, *ʿEni-ʿanabi*	*see Kiriath-anab*			11
Ḫinnatuna	*see* Hannathon			11
Hor, Mount (Lebanon)	Râs Shaqqah?		213402	3, 17
— (Negeb)	ʿImâret el-Khureisheh?		104017	13–14
Hormah	Kh. el-Meshâsh	T. Masos	146069	8, 13–15, 19–20, 28
Horonaim	el-ʿIrâq?		211055	26
Hosah	*see Usu*?			18, 21
Hukkok	Kh. el-Jemeijmeh?	H̲. Gamom	175252	18
Hushah	Ḥûsân?		162124	19
Ibleam	Kh. Belʿameh		177205	9, 15–18, 20, 22–3
Ije-abarim	el-Medeiyineh?		223041	14, 26
Ijon	T. ed-Dibbîn		205308	8–9, 15, 18, 20–1, 23, 30
Ir-nahash	Kh. en-Naḥâs		191010	14

Jaazer	Kh. eṣ-Ṣâr?		228150	14–15, 20–3
Jabesh-gilead	T. el-Maqlûb		214201	15, 20, 23
Jabneel (Naphtali)	T. en-Naʿam	T. Yinʿam	198235	18, 23
— (Judah)	Yebnā	Yavne	126141	18–19, 27
Jahaz, Jahazah	Kh. el-Medeiyineh?		236110	14, 22–3, 26
Janoah (Galilee)	Yānûḥ		173265	30
— (Ephraim)	Kh. Yānûn		184173	18, 29
Japhia, *Yapu*	Yâfā		176232	16, 18
Japho	*see* Joppa			
Jarmuth (Issachar)	*see* Remeth			
— (Judah)	Kh. el-Yarmûk	T. Yarmut	147124	6, 11, 15, 19, 28, 34
Jattir (Judah)	Kh. ʿAttîr	H̱. Yatir	151084	19–20, 22, 28
Jebus	*see* Jerusalem			15, 17
Jehud	el-Yehūdîyeh	Yehud	139159	23
Jericho	T. es-Sulṭân		192142	5–7, 14–15, 18, 25, 28, 32–4
Jerusalem	el-Quds	Jerusalem	172131	2–5, 7–8, 11, 21-25,27,28,30–4
Jeshanah	Burj el-Isâneh		174156	29
Jeshua	T. es-Saʿweh?	T. Jeshuʿa	149076	28, 34
Jezreel	Zerʿîn	T. Yizreʿel	181218	15–16, 18, 20, 23
Jogbehah	el-Jubeihât		231159	15, 20, 23
Jokmeam	T. el-Mazâr?		195171	22–3, 29
Jokneam	T. Qeimûn	T. Yoqneam	160230	9, 15–16, 18, 22–3
Joktheel	*see* Sela			
Joppa	Yâfā	Yafo	126162	2–5, 9, 11–12, 15, 17–21, 23–4, 27, 30–4
Jotbah, *Jotapata*	Kh. Jefât	H̱. Yodefat	176248	30, 33
Jotbathah	Ṭâbeh?		139878	13
Juttah	Yaṭṭā		158095	19, 22, 28
Kabul	Kābûl		170252	15–16, 18, 23
Kadesh	T. Nebī Mind		291444	3, 9–12

Ancient Name	Modern Arab Name	Modern Hebrew Name	Map Reference	Numbers of Maps
Kadesh-barnea	ʿAin el-Qudeirât		096006	1, 3–5, 7, 13–14, 17, 21, 24, 27
Kain	en-Nebī Yaqîn?		165100	28
Kamon	Qamm?		218221	15
Kanah (Asher)	Qânā		178290	16, 18, 23
Kanah (Galilee)	Kh. Qânā	H̱. Qana	178247	30
Karka, Karkaa	ʿAin el-Qeṣeimeh?		089007	3
Karnaim	Sheikh Saʿd		247249	7, 28, 30–1, 33
Karthan	*see* Rakkath?			22
Kedemoth	ʿAleiyân?		233104	14, 22–3, 26
Kedesh (Galilee)	T. Qades	T. Qedesh	199279	6, 8–9, 12, 15–16, 18, 20–3, 30, 33
— (Naphtali)	Kh. Qedîsh	H̱. Qedesh	202237	16
Keilah	Kh. Qîlā		150113	11, 19–20, 28, 34
Kenath, *Qanu*	Qanawât		302241	3–4, 8, 11, 17, 21
Kerioth (Moab)	el-Qereiyât		215105	23, 26
— (Negeb)	Kh. el-Qaryatein?	T. Qeriyot	161083	28
Kinah	Kh. Ṭaiyib	H̱. Tov	163081	
Kir-hareseth	el-Kerak		217066	20–1, 26–7, 30–1, 33
Kir of Moab	*see* Kir-hareseth			14
Kiriathaim (Reuben)	Qaryat el-Mekhaiyeṭ?		220128	7, 23, 26
Kiriath-anab, *H̱ini-anabi*	T. esh-Shihâb?		241233	12
Kiriath-baal	*see* Kiriath-jearim			
Kiriath-jearim	Deir el-ʿÂzar	T. Qiryat Yeʿarim	159135	18–20, 24, 28, 32, 34
Kiriath-sepher	*see* Debir			
Kishion	Kh. Qasyûn	T. Qishyon	187229	9, 22–3
Kozoh	Kh. Qûṣîn		167182	29
Kumidi	Kâmid el-Lôz		226337	9, 11
Laban	T. Abû Seleimeh?		065071	27
Labana	*see* Lebo-hamath			11

Lachish	T. ed-Duweir	T. Lachish	135108	5–7, 11, 15, 19–20, 25, 27, 30, 32–4
Laish	*see* Dan			6–9
Lebo-hamath, Lebo, *Labana*	Lebweh		277397	3, 8–10, 17, 21, 27, 31
Lebonah	el-Lubban		173164	19, 23, 29
Libnah	T. Bornâṭ?	T. Burna	138115	15, 19, 22, 28, 32
Libnath	T. Abû Huwâm?		152245	18
Lod	el-Ludd	Lod	140151	6, 8–9, 19, 23, 34
Lo-debar, Lidebir	Umm ed-Dabar?		207219	23, 27
Madmannah	Kh. Tatrît		143084	19, 28
Madmen	Kh. Dimneh?		217077	26
Mahanaim	T. edh-Dhahab el-Gharbi		214177	20–4, 30–1
Manahath	el-Mâlḥah	Manaḫat	167128	11, 19, 28
Maon	Kh. Maʿîn		162090	19–20, 28
Maralah	T. Thôrah?	T. Shor	166228	18
Mareshah	T. Ṣandaḥannah	T. Maresha	140111	5, 19, 25, 28, 32, 34
Medeba	Mâdeba		225124	15, 20–1, 23, 26–7, 30
Megiddo	T. el-Mutesellim	T. Megiddo	167221	1, 3–12, 15–18, 20–1, 23–4, 27 30–1, 33
Mephaath	T. Jâwah?		239140	22–3
Merom	T. el-Khirbeh?		190275	9, 15–16, 30
Michmash, Michmas	Mukhmâs		176142	19–20, 23, 32, 34
Michmethath	Kh. Makhneh el-Fôqā		175176	18, 29
Middin	Kh. Abū Ṭabaq?		188127	28
Migdal, *Migdal-yen* (Sharon)	T. edh-Dhurûr?	T. Zeror	147203	9
Migdal-gad	Kh. el-Mejdeleh?	Ḫ. Migdal Gad	140105	28
Migdal-yen	*see Migdal* (Sharon)			10
Mishal	T. Kīsân?	T. Kison	164253	8–9, 22–3
Mizpah, Mizpeh	T. en-Naṣbeh		170143	19–20, 23, 25, 28, 32, 34
Moladah	Khereibet el-Waṭen?	Ḫ. Yittan	142074	28, 34
Moresheth-gat	T. el-Judeideh?	T̄. Goded	141115	19, 25, 32

Ancient Name	Modern Arab Name	Modern Hebrew Name	Map Reference	Numbers of Maps
Motha	Imtân		301265	9
Mozah	Qâlunyah	Mevasseret Ziyyon	165134	19, 28
Muhhazi	Tell Abū Sulṭân?	T. Mahoz	125147	9
Naarath	T. el-Jisr		190144	18
Naveh	Nawā		248255	20
Neballat	Beit Nabâlā	H. Nevallat	146154	34
Nebo	Kh. ᶜAyûn Mûsā?		220131	14, 26, 33
Neiel	Kh. Yaᶜnîn	H. Yaᶜanin	171255	18
Nephtoah, Waters of	Liftā	Me-Neftoah	168133	18
Netophah	Kh. Bedd Fālûḥ?		171119	19, 34
Nezib	Kh. Beit Neṣîb		151110	19, 28
Nibshan	Kh. el Maqârī?		186123	28
Nob	el- ᶜIsāwîyeh?		173134	19, 32, 34
Nobah	*see* Kenath			
Ono	Kafr ᶜAnā	Ono	137159	9, 19, 34
Ophrah, ᶜ*pr* (Abiezer)	el-ᶜAffuleh?	ᶜAfula	177223	9, 18
Ophrah (Benjamin)	eṭ-Ṭaiyibeh		178151	19–20, 23, 28
Paran	Feirân		018792	13
Peḥel, *Pella*	Kh. Faḥil		207206	5, 8–9, 11–12, 16
Penuel	T. edh-Dhahab esh-Sherqîyeh		215176	15, 24
Peor	Kh. Fāghûr		163119	28
Pirathon	Farᶜatā		165177	29
Punon	Feinân		197004	14

Qanu	*see* Kenath			
Qaṭna	el-Mishrifeh		323471	1, 10
Rabbah (Ammon)	*see* Rabbath-ammon			
—, *Rubute* (Judah)	Kh. Ḥamîdeh		149137	24, 28
Rabbath-ammon	ᶜAmmân		238151	1, 4–5, 14–15, 17, 20–1, 23, 27, 30–1, 33
Rakkath, Karthan(?)	Kh. el-Quneiṭireh	T. Raqqat	199245	23
Ramah (Naphtali)	Kh. Zeitûn er-Râmeh (Kh. Jûl)		187259	16, 20, 23
— (Benjamin)	er-Râm		172140	19, 20, 23, 28, 32, 34
Ramath-mizpeh	Kh. Jelᶜad?		223169	23, 33
Ramoth (Issachar)	*see* Remeth			
Ramoth-gilead	T. Rāmîth		244210	15, 17, 20–3, 27, 30–1, 33
Ramoth-negeb	Kh. Ghazzah	H̱. ʿUzza	165068	
Raphia	T. Rafaḥ		077079	12, 24, 27
Raphon	er-Râfeh		258255	9
Rehob (Galilee)	T. el-Balâṭ?		177280	9, 16
— (Asher)	T. el-Bîr el-Gharbî?	T. Bira	166256	15–18, 22–3
Rehob (Beth-shean)	T. eṣ-Ṣârem	T. Reẖov	197207	6, 8, 10, 12, 16, 24
Rekem (Edom)	Umm el-Bayyâreh?		192971	14
Remeth	Kôkab el-Hawā?	Kokhav-Hayarden	199222	15–16, 22–3
Riblah, *Shabtuna* (?)	Ribleh		296427	31
Rimmon (Zebulun)	Rummâneh	H̱. Rimona	179243	18–22
Rogelim	Bersînyā?		223215	23
Rubute	*see* Rabbah (Judah)			9, 10–11
Rumah	Kh. er-Rûmeh	H̱. Ruma	177243	30, 33
Salchah	Ṣalkhad		311212	3, 17, 21
Samaria	Sebasṭiyeh		168187	5, 27, 29–31, 33, 34
Sansannah	Kh. esh-Shamsanīyât	H̱. Sansanna	140083	19, 28
Sarid (**Sadud*)	T. Shadûd		172229	18
Secacah	Kh. es-Samrah?		187125	28
Sela	es-Selaᶜ		205020	3, 14, 27
Sepher	Saffārîn		160185	29

Ancient Name	Modern Arab Name	Modern Hebrew Name	Map Reference	Numbers of Maps
Shaalbim, Shaalabbin	Selbît	T. Sha^{c}alevim	148141	15, 17–19, 23
Shabtuna	*see* Riblah?			9
Shamḫuna	*see* Shimron			11
Sharuhen	T. el-Fâr^{c}ah	T. Sharuẖen	100076	9, 19–21, 24
Shechem	T. Balâṭah		176179	4–6, 8, 11–12, 15, 17–18, 20–4, 29, 34
Shemesh-adam	*see* Adamah			9–10
Shikkeron	T. el-Fûl		132136	18
Shikimonah	T. es-Samak	T. Shiqmona	146247	
Shiloh	Kh. Seilûn		177162	5, 15, 17–19
Shim^{c}on	*see* Shimron			8–9
Shimron, *Shim^{c}on*, *Shamḫuna*	Kh. Sammûniyeh	T. Shimron	170234	15–16, 23
Shunem	Sôlem	Shunem	181223	9, 11, 16, 18, 23–4
Sidon	Ṣaidā		184329	1–3, 11–12, 17, 21, 27, 31
Siphtan	Shûfah?		157186	29
Sochoh, Socoh (Sharon)	Kh. Shuweiket er-Râs		153194	9–10, 15, 20, 23–4, 29
— (Shephelah)	Kh. ^{c}Abbâd	H̱. Sokho	147121	19–20, 25, 28, 30, 32
— (Mt. Judah)	Kh. Shuweikeh		150090	19, 28
Succoth	T. Deir ^{c}Allā		208178	15, 20, 23–4
Ṣumur	T. Kazel?		242453	1, 3, 9, 11–12, 17
Taanach	T. Ti^{c}innik		171214	5, 9–11, 15–16, 18, 20, 22–4
Taanath-shiloh	Kh. Ta^{c}nā el-Fôqā		185175	18, 29
Tamar	^{c}Ain Ḥuṣb	H̱aẕeva	173024	3–4, 7, 14, 17, 21, 24, 27, 31
Taphnith	Tibnîn		188288	9
Tappuah (Ephraim)	Sheikh Abū Zarad		172168	15, 18–19, 23, 29
Tekoa	Kh. Teqû^c		170115	19, 25, 28, 34
Teman	Ṭawīlân?		197971	14, 21, 27
Timnah	T. el-Baṭâshī	T. Baṭash	141132	18–19, 23, 32
Timnath-serah	Kh. Tibnah		160157	29
Tirzah	Kh. T. el-Fâr^{c}ah		182188	15, 18, 20, 23–4, 29

Tob	eṭ-Ṭaiyibeh		266218	9, 21
Tophel	eṭ-Ṭafîleh?		208027	14
Tyre	eṣ-Ṣûr		168297	1–6, 8–9, 11–12, 15–18, 20–3, 27, 30–1
Tyre of Tobiah	ᶜArâq el-Emîr		222148	34
Ullasa	el-Mînah?		240430	8, 11–12
Usu, Hosah(?)	T. Rashīdîyeh		170293	11–12
Yaḥam	Kh. Yemmā	T. Yaham	153197	9–10, 24
Yapu	*see* Japhia			11
Yashub	Yāsûf?		172168	18, 29
Yattir	Yaᶜtir		181284	9
Yazith	Yaṣîd		176189	29
Yenoam	el-ᶜAbeidîyeh		202232	9, 11–12
Yiron	Yārûn		189276	23, 30
Yoqereth	Iqrît	H. Yoqrat	176275	9
Yurza	T. Jemmeh?	T. Gamma	097088	9, 11, 19
Zalmonah	es-Salmaneh?		188021	14
Zanoah (Shephelah)	Kh. Zānûᶜ	H. Zanoah	150125	19, 28, 34
Zaphon	T. es-Saᶜīdîyeh		204186	11, 15, 20, 23–4
Zarephath	Ṣarafand		176316	12, 21
Zarethan	T. Umm Ḥamâd?		205172	8, 20, 23
Zedad	Ṣadâd		330420	3, 31
Zemaraim	Râs eṭ-Ṭāḥûneh?		170147	24, 28
Zephath (Sharon)	Kh. Sitt Leila	T. Zefi	150215	9
Zeredah	Deir Ghassâneh		159161	23, 29
Zereth-shahar	ez-Zārât?		203111	23
Ziklag	T. esh-Shārîᶜah?	T. Seraᶜ	119088	19–20, 28, 34
Ziph	T. Zîf		162098	19–20, 25, 28, 32
Ziphron	Ḥawwārîn		347407	3
Zoar	eṣ-Ṣâfī		194049	3, 7, 11, 14, 20–1, 26–7
Zobah	Ṣûbā?	T. Zova	162132	28
Zorah	Ṣarᶜah	T. Zor a	148131	11, 18–19, 25, 28, 34

LIST OF ABBREVIATIONS

AAAS	*Annales archéologiques arabes syriens*
AASOR	*Annual of the American Schools of Oriental Research*
Abel, *Géogr.*	F. M. Abel, *Géographie de la Palestine,* I-II, Paris 1933–8
Aharoni, *Settlement*	Y. Aharoni, *The Settlement of the Israelite Tribes in Upper Galilee,* Jerusalem, 1947 (Hebrew).
AJA	*American Journal of Archaeology.*
AJBA	*Australian Journal of Biblical Archaeology*
AJSL	*American Journal of Semitic Languages and Literatures.*
Albright, *APB*	W. F. Albright, *Archaeology of Palestine and the Bible,* New York, 1931 (3rd edition, 1935).
Albright, *SAC*	W. F. Albright, *From the Stone Age to Christianity,* Baltimore, 1940 (2nd edition, 1946).
Alt, *Kl. Schr.*	A. Alt, *Kleine Schriften zur Geschichte des Volkes Israel,* I-III, Munich, 1953–9.
ANEP	J. B. Pritchard, *The Ancient Near East in Pictures Relating to the Old Testament,* Princeton, 1954.
ANET	J. B. Pritchard, ed., *Ancient Near Eastern Texts Relating to the Old Testament,* Princeton, 1950 (2nd edition, 1955, 3rd edition, 1969 = *ANETS*).
ANETS	J. B. Pritchard, ed., *The Ancient Near East, Supplementary Texts and Pictures,* Princeton, 1969.
AOAT	*Alter Orient und Altes Testament*
AUSS	*Andrews University Seminary Studies.*
Avi-Yonah, *Historical Geography*	M. Avi-Yonah, *Historical Geography of Palestine,* Jerusalem, 1949 (3rd edition, 1962) (Hebrew).
BA	*Biblical Archaeologist.*
BASOR	*Bulletin of the American Schools of Oriental Research.*
BBSAJ	*Bulletin of the British School of Archaeology in Jerusalem.*
BIES	*Bulletin of the Israel Exploration Society* (Hebrew; continued as *Yediot*).
BJPES	*Bulletin of the Jewish Palestine Exploration Society* (Hebrew; continued as *BIES*).
Breasted, *AR*	J. H. Breasted, *Ancient Records of Egypt,* I–IV, Chicago, 1906–7.

Bright, *History*[2]	J. Bright, *A History of Israel,* 2nd ed., Philadelphia, 1973.
BZAW	*Beihefte zur Zeitschrift für die alttestamentliche Wissenschaft.*
CAD	*Assyrian Dictionary of the Oriental Institute of the University of Chicago.*
EA	*El-Amarna,* with tablet Nos.
EAEHL	*Encyclopaedia of Archaeological Excavations in the Holy Land,* Jerusalem 1975-.
Ed. Meyer, *Die Isr. u. i. Nachb.*	Ed. Meyer, *Die Israeliten und ihre Nachbarstämme,* Halle a/S., 1906.
EI	*Eretz-Israel* (mostly Hebrew).
Enc. Bib. (Hebrew)	*Encyclopaedia Biblica,* I–VII, Jerusalem, 1955–76 (Hebrew).
Galling, *BR*	K. Galling, *Biblisches Reallexikon,* Tübingen, 1937
Gardiner, *Anc. Eg. On.*	A. H. Gardiner, *Ancient Egyptian Onomastica,* I–II, Oxford, 1947.
Gardiner, *LEM*	A. H. Gardiner, *Late Egyptian Miscellanies,* Bruxelles, 1937.
Garstang, *Jos.-Judg.*	J. Garstang, *Joshua-Judges,* London, 1931.
Helck, *Beziehungen*[2]	W. Helck, *Die Beziehungen Aegyptens zu Vorderasien im 3. und 2. Jahrtausend v. Chr.,* 2nd ed., Wiesbaden, 1971.
HUCA	*Hebrew Union College Annual.*
IDB	G. A. Buttrick, ed., *The Interpreter's Dictionary of the Bible,* I–IV, Nashville, 1962.
IDB Suppl.	K. Crim *et al.,* eds., *The Interpreter's Dictionary of the Bible, Supplementary Volume,* Nashville, 1976.
IEJ	*Israel Exploration Journal.*
IOS	*Israel Oriental Studies.*
JANES	*Journal of the Ancient Near Eastern Society of Columbia University.*
JAOS	*Journal of the American Oriental Society*
JARCE	*Journal of the American Research Center in Egypt.*
JBL	*Journal of Biblical Literature.*
JCS	*Journal of Cuneiform Studies.*
JEA	*Journal of Egyptian Archaeology.*
JNES	*Journal of Near Eastern Studies.*
JPOS	*Journal of the Palestine Oriental Society.*
KUB	*Keilschrifturkunden aus Boghazköi.*
Luckenbill, *AR*	D. D. Luckenbill, *Ancient Records of Assyria and Babylonia,* I–II, Chicago, 1926–7.

Maisler, *Untersuchungen*	B. Maisler (Mazar), *Untersuchungen zur alten Geschichte und Ethnographie Syriens und Palästinas,* Giessen, 1929.
Maisler, *History*	B. Maisler (Mazar), *A History of Palestine,* I, Tel Aviv, 1934 (Hebrew).
NF	Neue Folge (New Series).
Noth, *Aufsätze*	M. Noth, *Aufsätze zur biblischen Landes- und Altertumskunde,* I–II, Neukirchen-Vluyn, 1971.
Noth, *Geschichte*	M. Noth, *Geschichte Israels,* Göttingen, 1948 (3rd ed., 1956).
Noth, *History*	M. Noth, *The History of Israel,* 2nd ed., Edinburgh, 1960.
Noth, *Josua*	M. Noth, *Das Buch Josua,* Tübingen, 1938 (2nd ed., 1953).
PEF An.	*Palestine Exploration Fund Annual.*
PEF QS	*Palestine Exploration Fund, Quarterly Statement.*
PEQ	*Palestine Exploration Quarterly*
PJb	*Palästina-Jahrbuch.*
QDAP	*The Quarterly of the Department of Antiquities in Palestine.*
RB	*Revue biblique.*
Rowley, *Jos.*-Josh.	H. H. Rowley, *From Joseph to Joshua,* London, 1950.
Saarisalo, *Boundary*	A. Saarisalo, *The Boundary between Issachar and Naphtali,* Helsinki, 1927.
Simons, *Handbook*	J. Simons, *Handbook for the Study of Egyptian Topographical Lists Relating to Western Asia,* Leiden, 1937.
UF	*Ugaritforschungen.*
VT	*Vetus Testamentum.*
VT Suppl.	*Vetus Testamentum Supplements.*
Wreszinski, *Atlas* II	W. Wreszinski, *Atlas zur altägyptischen Kulturgeschichte,* II, Leipzig, 1935.
ZAW	*Zeitschrift für die alttestamentliche Wissenschaft.*
ZDMG	*Zeitschrift der deutschen morgenländischen Gesellschaft.*
ZDPV	*Zeitschrift des deutschen Palästina Vereins.*

INDEX OF BIBLICAL REFERENCES

INDEX OF GEOGRAPHICAL NAMES

1. A name following a solidus is another name for the same place (e.g. Abdon/Ebron) and will usually have its own entry.
2. Matter in parentheses after a name is not part of the name, but serves to distinguish it in some way, e.g. Achzib (Asher).
3. The Index only gives map references for those places not included in the List of Site Identifications (pp. 429-43).
4. Sites are noted in square brackets, but only for places not included in the List of Site Identifications.